T0212771

Lecture Notes in Computer Science 9268

Commenced Publication in 1973
Founding and Former Series Editors:
Gerhard Goos, Juris Hartmanis, and Jan van Leeuwen

More information about this series at http://www.springer.com/series/7407

Sriram Sankaranarayanan · Enrico Vicario (Eds.)

Formal Modeling and Analysis of Timed Systems

13th International Conference, FORMATS 2015
Madrid, Spain, September 2–4, 2015
Proceedings

 Springer

Editors
Sriram Sankaranarayanan
University of Colorado
Boulder, CO
USA

Enrico Vicario
University of Florence
Florence
Italy

ISSN 0302-9743   ISSN 1611-3349   (electronic)
Lecture Notes in Computer Science
ISBN 978-3-319-22974-4   ISBN 978-3-319-22975-1   (eBook)
DOI 10.1007/978-3-319-22975-1

Library of Congress Control Number: 2015946098

LNCS Sublibrary: SL1 – Theoretical Computer Science and General Issues

Springer Cham Heidelberg New York Dordrecht London

Printed on acid-free paper

Springer International Publishing AG Switzerland is part of Springer Science+Business Media
(www.springer.com)

Preface

FORMATS 2015 was the 13th edition of the International Conference on Formal Modeling and Analysis of Timed Systems. It promoted the study and experimentation of fundamental and practical aspects of modeling and analysis of timed systems, and brought together researchers from different disciplines on various related topics, including:

- *Foundations and Semantics:* Theoretical foundations of timed systems and languages; comparison between different models (timed automata, timed Petri nets, hybrid automata, timed process algebra, max-plus algebra, probabilistic models).
- *Methods and Tools*: Techniques, algorithms, data structures, and software tools for analyzing timed systems and resolving temporal constraints (scheduling, worst-case execution time analysis, optimization, model checking, testing, constraint solving, etc.).
- *Applications:* Adaptation and specialization of timing technology in application domains for which timing plays an important role (real-time software, hardware circuits, and problems of scheduling in manufacturing and telecommunication).

FORMATS 2015 was held in Madrid, continuing the tradition of the events held in Florence (2014), Buenos Aires (2013), London (2012), Aalborg (2011), Klosterneuburg (2010), Budapest (2009), St Malo (2008), Salzburg (2007), Paris (2006), Uppsala (2005), Grenoble (2004), and Marseille (2003).

FORMATS 2015 was organized under the umbrella of Madrid Meet 2015 - a one-week event focussing on the areas of formal and quantitative analysis of systems, performance engineering, computer safety, and industrial critical applications. Co-located conferences included the 12th International Conference on Quantitative Evaluation of Systems (QEST 2015), the 26th International Conference on Concurrency Theory (CONCUR 2015), the 10th European Workshop on Performance Engineering (EPEW 2015), and various other associated workshops and symposia.

The Program Committee (PC) for FORMATS 2015 was formed by 36 experts plus the two PC chairs. A total of 42 full papers were submitted. All manuscripts received 4 reviews, with the exception of a single one which received 3. In this step, 81 additional subreviewers were involved. Reviews were discussed by the PC and the subreviewers using the EasyChair system. In the end, 19 papers were accepted. The conference program was then enriched with an invited talk by Jeremy Sproston (University of Turin, Italy) included in the proceedings of FORMATS, and an invited talk by Jozef Hooman (RU Nijmegen and TNO-ESI, The Netherlands) reported in the proceedings of QEST.

We sincerely thank all the authors who submitted papers for their interest in FORMATS and more generally for their involvement and contribution to the research in formal modeling and analysis of timed systems.We thank each member of the PC, and each sub-reviewer, for the high professionality and commitment shown in the elaboration of reviews and the following discussion. Their service was essential for continuinig the tradition of FORMATS. We thank the publicity chair Marco Paolieri and the webmaster Simone Mattolini for their precious service. We thank David De Frutos for the organization of the Madrid Meet event. We thank Oded Maler and Eugene Asarin for the help that they provided from a distance, and the Steering Committee of FORMATS for giving us the occasion to lead, for one step, this lively community.

June 2015   Sriram Sankaranarayanan
                                                                        Enrico Vicario

Organization

Program Committee

Bernard Berthomieu	LAAS/CNRS, Toulouse, France
Nathalie Bertrand	INRIA Rennes, France
Luca Bortolussi	University of Trieste, Italy
Marius Bozga	VERIMAG/CNRS, Grenoble, France
Victor Braberman	University of Buenos Aires/CONICET, Argentina
Thomas Brihaye	University of Mons, Belgium
Laura Carnevali	University of Florence, Italy
Franck Cassez	Macquarie University, Sydney, Australia
Krishnendu Chatterjee	Institute of Science and Technology, Austria
Goran Frehse	VERIMAG/University of Grenoble, France
Laurent Fribourg	LSV, ENS Cachan & CNRS, France
Martin Fränzle	Carl von Ossietzky University, Oldenburg, Germany
Kim G. Larsen	Aalborg University, Denmark
Radu Grosu	Institute of Computer Engineering, Vienna, Austria
Franjo Ivancic	Google, New York, USA
Xiaoqing Jin	Toyota Techinical Center, Los Angeles, USA
Joost-Pieter Katoen	RWTH Aachen University, Germany
Kai Lampka	Uppsala University, Sweden
Axel Legay	IRISA/INRIA, Rennes, France
Didier Lime	IRCCyN/École Centrale de Nantes, France
Giuseppe Lipari	Lille University, France
Oded Maler	Verimag/CNRS, Grenoble, France
Rahul Mangharam	University of Pennsylvania, USA
Nicolas Markey	LSV, CNRS & ENS Cachan, USA
Krishna S.	Indian Institute of Technology, Bombay, India
Cesar Sanchez	IMDEA Software Institute, Spain
Sriram Sankaranarayanan	University of Colorado Boulder, USA
Jeremy Sproston	University of Turin, Italy
Lothar Thiele	ETH Zurich, Switzerland
Ashish Tiwari	SRI International, USA
Louis-Marie Traonouez	IRISA/INRIA Rennes, France
Stavros Tripakis	Aalto University, Finland, and UC Berkeley, USA
Ashutosh Trivedi	Indian Institute of Technology, Bombay, India
Frits Vaandrager	Radboud University Nijmegen, The Netherlands
Enrico Vicario	University of Florence, Italy
Mahesh Viswanathan	University of Illinois, Urbana, USA

Additional Reviewers

Abbas, Houssam
Abdullah, Syed
  Md Jakaria
Adzkiya, Dieky
Akshay, S.
Andreychenko, Alexander
André, Étienne
Arechiga, Nikos
Asarin, Eugene
Baarir, Souheib
Ballabriga, Clément
Bartocci, Ezio
Bauer, Matthew S.
Bhave, Devendra
Biondi, Fabrizio
Bogomolov, Sergiy
Chatain, Thomas
Chen, Jian-Jia
Ciardo, Gianfranco
Dal Zilio, Silvano
Dalsgaard, Andreas
  Engelbredt
David, Nicolas
Dehnert, Christian
Estiévenart, Morgane
Fahrenberg, Uli
Fan, Chuchu
Fehnker, Ansgar

Ferrere, Thomas
Forget, Julien
Geeraerts, Gilles
Geltink, Gerben
Gretz, Friedrich
Haar, Stefan
Haddad, Axel
Jensen, Peter Gjøl
Jezequel, Loig
Jiang, Zhihao
Kekatos, Nikolaos
Kini, Dileep R.
Lanciani, Roberta
Markey, Nicolas
Mens, Irini-Eleftheria
Milios, Dimitrios
Minopoli, Stefano
Monmege, Benjamin
Morichetta, Andrea
Möhlmann, Eike
Ody, Heinrich
Olesen, Mads Chr.
Olmedo, Federico
Oortgiese, Arjan
Pagetti, Claire
Paolieri, Marco
Parker, David
Phawade, Ramchandra

Picaronny, Claudine
Poplavko, Peter
Praveen, M.
Quaas, Karin
Ratasich, Denise
Rodionova, Alena
Roohi, Nima
Roux, Olivier H.
Ruemmer, Philipp
S, Akshay
Samanta, Roopsha
Sankur, Ocan
Santinelli, Luca
Sassolas, Mathieu
Schobbens, Pierre-Yves
Seidner, Charlotte
Selyunin, Konstantin
Srivathsan, B
Stierand, Ingo
Sun, Jun
Taankvist, Jakob Haahr
van der Pol, Kevin
Volokitin, Sergei
Wille, Robert
Wognsen,
  Erik Ramsgaard
Zuliani, Paolo
Zutshi, Aditya

Contents

Verification and Control of Probabilistic Rectangular Hybrid Automata

Jeremy Sproston[✉]

Dipartimento di Informatica, University of Turin, Turin, Italy
sproston@di.unito.it

Abstract. Hybrid systems are characterised by a combination of discrete and continuous components. In many application areas for hybrid systems, such as vehicular control and systems biology, stochastic behaviour is exhibited. This has led to the development of stochastic extensions of formalisms, such as hybrid automata, for the modelling of hybrid systems, together with their associated verification and controller synthesis algorithms, in order to allow reasoning about quantitative properties such as "the vehicle's speed will reach 50kph within 10 seconds with probability at least 0.99". We consider verification and control of probabilistic rectangular hybrid automata, which generalise the well-known class of rectangular hybrid automata with the possibility of representing random behaviour of the discrete components of the system, permitting the modelling of the likelihood of faults, choices in randomised algorithms and message losses. Furthermore, we will also consider how probabilistic rectangular hybrid automata can be used as abstract models for more general classes of stochastic hybrid systems.

1 Background and Motivation

Verification and Control. The development of correct and reliable computer systems can benefit from formal verification and controller synthesis methods. Both of these kinds of methods necessitate the precise specification of a set of requirements that the system should satisfy: examples are the avoidance of an error state or the repeated completion of a task. A typical formal verification method is that of model checking [4,8], in which the system is modelled formally as a transition system (or in a high-level modelling formalism which has transition systems as its semantics), the requirements are modelled using temporal logic formulae or automata, and an algorithm determines whether the model of the system satisfies its requirements. Controller synthesis considers a partially-specified model of the system, which is subject to a method for restricting the behaviours of the system so that the restricted system satisfies a set of requirements. Controller synthesis is typically solved by representing the system as a two-player game, in which one player takes the role of the controller, which has the objective of

Supported by the MIUR-PRIN project CINA and the EU ARTEMIS Joint Undertaking under grant agreement no. 332933 (HoliDes).

S. Sankaranarayanan and E. Vicario (Eds.): FORMATS 2015, LNCS 9268, pp. 1–9, 2015.
DOI: 10.1007/978-3-319-22975-1_1

restricting system behaviours in order to achieve the requirements, and the other player takes the role of the system's environment [5,24,25]. A winning strategy of the first player constitutes a control mechanism that ideally can be used as a basis of an implementation, so that the system's behaviour is restricted in such a way as to satisfy the requirements.

Hybrid Automata. For the development of a wide range of computer systems, ranging from domestic appliances to vehicular controllers to medical devices, the interaction between the discrete behaviour of the digital system and the continuous behaviour of the environment in which the system operates is vital to understanding and reasoning about the overall system. Such systems are termed *hybrid systems. Hybrid automata* [1] have been introduced as a formalism for hybrid systems. A hybrid automaton consists of a finite directed graph and a set of real-valued variables, representing the discrete and continuous parts of the system, respectively. The discrete and continuous parts interact according to constraints on the continuous variables, and on their first derivatives, that label the nodes and edges of the graph. We refer to constraints on the first derivatives of variables as *flow constraints.* Variables can be *reset* to new values when an edge is traversed: resets are expressed as a relation between the previous value of the variable and its new value, and may involve nondeterministic choice (for example, a variable may be reset to any value in the interval $[1, 2]$ after taking an edge, where the choice of the new value is nondeterministic). For more information on hybrid automata, see [17,26].

The semantics of a hybrid automaton is represented by an infinite-state transition system: each state comprises a node and a valuation, that is a function associating a real value to each variable, and the transitions between states either correspond to the elapse of time or to the traversal of an edge of the hybrid automaton's graph. We say that the *continuous-time semantics* of hybrid automata corresponds to the case in which the durations of time-elapse transitions are taken from the set of non-negative reals, whereas the *discrete-time semantics* corresponds to the case in which time-elapse transitions can correspond to natural numbered durations (and duration 0) only.

Probabilistic Hybrid Automata. In many application contexts for hybrid systems, system behaviours may have dramatically varying degrees of likelihood. Examples of events that typically have a low probability include faults, message losses or extreme meteorological conditions. In such settings, the traditional formulation of verification and control problems, with their Boolean view of system correctness, is insufficient: for example, a message loss may be acceptable if the message can eventually be delivered within a specified deadline with high probability, and a lengthier journey of an automated vehicle may be acceptable in the case of uncharacteristically inclement weather. These facts have led to the development of the field of *stochastic hybrid systems.* In the literature, a number of formalisms have been considered, of which we mention piecewise-deterministic Markov processes [6,10], controlled discrete-time Markov processes [31] and stochastic hybrid automata [13,16]. In this paper, we consider *proba-*

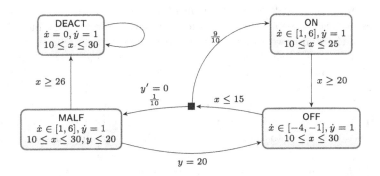

Fig. 1. A probabilistic hybrid automaton modelling a faulty thermostat

bilistic hybrid automata [27,28], which extend the classical hybrid automaton formalism with the possibility to associate probability to the edges of the model's graph. From another perspective, probabilistic hybrid automata can be viewed as finite-state Markov decision processes (for verification) or finite-state stochastic games (for control) extended with continuous variables and their associated constraints, in the same way that hybrid automata can be seen as finite-state graphs extended with variables and constraints. Probabilistic hybrid automata allow the modelling of probabilistic phenomena associated with the discrete part of the system, such as randomised choice between a finite number of alternatives of a digital controller, or the occurrence of a fault at the moment in which a discrete action is performed. The semantics of a probabilistic hybrid automaton is represented by an infinite-state Markov decision process (when considering verification) or stochastic game (when considering control). As for hybrid automata, either a continuous-time or discrete-time semantics can be considered.

An example of a probabilistic hybrid automaton modelling a faulty thermostat is shown in Figure 1. The ambient temperature is represented by the variable x, and variable y is a timer. When the heater is on (node ON or node MALF), the temperature increases at a rate between 1 and 6; when the heater is off (location OFF), the temperature changes at a rate between -4 and -1. The nodes ON and OFF corresponds to non-faulty behaviour, whereas the node MALF corresponds to the heater being on in the presence of a fault in the temperature sensor that means that the measurement of the temperature is temporarily unavailable. The system passes from ON to OFF, with probability 1, when the temperature is between 20 and 25, and from OFF to ON, with probability $\frac{9}{10}$, or to MALF, with probability $\frac{1}{10}$, when the temperature is between 10 and 15. The sensor fault means that the temperature can increase to a higher level in MALF than in ON. After a malfunction, either the system is deactivated if the temperature reaches an excessive level (location DEACT), or the system times-out exactly 20 time units after the location MALF was entered, in which case the heater is switched off. All edges of this example correspond to reaching a certain location with probability 1, apart from the probabilistically branching edge from OFF.

When considering verification problems of formalisms based on Markov decision processes, such as probabilistic hybrid automata, we must take into account the fact that there are two types of choice in the model, namely nondeterministic choice and probabilistic choice. A *strategy* is a function that, given a finite execution of the model, returns the next action to be performed from the set of possible actions that can be chosen nondeterministically in the final state of the execution. Hence, a strategy resolves the nondeterministic choice of the model, but not the probabilistic choice. Given a particular system requirement and a particular strategy, we can then reason about the probability of satisfying the requirement when the nondeterministic choice of the model is resolved by the strategy. In particular we are interested computing in the maximum or minimum probability of satisfying a requirement. Hence verification typically takes the form of considering a requirement φ (for example reachability, which specifies that a state with a node F is eventually reached, but more generally an ω-regular property), and a threshold $\lambda \in [0, 1]$, and then relies on determining whether the maximum probability of satisfying φ is at least λ. Controller synthesis approaches take a similar form although, recalling that control of probabilistic systems is typically stated in terms of a stochastic game [3,7], in that setting there are strategies belonging to each player. Hence we determine whether the controller player can guarantee that φ is satisfied with probability at least λ, regardless of the behaviour of the environment player.

2   Probabilistic Rectangular Hybrid Automata

Methods for the verification and control of probabilistic hybrid automata, like the associated methods for classical hybrid automata, must take into account the fact that the underling state space of the model is infinite; more precisely, the semantics of a probabilistic hybrid automaton is described in terms of an infinite-state Markov decision process or stochastic game. We can identify a number of techniques for the verification and control of probabilistic hybrid automata: in this paper, we will focus mainly on the approach of constructing a finite-state Markov decision process or stochastic game, which is then analysed using well-established methods. We also mention briefly alternative methods for verification of probabilistic hybrid automata: in [33], "symbolic" search through the state space of a probabilistic hybrid automaton using non-probabilistic methods is performed first, after which a finite-state Markov decision process is constructed and analysed; [14] uses stochastic satisfiability modulo theories to permit the verification of bounded requirements; [9] employs a stochastic semantics for more general stochastic hybrid systems, to which statistical model checking is applied.

Subclasses of hybrid automata are generally characterised in terms of the form of the constraints associated with the nodes and edges of the graph. In a similar way, we can characterise subclasses of probabilistic hybrid automata in terms of the form of constraints utilised. In particular, a *probabilistic rectangular automaton* is a probabilistic hybrid automaton for which the constraints on continuous variables take the form of conjunctions of comparisons of a variable with a constant, and flow constraints take the form of conjunctions of comparisons of a first derivative of a variable with a constant (that is, the constraints of probabilistic rectangular automata have the same form as the constraints used in non-probabilistic rectangular automata [19]). The example in Figure 1 is a probabilistic rectangular automaton. We say that a probabilistic rectangular automaton is *initialised* if the value of a variable is reset when making a transition between nodes with flow constraints on that variable.

We focus first on verification problems with the continuous-time semantics. Many verification problems for *probabilistic timed automata* [15,21], which are probabilistic rectangular automata for which variables increase at the same rate as real-time, are decidable. In particular, reachability verification for probabilistic timed automata is EXPTIME-complete [21,23]. These results can be generalised in the following way: letting $\mathcal{H}$ be a class of (non-probabilistic) hybrid automata, and letting $\mathcal{P}$ be the associated class of probabilistic hybrid automata (where $\mathcal{H}$ being associated with $\mathcal{P}$ means that the constraints used for both classes are of the same form), if the hybrid automata of the class $\mathcal{H}$ have finite bisimulation relations, then the probabilistic automata of the class $\mathcal{P}$ will have finite probabilistic bisimulation relations [30]. Given that, for an infinite-state Markov decision process with a finite probabilistic bisimulation relation, we can construct a finite-state Markov decision process that is equivalent with respect to a wide range of verification problems, this result means that a number of bisimulation-based decidability results for verification in the hybrid automata setting can be lifted to the probabilistic hybrid automata setting. For example, we can establish the decidability of a number of verification problems (including verification of requirements expressed as ω-regular properties or as probabilistic temporal logic formulae) for probabilistic hybrid automata that are probabilistic extensions of initialised multisingular automata [19] (a subclass of probabilistic rectangular automata), and also for classes incomparable to rectangular automata, such as o-minimal automata [22] and STORMED hybrid automata [32]. This result relies crucially on the fact that the hybrid automata considered have finite bisimulation relations: intuitively, bisimulation takes into account the branching structure of the system, which then allows results on bisimulation for hybrid automata to be lifted to the probabilistic case. Indeed, we note that the reduction from initialised rectangular automata to timed automata presented in [19], which results in a language equivalent and not necessarily bisimilar timed automaton, can be adapted to the probabilistic case [27,28], but obtains an over-approximate model, rather than a faithful representation of the original initialised probabilistic rectangular automaton.

Next we consider both verification and control of probabilistic rectangular automata with the discrete-time semantics. In this case, with the assumption that each variable is either non-decreasing (as time elapses) or remains within a bounded range throughout the model's execution, but without the assumption of initialisation, it is possible to obtain a finite probabilistic bisimulation relation of the model, and hence a finite-state Markov decision process or stochastic game [29]. Hence verification of many requirements, such as reachability, safety and

ω-regular properties, is EXPTIME-complete, whereas controller synthesis of the same classes of requirements can be done in NEXPTIME $\cap$ coNEXPTIME.

Instead, the problem of controller synthesis of probabilistic rectangular automata with the continuous-time semantics has received little attention so far. A notable exception is [12], in which a game version of probabilistic timed automata is considered.

3   Approximation with Probabilistic Hybrid Automata

A well-established approach in the field of modelling and verification is the construction of models that are amenable to verification and that over-approximate more faithful, but more difficult-to-verify models. In the context of classical hybrid automata, over-approximation generally consists of constructing a model whose set of observable behaviours contains all those of the original model. For example, rectangular automata have been used to approximate hybrid automata with more complex dynamics, in particular with respect to the constraints on the first derivatives of the variables [11,18]. In the context of probabilistic hybrid automata, or more general types of stochastic hybrid system, over-approximation generally consists of constructing a model for which, for any strategy σ of the original model, there exists a strategy σ' of the over-approximating model such that σ and σ' assign the same probability to observable events. This means that the maximum (minimum) probability of satisfying a certain requirement in the over-approximating model is no less than (no greater than) the probability of satisfying the requirement in the original model: that is, the maximum and minimum probabilities of a requirement in the over-approximating model bound those of the original model. Such an approach has been applied in the context of stochastic hybrid automata, in order to transform a model of a certain class of stochastic hybrid automata to a model of an more easily-analysed class of probabilistic hybrid automata. The applications of the approach have taken two forms: over-approximation of flows (which extends the results of [18] to the probabilistic setting) [2], and over-approximation of probabilistic resets. We concentrate our attention on the latter.

Recall that, in the probabilistic hybrid automaton framework described above, a variable can be reset when traversing an edge. The mechanism of resetting variables is generalised in [13,16,20] to allow the possibility to reset variables according to continuous probability distributions, such as the uniform or normal distributions, and thus allowing the modelling of an increased range of probabilistic phenomena, such as measurement errors and uncertain times of events. The resulting formalism is called stochastic hybrid automata. The approach taken in [13,16,20] to analyse a stochastic hybrid automaton S is to construct over-approximating probabilistic hybrid automaton P, where P is obtained from S by replacing the probabilistic choice involved in a probabilistic reset (over a continuous domain) by a discrete probabilistic choice (over a finite domain) between a number of intervals that cover the support of the probabilistic reset. After a probabilistic choice between the intervals, a nondeterministic choice is made within the chosen interval. For example, consider the probabilistic reset in which a variable x is updated according to a uniform distribution over $[1, 3]$. The probabilistic reset can be replaced by a discrete probabilistic choice over (for example) the intervals $[1, 2]$ and $[2, 3]$, each of which correspond to probability $\frac{1}{2}$, in accordance with the original uniform distribution, and which is then followed by a nondeterministic choice over the chosen interval. If, in all other respects (nodes, flows etc.), S and P are identical, then P over-approximates S.

The framework of over-approximation of probabilistic resets, with the aim of obtaining probabilistic rectangular automata, has been considered in [30]. In this context, stochastic hybrid automata are restricted as having rectangular-like constraints on flows and variables, although flows of the form $\dot{x} = y$, where y is constant as time passes, are allowed: this permits the modelling of situations in which the flow of a variable within a node is chosen according to a continuous probability distribution on entry to the node. With regard to the example of Figure 1, in node ON, rather than increase nondeterministically with a rate in $[1, 6]$, we could consider that the rate of increase of the temperature is chosen on entry to the node from the normal distribution with mean 3.5 and standard deviation 1, truncated to the interval $[1, 6]$. It is shown that such stochastic hybrid automata can be over-approximated by probabilistic rectangular automata.

References

1. Alur, R., Courcoubetis, C., Halbwachs, N., Henzinger, T.A., Ho, P.-H., Nicollin, X., Olivero, A., Sifakis, J., Yovine, S.: The algorithmic analysis of hybrid systems. TCS **138**(1), 3–34 (1995)
2. Assouramou, J., Desharnais, J.: Analysis of non-linear probabilistic hybrid systems. In: Proc. QAPL 2011. EPTCS, vol. 57, pp. 104–119 (2011)
3. Baier, C., Größer, M., Leucker, M., Bollig, B., Ciesinski, F.: Controller synthesis for probabilistic systems (extended abstract). In: Levy, J.-J., Mayr, E.W., Mitchell, J.C. (eds.) TCS 2004. IFIP, vol. 155, pp. 493–506. Springer, Heidelberg (2004)
4. Baier, C., Katoen, J.-P.: Principles of model checking. MIT Press (2008)
5. Büchi, J.R., Landweber, L.H.: Solving sequential conditions by finite-state strategies. Transactions of the AMS **138**, 295–311 (1969)
6. Bujorianu, M.L., Lygeros, J.: Reachability questions in piecewise deterministic Markov processes. In: Maler, O., Pnueli, A. (eds.) HSCC 2003. LNCS, vol. 2623, pp. 126–140. Springer, Heidelberg (2003)
7. Chatterjee, K., Henzinger, T.A.: A survey of stochastic omega-regular games. J. Comput. Syst. Sci. **78**(2), 394–413 (2012)
8. Clarke, E., Grumberg, O., Peled, D.: Model checking. MIT Press (2001)
9. David, A., Du, D., Larsen, K.G., Legay, A., Mikucionis, M., Poulsen, D.B., Sedwards, S.: Statistical model checking for stochastic hybrid systems. In: Proc. HSB 2012. EPTCS, vol. 92, pp. 122–136 (2012)
10. Davis, M.H.A.: Markov Models and Optimization. Chapman and Hall (1993)
11. Doyen, L., Henzinger, T.A., Raskin, J.-F.: Automatic rectangular refinement of affine hybrid systems. In: Pettersson, P., Yi, W. (eds.) FORMATS 2005. LNCS, vol. 3829, pp. 144–161. Springer, Heidelberg (2005)

12. Forejt, V., Kwiatkowska, M., Norman, G., Trivedi, A.: Expected reachability-time games. In: Chatterjee, K., Henzinger, T.A. (eds.) FORMATS 2010. LNCS, vol. 6246, pp. 122–136. Springer, Heidelberg (2010)
13. Fränzle, M., Hahn, E.M., Hermanns, H., Wolovick, N., Zhang, L.: Measurability and safety verification for stochastic hybrid systems. In: Proc. HSCC 2011, pp. 43–52. ACM (2011)
14. Fränzle, M., Teige, T., Eggers, A.: Engineering constraint solvers for automatic analysis of probabilistic hybrid automata. J. Log. Algebr. Program. **79**(7), 436–466 (2010)
15. Gregersen, H., Jensen, H.E.: Formal design of reliable real time systems. Master's thesis, Department of Mathematics and Computer Science, Aalborg University (1995)
16. Hahn, E.M.: Model checking stochastic hybrid systems. Dissertation, Universität des Saarlandes (2013)
17. Henzinger, T.A.: The theory of hybrid automata. In: Proc. LICS 1996, pp. 278–292. IEEE (1996)
18. Henzinger, T.A., Ho, P.-H., Wong-Toi, H.: Algorithmic analysis of nonlinear hybrid systems. IEEE TSE **43**, 540–554 (1998)
19. Henzinger, T.A., Kopke, P.W., Puri, A., Varaiya, P.: What's decidable about hybrid automata? J. Comput. Syst. Sci. **57**(1), 94–124 (1998)
20. Kwiatkowska, M., Norman, G., Segala, R., Sproston, J.: Verifying quantitative properties of continuous probabilistic timed automata. In: Palamidessi, C. (ed.) CONCUR 2000. LNCS, vol. 1877, pp. 123–137. Springer, Heidelberg (2000)
21. Kwiatkowska, M., Norman, G., Segala, R., Sproston, J.: Automatic verification of real-time systems with discrete probability distributions. TCS **286**, 101–150 (2002)
22. Lafferriere, G., Pappas, G., Sastry, S.: O-minimal hybrid systems. Mathematics of Control, Signals, and Systems **13**(1), 1–21 (2000)
23. Laroussinie, F., Sproston, J.: State explosion in almost-sure probabilistic reachability. IPL **102**(6), 236–241 (2007)
24. Pnueli, A., Rosner, R.: On the synthesis of a reactive module. In: Proc. POPL 1989, pp. 179–190. ACM Press (1989)
25. Ramadge, P.J., Wonham, W.M.: Supervisory control of a class of discrete-event processes. SIAM Journal of Control and Optimization **25**(1), 206–230 (1987)
26. Raskin, J.-F.: An introduction to hybrid automata. In: Handbook of Networked and Embedded Control Systems, pp. 491–518. Birkhäuser (2005)
27. Sproston, J.: Decidable model checking of probabilistic hybrid automata. In: Joseph, M. (ed.) FTRTFT 2000. LNCS, vol. 1926, pp. 31–45. Springer, Heidelberg (2000)
28. Sproston, J.: Model Checking for Probabilistic Timed and Hybrid Systems. PhD thesis, School of Computer Science, University of Birmingham (2001)
29. Sproston, J.: Discrete-time verification and control for probabilistic rectangular hybrid automata. In: Proc. QEST 2011, pp. 79–88. IEEE (2011)
30. Sproston, J.: Exact and approximate abstraction for classes of stochastic hybrid systems. In: Proc. AVOCS 2014. Electronic Communications of the EASST, pp. 79–88 (2014)
31. Tkachev, I., Mereacre, A., Katoen, J.-P., Abate, A.: Quantitative automata-based controller synthesis for non-autonomous stochastic hybrid systems. In: Proc. HSCC 2013, pp. 293–302. ACM (2013)

32. Vladimerou, V., Prabhakar, P., Viswanathan, M., Dullerud, G.E.: STORMED hybrid systems. In: Aceto, L., Damgård, I., Goldberg, L.A., Halldórsson, M.M., Ingólfsdóttir, A., Walukiewicz, I. (eds.) ICALP 2008, Part II. LNCS, vol. 5126, pp. 136–147. Springer, Heidelberg (2008)
33. Zhang, L., She, Z., Ratschan, S., Hermanns, H., Hahn, E.M.: Safety verification for probabilistic hybrid systems. European Journal of Control 18(6), 572–587 (2012)

Performance Evaluation of an Emergency Call Center: Tropical Polynomial Systems Applied to Timed Petri Nets

Xavier Allamigeon[2]([✉]), Vianney Bœuf[1,2,3], and Stéphane Gaubert[2]

[1] École des Ponts ParisTech, Marne-la-Vallée, France
[2] INRIA and CMAP, École polytechnique, CNRS, Palaiseau, France
{vianney.boeuf,xavier.allamigeon,Stephane.Gaubert}@inria.fr
[3] Brigade de sapeurs-pompiers de Paris, Paris, France

Abstract. We analyze a timed Petri net model of an emergency call center which processes calls with different levels of priority. The counter variables of the Petri net represent the cumulated number of events as a function of time. We show that these variables are determined by a piecewise linear dynamical system. We also prove that computing the stationary regimes of the associated fluid dynamics reduces to solving a polynomial system over a tropical (min-plus) semifield of germs. This leads to explicit formulæ expressing the throughput of the fluid system as a piecewise linear function of the resources, revealing the existence of different congestion phases. Numerical experiments show that the analysis of the fluid dynamics yields a good approximation of the real throughput.

1 Introduction

Motivations. Emergency call centers must handle complex and diverse help requests, involving different instruction procedures leading to the engagement of emergency means. An important issue is the performance evaluation of these centers. One needs in particular to estimate the dependence of quantities like throughputs or waiting times with respect to the allocation of resources, like the operators answering calls.

The present work originates from a case study relative to the current project led by Préfecture de Police de Paris (PP), involving the Brigade de sapeurs-pompiers de Paris (BSPP), of a new organization to handle emergency calls to Police (number 17), Firemen (number 18), and untyped emergency calls (number 112), in the Paris area. In addition to the studies and experimentation already carried out by PP and BSPP experts, we aim at developing formal methods, based on mathematical models. One would like to derive analytical formulæ or

The three authors were partially supported by the programme "Concepts, Systèmes et Outils pour la Sécurité Globale" of the French National Agency of Research (ANR), project "DEMOCRITE", number ANR-13-SECU-0007-01. The first and last authors were partially supported by the programme "Ingènierie Numérique & Sécurité" of ANR, project "MALTHY", number ANR-13-INSE-0003.

S. Sankaranarayanan and E. Vicario (Eds.): FORMATS 2015, LNCS 9268, pp. 10–26, 2015.
DOI: 10.1007/978-3-319-22975-1_2

performance bounds allowing one to confirm the results of simulation, to identify exceptional situations not easily accessible to simulations, and to obtain a general understanding of potential bottlenecks. In such applications, complex concurrency phenomena (available operators must share their time between different types of requests) are arbitrated by priority rules. The systems under study are beyond the known exactly solvable classes of Markov models, and it is desirable to develop new analytical results.

Contributions. We present an algebraic approach which allows to analyze the performance of systems involving priorities and modeled by timed Petri nets. Our results apply to the class of Petri nets in which the places can be partitioned in two categories: the routing in certain places is subject to priority rules, whereas the routing at the other places is free choice.

Counter variables determine the number of firings of the different transitions as a function of time. Our first result shows that, for the earliest firing rule, the counter variables are the solutions of a piecewise linear dynamical system (Sect. 3). Then, we introduce a fluid approximation in which the counter variables are real valued, instead of integer valued. Our main result shows that in the fluid model, the stationary regimes are precisely the solutions of a set of lexicographic piecewise linear equations, which constitutes a polynomial system over a tropical (min-plus) semifield of germs (Sect. 4). The latter is a modification of the ordinary tropical semifield. In essence, our main result shows that computing stationary regimes reduces to solving tropical polynomial systems.

Solving tropical polynomial systems is one of the most basic problems of tropical geometry. The latter provides insights on the nature of solutions, as well as algorithmic tools. In particular, the tropical approach allows one to determine the different congestion phases of the system.

We apply this approach to the case study of PP and BSPP. We introduce a simplified model of emergency call center (Sect. 2). This allows us to concentrate on the analysis of an essential feature of the organization: the two level emergency procedure. Operators at level 1 initially receive the calls, qualify their urgency, handle the non urgent ones, and transfer the urgent cases to specialized level 2 operators who complete the instruction. We solve the associated system of tropical polynomial equations and arrive at an explicit computation of the different congestion phases, depending on the ratio N_2/N_1 of the numbers of operators of level 2 and 1 (Sect. 5). Our analytical results are obtained only for the approximate fluid model. However, they are confirmed by simulations in which the original semantics of the Petri nets (with integer firings) is respected (Sect. 6).

Related work. Our approach finds its origin in the maxplus modeling of timed discrete event systems, introduced by Cohen, Quadrat and Viot and further developed by Baccelli and Olsder, see [1,2] for background. The idea of using counter variables already appeared in their work. However, the classical results only apply to restricted classes of Petri nets, like event graphs, or event graphs with weights as, for instance, in recent work by Cottenceau, Hardouin and Boimond [3]. The modeling of more general Petri nets by a combination of min-plus linear constraints and classical linear constraints was proposed by Cohen, Gaubert and Quadrat [4,5] and Libeaut and Loiseau (see [6]). The question of analyzing the behavior of the dynamical systems arising in this way was stated in a compendium of open problems in control theory [7]. A key discrepancy with the previously developed min-plus algebraic models lies in the *semantics* of the Petri nets. The model of [4,5] requires the routing to be based on open loop *preselection* policies of tokens at places, and it does not allow for priority rules. This is remedied in the present work: we show that priority rules can be written in a piecewise linear way, leading to a rational tropical dynamics.

Our approach is inspired by a work of Farhi, Goursat and Quadrat [8], who developed a min-plus model for a road traffic network. The idea of modeling priorities by rational min-plus dynamics first appeared there. By comparison, one aspect of novelty of the present approach consists in showing that this idea applies to a large class of Petri nets, mixing free choice and priority routing, so that its scope is not limited to a special class of road traffic models. Moreover, we provide a complete proof that these Petri nets follow the rational tropical dynamics, based on a precise analysis of the counter variables along an execution trace. Finally, the approach of [8] was developed in the discrete time case. A novelty of the present work consists in the treatment of the continuous time.

The analysis of timed Petri nets is a major question, which has been extensively studied. We refer to [9–12] for a non-exhaustive account on the topic, and to [13–15] for examples of tools implementing these techniques. An important effort has been devoted to the comparison of timed Petri nets with timed automata in terms of expressivity, see for instance [16,17]. The approaches developed in the aforementioned works aim at checking whether a given specification is satisfied (for instance, reachability, or more generally, a property expressed in a certain temporal logic), or at determining whether two Petri nets are equivalent in the sense of bisimulation. Hence, the emphasis is on issues different from the present ones: we focus on the performance analysis of timed Petri nets, by determining the asymptotic throughputs of transitions.

Acknowledgments. We thank Régis Reboul, from PP, in charge of the emergency call centers project, and Commandant Stéphane Raclot, from BSPP, for the information and insights they provided throughout the present work. We are grateful to the anonymous reviewers for their comments which helped to improve the presentation of this paper.

2   A Simplified Petri Net Model of an Emergency Call Center

In this section, we describe a call center answering to emergency calls according to a two level instruction procedure. In the new organization planned by PP together with BSPP [18], the emergency calls to the police (number 17), to

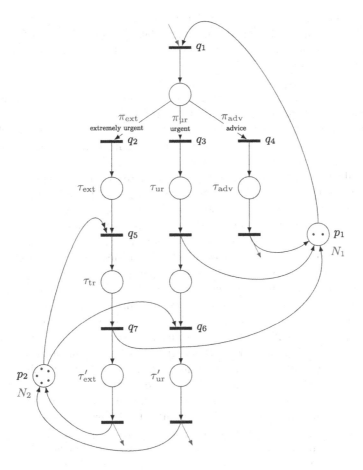

Fig. 1. Simplified Petri net model of the Parisian 17-18-112 emergency call center (organization in project). Blue arrows do not belong to the Petri net and symbolize the entrance and exit of calls in the system.

the firemen (18), and untyped emergency calls (European number 112) will be dealt with according to a unified procedure, allowing a strong coordination. Another important feature of this organization is that it involves a two level treatment. In the present paper, we limit our attention to the analysis of the two level procedure. We defer to a further work the analysis of the unification of the treatment of calls with heterogeneous characteristics. Hence, we discuss a simplified model, for academic purposes.

The first level operators filter the calls and assign them to three categories: extremely urgent (potentially life threatening situation), urgent (needing further instruction), and non urgent (e.g., call for advice). Non-urgent calls are dealt with entirely by level 1 operators. Extremely urgent and urgent calls are passed to level 2 operators. An advantage of this procedure lies in robustness considerations. In case of events generating bulk calls, the access to level 2 experts is protected by the filtering of level 1. This allows for better guarantees of service for the extremely urgent calls. Every call qualified as extremely urgent generates a 3-way conversation: the level 1 operator stays in line with the calling person when the call is passed to the level 2 operator. Such 3-way conversations were shown to contribute to the quality of the procedure [18]. Proper dimensioning of resources is needed to make sure that the synchronizations between level 1 and level 2 operators created by these 3-way conversations do not create bottlenecks. We focus on the case where the system is saturated, that is, there is an infinite queue of calls that have to be handled. We want to evaluate the performance of the system, i.e. the throughput of treatment of calls by the operators.

The call center is modeled by the timed Petri net of Fig. 1. We describe here the net in informal terms, referring the reader to Sect. 3 for more information on Petri nets and the semantics that we adopt. We use the convention that all transitions can be fired instantaneously. Holding times are attached to places.

Let us give the interpretation in terms of places and transitions. The number of operators of level 1 and 2 is equal to N_1 and N_2, respectively. The marking in places p_1 and p_2, respectively, represents the number of idle operators of level 1 or 2 at a given time. In particular, the number of tokens initially available in places p_1 and p_2 is N_1 and N_2. The initial marking of other places is zero. A firing of transition q_1 represents the beginning of a treatment of an incoming emergency call by a level 1 operator. The arc from place p_1 to transition q_1 indicates that every call requires one level 1 operator. The routing from transition q_1 to transitions q_2, q_3, q_4 represents the qualification of a call as extremely urgent, urgent, or non urgent (advice). The proportions of these calls are denoted by π_{ext}, π_{ur}, and π_{adv}, respectively, so that $\pi_{\text{ext}} + \pi_{\text{ur}} + \pi_{\text{adv}} = 1$. The proportions are known from historical data. The instruction of the call at level 1 is assumed to take a deterministic time τ_{ext}, τ_{ur}, or τ_{adv}, respectively, depending on the type of call.

After the treatment of a non urgent or urgent call at level 1, the level 1 operator is made immediately available to handle a new call. This is represented by the arcs leading to place p_1 from the transitions located below the places with holding times τ_{ur} and τ_{adv}. Before an idle operator of level 2 is assigned to the treatment of an urgent call, which is represented by the firing of transition q_6, the call is stocked in the place located above q_6. In contrast, the sequel of the processing of an extremely urgent call (transition q_5) requires the availability of a level 2 operator (incoming arc $p_2 \rightarrow q_5$) in order to initiate a 3-way conversation. The level 1 operator is released only after a time τ_{tr} corresponding to the duration of this conversation. This is represented by the arc $q_7 \rightarrow p_1$. The double arrow depicted on the arc $p_2 \rightarrow q_5$ means that level 2 operators are assigned to the treatment of extremely urgent calls (if any) in priority. The holding times τ'_{ext} and τ'_{ur} represent the time needed by a level 2 operator to complete the instruction of extremely urgent and urgent calls respectively.

3 Piecewise Linear Dynamics of Timed Petri Nets with Free Choice and Priority Routing

3.1 Timed Petri Nets: Notation and Semantics

A *timed Petri net* consists of a set $\mathcal{P}$ of places and a set $\mathcal{Q}$ of transitions, in which each place $p \in \mathcal{P}$ is equipped with a holding time $\tau_p \in \mathbb{R}_{>0}$ as well as an initial marking $M_p \in \mathbb{N}$. Given a place $p \in \mathcal{P}$, we respectively denote by p^{in} and p^{out} the sets of input and output transitions. Similarly, for all $q \in \mathcal{Q}$, the sets of upstream and downstream places are denoted by q^{in} and q^{out} respectively.

The semantics of the timed Petri net which we use in this paper is based on the fact that every token entering a place $p \in \mathcal{P}$ must stay at least τ_p time units in place p before becoming available for a firing of a downstream transition. More formally, a state of the semantics of the Petri net specifies, for each place $p \in \mathcal{P}$, the set of tokens located at place p, together with the age of these tokens since they have entered place p. In a given state σ, the Petri net can evolve into a new state σ' in two different ways:

(i) either a transition $q \in \mathcal{Q}$ is fired, which we denote $\sigma \xrightarrow{q} \sigma'$. This occurs when every upstream place contains a token whose age is greater than or equal to τ_p. The transition is supposed to be instantaneous. A token enters in each downstream place, and its age is set to 0;

(ii) or all the tokens remain at their original places, and their ages are incremented by the same amount of time $d \in \mathbb{R}_{\geq 0}$. This is denoted $\sigma \xrightarrow{d} \sigma'$.

In the initial state σ^0, all the tokens of the initial marking are supposed to have an "infinite" age, so that they are available for firings of downstream transitions from the beginning of the execution of the Petri net. The set of relations of the form $\xrightarrow{q}$ and $\xrightarrow{d}$ constitutes a timed transition system which, together with the initial state σ^0, fully describe the semantics of the Petri net. Note that in this semantics, transitions can be fired simultaneously. In particular, a given transition can be fired several times at the same moment. Recall that every holding time τ_p is positive, so that we cannot have any Zeno behavior.

In this setting, we can write any execution trace of the Petri net as a sequence of transitions of the form:

$$\sigma^0 \xrightarrow{d^0} \xrightarrow{q_1^0} \xrightarrow{q_2^0} \dots \xrightarrow{q_{n_0}^0} \sigma^1 \xrightarrow{d^1} \xrightarrow{q_1^1} \xrightarrow{q_2^1} \dots \xrightarrow{q_{n_1}^1} \sigma^2 \xrightarrow{d^2} \dots \tag{1}$$

where $d^0 \geqslant 0$ and $d^1, d^2, \dots > 0$. In other words, we consider traces in which we remove all the time-elapsing transitions of duration 0, except the first one, and in which time-elapsing transitions are separated by groups of firing transitions occurring simultaneously. We say that a transition q is *fired at the instant* t if there is a transition $\xrightarrow{q}$ in the trace such that the sum of the durations of the transitions of the form $\xrightarrow{d}$ which occur before in the trace is equal to t. The *state of the Petri net at the instant* t refers to the state of the Petri net appearing in the trace (1) after all transitions have been fired at the instant t.

In the rest of the paper, we stick to a stronger variant of the semantics, referred to as *earliest behavior* semantics, in which every transition q is fired

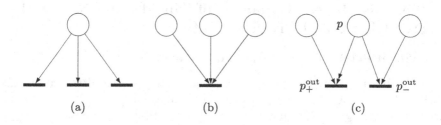

Fig. 2. Conflict, synchronization and priority configurations.

at the earliest moment possible. More formally, this means that in any state σ arising during the execution, a place p is allowed to contain a token of age (strictly) greater than τ_p only if no downstream transition can be fired (i.e. no transition $\xrightarrow{q}$ with $q \in p^{\text{out}}$ can be applied to σ). The motivation to study the earliest behavior semantics originates from our interest for emergency call centers, in which all calls are supposed to be handled as soon as possible.

3.2 Timed Petri Nets with Free Choice and Priority Routing

In this paper, we consider timed Petri nets in which places are free choice, or subject to priorities. This class of nets includes our model of emergency call center. Recall that a place $p \in \mathcal{P}$ is said to be *free choice* if either $|p^{\text{out}}| = 1$, or all the downstream transitions $q \in p^{\text{out}}$ satisfy $q^{\text{in}} = \{p\}$. The main property of such a place is the following: if one of the downstream transitions is activated (i.e. it can be potentially fired), then the other downstream transitions are also activated. A place is *subject to priority* if the available tokens in this place are routed to downstream transitions according to a certain priority rule. We denote by $\mathcal{P}_{\text{priority}}$ the set of such places. For the sake of simplicity, we assume that every $p \in \mathcal{P}_{\text{priority}}$ has precisely two downstream transitions, which we respectively denote by p_+^{out} and p_-^{out}. Then, if both transitions are activated, the tokens available in place p are assigned to p_+^{out} as a priority. Equivalently, in the execution trace of the Petri net, we have $\sigma \to^{p_-^{\text{out}}} \sigma'$ only if the transition $\to^{p_+^{\text{out}}}$ cannot be applied to the state σ. We remark that it is possible to handle multiple priority levels, up to making the presentation of the subsequent results more complicated.

To summarize, there are three possible place/transition patterns which can occur in the timed Petri nets that we consider, see Fig. 2. The first two ones involve only free choice places, and are referred to as *conflict* and *synchronization* patterns respectively. We denote by $\mathcal{P}_{\text{conflict}}$ the set of free choice places that have at least two output transitions, and by $\mathcal{Q}_{\text{sync}}$ the set of transitions such that every upstream place p satisfies $|p^{\text{out}}| = 1$. By definition, we have $\mathcal{P}_{\text{conflict}} \cap (\mathcal{Q}_{\text{sync}})^{\text{in}} = \emptyset$. The third configuration in Fig. 2 depicts a place p subject to priority. In order to distinguish p_+^{out} and p_-^{out}, we depict the arc leading to the transition p_+^{out} by a double arrow. We assume that p_+^{out} and p_-^{out} do not have edges coming from other places subject to priority. This allows to avoid inconsistency between priority rules (e.g. two priority places acting on the same transitions in a contradictory way). Consequently, as the non-priority places are free choice, the places $r \neq p$ located upstream p_+^{out} and p_-^{out} have only one output transition, as depicted in Fig. 2(c).

3.3   Piecewise Linear Representation by Counter Variables

Since we are interested in estimating the throughput of transitions in a Petri net, we associate with any transition $q \in \mathcal{Q}$ a counter variable z_q from $\mathbb{R}$ to $\mathbb{N}$ such that $z_q(t)$ represents the number of firings of transition q that occurred up to time t included. Similarly, given a place $p \in \mathcal{P}$, we denote $x_p(t)$ the number of tokens that have entered place p up to time t included. Note that the tokens initially present in place p are counted. More formally, $x_p(t)$ is given by the sum of the initial marking M_p and of the numbers of firings of transitions $q \in p^{\text{in}}$ which occurred before the instant t (included). We extend the counter variables x_p and z_q to $\mathbb{R}_{<0}$ by setting:

$$x_p(t) = M_p, \quad z_q(t) = 0, \quad \text{for all } t < 0 . \tag{2}$$

By construction, the functions x_p and z_q are non-decreasing. Besides, since they count tokens up to time t *included*, they are càdlàg functions, which means that they are right continuous and have left limits at any point. Given a càdlàg function f, we denote by $f(t^-)$ the left limit at the point t.

The goal of this section is to describe the dynamics of timed Petri nets with free choice and priority routing by means of a set of piecewise linear equality constraints over the counter variables. We provide an informal presentation of these constraints. First observe that we necessarily have:

$$\forall p \in \mathcal{P}, \quad x_p(t) = M_p + \sum_{q \in p^{\text{in}}} z_q(t), \tag{3}$$

as the initial marking M_p is counted in $x_p(t)$, and any token entering place p before the instant t must have been fired from an upstream transition $q \in p^{\text{in}}$ before. In a similar way, if $p \in \mathcal{P}_{\text{conflict}}$, the total number of times the downstream transitions have been fired before the instant t is necessarily equal to the number of tokens which entered place p before time $t - \tau_p$ (included). This is due to the fact that if a token enters p at the instant s, then it is consumed *exactly* at the instant $s + \tau_p$ (by definition of the earliest behavior semantics). This yields the identity:

$$\forall p \in \mathcal{P}_{\text{conflict}}, \quad \sum_{q \in p^{\text{out}}} z_q(t) = x_p(t - \tau_p). \tag{4}$$

Now consider a transition $q \in \mathcal{Q}_{\text{sync}}$. The number of times this transition is fired at the instant t is given by $z_q(t) - z_q(t^-)$. In each upstream place $p \in q^{\text{in}}$, the number of tokens which are available for firing q is equal to $x_p(t - \tau_p) - z_q(t^-)$. Indeed, since place p does not have any other output transition, the total number of tokens which have left place q until the instant t equals $z_q(t^-)$. By definition of the earliest behavior semantics, the number of firings of q at the instant t must be exactly equal to the minimum number of tokens available in places $p \in q^{\mathrm{in}}$. If we denote $\min(x, y)$ by $x \wedge y$, we consequently get:

$$\forall q \in \mathcal{Q}_{\mathsf{sync}}, \quad z_q(t) = \bigwedge_{p \in q^{\mathrm{in}}} x_p(t - \tau_p). \tag{5}$$

Finally, let us take a place $p \in \mathcal{P}_{\mathsf{priority}}$. Since the transition p_+^{out} has priority over p_-^{out}, the quantity $z_{p_+^{\mathrm{out}}}(t) - z_{p_+^{\mathrm{out}}}(t^-)$ must be equal to the minimal number of tokens available in the upstream places, including p. For every place $r \in (p_+^{\mathrm{out}})^{\mathrm{in}}$ distinct from p, the number of available tokens is given by $x_r(t - \tau_r) - z_{p_+^{\mathrm{out}}}(t^-)$ (recall that p_+^{out} is the only downstream transition of r). In contrast, the number of tokens available for firing in place p is equal to $x_p(t - \tau_p) - (z_{p_+^{\mathrm{out}}}(t^-) + z_{p_-^{\mathrm{out}}}(t^-))$. We deduce that we have:

$$\forall p \in \mathcal{P}_{\mathsf{priority}}, \quad z_{p_+^{\mathrm{out}}}(t) = \left(x_p(t - \tau_p) - z_{p_-^{\mathrm{out}}}(t^-) \right) \wedge \bigwedge_{\substack{r \in (p_+^{\mathrm{out}})^{\mathrm{in}} \\ r \neq p}} x_r(t - \tau_r). \tag{6}$$

The number of tokens from place p which are available for the transition p_-^{out} after the firings of p_+^{out} is given by $x_p(t - \tau_p) - (z_{p_+^{\mathrm{out}}}(t^-) + z_{p_-^{\mathrm{out}}}(t^-)) - (z_{p_+^{\mathrm{out}}}(t) - z_{p_+^{\mathrm{out}}}(t^-))$. Hence, we obtain:

$$\forall p \in \mathcal{P}_{\mathsf{priority}}, \quad z_{p_-^{\mathrm{out}}}(t) = \left(x_p(t - \tau_p) - z_{p_+^{\mathrm{out}}}(t) \right) \wedge \bigwedge_{\substack{r \in (p_-^{\mathrm{out}})^{\mathrm{in}} \\ r \neq p}} x_r(t - \tau_r). \tag{7}$$

We summarize the previous discussion by the following result:

Theorem 1. *Given any execution trace of a timed Petri net with free choice and priority routing, the counter variables x_p ($p \in \mathcal{P}$) and z_q ($q \in \mathcal{Q}$) satisfy the constraints (3)–(7) for all $t \geqslant 0$, together with the initial conditions (2).*

Notice that, if we do not restrict to the earliest behavior semantics, the constraints (4)–(7) are relaxed to inequalities.

So far, we have described the dynamics of timed Petri nets in the continuous time setting. However, since the Petri net of our case study is a model of a real system which is implemented in silico, we need to investigate the dynamics in discrete time as well. In more details, assuming that all the quantities τ_p are multiple of an elementary time step $\delta > 0$, the discrete-time version of the semantics of the Petri net restricts the transitions $\xrightarrow{d}$ to the case where d is a multiple of δ. In this case, on top of being càdlàg, the functions x_p and z_q are constant on any interval of the form $[k\delta, (k+1)\delta)$ for all $k \in \mathbb{N}$. Then, we can verify that the following result holds:

Proposition 1. *In the discrete time semantics, the counter variables x_p and z_q satisfy the constraints (3)–(7) for all $t \geqslant 0$, independently of the choice of the elementary time step δ.*

In other words, the dynamics in continuous-time is a valid representation of the dynamics in discrete time which allows to abstract from the discretization time step. We also note that we can refine the constraint given in (6) by replacing the left limit $z_{p_-^{out}}(t^-)$ by an explicit value:

$$\forall p \in \mathcal{P}_{priority}, \quad z_{p_+^{out}}(t) = \begin{cases} \left(x_p(t-\tau_p) - z_{p_-^{out}}(t-\delta)\right) \\ \quad \wedge \bigwedge_{r \in (p_+^{out})^{in}, r \neq p} x_r(t-\tau_r) & \text{if } t \in \delta\mathbb{N}, \\ \left(x_p(t-\tau_p) - z_{p_-^{out}}(t)\right) \\ \quad \wedge \bigwedge_{r \in (p_+^{out})^{in}, r \neq p} x_r(t-\tau_r) & \text{otherwise.} \end{cases} \quad (8)$$

(Here and below, we denote by $\delta\mathbb{N}$ the set $\{0, \delta, 2\delta, \dots\}$.) The system formed by the constraints (3)–(5), (7), (8) is referred to as the δ-*discretization of the Petri net dynamics*.

The only source of non-determinism in the model that we consider is the routing policy in the conflict pattern (Fig. 2(a)). In the sequel, we assume that the tokens are assigned according to a stationary probability distribution. Given a free choice place $p \in \mathcal{P}_{conflict}$, we denote by π_{qp} the probability that an available token is assigned to the transition $q \in p^{out}$. In the following, we consider a *fluid approximation of the dynamics* of the system, in which the x_p and z_q are nondecreasing càdlàg functions from $\mathbb{R}$ to itself, and the routing policy degenerates in sharing the tokens in fractions π_{qp}. Equivalently, the fluid dynamics is defined by the constraints (3)–(7) and the following additional constraints:

$$\forall p \in \mathcal{P}_{conflict}, \forall q \in p^{out}, \quad z_q(t) = \pi_{qp} x_p(t - \tau_p). \quad (9)$$

Note that the latter equation is still valid in the context of discrete time. By extension, the system formed by the constraints (3)–(5), (7)–(9) is referred to as the δ-*discretization of the fluid dynamics*.

Example 1. We illustrate Theorem 1 on the Petri net of Fig. 1. It can be shown that the fluid dynamics is described by the following reduced system

$$z_1(t) = N_1 + z_5(t - \tau_{tr}) + \pi_{ur} z_1(t - \tau_{ur}) + \pi_{adv} z_1(t - \tau_{adv})$$
$$z_5(t) = \left(N_2 + z_5(t - \tau_{tr} - \tau'_{ext}) + z_6(t - \tau'_{ur}) - z_6(t^-)\right) \wedge \pi_{ext} z_1(t - \tau_{ext}) \quad (10)$$
$$z_6(t) = \left(N_2 + z_5(t - \tau_{tr} - \tau'_{ext}) + z_6(t - \tau'_{ur}) - z_5(t)\right) \wedge \pi_{ur} z_1(t - \tau_{ur})$$

which involve the counter variables z_1, z_5 and z_6 only (here, z_i denotes z_{q_i} for brevity). These variables correspond to the key characteristics of the system. They respectively represent the number of calls handled at level 1, and the number of extremely urgent and urgent calls handled at level 2, up to time t. All the other counter variables can be easily obtained from z_1, z_5 and z_6.

We point out that in Fig. 1, we omitted to specify the holding time of some places. By default, this holding time is set to a certain $\tau_\varepsilon > 0$, and is meant to be negligible w.r.t. the other holding times. For the sake of readability, we slightly modified the holding times $\tau_t, \tau_{\mathrm{ur}}, \ldots$ to incorporate the effect of τ_ε, so that τ_ε does not appear in dynamics given in (10).

4   Computing Stationary Regimes

We investigate the stationary regimes of the fluid dynamics associated with Petri nets with free choice and priority routing. More specifically, our goal is to characterize the non-decreasing càdlàg solutions x_p and z_q of the dynamics which behave ultimately as affine functions $t \mapsto u + \rho t$ ($u \in \mathbb{R}$ and $\rho \in \mathbb{R}_{\geqslant 0}$). By *ultimately*, we mean that the property holds for t large enough. In this case, the scalar ρ corresponds to the asymptotic throughput of the associated place or transition. However, if the functions x_p and z_q are continuous, and a fortiori if they are affine, their values at points t and t^- coincide, and then, the effect of the priority rule on the dynamics vanishes (see (6)). Hence, looking for ultimately affine solutions of the continuous time equations might look as an ill posed problem, if one interprets it in a naive way. However, looking for the ultimately affine solutions of the δ-discretization of the fluid dynamics is a perfectly well posed problem. In other words, we aim at determining the solutions x_p and z_q of the discrete dynamics which coincide with affine functions at points $k\delta$ for all sufficiently large $k \in \mathbb{N}$. These solutions are referred to as the *stationary solutions* of the dynamics. As we shall prove in Theorem 2, the characterization of these solutions does not depend on the value of δ, leading to a proper definition of ultimately affine solutions of the continuous time dynamics.

In order to determine the stationary regimes, we use the notion of germs of affine functions. We introduce an equivalence relation $\sim$ over functions from $\mathbb{R}$ to itself, defined by $f \sim g$ if $f(t)$ and $g(t)$ are equal for all $t \in \delta\mathbb{N}$ sufficiently large. A *germ of function* (at point infinity) is an equivalence class of functions with respect to the relation $\sim$. For brevity, we refer to the germs of affine functions as *affine germs*, and we denote by (ρ, u) the germ of the function $t \mapsto u + \rho t$. In this setting, our goal is to determine the affine germs of the counter variables of the Petri net in the stationary regimes.

Given two functions f and g of affine germs (ρ, u) and (ρ', u') respectively, it is easy to show that $f(t) \leqslant g(t)$ for all sufficiently large $t \in \delta\mathbb{N}$ if, and only if, the couple (ρ, u) is smaller than or equal to (ρ', u') in the lexicographic order. Moreover, the affine germ of the function $f + g$ is simply given by the germ $(\rho + \rho', u + u')$, which we denote by $(\rho, u) + (\rho', u')$ by abuse of notation. As a consequence, affine germs provide an ordered group. Let us add to this group a greatest element $\top$, with the convention that $\top + (\rho, u) = (\rho, u) + \top = \top$. Then, we obtain the *tropical (min-plus) semiring of affine germs* $(\mathbb{G}, \wedge, +)$, where $\mathbb{G}$ is defined as $\{\top\} \cup \mathbb{R}^2$, and for all $x, y \in \mathbb{G}$, $x \wedge y$ stands for the minimum of x and y in lexicographic order (extended to $\top$). Since in $\mathbb{G}$, the addition plays the role of the multiplicative law, the additive inversion defined by $-(\rho, u) := (-\rho, -u)$ corresponds to a division over $\mathbb{G}$. This makes $\mathbb{G}$ a semifield, i.e., in loose terms, a structure similar to a field, except that the additive law has no inverse. Finally, we can define the multiplication by a scalar $\lambda \in \mathbb{R}$ by $\lambda(\rho, u) := (\lambda\rho, \lambda u)$. When $\lambda \in \mathbb{N}$, this can be understood as an exponentiation operation in $\mathbb{G}$.

Instantiating the functions x_p and z_q by affine asymptotics $t \mapsto u_p + t\rho_p$ and $t \mapsto u_q + t\rho_q$ in the δ-discretization of the fluid dynamics leads to the following counterparts of the constraints (3), (5), (7) and (9), the variables being now elements of the semifield $\mathbb{G}$ of germs:

$$\forall p \in \mathcal{P}, \qquad (\rho_p, u_p) = (0, M_p) + \sum_{q \in p^{\text{in}}} (\rho_q, u_q) \tag{11a}$$

$$\forall p \in \mathcal{P}_{\text{conflict}}, \forall q \in p^{\text{out}}, \qquad (\rho_q, u_q) = \pi_{qp}(\rho_p, u_p - \rho_p \tau_p) \tag{11b}$$

$$\forall q \in \mathcal{Q}_{\text{sync}}, \qquad (\rho_q, u_q) = \bigwedge_{p \in q^{\text{in}}} (\rho_p, u_p - \rho_p \tau_p) \tag{11c}$$

$$\forall p \in \mathcal{P}_{\text{priority}}, \qquad (\rho_{p_-^{\text{out}}}, u_{p_-^{\text{out}}}) = (\rho_p - \rho_{p_+^{\text{out}}}, u_p - \rho_p \tau_p - u_{p_+^{\text{out}}}) \tag{11d}$$

$$\wedge \bigwedge_{r \in (p_-^{\text{out}})^{\text{in}}, r \neq p} (\rho_r, u_r - \rho_r \tau_r)$$

Given $p \in \mathcal{P}_{\text{priority}}$, the transposition of (6) (or equivalently (8)) to germs is more elaborate due to the occurrence of the left limit $x_{p_-^{\text{out}}}(t^-)$. We obtain:

$$(\rho_{p_+^{\text{out}}}, u_{p_+^{\text{out}}}) = \begin{cases} (\rho_p - \rho_{p_-^{\text{out}}}, u_p - \rho_p \tau_p - u_{p_-^{\text{out}}}) \\ \quad \wedge \bigwedge_{r \in (p_+^{\text{out}})^{\text{in}}, r \neq p} (\rho_r, u_r - \rho_r \tau_r) \quad \text{if } \rho_{p_-^{\text{out}}} = 0, \\ \bigwedge_{r \in (p_+^{\text{out}})^{\text{in}}, r \neq p} (\rho_r, u_r - \rho_r \tau_r) \quad \text{otherwise.} \end{cases} \tag{11e}$$

The correctness of these constraints is stated in the following result:

Theorem 2. *The affine germs of the stationary solutions of the δ-discretization of the fluid dynamics are precisely the solutions of System (11) such that $\rho_p, \rho_q \geqslant 0$ ($p \in \mathcal{P}, q \in \mathcal{Q}$).*

Since the expressions at the right hand side of the constraints of System (11) involve minima of linear terms, these expressions can be interpreted as fractional functions over the tropical semifield $\mathbb{G}$. In this way, System (11) can be thought of as a set of tropical polynomial constraints (or more precisely, rational constraints).

The solutions of tropical polynomial systems is a topic of current interest, owing to its relations with fundamental algorithmic issues concerning classical polynomial system solving over the reals. Here, we describe a simple method to solve System (11), which is akin to *policy search* in stochastic control. Observe that System (11) corresponds to a fixpoint equation $(\rho, u) = f(\rho, u)$, where the function f can be expressed as the infimum $\bigwedge_\pi f^\pi$ of finitely many linear (affine) maps f^π. In more details, every function f^π is obtained by selecting one term for each minimum operation $\bigwedge$ occurring in the constraints (for instance, in (11c),

Table 1. The normalized throughputs ρ_1, ρ_5 and ρ_6 as piecewise linear functions of N_2/N_1.

	$0 \leqslant N_2/N_1 \leqslant r_1$	$r_1 \leqslant N_2/N_1 \leqslant r_2$	$r_2 \leqslant N_2/N_1$
ρ_1/ρ^*	$\dfrac{\bar{\tau}}{\pi_{\text{ext}}(\tau_{\text{tr}} + \tau'_{\text{ext}})} \dfrac{N_2}{N_1}$	1	1
ρ_5/ρ^*	$\dfrac{\bar{\tau}}{\tau_{\text{tr}} + \tau'_{\text{ext}}} \dfrac{N_2}{N_1}$	π_{ext}	π_{ext}
ρ_6/ρ^*	0	$\dfrac{\bar{\tau}}{\tau'_{\text{ur}}} \dfrac{N_2}{N_1} - \dfrac{\pi_{\text{ext}}(\tau_{\text{tr}} + \tau'_{\text{ext}})}{\tau'_{\text{ur}}}$	π_{ur}

we select one term $(\rho_p, u_p - \rho_p \tau_p)$ with $p \in q^{\text{in}}$). For every selection π, we can solve the associated linear system $(\rho, u) = f^\pi(\rho, u)$, and under some structural assumptions on the Petri net, the solution (ρ^π, u^π) is unique. If $f^\pi(\rho^\pi, u^\pi) = f(\rho^\pi, u^\pi)$, i.e. in every constraint, the term we selected is smaller than or equal to the other terms appearing in the minimum, then (ρ^π, u^π) forms a solution of System (11) associated with the selection π. Otherwise, the selection π does not lead to any solution. Iterating this technique over the set of selections provides all the solutions of System (11). Every iteration can be done in polynomial time. However, since there is an exponential number of possible selections, the overall time complexity of the method is exponential in the size of the Petri net.

5   Application to the Emergency Call Center

We now apply the results of Sect. 4 to determine the stationary regimes of the fluid dynamics associated with our timed Petri net model of emergency call center. As in Example 1, we consider the subsystem reduced to the variables z_1, z_5 and z_6. The corresponding system of constraints over the germ variables (u_1, ρ_1), (u_5, ρ_5) and (u_6, ρ_6) is given by:

$$(\rho_1, u_1) = \big(\rho_5 + \pi_{\text{ur}}\rho_1 + \pi_{\text{adv}}\rho_1, \tag{12a}$$
$$N_1 + (u_5 - \rho_5\tau_{\text{tr}}) + \pi_{\text{ur}}(u_1 - \rho_1\tau_{\text{ur}}) + \pi_{\text{adv}}(u_1 - \rho_1\tau_{\text{adv}})\big)$$

$$(\rho_5, u_5) = \begin{cases} \big(\rho_5, N_2 + u_5 - \rho_5(\tau_{\text{tr}} + \tau'_{\text{ext}})\big) \wedge \pi_{\text{ext}}(\rho_1, u_1 - \rho_1\tau_{\text{ext}}) & \text{if } \rho_6 = 0 \\ \pi_{\text{ext}}(\rho_1, u_1 - \rho_1\tau_{\text{ext}}) & \text{if } \rho_6 > 0 \end{cases}$$
$$\tag{12b}$$

$$(\rho_6, u_6) = \big(\rho_6, N_2 - \rho_5(\tau_{\text{tr}} + \tau'_{\text{ext}}) + (u_6 - \rho_6\tau'_{\text{ur}})\big) \wedge \pi_{\text{ur}}(\rho_1, u_1 - \rho_1\tau_{\text{ur}}) \tag{12c}$$

We solve System (12) using the method described previously, and report the value of the throughputs ρ_1, ρ_5 and ρ_6 in Table 1. We normalize these values by a quantity ρ^* which corresponds to the throughput (of transition q_1) in an "ideal" call center which involves as many level 2 operators as necessary, i.e. $N_2 = +\infty$. Then, the throughput ρ^* is given by $N_1/\bar{\tau}$, where $\bar{\tau} := \pi_{\text{ext}}(\tau_{\text{ext}} + \tau_{\text{tr}}) + \pi_{\text{ur}}\tau_{\text{ur}} + \pi_{\text{adv}}\tau_{\text{adv}}$ represents the average time of treatment at level 1.

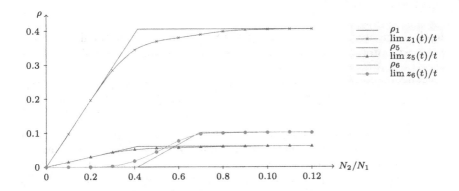

Fig. 3. Comparison of the throughputs of the real system with the theoretical throughputs (fluid model), for $(\tau_{\text{ext}}, \tau_{\text{ur}}, \tau_{\text{adv}}, \tau_{\text{tr}}, \tau'_{\text{ext}}, \tau'_{\text{ur}}) = (16, 20, 27, 7, 61, 28)$, $(\pi_{\text{ext}}, \pi_{\text{ur}}, \pi_{\text{adv}}) = (0.15, 0.25, 0.6)$ and $N_1 = 10$. In this case, $r_1 = 0.413$ and $r_2 = 0.688$.

As shown in Table 1, the ratios ρ_1/ρ^*, ρ_5/ρ^* and ρ_6/ρ^* are piecewise linear functions of the ratio N_2/N_1. The non-differentiability points are given by:

$$r_1 := \frac{\pi_{\text{ext}}(\tau_{\text{tr}} + \tau'_{\text{ext}})}{\bar{\tau}} \qquad r_2 := \frac{\pi_{\text{ext}}(\tau_{\text{tr}} + \tau'_{\text{ext}}) + \pi_{\text{ur}}\tau'_{\text{ur}}}{\bar{\tau}}.$$

They separate three phases:

(i) when N_2/N_1 is strictly smaller than r_1, the number of level 2 operators is so small that some extremely urgent calls cannot be handled, and no urgent call is handled. This is why the throughput of the latter calls at level 2 is null. Also, level 1 operators are slowed down by the congestion of level 2, since, in the treatment of an extremely urgent call, a level 1 operator cannot be released until the call is handled by a level 2 operator.

(ii) when N_2/N_1 is between r_1 and r_2, there are enough level 2 operators to handle all the extremely urgent calls, which is why the throughput ρ_5 is equal to ρ_1 multiplied by the proportion π_{ext} of extremely urgent calls. As a consequence, level 2 is no longer slowing down level 1 (the throughput ρ_1 reaches its maximal value ρ^*). However, the throughput of urgent calls at level 2 is still limited because N_2 is not sufficiently large.

(iii) if N_2/N_1 is larger than r_2, the three throughputs reach their maximal values. This means that level 2 is sufficiently well-staffed w.r.t. level 1.

This analysis provides a qualitative method to determine an optimal dimensioning of the system in stationary regimes. Given a fixed N_1, the number N_2 of level 2 operators should be taken to be the minimal integer such that $N_2/N_1 \geqslant r_2$. This ensures that the level 2 properly handles the calls transmitted by the level 1 (all calls are treated). Then, N_1 should be the minimal integer such that $\rho_1 = \frac{N_1}{\bar{\tau}}$ dominates the arrival rate of calls.

6   Experiments

We finally compare the analytical results of Sect. 5, obtained in the fluid setting, with the asymptotic throughputs of the Petri net provided by simulations.

Asymptotic behavior of the non-fluid dynamics. We have implemented the δ-discretization of the non-fluid dynamics (Equations (3)–(5), (7) and (8)) since this setting is the closest to reality. Recall that, in this case, tokens are routed towards transitions q_2, q_3 and q_4 randomly according to a constant probability distribution. We assume that holding times are given by integer numbers of seconds, so that we take $\delta = 1\,\mathrm{s}$. In this way, we compute the quantities $z_1(t)$, $z_5(t)$ and $z_6(t)$ by induction on $t \in \mathbb{N}$ using the equations describing the dynamics. In the simulations, we choose holding times and probabilities which are representative of the urgency of calls.

Figure 3 compares the limits when $t \to +\infty$ of the throughputs $z_1(t)/t$, $z_5(t)/t$, $z_6(t)/t$ of the "real" system, with the throughputs ρ_1, ρ_5 and ρ_6 of the stationary solutions which have been determined in Sect. 5. The latter are simply computed using the analytical formulæ of Table 1. We estimate the limits of the throughput $z_i(t)/t$ by evaluating the latter quantity for $t = 10^6\,\mathrm{s}$. As shown in Fig. 3, these estimations confirm the existence of three phases, as described in the previous section. The convergence of $z_i(t)/t$ towards the throughputs ρ_i is mostly reached in the two extreme phases. In the intermediate phase, the difference between the limit of $z_i(t)/t$ and the throughput ρ_i is more important. This originates from the stochastic nature of the routing, which causes more variations in the realization of the minima in the $z_i(t)$: the throughput of q_6 increases and the throughputs of q_1 and q_5 decrease.

Asymptotic behavior of the fluid dynamics. We also simulate the discrete-time fluid dynamics (using Equations (3)–(5) and (7)–(9)). In most cases, we observe that the corresponding asymptotic throughputs converge to the throughputs of the stationary solutions. However, there are also cases in which they slightly differ. In the experiments we have made, this happens only in the intermediate phase, when $r_1 < N_2/N_1 < r_2$. Such cases suggest the existence of other kinds of stationary regimes of the dynamics, in which the system oscillates between different phases. We remark that these phenomena appear to be related to the existence of arithmetical relationships between the holding times of places.

7   Concluding Remarks

We have shown that timed Petri nets with free choice and priority routing can be analyzed by means of tropical geometry. This allows us to identify the congestion phases in the fluid version of the dynamics of the Petri net. We have applied this method to a model of emergency call center. Numerical experiments indicate that these theoretical results are representative of the real dynamics.

In future work, we aim at comparing the behaviors of the fluid deterministic model and of the discrete stochastic one. We also plan to study uniqueness conditions of the stationary regimes, and conditions under which convergence of the fluid dynamics to a stationary regime can be shown. We will refine our Petri net model of emergency call center to take care of the heterogeneous nature of level 2 (calls to police and firemen require different instruction times). To this end, it will be helpful to implement an analysis tool determining automatically the stationary regimes of a timed Petri net given in input. Finally, we plan to analyze the treatment times of the system, on top of the throughputs.

References

1. Baccelli, F., Cohen, G., Olsder, G., Quadrat, J.: Synchronization and Linearity. Wiley (1992)
2. Heidergott, G., Olsder, G.J., van der Woude, J.: Max Plus at work. Princeton University Press (2006)
3. Cottenceau, B., Hardouin, L., Boimond, J.: Modeling and control of weight-balanced timed event graphs in dioids. IEEE Trans. Autom. Control **59**(5) (2014)
4. Cohen, G., Gaubert, S., Quadrat, J.: Asymptotic throughput of continuous timed Petri nets. In: 34th Conference on Decision and Control (1995)
5. Cohen, G., Gaubert, S., Quadrat, J.: Algebraic system analysis of timed Petri nets. In: Gunawardena, J. (ed.) Idempotency. Publications of the Isaac Newton Institute, pp. 145–170. Cambridge University Press (1998)
6. Libeaut, L.: Sur l'utilisation des dioïdes pour la commande des systèmes à événements discrets. Thèse, École Centrale de Nantes (1996)
7. Plus, M.: Max-plus-times linear systems. In: Open Problems in Mathematical Systems and Control Theory. Springer (1999)
8. Farhi, N., Goursat, M., Quadrat, J.P.: Piecewise linear concave dynamical systems appearing in the microscopic traffic modeling. Linear Algebra and Appl. (2011)
9. Berthomieu, B., Diaz, M.: Modeling and verification of time dependent systems using time Petri nets. IEEE Transactions on Software Engineering **17**(3) (1991)
10. Abdulla, P.A., Nylén, A.: Timed Petri nets and BQOs. In: Colom, J.-M., Koutny, M. (eds.) ICATPN 2001. LNCS, vol. 2075, pp. 53–70. Springer, Heidelberg (2001)
11. Gardey, G., Roux, O.H., Roux, O.F.: Using zone graph method for computing the state space of a time Petri net. In: Larsen, K.G., Niebert, P. (eds.) FORMATS 2003. LNCS, vol. 2791. Springer, Heidelberg (2004)
12. Jacobsen, L., Jacobsen, M., Møller, M.H., Srba, J.: Verification of timed-arc Petri nets. In: Černá, I., Gyimóthy, T., Hromkovič, J., Jefferey, K., Královič, R., Vukolić, M., Wolf, S. (eds.) SOFSEM 2011. LNCS, vol. 6543, pp. 46–72. Springer, Heidelberg (2011)
13. Berthomieu, B., Vernadat, F.: Time Petri nets analysis with TINA. In: QEST 2006. IEEE (2006)
14. Lime, D., Roux, O.H., Seidner, C., Traonouez, L.-M.: Romeo: a parametric model-checker for Petri nets with stopwatches. In: Kowalewski, S., Philippou, A. (eds.) TACAS 2009. LNCS, vol. 5505, pp. 54–57. Springer, Heidelberg (2009)
15. Byg, J., Jørgensen, K.Y., Srba, J.: TAPAAL: editor, simulator and verifier of timed-arc Petri nets. In: Liu, Z., Ravn, A.P. (eds.) ATVA 2009. LNCS, vol. 5799, pp. 84–89. Springer, Heidelberg (2009)

16. Bérard, B., Cassez, F., Haddad, S., Lime, D., Roux, O.H.: Comparison of the expressiveness of timed automata and time Petri nets. In: Pettersson, P., Yi, W. (eds.) FORMATS 2005. LNCS, vol. 3829, pp. 211–225. Springer, Heidelberg (2005)

17. Srba, J.: Comparing the expressiveness of timed automata and timed extensions of Petri nets. In: Cassez, F., Jard, C. (eds.) FORMATS 2008. LNCS, vol. 5215, pp. 15–32. Springer, Heidelberg (2008)

18. Raclot, S., Reboul, R.: Analysis of the new call center organization at PP and BSPP. Personal communication to the authors (2015)

Language Preservation Problems in Parametric Timed Automata

Étienne André[1] and Nicolas Markey[2]

[1] Université Paris 13, Sorbonne Paris Cité, LIPN, CNRS, Villetaneuse, France
[2] LSV, CNRS and ENS Cachan, Cachan, France

Abstract. Parametric timed automata (PTA) are a powerful formalism to model and reason about concurrent systems with some unknown timing delays. In this paper, we address the (untimed) language- and trace-preservation problems: *given a reference parameter valuation, does there exist another parameter valuation with the same untimed language (or trace)?* We show that these problems are undecidable both for general PTA, and even for the restricted class of L/U-PTA. On the other hand, we exhibit decidable subclasses: 1-clock PTA, and 1-parameter deterministic L-PTA and U-PTA.

1 Introduction

Timed Automata. Timed Automata (TA hereafter) were introduced in the 1990's [1] as an extension of finite automata with *clock variables*, which can be used to constrain the delays between transitions. Despite this flexibility, TA enjoy efficient algorithms for checking reachability (and many other properties), which makes them a perfect model for reasoning about real-time systems.

In TA, clock variables are compared to (integer) constants in order to allow or disallow certain transitions. The behaviour of a TA may heavily depend on the *exact* values of the constants, and slight changes in any constant may give rise to very different behaviours. In many cases however, it may be desirable to optimise the values of some of the constants of the automaton, in order to exhibit better performances. The question can then be posed as follows: *given a TA and one of the integer constant in one of the clock constraints of this TA, does there exist another value of this constant for which the TA has the exact set of (untimed) behaviours?* We call this problem the *language-preservation problem*.

A special case of this problem occurs naturally in recent approaches for dealing with *robustness* of timed automata [7,11,12]. The question asked there is whether the behaviour of a timed automaton is preserved when the clock constraints are slightly (parametrically) enlarged. In most of those cases, the existence of a parametric enlargement for which the behaviours are the same as in the original TA has been proved decidable.

This work is partially supported by the ANR national research program PACS (ANR-14-CE28-0002), and by European projects ERC EQualIS (308087) and FET Cassting (601148).

S. Sankaranarayanan and E. Vicario (Eds.): FORMATS 2015, LNCS 9268, pp. 27–43, 2015.
DOI: 10.1007/978-3-319-22975-1_3

For the general problem however, the decidability status remains open. To the best of our knowledge, the only approach to this problem is a procedure (called the *inverse method* [3]) to compute a dense set of parameter valuations around a reference valuation v_0.

Parametric Timed Automata. In this paper, we tackle the language-preservation problem using *Parametric Timed Automata* (PTA) [2]. A PTA is a TA in which some of the constants in clock constraints are replaced by variables (a.k.a. parameters), whose value is not fixed a priori. The classical problem (sometimes called the *EF-emptiness problem*) in PTA asks whether a given target location of a PTA is reachable for some valuation of the parameter(s). This problem was proven undecidable in various settings: for integer parameter valuations [2], for bounded rational valuations [10], etc. The proofs of these results exist in many different flavours, with various bounds on the number of parameters and clocks needed in the reductions.

To the best of our knowledge, the only non-trivial syntactic subclass of PTA with decidable EF-emptiness problem is the class of L/U-PTA [8]. These models have the following constraint: each parameter may only be used either always as a lower bound in the clock constraints, or always as an upper bound. For those models, the problems of the emptiness, universality and finiteness (for integer-valued parameters) of the set of parameters under which a target location is reachable, are decidable [6,8]. In contrast, the AF-emptiness problem (*"does there exist a parameter valuation for which a given location is eventually visited along any run?"*) is undecidable for L/U-PTA [9].

Our Contributions. In this paper, we first prove that the language-preservation problem (and various related problems) is undecidable in most cases. While it might not look surprising given the numerous undecidability results about PTA, it contrasts with the decidability results proved so far for robustness of TA.

Our second contribution is to devise a semi-algorithm that solves the language- and trace-preservation problems (and actually synthesizes all parameter valuations yielding the same untimed language (or trace) as a given reference valuation), in the setting of *deterministic* PTA. Finally, we also study the decidability of these emptiness problems for subclasses of PTA: we prove decidability for PTA with a single clock, undecidability for L/U-PTA, and decidability for two subclasses of L/U-PTA with a single parameter.

A long version of this paper, with detailed proofs, is available as [4].

2   Definitions

Constraints. We fix a finite set $X = \{x_1, \ldots, x_H\}$ set of real-valued variables (called *clocks* in the sequel). A clock valuation w is a function $w\colon X \to \mathbb{R}_{\geq 0}$. We define two operations on clock valuations: for $d \in \mathbb{R}_{\geq 0}$ and a clock valuation w, we let $w + d$ be the valuation w' such that $w'(x) = w(x) + d$ for all $x \in X$. Given a set $R \subseteq X$ and a valuation w, we let $w[R \mapsto 0]$ be the clock valuation w' such that $w'(x) = 0$ if $x \in R$, and $w'(x) = w(x)$ otherwise. We also fix a finite set $P = \{p_1, \ldots, p_M\}$ of rational-valued variables called *parameters*. A parameter valuation v is a function $v \colon P \to \mathbb{Q}_{\geq 0}$. In the sequel, we will have to handle clocks and parameters together. A valuation is a function $u \colon X \cup P \to \mathbb{R}_{\geq 0}$ such that $u_{|X}$ is a clock valuation and $u_{|P}$ is a parameter valuation.

An *atomic constraint* over X and P is an expression of the form either $x \prec p + c$ or $x \prec c$ or $p \prec c$, where $\prec \in \{<, \leq, =, \geq, >\}$, $x \in X$, $p \in P$ and $c \in \mathbb{Z}$. The symbols $\top$ and $\bot$ are also special cases of atomic constraints. Notice that our constraints are a bit more general than in the setting of [2], where only atomic constraints of the form $x \prec p$ and $x \prec c$ (and $\top$ and $\bot$) were allowed. A *constraint* over X and P is a conjunction of atomic constraints. An *(atomic) diagonal constraint* is a constraint of the form $x - x' \prec p + c$ or $x - x' \prec c$, where x and x' are two clocks and $\prec$, p and c are as in plain atomic constraints. A *generalized constraint* over X and P is a conjunction of atomic constraints and atomic diagonal constraints.

Remark 1. We mainly focus here on continuous time (clock valuations take real values) and rational-valued parameters, as defined above. However, several of our results remain valid for discrete time (clock valuations take integer values) and integer-valued parameters. We will mention it explicitly when it is the case.

A valuation u satisfies an atomic constraint $\varphi \colon x \prec p + c$, which we denote $u \models \varphi$, whenever $u(x) \prec u(p) + c$. The definition for diagonal constraints is similar. All valuations satisfy $\top$, and none of them satisfies $\bot$. A valuation u satisfies a constraint Φ, denoted $u \models \Phi$ if, and only if, it satisfies all the conjuncts of Φ. A constraint Φ is said to depend on $D \subseteq X \cup P$ whenever for any two valuations u and u' such that $u(d) = u'(d)$ for all $d \in D$, it holds $u \models \Phi$ if, and only if, $u' \models \Phi$. A parameter constraint is a constraint that depends only on P.

Given a partial valuation u and a constraint Φ, we write $u(\Phi)$ for the constraint obtained by replacing each $z \in \text{dom}(u)$ in Φ with $u(z)$. The resulting constraint depends on $(X \cup P) \setminus \text{dom}(u)$.

We denote by $\Phi{\downarrow}_V$ the *projection* of constraint Φ onto $V \subseteq X \cup P$, *i.e.* the constraint obtained by eliminating the clock variables. This projection has the property that $v \models \Phi{\downarrow}_P$ if, and only if, there is an extension u of v to $X \cup P$ such that $u \models \Phi$. Such projections can be computed *e.g.* using Fourier-Motzkin elimination. We also define the *time elapsing* of Φ, denoted by $\Phi^{\uparrow}$, as the *generalized constraint* over X and P obtained from C by delaying an arbitrary amount of time. The time-elapsing of a constraint Φ is obtained by preserving all differences between any pair of clocks, preserving lower bounds, and relaxing upper bounds on atomic (single-clock) constraints. Given $R \subseteq X$, we define the *reset* of Φ, denoted $[\Phi]_R$, as the constraint obtained from Φ by resetting the clocks in R, and keeping the other clocks unchanged. This is computed in the same way as projection above (*i.e.*, it corresponds to an existential quantification), and then adding constraints $x = 0$ on the clocks being reset.

Parametric Timed Automata. Parametric timed automata are an extension of the class of timed automata to the parametric case, where parameters can be used within guards and invariants in place of constants [2].

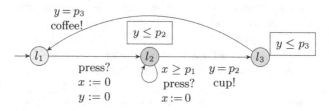

Fig. 1. An example of a coffee machine

Definition 2. *A* parametric timed automaton *(PTA for short) is a tuple* $A = \langle \Sigma, L, l_{init}, X, P, I, \rightarrow \rangle$, *where:* Σ *is a finite set of actions;* L *is a finite set of locations;* $l_{init} \in L$ *is the initial location;* X *is a set of clocks;* P *is a set of parameters;* I *assigns to every* $l \in L$ *a constraint* $I(l)$, *called the* invariant *of* l; $\rightarrow$ *is a set of edges* (l, g, a, R, l'), *also denoted by* $l \xrightarrow{g,a,R} l'$, *where* $l, l' \in L$ *are the source and destination locations,* g *is a constraint (called* guard *of the transition),* $a \in \Sigma$, *and* $R \subseteq X$ *is a set of clocks to be reset.*

For example, the PTA in Fig. 1 has 3 locations, 3 parameters p_1, p_2, p_3 and 2 clocks x, y.

A PTA is *deterministic* if, for all $l \in L$, for all $a \in \Sigma$, there is at most one edge $(l', g, a', R, l'') \in \rightarrow$ with $l' = l$ and $a' = a$.

Given a PTA $A = \langle \Sigma, L, l_{init}, X, P, I, \rightarrow \rangle$, and a parameter valuation v, $v(A)$ denotes the automaton obtained from A by substituting every occurrence of a parameter p_i by the constant $v(p_i)$ in the guards and invariants. Then $v(A)$ is a timed automaton [1], whose semantics is defined as follows:

Definition 3. *Given a PTA* $A = \langle \Sigma, L, l_{init}, X, P, I, \rightarrow \rangle$, *and a parameter valuation* v, *the semantics of* $v(A)$ *is given by the timed transition system* $\langle Q, q_{init}, \Rightarrow \rangle$ *where* $Q = \{(l, w) \in L \times (\mathbb{R}_{\geq 0})^X \mid w(v(I(l)))$ *evaluates to true*$\}$, *with initial state* $q_{init} = (l_{init}, \mathbf{0}_X)$, *and* $((l, w), (d, e), (l', w')) \in \Rightarrow$ *whenever* e *is a transition* $(l, g, a, R, l') \in \rightarrow$ *such that* $(l, w + d) \models I(l) \wedge g$ *and* $w' = (w + d)[R \mapsto 0]$.

A run of a TA is a maximal sequence of consecutive transitions of the timed transition system associated with the TA. For the sake of readability, we usually write runs as $s_0 \xrightarrow{d_0, e_0} s_1 \xrightarrow{d_1, e_1} \cdots \xrightarrow{d_{m-1}, e_{m-1}} s_m \cdots$. With *maximal*, we mean that a run may only be finite if its last state has no outgoing transition. The timed word associated to a run $s_0 \xrightarrow{d_0, e_0} s_1 \xrightarrow{d_1, e_1} \cdots \xrightarrow{d_{m-1}, e_{m-1}} s_m \cdots$ is the (finite or infinite) sequence $(d_i, a_i)_i$ such that for all i, a_i is the action of edge e_i. The corresponding untimed word is the word $(a_i)_i$. The timed (resp. untimed) language of a TA A, denoted by $Lang^t(A)$ (resp. $Lang(A)$), is the set of timed (resp. untimed) words associated with maximal runs of this automaton. Similarly, the untimed trace associated with the run $s_0 \xrightarrow{d_0, e_0} s_1 \xrightarrow{d_1, e_1} \cdots \xrightarrow{d_{m-1}, e_{m-1}} s_m \cdots$ is the sequence $(l_i, a_i)_i$ s.t. l_i is the location of s_i and a_i is the action of edge e_i. The set of untimed traces of A is denoted by $Traces(A)$.

Given a state $s = (l, w)$, state s is said reachable in A under valuation v if s belongs to a run of $v(A)$; a location l is reachable if some state (l, w) is.

Following [8], we now define a symbolic semantics for PTA:

Definition 4 (Symbolic State). *A symbolic state of a PTA A is a pair (l, C) where $l \in L$ is a location, and C is a generalized constraint.*

Given a parameter valuation v, a state $s = (l, C)$ is v-compatible if $v \models C{\downarrow}_P$. The computation of the state space relies on the Succ operation. The initial state of A is $s_{init} = (l_{init}, (X = 0)^{\uparrow} \wedge I(l_{init}))$. Given a symbolic state $s = (l, C)$ and a transition $e = (l, g, a, R, l')$, we let $\mathsf{Succ}_e(s) = \{(l', C') \mid C' = ([(C \wedge g)]_R)^{\uparrow} \cap I(l')\}$ (notice that this is a singleton); we write $\mathsf{Succ}(s) = \bigcup_{e \in \rightarrow} \mathsf{Succ}_e(s)$. By extension, given a set S of states, $\mathsf{Succ}(S) = \{s' \mid \exists s \in S \text{ s.t. } s' \in \mathsf{Succ}(s)\}$. Again, this gives rise to an infinite-state transition system, called the *parametric zone graph* later on. A symbolic run of a PTA from some symbolic state s_0 is an infinite sequence of edges $(e_i)_i$ such that there exists a sequence of symbolic states $(s_i)_i$ such that $s_{i+1} = \mathsf{Succ}_{e_i}(s_i)$. Two runs are said *equivalent* when they correspond to the same sequences of edges (hence the same sequences of locations), but may visit different symbolic states. In this paper, we address the following two problems:

Definition 5. *Given a PTA A and a parameter valuation v,*

- *the* language preservation problem *asks whether there exists another parameter valuation v' giving rise to the same untimed language (i.e. such that $Lang(v(A)) = Lang(v'(A))$);*
- *the* trace preservation problem *asks whether there exists another parameter valuation v' giving rise to the same set of traces (i.e. such that $Traces(v(A)) = Traces(v'(A))$) [3].*

The continuous *versions of those problems additionally require that the language (resp. set of traces) is preserved under any intermediary valuation of the form $\lambda \cdot v + (1 - \lambda) \cdot v'$, for $\lambda \in [0, 1]$ (with the classical definition of addition and scalar multiplication).*

3 Undecidability of the Preservation Problems in General

3.1 Undecidability of the Language Preservation Problem

Theorem 6. *The language preservation problem for PTA with one parameter is undecidable (both over discrete and continuous time, and for integer and rational parameter valuations).*

Proof. The proof proceeds by a reduction from the halting problem for two-counter machines. We begin with reducing this problem into the classical problem of reachability emptiness ("EF-emptiness") in parametric timed automata ("*does there exist a valuation of the parameters under which the target location is reachable?*"). We then extend the construction in order to prove the result.

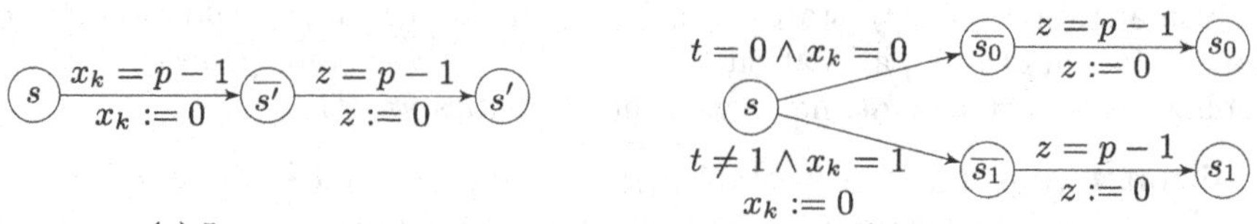

(a) Incrementing c_k

(b) Decrementing c_k

Fig. 2. Encoding a 2-counter machine

Fix a deterministic two-counter machine $\mathcal{M} = \langle S, T \rangle$. Our reduction requires four clocks: clock t will serve as a tick (it will be reset exactly every p time units, where p is the parameter), and we will have a correspondence between a configuration of the timed automaton and a configuration of the two-counter machine exactly when $t = 0$; clocks x_1 and x_2 are used to store the values of counters c_1 and c_2 of $\mathcal{M}$, with the correspondence $x_1 = c_1$ and $x_2 = c_2$ when $t = 0$; finally, clock z is used to count the number of steps of the two-counter machine: this is where our construction differs from the classical ones (e.g., [2,9]), as we use the parameter p to bound the length (number of step) of the possible halting computation of the two-counter machine. As the number of steps is bounded by p, we know that both c_1 and c_2 are also bounded by p. The parametric timed automaton A associated with $\mathcal{M}$ is defined as follows:

- its set of states has two copies of the set S of states of $\mathcal{M}$: for each $s \in S$, there is a *main state* with the same name s, and an *intermediary state* named $\overline{s}$;
- each state of A carries four self-loops, associated with each of the four clocks and resetting that clock when it reaches value p. This requires a global invariant enforcing the clocks t, x_1 and x_2 to remain below p, and clock z to remain below $p - 1$.
  Then each transition $(s, c_k + +, s')$ incrementing counter c_k in $\mathcal{M}$ gives rise to a transition from state s to state $\overline{s'}$, with guard is $x_k = p - 1$, and resetting clock x_k (see Figure 2a). Each transition of the form $(s, c_k - -, s_0, s_1)$ is handled similarly, but gives rise to two transitions: one transition from s to $\overline{s_0}$ with guard $t = 0 \wedge x_k = 0$, and one transition from s to $\overline{s_1}$ with guard $x_k = 1$ and resetting clock x_k. Then, from each state $\overline{s}$ of A, there is a transition to the corresponding state s with guard $z = p - 1$ and resetting z (see Figure 2b).

This construction works as we expect (assuming p is an integer, which is easily checked by a simple initial module): clock t is reset every p time units (which cannot be seen in Figure 2 because we omitted the self-loops); clocks x_1 and x_2 keep track the values of c_1 and c_2, with the correspondence $x_k = c_k$ when $t = 0$; finally, clock z counts the number of steps (when considering the value of this clock when $t = 0$, it encodes a counter that is incremented at every transition of $\mathcal{M}$). Notice that clock z counts, but for the moment, it does not impose any constraint on the length of the simulation. Notice also that this construction currently does *not* correctly encode the runs of $\mathcal{M}$, since the counters are encoded modulo p.

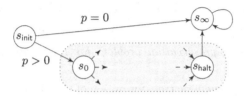

Fig. 3. Encoding the halting problem into the language-preservation problem

We modify our construction by adding the extra condition that $0 < t < p$ (or equivalently $1 \leq t \leq p-1$) to the guards $z = p-1$ of the transitions leaving the intermediary states. This way, when z (seen as a counter) has value $p-1$, no transition is available from any state s (or a transition to a sink state can be added), so that the encoding stops after mimicking $p-1$ steps of the execution of $\mathcal{M}$. With this reduction, we have:

Lemma 7. *The two-counter machine $\mathcal{M}$ has a computation of length at most $p-1$ reaching s_{halt} from $(s_0, (c_1 = 0, c_2 = 0))$ if, and only if, there is a run reaching the corresponding state s_{halt} from $(s_0, (t = 0, x_1 = 0, x_2 = 0, z = 0))$ in $v(\mathsf{A})$.*

We now explain how to adapt this construction to the language preservation problem. The idea is depicted on Figure 3 (where all transitions are labeled with the same letter a): when $p = 0$, the automaton accepts the untimed language $\{a^\omega\}$. Notice that the guard $p = 0$ in the automaton can be encoded by requiring $t = 0 \wedge t = p$. On the other hand, when $p > 0$, we have to enter the main part of the automaton A, and mimic the two-counter machine. From our construction above, the untimed language is the same if, and only if, the halting location is reachable.

Finally, notice that our reduction is readily adapted to the discrete-time setting, and/or to integer-valued parameters. □

Remark 8. Our construction uses both p and $p-1$ in the clock constraints, as well as parametric constraints $p = 0$ and $p > 0$. This was not allowed in [2] (where three parameters were needed to compare the clocks with p, $p-1$ and $p+1$). Our construction could be adapted to only allow comparisons with $p-1$, while keeping the number of clocks unchanged:

- the parametric constraints $p = 0$ and $p > 0$ could be respectively encoded as $(x = p) \wedge (x = 0)$ and $(x < p) \wedge (x = 0)$;
- transitions guarded by $x = p$ (which always reset the corresponding clock x) would then be encoded by a first transition with $x = p-1$ resetting x and moving to a copy of A where we *remember* that the value of x should be shifted up by $p-1$. All locations have invariant $x \leq 1$, and transitions guarded with $x = 1$, resetting x and returning to the main copy of A. The same can be achieved for the other clocks, even if it means duplicating A 16 times (twice for each clock).

3.2   Undecidability of the Trace Preservation Problem.

In this section, we provide two proofs of the following result:

Theorem 9. *The trace-preservation problem for PTA with one parameter is undecidable.*

The first proof is by a generic transformation of timed automata without zero-delay cycle into one-location timed automata; it involves diagonal constraints, but only a fixed number of parametric clocks. The second proof does not involve diagonal constraints, but it uses an unbounded number of parametric clocks.

Encoding Timed Automata into One-Location Timed Automata. Our first proof relies on the encoding of TA (with the restriction that no sequence of more than k transitions may occur in zero delay, for some k; equivalently, those timed automata may not contain zero-delay cycles) into an equivalent TA with a single location; this reduction uses $k \times |L|$ additional clocks (where $|L|$ denotes the number of clocks of A) and requires diagonal constraints, *i.e.* constraints comparing clocks with each other (of the form $x_1 - x_2 \prec c$).

This result extends to PTA, and the additional clocks are non-parametric. Using this reduction, the undecidability of the language preservation (Theorem 6) trivially extends to trace preservation. Let us first show the generic result for TA.

Proposition 10. *Let A be a TA in which, for some k, no sequence of more than k transitions occur in zero delay. Then there exists an equivalent TA A′ with only one location and $k \times |A| + 1$ additional clocks, such that the timed languages of A and A′ are the same.*

Proof. We begin with the intuition behind our construction: each location ℓ of the automaton A is encoded using an extra clock x_ℓ, with the following property: when location ℓ is entered, the clock x_ℓ is reset. An extra clock x_0 is reset along each transition. Then when the automaton is visiting ℓ, it holds $x_\ell - x_0 = 0$. However, the converse does not hold, because several transitions may be taken in zero delay.

To overcome this difficulty, we use $k+1$ copies of x_ℓ, numbered x_ℓ^1 to x_ℓ^{k+1}. The exact encoding is then as follows: each transition (ℓ, g, a, R, ℓ') is encoded as several self-loops on the single location of A′:

- one self-loop is guarded with the conjunction of the guard g and of the constraint $x_0 > 0 \land \bigvee_{i \geq 1} \left[x_\ell^i - x_0 = 0 \land \bigwedge_{\ell'' \in L} x_{\ell''}^{i+1} - x_0 > 0 \right]$; it is labeled with a, and resets the clocks in R as well as x^0 and $x_{\ell'}^1$.
- for each $1 \leq i \leq k$, one self-loop is guarded with the conjunction of g and $x_0 = 0 \land \left[x_\ell^i = 0 \land \bigwedge_{\ell'' \in L} x_{\ell''}^{i+1} > 0 \right]$; it is labeled with a and resets the clocks in R and $x_{\ell'}^{i+1}$.

With this transformation, we get a one-to-one correspondence between the run in A and in A′, so that both automata have the same timed language.   □

The above transformation can be applied to a PTA, with the property that the timed language is preserved for any valuation of the parameters. Proposition 10 can be extended to PTA as follows:

Proposition 11. *Let* A *be a PTA with no zero-delay cycle (for any valuation of the parameters). Then there exists an equivalent PTA* A′ *with only one location and* $k \times |A| + 1$ *additional clocks such that for any parameter valuation* v, *the timed languages of* $v(A)$ *and* $v(A′)$ *coincide.*

Now, for one-location automata, the untimed languages and the sets of untimed traces coincide. Applying this to our construction of Theorem 6 proves our result.

An Ad-Hoc Proof Avoiding Diagonal Constraints. We propose a second proof, where we avoid the use of diagonal constraints, at the expense of using unboundedly many parametric clocks. This proof follows the reduction of the proof of Theorem 6, but with only four states: one state is used to initialize the computation, and the other three states are then visited cyclically, in order to first update the information about the counters and then about the state of the two-counter machine. The location of the machine is then stored using as many clocks as the number of locations of the machine: the clock with least value (less than or equal to p) corresponds to the current location.

Formally, from a deterministic two-counter machine $\mathcal{M}$ with n states, we build a PTA with $n + 4$ (parametric) clocks: n clocks q_1 to q_n are used to store the current location of $\mathcal{M}$ (the only clock with value less than or equal to p corresponds to the current state of $\mathcal{M}$), two clocks x_1 and x_2 store the values of the two counters, clock t measures periods of p time units (where p is the parameter), and an extra clock r stores temporary information along the run. Intuitively, the PTA cycles between two main states: it goes from the first one to the second one for updating the values of the counters, and from the second one back to the first one for updating clocks encoding the location of $\mathcal{M}$.

This is a direct encoding of a two-counter machine as a PTA. It is easily adapted to follow the reduction scheme of Theorem 6, which entails our result. Note that by adding two extra clocks and two intermediary locations, we can get rid of comparisons with $p-1$ and $p+1$, and use only constraints of the form $x \sim p$.

3.3   Undecidability of the Robust Language-Preservation Problem

The robust language-preservation problem extends discrete one by additionally requiring that the language is preserved on a "line" of valuations originating from the reference valuation. This is not the case of our previous proofs, which require the parameter to take integer values for the reduction to be correct. In this section, we depart from the "discrete" setting of the previous section, and use rational-valued parameters and the full power of real-valued clocks.

Theorem 12. *The robust language preservation problem for PTA with one (possibly bounded) parameter is undecidable.*

Proof. We begin with a reduction[1] of the halting problem for counter machines to the EF-emptiness problem for 1-parameter PTA. The proof is then adapted to the language-preservation problem in the same way as for the proof of Theorem 9.

---

[1] This reduction for the EF problem we present here is an unpublished proof by Didier Lime; we develop the reduction here for our paper to be self-contained.

The encoding of the two-counter machine is as follows: it uses one rational-valued parameter p, one clock t to tick every time unit, and one parametric clock x_i for storing the value of each counter c_i, with $x_i = 1 - p \cdot c_i$ when $t = 0$.

An initial transition is used to initialize the values of x_1 and x_2 to 1, while it sets t to zero. It also checks that the value of p is in $(0, 1)$. Zero-tests are easily encoded by checking whether $x_i = 1$ while $t = 0$. Incrementation is achieved by resetting clock x_i when it reaches $1 + p$, while the other clocks are reset when they reach 1. This way, exactly one time unit elapses in this module, and clock x_i is decreased by a, which corresponds to incrementing c_i. Decrementing is handled similarly. Finally, notice that the use of the constraint $x_i = 1 + p$ can be easily avoided, at the expense of an extra clock.

One easily proves that if a (deterministic) two-counter machine $\mathcal{M}$ halts, then by writing P for the maximal counter value reached during its finite computation, the PTA above has a path to the halting location as soon as $0 < p \leq 1/P$. Conversely, assume that the machine does not halt, and fix a parameter value $0 < p < 1$. If some counter of the machine eventually exceeds $1/p$, then at that moment in the corresponding execution in the associated PTA, the value of t when $x_i = 1 + p$ will be larger than 1, and the automaton will be in a deadlock. If the counters remain bounded below $1/p$, then the execution of the two-counter machine will be simulated correctly, and the halting state will not be reached.

We now adapt this construction to our language preservation problem. We have to forbid the infinite non-halting run mentioned above. For this, we add a third counter, which will be incremented every other step of the resulting three-counter machine, in the very same way as in the proof of Theorem 9. We then have the property that if $\mathcal{M}$ does not halt, the simulation in the associated PTA will be finite. Adding states s_{init} and s_∞ as in Fig. 3, we get the result that the two-counter machine $\mathcal{M}$ halts if, and only if, there is a parameter value $v_0(p) > 0$ such that all values $v(p)$ between 0 and $v_0(p)$ give rise to timed automata $v(\mathsf{A})$ accepting the same language. □

3.4 Undecidability of the Robust Trace Preservation Problem

Combining Theorem 12 and the arguments of Section 3.2, we get:

Theorem 13. *The robust trace-preservation problem is undecidable for PTA with one (possibly bounded) parameter.*

4 A Semi-algorithm for the Trace Preservation Synthesis

In this section, we propose a semi-algorithm that solves the following *parameter-synthesis* problem: *"given a PTA* A *and a parameter valuation* v, *synthesize parameter valuations that yield the same language (or trace set) as* v*".*

The inverse method proposed in [3] outputs a parameter constraint that is a correct but non-complete answer to the trace-preservation problem. Below, we rewrite this algorithm so that, whenever it terminates, it outputs a correct answer for any PTA, and a complete answer for deterministic PTA.

We give TPSynth(A, v) in Algorithm 1. TPSynth maintains two constraints: K_{good} is the intersection of v-compatible states met, whereas K_{bad} is the union[2] of all v-incompatible states. TPSynth also maintains two sets of states, *viz.* the set S of all states met, and the set S_{new} of states met at the latest iteration of the **while** loop. TPSynth is a breadth-first search algorithm, that iteratively explores the symbolic state space. Whenever a new state is met, its v-compatibility is checked (line 4). If it is v-compatible, its projection onto the parameters is added to K_{good} (line 4). Otherwise, its projection onto the parameters is added to K_{bad} (line 5), and the state is discarded from S_{new} (line 5), *i.e.* its successors will not be explored. When no new states can be explored, *i.e.* the set S_{new} is either empty or contains only states explored earlier (line 6), the intersection of v-compatible parametric constraints and the negation of the v-incompatible parametric constraints is returned (line 6). Otherwise, the algorithm explores one step further in depth (line 7).

Algorithm 1. TPSynth(A, v)

---

    input   : PTA A, parameter valuation v
    output : Constraint K over the parameters

1 $K_{good} \leftarrow \top$; $K_{bad} \leftarrow \bot$; $S_{new} \leftarrow \{s_{\text{init}}\}$; $S \leftarrow \varnothing$
2 **while true do**
3 | **foreach** *state* $(l, C) \in S_{new}$ **do**
4 | | **if** $v \models C{\downarrow}_P$ **then** $K_{good} \leftarrow K_{good} \wedge C{\downarrow}_P$;
5 | | **else** $K_{bad} \leftarrow K_{bad} \vee C{\downarrow}_P$; $S_{new} \leftarrow S_{new} \setminus \{(l, C)\}$;
6 | **if** $S_{new} \subseteq S$ **then return** $K_{good} \wedge \neg K_{bad}$;
7 | $S \leftarrow S \cup S_{new}$; $S_{new} \leftarrow \mathsf{Succ}(S_{new})$

Theorem 14 states that, in case TPSynth(A, v) terminates, its result is correct.

Theorem 14 (correctness of TPSynth). *Let A be a PTA, let v be a parameter valuation. Assume TPSynth(A, v) terminates with constraint K. Then $v \models K$, and for all $v' \models K$, Traces$(v'(A)) =$ Traces$(v(A))$.*

We now state the completeness of TPSynth for *deterministic* PTA.

Theorem 15 (completeness of TPSynth). *Let A be a deterministic PTA, let v be a parameter valuation. Assume TPSynth(A, v) terminates with constraint K. Then $v' \models K$ iff Traces$(v'(A)) =$ Traces$(v(A))$.*

Remark 16. The incompleteness of TPSynth for nondeterministic PTA is easily seen: consider a PTA with two states l and l', and two transitions from l to l' labeled with a and guarded with $x = p \wedge x \geq 5$ and $x = p \wedge x \leq 2$. Consider v such that $p = 0$. TPSynth(A, v) outputs $p \leq 2$, whereas the complete set of parameter valuations with the same trace set as $v(A)$ is in fact $p \leq 2 \vee p \geq 5$.

---

[2] This union of a constraints can be seen (and implemented) as a finite list of convex constraints.

5 Decidability Results for Subclasses of PTA

In this section, we first prove the finiteness of the parametric zone graph of 1-clock PTA over both discrete and rational time (Section 5.1). We then study the (un)decidability of the language and trace preservation emptiness problems for deterministic 1-clock PTA (Section 5.2), L/U-PTA (Section 5.3) and deterministic 1-parameter L-PTA and U-PTA (Section 5.4).

5.1 1-Clock PTA

In this section, we restrict the number of clocks of a PTA, without any restriction on the number of parameters. In fact, we even slightly extend the definition of PTA, by allowing parametric linear terms in guards and invariants.

Definition 17. *An extended 1-clock PTA (1cPTA for short) is a PTA with only one clock and possibly several parameters, and allowing guards and invariants of the form $x \prec \sum_i \alpha_i p_i + c$, with $p_i \in P$ and $\alpha_i \in \mathbb{Z}$.*

We show below that the parametric zone graph for 1cPTA is finite. In [2], it is shown that the set of parameters reaching some location can be computed for PTA over discrete time with only one parametric clock and arbitrarily many non-parametric clocks. Here, we lift the assumption of discrete time, we allow more general guards and invariants, and the finiteness of the parametric zone graph allows to synthesize valuations for more complex properties than pure reachability; however, we only consider a single (parametric) clock. Eliminating non-parametric clocks in this setting is the subject of future work.

Definition 18. *Given a 1cPTA A, a 1-clock symbolic constraint is a constraint over $X \cup P$ of the form $\bigwedge_i (<_i \sim x) \wedge \bigwedge_j (<_j^1 \sim <_j^2)$, where $i, j \in \mathbb{N}$, x is the unique clock of A, and $<_i, <_j^1, <_j^2$ are parametric linear terms either (i.e. of the form $\sum_i \alpha_i p_i + c$) appearing in guards and invariants of A, or equal to 0, and such that $<_j^1, <_j^2$ are all different from each other. We denote by 1CSC(A) the set of 1-clock symbolic constraints of A.*

Lemma 19. *Let A be a 1cPTA. Let (l, C) be a reachable symbolic state of A. Then $C \in 1CSC(A)$.*

Proof sketch. We reason by induction on the length of the runs. For the base case, the initial state is obviously in 1CSC(A). Then, for any state, we compute one of its successors using the Succ relation; and we show that each operation (intersection with the guard, resetting clocks, time elapsing, intersection with the invariant) makes the resulting constraint still belong to 1CSC(A). □

Theorem 20. *The parametric zone graph of a 1cPTA is finite.*

Proof. From Lemma 19, each symbolic state of a 1cPTA A belongs to 1CSC(A). Due to the finite number of linear terms in the guards and invariants in A and the finite number of locations of A, there is a finite number of possible symbolic states reachable in A.   □

Let us compute below an upper bound on the size of this symbolic graph. In the following, $|LT|$ denotes the number of different parametric linear terms (*i.e.* the number of guards and invariants) used in A.

Proposition 21. *The parametric zone graph of a 1cPTA is in* $|L| \times 2^{|LT|(|LT|+1)}$.

5.2 Decidability and Synthesis for Deterministic 1-Clock PTA

We show here that the language- and trace-preservation problems are decidable for deterministic 1cPTA. These results rely on the correctness and completeness of Algorithm 1 and on the finiteness of the parametric zone graph of 1cPTA.

Theorem 22 (trace-preservation synthesis). *Let* A *be a deterministic 1cPTA and* v *be a parameter valuation. The set of parameters for which the trace set is the same as in* v(A) *is computable in* $|L| \times 2^{|LT|(|LT|+1)}$.

Proof. Since A is a 1cPTA, then its parametric zone graph is finite from Theorem 20. Hence TPSynth(A, v) terminates. Furthermore, since A is deterministic, from Theorems 14 and 15, TPSynth(A, v) returns all parameter valuations v' such that $Traces(v'(A)) = Traces(v(A))$.

Concerning the complexity, in the worst case, all symbolic states of A are v-compatible, and TPSynth(A, v) needs to explore the entire parametric zone graph, which is of size $|L| \times 2^{|LT|(|LT|+1)}$.   □

Theorem 23 (language-preservation synthesis). *Let* A *be a deterministic 1cPTA and* v *be a parameter valuation. The set of parameters for which the language is the same as in* v(A) *is computable in* $|L| \times 2^{|LT|(|LT|+1)}$.

Proof. Since A is deterministic, the set of parameter valuations v' such that $Lang(v'(A)) = Lang(v(A))$ is the same as the set of parameter valuations v' such that $Traces(v'(A)) = Traces(v(A))$. Hence one can directly apply TPSynth(A, v) to compute the parameter valuations with the same language as $v(A)$.   □

As direct corollaries of these results, the language- and trace-preservation problems are decidable for deterministic 1cPTA.

5.3 Undecidability for L/U-PTA

We showed so far that the language- and trace-preservation problems are undecidable for general PTA (Section 3) and decidable for (deterministic) 1-clock PTA (Section 5.2). These results match the EF-emptiness problem, also undecidable for general PTA [2] and decidable for 1-clock PTA (at least over discrete time). We now show that the situation is different for L/U-PTA (PTA in which each parameter is always either used as a lower bound or always as an upper bound [8]): while EF-emptiness is decidable for L/U-PTA [6,8], we show that the language- and trace-preservation problems are not.

Constraining Parameter Equality.
We first show how to encode equality of a lower-bound parameter and an upper-bound parameter in a L/U-PTA, using language preservation. Consider the PTA gadget depicted in Figure 4. Assume a parameter valuation v such that $p_l = p_u$. Note that since $p_l = p_u$, no time can elapse in l_1, and the b transition can never be taken. In fact, we have that the language of this gadget is aa iff $p_l = p_u$.

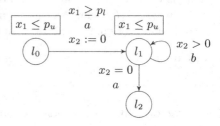

Fig. 4. PTA gadget ensuring $p_l = p_u$

Now, one can rewrite the 2CM encoding of Section 3.1 using an L/U-PTA which, together with the previous gadget, gives the following undecidability result.

Theorem 24. *The language-preservation problem is undecidable for L/U-PTA with at least one lower-bound and at least one upper-bound parameter.*

This reasoning can be reused to prove the undecidability for L/U-PTA of the other problems considered in Section 3. It follows:

Theorem 25. *1. The trace-preservation problem is undecidable for L/U-PTA with at least one lower-bound and at least one upper-bound parameter.*
2. The robust language- and trace-preservation problems are undecidable for L/U-PTA with at least one lower-bound and at least one upper-bound parameter.

5.4   A Decidability Result for 1-Parameter L-PTA and U-PTA

In [6], a bound is exhibited for both L-PTA and U-PTA (*i.e.* PTA with only lower-bound, resp. upper-bound, parameters) such that either all parameter valuations beyond this threshold have an accepting run, or none of them has. This provides an algorithm for synthesizing all integer parameter valuations for which there exists an accepting run, by considering this bound, and then enumerate all (integer) valuations below this bound.

Unfortunately, such a bound for U-PTA (and L-PTA) does not exist for the language, as witnessed by the U-PTA of Fig. 5: given $p \in \mathbb{N}$, the accepted language is $a^{\leq p}b^\omega$. A similar L-PTA example is easily obtained.

We now show that the trace-preservation problem is decidable for deterministic L-PTA and U-PTA with a single integer parameter and

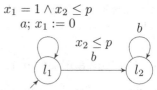

Fig. 5. An U-PTA with different language for each parameter valuation

arbitrarily many clocks: given a reference integer parameter valuation v, it suffices to check $v + 1$ and $v - 1$ to decide whether another parameter valuation yields the same trace set as v.

Theorem 26. *The trace-preservation problem is decidable for deterministic U-PTA and deterministic L-PTA with a single integer-valued parameter.*

Proof. Let A be a deterministic U-PTA with a single integer-valued parameter p (the reasoning is dual for L-PTA). Let v be a valuation of p. Construct the trace set of $v(A)$. Consider the valuation $v + 1$ (*i.e.* the smallest integer valuation larger than v). It is known that increasing a parameter in a U-PTA can only *add* behaviors. Suppose $v + 1(A)$ adds a behavior, *i.e.* enables a transition that was not enabled in $v(A)$. Since A is deterministic, then necessarily $v + 1(A)$ contains a transition $l_1 \overset{a}{\Rightarrow} l_2$ that did not exist in $v(A)$. Hence the trace set of $v + 1(A)$ strictly contains the trace set of $v(A)$, and the trace set of any valuation greater or equal to $v + 1$ will again strictly contain the trace set of $v(A)$. Hence, deciding whether there exists a valuation greater than v for which the trace set is the same as $v(A)$ is equivalent to checking whether the trace set of $v + 1(A)$ is the same as the trace set of $v(A)$.

The proof for $v - 1$ is symmetric. Hence it is decidable whether there exists a valuation different from v for which the trace set is the same as $v(A)$. □

Since we have a direct correspondence between trace sets and languages in deterministic automata, we get:

Theorem 27. *The language-preservation problem is decidable for deterministic U-PTA and deterministic L-PTA with a single integer-valued parameter.*

Theorem 27 cannot be lifted to the language for non-deterministic L- and U-PTA. Consider the U-PTA in Fig. 6: for $p = 1$, the language is ab^ω. For $p = 2$, the language is $ab^\omega | a$, which is different from $p = 1$. But then for $p \geq 3$, the language is again ab^ω. Hence testing only $v + 1 = 2$ is not enough.

Similarly, a counter-example to the extension of Theorem 26 to non-deterministic L- and U-PTA can be obtained easily.

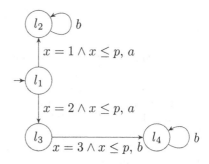

Fig. 6

6   Conclusion and Perspectives

In this paper, we studied the decidability of the language and trace preservation emptiness. We summarize in Table 1 our (un)decidability results for PTA and its subclasses with arbitrarily many clocks; an italicized cell denotes undecidability.

Table 1. Undecidability of preservation emptiness problems for subclasses of PTA

Preservation	1ip-dL&U-PTA	L&U-PTA	bL/U-PTA	L/U-PTA	bPTA	PTA
Language	Th. 27	open	Th. 25	Th. 24	Th. 13	Th. 6
Trace	Th. 26	open	Th. 25	Th. 25	Th. 13	Th. 9
Robust language	open	open	Th. 25	Th. 25	Th. 12	Th. 12
Robust trace	open	open	Th. 25	Th. 25	Th. 13	Th. 13

(1ip-dL&U-PTA stand for deterministic L-PTA, resp. U-PTA, with one integer-valued parameter; L&U-PTA stand for L-PTA and U-PTA; bPTA stand for PTA with bounded parameters.) We also showed that both problems are decidable for deterministic PTA with a single clock.

Future Works. First, we used an *ad-hoc* encoding of a 2-counter machine for our proofs of undecidability, using four parametric clocks. In contrast, a new encoding of a 2-counter machine using PTA was proposed very recently in [5], that makes use of only three parametric clocks. We assume that our proofs could be rewritten using that encoding, proving the undecidability of the problems considered in this paper with as few as three clocks.

A promising direction to find decidability results consists in considering L-PTA and U-PTA. Furthermore, our results are linked to the robustness of timed systems; future works consist in finding the boundary between expressive models of robustness (with many parameter dimensions), that are undecidable, and less expressive models (usually with a single parameter), that are decidable.

Acknowledgments. We thank Didier Lime for telling us about the reduction we used in the proof of Theorem 12.

References

1. Alur, R., Dill, D.: Automata for modeling real-time systems. In: Paterson, M.S. (ed.) Automata, Languages and Programming. LNCS, vol. 443, pp. 322–335. Springer, Heidelberg (1990)
2. Alur, R., Henzinger, T.A., Vardi, M.Y.: Parametric real-time reasoning. In: STOC, pp. 592–601. ACM Press (1993)
3. André, É., Chatain, T., Encrenaz, E., Fribourg, L.: An inverse method for parametric timed automata. IJFCS **20**(5), 819–836 (2009)
4. André, É., Markey, N.: Language preservation problems in parametric timed automata. Research Report LSV-15-05, Laboratoire Spécification et Vérification, ENS Cachan, France, June 2015
5. Beneš, N., Bezděk, P., Larsen, K.G., Srba, J.: Language emptiness of continuous-time parametric timed automata. In: Halldórsson, M.M., Iwama, K., Kobayashi, N., Speckmann, B. (eds.) ICALP 2015. LNCS, vol. 9135, pp. 69–81. Springer, Heidelberg (2015)
6. Bozzelli, L., La Torre, S.: Decision problems for lower/upper bound parametric timed automata. FMSD **35**(2), 121–151 (2009)
7. De Wulf, M., Doyen, L., Markey, N., Raskin, J.-F.: Robust safety of timed automata. FMSD **33**(1–3), 45–84 (2008)

8. Hune, T., Romijn, J., Stoelinga, M., Vaandrager, F.: Linear parametric model checking of timed automata. Journal of Logic and Algebraic Programming **52–53**, 183–220 (2002)
9. Jovanović, A., Lime, D., Roux, O.H.: Integer parameter synthesis for timed automata. IEEE Transactions on Software Engineering **41**(5), 445–461 (2015)
10. Miller, J.S.: Decidability and complexity results for timed automata and semi-linear hybrid automata. In: Lynch, N.A., Krogh, B.H. (eds.) HSCC 2000. LNCS, vol. 1790, pp. 296–309. Springer, Heidelberg (2000)
11. Sankur, O.: Untimed language preservation in timed systems. In: Murlak, F., Sankowski, P. (eds.) MFCS 2011. LNCS, vol. 6907, pp. 556–567. Springer, Heidelberg (2011)
12. Sankur, O.: Robustness in Timed Automata: Analysis, Synthesis, Implementation. Thèse de doctorat, Laboratoire Spécification & Vérification, ENS Cachan, France (2013)

Timed Symbolic Dynamics

Nicolas Basset[(✉)]

Department of Computer Science, University of Oxford, Oxford, UK
nicolas.basset@cs.ox.ac.uk

Abstract. We introduce a theory of timed symbolic dynamics unifying results from timed automata theory and symbolic dynamics. The timed sofic shift spaces we define are a way of seeing timed regular languages as shift spaces on general alphabets (in classical symbolic dynamics, sofic shift spaces correspond to regular languages). We show that morphisms of shift spaces on general alphabets can be approximated by sliding block codes resulting in a generalised version of the so-called Curtis-Hedlund-Lyndon Theorem. We provide a new measure for timed languages by characterising the Gromov-Lindenstrauss-Weiss metric mean dimension for timed shift spaces and illustrate it on several examples. We revisit recent results on volumetry of timed languages in terms of timed symbolic dynamics. In particular we explain the discretisation of timed shift spaces and their entropy.

1 Introduction

Timed automata were introduced in the early 1990's to model continuous time behaviours in a verification context [1]. Since then they have been thoroughly studied from a theoretical standpoint, a common challenge being the lifting of results from the well established automata theory.

The theory of symbolic dynamics was developed since the beginning of the 20th century as a method to study, in a symbolic fashion, general dynamical systems like ordinary differential equations. The method consists in associating an (infinite) sequence of symbols to every (infinite) trajectory of the dynamical system. The symbols represents regions of a finite partition of the state space that are visited along trajectories at discrete time steps. Departing from its topological origins, symbolic dynamics has a lot of applications in channel-coding theory and data storage, number theory, and linear algebra (see [19] and reference therein). It is also used in the context of analysis of algorithm (see e.g. [26]).

Thus, as automata theory, symbolic dynamics is a broad research field that can provide a source of interesting results to lift to the timed world. Indeed, this theory has three interesting characteristics. (i) It is really close to automata theory and dealing with object very similar to regular languages (namely the set of

This research is supported in part by ERC Advanced Grant VERIWARE and was also supported by the ANR project EQINOCS (ANR-11-BS02-004). The present article is an improved and shortened version of Chapter 5 of the PhD thesis [10]. Omitted proofs and extra details can be found in the technical report [12].

© Springer International Publishing Switzerland 2015
S. Sankaranarayanan and E. Vicario (Eds.): FORMATS 2015, LNCS 9268, pp. 44–59, 2015.
DOI: 10.1007/978-3-319-22975-1_4

allowed block of sofic shifts) and having similar results such as determinisation, minimisation, pumping lemma, etc. (ii) Symbolic dynamics provides a quantitative analysis of regular languages with the notion of entropy. Entropy measures the growth rate of the languages with respect to the size of words considered. (iii) Symbolic dynamics considers regular languages as dynamical systems called shift spaces and provides a topological point of view. For instance the entropy of a shift space is a particular case of the so-called topological entropy defined for general dynamical systems (see e.g. [16]). Thus this theory is nicely placed within broad mathematical theories developed by the pioneers Markov, Shannon, Kolmogorov.

Volumes and volumetric entropy were recently introduced [4,6] to quantify the size of timed languages and the information content of their elements. These exploratory works were inspired by the symbolic dynamics' notion of entropy but left open several questions. What is the notion of shift space for timed automata? How is the topological entropy of such an hypothetical shift space linked to the volumetric entropy? What are the others quantitative results that can be borrowed from symbolic dynamics?

Contributions. Here, we propose a theory of timed symbolic dynamics that sheds a new light on the underlying dynamics of timed regular languages (the languages recognised by timed automata). The main difficulty here is that the natural shift space for a timed language has an infinite, and even uncountable, alphabet. Such shift spaces are quite different from those usually studied in symbolic dynamics. Thus we first define and characterise shift spaces on general alphabets that are compact, metric and measurable spaces. Then we associate general alphabet shift spaces to timed languages and study their properties; we call timed sofic shift such shift spaces. As for size/complexity measures for timed sofic shift, the standard approach based on topological entropy cannot work: this entropy is infinite, and we study more relevant characteristics. The first one is the Gromov-Lindenstrauss-Weiss metric mean dimension [20] that we characterise for timed sofic shift. The second one is obtained by "renormalisation" of topological entropy, and turns out to coincide with volumetric entropy of timed languages (thus we justify in terms of symbolic dynamics the somewhat ad hoc definitions from [4,6]). We also investigate morphisms for general alphabet shift spaces, namely, we state a generalisation of the Curtis-Hedlund-Lyndon theorem after proving that the classical statement cannot hold for general alphabet shift spaces.

Related work and possible applications. This article is designed for readers with a basic knowledge of automata theory or of symbolic dynamics. No specific knowledge of these fields is required to read the paper. We refer the reader to [19] for an extensive introduction to symbolic dynamics and to [14] for an exposition of this theory in the context of automata theory. The seminal paper on timed automata is [1].

In [27], deterministic continuous dynamical systems are abstracted by timed automata. Hence the state space is discretised as in symbolic dynamics while the timing behaviours are made non-deterministic because of the abstraction. It would be very interesting to use symbolic dynamics methods in this context.

We introduced the basis of a timed theory of channel coding in [2]. Algorithms and result of this latter paper were inspired by the theory of symbolic dynamics and coding. We think that the formal exposition of timed symbolic dynamics in the present paper will probably lead to new developments of the timed theory of channel coding.

Metric mean dimension can be interpreted in terms of robustness analysis as follows: it tells us how often arbitrary precision is required to encode delays along timed words. For instance a timed automaton with metric mean dimension $1/3$ means that $2/3$ of the delays must be chosen with arbitrary precision. A more detailed discussion with related work is given in the conclusion (Section 5).

Article structure. After giving preliminaries in Section 2, we characterise properties of general alphabet shift spaces in Section 3. In particular, we explain why several key results of symbolic dynamics do not hold in this more general settings (Fact 1 and 2) and what are the suitable generalisations of these results (definition of the volumetric entropy and Theorem 3). In Section 4, we associate general alphabet shift spaces to timed automata and study there quantitative properties (entropy, metric mean dimension). In Section 5 we discuss the results obtained in this paper and the perspectives.

2   Preliminaries

In this section we give topological definitions of shift spaces from symbolic dynamics (see [16, 19]) except that we generalise definitions from finite to compact metric alphabets in Section 2.3. We use classical topology concepts whose definitions and properties can be found in books such as [21].

2.1   Dynamical Systems

Let (X, d) be a compact metric space. A subset $Y \subseteq X$ is an ε-*net* of X if every element of X is at most ε far apart from an element of Y ($\forall x \in X$, $\exists y \in Y$ such that $d(x, y) \leq \varepsilon$). In a compact set, for all $\varepsilon > 0$, there exists a finite ε-net of it. We denote by $\mathcal{N}_\varepsilon(X, d)$ the minimal cardinality of ε-net of X. A subset $Y \subseteq X$ is ε-*separated* if all two different elements of Y are at least ε far apart from each other ($\forall x, y \in Y$, $x \neq y \Rightarrow d(x, y) > \varepsilon$). In a compact set, all ε-separated set are of finite cardinality. We denote by $\mathcal{S}_\varepsilon(X, d)$ the maximal cardinality of ε-separated sets of X.

Lemma 1 ([18], see also [16] for an English version). *Given a compact metric space X the followings inequalities hold* $\mathcal{S}_{2\varepsilon}(X, d) \leq \mathcal{N}_\varepsilon(X, d) \leq \mathcal{S}_\varepsilon(X, d)$.

A *discrete time dynamical system* (just called dynamical system thereafter) is a couple $((X, d), f)$ where (X, d) is a compact metric space and f is a homeomorphism of X i.e. a continuous bijection from X to X. Informally, we can see X as the state space of the system. The function f is the evolution law of the system, it gives the dynamics: given a starting state x_0, the states $f(x_0), f^2(x_0), \ldots$

are the successors of x, $f^n(x_0)$ is the state at the "moment" n. The function f^{-1} permits one to go back in the past. A continuous function ϕ from a dynamical system $((X,d),f)$ to another $((X',d'),f')$ that commutes with the dynamics (i.e. $f' \circ \phi = \phi \circ f$) is called a *morphism*.

2.2 ε-Entropies and Topological Entropy

The topological entropy permits one to measure the complexity of a system. Intuitively a system is complex when it is sensitive to initial conditions. There are several equivalent ways to define topological entropy, here we give a definition due to Bowen [15]. Let $((X,d),f)$ be a dynamical system. For all positive integer n we define the distance between the n first iterations of f on $x,y \in X$ by:

$$d_n(x,y) = \max_{0 \leq k \leq n-1} d(f^k(x), f^k(y)).$$

The idea is that two points x and y are ε far apart for d_n if when iterating f at most n times, we can distinguish them with a precision ε. An ε-net[1] for d_n is thus an approximation of the system during n iterations and with precision ε. The N-ε entropy $h_\varepsilon^N(X)$ measures the growth rate of these sets wrt. n:

$$h_\varepsilon^N(X) = \limsup_{n \to \infty} \frac{1}{n} \log_2(\mathcal{N}_\varepsilon(X, d_n)).$$

Similarly the S-ε-entropy is:

$$h_\varepsilon^S(X) = \limsup_{n \to \infty} \frac{1}{n} \log_2(\mathcal{S}_\varepsilon(X, d_n)).$$

The topological entropy is:

$$h_{\text{top}}(X) \stackrel{\text{def}}{=} \lim_{\varepsilon \to 0} h_\varepsilon^N(X) = \lim_{\varepsilon \to 0} h_\varepsilon^S(X). \tag{1}$$

The second equality is due to Lemma 1. A real ε is called a *discretisation step* if it is the inverse of a positive integer. In the following we consider wlog. only reals ε that are discretisation steps (they provide sequences that tend to 0).

2.3   Shift Spaces on General Alphabet

In the broad field of research of symbolic dynamics (see [19]), the shift spaces considered are on finite alphabets (we give an example in Section 2.4 below). Here, we present shift spaces in a version extended to general alphabets being compact metric spaces. The main instantiation in the following is the *timed alphabet* $[0,M] \times \Sigma$ where $M \in \mathbb{N}$ and Σ is finite, with metric $d((t,a),(t',a')) = |t - t'| + 1_{a \neq a'}$. In the rest of the article $(\mathcal{C}, d)$ is a compact metric alphabet. We denote by $\mathcal{C}^{\mathbb{Z}}$ the set of bi-infinite words over $\mathcal{C}$ (i.e. words of the form $x = (x_i)_{i \in \mathbb{Z}}$

---

[1] (X, d_n) is a metric compact space when (X, d) is; so, one can consider ε-net of it.

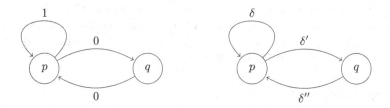

Fig. 1. A labelled graph (left) and its unlabelled version (right)

with $x_i \in \mathcal{C}$). One can define a metric $\bar{d}$ on $\mathcal{C}^{\mathbb{Z}}$ by $\bar{d}(x, x') = \sup_{i \in \mathbb{Z}} \frac{d(x_i, x_i')}{2^{|i|}}$. The *shift map* σ is defined by $y = \sigma(x)$ when for all $i \in \mathbb{Z}$, $y_i = x_{i+1}$.

It can easily be shown that $((\mathcal{C}^{\mathbb{Z}}, \bar{d}), \sigma)$ is a dynamical system, we call it the *full shift space* on $\mathcal{C}$ and just denote it by $\mathcal{C}^{\mathbb{Z}}$ when d and σ are clear from the context. A subspace X of $\mathcal{C}^{\mathbb{Z}}$ is called a *sub-shift space* of $\mathcal{C}^{\mathbb{Z}}$ whenever it is topologically closed and shift invariant: $\sigma(X) = X$. We often just call shifts (or shift spaces) the sub-shift spaces of full shift spaces.

Given a bi-infinite word $x \in \mathcal{C}^{\mathbb{Z}}$ and two indices $i, j \in \mathbb{Z}$ with $i \leq j$, the finite word $x_i x_{i+1} \cdots x_j$ is called a *factor* of x and is denoted by $x_{[i..j]}$. For a shift space X, the set of factors of length n of bi-infinite words of X is denoted by $X_n \stackrel{\text{def}}{=} \{x_{[i+1..i+n]} \mid x \in X, \ i \in \mathbb{Z}\}$.

2.4 Edge and Sofic Shifts from Classical Symbolic Dynamics

Here, we recall the definitions of edge and sofic shift central in symbolic dynamics. These definitions will be lifted to the timed setting in Section 4.

Let $G = (Q, \Delta)$ be a finite graph with possibly multiple edges between two vertices. Any edge $\delta \in \Delta$ has an *origin* $\delta^- \in Q$ and a *destination* $\delta^+ \in Q$. Let Σ be a finite alphabet and $\mathtt{Lab} : \Delta \to \Sigma$ a labelling function on edges. The pair $(G, \mathtt{Lab})$ is called a *labelled graph*.

A finite (resp bi-infinite) path of G is a finite (resp bi-infinite) sequence of consecutive edges δ_i such that for all $i \in \{1, \ldots, n-1\}$ (resp $i \in \mathbb{Z}$) $\delta_i^+ = \delta_{i+1}^-$.

The set of bi-infinite paths of a graph G is a sub-shift of $\Delta^{\mathbb{Z}}$ called the *edge shift* of G. The *sofic shift* of a labelled graph $A = (G, \mathtt{Lab})$ is the set of bi-infinite words that label bi-infinite paths of A: $[A] \stackrel{\text{def}}{=} \{(\mathtt{Lab}(\delta_i))_{i \in \mathbb{Z}} \mid \forall i \in \mathbb{Z}, \delta_i^+ = \delta_{i+1}^-\}$. It is a sub-shift of $\Sigma^{\mathbb{Z}}$. A labelled graph is called *right-resolving* whenever for every vertex q, all edges starting from q have distinct labels.

Example 1. Consider the graph G on the right of figure 1 and $\mathtt{Lab}$ the labelling function defined by $\mathtt{Lab}(\delta) = 1$ and $\mathtt{Lab}(\delta') = \mathtt{Lab}(\delta'') = 0$. The labelled graph $(G, \mathtt{Lab})$ is depicted on the left of figure 1, it is right-resolving and its sofic shift is composed by the bi-infinite words such that the number of 0 between every two consecutive 1 is even.

Note that vertices without incoming edges or without outgoing edges cannot be visited by a bi-infinite words and can hence be deleted without loss of generality. The resulted graph is called *pruned*.

2.5   Comparison with Finite State Automata

A *non-deterministic finite state automaton* (NFA) $B = (Q, \Delta, \mathsf{Lab}, I, F)$ is a labelled graph (with vertices called states) augmented with sets of initial and final states I and F. The set of words that label paths leading from initial states to final states is the language of B (such language is called *regular*). One can see that sets of allowed factors $\cup_{n \in \mathbb{N}}[A]_n$ of sofic shifts A correspond to regular languages L that are *factorial* (every factor of a word of L is a word of L), *left-* and *right-extensible* (if $w \in L$ then there exists $a, b \in \Sigma$ such that $aw \in L$ and $wb \in L$). Being factorial and extensible are suitable properties in the classical context of constrained-channel coding (for which symbolic dynamics offer a meaningful framework). We already motivated these properties for timed languages in [2] where we built the basis of a timed theory of channel coding.

There exists a variation of the theory of symbolic dynamics based on mono-infinite words rather than bi-infinite words, that is, indexed by $\mathbb{N}$ rather than $\mathbb{Z}$ (see §13.8 of [19]). The "one-sided" shift spaces of this theory are exactly the omega-regular languages recognised by Büchi automata with all states initial and final.

3   Factor Based Characterisations

In the previous section, we gave topological definitions of shift spaces, their entropies and morphisms. Simpler characterisations of these objects based on factors are available in symbolic dynamics (i.e. when the alphabet is finite). In this section we generalise these characterisations to general alphabet shift spaces. We carefully replace properties that implicitly use finite cardinality of sets in symbolic dynamics by similar properties involving compactness or finite measure of corresponding sets in our more general setting.

3.1   Factor Based Characterisation of General Alphabet Shift Spaces

We recall that the alphabet $\mathcal{C}$ considered in the following is a compact metric space.

Definition 1. *Given a family $O = (O_n)_{n \in \mathbb{N} \setminus \{0\}}$ where all O_n are open sets of $\mathcal{C}^n$, we denote by $\mathcal{F}(O)$ the set of bi-infinite words not having factors in O :* $\mathcal{F}(O) = \{x \in \mathcal{C}^{\mathbb{Z}} \mid \forall i \in \mathbb{Z}, \forall n \in \mathbb{N} \setminus \{0\}, x_{[i..i+n-1]} \notin O_n\}.$

We have also the dual definition

Definition 2. *Given a family $F = (F_n)_{n \in \mathbb{N} \setminus \{0\}}$ where all F_n are closed sets of $\mathcal{C}^n$, we denote by $\mathcal{B}(F)$ the set of bi-infinite words whose allowed factors are those of F :* $\mathcal{B}(F) = \{x \in \mathcal{C}^{\mathbb{Z}} \mid \forall i \in \mathbb{Z}, \forall n \in \mathbb{N} \setminus \{0\}, x_{[i..i+n-1]} \in F_n\}$

Theorem 1. *A subset of $\mathcal{C}^{\mathbb{Z}}$ is a shift space iff it can be defined as a $\mathcal{F}(O)$ iff it can be defined as a $\mathcal{B}(F)$.*

Note that, in symbolic dynamics (for which $\mathcal{C}$ is finite), there is no need of specifying which sets are open or closed as all finite sets satisfy both properties.

Example 2. We introduce five running examples (indexed with roman number).

Let $\mathcal{C}^{\mathrm{I}} \stackrel{\text{def}}{=} [0,1] \times \{a\}$ and the set of forbidden factors be given by $O_2^{\mathrm{I}} \stackrel{\text{def}}{=} \{(t,a)(t',a) \mid t + t' > 1\}$. The shift space $X^{\mathrm{I}} \stackrel{\text{def}}{=} \mathcal{F}(O^{\mathrm{I}})$ is the set $\{(t_i,a)_{i\in\mathbb{Z}} \mid t_i + t_{i+1} \leq 1\}$.

Let $\mathcal{C}^{\mathrm{II}} \stackrel{\text{def}}{=} [0,1] \times \{a\}$ and $O_1^{\mathrm{II}} \stackrel{\text{def}}{=} \{(t,a) \mid t < 1\}$. The only element of the shift space $X^{\mathrm{II}} \stackrel{\text{def}}{=} \mathcal{F}(O^{\mathrm{II}})$ is $(1,a)^{\mathbb{Z}}$.

Let $\mathcal{C}^{\mathrm{III}} \stackrel{\text{def}}{=} [0,1] \times \{a,b\}$ and[2] $O_2^{\mathrm{III}} \stackrel{\text{def}}{=} \{(t,a)(t',b) \mid t < 1, t' \in [0,1]\} \cup \{(t,l)(t',l) \mid l \in \{a,b\}, t,t' \in [0,1]\}$. The shift space $X^{\mathrm{III}} \stackrel{\text{def}}{=} \mathcal{F}(O^{\mathrm{III}})$ is the set of bi-infinite words of the form $[(t_i,a_i)(t_{i+1},b_{i+1})]_{i\in 2\mathbb{Z}}$ or $[(t_i,a_i)(t_{i+1},b_{i+1})]_{i\in 2\mathbb{Z}+1}$ with $t_i = 1$ and $t_{i+1} \in [0,1]$.

Let $\mathcal{C}^{\mathrm{IV}} \stackrel{\text{def}}{=} [0,1] \times \{b\}$ and $O_n^{\mathrm{IV}} \stackrel{\text{def}}{=} \{(t_1,b)\cdots(t_n,b) \mid t_1 + \ldots + t_n > 1\}$. The shift space $X^{\mathrm{IV}} \stackrel{\text{def}}{=} \mathcal{F}(O^{\mathrm{IV}})$ is the set of bi-infinite words $(t_i,b)_{i\in\mathbb{Z}}$ satisfying the (bi-infinite) *Zeno condition* $\sum_{i\in\mathbb{Z}} t_i \leq 1$.

Let $\mathcal{C}^{\mathrm{V}} \stackrel{\text{def}}{=} [0,1] \times \{a,b\}$ and $O_1^{\mathrm{V}} \stackrel{\text{def}}{=} \{(t,a) \mid t < 1\}$ and $O_n^{\mathrm{V}} \stackrel{\text{def}}{=} \{(t_1,b)\cdots(t_n,b) \mid t_1 + \ldots + t_n > 1\}$. Every bi-infinite words of $X^{\mathrm{V}} \stackrel{\text{def}}{=} \mathcal{F}(O^{\mathrm{V}})$ has its delays corresponding to events a equal to 1 (as for X^{II}) and the sum of delays of blocks of consecutive b bounded by 1 (as for X^{IV}).

3.2   Entropies for General Alphabet Shift Spaces

Topological entropy is very useful to compare dynamical systems. Unfortunately it is infinite for shift spaces on infinite alphabet as remarked in [20].

Fact 1. *Let $\mathcal{C}$ be an infinite compact metric space then $h_{\text{top}}(\mathcal{C}^{\mathbb{Z}}) = +\infty$.*

A first approach to circumvent this issue is to generalise the following characterisation of the entropy that holds for finite alphabet shift space X (see [19]),

$$h_{\text{top}}(X) = \lim_{n\to+\infty} \frac{1}{n} \log_2 |X_n|. \tag{2}$$

Asarin and Degorre replaced cardinality measures by volume measures (explained below) to define an ad hoc notion of entropy for timed automata in [5] called volumetric in later papers [2–4]. Here, we describe both entropies (classical and volumetric) in a unified and more general framework.

The compact metric spaces $\mathcal{C}$ considered in this paper are endowed with a "natural" measure μ and hence the set $\mathcal{C}^n$ has the product measure μ^n. For example the measure on Σ^n, for finite Σ, is the counting measure; the measure on $[0,M]^n$ is the n-dimensional volume (aka. Lebesgue measure); and the measure on $([0,M] \times \Sigma)^n \cong [0,M]^n \times \Sigma^n$ also called volume is the product of the two

---

[2] We recall that a set A is open in $[0,1]$ if it is of the form $A = B \cap [0,1]$ with B an open set of $\mathbb{R}$ (i.e. a union of open intervals). In particular $[0,1]$ is open in $[0,1]$.

preceding measures. More precisely, a subset E of $([0, M] \times \Sigma)^n$ can be seen as a formal sum of subsets $E^{|w} \subseteq [0, M]^n$ associated with $w \in \Sigma^n$ as follows $E^{|w} = \{(t_1, \ldots, t_n) \mid (t_1, w_1) \ldots (t_n, w_n) \in E\}$. The volume of E is just the sum of the volumes of $E^{|w}$: $\mathtt{Vol}(E) = \sum_{w \in \Sigma^n} \mathtt{Vol}(E^{|w})$.

We now give our general definition of entropy for general alphabet shift spaces:

Definition 3. *Given a compact metric space $\mathcal{C}$ and a measure μ on it, the entropy of a subshift $X \subseteq \mathcal{C}^{\mathbb{Z}}$ is*

$$\mathcal{H}(X) = \lim_{n \to +\infty} \frac{1}{n} \log_2 \mu^n(X_n) \quad \text{(with } X_n \stackrel{\text{def}}{=} \{x_{[i+1..i+n]} \mid x \in X, \ i \in \mathbb{Z}\}\text{)}. \quad (3)$$

Applying Fekete's lemma ([17]) on sub-additive sequence to $(\log_2 \mu^n(X_n))_{n \in \mathbb{N}}$ ensures that the limit exists in $\mathbb{R} \cup \{-\infty, +\infty\}$.

Another way of circumventing the problem of the infinite topological entropy is to consider an asymptotic expansion of the ε-entropy instead of its limit when ε tends to 0 in Equation (1). This has been done fruitfully for volumetric entropy of timed automata in [13] (recalled in Theorem 7 below).

3.3 Sliding Block Codes for General Alphabet Shift Spaces

In this section $\mathcal{C}$ and $\mathcal{C}'$ denote two compact metric spaces, X and Y denote subshifts of $\mathcal{C}^{\mathbb{Z}}$ and $\mathcal{C}'^{\mathbb{Z}}$ respectively. Given a function ψ from X to $\mathcal{C}'$ we denote by $\psi^\infty : X \to \mathcal{C}'^{\mathbb{Z}}$ the function defined by $(\psi^\infty(x))_i = \psi(\sigma^i(x))$. Such functions are those that commute with the shifts (i.e. $\sigma \circ \phi = \phi \circ \sigma$) and are thus morphisms if and only if continuous.

We say that ψ is a $(2m+1)$-block function when for every x, $\psi(x)$ depends only on the $(2m+1)$-central factor $x_{[-m..m]}$, i.e. there exists a function $f : \mathcal{C}^{2m+1} \to \mathcal{C}'$ such that for every x, $\psi(x) = f(x_{[-m..m]})$. One can remark that ψ is continuous iff so is f. A function ϕ that is equal to some ψ^∞ with ψ a (continuous) block function is called a *(continuous) sliding block code*.

The following famous theorem gives a characterization of the morphisms of finite-alphabet shift spaces as sliding block codes.

Theorem 2 (Curtis-Hedlund-Lyndon). *Let X and Y be two finite alphabet shift spaces. A function $\varphi : X \to Y$ is a morphism if and only if it is a sliding block code.*

This Theorem cannot be extended to the case of general alphabets shift spaces as highlighted by the following fact:

Fact 2. *There are endomorphisms of $[0, 1]^{\mathbb{Z}}$ which are not sliding block codes.*

Proof (Sketch). Let $\psi : [0, 1]^{\mathbb{Z}} \to [0, 1]$ be defined by $\psi(x) = \frac{1}{3} \sum_{i \in \mathbb{Z}} \frac{x_i}{2^{|i|}}$. One can show that ψ^∞ is an endomorphism of $[0, 1]^{\mathbb{Z}}$ which is not a sliding block code.

An adapted version of Theorem 2 can however be stated as follows.

Theorem 3. *Every morphism ϕ from a shift space X to a full shift $\mathcal{C}^{\mathbb{Z}}$ is the uniform limit of a sequence of continuous sliding block codes $(\phi_m)_{m \in \mathbb{N}}$ from X to $\mathcal{C}^{\mathbb{Z}}$, that is $\sup_{x \in X} \overline{d}(\phi(x), \phi_m(x)) \rightarrow_{m \to +\infty} 0$ where $\overline{d}$ is the metric on $\mathcal{C}^{\mathbb{Z}}$.*

Proof (Sketch). We first characterise every morphism as a function of the form ψ^{∞} with ψ a continuous function from X to $\mathcal{C}$. We then show that every continuous function from X to $\mathcal{C}$ is a uniform limit of continuous block functions from X to $\mathcal{C}$. Theorem 3 can then be proved by combining these two last results.

4   Timed Shift Spaces and Their Measures

In this section we define and study timed sofic shifts which are a way to see regular timed languages [1] as (general alphabet) shift spaces.

4.1   Timed Shift Spaces

Timed Graphs. Informally, a timed graph is to a timed automaton what a graph is to an automaton: an automaton without initial, final states as well as labels on transitions. Formally, a *timed graph* (TG) is a tuple $\mathcal{G} = (C, Q, \Delta)$ such that

- C is a finite set of bounded *clocks* which are variables ranging over $[0, M]$ with $M \in \mathbb{N}$;
- Q is a finite set of *locations*;
- Δ is a finite set of *transitions*. Any transition $\delta \in \Delta$ has an *origin* $\delta^- \in Q$; a *destination* $\delta^+ \in Q$; a *closed guard* $\mathfrak{g}_\delta$, that is a conjunction of inequalities of the form $x \sim c$ or $x \sim y + c$, where x and y are clocks, $\sim \in \{\leq, =, \geq\}$ and $c \in \{0, \ldots, M\}$; and a *reset* function $\mathfrak{r}_\delta$ determined by a subset of clocks $B \subseteq C$: it resets to 0 all the clocks in B and does not modify the value of the other clocks.

States, Timed Transitions and Successor Actions. We denote by , the set of *states* which are couples of a location and a clock vector $\mathbb{S} \overset{\text{def}}{=} Q \times [0, M]^C$. A *timed transition* is an element (t, δ) of $\mathbb{A} \overset{\text{def}}{=} [0, M] \times \Delta$. The *time delay* t represents the time before firing the transition δ.

Given a state $s = (q, \boldsymbol{x}) \in \mathbb{S}$ and a timed transition $\alpha = (t, \delta) \in \mathbb{A}$ the *successor* of s by α is denoted by $s \triangleright \alpha$ and defined as follows. If $\delta^- = q$ and $\boldsymbol{x} + t$ satisfies the guard $\mathfrak{g}_\delta$ then $s \triangleright \alpha = (\delta^+, \mathfrak{r}_\delta(\boldsymbol{x} + t))$ else $s \triangleright \alpha = \bot$. Here and in the rest of the paper $\bot$ represents undefined states.

Runs and Their Shifts. A *bi-infinite run* of a timed graph $\mathcal{G}$ is a bi-infinite word $(s_i, \alpha_i)_{i \in \mathbb{Z}} \in (\mathbb{S} \times \mathbb{A})^{\mathbb{Z}}$ such that $s_{i+1} = s_i \triangleright \alpha_i \neq \bot$ for all $i \in \mathbb{Z}$. Consider the timed graph $\mathcal{G}^{\mathrm{I}}$ depicted on Figure 2 (left) and a bi-infinte words whose ith letter is $\alpha_i = (t_i, \delta_i)$ with $\delta_i = \delta$ if i is even and $\delta_i = \delta'$ otherwise and such that $t_i + t_{i+1} \in [0, 1]$ for every $i \in \mathbb{Z}$; define for even i, $s_i = (p, (t_{i-1}, 0))$ and $s_{i+1} = (q, (0, t_i))$ then $(s_i, \alpha_i)_{i \in \mathbb{Z}}$ is a run of $\mathcal{G}^{\mathrm{I}}$.

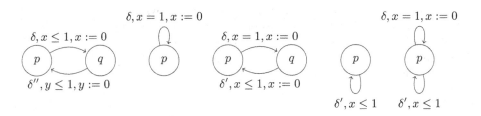

Fig. 2. From left to right LTGs $\mathcal{A}^i = (\mathcal{G}^i, \mathsf{Lab})$ for $i = \mathrm{I..V}$ with $\mathsf{Lab}(\delta) = \mathsf{Lab}(\delta'') = a$ and $\mathsf{Lab}(\delta') = b$. They recognise timed sofic shift of Example 2.

Proposition 1. *The set of bi-infinite runs of $\mathcal{G}$ is a sub-shift of $(\mathbb{S} \times \mathbb{A})^{\mathbb{Z}}$.*

Timed Edge Shift and Timed Sofic Shift. We are now ready to define the timed generalisation of edge shift and sofic shift.

Proposition-definition 1 (Timed edge shift). *The following set is a sub-shift of $\mathbb{A}^{\mathbb{Z}}$ called the* timed edge shift *of $\mathcal{G}$ and denoted by $[\mathcal{G}]$:*

$$[\mathcal{G}] = \{(\alpha_i)_{i \in \mathbb{Z}} \mid \exists (s_i)_{i \in \mathbb{Z}} \in \mathbb{S}^{\mathbb{Z}}, \ \forall i \in \mathbb{Z}, s_{i+1} = s_i \rhd \alpha_i\}$$

When adding to a TG $\mathcal{G}$ a labelling function $\mathsf{Lab} : \Delta \rightarrow \Sigma$ from the set of transition Δ to a finite alphabet of event Σ we obtain a *labelled timed graph* (LTG) $\mathcal{A} = (\mathcal{G}, \mathsf{Lab})$. Abusing the notation we extend the labelling function to timed transitions and runs as follows: $\mathsf{Lab}(\alpha) = (t, \mathsf{Lab}(\delta))$ when $\alpha = (t, \delta)$ and $\mathsf{Lab}((s_i, \alpha_i)_{i \in \mathbb{Z}}) = (s_i, \mathsf{Lab}(\alpha_i))_{i \in \mathbb{Z}}$. Thus we use two kinds of *timed alphabet*: alphabet of timed transitions $\mathbb{A} = [0, M] \times \Delta$ and alphabets of *timed letters* $\mathsf{Lab}(\mathbb{A}) = [0, M] \times \mathsf{Lab}(\Delta)$.

Proposition-definition 2 (Timed sofic shift). *Let $\mathcal{A} = (\mathcal{G}, \mathsf{Lab})$ be a labelled closed timed graph then the set $[\mathcal{A}] = \{\mathsf{Lab}((\alpha_i)_{i \in \mathbb{Z}}) \mid (\alpha_i)_{i \in \mathbb{Z}} \in [\mathcal{G}]\}$ is a sub-shift of $(\mathsf{Lab}(\mathbb{A}))^{\mathbb{Z}}$ called the* timed sofic shift *of $\mathcal{A}$.*

An LTG is called *right resolving* if every two different transitions labelled by the same letter and starting from the same location have pairwise incompatible guards. As for classical symbolic dynamics, being right-resolving is the same thing as being deterministic less the property of having a unique initial state (see [1] for the usual definition of determinism in timed automata context). The LTGs of Figure 2 are right-resolving, they recognise the shift spaces of Example 2.

4.2 Discretisation of Shift Spaces and Their Entropy

Several definitions of ε-entropy for compact metric alphabet shift spaces were recalled in Section 2.2. Here, we give a simpler definition of ε-entropy for timed shift spaces which is asymptotically linked to the other ε-entropies in Proposition 3. This new definition of ε-entropy is based on discretisation of the timed shift space we explore now.

We call ε-*discrete* the different objects involving delays and clocks multiple of ε (i.e vector of delays of $\mathbb{R}^n$, timed words, bi-infinite timed words, runs, etc.). The ε-*discretisation* of a set B denoted by B_ε is the set of its ε-discrete elements. For instance, for $\mathbb{A} = [0, M] \times \Delta$, $\mathbb{A}_\varepsilon = \{0, \varepsilon, \dots, M\} \times \Delta$; for $X \subseteq \mathbb{A}^{\mathbb{Z}}$, $X_\varepsilon = X \cap \mathbb{A}_\varepsilon^{\mathbb{Z}}$.

The following proposition states a discretisation of timed shift spaces, the resulting shift space being a finite alphabet shift space.

Proposition 2. *If X is a sub-shift of $\mathbb{B}^{\mathbb{Z}}$ where $\mathbb{B}$ is a timed alphabet, then X_ε is a sub-shift of $\mathbb{B}_\varepsilon^{\mathbb{Z}}$.*

We define the ε-entropy of a shift $X \subseteq \mathbb{B}^{\mathbb{Z}}$ as the entropy of the shift $X_\varepsilon \subseteq \mathbb{B}_\varepsilon^{\mathbb{Z}}$:

$$h_\varepsilon(X) \overset{\text{def}}{=} h_{\text{top}}(X_\varepsilon) = \lim_{n \to \infty} \frac{1}{n} \log_2 |X_{\varepsilon,n}|.$$

Proposition 3. *For every two discretisation steps $\varepsilon' \geq \varepsilon$, for every timed sofic shift X, it holds that $h_{2\varepsilon'}(X) \leq h_{2\varepsilon}^S(X) \leq h_\varepsilon^N(X) \leq h_\varepsilon(X)$.*

Let $\mathcal{A} = (\mathcal{G}, \text{Lab})$ be a right-resolving LTG. The discretisation of the timed sofic shift $[\mathcal{A}]$ is the sofic shift of a right-resolving finite labelled graph $\mathcal{A}_\varepsilon$ obtained from $\mathcal{A}$ by a discretisation of its timed transitions and states as follows: $\mathcal{A}_\varepsilon = ((Q_\varepsilon, \Delta'), \text{Lab}')$ with $Q_\varepsilon = \mathbb{S} \cap (Q \times \{0, \varepsilon, \dots, M\}^d)$, $\text{Lab}' : \Delta' \to \text{Lab}(\mathbb{A}_\varepsilon)$ and there is a transition $\delta_{s,\alpha,s'} \in \Delta'$ going from $\delta_{s,\alpha,s'}{}^- \overset{\text{def}}{=} s$ to $\delta_{s,\alpha,s'}{}^+ \overset{\text{def}}{=} s'$ and labelled by $\text{Lab}'(\delta_{s,\alpha,s'}) \overset{\text{def}}{=} \text{Lab}(\alpha)$ iff $s \triangleright \alpha = s'$.

Proposition 4. *Let $\mathcal{A}$ be a right-resolving LTG, then $[\mathcal{A}_\varepsilon] = [\mathcal{A}]_\varepsilon$.*

As a corollary the computation of the ε-entropy of a timed sofic shift reduces to the computation of the entropy of a (finite alphabet) sofic shift.

Corollary 1. *Let $\mathcal{A} = (\mathcal{G}, \text{Lab})$ be a right-resolving LTG, its ε-entropy is the topological entropy of the sofic shift of $\mathcal{A}_\varepsilon$: $h_\varepsilon([\mathcal{A}]) = h_{\text{top}}([\mathcal{A}_\varepsilon])$. In particular, $h_\varepsilon([\mathcal{A}])$ can be computed as the logarithm of the spectral radius of the adjacency matrix of $\mathcal{A}_\varepsilon$ (This matrix has order $O(|Q|/\varepsilon^{|C|})$) where C is the set of clocks).*

In [6], a similar approach was used to over- and under-approximate the quantity $\mathcal{H}(\mathcal{A}) + \log_2(1/\varepsilon)$ for a timed automaton $\mathcal{A}$ without guarantee of convergence. The asymptotic equality of this quantity with the ε-entropy was later proved in [13] (Theorem 7 below).

The following theorem justifies that one can focus on TGs rather than right-resolving LTGs without loss of generality for the entropies.

Theorem 4. *Let $\mathcal{A} = (\mathcal{G}, \text{Lab})$ be a right-resolving LTG, then $\mathcal{H}([\mathcal{A}]) = \mathcal{H}([\mathcal{G}])$ and $h_\varepsilon([\mathcal{A}]) = h_\varepsilon([\mathcal{G}])$.*

Proof (Sketch). We use the following chain of equalities $h_\varepsilon([\mathcal{A}]) = h_{\text{top}}([\mathcal{A}_\varepsilon]) = h_{\text{top}}([\mathcal{G}_\varepsilon]) = h_\varepsilon([\mathcal{G}])$ where the first and third equalities are given by Corollary 1 and the second equality follows from a classical correspondence of entropy between finite alphabet sofic shift and their underlying edge shift (see [19]).

To prove that $\mathcal{H}([\mathcal{A}]) \leq \mathcal{H}([\mathcal{G}])$, we use the fact that for every word $w \in \Sigma^*$, $[\mathcal{A}]_n^{|w} = \cup_{\pi \in \mathtt{Lab}^{-1}(w)}[\mathcal{G}]_n^{|\pi}$, pass to volumes: $\mathtt{Vol}([\mathcal{A}]_n^{|w}) \leq \sum_{\pi \in \mathtt{Lab}^{-1}(w)} \mathtt{Vol}([\mathcal{G}]_n^{|\pi})$ and apply operator $\lim_{n \to \infty} \frac{1}{n} \log_2 \sum_{w \in \Sigma^n} (\ )$. The converse inequality $\mathcal{H}([\mathcal{A}]) \geq \mathcal{H}([\mathcal{G}])$ is more involved since the sets $[\mathcal{G}]_n^{|\pi}$ for $\pi \in \mathtt{Lab}^{-1}(w)$ can overlap. However, using the fact that $\mathcal{A} = (\mathcal{G}, \mathtt{Lab})$ is right-resolving, one can show that the volume of the overlap does not contribute to the entropy as it decreases too fast when $n \to \infty$ and hence $\mathcal{H}([\mathcal{A}]) \geq \mathcal{H}([\mathcal{G}])$ also holds. □

4.3 Metric Mean Dimension of Timed Sofic Shifts

Given a timed graph $\mathcal{G}$, a path π and $n = |\pi|$, it is well known that the set of delay vectors $[\mathcal{G}]_n^{|\pi} \overset{\text{def}}{=} \{(t_1, \ldots, t_n) \mid (t_1, \pi_1) \ldots (t_n, \pi_n) \in [\mathcal{G}]_n\}$ is a polytope. One can define the dimension $\dim(\pi)$ of a path, as the affine dimension of its polytope, that is, the maximal number of affinely independent points in the polytope minus 1 (see also [8]). A TG $\mathcal{G}$ is *fleshy* whenever all its path are full dimensional, that is $\dim(\pi) = |\pi|$ for every paths π of $\mathcal{G}$. It can happen that when the length of paths considered tends to infinity the delays are more and more constrained resulting in a null average choice. This kind of phenomena is measured by metric mean dimension defined and illustrated on several examples below.

The *metric mean dimension* [20] of a dynamical system $((X, d), f)$ is:

$$\mathbf{mdim}(X) = \liminf_{\varepsilon \to 0} \frac{\log_2 h_\varepsilon^S(X)}{\log_2(1/\varepsilon)} = \liminf_{\varepsilon \to 0} \frac{\log_2 h_\varepsilon^N(X)}{\log_2(1/\varepsilon)}$$

The second equality is due to Lemma 1. As a corollary of Proposition 3, we can characterise the metric mean dimension of timed sofic shift explicitly in terms of their ε-entropy as follows:

Corollary 2. *The metric mean dimension of a timed sofic shift X is:*

$$\mathbf{mdim}(X) = \liminf_{\varepsilon \to 0} \frac{\log_2 h_\varepsilon(X)}{\log_2(1/\varepsilon)} \tag{4}$$

Note that if $X \subseteq Y$ then $\mathbf{mdim}(X) \leq \mathbf{mdim}(Y)$ and that $\mathbf{mdim}(\mathbb{B}^\mathbb{Z}) = 1$ for every timed alphabet $\mathbb{B}$. Thus $\mathbf{mdim}(X) \leq 1$ for every sub-shift X of $\mathbb{B}^\mathbb{Z}$.

Example 3 (Example 2 and Figure 2 continued). The shift space X^{I} has metric mean dimension 1 since all the delays can be chosen independently in the interval $[0, 1/2]$. The shift space X^{II} contains only one element and has thus metric mean dimension 0. The metric mean dimension of X^{III} is $1/2$. This corresponds to the intuition that a full choice can be made half of the time, since delays before edges δ are always in the 0-dimensional singleton $\{1\}$ while delays before edges δ' are to be chosen in the 1-dimensional interval $[0, 1]$. The number of ε-discrete points in the polytope $[\mathcal{G}^{\mathrm{IV}}]_n^{|\pi}$ for the only path π of length n is $\binom{n+1/\varepsilon}{n}$ (Lemma 2 below) and thus the metric mean dimension of X^{IV} is null. Intuitively, there are less and less choices as n increases. Every path of $\mathcal{G}^\mathsf{V}$ containing a δ yields a volume 0, the only path of length n that yields a non-null volume is δ'^n. This volume is $\mathsf{Vol}(X_n^\mathsf{V}) = 1/n!$ and hence the entropy is $\mathcal{H}(X^\mathsf{V}) = -\infty$. The metric mean dimension of X^V is 1. Indeed, for every positive integer m, the paths in $(\delta^{m-1}\delta')^*$ yield a metric mean dimension equal to $(m-1)/m$ and thus $\mathbf{mdim} \geq 1 - 1/m$ for every $m > 0$.

Lemma 2 (Few points in a simplex). *The number of ε-discrete points in a simplex described by inequalities $0 \leq u_1 \leq \cdots \leq u_n \leq M$ (resp. by inequalities $\sum_{i=1}^{n} u_i \leq M$ and $u_i \geq 0$) is $\binom{n+M/\varepsilon}{n}$ and $(1/n) \log_2 \left[\binom{n+M/\varepsilon}{n} \right] \to_{n \to +\infty} 0$.*

One can generalise $\mathcal{G}^{\mathrm{III}}$ by defining a cycle with k transition b and $l-k$ transition a for every naturals $1 \leq k \leq l$. The resulting timed sofic shift has metric mean dimension k/l. More surprisingly arbitrary rational metric mean dimensions lower than 1 can be obtained from timed graph that have full dimensional sets of factors X_n for every length n.

Theorem 5. *For every rational $r \in \mathbb{Q} \cap [0, 1]$, there exists a timed sofic shift X recognised by a right-resolving fleshy LTG such that $\mathbf{mdim}(X) = r$.*

Proof (sketch). Examples of fleshy timed graph with metric mean dimension 0 or 1 have already been treated ($\mathcal{G}^\mathrm{I}$ and $\mathcal{G}^\mathrm{II}$). For every $a, b \in \mathbb{N}$ such that $0 < a < b$, we describe a cyclic timed graph with $2b$ edges and metric mean dimension $a/b \in \mathbb{Q} \cap (0, 1)$. The edges are $q_i \xrightarrow{x \in [i, i+1]} q_{i+1}$ for $i = 0..2a - 1$; $q_i \xrightarrow{y \geq 2a+1, x \in [2a, 2a+1]} q_{i+1}$ for $i = 2a..2b - 3$; $q_{2b-2} \xrightarrow{y \geq 2a+1, x \in [2a, 2a+1], y := 0} q_{2b-1}$; $q_{2b-1} \xrightarrow{x \in [2a, 2a+1], x := 0} q_0$. One can see that each edge of the first form yields a full dimension ($i = 0..2a - 1$). The other edges impose stringent constraints on clocks and delays like in a simplex. This yields a null mean dimension for these edges (Lemma 2). At the end for each cycle of length $2b$ there are $2a$ full dimensional edges and thus $\mathbf{mdim} = 2a/2b = a/b$.

The Thick Timed Sofic Shifts. In [13], we characterised precisely a dichotomy between *thin* and *thick* timed automata based on entropy, the former having infinite entropy ($\mathcal{H} = -\infty$) while the latter having a finite one ($\mathcal{H} > -\infty$). Beyond its entropy based definition we argued that this dichotomy is between bad behaving and well behaving TA. The former are in some weak sense Zeno, are non robust against clock perturbations, cannot be discretised well, etc. while the latter enjoy better properties such as a good discretisation, a quantitative pumping lemma and the existence of so-called forgetful cycles.

The metric mean dimension measurement gives a novel characterisation of thickness in terms of maximal metric mean dimension:

Theorem 6. *For timed sofic shifts X recognised by fleshy LTGs, thickness is equivalent to maximal metric mean dimension: $\mathcal{H}(X) > -\infty$ iff $\mathbf{mdim}(X) = 1$.*

Note that X^V satisfies both $\mathcal{H}(X^V) = -\infty$ and $\mathbf{mdim}(X^V) = 1$. This means that fleshiness is necessary in Theorem 6. Remark that regarding thickness, fleshiness is assumed wlog. since pruning the transitions involving punctual guards (e.g. $x = 1$) does not change the volume nor the entropy.

Beyond the pure dichotomy between thin and thick timed languages [13], Theorem 5 and 6 provide a deeper insight of convergence phenomena among thin timed languages. There is a whole continuum of thin timed languages between the extremely narrow ones of metric mean dimension 0 where all delays of timed words are constrained in a very stringent way, and the ones of dimension almost 1 for which full freedom in the delay is available at almost each transition.

For the sake of completness we recall one of the main theorems of our previous work [13] in terms of timed symbolic dynamics. This theorem ensures that the approximation of the entropy by discretisation initiated in [6] converges.

Theorem 7 (A symbolic dynamics version of Theorem 4 of [13]). *Let $\mathcal{A}$ be a right-resolving fleshy thick LTG then its volumetric entropy can be approximated by its ε-entropy as follows: $h_\varepsilon([\mathcal{A}]) = \log_2(1/\varepsilon) + \mathcal{H}([\mathcal{A}]) + o(1)$.*

One can interpret as in [2,6] $\mathcal{H}([\mathcal{A}])$ as the average information per event and $\log_2(1/\varepsilon)$ as the information necessary to represents with precision ε the time between two events.

5 Conclusion and Perspectives

In this paper, we introduced a theory of timed symbolic dynamics. We revisited previous works on volumetry of timed languages [5,6,13] within this new theory. We adapted to timed sofic shifts the metric mean dimension of Lindenstrauss, Weiss and Gromov [20]. We also stated a generalisation of the Curtis-Hedlund-Lyndon theorem for shift spaces on alphabets that are compact metric spaces.

Fundamental objects of classical symbolic dynamics are so-called shifts of finite types (SFT): the shift spaces that can be defined with a finite set of forbidden factors. In fact, such shifts are conjugated to edge shifts. That is why we are able to lift results from classical symbolic dynamics to the timed case without referring to SFTs (but referring to graphs and edge shifts). The entropy of probability measures on shift spaces is well studied in symbolic dynamics. The entropy of a probability measure on an edge shift (or equivalently SFT) is always bounded from above by the entropy of its underlying graph. An important result obtained by Parry [23] is that for every edge shift associated to a strongly connected graph, there is a unique probability measure whose entropy is equal to that of the edge shift. This probability measure is given by a Markov chain on the graph of the edge shift (originally described by Shannon [25]). We already generalised such a Shannon-Parry Markov chain to the timed settings motivated by verification purposes [9,11]. However, we left open the question of uniqueness. Symbolic dynamics techniques (as those of Parry) could hence be useful to address this problem.

In [7], Asarin and Degorre introduced a mean dimension (that we call *syntactic*) for timed automata and proposed an algebraic characterisation of it.

However this dimension only measures the proportion of non-punctual transitions along runs but not the Zeno behaviours. For instance, every fleshy timed graph has syntactic mean dimension 1 including $\mathcal{G}^{IV}$. It seems easy to show that the syntactic mean dimension is upper bounded by the metric mean dimension. The case of equality is more involved and still needs to be investigated.

Metric mean dimension and controllability. In robust control [22,24], the goal is to design a controller that chooses step by step an infinite timed word satisfying a Büchi condition even if every delay is slightly perturbed. As every transition can be perturbed, the part that is robustly controllable does not contain punctual guards (fleshiness). Robust controllability is equivalent to the reachability (through fleshy transitions) of a forgetful cycle satisfying the Büchi condition [22,24]. It would be interesting to relax the condition that every transition must be robustly controllable and consider a framework where in some steps delays with arbitrary precision are chosen. In such a framework we would like to prove that timed automata with metric mean dimension α are the timed automata that can be robustly controlled with a frequency of α and that require arbitrary precision with frequency $1 - \alpha$.

Acknowledgment. We gratefully acknowledge Eugène Asarin, Aldric Degorre and Dominique Perrin for motivating discussions.

References

1. Alur, R., Dill, D.L.: A theory of timed automata. TCS **126**(2), 183–235 (1994)
2. Asarin, E., Basset, N., Béal, M.-P., Degorre, A., Perrin, D.: Toward a timed theory of channel coding. In: Jurdziński, M., Ničković, D. (eds.) FORMATS 2012. LNCS, vol. 7595, pp. 27–42. Springer, Heidelberg (2012)
3. Asarin, E., Basset, N., Degorre, A.: Spectral gap in timed automata. In: Braberman, V., Fribourg, L. (eds.) FORMATS 2013. LNCS, vol. 8053, pp. 16–30. Springer, Heidelberg (2013)
4. Asarin, E., Basset, N., Degorre, A.: Entropy of regular timed languages. Information and Computation **241**, 142–176 (2015)
5. Asarin, E., Degorre, A.: Volume and entropy of regular timed languages: analytic approach. In: Ouaknine, J., Vaandrager, F.W. (eds.) FORMATS 2009. LNCS, vol. 5813, pp. 13–27. Springer, Heidelberg (2009)
6. Asarin, E., Degorre, A.: Volume and entropy of regular timed languages: discretization approach. In: Bravetti, M., Zavattaro, G. (eds.) CONCUR 2009. LNCS, vol. 5710, pp. 69–83. Springer, Heidelberg (2009)
7. Asarin, E., Degorre, A.: Two size measures for timed languages. In: FSTTCS. LIPIcs, vol. 8, pp. 376–387. Schloss Dagstuhl - Leibniz-Zentrum fuer Informatik (2010)
8. Baier, C., Bertrand, N., Bouyer, P., Brihaye, T., Größer, M.: Probabilistic and topological semantics for timed automata. In: Arvind, V., Prasad, S. (eds.) FSTTCS 2007. LNCS, vol. 4855, pp. 179–191. Springer, Heidelberg (2007)
9. Basset, N.: A maximal entropy stochastic process for a timed automaton. In: Fomin, F.V., Freivalds, R., Kwiatkowska, M., Peleg, D. (eds.) ICALP 2013, Part II. LNCS, vol. 7966, pp. 61–73. Springer, Heidelberg (2013)

10. Basset, N.: Volumetry of Timed Languages and Applications. PhD thesis, Université Paris-Est, France (2013)
11. Basset, N.: A maximal entropy stochastic process for a timed automaton. Information and Computation **243**, 50–74 (2015)
12. Basset, N.: Timed symbolic dynamics. hal-01094105 (2015). https://hal. archives-ouvertes.fr/hal-01094105
13. Basset, N., Asarin, E.: Thin and thick timed regular languages. In: Fahrenberg, U., Tripakis, S. (eds.) FORMATS 2011. LNCS, vol. 6919, pp. 113–128. Springer, Heidelberg (2011)
14. Béal, M.-P., Berstel, J., Eilers, S., Perrin, D.: Symbolic dynamics. CoRR, abs/1006.1265 (2010)
15. Bowen, R.: Entropy for group endomorphisms and homogeneous spaces. Transactions of the American Mathematical Society **153**, 401–414 (1971)
16. Brin, M., Stuck, G.: Introduction to Dynamical Systems. Cambridge University Press, New York (2002)
17. Fekete, M.: Uber die verteilung der wurzeln bei gewissen algebraischen gleichungen mit ganzzahligen koeffizienten. Mathematische Zeitschrift **17**, 228–249 (1923)
18. Kolmogorov, A.N., Tikhomirov, V.M.: ε-entropy and ε-capacity of sets in function spaces. Uspekhi Mat. Nauk **14**(2), 3–86 (1959)
19. Lind, D., Marcus, B.: An introduction to symbolic dynamics and coding. Cambridge University Press (1995)
20. Lindenstrauss, E., Weiss, B.: Mean topological dimension. Israel J. of Math. **115**, 1–24 (2000)
21. Munkres, J.R.: Topology. Prentice Hall, Incorporated (2000)
22. Oualhadj, Y., Reynier, P.-A., Sankur, O.: Probabilistic robust timed games. In: Baldan, P., Gorla, D. (eds.) CONCUR 2014. LNCS, vol. 8704, pp. 203–217. Springer, Heidelberg (2014)
23. Parry, W.: Intrinsic Markov chains. Transactions of the American Mathematical Society, 55–66 (1964)
24. Sankur, O., Bouyer, P., Markey, N., Reynier, P.-A.: Robust controller synthesis in timed automata. In: D'Argenio, P.R., Melgratti, H. (eds.) CONCUR 2013. LNCS, vol. 8052, pp. 546–560. Springer, Heidelberg (2013)
25. Shannon, C.E.: A mathematical theory of communication. Bell Sys. Tech. J. **27**(379–423), 623–656 (1948)
26. Vallée, B.: Dynamical analysis of a class of euclidean algorithms. Theor. Comput. Sci. **297**(1–3), 447–486 (2003)
27. Wisniewski, R., Sloth, C.: Completeness of Lyapunov Abstraction. Electronic Proceedings in Theoretical Computer Science **124**, 26–42 (2013)

Timed-Automata Abstraction of Switched Dynamical Systems Using Control Funnels

Patricia Bouyer[1], Nicolas Markey[1], Nicolas Perrin[2,3][✉],
and Philipp Schlehuber-Caissier[2]

[1] Laboratoire Spécification and Vérification, CNRS and ENS Cachan, Cachan, France
[2] Sorbonne Universités, UPMC Univ Paris 06, UMR 7222, ISIR, 75005 Paris, France
[3] CNRS, UMR 7222, ISIR, 75005 Paris, France
perrin@isir.upmc.fr

Abstract. The development of formal methods for control design is an important challenge with potential applications in a wide range of safety-critical cyber-physical systems. Focusing on switched dynamical systems, we propose a new abstraction, based on time-varying regions of invariance (the *control funnels*), that models behaviors of systems as timed automata. The main advantage of this method is that it allows automated verification of formal specifications and reactive controller synthesis without discretizing the evolution of the state of the system. Efficient constructions are possible in the case of linear dynamics. We demonstrate the potential of our approach with two examples.

1 Introduction

Verification and synthesis are notoriously difficult for hybrid dynamical systems, i.e. systems that allow abrupt changes in continuous dynamics. For instance, reachability is already undecidable for 2-dimensional piecewise-affine maps [14], or for 3-dimensional dynamical systems with piecewise-constant derivatives [2].

To enable automated logical reasoning on switched dynamical systems, most methods tend to entirely discretize the dynamics, for example by approximating the behavior of the system with a finite-state machine. Alternatively, early work pointed out links between hybrid and timed systems [20], and several methods have been designed to create formal abstractions of dynamical systems that do not rely on a discretization of time. In [11], a finite maneuver automaton is constructed from a library of motion primitives, and motion plans correspond to timed words. In [12,16], switched controller synthesis and stochastic optimal control are realized via metric temporal logic (MTL) or metric-interval temporal logic (MITL) specifications. In [19,22], grid-based abstractions and timed automata are used for motion planning or to check timed properties of dynamical systems. In [24], a subdivision of the state space created from sublevel sets of Lyapunov functions leads to an abstraction of dynamical systems by timed

This work has been partly supported by ERC Starting grant EQualIS (FP7-308087) and by European FET project Cassting (FP7-601148).

© Springer International Publishing Switzerland 2015
S. Sankaranarayanan and E. Vicario (Eds.): FORMATS 2015, LNCS 9268, pp. 60–75, 2015.
DOI: 10.1007/978-3-319-22975-1_5

automata that enables verification and falsification of safety properties. The same kind of abstraction is used in [23] for controller design via timed games, but the update map of the timed games obtained is such that synthesis cannot be realized using existing tools. In [8], the state space of each mode of a piecewise-affine hybrid system is portioned into polytopes, and thanks to control laws that prevent the system from exiting through a given facet, or that force the system to exit through a facet in finite time, reactive control problems can be solved as timed games on timed automata.

Our contribution is a novel timed-automata abstraction of switched dynamical systems based on a particular kind of time-varying regions of invariance: control funnels. Recent results have shown that these invariants are very useful for robust motion planning and control [17,18,26], and that funnels or similar concepts related to the notion of Lyapunov stability can be used for formal verification of hybrid systems [10,13], and for reactive controller synthesis [9].

The paper is organized as follows: Section 2, describes how control funnels, especially for trajectory tracking controllers, can be used to create timed transition systems that abstract the behavior of a given switched dynamical system, and as a result can potentially allow the use of verification tools for motion planning. In Section 3, we show how these timed transition systems can be encoded as timed automata. In Section 4, we consider the case of linear dynamics and introduce the notion of fixed size LQR funnel. In Section 5, we present two examples of application and efficient algorithms that manipulate these LQR funnels. In the first one, a timed game is solved by the tool Uppaal-Tiga [5] for the synthesis of a controller that can reactively adjust the phase of a sine wave controlled in acceleration. In the second example, we show that, using our timed-automata abstraction with LQR funnels along constant velocity trajectories, a non-trivial solution to a pick-and-place problem can be computed by the model checker Uppaal [6]. Section 6 concludes and presents avenues for future work.

2   Graphs of Control Funnels

2.1   Control Funnels

Consider a controlled dynamical system governed by the following equation:

$$\dot{x} = f(x, t, u(x, t)), \tag{1}$$

where $x \in \mathbb{R}^d$ is the state of the system (which can contain velocities[1]), $t \in \mathbb{R}^+$ is a real (clock) value corresponding to time (we restrict ourselves to nonnegative time values), $u \colon \mathbb{R}^d \times \mathbb{R}^+ \to \mathbb{R}^k$ is the control input function, and f is a continuously differentiable function from $\mathbb{R}^d \times \mathbb{R}^+ \times \mathbb{R}^k$ to $\mathbb{R}^d$ (which ensures

---

[1] In this paper, we mostly consider state spaces that describe the position and velocity of systems controlled in acceleration. The continuity of trajectories in the state space ensures that the position is always a continuously differentiable function of time.

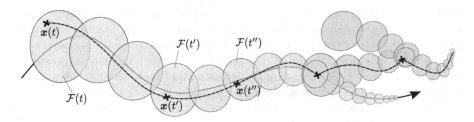

Fig. 1. An example of control funnel for a controller tracking a reference trajectory. The dashed line is a trajectory of the controlled system in the state space. On the right side, switching transitions between control funnels are depicted.

the uniqueness of the solution for given initial conditions). Assuming that the function u is fixed, we also use the following notation for Equation (1):

$$\dot{x} = f_u(x, t). \tag{2}$$

A *control funnel* for the above dynamical system is a function $\mathcal{F}: I \to 2^{\mathbb{R}^d}$ such that $I \subseteq \mathbb{R}^+$ and for any solution $x(t)$ of (2), the following property holds:

$$\forall t_1 \in I.\ \forall t_2 \in I.\ (t_2 > t_1 \text{ and } x(t_1) \in \mathcal{F}(t_1)) \Rightarrow x(t_2) \in \mathcal{F}(t_2). \tag{3}$$

It corresponds to time-varying regions of invariance.

Example 1. A typical example of a control funnel based on a trajectory tracking controller (that is, a control funnel asymptotically converging towards a reference trajectory in the state space) is shown in Fig. 1.

Example 2. For a concrete example, consider the simple system whose trajectories are of the form $e^{-t} \cdot x_0$. Then any set $W \subseteq \mathbb{R}^d$ defines a control funnel $\mathcal{F}_W: t \mapsto \{e^{-t} \cdot w \mid w \in W\}$.

The notion of funnel was popularized by Mason [21], and it usually specifically refers to operations that eliminate uncertainty (as is the case in the example of Fig. 1) by collapsing a large set of initial conditions into a smaller set of final conditions (see for instance [26]). In our case, the control funnel may or may not reduce uncertainty, and it is important to note that the set $\mathcal{F}(t)$ does not have to decrease in size over time. This more general concept is closer to the definition of *viability tubes* [4], but we nevertheless use the term control funnel as some reduction of uncertainty is often essential to the usefulness of our abstractions. We address the computation of control funnels in Section 4, and leave them as relatively abstract objects for now.

2.2 Motion Planning

Let us suppose that we have a finite set U of control laws $u_1(x, t)$, $u_2(x, t)$, ..., $u_n(x, t)$ that respectively set the dynamics of a given system to $\dot{x} = f_{u_1}(x, t)$, $\dot{x} = f_{u_2}(x, t)$, ..., $\dot{x} = f_{u_n}(x, t)$.

We say that the system can switch to the control law $u_i(\boldsymbol{x}, t)$ at some state $\widetilde{\boldsymbol{x}}$ whenever there is $t_0 \in \mathbb{R}^+$ and a solution $\boldsymbol{x}(t)$ of $\dot{\boldsymbol{x}} = f_{u_i}(\boldsymbol{x}, t)$ with initial condition $\widetilde{\boldsymbol{x}} = \boldsymbol{x}(t_0)$. Typically, if $u_i(\boldsymbol{x}, t)$ corresponds to a trajectory tracking controller, t_0 identifies the point of the trajectory where the tracking is triggered.

Informally, the *motion planning* problem asks, given a finite set of control laws as above, an initial point $\boldsymbol{x}_0$, a target zone $T_f \subseteq \mathbb{R}^d$, and an obstacle $\Omega \subseteq \mathbb{R}^d$, whether there exists a sequence of control law switches that generates a trajectory from $\boldsymbol{x}_0$ to T_f while avoiding the obstacle Ω. Several variants of this problem can be considered, that vary on the objective (for instance some tasks can be expressed as ω-regular objectives), but we focus here on a reachability with avoidance objective.

More formally, motion planning asks for a finite sequence of time values $t_0^1 < t_1^1, t_0^2 < t_1^2, \ldots, t_0^P < t_1^P$, a finite sequence of control laws indices $k_1, \ldots, k_P$, and a finite sequence $\boldsymbol{x}_1, \ldots, \boldsymbol{x}_P \in T_f$ of points in $\mathbb{R}^d$, such that:

(a) for every $1 \leq p \leq P$, if $\boldsymbol{x}^p$ is the unique solution to $\dot{\boldsymbol{x}} = f_{u_{k_p}}(\boldsymbol{x}, t)$ with initial condition $\boldsymbol{x}^p(t_0^p) = \boldsymbol{x}_{p-1}$, then $\boldsymbol{x}^p(t_1^p) = \boldsymbol{x}_p$.

(b) for every $1 \leq p \leq P$, for every $t_0^p \leq t \leq t_1^P$, $\boldsymbol{x}^p(t) \notin \Omega$.

Intuitively, this means that we can switch conveniently between all the control laws, causing discrete changes in the system dynamics, and ensure the global (reachability with avoidance) objective. The continuous trajectory generated by the solution above is the concatenation of the trajectory portions $\{x^p(t) \mid t_0^p \leq t \leq t_1^p\}$ for $1 \leq p \leq P$.

2.3 Motion Planning with Graphs of Control Funnels

We now explain how the motion planning problem can be abstracted using timed transition systems based on control funnels.

For each control law $u_i(\boldsymbol{x}, t)$, we assume that we have a finite set of control funnels $\mathcal{F}_i^1, \mathcal{F}_i^2, \ldots, \mathcal{F}_i^{m_i}$, respectively defined over $I_i^1 \subseteq \mathbb{R}^+, I_i^2 \subseteq \mathbb{R}^+, \ldots, I_i^{m_i} \subseteq \mathbb{R}^+$. We assume that for every $1 \leq i \leq n$, for every $1 \leq j \leq m_i$, for every $t \in I_i^j$, it holds $\mathcal{F}_i^j(t) \cap \Omega = \varnothing$, which means that trajectories contained in these funnels always avoid the obstacle Ω.

Consider a control law switch at position $\widetilde{\boldsymbol{x}}$ to law $u_i(\boldsymbol{x}, t)$ with clock value t_0. If there exists a control funnel $\mathcal{F}_i^j$ such that $t_0 \in I_i^j$, and $\widetilde{\boldsymbol{x}} \in \mathcal{F}_i^j(t_0)$, then we know that the state of the system will remain inside $\mathcal{F}_i^j(t)$ for any $t > t_0$ in I_i^j (as long as control law $u_i(\boldsymbol{x}, t)$ is used). To always keep the system inside one of the control funnels, we can impose sufficient conditions on the switches. For instance, if the state is inside $\mathcal{F}_i^j(t_0)$, and if for some future clock value t_1, there exists a control funnel $\mathcal{F}_k^l$ and $t_2 \in I_k^l$ such that $\mathcal{F}_i^j(t_1) \subseteq \mathcal{F}_k^l(t_2)$, then when the clock value is t_1 we can safely switch to the control law $u_k(\boldsymbol{x}, t)$ while setting the clock to t_2. Indeed, we know that the state of the system at the switch instant will be inside $\mathcal{F}_k^l(t_2)$, and therefore it will remain inside $\mathcal{F}_k^l(t)$ after the switch. Such transitions from a funnel to another are illustrated on the right side of Fig. 1. It is worth noting that similar transitions could be achieved with, instead of control funnels, controller specifications as introduced in [15]. For some control funnels $\mathcal{F}_i^j$ and $\mathcal{F}_i^k$ associated to the same control law, it is the case (see Section 4) that when funnel $\mathcal{F}_i^j$ is entered at time t, then at any time $t' \geq t + h_i^{j \to k}$ (where $h_i^{j \to k}$ is a constant), the state of the system is inside $\mathcal{F}_i^k(t')$. In that case, we say that the funnel $\mathcal{F}_i^k$ $h_i^{j \to k}$-absorbs the funnel $\mathcal{F}_i^j$.

These rules for navigating between control funnels give to the set of control funnels the structure of an infinite graph, or, more precisely, of a timed transition system with real-valued clocks. One of the clocks of this timed transition system is c_t, the *controller clock*. We add two other clocks: a global clock c_g, and a local clock c_h.

The *funnel timed transition system* $\mathcal{T}_{U,F}$ associated with the family of laws $U = (u_i(x,t))_{1 \leq i \leq n}$ and the family of funnels $F = ((\mathcal{F}_i^j, I_i^j))_{1 \leq i \leq n, 1 \leq j \leq m_i}$ is defined as follows. The configurations are pairs $(\mathcal{F}_i^j, v)$ where v assigns a non-negative real value to each of the clocks c_t, c_g and c_h, with $v(c_t) \in I_i^j$, and its transition set contains three types of elements:

- the *time-elapsing transitions*: $(\mathcal{F}_i^j, v) \to (\mathcal{F}_i^j, v + \Delta)$ whenever $[v(c_t), v(c_t) + \Delta] \subseteq I_i^j$ (where $v + \Delta$ denotes the valuation that maps each clock c to $v(c) + \Delta$);
- the *switching transitions*: $(\mathcal{F}_i^j, v) \to (\mathcal{F}_k^l, v')$ whenever $v'(c_g) = v(c_g)$, $v'(c_h) = 0$, $v(c_t) \in I_i^j$, $v'(c_t) \in I_k^l$, and $\mathcal{F}_i^j(v(c_t)) \subseteq \mathcal{F}_k^l(v'(c_t))$);
- the *absorbing transitions*: $(\mathcal{F}_i^j, v) \to (\mathcal{F}_i^k, v')$ whenever $\mathcal{F}_i^k$ $h_i^{j \to k}$-absorbs $\mathcal{F}_i^j$, $v(c_h) \geq h_i^{j \to k}$, $v'(c_h) = 0$, $v'(c_g) = v(c_g)$ and $v'(c_t) = v(c_t)$.

A run in this timed transition system is a finite sequence of configurations $((\mathcal{F}_{i_0}^{j_0}, v_0), (\mathcal{F}_{i_1}^{j_1}, v_1), \ldots, (\mathcal{F}_{i_P}^{j_P}, v_P))$ such that $v_0(c_h) = v_0(c_g) = 0$, $v_0(c_t) \in I_{i_0}^{j_0}$, and all the transitions $(\mathcal{F}_{i_p}^{j_p}, v_p) \to (\mathcal{F}_{i_{p+1}}^{j_{p+1}}, v_{p+1})$ for $0 \leq p < P$ are valid transitions that belong to $\mathcal{T}_{U,F}$.

Such a run is of total duration $v_P(c_g)$, and it corresponds to a schedule of control law switches that results from the following rules: initially, the control law is set to $u_{i_0}(x,t)$, and the controller clock c_t is set to $v_0(c_t)$. For every time-elapsing transition $(\mathcal{F}_i^j, v) \to (\mathcal{F}_i^j, v + \Delta)$, the same control law $u_i(x,t)$ is kept for a duration of Δ time units, and for every switching transition $(\mathcal{F}_i^j, v) \to (\mathcal{F}_k^l, v')$, the control law is switched from $u_i(x,t)$ to $u_k(x,t)$, with an initialization of the controller clock to $v'(c_t)$. Absorbing transitions are discarded, as they just correspond to an instantaneous change of funnels for the same control law. Let us denote this sequence of switches by r. Then, it is fundamental to notice that for every $x \in \mathcal{F}_{i_0}^{j_0}(v_0(c_t))$, if we follow the schedule of control law switches just described, then the system remains inside control funnels and reaches at the end of the run a unique point of $\mathbb{R}^d$, that we denote $r(x)$. The trajectory going from x to $r(x)$ is also uniquely defined.

The funnel timed transition system $\mathcal{T}_{U,F}$ satisfies the following property:

Theorem 1. *Let* $r = ((\mathcal{F}_{i_0}^{j_0}, v_0), (\mathcal{F}_{i_1}^{j_1}, v_1), \ldots, (\mathcal{F}_{i_P}^{j_P}, v_P))$ *be a run in* $\mathcal{T}_{U,F}$. *If* $x \in \mathcal{F}_{i_0}^{j_0}(v_0(c_t))$, *then* $r(x) \in \mathcal{F}_{i_P}^{j_P}(v_P(c_t))$.

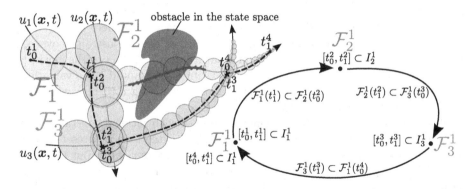

Fig. 2. Run of a funnel timed transition system with three control funnels: $r = ((\mathcal{F}_1^1, v_0^1), (\mathcal{F}_1^1, v_1^1), (\mathcal{F}_2^1, v_0^2), (\mathcal{F}_2^1, v_1^2), (\mathcal{F}_3^1, v_0^3), (\mathcal{F}_3^1, v_1^3), (\mathcal{F}_4^1, v_0^4), (\mathcal{F}_4^1, v_1^4))$, with: $\forall 1 \le i \le 4, v_0^i(c_t) = t_0^i, v_1^i(c_t) = t_1^i, v_0^i(c_h) = 0, v_1^i(c_h) = t_1^i - t_0^i, v_1^i(c_g) = v_0^i(c_g) + v_1^i(c_h)$, and $v_0^1(c_g) = 0$, and $\forall 2 \le i \le 4, v_0^i(c_g) = v_1^{i-1}(c_g)$.

In some sense, the funnel timed transition system $\mathcal{T}_{U,F}$ is a correct abstraction of trajectories that can be generated by the set of control laws: if $x_0 \in \mathcal{F}_{i_0}^{j_0}(v_0(c_t))$ and $\mathcal{F}_{i_P}^{j_P}(v_P(c_t)) \subseteq T_f$, then such a run witnesses a solution to the motion planning problem. However, this abstraction is obviously not complete.

Example 3 (An example with obstacles). The example in Fig. 2 shows a run with three control laws $u_1(x,t)$, $u_2(x,t)$ and $u_3(x,t)$, three control funnels $\mathcal{F}_1^1$, $\mathcal{F}_2^1$ and $\mathcal{F}_3^1$, and an obstacle in the state space. The domains of definition of the control funnels I_1^1, I_2^1 and I_3^1 are such that for all $\alpha \in \{1,2,3\}$ and all $t \in I_\alpha^1$, $\mathcal{F}_\alpha^1(t)$ does not intersect the obstacles.

With the previous property, any run in the corresponding funnel timed transition system leads to a trajectory that avoids the obstacles. The example of Fig. 2, where reaching $\mathcal{F}_1^1(t_1^4)$ from $\mathcal{F}_1^1(t_0^1)$ requires a series of switches between the different control funnels, shows the potential interest of automated verification in timed transition systems, as it can result in the generation of obstacle-free dynamic trajectories via appropriate control law switches.

3   Reduction to Timed Automata

Timed automata [1] are a timed extension of finite-state automata, with a well-understood theory. They provide an expressive formalism for modelling and reasoning about real-time systems, and enjoy decidable reachability properties; much efforts have been invested over the last 20 years for the development of efficient algorithms and tools for their automatic verification (such as the tool Uppaal [6], which we use in this work).

Let C be a finite set of real-valued variables called *clocks*. A *clock valuation* over a finite set of clocks C is a mapping $v \colon C \to \mathbb{R}^+$. We write $\mathbb{R}^C$ for the set of clock valuations over C. If $\Delta \in \mathbb{R}^+$, we write $v + \Delta$ for the clock valuation defined by $(v + \Delta)(c) = v(c) + \Delta$ for every $c \in C$. A *clock constraint* over C is a boolean combination of expressions of the form $c \sim \alpha$ where $\alpha \in \mathbb{Q}$, and $\sim \in \{\leq, <, =, >, \geq\}$. We denote by $\mathcal{C}(C)$ the set of clock constraints over C. We write $v \models g$ if v satisfies g (defined in a natural way). A reset of the clocks is an element res of $(\mathbb{Q} \cup \{\bot\})^C$ (which we may write $R(C)$), and if v is a valuation, its image by res, denoted $\mathsf{res}(v)$, is the valuation mapping c to $v(c)$ whenever $\mathsf{res}(c) = \bot$, and to $\mathsf{res}(c) \in \mathbb{Q}$ otherwise.

We define a slight extension of timed automata with rational constants, general boolean combinations of clock constraints and extended clock resets; those timed automata are as expressive as standard timed automata [7], but they will be useful for expressing funnel timed transition systems. A *timed automaton* is a tuple $\mathcal{A} = (L, L_0, L_F, C, E, \mathsf{Inv})$ where L is a finite set of locations, $L_0 \subseteq L$ is a set of initial locations, $L_F \subseteq L$ is a set of final locations, C is a finite set of clocks, $E \subseteq L \times \mathcal{C}(C) \times R(C) \times L$ is a set of edges, and $\mathsf{Inv} \colon L \to \mathcal{C}(C)$ is an invariant labelling function.

A configuration of $\mathcal{A}$ is a pair $(\ell, v) \in L \times \mathbb{R}^C$ such that $v \models \mathsf{Inv}(\ell)$, and the timed transition system generated by $\mathcal{A}$ is given by the following two rules:

- *time-elapsing transition:* $(\ell, v) \to (\ell, v + \Delta)$ whenever $v + \delta \in \mathsf{Inv}(\ell)$ for every $0 \leq \delta \leq \Delta$;
- *switching or absorbing transition:* $(\ell, v) \to (\ell', v')$ whenever there exists $(\ell, g, \mathsf{res}, \ell') \in E$ such that $v \models g \wedge \mathsf{Inv}(\ell)$, $v' = \mathsf{res}(v)$, and $v' \in \mathsf{Inv}(\ell')$.

A run in $\mathcal{A}$ is a sequence of consecutive transitions. The most fundamental result about timed automata is the following:

Theorem 2 ([1]). *Reachability in timed automata is PSPACE-complete.*

We consider again the family of control laws $U = (u_i(\boldsymbol{x}, t))_{1 \leq i \leq n}$, and the family of funnels $F = ((\mathcal{F}_i^j, I_i^j))_{1 \leq i \leq n, 1 \leq j \leq m_i}$, as in the previous section. For every pair $1 \leq i, k \leq n$, and every $1 \leq j \leq m_i$ and $1 \leq l \leq m_k$, we select finitely many tuples $(\mathsf{switch}, [\alpha, \beta], (i, j), \gamma, (k, l))$ with $\alpha, \beta, \gamma \in \mathbb{Q}$ such that (i) $[\alpha, \beta] \subseteq I_i^j$, (ii) $\gamma \in I_k^l$, and (iii) for every $t \in [\alpha, \beta]$, $\mathcal{F}_i^j(t) \subseteq \mathcal{F}_k^l(\gamma)$. This allows us to under-approximate the possible switches between funnels. For every $1 \leq i \leq n$, for every pair $1 \leq j, k \leq m_i$, we select at most one tuple $(\mathsf{absorb}, \nu, (i, j, k))$ such that $\nu \in \mathbb{Q}$ and $\mathcal{F}_i^k(t)$ ν-absorbs $\mathcal{F}_i^j(t)$. This allows us to under-approximate the possible absorbing transitions. For every $1 \leq i \leq n$ and every $1 \leq j \leq m_i$, we fix a finite set of tuples $(\mathsf{initial}, \alpha, (i, j))$ such that $\alpha \in \mathbb{Q}$ and $\boldsymbol{x}_0 \in \mathcal{F}_i^j(\alpha)$. This allows us to under-approximate the possible initialization to a control funnel containing the initial point $\boldsymbol{x}_0$. For every $1 \leq i \leq n$ and $1 \leq j \leq m_i$, we fix finitely many tuples $(\mathsf{invariant}, S_{i,j}, (i, j))$, where $S_{i,j} \subseteq I_i^j$ is a finite set of closed intervals with rational bounds. This allows us to under-approximate the definition set of the funnels. Finally, for every $1 \leq i \leq n$ and $1 \leq j \leq m_i$, we fix finitely many tuples $(\mathsf{target}, [\alpha, \beta], (i, j))$, where $\alpha, \beta \in \mathbb{Q}$ and $[\alpha, \beta] \subseteq I_i^j \cap \{t \mid \mathcal{F}_i^j(t) \subseteq T_f\}$. This allows us to under-approximate the target zone. We denote by K the set of all tuples we just defined.

We can now define a timed automaton that conservatively computes the runs generated by the funnel timed transition system. It is defined by $\mathcal{A}_{U,F,K} = (L, L_0, L_F, C, E, \mathsf{Inv})$ with:

- $L = \{\mathcal{F}_i^j \mid 1 \leq i \leq n,\ 1 \leq j \leq m_i\} \cup \{\mathsf{init}, \mathsf{stop}\}$; $L_0 = \{\mathsf{init}\}$; $L_F = \{\mathsf{stop}\}$;
- $C = \{c_t, c_g, c_h\}$;
- E is composed of the following edges:
  - for every $(\mathsf{initial}, \alpha, (i,j)) \in K$, we have an edge $(\mathsf{init}, \mathsf{true}, \mathsf{res}, \mathcal{F}_i^j)$ in E, with $\mathsf{res}(c_t) = \alpha$ and $\mathsf{res}(c_g) = \mathsf{res}(c_h) = 0$;
  - for every $(\mathsf{switch}, [\alpha, \beta], (i,j), \gamma, (k,l)) \in K$, we have an edge $(\mathcal{F}_i^j, \alpha \leq c_t \leq \beta, \mathsf{res}, \mathcal{F}_k^l)$ with $\mathsf{res}(c_t) = \gamma$, $\mathsf{res}(c_h) = 0$ and $\mathsf{res}(c_g) = \bot$;
  - for every $(\mathsf{target}, [\alpha, \beta], (i,j)) \in K$, we have an edge $(\mathcal{F}_i^j, \alpha \leq c_t \leq \beta, \mathsf{res}, \mathsf{stop})$ in E, with $\mathsf{res}(c_t) = \mathsf{res}(c_g) = \mathsf{res}(c_h) = \bot$;
  - for every $(\mathsf{absorb}, \nu, (i,j,k)) \in K$, we have an edge $(\mathcal{F}_i^j, c_h \geq \nu, \mathsf{res}, \mathcal{F}_i^k)$ with $\mathsf{res}(c_h) = 0$ and $\mathsf{res}(c_t) = \mathsf{res}(c_g) = \bot$;
- for every $(\mathsf{invariant}, S_{i,j}, (i,j)) \in K$, we let $\mathsf{Inv}(\mathcal{F}_i^j) \triangleq \bigvee_{[\alpha,\beta] \in S_{i,j}} (\alpha \leq c_t \leq \beta)$.

We easily get the following result:

Theorem 3. *Let* $(\mathsf{init}, v_0) \to (\ell_1, v_1) \to \cdots \to (\ell_P, v_P) \to (\mathsf{stop}, v_P)$ *be a run in* $\mathcal{A}_{U,F,K}$ *such that* v_0 *assigns* 0 *to every clock. Then* $r = ((\ell_1, v_1), \ldots, (\ell_P, v_P))$ *is a run of the funnel timed transition system* $\mathcal{T}_{U,F}$ *that brings* x_0 *to* $r(x_0) \in T_f$ *while avoiding the obstacle* Ω.

This shows that the reachability of stop in $\mathcal{A}_{U,F,K}$ implies that there exists an appropriate schedule of control law switches that safely brings the system to the target zone. Of course, the method is not complete, not all schedules can be obtained using the timed automaton $\mathcal{A}_{U,F,K}$. But if $\mathcal{A}_{U,F,K}$ is precise enough, it will be possible to use automatic verification techniques for dynamic trajectory generation.

Remark 1. We could be more precise in the modelling as a timed automaton, if we could use non-deterministic clock resets [7]; but we should then be careful with decidability issues. Additionally, non-deterministic resets are not implemented in Uppaal, which is why we have chosen timed automata with deterministic resets only.

Remark 2. As we show with some examples in Section 5, our timed-automata abstraction can be used for other types of objectives than just reachability with avoidance. In particular, the approach can be extended to *timed games* [3], where special uncontrollable transitions model uncertainty in the environment. In that case, the aim is not to synthesize one single run in the system, but rather a *strategy* that dictates how the system should be controlled, depending on how the environment evolves. It is worth knowing that winning strategies can be computed in exponential time in timed games, and that the tool Uppaal-Tiga [5] computes winning strategies. In Section 5.1, we give an example of application where timed games and Uppaal-Tiga are used.

4 LQR Funnels

In this section we consider the particular case of linear time-invariant stabilizable systems whose dynamics are described by the following equation:

$$\dot{x} = Ax + Bu, \tag{4}$$

where $A \in \mathbb{R}^{d \times d}$ and $B \in \mathbb{R}^{d \times k}$ are two constant matrices, and $u \in \mathbb{R}^k$ is the control input. We also consider reference trajectories that can be realized with controlled systems described by Eq. (4), i.e. trajectories $x_{\text{ref}}(t)$ for which there exists $u_{\text{ref}}(x, t)$ such that $\dot{x}_{\text{ref}} = Ax_{\text{ref}} + Bu_{\text{ref}}$. We can combine this equation with (4) and get $\dot{x} - \dot{x}_{\text{ref}} = A(x - x_{\text{ref}}) + B(u - u_{\text{ref}})$, which rewrites

$$\dot{x}_\Delta = Ax_\Delta + Bu_\Delta. \tag{5}$$

To track $\dot{x}_{\text{ref}}$, we compute u_Δ as an infinite-time linear quadratic regulator (LQR, see [25]), i.e. a minimization of the cost: $J = \int_0^\infty \left(x_\Delta^\mathsf{T} Q x_\Delta + u_\Delta^\mathsf{T} R u_\Delta \right) dt$, where Q and R respectively are positive-semidefinite and positive-definite matrices. The solution is $u_\Delta = -Kx_\Delta$, with $K = R^{-1}B^\mathsf{T}P$ and P being the unique positive-definite matrix solution of the continuous time algebraic Riccati equation: $PA + A^\mathsf{T}P - PBR^{-1}B^\mathsf{T}P + Q = 0$.

The dynamics can be rewritten $\dot{x}_\Delta = (A - BK)x_\Delta = \bar{A}x_\Delta$, i.e.:

$$\dot{x} = \dot{x}_{\text{ref}} + \bar{A}(x - x_{\text{ref}}), \tag{6}$$

and the matrix $\bar{A}$ is Hurwitz, i.e. all its eigenvalues have negative real parts. Additionally, $V : x_\Delta \mapsto x_\Delta^\mathsf{T} P x_\Delta$ is a Lyapunov function ($V(0) = 0$ and for all $x_\Delta \neq 0$, it holds $V(x_\Delta) > 0$ and $\dot{V}(x_\Delta) < 0$). The solutions of Eq. (6) can be written: $x(t) = x_{\text{ref}}(t) + e^{\bar{A}(t-t_0)}x_\Delta(t_0)$. Since $\bar{A}$ is Hurwitz, the term $e^{\bar{A}(t-t_0)}$ tends to 0 exponentially fast, and the tracking asymptotically converges towards the reference trajectory $x_{\text{ref}}(t)$. The Lyapunov function V can be used to define control funnels as follows. For $\alpha > 0$, we let:

$$\mathcal{F}_\alpha(t) = \{x_{\text{ref}}(t) + x_\Delta \mid V(x_\Delta) \leq \alpha\} \tag{7}$$

$\mathcal{F}$ is a control funnel defined over $\mathbb{R}$: if $x_\Delta(t) = x(t) - x_{\text{ref}}(t)$ is a solution of Eq. (5) such that $x(t_1) \in \mathcal{F}_\alpha(t_1)$, then for any $t_2 > t_1$, since $V(x_\Delta)$ only decreases, $V(x_\Delta(t_2)) \leq V(x_\Delta(t_1)) \leq \alpha$, and thus $x(t_2) = x_{\text{ref}}(t_2) + x_\Delta(t_2) \in \mathcal{F}_\alpha(t_2)$.

$\mathcal{F}_\alpha(t)$ is a fixed d-dimensional ellipsoid centered at $x_{ref}(t)$. Without going into details, it is possible to get lower bounds on the rate of decay of $V(x_\Delta)$, and effectively compute $\beta > 0$ such that, for any solution $x_\Delta(t)$ of Eq. (5):

$$\forall t \in \mathbb{R}, \forall \delta t \in \mathbb{R}^+, \; V(x_\Delta(t + \delta t)) \leq e^{-\beta.\delta t}V(x_\Delta(t)) \tag{8}$$

This proves that if the system is inside the control funnel $\mathcal{F}_\alpha(t)$ at a given instant, then after letting time elapse for a duration of δt, the system will be inside the control funnel $\mathcal{F}_{\alpha e^{-\beta.\delta t}}(t)$. Using the terminology of Section 2.3, this

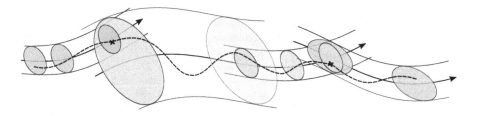

Fig. 3. An absorbing transition (in green) between two switching transitions.

can be equivalently stated as follows: for $0 < \alpha' < \alpha$, the control funnel $\mathcal{F}_{\alpha'}(t)$ $\left[\frac{1}{\beta}\log(\frac{\alpha}{\alpha'})\right]$-absorbs the control funnel $\mathcal{F}_{\alpha}(t)$. Thanks to this property, for a given LQR controller and a reference trajectory $x_{\mathrm{ref}}(t)$, we can define a finite set of fixed-size control funnels $\mathcal{F}_{\alpha_0}(t), \mathcal{F}_{\alpha_1}(t), \ldots, \mathcal{F}_{\alpha_q}(t)$, with $\alpha_0 > \alpha_1 > \cdots > \alpha_q > 0$, and absorbing transitions between them in the corresponding timed automaton.

In the remainder of the article, we will only use this kind of fixed size control funnels, which we call "LQR funnels". They are convenient because the larger ones can be used to "catch" other control funnels, and the smaller ones can easily be caught by other control funnels. Figure 3 depicts a typical sequence, where first a large control funnel (in green) catches the system, then after some time, an absorbing transition can be triggered, and finally, a new transition brings the system to a larger control funnel (in blue) on another trajectory. Besides that, testing for inclusion between fixed-size ellipsoids is easy, and therefore LQR funnels allow relatively efficient algorithms for the computation of the tuples needed for the timed-automaton reduction $((\mathsf{switch}, [\alpha, \beta], (i, j), \gamma, (k, l))$, $(\mathsf{invariant}, S_{i,j}, (i, j)), \ldots$, see Section 3).

It should be noted that the concepts of fixed size control funnels and absorbing transitions, introduced here for linear systems, are also suitable for general nonlinear systems. Lyapunov functions in general, and quadratic ones in particular, can be computed via optimization, for example with Sum-of-Squares techniques as shown in [17]. By imposing specific constraints on the optimization, fixed size control funnels with exponential convergence can be obtained inducing the same kind of absorbing transitions as introduced in the last paragraph.

5   Examples of Application

5.1   Synchronization of Sine Waves

In this example, there is a unique reference trajectory: $x_{\mathrm{ref}}(t) = \sin(\frac{2\pi}{\tau}t)$, for $t \in [0, \tau]$ and $\tau \in \mathbb{Q}$, and a unique LQR controller tracking this trajectory. We define two fixed size LQR funnels $\mathcal{F}^1$ (the large one) and $\mathcal{F}^2$ (the small one) defined over $[0, \tau]$ such that $\mathcal{F}^2$ γ-absorbs $\mathcal{F}^1$ for some $\gamma \in \mathbb{Q}$. The size of $\mathcal{F}^1$ is

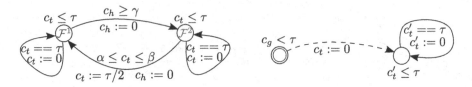

Fig. 4. *On the left:* the timed automaton for the controlled signal (the system). *On the right:* the timed automaton used to model the target signal with an initially unknown phase φ_0. The opponent transition (dashed) is the one used to set φ_0.

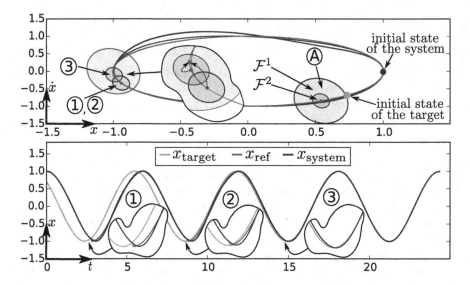

Fig. 5. The reactive controller performs three switching transitions to exactly adjust its phase to that of the target signal.

computed so that an upper bound on the acceleration is always ensured, as long as the state of the system remains inside the control funnel.

The set $\mathcal{F}^1(\tau/2)$ contains the smaller control funnel $\mathcal{F}^2(t)$ for a range of time values $[\alpha, \beta]$ for some $\alpha < \frac{\tau}{2} \in \mathbb{Q}$ and $\beta > \frac{\tau}{2} \in \mathbb{Q}$. This allows switching transitions from $\mathcal{F}^2$ to $\mathcal{F}^1$ with abrupt modifications of the controller clock c_t. Together with the absorbing transition and "cyclic transitions" that come from the equalities $\mathcal{F}^1(0) = \mathcal{F}^1(\tau)$ and $\mathcal{F}^2(0) = \mathcal{F}^2(\tau)$, it results in an abstraction by the timed automaton shown on the left side of Fig. 4. The goal is to synchronize the controlled signal to a fixed signal $\sin(\frac{2\pi}{\tau}t + \varphi_0)$. The phase φ_0 is initially unknown, which we model using an adversary: we use a new clock c_t', and an opponent transition as in the timed automaton on the right side of Fig. 4.

With these two timed automata, we can use the tool Uppaal-Tiga to synthesize a controller that reacts to the choice of the adversary, and performs adequate switching transitions until $c_t = c_t'$. It is even possible to generate a strategy that guarantees that the synchronization can always be performed in a

Fig. 6. The figure on the left shows the set-up. The black dots correspond to the position of the lanes. On the right are shown some LQR funnels along the constant velocity reference trajectories in the state space.

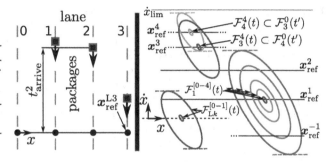

bounded amount of time. We show in Fig. 5 a trajectory generated by the synthesized reactive controller. In this example, the phase chosen by the adversary is such that it is best to accelerate the controlled signal. Therefore, the controller uses twice the switching transition from $\mathcal{F}^2$ to $\mathcal{F}^1$ with a reset of the controller clock from α to $\tau/2$ (① and ② in Fig. 5). Between these switching transitions, an absorbing transition is taken to go back to the control funnel $\mathcal{F}^2$ (Ⓐ in Fig. 5). After the first two switching transitions, the remaining gap ε between c_t and c'_t is smaller than $\frac{\tau}{2} - \alpha$, and therefore the controller waits a bit longer (until $\frac{\tau}{2} - \varepsilon$) to perform the switching transition that exactly synchronizes the two signals (③ in Fig. 5).

This example shows that our abstraction can be used for reactive controller synthesis via timed games. The main advantage of our approach over methods based on full discretization is that, since a continuous notion of time is kept in our abstraction, the reactive strategy is theoretically able to *exactly* synchronize the controlled signal to any real value of φ_0. One of our hopes is that extensions of this result can lead to a general formal approach for signal processing.

5.2   A 1D Pick-and-Place Problem

In this second example, we show that timed-automata abstractions based on control funnels can be used to perform non-trivial planning. We propose a one-dimensional pick-and-place scenario. The set-up consists of a linear system controlled in acceleration moving along a straight line. On this line, four positions are defined as lanes (see Fig. 6). On three of these lanes (1, 2 and 3), packages arrive that have to be caught at the right time by the system and later delivered to lane 0. The system has limited acceleration and velocity, and can carry at most two packages at a time.

The LQR funnels in this example are constructed based on 12 reference trajectories. The first four have different constant positive velocities (x_{ref}^i with $i \in \{1, \ldots, 4\}$, the fastest one being x_{ref}^4, and the slowest one x_{ref}^1). The next four are the same trajectories with negative velocities. On each of these reference trajectories, five different control funnels of constant size are defined ($\mathcal{F}_i^j$ for $j \in \{0, \ldots, 4\}$, the largest one being $\mathcal{F}_i^0$). The control funnels with negative constant velocity are the mirror image of those with positive velocity.

72   P. Bouyer et al.

Fig. 7. In order to define the tuples (switch, $[\alpha, \beta], (i,j), \gamma, (k,l)$) (see Section 3), N regularly spaced points are chosen in x^k_{ref} (defining the ellipses $\mathcal{F}^l_k(t_n)$ for $n \in \{1, \ldots, N\}$), and for each n, we set $\gamma = t_n$, and if a point $x^i_{ref}(t)$ such that $\mathcal{F}^j_i(t) \subset \mathcal{F}^l_k(\gamma)$ is found, an incremental search is performed to define a range $[\alpha, \beta]$ such that $\forall t \in [\alpha, \beta]$, $\mathcal{F}^j_i(t) \subset \mathcal{F}^l_k(\gamma)$.

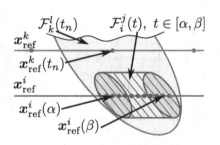

Additionally, four stationary trajectories x^{Lk}_{ref} (with $k \in \{0, \ldots, 3\}$) at the positions of the lanes are defined. The controllers associated to these trajectories simply stabilize the system at lane positions. For each of these trajectories a small ($j = 0$) and a large ($j = 1$) control funnel are constructed. They are denoted by $\mathcal{F}^j_{Lk}$. By construction, neighboring trajectories (e.g. x^3_{ref} and x^2_{ref} or x^1_{ref} and x^{-1}_{ref}) are connected, meaning that for two neighboring trajectories x^i_{ref} and x^k_{ref}, $\forall t \in I_i$, $\exists t' \in I_k$ s.t. $\mathcal{F}^4_i(t) \subset \mathcal{F}^0_k(t')$ (see Fig. 6). This allows the system to reach a higher or lower velocity without the need of an explicitly defined acceleration trajectory. While the abstraction based on these control funnels does not represent all the possible behaviors of the system (it is not complete), switching between different velocity references allows the system to perform a great variety of trajectories with continuous and bounded velocity and bounded acceleration.

To fully specify the timed-automata abstraction, the tuples defining the transition guards must be computed (see Section 3). Here, the regions of invariance defining the funnels are identically-shaped ellipses (only translated along a reference trajectory and scaled), thus the test for inclusion is computationally very cheap. Therefore, many points can be tested for inclusion on each trajectory, as depicted in Fig. 7, which leads to precise ranges for the switching transitions. Since the funnels are fixed sets translated along reference trajectories, knowing velocity or acceleration bounds on these references, and using offsets in the inclusion tests, we can ensure inclusion on the whole range of a switching transition with only a finite number of inclusion tests.

We consider an example where three packages respectively arrive on lanes 3, 2 and 1 at times $t^1_{arrive} = 40$, $t^2_{arrive} = 111$ and $t^3_{arrive} = 122$ (corresponding equality tests on c_g can be used to refer to these moments in the timed automaton abstraction). The goal is to find a trajectory that catches all the packages and delivers them to lane 0. At the moment of the catch ($c_g = t^p_{arrive}$), the reference x^i_{ref} tracked by the system must be exactly at the correct position (i.e. on the lane of the arriving package). Depending on the reference trajectory, this corresponds to a particular value of c_t. We add the following constraints on the catches: an upper bound on velocity such that the system cannot be tracking x^4_{ref}, x^3_{ref}, x^{-3}_{ref} or x^{-4}_{ref} when it catches a package, and a bound on uncertainty such that the system must be in a small control funnel to catch a package. Using additional constructions in our timed automaton abstraction (for example a bounded counter that keeps track of the number of packages being carried by

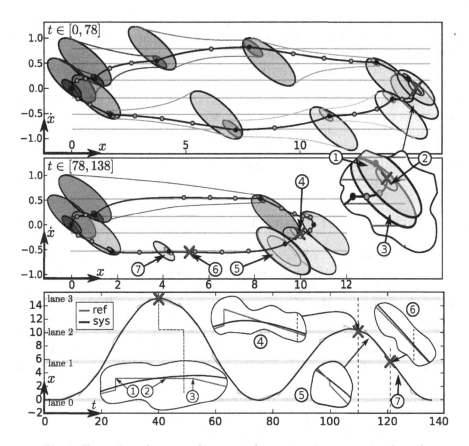

Fig. 8. Execution of a succeeding control strategy given as a timed word.

the system), it is easy to specify these constraints and the objective as a reachability specification that can be checked by Uppaal. Uppaal outputs a timed word that corresponds to the schedule of control law switches and the trajectory shown on Fig. 8, which successfully catches the packages and delivers them to lane 0.

The two upper graphs of Fig. 8 show the evolution of the system in its state space and some of the regions of invariance when taking a *switching transition* (colored ellipses). The green dots mark positions at which *absorbing transitions* take place ($\mathcal{F}_i^j \rightarrow \mathcal{F}_i^{j+1}$). Purple crosses represent a package. The lower graph compares the evolution of the position of the real system with the reference. One can see that even though the reference velocity can only take seven different values, a relatively smooth trajectory is realized. Before catching the first package, the system switches from $\mathcal{F}_1^4$ to $\mathcal{F}_{L3}^0$ ①. It then converges to $\mathcal{F}_{L3}^1$ ② just before the catch. The difference between the real system position and the reference is very small at that point in time. The system then switches to $\mathcal{F}_{-1}^0$ ③ in order to return to lane 0. It is interesting to notice that the system chooses to return to lane 0 after having picked only one package, therefore adopting a non-greedy strategy. This is because it wouldn't have time to perform a delivery to lane 0 between the arrival of the second and third packages.

When the second package arrives on lane 2, the system catches it while being in $\mathcal{F}^4_{-1}$ ④. This is again a non-trivial behavior: in order to get both the second and the third packages, the system has to first go a little bit further than lane 2 so as to be able to catch the two packages without violating the limit on acceleration. A slight adjustment of the reference position ⑤ has to be done to catch the third package exactly on time ⑥. After that, the system performs a local acceleration ⑦ to reach lane 0 as soon as possible, and delivers the two packages.

6   Conclusion and Future Work

We have presented a timed-automata abstraction of switched dynamical systems based on control funnels, i.e. time-varying regions of invariance. Applying verification tools (such as Uppaal) on this abstraction, one can solve motion planning or more complicated problems with timing requirements. In the example of Section 5.2, we are able to generate a non-trivial solution for a pick-and-place problem. Synthesis of controllers that react to the environment can be done by solving timed games, and in the example of Section 5.1 we use Uppaal-Tiga to generate a controller that can reactively adjust the phase of a signal controlled in acceleration.

To go further and improve our abstraction, as mentioned in Section 3 (Remark 1), we could use non-deterministic clock updates and study the related decidability issues. We could also exploit the specific structure of the timed automata used in our abstraction and design dedicated verification and synthesis algorithms. Indeed, the timed automata of our model have three clocks, and there is non-determinism for only one of them (c_t). This makes us believe that we could potentially outperform the general algorithms of Uppaal and Uppaal-Tiga and solve more complex problems. Finally, in this quest to scale our approach up to larger models and more advanced specifications, we also plan to combine it to numerical and optimization methods.

References

1. Alur, R., Dill, D.L.: A theory of timed automata. Theor. Computer Science **126**(2), 183–235 (1994)
2. Asarin, E., Maler, O., Pnueli, A.: Reachability analysis of dynamical systems having piecewise-constant derivatives. Theor. Computer Science **138**(1), 35–65 (1995)
3. Asarin, E., Maler, O., Pnueli, A., Sifakis, J.: Controller synthesis for timed automata. In: SSSC 1998, pp. 469–474. Elsevier (1998)
4. Aubin, J.P.: Viability tubes. In: Byrnes, C.I., Kurzhanski, A.B. (eds.) Modelling and Adaptive Control. LNCIS, vol. 105, pp. 27–47. Springer, Heidelberg (1988)

5. Behrmann, G., Cougnard, A., David, A., Fleury, E., Larsen, K.G., Lime, D.: UPPAAL-Tiga: time for playing games!. In: Damm, W., Hermanns, H. (eds.) CAV 2007. LNCS, vol. 4590, pp. 121–125. Springer, Heidelberg (2007)

6. Behrmann, G., David, A., Larsen, K.G., Håkansson, J., Pettersson, P., Yi, W., Hendriks, M.: Uppaal 4.0. In: QEST 2006, pp. 125–126. IEEE, September 2006

7. Bouyer, P., Dufourd, C., Fleury, E., Petit, A.: Updatable timed automata. Theor. Computer Science **321**(2–3), 291–345 (2004)

8. David, A., Grunnet, J.D., Jessen, J.J., Larsen, K.G., Rasmussen, J.I.: Application of model-checking technology to controller synthesis. In: Aichernig, B.K., de Boer, F.S., Bonsangue, M.M. (eds.) FMCO 2010. LNCS, vol. 6957, pp. 336–351. Springer, Heidelberg (2011)

9. DeCastro, J., Kress-Gazit, H.: Synthesis of nonlinear continuous controllers for verifiably-correct high-level, reactive behaviors. IJRR **34**(3), 378–394 (2014)

10. Duggirala, P.S., Mitra, S., Viswanathan, M.: Verification of annotated models from executions. In: EMSOFT 2013, pp. 1–10. IEEE, September 2013

11. Frazzoli, E., Dahleh, M.A., Feron, E.: Maneuver-based motion planning for nonlinear systems with symmetries. IEEE Trans. Robotics **21**(6), 1077–1091 (2005)

12. Fu, J., Topcu, U.: Computational methods for stochastic control with metric interval temporal logic specifications. Tech. Rep. 1503.07193, ArXiv, Mar 2015

13. Julius, A.A., Pappas, G.J.: Trajectory based verification using local finite-time invariance. In: Majumdar, R., Tabuada, P. (eds.) HSCC 2009. LNCS, vol. 5469, pp. 223–236. Springer, Heidelberg (2009)

14. Koiran, P., Cosnard, M., Garzon, M.: Computability with low-dimensional dynamical systems. Theor. Computer Science **132**(1), 113–128 (1994)

15. Le Ny, J., Pappas, G.J.: Sequential composition of robust controller specifications. In: ICRA 2012, pp. 5190–5195. IEEE, May 2012

16. Liu, J., Prabhakar, P.: Switching control of dynamical systems from metric temporal logic specifications. In: ICRA 2014, pp. 5333–5338. IEEE, May 2014

17. Majumdar, A., Ahmadi, A.A., Tedrake, R.: Control design along trajectories with sums of squares programming. In: ICRA 2013, pp. 4054–4061. IEEE, May 2013

18. Majumdar, A., Tedrake, R.: Robust online motion planning with regions of finite time invariance. In: WAFR 2012. STAR, vol. 86, pp. 543–558. Springer, Heidelberg (2013)

19. Maler, O., Batt, G.: Approximating continuous systems by timed automata. In: Fisher, J. (ed.) FMSB 2008. LNCS (LNBI), vol. 5054, pp. 77–89. Springer, Heidelberg (2008)

20. Maler, O., Manna, Z., Pnueli, A.: From timed to hybrid systems. In: de Bakker, J.W., Huizing, C., de Roever, W.P., Rozenberg, G. (eds.) Real-Time: Theory in Practice. LNCS, vol. 600, pp. 447–484. Springer, Heidelberg (1992)

21. Mason, M.T.: The mechanics of manipulation. In: ICRA 1985, vol. 2, pp. 544–548. IEEE , March 1985

22. Quottrup, M.M., Bak, T., Zamanabadi, R.I.: Multi-robot planning : a timed automata approach. In: ICRA 2004, vol. 5, pp. 4417–4422. IEEE, April 2004

23. Sloth, C., Wisniewski, R.: Timed game abstraction of control systems. Tech. Rep. 1012.5113, ArXiv, December 2010

24. Sloth, C., Wisniewski, R.: Complete abstractions of dynamical systems by timed automata. Nonlinear Analysis: Hybrid Systems **7**(1), 80–100 (2013)

25. Sontag, E.D.: Mathematical control theory: deterministic finite dimensional systems. Springer (1998)

26. Tedrake, R., Manchester, I.R., Tobenkin, M., Roberts, J.W.: LQR-trees: Feedback motion planning via sums-of-squares verification. IJRR **29**(8), 1038–1052 (2010)

Quantitative Analysis of Communication Scenarios

Clemens Dubslaff[(⊠)] and Christel Baier

Faculty of Computer Science, Technische Universität Dresden, Dresden, Germany
{dubslaff,baier}@tcs.inf.tu-dresden.de

Abstract. Message sequence charts (MSCs) and their higher-order formalism in terms of message sequence graphs (MSGs) provide an intuitive way to describe communication scenarios. Naturally, quantitative aspects such as the probability of failure, maximal latency or the expected energy consumption play a crucial role for communication systems. In this paper, we introduce quantitative MSGs with costs or rewards and stochastic timing information in terms of rates. To perform a quantitative analysis, we propose a branching-time semantics for MSGs as possibly infinite continuous-time Markov chains (CTMCs) interpreting delayed choice on the partial-order semantics of MSGs. Whereas for locally synchronized MSGs a finite-state bisimulation quotient can be found and thus, standard algorithms for CTMCs can be applied, this is not the case in general. However, using a truncation-based approach we show how approximative solutions can be obtained. Our implementation shows feasibility of this approach exploiting reliability, resilience and energy consumption.

1 Introduction

Nowadays, communication protocols have to face many non-functional requirements to be considered during their design process. For instance, the next-generation wireless communication standard 5G will rely on time-bounded requirements concerning latency, energy consumption, and outage probability [28]. To avoid costly and timely redesign steps, these requirements should be considered already in early design phases [32]. An intuitive formalism to describe communication systems widely used in

Fig. 1. An MSC

early stages of development is provided by *message sequence charts (MSCs)*, standardized by the ITU [22]. Figure 1 shows an example MSC where a sender s sends two data packages that are in turn acknowledged by a receiver r. The partial-order semantics for MSCs arises from the time-line orderings of each process and the condition that each send event must precede the corresponding receive event.

The authors are supported by Deutsche Telekom Stiftung, the DFG through the collaborative research centre HAEC (SFB 912), the Excellence Initiative by the German Federal and State Governments (cluster of excellence cfAED and Institutional Strategy), the Graduiertenkolleg QuantLA (1763), the 5G Lab Germany, and the DFG/NWO-project ROCKS, and the EU-FP-7 grant MEALS (295261).

S. Sankaranarayanan and E. Vicario (Eds.): FORMATS 2015, LNCS 9268, pp. 76–92, 2015.
DOI: 10.1007/978-3-319-22975-1_6

In order to specify collections of MSCs, the standard higher-order formalism is given in terms of *high-level MSCs* [22]. In this paper, we deal with *message sequence graphs (MSGs)*, the simplest form of high-level MSCs that are, however, expressively equivalent to high-level MSCs [5]. MSGs can be seen as finite automata over MSCs where the collections of scenarios arise from composing MSCs along accepting paths. The composition of MSCs is performed by glueing the time lines of the processes together and possibly matching unmatched send events and corresponding receive events [14,15]. The verification of MSGs and linear-time requirements has been extensively studied (cf. surveys [23,30]), but most verification problems turn out to be undecidable. However, for MSGs where processes locally synchronize, the execution language can be represented by a finite-state automaton, which renders many linear-time verification problems decidable for this class of MSGs. Also when directly reasoning about the graph structure of the MSCs defined by an MSG, decidability results can be established [25,26,30].

This paper aims to establish a probabilistic model-checking approach for the quantitative analysis of MSGs with annotated costs and stochastic timing information in terms of rates. In order to apply probabilistic model-checking techniques, a branching-time view on (quantitative) MSGs is required, where choices are resolved probabilistically. In the ITU standard [21,22], an interleaving branching-time semantics was specified which relies on *delayed choice*, where any resolution of a choice between the communication scenarios specified by the MSG is avoided until it is inevitable:

> "In the case where alternative MSC sections have common preamble, the choice of which MSC section will be executed is performed after the execution of the common preamble."

Using process algebra, the concept of delayed choice was specified by an intrinsic linear-time operator $\mp$ [27] (cf. the rules **(DC1)** and **(DC2)** below).

$$\frac{x \xrightarrow{\alpha} x' \land y \xdcancelarrow{\beta}}{(x \mp y) \xrightarrow{\alpha} x'} \textbf{(DC1)} \qquad \frac{x \xrightarrow{\alpha} x' \land y \xrightarrow{\alpha} y'}{(x \mp y) \xrightarrow{\alpha} (x' \mp y')} \textbf{(DC2)}$$

For formal reasoning about MSGs, the process-algebraic semantics proposed in the standard is, however, difficult to use since it includes all facets of the modeling formalism and an algorithmic analysis turns out to be very challenging [34].

Our Contribution. First, we propose a branching-time semantics for MSGs in terms of transition systems by interpreting delayed choice directly on the partial-order semantics of MSGs. With the partial-order semantics of MSGs as an intermediate step, we obtain a uniform approach to support many variants of MSGs that have been proposed in the literature, such as causal MSGs [13] (required, e.g., to specify TCP/IP protocol scenarios) and compositional MSGs [9,15,26] (required, e.g., to specify scenarios of the alternating-bit or stop-and-wait protocol [36]). As an MSG may exhibit infinite communication scenarios, our transition-system semantics cannot be fully constructed in general. However, we show that the transition system of an MSG can be constructed on-the-fly, crucial for an algorithmic analysis.

Second, according to the (hardware and software) characteristics of the communication system modeled, we annotate communication actions by costs and rates. The arising *quantitative MSG* constitutes a *continuous-time Markov chain (CTMC) semantics*, where the underlying transition system coincides with our branching-time semantics for (non-quantitative) MSGs. The CTMC semantics enables for a quantitative analysis using probabilistic model-checking techniques to reason, e.g., about the communication system's resilience, expected energy costs and the probability of failure.

Third, we investigate applicability of algorithmic analysis on the transition-system and CTMC semantics. Given the undecidability results for linear-time properties and the fact that the transition system of MSGs can be infinite, the undecidability of even basic reachability properties is as expected. However, when the MSG is locally synchronized, its transition system (or CTMC, respectively) has a finite bisimulation index. Then, a bisimilar finite-state transition system (CTMC, respectively) can be constructed and analyzed using standard (probabilistic) model-checking algorithms. For general (not necessarily locally synchronized) MSGs, we show that the probabilities for time-bounded reachability properties are approximable up to an arbitrary precision by constructing the CTMC on-the-fly up to a sufficient depth.

Fourth, we implemented the construction of the CTMC semantics for quantitative MSGs up to a given truncation bound and applied approximative methods to reason about performance measures. This implementation is used to carry out a case study investigating non-functional properties of scenarios from the USB 1.1 protocol and two variants of a classical stop-and-wait protocol. State aggregation with respect to bisimulation equivalence (a.k.a. lumpability for CTMCs) based on the structure of the MSGs allows to establish results within a reasonable time, whereas without such bisimulation techniques we run into timeouts.

Related Work. Several branching-time semantics have been proposed for subclasses of MSGs [10,17,25], however not focusing on delayed choice and without the support for compositional MSGs. Also the automata constructions to describe the execution language of locally synchronized MSGs [5,9,13,29] define inherently a branching-time semantics. These semantics are directly defined on a fixed communication architecture and have to be redefined when the underlying partial-order semantics changes [4].

Within *time-constrained MSGs*, time intervals are annotated to pairs of actions to specify the time horizon in which the second action of the pair has to be performed after the first one [1,2,24]. Similar as within locally synchronized MSGs in the untimed case, subclasses of time-constrained MSGs exhibit a timed automata which accepts the language of timed words satisfying the constraints imposed on action pairs. Also in this paper we annotate timing information to actions of MSGs. However, our approach is orthogonal, as the timing information on actions is modeled stochastically. A simulation-based stochastic analysis of MSCs with annotated rates has been undertaken by [37] using the trace-generation engine of the tool MÖBIUS [11]. However, a formal framework for a CTMC semantics of MSGs was not specified in [37]. Finite-state discrete-time Markov chains synthesized from from the local views of each process in an MSG annotated with reliability probabilities has been presented by [35]. Their approach disregards the global control of MSGs and could thus be applied for locally synchronized MSGs which are implementable [3].

Probabilistic model checking of infinite-state CTMCs is challenging already independent from the context of MSGs. Model-checking algorithms for highly structured infinite CTMCs (including Jackson queuing networks and quasi-birth-death processes) and properties in *continuous stochastic logic (CSL)* [7] have been presented by Remke et al. (see, e.g., [33]). In order to approximate properties of infinite CTMCs arising from biological systems, [18] presented on-the-fly analysis techniques. Similarly, [16] established approximation methods for arbitrarily structured infinite CTMCs with possible unbounded rates and time-bounded CSL properties.

Outline. We recall basics on modeling communication systems, including MSCs and MSGs in Section 2. Section 3 is advocated to our branching-time semantics for MSGs, its consistency within the standard, and related model-checking problems. Quantitative MSGs and their properties are introduced in Section 4. We illustrate our approach towards approximative performance measures by a case study within our implementation in Section 5 and conclude with Section 6.

2   Preliminaries

We denote by A^∞ ($A^\star$, A^+, A^ω) the set of all (finite, non-empty finite, infinite) *words* over an alphabet A. By w_i we denote the $(i{+}1)$-th symbol of a word w and by $|w|$ the length of w ($|w| = \infty$ if $w \in A^\omega$). The *concatenation* of languages, i.e., subsets of A^∞, is defined as the union of element-wise concatenation of their words. *Atomic actions* are tasks of some process of $P = \{p_1, p_1, ..., p_k\}$ indivisible on the abstraction level of the model and collected in $\Sigma = \bigcup_{p \in P} \Sigma_p$. Here, $\Sigma_p = \{p\} \times (\{!, ?\} \times P \backslash \{p\} \times \Gamma \cup \Lambda)$, where Γ and Λ are sets of message and local action labels, respectively. The action $p!q(m) \in \Sigma$ stands for sending a message m from process p to process q, $p?q(m) \in \Sigma$ for p receiving m from q, and $p(a) \in \Sigma$ for a local action a. *Events* are occurrences of atomic actions collected in a set E and assigned to actions through a labeling function $\lambda \colon E \to \Sigma$. We partition E into the set of send events $E_!$, receive events $E_?$, and local events E_l. By E_p we denote the set of events of process p, i.e., $E_p = \{e \in E \colon \lambda(e) \in \Sigma_p\}$. A *(labeled) partial order* is a tuple $\mathcal{P} = (E, \leq, \lambda)$, where $\leq$ is an asymmetric, reflexive and transitive binary relation over E. Isomorphic labeled partial orders are identified. $\mathcal{P}$ is called *total* if for all $e, e' \in E$ with $e \neq e'$ we have either $e < e'$ or $e > e'$. A linearization of $\mathcal{P}$ is a word $w \in \Sigma^\infty$ where there is a bijection $f \colon N \to E$ with $N \subseteq \mathbb{N}$ such that for all $i, j \in N \colon \lambda(f(i)) = w_i$ and if $i < j$ then $f(i) \not\geq f(j)$. We define the *language of* $\mathcal{P}$ as the set of linearizations $\mathrm{L}(\mathcal{P}) \subseteq \Sigma^\infty$. The *downward closure* $\downarrow F$ on sets of events F is defined as $\{e \in E \colon \exists f \in F.e \leq f\}$. We call $\mathcal{P}$ *prefinite* if $\downarrow e = \downarrow \{e\}$ is finite for all $e \in E$. Besides $\mathcal{P}$, let $\mathcal{P}' = (E', \leq', \lambda')$ be another partial order. If E' is a finite downward-closed subset of E, $\leq' = \leq \cap$ $(E \times E')$ and $\lambda' = \lambda|_{E'}$, then $\mathcal{P}'$ is called a *prefix* of $\mathcal{P}$. The set of all prefixes of $\mathcal{P}$ is denoted by $\mathrm{Pref}(\mathcal{P})$. Concurrent systems are modeled by sets $\mathcal{F}$ of partial orders, called *partial-order families*. Notations for partial orders defined above extend to partial-order families as expected, e.g., the set of all prefixes of $\mathcal{F}$ is $\mathrm{Pref}(\mathcal{F}) = \{\mathcal{P}' \colon \exists \mathcal{P} \in \mathcal{F}.\mathcal{P}' \in \mathrm{Pref}(\mathcal{P})\}$.

2.1 Branching-Time Models and Quantitative Annotations

A *transition system (TS)* is a tuple $(S, s_0, \longrightarrow)$, where S is a countable set of states, $s_0 \in S$ is an initial state, and $\longrightarrow \subseteq S \times \Sigma \times S$ is a transition relation. We denote by $En(s)$ the set of enabled actions in s, i.e., the set of all $\alpha \in \Sigma$ where there is an s' with $s \xrightarrow{\alpha} s'$. $\mathcal{T}$ is *deterministic* if for all $s \xrightarrow{\alpha} s'$, $s \xrightarrow{\alpha} s''$ follows $s' = s''$. Likewise, an *execution* is a sequence $\eta = s_0\alpha_0s_1\alpha_1\ldots \in S \times (\Sigma \times S)^\infty$, where $s_i \xrightarrow{\alpha} s_{i+1}$ for all $i < |\eta|-1$. A *path* is an execution where transition actions are omitted. If $\mathcal{T}$ is deterministic, we identify executions with their projections onto actions and define the language $\mathrm{L}(\mathcal{T}) \subseteq \Sigma^\infty$ as the set of maximal executions. When $C \subseteq S$, we denote by $\Diamond C$ the set of all finite paths π such that $s_{|\pi|-1} \in C$ and $s_i \notin C$ for all $i < |\pi|-1$.

Quantitative Annotations. A *continuous-time Markov chain (CTMC)* [7] is a tuple $\mathcal{C} = (\mathcal{T}, \mathbf{R}, \mathbf{C})$, where $\mathcal{T} = (S, s_0, \longrightarrow)$ is a transition system, and $\mathbf{R} \colon S \times \Sigma \times S \to \mathbb{Q}_{\geq 0}$ and $\mathbf{C} \colon S \cup S \times \Sigma \times S \to \mathbb{Q}_{\geq 0}$ assign *rates* and *costs*, respectively. For a state $s \in S$ and a set of states $C \subseteq S$, we denote by $\mathbf{Q}(s, s') = \sum_{\alpha \in \Sigma} \mathbf{Q}(s, \alpha, s')$ and $\mathbf{Q}(s, C) = \sum_{s' \in C} \mathbf{Q}(s, s')$, where $\mathbf{Q}$ is either $\mathbf{R}$ or $\mathbf{C}$. We assume that the *exit rate* $\mathbf{E}(s) = \mathbf{R}(s, S)$ converges for all $s \in S$. According to the rates, a race between the outgoing transitions from state s exists, where the probability of state s' winning the race is $\mathbf{P}(s, s') = \mathbf{R}(s, s')/\mathbf{E}(s)$. Paths in $\mathcal{T}$ annotated with exit time points are *timed paths*, i.e., sequences of the form $\vartheta = s_0t_0s_1t_1\ldots \in S \times (\mathbb{R}_{>0} \times S)^\infty$. The *accumulated costs* along ϑ is defined as

$$\mathbf{C}(\vartheta) \;=\; \textstyle\sum_{i < |\pi|-1}\big(\mathbf{C}(s_i) \cdot t_i + \mathbf{C}(s_i, s_{i+1})\big).$$

For $s, s' \in S$, and $u, v \in \mathbb{R}_{\geq 0}$ with $u \leqslant v$, the probability of moving from s to s' after at least time t and at most time T is given by transition probabilities

$$\mathbf{P}(s, [t, T], s') \;=\; \mathbf{P}(s, s') \cdot \big(e^{-\mathbf{E}(s)t} - e^{-\mathbf{E}(s)T}\big)$$

We write $\Theta = s_0I_0s_1I_1\ldots I_{n-1}s_n$ for the set of all timed paths $s_0t_0s_1\ldots t_{n-1}s_n\ldots$ with $t_i \in I_i$ and refer to Θ as a *trajectory*. As usual, we define a probability measure $\mathrm{Pr}_s(\Theta)$ for a state s as product of the transition probabilities for the intervals I_i, $i = 0, \ldots, n-1$ [7]. *Expected accumulated costs* $\mathrm{Ex}(\Diamond^{\leq t}C)$ are defined as the expectation of the random variable which assigns to some timed path the minimal accumulated costs of either reaching $C \subseteq S$ or the time bound $t \in \mathbb{Q}_{>0}$.

2.2 Scenarios Specifying Communication Systems

To model communication systems, we focus on *message sequence charts (MSCs)* with lost and found messages [22] (also known as *compositional MSCs*) and their higher-order formalism in terms of *message sequence graphs (MSGs)*, defining possibly infinite collections of MSCs [14,15].

Definition 1 (MSC). *An* MSC *is a prefinite partial order* $\mathcal{M} = (E, \leq, \lambda, \mu)$, *equipped with an injective function* $\mu\colon M \to E_?$ *matching corresponding send events* $M \subseteq E_!$ *and receive events in* $E_?$ *such that* $\leq_\mu = \{(e, \mu(e))\colon e \in M\}$ *is contained in* $\leq$ *and for all* $e \in M$ *with* $\lambda(e) = p!q(m)$ *we have* $\lambda(\mu(e)) = q?p(m)$. *Furthermore, we require* $\leq|_{E_p}$ *to be total for all* $p \in P$.

An event not contained in M, $\mu(M)$, or E_l is called *unmatched*. $\mathcal{M}$ is called *basic* if λ is injective, *left-closed* if there are no unmatched receive events, and *closed* if $\mathcal{M}$ is left-closed and there are no unmatched send events. We denote by MSC the set of MSCs and by bMSC the set of basic MSCs. If any confusion is excluded, we abbreviate the empty MSC by ε and the MSC containing only one event labeled by $\alpha \in \Sigma$ by α.

MSC Families, Systems and Graphs. MSCs are composed by "glueing" their process lines together, and possibly matching send and receive events [14,21]. Formally, let $\mathcal{M}_i = (E_i, \leq_i, \lambda_i, \mu_i)$ for $i = 1, 2$ be two disjoint MSCs and let M_i as in Definition 1. The *composition* $\mathcal{M}_1 \cdot \mathcal{M}_2$ is the family of all MSCs $\mathcal{M} = (E, \leq, \lambda, \mu)$ with $E = E_1 \cup E_2$, where (1) $\mathcal{M}|_{E_i} = \mathcal{M}_i$ for $i = 1, 2$ and (2) for all $e \in E_2, e' \in E$ holds $e \leq e' \Rightarrow e' \in E_2$. The latter condition (2) implies that send events in $\mathcal{M}_2$ are not matched with receive events in $\mathcal{M}_1$ and that the events of each process in $\mathcal{M}_1$ are all lower than the events of the same process in $\mathcal{M}_2$. Collections of MSCs are composed through the union of element-wise composition of the MSCs in the families, i.e.,

$$\mathcal{F}_1 \cdot \mathcal{F}_2 \ = \ \{\mathcal{M} \in \mathcal{M}_1 \cdot \mathcal{M}_2 \colon \mathcal{M}_1 \in \mathcal{F}_1, \mathcal{M}_2 \in \mathcal{F}_2\}.$$

We define the composition along a word over basic MSCs $\pi \in \text{bMSC}^\infty$ by $\mathcal{F}_0 = \{\pi_0\}$ and $\mathcal{F}_i = \mathcal{F}_{i-1} \cdot \pi_i$ for each $0 < i < |\pi|$. This naturally extends to languages $\mathcal{L} \subseteq \text{bMSC}^\infty$ as the union of all MSC families arising from compositions along $\pi \in \mathcal{L}$. To ease notations, we identify with $\pi \in \text{bMSC}^\infty$ ($\mathcal{L} \subseteq \text{bMSC}^\infty$, respectively) the MSC family arising by composition along π ($\mathcal{L}$, respectively). If $\mathcal{L}$ is left-closed, we call $\mathcal{L}$ an *MSC system*. Regular MSC systems are usually provided by *message sequence graphs (MSGs)* [22], which are in essential finite automata over basic MSCs.

Definition 2 (MSG). *An* MSG *is a tuple* $\mathcal{G} = (N, n_0, \to)$, *where* N *is a set of nodes,* $n_0 \in N$ *an initial node, and* $\to \subseteq N \times \text{bMSC} \times N$ *a transition relation.*

We may employ the same terminology as for transition systems. An MSC $\mathcal{M}$ is accepted by $\mathcal{G}$ if there is a composition along a maximal execution containing $\mathcal{M}$. The MSC system containing all left-closed MSCs accepted by $\mathcal{G}$ is denoted by $\mathcal{S}(\mathcal{G})$. When not stated differently, we assume an MSG to be *safe*, i.e., every accepting execution contains a left-closed MSC (which can be decided [23]).

Example 1. The MSG $\mathcal{G}_{\text{usb}}$ depicted in Figure 2, which is taken from [14], formalizes scenarios of transactions according to the USB 1.1 protocol. The MSG

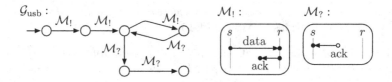

Fig. 2. Scenarios of USB 1.1 transactions by the MSG $\mathcal{G}_{usb}$

is shown on the left, the assigned MSC labels on the right. A sender s continuously sends data to a receiver r, which returns an acknowledgement directly after it received the data package. However, the sender has some advance by 2-3 messages. The smallest scenario described by $\mathcal{G}_{usb}$ is the only left-closed MSC contained in the execution $\mathcal{M}_!\mathcal{M}_!\mathcal{M}_?\mathcal{M}_?$ shown in Figure 1.

Locally Synchronized MSGs. For MSGs over closed basic MSCs, [5] and [29] independently stated a syntactic criterion such that a finite automaton accepting the linearizations of the partial-order semantics can be constructed. We deal here with a similar criterion based on [14,15]. For an MSC $\mathcal{M} = (E, \leq, \lambda, \mu)$, the *communication graph* $H_\mathcal{M}$ is defined as the directed graph $(P, \rightarrow)$, where $p \rightarrow q$ iff there exists an event e in $\mathcal{M}$ with $\lambda(e) = p!q(m)$ for some $m \in \Gamma$ or $p = q$ and $\lambda(e) = p(a)$ for some $a \in \Lambda$. The *deficit* $D_\mathcal{M} \colon P \times P \times \Lambda \rightarrow \mathbb{Z}$ is defined as the number of messages in the communication channels after executing $\mathcal{M}$:

$$D_\mathcal{M}(p, q, m) = |\{e \in E \colon \lambda(e) = p!q(m)\}| - |\{e \in E \colon \lambda(e) = q?p(m)\}|$$

If for every $\mathcal{M}$ contained in a composition along cycles in an MSG $\mathcal{G}$ the communication graph $H_\mathcal{M}$ consists of a single non-trivial strongly connected component and $D_\mathcal{M}(p, q, m) = 0$ for all $p, q \in P$, $m \in \Lambda$, then $\mathcal{G}$ is called *locally synchronized*. Note that the MSG in Example 1 is locally synchronized.

3   Branching-Time Semantics

The semantics of an MSG with quantitative annotations in form of rates and costs for actions will be given as an infinite-state continuous-time Markov chain. To define this CTMC, we first provide a (non-probabilistic) transition-system semantics for MSGs that is compatible with the ITU standard and the delayed choice interpretations of branchings [21,22]. The transition system will serve as basis for the CTMC semantics, but might be also useful for other (non-stochastic) purposes as well. First, we transfer the concept of delayed choice to the setting of an MSC system $\mathcal{S}$. The set of communication scenarios in $\mathcal{S}$ according to which a common preamble[1] $w \in \Sigma^*$ could have been executed is

$$\mathcal{S}(w) = \{\mathcal{P} \in \mathcal{S} \colon w \in \mathrm{Pref}(\mathrm{L}(\mathcal{P}))\}.$$

---

[1] Check for the definition of delayed choice provided in the introduction.

Hence, interpreting delayed choice for $\mathcal{S}$ reveals that during the execution of w, no choice between the scenarios in $\mathcal{S}(w)$ is made. Furthermore, any reordering $\hat{w}$ of w where $\mathcal{S}(w) = \mathcal{S}(\hat{w})$ yields the same global state of the system. Such reorderings are exactly executions of partial-order prefixes of $\mathcal{S}(w)$ containing only events executed by w and thus can be represented by w-*configurations*

$$\mathrm{Conf}(\mathcal{S}, w) = \{\mathcal{P} \in \mathrm{Pref}(\mathcal{S}) \colon w \in \mathrm{L}(\mathcal{P})\}.$$

The set of all configurations in $\mathcal{S}$ is then defined as

$$\mathrm{Conf}(\mathcal{S}) = \bigcup_{w \in \mathrm{Pref}(\mathrm{L}(\mathcal{S}))} \mathrm{Conf}(\mathcal{S}, w).$$

This yields an operational transition-system semantics for MSC systems $\mathcal{S}$ as

$$\mathcal{T}_{\mathcal{S}} = (\mathrm{Conf}(\mathcal{S}), \{\varepsilon\}, \longrightarrow),$$

where $\longrightarrow$ is defined through $\mathrm{Conf}(\mathcal{S}, w) \overset{\alpha}{\longrightarrow} \mathrm{Conf}(\mathcal{S}, w\alpha)$ for any $w \in \Sigma^{\star}$ with $\mathrm{Conf}(\mathcal{S}, w\alpha) \neq \emptyset$. Recall that ε stands for the empty MSC. Due to delayed choice, $\mathcal{T}_{\mathcal{S}}$ is deterministic. As the *level* $\ell vl(\mathcal{K}) = \{|\mathcal{P}| \colon \mathcal{P} \in \mathcal{K}\}$ of configurations $\mathcal{K}$ along paths in $\mathcal{T}_{\mathcal{S}}$ increase within each transition, $\mathcal{T}_{\mathcal{S}}$ is also acyclic. Furthermore, $\mathcal{T}_{\mathcal{S}}$ is infinite if $\mathcal{S}$ contains an infinite MSC, such that it cannot be fully constructed in general, e.g., $\mathcal{T}_{\mathcal{S}(\mathcal{G})}$ is infinite for an MSG $\mathcal{G}$ containing loops. This transition-system semantics is language consistent with the partial-order semantics in the sense that prefixes of executions agree with the one of $\mathcal{S}(\mathcal{G})$:

Proposition 1. *When $\mathcal{S}$ is an MSC system, $\mathrm{Pref}(\mathrm{L}(\mathcal{S})) = \mathrm{Pref}(\mathrm{L}(\mathcal{T}_{\mathcal{S}}))$.*

Example 2. Let us consider a simple stop-and-wait protocol [36,37] described through the MSG $\mathcal{G}_{\mathrm{stoc}}$ depicted on the left in Figure 3. A sender s sends a data package to a receiver r over an unreliable channel. The receiver provides an acknowledgement "ack" if the data has been transmitted successfully and a negative acknowledgement "nak" if not. A message is considered to be lost after a timeout "to" has been risen on the sender's side. Note that this MSG is neither locally synchronized nor realizable in the sense of [3]. In the center, a part of the infinite-state transition system $\mathcal{T}_{\mathcal{S}(\mathcal{G}_{\mathrm{stoc}})}$ is shown (event labels are abbreviated, e.g., "s!r(data)" by "!d"). Due to delayed choice, the triangular states do not agree: The state reached by !d·to·?d·!d surely matches the first send and receive event. Differently, the filled triangle state reachable through !d·to·!d·?d could match ?d with either one of the both !d events and thus, its configuration has two elements. For further illustrating the impact of delayed choice, we depicted the configurations after an action !n on the right – dashed arrows indicate possible matches of events (i.e., which yield several elements in the configuration) and solid ones indicate sure matchings.

3.1 Model Checking Branching-Time Requirements

Our transition-system semantics for MSGs enables to reason about branching-time properties. However, even basic reachability problems are undecidable:

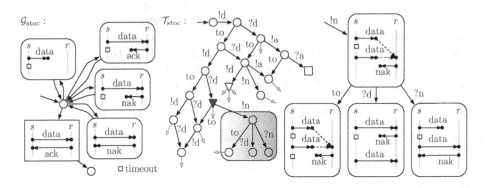

Fig. 3. Stop-and-wait protocol scenarios by the MSG $\mathcal{G}_{\mathrm{stoc}}$ and its TS semantics

Theorem 1. *The* action-enabled reachability problem *for an MSG $\mathcal{G}$ and $A \subseteq \Sigma$, asking whether there is a state $\mathcal{K}$ reachable in $\mathcal{T}_{\mathcal{G}}$ with $En(\mathcal{K}){=}A$, is undecidable.*

The proof of this theorem relies on a reduction from the Post's Correspondence Problem as presented in [30] for the linear-time setting and matchings of executions due to delayed choice. Clearly, Theorem 1 renders model checking MSGs against branching-time logics such as ACTL [12] undecidable. However, when $\mathcal{G}$ is locally synchronized, a finite transition system bisimilar to $\mathcal{T}_{\mathcal{S}(\mathcal{G})}$ can be constructed, which enables to apply standard algorithms to reason about branching-time requirements on $\mathcal{G}$. To see this, we use a similar construction as presented in [29], where a finite-state automaton $\mathcal{A}_{\mathcal{G}}$ has been constructed which accepts the executions $\mathrm{L}(\mathcal{S}(\mathcal{G}))$ of $\mathcal{G}$. Performing a determinization on $\mathcal{A}_{\mathcal{G}}$ yields a finite transition system, which is bisimilar to $\mathcal{T}_{\mathcal{S}(\mathcal{G})}$ since trace equivalence coincides with bisimulation equivalence for deterministic systems [8].

Theorem 2. *For a locally synchronized MSG $\mathcal{G}$, $\mathcal{T}_{\mathcal{S}(\mathcal{G})}$ has a finite bisimulation quotient which can be effectively constructed.*

Note that $\mathcal{T}_{\mathcal{S}(\mathcal{G})}$ having a finite bisimulation quotient does not necessarily imply that $\mathcal{G}$ is locally synchronized.

4   Quantitative Message Sequence Graphs

We now introduce MSGs with quantitative annotations and a suitable CTMC semantics based on the transition-system semantics of the last section. As we consider events in an MSC as instances of actions, i.e., tasks indivisible on the abstraction level, it is rather natural to extend this interpretation to quantitative annotations on MSC systems. That is, quantitative annotations are mappings from actions to rational values. We focus here on annotation structures we call *profiles*, formalizing the specification of different (hardware or software) setups.

Definition 3. *A profile is a tuple $\mathcal{I} = (\mathbf{r}, \mathbf{c}, \sigma)$, where $\mathbf{r}\colon \Sigma \to \mathbb{Q}_{>0}$ assigns rates, $\mathbf{c}\colon \Sigma \to \mathbb{Q}_{\geq 0}$ costs and $\sigma \in \mathbb{Q}_{>0}$ specifies stationary costs.*

The rates $\mathbf{r}$ contain stochastic timing information about the frequency actions are executed. Costs are given by $\mathbf{c}$, formalizing the costs of executing an action, and by σ, formalizing the stationary costs required keep the system operational for one time unit. We call an MSG $\mathcal{G}$ amended with a profile $\mathcal{I}$ *quantitative MSG*.

Definition 4. *Let $\mathcal{G}$ be an MSG with $\mathcal{T}_{\mathcal{S}(\mathcal{G})} = (S, s_0, \longrightarrow)$ and $\mathcal{I} = (\mathbf{r}, \mathbf{c}, \sigma)$ a profile. The CTMC semantics $\mathcal{C}_{\mathcal{G}} = (\mathcal{T}_{\mathcal{S}(\mathcal{G})}, \mathbf{R}, \mathbf{C})$ of the quantitative MSG $(\mathcal{G}, \mathcal{I})$ is defined as follows: $\mathbf{R}(s, \alpha, s') = \mathbf{r}(\alpha)$, $\mathbf{C}(s, \alpha, s') = \mathbf{c}(\alpha)$, and $\mathbf{C}(s) = \sigma$ for all $s, s' \in S$, $\alpha \in \Sigma$ if $s \xrightarrow{\alpha} s'$ and $\mathbf{R}(s, \alpha, s') = \mathbf{C}(s, \alpha, s') = 0$ otherwise.*

Note that these assignments to the transition system of an MSG still obey the rules of delayed choice. The same rate $\mathbf{r}(\alpha)$ is attached to all transitions labeled by α, no matter whether the transitions arise by "merging" two or more α-events according to the rules for delayed choice. This is in contrast to the choice operator $+$ of PEPA [19] and other stochastic process algebras, where $\alpha.x + \alpha.y$ implies a race between two α-labeled transitions. In particular, the exit rate of $\alpha.x + \alpha.y$ is $2 \cdot \mathbf{r}(\alpha)$, whereas for the delayed choice operator $\mp$, the process $\alpha.x \mp \alpha.y$ is (bisimulation) equivalent to $\alpha.(x \mp y)$ and has the exit rate $\mathbf{r}(\alpha)$.

Example 3. Let us assume that both, the USB 1.1 scenario given in Example 1 and the stop-and-wait protocol of Example 2 use a low-speed USB 1.1 data connection for the communication between sender and receiver. To exemplify how statistical data can be included into early design steps for communication protocols, we define a profile $\mathcal{I} = (\mathbf{r}, \mathbf{c}, \sigma)$ with timings and costs in terms of

	s!r(data)	r?s(data)	s(timeout)	r!s(ack)	s?r(ack)	r!s(nak)	s?r(nak)
rates $\mathbf{r}(\cdot)$	1	1	0.1	10	10	0.5	10
energy $\mathbf{c}(\cdot)$	0.0323	0.0323	0	0.0032	0.0032	0.0032	0.0032

energy consumption within several assumptions inspired by measurements for USB 1.1 devices [31]. Rates are scaled upon sending/receiving one data package which comprises 8 bytes of data, 1 byte package identifier and 2 bytes CRC. Acknowledgements (positive and negative ones) have a package size of 1 byte. With probability 0.05 data is corrupted and with probability 0.01 totally lost. The energy-cost rate is fixed to be constantly $\sigma = 0.0597$, representing the power consumption of an idling USB device. Action energy costs stand for the additional power required to perform an action.

4.1   Model Checking Quantitative Requirements

In the following, let us fix the CTMC semantics $\mathcal{C}_{\mathcal{G}}$ for a quantitative MSG $(\mathcal{G}, \mathcal{I})$. Due to the undecidability result by Theorem 1, we cannot expect decidability for model checking $\mathcal{C}_{\mathcal{G}}$ against even basic qualitative reachability requirements.

Corollary 1. *Given a quantitative MSG $(\mathcal{G}, \mathcal{I})$, $A \subseteq \Sigma$, and a time bound $t \in \mathbb{Q}_{>0}$, the decision problems for $\mathcal{C}_{\mathcal{G}}$ whether $\Pr(\Diamond^{\leq t} D) > 0$ and whether $\Pr(\Diamond D) > 0$ with $D = \{\mathcal{K} \in \mathrm{Conf}(\mathcal{S}(\mathcal{G})): En(\mathcal{K}) = A\}$ are undecidable.*

This result directly yields undecidability of model checking quantitative MSGs against action-based CSRL requirements [6]. However, if $\mathcal{G}$ is locally synchronized, Theorem 2 yields that the underlying transition system of $\mathcal{C}_\mathcal{G}$ has a finite bisimulation quotient. Thus, also $\mathcal{C}_\mathcal{G}$ itself has a finite bisimulation quotient as rates and costs only depend on the actions assigned to transitions and $\mathcal{T}_{\mathcal{S}(\mathcal{G})}$ is deterministic. In this case, standard CTMC techniques are applicable.

Time-Bounded Reachability. Towards approximative solutions for arbitrary, possibly infinite $\mathcal{C}_\mathcal{G}$, we exploit the fact that $\mathcal{C}_\mathcal{G}$ is finitely branching and rates and costs are bounded. Thus, the probability and expectation of time-bounded reachability properties can be approximated by investigating only that part of $\mathcal{C}_\mathcal{G}$ which is reachable within a sufficient *truncation depth* [16].

Theorem 3. *Given a quantitative MSG* $(\mathcal{G}, \mathcal{I})$, *a decidable set of target states* D *in* $\mathcal{C}_\mathcal{G}$, *a time bound* $t \in \mathbb{Q}_{>0}$ *and a precision* $\delta \in \mathbb{Q}_{>0}$, *one can compute* $x \in \mathbb{Q}_{\geq 0}$ *such that* $|\Pr(\Diamond^{\leq t} D) - x| \leq \delta$.

Let us go more into detail. For a set of states $X \subseteq S$, we denote by X_i the set of states $\mathcal{K} \in X$ where $\mathit{lvl}(\mathcal{K}) = i$ for $i \in \mathbb{N}$. We define $X_{\leq i} = \bigcup_{k=0}^{i} X_i$ and $\mathcal{C}_{\leq i}^{D}$ as the projection of $\mathcal{C}_\mathcal{G}$ onto $S_{\leq i}$ where all states in $S_i \cup D_{\leq i}$ are made absorbing without any rates or costs assigned. It is clear that by iteratively composing MSCs along paths in $\mathcal{G}$ in a breadth-first fashion and computing their prefixes, executions and configurations, $\mathcal{C}_{\leq i}^{D}$ can be effectively computed. Starting from $i=0$ we step-wise increment i and compute the probability $\delta_i = \Pr(\Diamond^{\leq t} S_i)$ in $\mathcal{C}_{\leq i}^{D}$, using standard methods for finite CTMCs. If $\delta_i \leq \delta$, we are done by computing $x = \Pr(\Diamond^{\leq t} D_{\leq i})$ in $\mathcal{C}_{\leq i}^{D}$, again by using standard methods.

Similarly, the *expected cumulative costs* $\mathrm{Ex}(\Diamond^{\leq t} D)$ for reaching D or the time bound $t \in \mathbb{Q}_{>0}$ can be approximated up to precision $\delta \in \mathbb{Q}_{>0}$. To see this, let $\mathcal{C}_{\leq i}^{+}$ arise from $\mathcal{C}_{\leq i}^{D}$ by making all states $s \in S_i \backslash D$ absorbing with $\mathbf{R}(s,s) = \sum_{\alpha \in \Sigma} \mathbf{r}(\alpha)$, $\mathbf{C}(s,s) = \max_{\alpha \in \Sigma} \mathbf{c}(\alpha)$, and $\mathbf{C}(s) = \sigma$. When Ex^{-}, Ex, and Ex^{+} are the expectations in $\mathcal{C}_{\leq i}^{D}$, $\mathcal{C}_\mathcal{G}$, and $\mathcal{C}_{\leq i}^{+}$, respectively, we obtain

$$\eta^{-} = \mathrm{Ex}^{-}(\Diamond^{\leq t} D_{\leq i}) \leq \mathrm{Ex}(\Diamond^{\leq t} D) \leq \mathrm{Ex}^{+}(\Diamond^{\leq t} D_{\leq i}) = \eta^{+}$$

Again, we compute these expectations in the finite CTMCs $\mathcal{C}_{\leq i}^{D}$ for increasing i until $\eta_i^{+} - \eta_i^{-} \leq \delta$ and choose η_i^{-} as approximation.

Limitations of the Approach. For time-bounded reachability of undecidable target sets D, our truncation-based approach clearly does not guarantee to succeed. This is the case, e.g., if $D = \{s \in S: \Pr_s(\Diamond^{\leq t} U) \geq \tau\}$ for some probability threshold $\tau \in [0,1]$ and a decidable set of states U (see Corollary 1). Such a pattern is useful, e.g., to approximate requirements stated within nested (action-based) CSRL formulas. To evaluate such nested formulas, we can apply a top-down approach that approximates nested probability constraints on-the-fly by possibly further increasing truncation depths [16]. For the above pattern, this requires, e.g., that during the step-wise construction of $\mathcal{C}_{\leq i}^{D}$ there is a precision $\gamma \in \mathbb{Q}_{>0}$ such that for all $s \in S_{\leq i}$ we have $\Pr_s(\Diamond^{\leq t} U) \geq \tau$ if $\Pr_s(\Diamond^{\leq t} U) \geq \tau - \gamma$. Also for unbounded reachability probabilities of the form $\Pr(\Diamond D)$, our approach is not applicable in general, as there might be a "drift away from D" such that in $\mathcal{C}^{D}_{\leq i}$ the probability $\Pr(\Diamond S_i)$ does not converge to 0 when i tends to infinity (e.g., for $\mathcal{G}_{\text{stoc}}$ of Example 2 with a profile where actions of s have much higher rates than actions of r). However, in the case of convergence with limit 0, the approach presented for time-bounded reachability properties yields an approximation technique also for the time-unbounded case.

5   Implementation and Case Study

We implemented the breadth-first level-wise construction of our transition-system semantics for MSGs, the annotation of profiles and the finite-state projection approach [16] to approximate action-based CSL properties [6] using the probabilistic model checker PRISM [20]. As PRISM does not natively support action-based requirements to reason about, we included the option to encode the last action fired as a state variable in the target state [6]. Clearly, this yields a linear blow-up of the state space in the number of actions not apparent when using specialized action-based model-checking algorithms. The key in our implementation is an efficient construction of the transition-system semantics in a

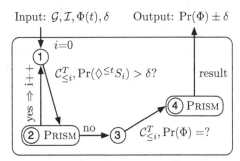

Fig. 4. The general tool scheme

breadth-first fashion to obtain truncations. Given an MSG $\mathcal{G}$, we first implemented the construction directly on the partial-order prefixes of $\mathcal{S}(\mathcal{G})$ generated by compositions along paths in $\mathcal{G}$ up to a sufficient depth. This construction turned out to be very time-consuming, as the sufficient length of paths in $\mathcal{G}$ can be very long due to concurrent behaviors between basic MSCs in $\mathcal{G}$. We thus replaced this approach by generating candidates for enabled actions α in a configuration $\mathcal{K}$ from the local views of each process (cf., e.g., [3]) and then omitted those MSCs in $\mathcal{K}{\cdot}\alpha$ which are not prefixes of $\mathcal{S}(\mathcal{G})$, i.e., let the global control imposed by the $\mathcal{G}$ rule out only locally enabled actions. The general computation scheme of our tool is depicted in Figure 4. At each constructed truncation ①, we feed PRISM with the truncation (but without encoding actions to avoid the linear blow-up) and compute the probability of reaching the states added in the last truncation step within the given time bound ②. When this probability is not greater than the desired precision δ anymore ③, the PRISM evaluates the property under consideration ④. Here, we choose the model where the last action performed is encoded into the states to allow reasoning about state-based CSRL formulas containing action-based information.

5.1   Models and Requirements in our Case Study

We evaluated our implementation based on the quantitative MSGs provided in Example 3. Besides the CTMCs for $\mathcal{G}_{\text{usb}}$ and $\mathcal{G}_{\text{stoc}}$, we consider a variant $\mathcal{G}_{\text{rstoc}}$ of

Table 1. Results of the truncation-based quantitative analysis

MSG	property	result	depth i $\mathcal{C}_\mathcal{G}$	$\mathcal{C}_\mathcal{G}/\equiv$	#states $\mathcal{C}_\mathcal{G}$	$\mathcal{C}_\mathcal{G}/\equiv$	overall time $\mathcal{C}_\mathcal{G}$	$\mathcal{C}_\mathcal{G}/\equiv$	analysis time $\mathcal{C}_\mathcal{G}$	$\mathcal{C}_\mathcal{G}/\equiv$
$\mathcal{G}_\text{usb}$	success	0.966	38	16	145 (231)	43 (65)	1.3s	0.6s	0.8s	0.3s
	energy	0.351	37	16	141 (226)	43 (65)	1.4s	0.6s	0.8s	0.3s
$\mathcal{G}_\text{rstoc}$	success	0.946	22	11	3252 (5158)	26 (53)	6.5s	0.3s	1.8s	0.2s
	energy	0.225	21	11	2524 (4067)	26 (53)	4.8s	0.3s	1.4s	0.2s
	resilience	0.995	>40	11+1	>400000	28 (58)	>12h	0.4s	–	0.2s
$\mathcal{G}_\text{stoc}$	success	0.955	21	21	12513 (17824)	4124 (6177)	84.7s	39.2s	5.6s	2.1s
	energy	0.221	21	21	12513 (17824)	4124 (6177)	86.4s	41.0s	10.0s	3.9s
	resilience	0.999	>40	29+0	>400000	69084 (99505)	>12h	1.3h	–	38.2s

$\mathcal{G}_\text{stoc}$ where the data channel is reliable, i.e., the upper left transition in Figure 3 is omitted. We also exploit the regular structure of the MSGs and introduce backward transitions to bisimilar states on-the-fly during the construction of the truncations, based on the following observations for configurations $\mathcal{K}$:

(usb) Fully executed loops do not have any impact on future behaviors, i.e., if the uniquely defined prefix in $\mathcal{K}$ has the form $\mathcal{M}_!\mathcal{M}_!\mathcal{M}_?\mathcal{N}$, then $\mathcal{K}$ is bisimilar to the configuration $\{\mathcal{M}_!\mathcal{M}_!\mathcal{N}\}$.[2]

(stoc, rstoc) Matches not affected by delayed choice synchronize. That is, if there is a message matched in each prefix $K \in \mathcal{K}$ at the same position, removing preceding events in all prefixes of $\mathcal{K}$ yields a bisimilar configuration.

As requirements for the performance analysis, we investigated the following properties expressed in an action-based CSRL fashion [6]:

(success) $\Pr(\Diamond^{\leq 6}\text{s?r(ack)})$: What is the probability of a successful communication within 6 time units?

(energy) $\text{Ex}_\text{energy}(\Diamond^{\leq 6}\text{s?r(ack)})$: What is the expected energy consumed towards a successful communication or reaching the deadline of 6 time units?[3]

(resilience) $\Pr(\Box((\text{s?r(nak)}\vee\text{s(timeout)}) \Rightarrow \mathsf{P}_{\geq 0.9}(\Diamond^{\leq 6}\text{s?r(ack)})))$: What is the probability that always after an unsuccessful communication, with probability at least 0.9 the communication is successful within 6 time units?

The latter **resilience** property can only be expressed by a nested formula, where evaluating the inner probability operator is undecidable in general (see Corollary 1). Furthermore, the property contains a time-unbounded reachability modality, such that our approach is not a priori successful. Fortunately, for the quantitative MSGs we considered in our case study, our approach is still applicable (cf. last paragraph of Section 4).

---

[2] Cutting off fully executed loops of configurations is in the spirit of [10], however, does not always yield a bisimular configuration in general due to delayed choice.

[3] This property corresponds to the PRISM query R=? [C<=6] on the transformed model $\mathcal{C}'_\mathcal{G}$ as described in Section 4, where all states are terminal after an s?r(ack) action.

5.2   Evaluation

For carrying out the case study, we used PRISM version 4.2 on a computer with Intel i7-3720QM processor running at 2.6 Ghz with 8 GBytes of memory. The required truncation depth i is computed for a precision of $\delta = 10^{-6}$ and we chose a precision of $\epsilon = 10^{-12}$ for the PRISM computations. In Table 1, we summarize our results, where $\mathcal{C}_\mathcal{G}/\equiv$ stands for the bisimulation quotient constructed with respect to the bisimulation relations identified above. The number of states are those of the final CTMC and we indicated the number of states in the action-encoded model (required for the final PRISM computation) in brackets. As shown also in the table, generating the truncations of the CTMC semantics of quantitative MSGs is very time-consuming and bisimulation techniques are very promising. This is especially the case for the most simple quantitative MSG $\mathcal{G}_{\text{usb}}$, which is locally synchronized and where after a truncation depth $i = 16$, the bisimulation quotient does not change anymore (see Theorem 2). The **resilience** property is not considered for $\mathcal{G}_{\text{usb}}$, as the channels of the communication scenarios generated are all reliable. We indicated the further truncation steps j required to guarantee correct approximations of the nested action-based CSRL formula for the **resilience** property separately, indicated by $i + j$. Without employing bisimulation techniques, we run into timeouts in all **resilience** experiments.

Remark 1. Besides the *finite-state projection* we applied in our approach, [16] presented other heuristics to compute sufficient truncation depths and saving analysis time. We evaluated their unichain and layered-chain method, but got high truncation depths where the truncation could not be constructed anymore. This is not surprising, as the analysis step is not the bottleneck in our approach, rather than the construction of the truncation (see timings in Table 1).

6   Conclusion

We presented a transition-system semantics for MSGs, which obeys delayed choice and thus follows the ITU standard for MSGs [22]. Different to other branching-time semantics for MSGs, our semantics can be interpreted on all kinds of MSGs where a partial-order semantics is defined, including compositional MSGs [9,15,26] and causal MSGs [13]. Our semantics opens the door towards probabilistic operational semantics for MSGs which may arise by an annotation of stochastic information. Such annotations enable to reason about performance measures, which can trigger redesign steps in early communication protocol development. In this paper, we focused on annotations in terms of stochastic timing information and costs and presented a (possibly infinite) CTMC semantics for MSGs. We showed that already a simple qualitative time-bounded reachability problem is undecidable, whereas approximative solutions can be obtained choosing a truncation-based approach. By an implementation and a case study we demonstrated that practical relevant properties such as the probability of failure, the expected energy consumption and a probabilistic resilience measure can be approximated using our approach.

Our transition-system semantics as well as the CTMC semantics can be used for many other purposes. For instance, states could be annotated with atomic propositions defined through MSO formulas over MSCs (which are decidable [26]). This enables to reason about state-based branching-time properties aimed already for in [25] but now with obeying delayed choice. More sophisticated annotations for stationary costs can also be imagined, depending for instance on the local state of each process in the spirit of [3] or histories of actions performed to reach the state. We noticed in our case study that bisimulation techniques play an important role for analyzing MSGs. However, finding a suitable bisimulation is not as easy (e.g., cutting of fully executed loops as presented by [10] does not maintain language consistency within a delayed choice semantics). Establishing generic approaches towards bisimulations are left for further work.

References

1. Akshay, S., Gastin, P., Mukund, M., Kumar, K.N.: Model checking time-constrained scenario-based specifications. In: FSTTCS 2010, pp. 204–215 (2010)
2. Akshay, S., Genest, B., Hélouët, L., Yang, S.: Regular set of representatives for time-constrained MSC graphs. Inf. Process. Lett. **112**(14–15), 592–598 (2012)
3. Alur, R., Etessami, K., Yannakakis, M.: Inference of message sequence charts. IEEE Transactions on Software Engineering **29**(7), 623–633 (2003)
4. Alur, R., Holzmann, G.J., Peled, D.: An analyzer for message sequence charts. In: Software Concepts and Tools, pp. 304–313 (1996)
5. Alur, R., Yannakakis, M.: Model checking of message sequence charts. In: Baeten, J.C.M., Mauw, S. (eds.) CONCUR 1999. LNCS, vol. 1664, pp. 114–129. Springer, Heidelberg (1999)
6. Baier, C., Cloth, L., Haverkort, B., Kuntz, M., Siegle, M.: Model checking Markov chains with actions and state labels. IEEE Transactions on Software Engineering **33**(4), 209–224 (2007)
7. Baier, C., Haverkort, B., Hermanns, H., Katoen, J.: Model-checking algorithms for continuous-time Markov chains. IEEE Transactions on Software Engineering **29**(6), 524–541 (2003)
8. Baier, C., Katoen, J.-P.: Principles of model checking. The MIT Press (2008)
9. Bollig, B., Leucker, M., Lucas, P.: Analysing message sequence graph specifications. In: Baaz, M., Voronkov, A. (eds.) LPAR 2002. LNCS (LNAI), vol. 2514, pp. 68–85. Springer, Heidelberg (2002)
10. Chakraborty, J., D'Souza, D., Narayan Kumar, K.: Analysing message sequence graph specifications. In: Margaria, T., Steffen, B. (eds.) ISoLA 2010, Part I. LNCS, vol. 6415, pp. 549–563. Springer, Heidelberg (2010)
11. Daly, D., Deavours, D.D., Doyle, J.M., Webster, P.G., Sanders, W.H.: Möbius: an extensible tool for performance and dependability modeling. In: Haverkort, B.R., Bohnenkamp, H.C., Smith, C.U. (eds.) TOOLS 2000. LNCS, vol. 1786, pp. 332–336. Springer, Heidelberg (2000)

12. Fantechi, A., Gnesi, S., Ristori, G.: Model checking for action-based logics. Formal Methods in System Design **4**(2), 187–203 (1994)
13. Gazagnaire, T., Genest, B., Hélouët, L., Thiagarajan, P.S., Yang, S.: Causal message sequence charts. Theor. Comput. Sci. **410**(41), 4094–4110 (2009)
14. Genest, B., Kuske, D., Muscholl, A.: A Kleene theorem and model-checking algorithms for existentially bounded communicating automata. Inf. Comput. **204**(6)
15. Gunter, E.L., Muscholl, A., Peled, D.A.: Compositional message sequence charts. In: Margaria, T., Yi, W. (eds.) TACAS 2001. LNCS, vol. 2031, pp. 496–511. Springer, Heidelberg (2001)
16. Hahn, E.M., Hermanns, H., Wachter, B., Zhang, L.: Time-bounded model checking of infinite-state continuous-time markov chains. Fundamenta Informaticae **95**(1), 129–155 (2009)
17. Hélouët, L., Jard, C., Caillaud, B.: An event structure based semantics for high-level message sequence charts. Math. Struct. in CS **12**(4), 377–402 (2002)
18. Henzinger, T.A., Mateescu, M., Wolf, V.: Sliding window abstraction for infinite markov chains. In: Bouajjani, A., Maler, O. (eds.) CAV 2009. LNCS, vol. 5643, pp. 337–352. Springer, Heidelberg (2009)
19. Hillston, J.: A Compositional Approach to Performance Modelling. Cambridge University Press (1996)
20. Hinton, A., Kwiatkowska, M., Norman, G., Parker, D.: PRISM: A tool for automatic verification of probabilistic systems. In: Hermanns, H., Palsberg, J. (eds.) TACAS 2006. LNCS, vol. 3920, pp. 441–444. Springer, Heidelberg (2006)
21. ITU-T. Annex b: Formal semantics of message sequence charts. Z.120, v2.2 (1998)
22. ITU-T. Message Sequence Chart (MSC). Z.120, Edition 5.0 (2011)
23. Kumar, K.N.: The theory of message sequence charts. In: Modern Applications of Automata Theory, pp. 289–324 (2012)
24. Lucas, P.: Timed semantics of message sequence charts based on timed automata. Electronic Notes in Theoretical Computer Science **65**(6), 160–179 (2002)
25. Madhusudan, P.: Reasoning about sequential and branching behaviours of message sequence graphs. In: Orejas, F., Spirakis, P.G., van Leeuwen, J. (eds.) ICALP 2001. LNCS, vol. 2076, pp. 809–820. Springer, Heidelberg (2001)
26. Madhusudan, P., Meenakshi, B.: Beyond message sequence graphs. In: Hariharan, R., Mukund, M., Vinay, V. (eds.) FSTTCS 2001. LNCS, vol. 2245, pp. 256–267. Springer, Heidelberg (2001)
27. Mauw, S., Reniers, M.A.: High-level message sequence charts. In: SDL, Forum, pp. 291–306 (1997)
28. Mousa, A.M.: Prospective of fifth generation mobile communications. International Journal of Next-Generation Networks (2012)
29. Muscholl, A., Peled, D.: Message sequence graphs and decision problems on mazurkiewicz traces. In: Kutyłowski, M., Pacholski, L., Wierzbicki, T. (eds.) MFCS 1999. LNCS, vol. 1672, pp. 81–91. Springer, Heidelberg (1999)
30. Muscholl, A., Peled, D.A.: Deciding properties of message sequence charts. In: Leue, S., Systä, T.J. (eds.) Scenarios: Models, Transformations and Tools. LNCS, vol. 3466, pp. 43–65. Springer, Heidelberg (2005)
31. O'Brien, K., Salyers, D., Striegel, A., Poellabauer, C.: Power and performance characteristics of usb flash drives. In: WoWMoM 2008, pp. 1–4, June 2008
32. Pooley, R., King, P.: The unified modeling language and performance engineering. IEEE Proceedings - Software **149**, 2–10 (1999)

33. Remke, A., Haverkort, B.R.: CSL model checking algorithms for infinite-state structured markov chains. In: Raskin, J.-F., Thiagarajan, P.S. (eds.) FORMATS 2007. LNCS, vol. 4763, pp. 336–351. Springer, Heidelberg (2007)
34. Reniers, M.A.: Message Sequence Chart: Syntax and Semantics. PhD thesis, Eindhoven University of Technology, June 1999
35. Hammouda, I., Hautamäki, J., Pussinen, M., Koskimies, K.: Managing variability using heterogeneous feature variation patterns. In: Cerioli, M. (ed.) FASE 2005. LNCS, vol. 3442, pp. 145–159. Springer, Heidelberg (2005)
36. Tanenbaum, A.S., Wetherall, D.J.: Computer Networks, 5th edn. Prentice Hall (2011)
37. Zhou, Z., Sheldon, F.T., Potok, T. E.: Modeling with stochastic message sequence charts. In: IIIS Proceedings of the International Conference on Computer, Communication, and Control Technology (CCCT 2003) (2003)

Multi-objective Parameter Synthesis in Probabilistic Hybrid Systems

Martin Fränzle[1,2], Sebastian Gerwinn[2(✉)], Paul Kröger[1], Alessandro Abate[3], and Joost-Pieter Katoen[4]

[1] Department of Computing Science, Carl von Ossietzky University, Oldenburg, Germany
{fraenzle,paul.kroeger}@informatik.uni-oldenburg.de
[2] OFFIS Institute for Information Technology, Oldenburg, Germany
sebastian.gerwinn@offis.de
[3] Department of Computer Science, Oxford University, Oxford, UK
aabate@cs.ox.ac.uk
[4] Department of Computer Science, RWTH Aachen University, Aachen, Germany
katoen@cs.rwth-aachen.de

Abstract. Technical systems interacting with the real world can be elegantly modelled using probabilistic hybrid automata (PHA). Parametric probabilistic hybrid automata are dynamical systems featuring hybrid discrete-continuous dynamics and parametric probabilistic branching, thereby generalizing PHA by capturing a family of PHA within a single model. Such system models have a broad range of applications, from control systems over network protocols to biological components. We present a novel method to synthesize parameter instances (if such exist) of PHA satisfying a multi-objective bounded horizon specification over expected rewards. Our approach combines three techniques: statistical model checking of model instantiations, a symbolic version of importance sampling to handle the parametric dependence, and SAT-modulo-theory solving for finding feasible parameter instances in a multi-objective setting. The method provides statistical guarantees on the synthesized parameter instances. To illustrate the practical feasibility of the approach, we present experiments showing the potential benefit of the scheme compared to a naive parameter exploration approach.

1 Introduction

Systems engineering frequently calls for finding parameters on event probabilities, like frequencies of inspections or halts for maintenance, under constraints on expected values of costs and rewards, like expected maintenance cost and expected loss due to unscheduled downtime. In this article, we propose a method which can systematically address this problem for probabilistic hybrid automata

This work is funded by the EU FP7 projects MoVeS, SENSATION and AMBI, by the DFG through the collaborative research center SFB-TR 14 AVACS, and by the John Fell OUP Research Fund.

S. Sankaranarayanan and E. Vicario (Eds.): FORMATS 2015, LNCS 9268, pp. 93–107, 2015.
DOI: 10.1007/978-3-319-22975-1_7

featuring parametric discrete probability distributions governing choices within the automaton's control flow. We are able to devise instances of the parametric distribution guaranteeing multi-objective specifications concerning expected costs and rewards over a bounded horizon, i.e., enforcing that expectations on a multi-dimensional vector of costs/rewards incurred within the bounded horizon satisfy a first-order specification over these costs and rewards. Such specifications may place bounds on individual costs/rewards as well as relate them arithmetically, e.g., enforcing a relation between maintenance costs and system availability. The bounded horizon may deal with a number of computation steps or with a time bound, provided the system is non-Zeno.

For confined settings, such parameter fitting could be reduced to SAT modulo theory (SMT) solving, based on a parametric extension of the encodings pioneered by Wimmer *et al.* [23]. This would, however, require that both the system dynamics and the reward functions, as well as their dependency on probabilistic choices, can be encoded in the arithmetic theory supported by the SMT solver, and that the bounded horizon is given in terms of a step bound in order to facilitate a symbolic unravelling of the transition tree. Such an approach would for example require SMT over polynomials to deal with parametric probabilistic linear hybrid automata (featuring piecewise constant differential equations, linear guards, etc.). It is thus confined to systems with rather simple dynamics and, given the complexity of polynomial constraint solving, of rather small size under rather restrictive bounds on the temporal horizon.

To overcome these shortcomings, our method is based on ideas from *statistical model checking* (SMC) [24], which in its traditional setup deals with non-parametric probabilistic (hybrid) systems. The strength of SMC is that it can tackle arbitrary system dynamics, as long as a simulator is available, and is rather insensitive to system size. The underlying principle is to run a number of simulations of the system under investigation within a simulator faithfully representing the — then necessarily non-parametric — probabilistic choices in the system as well as its state dynamics, and to exploit the set of traces obtained from the simulations for computing an estimate of the expected values of reward or cost variables by means of averaging over the individual traces.

Extensions of SMC to parametric probabilistic hybrid systems could in principle be addressed by sampling the parameter space, yet this would induce the curse of dimensionality, confining such a method to fitting isolated parameters. We avoid this problem by adequately adapting the concept of *importance sampling*, which permits factoring out the parameter dependency of the distributions by sampling a fixed substitute distribution instead. The method is based on a combination of statistical model checking of a substitute model devoid of parametricity, a symbolic version of importance sampling providing an *SMT representation of the parameter dependencies*, and SMT solving for finding feasible parameter instances satisfying the constraints imposed on expected values.

Organization of the Paper. Section 2 introduces parametric probabilistic hybrid automata and multi-objective specifications on expected rewards. Section 3 explains importance sampling for parametric distributions and presents the

equations that are key to our approach. Section 4 considers the specific case
of parametric distributions in (finite- or infinite-state) Markov chains and provides statistical guarantees in the form of confidence intervals. Section 5, finally,
sketches how SMT solving can be applied so as to find (a) feasible parameter instances satisfying the multi-objective specification and (b) the confidence
in the provided solution. We close with discussing related work and general
conclusions.

2   Parametric Probabilistic Hybrid Automata

*Probabilistic hybrid automata
(PHA).* [19] extend hybrid
automata with discrete probabilistic branching. This enables modeling of, e.g., random
component failures and data
packet losses. Similar to hybrid
automata, PHA feature a
finite set of discrete locations
(or modes), each of which
comes decorated with a differential equation governing the
dynamics of a vector of continuous variables while resid-
ing in that mode. Modes
change through instantaneous
transitions guarded by conditions on the current values
of the continuous variables,
and may yield discontinu-
ous updates of the continuous variables. Aiming at
simulation-based evaluation

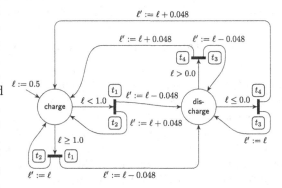

Fig. 1. PPHA model of a charging station. Modes
are labeled with labels `charge` and `discharge` abbre-
viating ODE (not shown explicitly) representing
corresponding dynamics over a continuous capacity
ℓ. Modes can switch according to guarded transitions leading to a probabilistic branch. Probabilities
are summarized as terms $t_1, \ldots, t_4$ indicating their
parameter dependencies.

methods as in SMC, transition selection here is assumed to be deterministic,
i.e., guard conditions at each mode are mutually exclusive. To prevent non-
determinism between possible time flows and transitions, we also assume that
transitions are urgent, i.e., they are taken as soon as they are enabled (which furthermore renders mode invariants redundant). In addition to these mechanisms
from deterministic hybrid automata, PHA allow for the probabilistic selection of
a transition variant based on a discrete random experiment. Following the idea
of Sproston [19,20], the selected transition entails a randomized choice between
transition variants according to a discrete probability distribution. The different
transition variants can lead to different follow-up locations and different continuous successors, as depicted in Figure 1, where the guard condition determining
transition selection is depicted along the straight arrows leading to a potential
branching annotated with probability terms denoting the random experiment.

Parametric probabilistic hybrid automata (PPHA) extend PHA with the presence of parameters. Whereas in PHA the probability distributions are constants, PPHA allow the branching probabilities to be terms over a set *Param* of parameter names. The viable parameter instantiations $\theta : Param \to \mathbb{R}$ are constrained by an arithmetic first-order predicate ϕ over *Param*, defining their mutual relation. Let $\Theta = \{\theta : Param \to \mathbb{R} \mid \theta \models \phi\}$ denote the set of all viable parameterizations. Arithmetic terms over *Param* are subject to the constraint that for all viable parameter valuations $\theta \models \phi$, the sum of outgoing probabilities assigned to each transition is one, i.e., $\phi \implies \sum_{i=1}^{n} t_i(\theta) = 1$ holds for the probability terms $t_1, \ldots, t_n$ associated to each transition t. Note that the probability terms need not contain free variables θ: ordinary non-parametric distributions are thus special cases of parametric distributions and do not require special treatment.

2.1   Interpretation as Parametric Infinite-State Markov Chain

A PPHA engages in a sequence of continuous flows and discrete jumps. The continuous flows are solutions of the ordinary differential equations assigned to the current location. The discrete jumps originate from taking enabled transitions, thereby eliciting a transition as soon as it is triggered, and then probabilistically deciding among the different transition variants, with their associated target locations and resets to continuous variables. For the sake of formal analysis, we formalize the semantics of PPHA through a reduction to a parametric infinite-state Markov chain. For a PPHA with location set Λ and continuous variables $x_1, \ldots, x_D$, the states of the Markov chain are given by $\Sigma = \Lambda \times \mathbb{R}^D$ and the initial state distribution is inherited from the PPHA. Each state $\sigma = (l, \boldsymbol{x}) \in \Sigma$ gives rise to a parameter-dependent distribution[1] $p_\sigma : \Sigma \times \Theta \to [0, 1]$ of successor states:

$$p_\sigma(\sigma', \theta) = \begin{cases} t(\theta) & \text{if a transition } (\sigma, \sigma') \text{ labeled with probability term } t \text{ is enabled,} \\ 1 & \text{if } \sigma' = (l, g(t)), \text{ where } g \text{ is a solution to the ODE associated to} \\ & l \in \Lambda \text{ with } g(0) = \boldsymbol{x}, \text{ no transition is enabled in } (l, g(t')) \text{ for any} \\ & t' \in [0, t[, \text{ and a transition is enabled in } \sigma' = (l, g(t)), \\ 0 & \text{otherwise.} \end{cases}$$

Given a parametric infinite-state Markov chain M with its initial (state) distribution given by a density $\iota : \Sigma \to \mathbb{R}_{\geq 0}$ and a parametric next-state distribution $p_\sigma : \Sigma \times \Theta \to [0, 1]$, the *density function associated to finite runs* $\langle \sigma_0, \sigma_1, \ldots, \sigma_k \rangle \in \Sigma^*$ *given a parameter instance* $\theta \in \Theta$ is

$$p_M(\langle \sigma_0, \sigma_1, \ldots, \sigma_k \rangle; \theta) = \iota(\sigma_0) \cdot \prod_{i=0}^{k-1} p_{\sigma_i}(\sigma_{i+1}, \theta).$$

Note that while we represented the parametric dependence by a single parameter θ, this can be vector valued, thereby encoding potentially different dependencies for different nodes.

---

[1] Note that due to the finite probabilistic branching in PPHA, we deal with distributions rather than densities here.

2.2   Parameter Synthesis

Let $f : \Sigma \to \mathbb{R}$ be a scalar function on states, to be evaluated on the last state of a run and called the *reward* f of the run,[2] and let $k \in \mathbb{N}$. The *k-bounded expected reward for f in a parameter instance $\theta \in \Theta$* is

$$\mathcal{E}_{M,k}[f;\theta] = \int_{\Sigma^k} f(\sigma_{k-1}) p_M(\langle\sigma_0,\sigma_1,\dots,\sigma_{k-1}\rangle;\theta) \, \mathrm{d}\langle\sigma_0,\sigma_1,\dots,\sigma_{k-1}\rangle,$$

where Σ^k denotes the sequences over Σ of length k. We will subsequently drop the index M in $\mathcal{E}_{M,k}$ and p_M whenever it is clear from the context.

Rewards represent quantitative measures of the system's performance, and therefore mutual constraints on their values can be used for capturing design goals. The design problem we are thus facing is, given a vector $f_1,\dots,f_n : \Sigma \to \mathbb{R}$ of rewards in Markov chain M, to ensure via adequate instantiation of the parameter that the expected rewards meet the design goal. The following definition captures this intuition.

Definition 1 (Parameter Synthesis Problem). *Let $f_1,\dots,f_n : \Sigma^k \to \mathbb{R}$ be a vector of rewards in a Markov chain M and let C be a design goal in the form of a constraint on the expected rewards, i.e., an arithmetic predicate containing $f_1,\dots,f_n$ as free variables. A parameter instance $\theta : Param \to \mathbb{R}$ is* feasible *(wrt. M and C) iff*

$$\theta \models \phi \quad and \quad [f_1 \mapsto \mathcal{E}_{M,k}(f_1;\theta),\dots,f_n \mapsto \mathcal{E}_{M,k}(f_n;\theta)] \models C.$$

The multi-objective parameter synthesis problem *is to find a feasible parameter instance θ, if it exists, or to prove its absence otherwise.*

Stated in words, a parameter instance θ is feasible wrt. ϕ and C iff the parameters are in the range defined by ϕ and the expected rewards resulting from the instantiation meet the multi-objective C. Note that the aim is to find a parameter instance meeting our design goal; we are not considering determining all instantiations. In the sequel, we will focus on a single reward f rather than n such functions and indicate whenever appropriate how to deal with a vector.

3   Estimating Expectations by Sampling

In order to introduce the general concept of importance sampling [21], we mostly abstract from our PPHA setting in this section. We instead assume that the parametric probability distribution of the random variable $x \in X$ is given in terms of a density function $p(\cdot;\theta)$ which depends on a vector θ of bounded real-valued parameters. Permissible values of θ are defined by a first-order constraint ϕ.

---

[2] Despite the generality of the PPHA model, defining rewards exclusively on the final state σ_k of a run $\langle\sigma_0,\sigma_1,\dots,\sigma_k\rangle \in \Sigma^*$ is as expressive as defining them via functions $f(\langle\sigma_0,\sigma_1,\dots,\sigma_k\rangle)$, where $f : \Sigma^{k+1} \to \mathbb{R}$. Such rewards can be alternatively encoded by augmenting the state-space of the PPHA model with additional variables accumulating the quantities of interest along the trajectory.

Classical Sampling. Given an arbitrary (bounded) function $f : X \rightarrow \mathbb{R}$, we are interested in estimating expected values of f under all parameter values $\theta \models \phi$. The expectation $\mathcal{E}[f; \theta]$ for reward f given parameter vector θ is

$$\mathcal{E}[f; \theta] = \int_X f(x)p(x; \theta)\,\mathrm{d}x \ . \tag{1}$$

Given a specific parameter instance θ^* and a process sampling x_i according to the distribution $p(\cdot; \theta^*)$, the expectation $\mathcal{E}[f; \theta^*]$ can be estimated by

$$\tilde{\mathcal{E}}[f; \theta^*] = \frac{1}{N} \sum_{i=1}^{N} f(x_i) \ , \tag{2}$$

which is the empirical mean of the sampled f-values. In our PPHA setting, a reasonable process for generating such samples x_i according to the distribution $p(\cdot; \theta^*)$ would be a simulator for non-parametric PHA, applied to the instance of the PPHA under investigation obtained by substituting θ^* for the free parameters.

For sufficiently large N, we expect $\mathcal{E}[f; \theta^*] \approx \tilde{\mathcal{E}}[f; \theta^*]$ due to the law of large numbers. We can quantify the quality of the approximation in (2) using Hoeffdings inequality [13], provided that f has a bounded support $[a_f, b_f]$:

$$P\left(\mathcal{E}[f; \theta^*] - \tilde{\mathcal{E}}[f; \theta^*] \geq \varepsilon\right) \leq \exp\left(-2\frac{\varepsilon^2 N}{(b_f - a_f)^2}\right) \geq P\left(\tilde{\mathcal{E}}[f; \theta^*] - \mathcal{E}[f; \theta^*] \geq \varepsilon\right) \tag{3}$$

Therefore, the empirical mean (2) yields a very reliable estimate of the actual expectation when the number of samples is large, with the accuracy given by (3).

Importance Sampling. While determining the empirical mean (2) by repeated simulation is an adequate procedure for assessing non-parametric PHA, it is bound to fail for PPHA when applied naïvely, as it would require to sufficiently densely cover the parameter space Θ with parameter instances θ_j^* and generating $j = 1, \ldots, N$ samples for each instance θ_j^*. This is thus subject to the curse of dimensionality. Fortunately, importance sampling [21] provides a means of using substitute probability distributions in sampling processes. We will exploit this for dealing with parameters. Importance sampling was originally designed to enhancing the quality of empirical estimates by artificially drawing according to their (assumed) importance for the estimate and later correcting the estimate by weighting the individual samples by that importance. In our setting, we will use importance sampling for estimating the parameter-dependent expectation $\mathcal{E}[f; \theta]$ defined in equation (1). Instead of sampling X according to the distribution p, importance sampling uses a different distribution q to sample from. It then calculates the empirical mean of the samples (over q), but weighs each sample x_i by its importance weight $\frac{p(x_i)}{q(x_i)}$, in order to obtain an estimate of the expectation under the original distribution p. Applying this idea to our parametric setting, we can pursue a single round of sampling wrt. some non-parametric distribution

q and estimate the expected value $\mathcal{E}[f; \theta]$ for arbitrary θ as follows:

$$\mathcal{E}[f; \theta] = \int_X f(x)p(x; \theta)\, \mathrm{d}x = \int_X \frac{f(x)p(x; \theta)}{q(x)} q(x)\, \mathrm{d}x$$

$$\approx \frac{1}{N} \sum_{i=1}^{N} \frac{f(x_i)p(x_i; \theta)}{q(x_i)} =: \hat{\mathcal{E}}[f; \theta], \qquad \text{where } x_i \sim q. \tag{4}$$

Note that all the samples $\{x_1, \ldots, x_N\}$ are drawn according to the substitute[3] distribution q (indicated by $x_i \sim q$); nevertheless, (4) still keeps the parameter dependence $\hat{\mathcal{E}}[f; \theta]$ for arbitrary values of θ.

4   Symbolic Representation of Importance Sampling

The purpose of this section is to derive a symbolic characterization of a solution to our parameter synthesis problem. This is achieved by using samples drawn from the proposal distribution to construct a symbolic constraint system by means of the importance sampling expression for the expectation.

A Symbolic Constraint System. Let $p(x; \theta)$ have a closed-form representation given as term t. (Typically t contains one or more free occurrences of x and θ.) A symbolic representation of the parameter dependency of $\hat{\mathcal{E}}[f; \theta]$, and (due to the sampling error) an approximate symbolic representation of the parameter dependency of $\mathcal{E}[f; \theta]$ can now readily be obtained as follows. We replace all occurrences of $p(x_1; \theta)$ through $p(x_N; \theta)$ in (4) by the terms $t[x_1/x]$ through $t[x_N/x]$ respectively, and substitute the concrete values for N, $(x_i)_{i=1\ldots N}$, and $(f(x_i))_{i=1\ldots N}$. The resulting term, referred to as η, is a large sum with multiple occurrences of θ in different instances of the sub-term t. Let C be a constraint on the expected reward $\mathcal{E}$, i.e., C is a formula with free variable f formalizing the requirements on the expectation $\mathcal{E}[f; \theta]$. A parameter instance $\theta \models \phi$ statistically guaranteeing C can now in principle be found — or conversely, the infeasibility of C over ϕ be established — by solving the constraint system

$$(\mathcal{E}[f; \theta] = \eta[f; \theta]) \wedge \phi \wedge C \tag{5}$$

using an appropriate constraint solver. Note that (5) enforces $\theta \models \phi$ through the conjunct ϕ and guarantees $[f \mapsto \hat{\mathcal{E}}[f; \theta]] \models C$ due to the construction of η and the presence of the constraints $\mathcal{E} = \eta$ and C.

As $\hat{\mathcal{E}}[f; \theta] \approx \mathcal{E}[f; \theta]$, the instance θ of the parameterized system under investigation then intuitively is likely to also satisfy $\mathcal{E}[f; \theta] \models C$, as desired. However, the resulting parameter instances might suffer from being biased towards the particular samples, which will be investigated in detail in the next section.

The generalization of (5) to multiple rewards $f_j : X \to \mathbb{R}$ and a corresponding multi-objective constraint C containing arbitrary arithmetic and Boolean combinations of the expected rewards is straightforward, albeit potentially higher in computational cost.

---

[3] In principle, an arbitrary distribution q can serve as a substitute. In our setting, it is natural to use an instance $q = p(\cdot; \theta^*)$ of the parametric distribution, where $\theta^* \models \phi$.

Simplified Constraint System. In practice, the constraint (5) may become unwieldy due to the large number of samples x_i necessary for obtaining a sufficiently tight confidence bound in equation (3), as the number of samples directly translates into a corresponding number of summands in η. This problem can be alleviated in our setting as we consider Markov processes.

For the sake of illustration, let us assume that there is a (non-empty) subset Δ of the state set Σ of the Markov chain M, where the chain has a parameter-dependent probabilistic choice between just two transition alternatives, taking alternative one with probability t, where t is a term dependent on θ, and alternative two with probability $1 - t$, and that all other states in $\Sigma \setminus \Delta$ feature non-parametric distributions.[4] During sampling, we substitute these parameter-dependent probabilities t and $1-t$ by the static substitute probabilities q and $1-q$, respectively, where $q \in \,]0,1[$ is a constant.

During a simulation providing N samples, we now keep track of how many times a run takes transition alternatives one and two. Let $T_{n,m}$ denote the set of simulated trajectories taking n times alternative one and m times alternative two. Note that there are finitely many $T_{n,m} \neq \emptyset$, and that in practice the number of non-empty $T_{n,m}$ is considerably smaller than N. Let $\Sigma_{n,m} = \sum_{x_i \in T_{n,m}} f(x_i)$ denote the sum of the rewards seen on all trajectories in $T_{n,m}$. This quantity can easily be computed during sampling. With these notations in place, we can partition the sum (4) in terms of the necessarily pairwise disjoint sets $T_{n,m}$, obtaining the following equivalent formulation of (4):

$$\hat{\mathcal{E}}[f;\theta] = \frac{1}{N} \sum_{n,m \in \mathbb{N}} \left(\Sigma_{n,m} \left(\frac{t}{q}\right)^n \left(\frac{1-t}{1-q}\right)^m \right) \tag{6}$$

Note that θ freely occurs in the right-hand side of (6), as it does so in t. If the number of non-empty $T_{n,m}$ is considerably smaller than N, the right-hand side of equation (6), after dropping summands for which $T_{n,m} = \emptyset$ and thus $\Sigma_{n,m} = 0$, provides us with a much shorter sum than (4), which still characterises $\hat{\mathcal{E}}[f;\theta]$. A symbolic representation η of the parameter-dependency of $\hat{\mathcal{E}}[f;\theta]$ can again be obtained by substituting the specific values for N, q, and $\Sigma_{n,m}$ into (6). Based on the resulting expression η, we can construct a logically equivalent, yet syntactically shorter formulation of the constraint (5):

$$\left(\varepsilon = \frac{1}{N} \sum_{n,m \in \mathbb{N}} \left(\Sigma_{n,m} \left(\frac{t}{q}\right)^n \left(\frac{1-t}{1-q}\right)^m \right) \right) \wedge \phi \wedge C. \tag{7}$$

This constraint expresses $[f \mapsto \hat{\mathcal{E}}[f;\theta]] \models C$ subject to $\theta \models \phi$, and thus approximates the feasibility condition on θ up to the inaccuracies incurred through sampling and rescaling due to importance sampling. In Sect. 6, we will demonstrate that (7) is amenable to constraint solving for a set of interesting PPHA.

---

[4] The generalization to arbitrary discrete distributions (fan-out larger than two) controlled by a finite-dimensional vector of parameters is straightforward, as is tackling multiple different subsets $\Delta_i \subset \Sigma$.

5   Existence or Absence of Parameter Instances

As constraint (7) is an arithmetic constraint containing addition, multiplication, and the operations found in the term t as well as in the parameter domain constraint ϕ and the design goal C, it can be solved by SMT solvers addressing the corresponding subset of arithmetic, e.g., iSAT [8]. This provides an automatic feasibility check for (7), i.e., a test whether there is a parameter instance within the domain defined by ϕ which guarantees (modulo sampling errors) satisfaction of constraint C over the expectations. Should this test succeed, it will also deliver a parameter instance. Additional optimization wrt. the expectation $\mathcal{E}[f; \theta]$ can be added on top by a branch-and-prune algorithm, as available in the HySAT II tool [12]. It is, however, obvious that a solution to (7), if existing, guarantees the approximate feasibility condition $[f \mapsto \hat{\mathcal{E}}[f; \theta]] \models C$ only, rather than the desired $[f \mapsto \mathcal{E}[f; \theta]] \models C$. Therefore, we have to account for the statistical approximation error associate to the empirical estimate.

For the sake of simplicity, assume in the sequel that the constraint C on the expectation $\mathcal{E}[f; \theta]$ is of the form $\mathcal{E}[f; \theta] < c$, for some constant $c \in \mathbb{R}$. The generalization to arbitrary constraints, including constraints on multiple different expectations, is straightforward by adopting the concept of δ-weakening discussed in the context of robust interpretations of arithmetic logics [17].

In the following, we consider the case that symbolic checking of the empirical constraint system (7) could not be satisfied. In this case, we know that $\min_\theta \hat{\mathcal{E}}[f; \theta] > c + \varepsilon$, with an additional slackness ε to be defined shortly. We are then interested in the probability that there nevertheless exists a θ' with $\mathcal{E}[f; \theta'] < c$, i.e., $\min_{\theta'} \mathcal{E}[f; \theta'] < c$. To quantify this, let the subindex $S = (X_1, \ldots, X_N)$ indicate the dependency of the estimated expectation on the ensemble of samples drawn from the proposal q, i.e., $\hat{\mathcal{E}}_S[f; \theta] = \frac{1}{N} \sum_i f(x_i) \frac{p(x_i; \theta)}{q(x_i)}$:

$$P_S \left(\min_\theta \hat{\mathcal{E}}_S[f; \theta] \geq \varepsilon + c \;\wedge\; \min_\theta \mathcal{E}[f; \theta] < c \right) \leq P_S \left(\min_\theta \hat{\mathcal{E}}_S[f; \theta] \geq \min_\theta \mathcal{E}[f; \theta] + \varepsilon \right)$$

$$\overset{\text{Jensen ineq.}}{\leq} P_S \left(\underbrace{\min_\theta \hat{\mathcal{E}}_S[f; \theta]}_{=:g(S)} - \mathcal{E} \left[\min_\theta \hat{\mathcal{E}}_S[f; \theta] \right] \geq \varepsilon \right) = P_S \left(g(S) - \mathcal{E}\left[g(S) \right] \geq \varepsilon \right)$$

$$\overset{\text{McDiarmid ineq.}}{\leq} \exp\left(-\frac{\varepsilon^2 N}{4B^2} \right) =: \delta; \; B := \max_{x, \theta} \frac{p(x; \theta)}{q(x)} \overset{\text{Markov}}{\leq} \left(\max_\theta \left\{ \frac{p_\theta}{q}, \frac{1 - p_\theta}{1 - q} \right\} \right)^{k-1}$$

$$\tag{8}$$

The last of these inequalities is specific to our case of a binary Markov chain with samples consisting of k probabilistic transitions.

Therefore, if we are aiming for a confidence of $1 - \delta$, we can use equation (8) and check the symbolic constraint system with an adapted threshold $c' = c + \varepsilon(\delta, N) = \sqrt{\frac{\log(\frac{1}{\delta})}{N}} 2B$. If this constraint system is unsatisfiable, we know with probability at least $1 - \delta$ that the original constraint system is also unsatisfiable.

Obtaining similar bounds in case we have found a parameter instance for which the empirical constraint system is indeed satisfiable is more involved.

In fact, these bounds are tightly coupled to the generalization bounds within statistical learning theory (see [1,5,22]). Therefore, in case we find a potential satisfying parameter setting using the symbolic constraint system, we simply check the validity of this parameter statistically using another round of naïve sampling, similar to [25], thereby avoiding restricting ourselves to particular function classes for the parameter dependence of the terms t.

Using the above two tests, we can iteratively solve for a parameter satisfying the desired constraint system until one of the tests succeeds, giving us a (statistically) reliable answer. If a parameter instance satisfying (7) is found that nevertheless fails to pass the statistical check, we use the fresh samples to build another symbolic constraint system as in equation (7). We can then use this constraint system to solve for a new parameter value, which we can then check subsequently. To use as much information as possible from the samples, instead of building a completely fresh symbolic constraint system, we simply add the newly constructed constraint system to the previous one (see Algorithm 1). To retain the confidence statement with respect to unsatisfiability when adding more clauses to the constraint system, we have to account for sequential hypothesis testing. This can be achieved by using a Bonferroni correction, i.e., requiring the individual tests to be more confident, relative to the maximal amount of tests to be performed ($\delta^c = \frac{\delta}{I}$ in Algorithm 1).

Algorithm 1. Parameter Fitting by Symbolic Importance Sampling

---

function SYM-IMP(ϕ, C, confidence δ, number of samples N, max. iterations I)

    $\delta^c \leftarrow \frac{\delta}{I}$; $\theta_0 \leftarrow$ DRAWUNIFORM(Θ); $\varepsilon \leftarrow \sqrt{\frac{\log(\frac{1}{\delta^c})}{N}}2B$; $n \leftarrow 0$; $\hat{\phi}_0 \leftarrow \phi$

    while $n \leq I$ **do**

        $q \leftarrow p(\cdot; \theta_n)$

        $S = (x_1, \ldots, x_N) \leftarrow$ DRAWSAMPLES(q, N)

        if CHECKSAMPLES(S, δ, ϕ, C) **then**

            return θ_n ▷ Found parameterization satisfying C with prob. $\geq 1 - \delta$

        else

            $\hat{\phi}_{n+1} \leftarrow \hat{\phi}_n \wedge (\eta(S) < c + \varepsilon)$ ▷ Add samples to empirical system

            $\theta_{n+1} \leftarrow$ SOLVECONSTRAINTSYSTEM($\hat{\phi}_{n+1}$)

            if $\hat{\phi}_{n+1}$ is unsatisfiable **then**

                return Unsat   ▷ Original system is unsatisfiable with prob. $\geq 1 - \delta$

            else $n \leftarrow n + 1$

            end if

        end if

    end while

    return Unknown   ▷ Reached maximal iterations I

end function

Altogether, we arrive at Algorithm 1 which upon termination within the specified maximal number of iterations either delivers a parameter instance satisfying the design objective with the desired confidence or proves with the desired confidence that no such instance exists.

6   Experiments

In this section, we explore the potential and limitations of the presented app-roach, exemplified on the PPHA depicted in Figure 1. The PPHA simplistically models a battery being charged and discharged, where switching between those two modes happens randomly, thereby reflecting external influences like weather on a solar panel. As the climatic conditions might change depending on the region, the probabilistic transitions are parameterized. Initially, the battery is in charge mode. As long as its capacity has not reached its maximal value (guard: $\ell < 1$), it can switch randomly with probability t_1 to the discharge mode. During the transition from charge to discharge mode, the capacity is reduced. For simplicity, we assume a fixed value of 0.048 (see Figure 1), which reduces the continuous variable ℓ to the new value after the transition to ℓ'. For the probabilistic transitions, we assume the following parametric dependence to include non-linear dependence of the parameters h: $t_1 = t_3 = \sin(h)$, and $t_2 = t_4 = 1 - t_1$, where $h \in [0.0, 0.1]$ is the parameter of interest. As an illus-trative objective for this PPHA, we are interested in finding a parameter value such that the charge of the battery reaches a sufficient level at a certain time, e.g., exceeding a threshold level at sunset which provides sufficient power for the following night. This property can be formalized as follows:

> **Goal:** The battery is sufficiently charged at sunset (indicated by time step K) in 90% of the days. The corresponding reward function takes the current time into account: it evaluates to 1 if $\ell \geq 0.98$ at time K, and 0 otherwise. We require this condition to hold with probability $c \geq 0.9$.

Using this formalization, we evaluate the presented approach in terms of both accuracy and efficiency. Using Algorithm 1, we can obtain the following results from our solver characterizing the solution: 'unknown', 'candidate solution', 'unsatisfiable'. If the problem is satisfiable, we expect the solver to return, either 'unknown' or 'candidate solution' due to the general undecidable nature of the problem. However, if the solver returns 'unsatisfiable', we know that with a high likelihood $(1 - \delta)$ there is no parameter value within the given domain, such that the constraint system is satisfiable.

Fortunately, the simplicity of the model allows us to calculate maximal and minimal values for the expected values as a function of the parameter quite accurately, thereby enabling us to determine the satisfiability of the problem analytically in some of the settings. Using this analytical result we can determine the fraction of simulations in which we have obtained the most informative result with respect to these analytically obtained satisfiability statements.

For the model described above, we are able to compute the satisfiability for both constraint variants by calculating the expected values using $h = 0.0$ and $h = 0.1$, due to the monoticity of the properties: From these expectations, we can conclude on the existence of a parameter instances for which $\theta \models C$ or $\theta \not\models C$

holds[5]. Using these bounds we evaluate the frequency with which the algorithm found the most informative solution as a proxy for the accuracy of the approach.

To judge the improvement of the presented approach, we compare the sampling based verification with a parameter-state exploration approach. As we are considering a bounded model checking approach within a Markov transition system, we can fully unroll the probabilistic transitions and use the same SMT solver to check the existence of a parameter value that result in a satisfaction of the desired property. As the complexity of the satisfaction property increases with increasing unrolling depth, we vary the maximal number of transitions as well as the level of confidence. As we expect the choice of the proposal distribution to crucially influence the effectiveness of the approach, we compare two different choices: one minimizing the possible range B of the fraction $\frac{q(x)}{p(x;\theta)}$ (as a function of the parameter as well as a function of the sampled path x, cf. (8)), and a slightly perturbed version. As a backend SMT solver, we used iSAT3[6].

In Figure 2, we compare the accuracy as well as the run-time of our sampling-based method against a full exploration approach. In the left panel, the obtained (and averaged obtained) result are plotted for either method. For the sampling based method the results are averaged across 50 repetitions, for each of which we used a confidence of $1 - \delta = 0.7$, $N = 15000$ samples, and a maximal number of $I = 3$ iterations. Although none of the algorithms, both sampling and unwinding based, produced any wrong results, the sampling-based algorithm was able to provide more informative results for models with large complexity. Although we know the problem for the settings with higher unrolling depth (≥ 16) to be satisfiable, only the sampling based approach was able to provide a corresponding certificate, while the unwinding scheme returned a 'potentially satisfiable' result, indicated by the UNKNOWN result. The drop in accuracy around unrolling depth $K \approx 15$ can be explained by the fact that the range of possible expected values $\mathcal{E}$ as a function of the parameters overlaps with the confidence interval, rendering the problem harder to answer. As the problem size for naïve scheme of fully unwinding the transition system grows exponentially with the maximal length of paths (K), we expect the speedup compared to the run-time of the sampling based scheme also to be exponential as a function of K. It can be observed that the speedup in the run-time increases with the complexity, as shown in Figure 2b. However, for settings with small number of possible paths, the speedup is less pronounced. In fact, it could also happen that the speedup is below 1 (a slower performance), as the sampling based approach needs to simulate more than actual possible paths for small unrolling depths, leading to an overhead in computation.

---

[5] These regions are indicated in Figure 2 in green and red respectively. For the region inbetween, we could not analytically calculate the true result. As the sampling-based method returned some satisfiable parameter values, it suggests the satisfiable region to be larger than depicted in the Figure.

[6] https://projects.avacs.org/projects/isat3

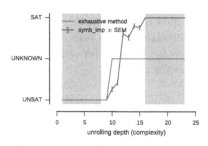
(a) Solution found by either method

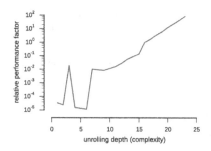
(b) Sampling-based speed-up

Fig. 2. Comparison of exhaustive and sample based method wrt. accuracy and running-time. For the accuracy (left panel), the analytically guaranteed UNSAT and SAT regions are marked red (left) and green (right) respectively. For the sample-based algorithm an interpolated average ± 1 standard error is plotted.

7 Related Work

The verification of parametric probabilistic models in which certain transition probabilities are given as parameters (or functions thereof) has received considerable attention recently. Most approaches focus on parameter synthesis: for which parameter instances does a given (LTL or probabilistic CTL) formula hold? This question has been tackled in several different settings, varying in the properties, the forms of parameter dependence, as well as the class of systems considered. Han *et al.* [3,11] considered the problem for timed reachability in continuous-time Markov chains, Hahn *et al.* [9] and Pugelli *et al.* [18] for discrete-state Markov decision processes (MDPs). Benedikt *et al.* [2] considered the parameter synthesis as a maximization problem for the probability of satisfying ω-regular properties within an interval Markov chain without further constraints on the parameter dependence. Hahn *et al.* [10] provide an algorithm for computing the rational function of the parameters expressing the probability of reaching a given set of states in a parametric (reward) MDP based on exploiting regular expressions, as initially proposed by Daws [6]. For non-probabilistic systems and linear arithmetic dependence on parameters, the synthesis (i.e., reachability as the dual problem) has been analyzed in [4]. Similarly, in [15] and [14] reachability is analyzed for parametric probability distribution in a finite-state Markov chain. To increase the efficiency of the synthesis problem, [14] restricted the parametric dependence to rational functions. Zhang *et al.*, [25] considered the following problem: Find parameters u such that for a given black box function r, the following holds: $P_X(r(u, x) \in [a, b]) \geq \theta$. For this single objective the probability distribution of x needs to be known and independent of the design parameters u. The presented procedure is similar, as it iterates between optimization and a simulation-based verification step, however, it cannot provide an unsatisfiability statement. The parametric dependence of the probability distributions presented in this paper can also be integrated into a hierarchical optimization procedure, see [7] for more details. There however, only single objectives were considered instead of multiple constraints as specified in equation (5).

To the best of our knowledge, synthesis wrt. arbitrary first-order objectives over expected rewards has not been considered so far. Parameter synthesis in PHA also seems to be a mostly unexplored research arena.

8   Conclusion

We have discussed a method for automatically finding parameter instances satisfying arbitrary first-order, multi-objective specifications on expected rewards, given a probabilistic hybrid system with parametric probability distributions. Although our approach is based on simulations and hence can only provide statistical guarantees of the property being satisfied, we found that such an approach can rapidly find parameter instances at similar or even better accuracy than exhaustive, safely overapproximating procedures. The probable reason is that the overall number of paths to be analyzed is drastically reduced by the sampling process, thereby rendering the approach less sensitive to the overapproximations typically used by the internal mechanics of the solver used.[7] For this reason, it is to be expected that this accuracy benefit gets even more pronounced for higher-dimensional optimization problems. As our approach effectively tames the dimensionality barrier, which inevitably is hit by both exhaustive procedures and procedures sampling the parameter space, by employing a form of symbolic importance sampling it should scale well to such higher-dimensional problems. This, however, remains subject to future investigations.

References

1. Bartlett, P.L., Mendelson, S.: Rademacher and gaussian complexities: Risk bounds and structural results. J. of Machine Learning Research **3**, 463–482 (2003)
2. Benedikt, M., Lenhardt, R., Worrell, J.: LTL model checking of interval Markov chains. In: Piterman, N., Smolka, S.A. (eds.) TACAS 2013 (ETAPS 2013). LNCS, vol. 7795, pp. 32–46. Springer, Heidelberg (2013)
3. Češka, M., Dannenberg, F., Kwiatkowska, M., Paoletti, N.: Precise parameter synthesis for stochastic biochemical systems. In: Mendes, P., Dada, J.O., Smallbone, K. (eds.) CMSB 2014. LNCS, vol. 8859, pp. 86–98. Springer, Heidelberg (2014)
4. Cimatti, A., Griggio, A., Mover, S., Tonetta, S.: Parameter synthesis with IC3. In: FMCAD (2013)
5. Cortes, C., Mansour, Y., Mohri, M.: Learning bounds for importance weighting. In: Advances in Neural Information Processing Systems (NIPS), pp. 442–450 (2010)
6. Daws, C.: Symbolic and parametric model checking of discrete-time Markov chains. In: Liu, Z., Araki, K. (eds.) ICTAC 2004. LNCS, vol. 3407, pp. 280–294. Springer, Heidelberg (2005)
7. Ellen, C., Gerwinn, S., Fränzle, M.: Statistical model checking for stochastic hybrid systems involving nondeterminism over continuous domains. International Journal on Software Tools for Technology Transfer **17**(4), 485–504 (2015)

---

[7] The iSAT solver we used for the experiments uses interval arithmetics. Its internal mechanics [8] is closely akin to, yet predates δ-decision procedures [16].

8. Fränzle, M., Herde, C., Teige, T., Ratschan, S., Schubert, T.: Efficient Solving of Large Non-linear Arithmetic Constraint Systems with Complex Boolean Structure. JSAT **1**, 209–236 (2007)

9. Hahn, E.M., Han, T., Zhang, L.: Synthesis for PCTL in parametric Markov decision processes. In: Bobaru, M., Havelund, K., Holzmann, G.J., Joshi, R. (eds.) NFM 2011. LNCS, vol. 6617, pp. 146–161. Springer, Heidelberg (2011)

10. Hahn, E.M., Hermanns, H., Zhang, L.: Probabilistic reachability for parametric Markov models. STTT **13**(1), 3–19 (2011)

11. Han, T., Katoen, J.-P., Mereacre, A.: Approximate parameter synthesis for probabilistic time-bounded reachability. In: IEEE Real-Time Systems Symposium (RTSS), pp. 173–182. IEEE Computer Society (2008)

12. Herde, C., Eggers, A., Fränzle, M., Teige, T.: Analysis of hybrid systems using HySAT. In: Third International Conference on Systems, ICONS 2008, pp. 196–201. IEEE (2008)

13. Hoeffding, W.: Probability inequalities for sums of bounded random variables. Journal of the American Statistical Association, 13–30 (1963)

14. Jansen, N., Corzilius, F., Volk, M., Wimmer, R., Ábrahám, E., Katoen, J.-P., Becker, B.: Accelerating parametric probabilistic verification. In: Norman, G., Sanders, W. (eds.) QEST 2014. LNCS, vol. 8657, pp. 404–420. Springer, Heidelberg (2014)

15. Lanotte, R., Maggiolo-Schettini, A., Troina, A.: Parametric probabilistic transition systems for system design and analysis. Formal Aspects of Computing **19**(1), 93–109 (2007)

16. Liu, B., Kong, S., Gao, S., Zuliani, P., Clarke, E.M.: Parameter synthesis for cardiac cell hybrid models using δ-decisions. In: Mendes, P., Dada, J.O., Smallbone, K. (eds.) CMSB 2014. LNCS, vol. 8859, pp. 99–113. Springer, Heidelberg (2014)

17. Liu, J., Ozay, N.: Abstraction, discretization, and robustness in temporal logic control of dynamical systems. In: Proceedings of the 17th International Conference on Hybrid Systems: Computation and Control, pp. 293–302. ACM (2014)

18. Puggelli, A., Li, W., Sangiovanni-Vincentelli, A.L., Seshia, S.A.: Polynomial-time verification of PCTL properties of MDPs with convex uncertainties. In: Sharygina, N., Veith, H. (eds.) CAV 2013. LNCS, vol. 8044, pp. 527–542. Springer, Heidelberg (2013)

19. Sproston, J.: Decidable model checking of probabilistic hybrid automata. In: Joseph, M. (ed.) FTRTFT 2000. LNCS, vol. 1926, pp. 31–45. Springer, Heidelberg (2000)

20. Sproston, J.: Model Checking for Probabilistic Timed and Hybrid Systems. PhD thesis, School of Computer Science, The University of Birmingham (2001)

21. Tokdar, S.T., Kass, R.E.: Importance sampling: a review. Wiley Interdisciplinary Reviews: Computational Statistics **2**(1), 54–60 (2010)

22. Vapnik, V.N.: Statistical learning theory, vol. 1. Wiley, New York (1998)

23. Wimmer, R., Derisavi, S., Hermanns, H.: Symbolic partition refinement with dynamic balancing of time and space. In: Rubino, G. (ed.) Quantitative Evaluation of Systems (QEST), pp. 65–74. IEEE Computer Science Press (2008)

24. Younes, H.L.S., Kwiatkowska, M., Norman, G., Parker, D.: Numerical vs. statistical probabilistic model checking. International Journal on Software Tools for Technology Transfer (STTT) **8**(3), 216–228 (2006)

25. Zhang, Y., Sankaranarayanan, S., Somenzi, F.: Statistically sound verification and optimization for complex systems. In: Cassez, F., Raskin, J.-F. (eds.) ATVA 2014. LNCS, vol. 8837, pp. 411–427. Springer, Heidelberg (2014)

On the Scalability of Constraint Solving for Static/Off-Line Real-Time Scheduling

Raul Gorcitz[2]($\boxtimes$), Emilien Kofman[4,5]($\boxtimes$), Thomas Carle[3],
Dumitru Potop-Butucaru[1]($\boxtimes$), and Robert de Simone[5]

[1] INRIA, Rocquencourt, France
dumitru.potop_butucaru@inria.fr
[2] CNES, Paris, France
raul.gorcitz@inria.fr
[3] Brown University, Providence, USA
[4] CNRS/UNS, Sophia-Antipolis, France
[5] INRIA, Sophia-Antipolis Méditerranée, France
emilien.kofman@inria.fr

Abstract. Recent papers have reported on successful application of constraint solving techniques to off-line real-time scheduling problems, with realistic size and complexity. Success allegedly came for two reasons: major recent advances in solvers efficiency and use of optimized, problem-specific constraint representations. Our current objective is to assess further the range of applicability and the scalability of such constraint solving techniques based on a more general and agnostic evaluation campaign. For this, we have considered a large number of synthetic scheduling problems and a few real-life ones, and attempted to solve them using 3 state-of-the-art solvers, namely CPLEX, Yices2, and MiniZinc/G12. Our findings were that, for all problems considered, constraint solving does scale to a certain limit, then diverges rapidly. This limit greatly depends on the specificity of the scheduling problem type. All experimental data (synthetic task systems, SMT/ILP models) are provided so as to allow experimental reproducibility.

Keywords: Real-time scheduling · Satisfiability modulo theories · Constraint solving · Repeatable

1 Introduction

Multi-processor scheduling is a vast, difficult and still open topic. It is addressed in several research areas (real-time scheduling, parallel compilation,...), using various formal resolution approaches (from operations research to dedicated algorithmics). Still, regardless of the area or the solving approach, the majority of multiprocessor scheduling problems are NP-hard [8,15]. Only a few utterly simple cases have polynomial solutions [6].

While NP-hard complexity is usually *bad news*, because some medium-size problem instances may be found to be intractable, it is not always so. And, because of the regularity induced by human-made specifications, the tough

S. Sankaranarayanan and E. Vicario (Eds.): FORMATS 2015, LNCS 9268, pp. 108–123, 2015.
DOI: 10.1007/978-3-319-22975-1_8

complexity sometimes only occur in accidental pathological descriptions. In fact, many instances of NP-hard problems can be rapidly solved in practice using exact algorithms [11]. This led to a renewal of interest in the improvement of solvers to increase their efficiency, a topic once thought as almost closed decades ago. And these recent improvements in solver power in turn led researchers for a renewed interest in using these exact techniques for solving problems such as multi-processor scheduling (whose need in part motivated the solver's improvements, so that everything gets quite intricated in the end).

Another avenue of research in this area was (and still is) the definition of insightful *heuristics* for fast scheduling, with generally admittedly good results. We shall not consider heuristic approaches here, partly because they are by definition non-optimal (meaning that they have no guarantee to find a schedule when one exists, or that their solution is close or not to being optimal), but mostly because the current relevance of exact scheduling techniques relying on top-class constraint solvers is our actual research concern in this paper. It is therefore always interesting to determine when exact/optimal techniques work. This is exactly our objective here: to determine the limits of applicability of exact solving techniques for various multi-processor scheduling problems. In other terms, we seek to determine the empirical practical complexity [11] of such problems.

Our approach considers static (off-line) real-time multi-processor scheduling problems, encoded as specifications made for satisfiability modulo theories (SMT), integer linear programming (ILP), or more general constraint programming (CP). The encodings themselves cover a range of scheduler features: single-period vs. multi-period, non-preemptive vs. preemptive, non-dependent vs. dependent tasks, heterogenous architectures vs. homogenous architectures, schedulability verification vs. optimization. For each scheduling problem we study the evolution of resolution time as number of tasks and processors grow, under different system loads. We deduce in a systematic way for which range of values exact constraint resolution can be applied within reasonable time, and where are the actual limits of tools and methods.

The problem instances we consider include (mostly) synthetic and (a few) real-life examples. Constraints are generated from tasks graphs in a systematic way [7]. Tasks graphs are usually displaying some amount of parametric symmetry which allows us to produce even more constraints [14] (see Section 4.2). This allows to select one solution out of a stable symetric class and thus cuts down the search space complexity.

We solve the resulting specifications using 3 state-of-the-art solvers: CPLEX for ILP specifications, Yices2 for SMT, and MiniZinc/G12 for the CP programs. We thus determine the (average) time required to solve instances of the scheduling problems for each type of problem and for each choice of parameters (number of tasks/processors and system load).

Our results indicate that, for most problems we considered, exact resolution works very efficiently for small to medium-size instances, but an abrupt combinatorial explosion systematically occurs at some point. It is thus interesting to figure what is the range of values for which the exact solution scales up. The limit largely depends on the particular scheduling features as described above, and on the system load (from less than 20 tasks for the optimal scheduling of average-load dependent tasks to more than 150 tasks in the schedulability analysis of single-period non-dependent, non-preemptive task systems with low system load).

By exploring the applicability limits of exact solving over multiple classes of scheduling problems, we provide insight into which characteristics of a scheduling problem make it more or less difficult to solve in practice. For instance, our results show that it is generally easier to build schedules when system utilization is low or, on the opposite, to prove unsatisfiability when load is very high.

Our experimental setting can be seen as a real-life effort at reconciling the seemingly contradictory conclusions found in two series of papers:

- Papers recording unsuccessful previous attempts at using exact techniques for off-line real time scheduling, such as [9]. This pessimistic view has recently been reinforced by evidences that it is still unfeasible to map relatively simple parallelized applications onto many-cores (cf. Section 5) or to map complex embedded control applications modeled as real-time dependent task systems onto bus-based multiprocessors when both allocation and scheduling must be computed [4]. We do *not* consider in this category the many other papers which discard exact solving techniques based on theoretical considerations, rather than experimental ones, because the issue is indeed to consider the potential gap between the two.
- A few recent papers reporting the successful application of modern constraint solving tools to realistic real-time scheduling and compilation problems[7,13], due to increase in solver efficiency.

As suggested by our experiments, the brute-force application of exact methods to any-size problems shall certainly comfort the first point-of-view (generally the one shared amongst the real-time scheduling and compilation communities). But, still, if one gets conscious of the boundaries as well as of the care and attention that must be taken in modeling the problems to be presented to the solvers, there is now a growing range of applications that can indeed fall into the scope of these methods. And this includes already a number of problems of practical relevance, especially those displaying certain features such as low system utilization, non-preemptive execution model, few dependencies,... as shown in our results.

Outline. The remainder of the paper is structured as follows. Section 2 reviews related work. Section 3 fully defines the ILP/SMT/CP encoding schemes used on the various scheduling problems we cover. Section 4 details the composition of our testbench, *i.e.* the generation rules for the synthetic examples and the structure of the non-synthetic ones. Section 5 provides and interprets the results, and Section 6 concludes.

2   Related Work

One major inspiration came from previous work by Leyton-Brown *et al.* [11] on understanding the empirical hardness of NP-complete problems, and in particular SAT. Their paper points out that SAT solving is simple(r) when either the number of constraints per variable is low (thus allowing the rapid construction of a solution) or when it is high, in which case unsatisfiability can be rapidly determined. Our paper provides a similar conclusion when the number of constraints per variable is replaced with the average real-time system load. Our paper also provides a more practical evaluation of when exact solving is usable, through criteria such as solving time and timeout ratio.

Our paper also develops over previous work on applying exact solving techniques (ILP/SMT/CP, more classical branch-and-cut, model checking) to off-line real-time scheduling problems [7,9,13]. These previous results all focus on either the (improved) modeling of a given scheduling problem or on the improvement of the solver algorithm. Our objective was quite different: to evaluate the limits of applicability of existing techniques and to determine global patterns that hold for all scheduling problems, and which should guide the search for efficient solutions in particular cases.

Previous work also exhibits handcrafted operations research backtracking algorithms for specific scheduling problems [2] with finely tuned branching and constraint propagation policies. Our work assumes a more generic approach and uses the policies of the solvers. Depending on the tool it is sometimes possible to guide the solver in order to change those policies. Because of the variety of the studied models and tools we did not investigate those possible optimizations.

Our paper is not directly related to previous work on heuristic solving of scheduling problems. This includes work on the heuristic use of exact solving methods, such as the use of intermediate non-optimal solutions provided by optimizaton tools, or the use of exact techniques to separately solve parts of a scheduling problem (*e.g.* communications scheduling). However, our work suggests that solving complex scheduling problems is likely to require heuristics for some time, especially given the trend of considering larger systems and adding more and more detail (non-functional requirements).

Finally, in the SMT/ILP/CP modeling of this paper we have neglected the modeling approach associated with fluid scheduling [12]. While this modeling technique bears a promise of reduced complexity, it is not clear yet whether it can deal with dependent tasks, which we consider central for the future of real-time scheduling.

3   ILP/SMT/CP Modeling of Scheduling Problems

This section formally introduces the scheduling problems we consider and then formally defines the encodings as SMT/ILP/CP constraint systems. We consider scheduling problems of two main types: schedulability verification and optimization. Schedulability verification consists here in determining if a schedule exists when the periods and durations of the various tasks are fixed. All optimization problems we consider concern single-period task systems. There, the objective is to compute the smallest period ensuring the existence of a schedule. Only the durations of the tasks are an input to the optimization problems. In all cases, deadlines are implicit (equal to the periods). Among the 3 solvers we use, CPLEX and MiniZinc/G12 can natively solve optimization problems, whereas Yices2 cannot.

As a baseline, we employ for all problems classical encodings, similar to the one of [7]. In the case of parallelized code running on homogenous architectures, this encoding is enriched with state-of-the-art symmetry-breaking constraints [14] that largely reduce solving time. The symmetry-breaking constraints are introduced later, in Section 4.2, after an application example has been introduced (to allow intuitive presentation).

Our encoding will assume that all time values used in the definition of the scheduling problem are a multiple of a given time base. This must hold for problem inputs, like the worst-case durations of tasks, and also for problem results (computed start dates and, for optimization problems, the period). All these time values are represented using integer constants and variables.

We directly present here only the SMT/CP encoding of the problems. The ILP encoding requires representing the Boolean logic parts of the rules with integer linear constraints. This straightforward translation is not detailed here.

3.1   Single-Period Dependent Tasks, Heterogenous Architecture

The first problem we consider is that of non-preemptive distributed scheduling of a set of dependent tasks having all the same period on a heterogenous set of processors connected using a single broadcast bus. The abstract formal definition of such a scheduling problem, known as a task model, must provide the following objects:

- The sets of tasks, task dependencies, and processors, respectively denoted with $\mathcal{T}$, $\mathcal{D}$, and $\mathcal{P}$. We assume that each dependecy $d \in \mathcal{D}$ connects exactly one source task denoted $\mathrm{Src}(d)$ and one destination task denoted $\mathrm{Dst}(d)$. The elements of the task and dependency sets are totally ordered, so that we can write $\tau_1 > \tau_2$ or $d_1 < d_2$ (any total order is good).
- For each $\tau \in \mathcal{T}$ and $p \in \mathcal{P}$, $\mathrm{CanExec}(\tau, p)$ is a Boolean defining whether processor p can execute task τ. Whenever $\mathrm{CanExec}(\tau, p)$ is true, the value $\mathrm{WCET}(\tau, p)$ is defined as a safe upper bound of the worst-case execution time of τ on p. $\mathrm{WCET}(\tau, p)$ is a finite integer positive value.
- For each $d \in \mathcal{D}$, $\mathrm{WCCT}(d)$ is a safe upper bound of the worst-case duration of transmitting over the bus the data communication associated with d. $\mathrm{WCCT}(d)$ is always a positive value. We make the assumption that the bus can perform data communications associated with any d.

SMT/CP encoding: Variables and bounds.

- $Alloc(\tau, p)$ is a Boolean variable. It is true when task τ is allocated on processor p. It is only defined and used in constraints when $\mathrm{CanExec}(\tau, p)$ is true.

- *BusAlloc(d)* is a Boolean variable. It is true when a bus communication is allocated for dependency d. It must be true when the source and destination tasks of d are allocated on different processors.
- *Before*(τ_1, τ_2) is a Boolean variable. If true, it requires that task τ_1 is scheduled before task τ_2, in which case τ_2 starts after τ_1 ends.
- *Before*(d_1, d_2) is a Boolean variable. It is true when the bus communication of dependency d_1 is scheduled before the communication of d_2, in which case we will require that whenever both communications are scheduled on the bus, d_2 starts after d_1 ends.
- *Start*(τ) and *Start*(d) are non-negative integers providing respectively the start dates of task τ (on a processor) and communication associated with dependency d (on the bus). The value of *Start*(d) should only be used when *BusAlloc(d)* is true.
- T is the length of the schedule table, which gives the maximum period of the resulting schedule. It can be either an input of the problem, when the period is fixed, or an output, for optimization problems.

SMT/CP encoding: Constraints. The 8 following rules are used as constraint constructors for both optimization and schedulability problems. Note that considering only rules [1], [2], [3], and [8] corresponds to encoding of single-period, *non-dependent* tasks.

[1] Each task is allocated on exactly one processor.

for all $\tau \in \mathcal{T}$ **do**
$$\sum_{\substack{p \in \mathcal{P} \\ \mathrm{CanExec}(\tau,p)=true}} Alloc(\tau, p) = 1$$

[2] If two tasks are ordered, the second starts after the first ends.

for all $p \in \mathcal{P}$ **do**
    for all $(\tau_1, \tau_2) \in \mathcal{T}^2$ with $\mathrm{CanExec}(\tau_1, p) = true$ and $\tau_1 \neq \tau_2$ **do**
      $Before(\tau_1, \tau_2) \wedge Alloc(\tau_1, p) \Rightarrow Start(\tau_1) + \mathrm{WCET}(\tau_1, p) \leq Start(\tau_2)$

[3] If two tasks are allocated on the same processor, they must be ordered.

for all $p \in \mathcal{P}$ **do**
    for all $\tau_1, \tau_2 \in \mathcal{T}$ with $\mathrm{CanExec}(\tau_i, p) = true$, $i = 1, 2$ and $\tau_1 < \tau_2$ **do**
      $Alloc(\tau_1, p) \wedge Alloc(\tau_2, p) \Rightarrow Before(\tau_1, \tau_2) \vee Before(\tau_2, \tau_1)$

[4] The source and destination of a dependency must be ordered.

for all $d \in \mathcal{D}$ **do**
    $Before(\mathrm{Src}(d), \mathrm{Dst}(d)) \wedge \neg Before(\mathrm{Dst}(d), \mathrm{Src}(d))$

[5] The bus communication associated with a dependency (if any) must start after the source task ends and must end before the destination task starts.

for all $(d, p) \in \mathcal{D} \times \mathcal{P}$ **do**
    if $\mathrm{CanExec}(\mathrm{Src}(d), p) = true$ **then**
      if $\mathrm{CanExec}(\mathrm{Dst}(d), p) = true$ **then**
        $Alloc(\mathrm{Src}(d), p) \wedge \neg Alloc(\mathrm{Dst}(d), p) \Rightarrow$
             $Start(\mathrm{Src}(d)) + \mathrm{WCET}(\mathrm{Src}(d), p) \leq Start(d)$
        $Alloc(\mathrm{Src}(d), p) \wedge \neg Alloc(\mathrm{Dst}(d), p) \Rightarrow Start(d) + \mathrm{WCCT}(d) \leq Start(\mathrm{Dst}(d))$
        $Alloc(\mathrm{Src}(d), p) \wedge \neg Alloc(\mathrm{Dst}(d), p) \Rightarrow BusAlloc(d)$
      else

$$Alloc(\mathrm{Src}(d), p) \Rightarrow Start(\mathrm{Src}(d)) + \mathrm{WCET}(\mathrm{Src}(d), p) \leq Start(d)$$
$$Alloc(\mathrm{Src}(d), p) \Rightarrow Start(d) + \mathrm{WCCT}(d) \leq Start(\mathrm{Dst}(d))$$
$$Alloc(\mathrm{Src}(d), p) \Rightarrow BusAlloc(d)$$

[6] When two dependencies require both a bus communication, these communications must be ordered.

for all $(d_1, d_2) \in \mathcal{D}^2$ with $d_1 < d_2$ **do**
$$BusAlloc(d_1) \wedge BusAlloc(d_2) \Rightarrow Before(d_1, d_2) \vee Before(d_2, d_1)$$

[7] If two dependencies are ordered, the first must end before the second starts.

for all $(d_1, d_2) \in \mathcal{D}^2$ with $d_1 \neq d_2$ **do**
$$Before(d_1, d_2) \Rightarrow Start(d_1) + \mathrm{WCCT}(d_1) \leq Start(d_2)$$

[8] All tasks must end at a date smaller or equal than the schedule length.

for all $(p, \tau) \in \mathcal{P} \times \mathcal{T}$ with $\mathrm{CanExec}(\tau, p) = true$ **do**
$$Alloc(\tau, p) \Rightarrow Start(\tau) + \mathrm{WCET}(\tau, p) \leq \mathrm{T}$$

3.2   Simplified Encoding for the Homogenous Case

In the homogenous case, all processors have the same computing power, so that for each task τ we only need to define a single duration $\mathrm{WCET}(\tau)$. We still allow some allocation constraints: A task τ has either fixed allocation, in which case $\mathrm{CanExec}(\tau, p)$ is *true* for exactly one of the processors p, or can be executed on all processors, in which case $\mathrm{CanExec}(\tau, p)$ is *true* for all p. The constraint rules [2], [5], and [8] need to be replaced with the following simplified rules.

[2hom] If two tasks are ordered, the second starts after the first ends.

for all $p \in \mathcal{P}$ **do**
  for all $(\tau_1, \tau_2) \in \mathcal{T}^2$ with $\mathrm{CanExec}(\tau_1, p) = true$ and $\tau_1 \neq \tau_2$ **do**
$$Before(\tau_1, \tau_2) \wedge Alloc(\tau_1, p) \Rightarrow Start(\tau_1) + \mathrm{WCET}(\tau_1) \leq Start(\tau_2)$$

[5hom] The bus communication associated with a dependency (if any) must start after the source task ends and must end before the destination task starts.

for all $(d, p) \in \mathcal{D} \times \mathcal{P}$ **do**
  if $\mathrm{CanExec}(\mathrm{Src}(d), p) = true$ **then**
    if $\mathrm{CanExec}(\mathrm{Dst}(d), p) = true$ **then**
      $Alloc(\mathrm{Src}(d), p) \wedge \neg Alloc(\mathrm{Dst}(d), p) \Rightarrow Start(\mathrm{Src}(d)) + \mathrm{WCET}(\mathrm{Src}(d)) \leq Start(d)$
      $Alloc(\mathrm{Src}(d), p) \wedge \neg Alloc(\mathrm{Dst}(d), p) \Rightarrow Start(d) + \mathrm{WCCT}(d) \leq Start(\mathrm{Dst}(d))$
      $Alloc(\mathrm{Src}(d), p) \wedge \neg Alloc(\mathrm{Dst}(d), p) \Rightarrow BusAlloc(d)$
    else
      $Alloc(\mathrm{Src}(d), p) \Rightarrow Start(\mathrm{Src}(d)) + \mathrm{WCET}(\mathrm{Src}(d)) \leq Start(d)$
      $Alloc(\mathrm{Src}(d), p) \Rightarrow Start(d) + \mathrm{WCCT}(d) \leq Start(\mathrm{Dst}(d))$
      $Alloc(\mathrm{Src}(d), p) \Rightarrow BusAlloc(d)$

[8hom] All tasks have release date 0 and implicit deadline (equal to the period), so that they must end at a date smaller or equal than the schedule length.

for all $\tau \in \mathcal{T}$ **do**
$$Start(\tau) + \mathrm{WCET}(\tau) \leq \mathrm{T}$$

3.3 Multi-period, Non-preemptive, Non-dependent Tasks

The scheduling problem has now a new input: For each task $\tau \in \mathcal{T}$, we define its period, denoted $T(\tau)$. It must be a positive integer. Unlike in the single-period case, the release date is not an input of the problem (it is assumed equal to the start date that is computed). The deadline of each task (equal to its period) is therefore trivially respected as soon as task WCET is smaller than the period.

As it is classically done in off-line real-time scheduling, the encoding of the problem assumes that all task instances share the same start date. This property, known as strict periodicity, has a negative impact on schedulability, but has the advantage of producing more compact schedules. For cases where strict periodicity is not desired, analysis can be done by first translating the multi-period problem into a single-period one, by means of a *hyper-period expansion* [5].

We provide here only the encoding for the heterogenous architecture case. The homogenous case can be easily derived. The encoding uses the same variables as for single-period tasks. To account for the multi-period case, the upper bound for $Start(\tau)$ is set to $T(\tau) - 1$ for all τ. Among the constraints, we use unmodified rule [1]. Rules [4]-[7] are not used here, because we have no dependencies. Rule [8] is no longer needed because tasks do not have release date 0. Rules [2] and [3] are replaced by a single rule (LCM denotes here the least common multiple of two integers):

[**2mpnp**] Instances of two different tasks cannot overlap.

> **for all** $(p, \tau_1, \tau_2) \in \mathcal{P} \times \mathcal{T} \times \mathcal{T}$ with $CanExec(\tau_i, p) = true$, $i = 1, 2$ and $\tau_1 < \tau_2$ **do**
> > **for all** $-1 \leq \alpha < LCM(T(\tau_1), T(\tau_2))/T(\tau_1)$ **do**
> > > **for all** $-1 \leq \beta < LCM(T(\tau_1), T(\tau_2))/T(\tau_2)$ **do**
> > > $Alloc(\tau_1, p) \wedge Alloc(\tau_1, p) \Rightarrow$
> > > $(Start(\tau_1) + \alpha * T(\tau_1) + WCET(\tau_1, p) \leq Start(\tau_2) + \beta * T(\tau_2)) \vee$
> > > $(Start(\tau_2) + \beta * T(\tau_2) + WCET(\tau_2, p) \leq Start(\tau_1) + \alpha * T(\tau_1))$

3.4 Multi-period, Preemptive, Non-dependent Tasks

In the preemptive model, a task can be interrupted and resumed. In our off-line scheduling context, the date of all interruptions and resumptions is an output of the scheduling problem. These dates are taken in the same integer time base as the start dates, periods... For simplicity, we consider non-dependent tasks, and we only provide here the encoding for heterogenous architectures. Preemption costs are neglected (as often in real-time scheduling). Migrations are not allowed.

The encoding basically replaces each preemptable task with a sequence of non-preemptable tasks of duration 1 which must be all allocated on the same processor. The output of the scheduling problem consists in one start date for each unit task. We denote with $Start(\tau, p, i)$ the start of the ith unit task of task τ on processor p, where i ranges from 0 to $WCET(\tau, p) - 1$. The bounds for $Start(\tau, p, i)$ are the same as for $Start(\tau)$ in the non-preemptive multi-period case. Among the constraints, we preserve unchanged only rule [1]. Rules [4]-[8] are not needed (as explained for the non-preemptive case). Rules [2] and [3] are modified as follows:

[2mpp] Unit task instances of different tasks do not overlap.

for all $(p, \tau_1, \tau_2) \in \mathcal{P} \times \mathcal{T}^2$ with $\text{CanExec}(\tau_1, p)$ and $\text{CanExec}(\tau_2, p)$ and $\tau_1 < \tau_2$ **do**
  for all $0 \le \alpha < \text{LCM}(\text{T}(\tau_1), \text{T}(\tau_2))/\text{T}(\tau_1)$ **do**
    for all $0 \le \beta < \text{LCM}(\text{T}(\tau_1), \text{T}(\tau_2))/\text{T}(\tau_2)$ **do**
      for all $0 \le i < \text{WCET}(\tau_1, p)$ and $0 \le j < \text{WCET}(\tau_2, p)$ **do**
      $Alloc(\tau_1, p) \wedge Alloc(\tau_1, p) \Rightarrow$
      $$Start(\tau_1, p, i) + \alpha * \text{T}(\tau_1) \ne Start(\tau_2, p, j) + \beta * \text{T}(\tau_2)$$

[3mpp] Multiple reservations made for a given task cannot overlap.

for all $(p, \tau) \in \mathcal{P} \times \mathcal{T}$ with $\text{CanExec}(\tau, p) = true$ **do**
  for all $0 \le i < \text{WCET}(\tau, p) - 1$ **do**
  $Start(\tau, p, i) < Start(\tau, p, i + 1)$

4 Test Cases

As often in real-time scheduling, we perform measurements on large numbers of synthetic test cases. In addition, we consider two real-life signal processing applications (an implementation of the Fast Fourier Transform, and an automotive platooning application), typical for the field of real-time implementation of data-parallel applications.

4.1 Test Case Generation

Synthesizing test cases posed significant challenges, because we must allow for meaningful comparisons between a variety of scheduling problems. For instance, we could not use the state-of-the-art algorithm UUniFast of Bini and Buttazzo [3] because it does not cover heterogenous architectures. Finally, we decided to use two synthesis algorithms.

The first one, used in comparisons involving non-dependent tasks, can be seen as an extension of UScaling [3]. For each type of scheduling problem and choice of system load, we generate examples with number of taks n ranging from 7 to 147 tasks, with an increment of 5. For each task size, we generate 40 problem instances (reduced to 25 instances for the more complex multiperiodic preemptive case). For each instance of a multi-period problem, periods are randomly assigned to the tasks uniformly in the set $\{5, 10, 15, 20, 30, 60\}$. For single-period schedulability problems, the period of all tasks is set to 60. In all cases, the number of processors is set to $\lceil n/5 \rceil$.

The choice of system load is done by setting the maximal per-task processor usage value u. For a task τ of period $\text{T}(\tau)$, WCET values are chosen randomly, with a uniform distribution, in the interval $[1..\lfloor u * \text{T}(\tau) \rfloor]$. For single-period optimization problems $\text{T}(\tau)$ is replaced in the formula by 60 for all tasks. Our measurements will use values of u ranging in the set $\{0.1, 0.3, 0.35, 0.5\}$. Given the way the number of processors is computed, this respectively corresponds to *average* system loads of approximately 25%, 75%, 87.5%, and 125%, and to *maximal* system loads of 50%, 150%, 175%, and 250%.

Each task is designated, with a 30% probability, a fixed-allocation task. In this case, a processor is randomly allocated to it (with uniform distribution), and a WCET value is only assigned for the task on this processor. In the heterogenous case, for each task τ that does not have fixed allocation, and for each processor p, we decide with 70% probability that τ can be executed on p, in which case we generate $WCET(\tau, p)$ as explained above.

The second generation algorithm is used in the comparison involving single-period dependent task systems. We use here the algorithm proposed by Carle and Potop [4] (in section 6). We use this algorithm to synthesize a single set of 40 random test cases. For each of these examples we create one SMT system including the dependence-related constraints, and one without these constraints.

4.2   Signal Processing Case Studies

FFT. The first application is a parallelized version of the Cooley-Tukey implementation of the integer 1D radix 2 FFT [1]. The FFT has a recursive nature, as the task graph of the FFT on 2^{n+1} inputs is obtained by instantiating twice the FFT on 2^n inputs and then adding 2^n tasks. For instance, the task graph of an 8-input FFT, provided in Fig. 1(middle) can be obtained by instantiating twice the task graph of the 4-input FFT, and then adding the 4 tasks of the bottom row. In each of the 3 task graphs of Fig. 1, nodes are tasks and arcs are data dependencies. All dependencies in an FFT transmit the same amount of data.

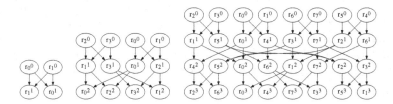

Fig. 1. From left to right: FFT task graphs for 4, 8 and 16 inputs

Platooning. This application is run by one car in order to automatically follow the car in front of it. It takes input from an embedded camera and controls the speed and steering of the car. It uses a Sober filter and a histogram search in order to detect the front car in the captured images. The detection and correction function uses this data to correct car speed and steering. It also adjusts image capture parameters, which creates a feedback loop in the model. The feedback dependency arc initially contains 2 tokens.

The image processing part of the application can be parallelized, by splitting the image into regions which can be processed independently. The task graph of the application (after parallelization) is provided in Fig. 2. The parallelism (of split/merge type) can be raised or decreased by changing the value of X. This means that the application exibhits both task parallelism (breadth) and pipeline parallelism (depth).

Encoding of the Examples and Symmetry Breaking. The task graphs of the 2 examples are transformed into a set of constraints by assuming that implementation is done on 3 homogenous processors connected by a bus, according to the rules of Section 3.2. But our examples feature multiple identical processors and split/merge parallelism defining groups of identical tasks [14]. Thus, the resulting SMT/CP encoding is not very efficient, a solver being forced to spend a lot of time traversing many equivalent configurations that are identical up to a permutation of identical tasks or processors. This can be avoided by adding *symmetry-breaking* constraints to the initial constraint system.

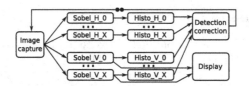

Fig. 2. Platooning application dataflow graph with X-way split/merge parallelism

In mapping the platooning application, a solver will explore the configurations where task *Sobel_H_0* starts before *Sobel_H_1*, but also those where *Sobel_H_1* starts before *Sobel_H_0*. However these two tasks have symmetric dependencies and have the same cost so that exploring only one of the cases is enough to solve the constraint system. This also means that one can swap them (and their *Histo* dependency) without violating any dependency and without modyfing the resulting makespan. Formally, if T_s is a set of symmetric tasks in T (as defined in [14]), then we add to the constraint system the following rule:

[9] Start dates of symmetric tasks are ordered.

> **for all** $(\tau_1, \tau_2) \in T_s^2$ with $\tau_1 < \tau_2$ **do**
> $Start(\tau_1) \leq Start(\tau_2)$

Like task symmetries, core symmetries can be exploited by constraining the allocation of tasks to processors, as explained in [14].

5   Experimental Results

We have run the SMT/ILP/CP specifications of the previous section respectively through the Yices 2, CPLEX, and MiniZinc/G12 solvers on 8-core Intel Xeon workstations. Solving was subject to a timeout of 3600 seconds (1 hour) for synthetic test cases and 1800 seconds for the FFT and platooning applications. For all synthetic schedulability problems we have used both Yices 2 and CPLEX. Scalability findings are similar for the two solvers,[1] so we will always plot only one of the result sets. Comparisons are only made between figures obtained using the same solver. For the FFT and platooning applications we have used MiniZinc/G12.

---

[1] We found differences between solvers, but they do not affect scalability and for space reasons we cannot present them here.

5.1   Synthetic Test Cases

For the test cases obtained using the first algorithm of Section 4.1, the solving times for instances of the same scheduling problem with the same load and the same number of tasks are averaged. The resulting average values are plotted separately for each scheduling problem and load value against the number of tasks. The resulting curve for preemptive, multi-periodic, heterogenous systems with 75% average load, under schedulability analysis, is provided in Fig. 3(left graph, dotted blue curve).

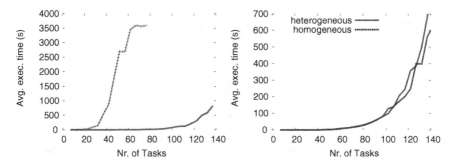

Fig. 3. Left: Single-period, non-preemptive (solid line) vs. Multi-period, preemptive (dotted line). Right: Heterogenous (solid) vs. homogenous (dotted)

To give a better feeling of how this graph is built, we plotted in Fig. 4(left) the results of each problem instance. Values with the same abscissa are averaged to obtain the blue line. Fig. 4(right) provides the evolution of timeouts as a function of task number. From 50 tasks on, solving has a timeout rate of more than 40%, making it unusable in practice. By comparison, Fig. 3(left graph, solid red curve) shows the results for the single-period, non-preemptive problems of the

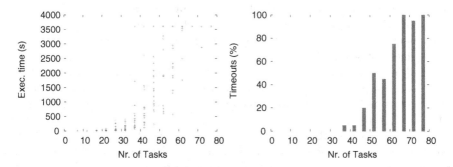

Fig. 4. Results for preemptive, multi-periodic, heterogenous systems, 75% load

same average load (schedulability analysis). Clearly, solving scales much better for the second problem. Intuitively, our experiments show that multi-periodic problems are more complex than single-period ones, and preemptive problems are more complex than non-preemptive ones.

Fig. 3(right graph) provides the results for single-period, non-preemptive task systems with 25% average load in the heterogenous and homogenous case (without symmetry breaking). The graph shows no significant differences, but we shall see later that the use of symmetry breaking should allow a significant reduction of the solving time in the homogenous case if split/merge parallelism is used (so that some homogenous problems are a lot easier to solve).

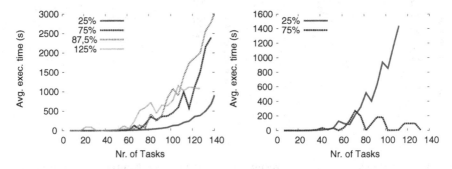

Fig. 5. Complexity as a function of system load. Single-period, non-preemptive, heterogenous (left), Multi-period, non-preemptive, heterogenous (right).

Fig. 5 shows the evolution of the empyric complexity of a problem as a function of the system load. The left graph show that for single-period, non-preemptive, heterogenous schedulability problems, solving scales very well for systems with either very low load (25% on average, solid red line) or very high (over-)load (125% on average, solid green line). In the first case, it is very easy to find solutions. In the second case, non-schedulability is rapidly determined. The remaining two lines correspond to systems with average load, where solving does not scale well. The right graph of the figure considers the multi-period, non-preemptive, heterogenous schedulability problem, where at 75% load solving scales indefinitely (most problems are non-schedulable), whereas at 25% load solving does not scale well.

Fig. 6(left) compares the scalability of schedulability analysis (red solid line) with that of period optimization (blue dotted line). The optimization problem is far more complex and does not scale beyond 25 tasks, where the timeout rate is 40% (cf. right graph).

For the test cases obtained using the second algorithm of Section 4.1, we first determined that the solving time for a dependent task problem is *always* greater or equal that the solving time for the corresponding problem without the dependence-related constraints. Furthermore, the global timeout rate for dependent tasks is 55%, whereas for non-dependent tasks is only 13% (due to the high timeout rate, we consider that comparing the durations is not meaningful).

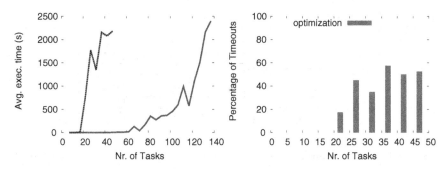

Fig. 6. Left: Schedulability analysis (solid line) vs. optimization (dotted line) for single-period, non-preemptive, heterogenous at 75% average load. Right: Percentage of time-outs for the optimization runs.

5.2   Signal Processing Case Studies

FFT. The solver was only able to produce optimal schedules for small problems (12 tasks and 16 dependencies), which is consistent with our synthetic example experiments. Note that we were unable to exploit here the symmetry breaking technique, because the FFT task graph does not use split/merge parallelism.

Table 1. Fast Fourier Transform CP resolution time at different levels of the recursion

FFT size (n. of inputs)	n. of tasks (messages)	opt. time (s)	mem. peak (MB)
2	1(0)	0.5	4
4	4(4)	1	4
8	12(16)	2	18
16	32(48)	> 1800	271
32	80(128)	> 1800	> 8000
64	192(320)	> 1800	> 8000

Platooning. The experiments show that the solver handles better a very deep task graph than a very large graph. Given the results, a problem with higher depth is expected to be solved within reasonable time as long as the memory of the machine is not exhausted. On contrary, with a problem of large breadth, the solver will not fill the memory of the machine, but will fail to return a solution within reasonable time. Symetry breaking is not trivial in this application graph but can still be achieved if the lexicographic order is the same for *Sobel_H_X* and *Histo_H_X*.

Table 2. CP solver optimisation: *time(s), memory(MB) problem performance when raising the breadth of the graph*

X (p=1)	n.of tasks (messages)	Symmetry breaking							
		None		Task		CPU		Both	
0	7 (7)	0.7	2	0.7	2	0.7	2	0.7	2
1	11 (14)	0.9	18	0.7	7	0.7	5	0.6	5
2	15 (21)	5.4	28	1.5	28	2.9	26	1.1	20
3	19 (28)	> 1800	80	159	58	> 1800	81	50	33

Table 3. CP solver optimisation problem performance when raising the depth of the graph

p (X=0)	1	2	3	4	5	6	7	8	9	10	11	12	13
n.of tasks	7	14	21	28	35	42	49	56	63	70	77	84	91
n.of messages	7	14	22	30	38	46	54	62	70	78	86	94	102
opt time(s)	0.4	0.8	1.2	2	3.2	4.9	7.2	11.3	17.6	21	26	28	> 300
mem peak (MB)	4	10	21	89	199	426	701	1195	1882	2936	4143	5872	> 8000

6   Conclusion

There is a constant mutual challenge between solvers efficiency and problems complexity: new needs from scheduling theory (in temporal correctness) and formal verification theory (functional correctness) raise new interest in resolution techniques, which at some points in history prompt advances in tool power (BDD symbolic representation, SAT/SMT solvers, partial-order and symmetry-based problem reductions,...). One is thus bound to periodically revise judgements on whether the current state-of-affairs in solvers allows to cope with reasonable size specifications, or how far it does.

We tried to provide an empirical answer of that sort (valid as of today), by checking a number of real-time scheduling problems, with typical features representative of real case-studies. We submitted them to state-of-the art constraint solvers, using optimizing symmetry assumptions, and got answers beyond a simple yes/no, showing that exact computation techniques can indeed be currently attempted on certain problems, provided much care is taken into the solver-aware specification encoding. At the same time, solving complex scheduling problems is likely to require heuristics for some time, especially given the trend of considering larger systems and adding more detail to the specifications.

Our empyrical evaluation can be significantly improved. First of all, we need to extend and improve our task generation techniques. For instance, we do not currently have a way to synthesize data-parallel task systems with symmetry. Our code generators should also allow more architectural exploration, for instance by considering the bus or shared memory load as a parameter, or by varying the set of admissible periods.

Recently the Boolean satisfaction *modulo theory* priniciple was extended to ILP modulo theory [10]. One could wonder at that point how our current contribution could fit in a (much more ambitious) idea of a general Constraint modulo theory.

To allow reproduction and extension, all test cases (many gigabytes of data) and generation scripts can be obtained by request to dumitru.potop@inria.fr.

References

1. Bahn, J.H., Yang, J., Bagherzadeh, N.: Parallel fft algorithms on network-on-chips. In: Proceedings ITNG 2008, April 2008
2. Baptiste, P., Le Pape, C., Nuijten, W.: Constraint-based scheduling: applying constraint programming to scheduling problems, vol. 39. Springer Science & Business Media (2001)
3. Bini, E., Buttazzo, G.: Measuring the performance of schedulability tests. Real Time Systems **30**, 129–154 (2005)
4. Carle, T., Potop-Butucaru, D.: Predicate-aware, makespan-preserving software pipelining of scheduling tables. TACO **11**(1), 12 (2014)
5. Carle, T., Potop-Butucaru, D., Sorel, Y., Lesens, D.: From dataflow specification to multiprocessor partitioned time-triggered real-time implementation. Research Report RR-8109 (2012). https://hal.inria.fr/hal-00742908
6. Coffman Jr., A.P.E., Graham, R.L.: Optimal scheduling for two-processor systems. Acta informatica **1**(3), 200–213 (1972)
7. Craciunas, S., Oliver, R.S.: SMT-based task- and network-level static schedule generation for time-triggered networked systems. In: Proceedings RTNS 2014. pp. 45:45–45:54. ACM, New York (2014). http://doi.acm.org/10.1145/2659787.2659812
8. Garey, M., Johnson, D.: Complexity results for multiprocessor scheduling under resource constraints. SIAM Journal of Computing **4**(4), 397–411 (1975)
9. Gu, Z., He, X., Yuan, M.: Optimization of static task and bus access schedules for time-triggered distributed embedded systems with model-checking. In: 44th ACM/IEEE Design Automation Conference, DAC 2007, pp. 294–299, June 2007
10. Hang, C., Manolios, P., Papavasileiou, V.: Synthesizing cyber-physical architectural models with real-time constraints. In: Gopalakrishnan, G., Qadeer, S. (eds.) CAV 2011. LNCS, vol. 6806, pp. 441–456. Springer, Heidelberg (2011)
11. Leyton-Brown, K., Hoos, H.H., Hutter, F., Xu, L.: Understanding the empirical hardness of np-complete problems. Commun. ACM **57**(5), 98–107 (2014). http://doi.acm.org/10.1145/2594413.2594424
12. Megel, T., Sirdey, R., David, V.: Minimizing task preemptions and migrations in multiprocessor optimal real-time schedules. In: 2010 IEEE 31st Real-Time Systems Symposium (RTSS), pp. 37–46, November 2010
13. Nowatzki, T., Sartin-Tarm, M., Carli, L.D., Sankaralingam, K., Estan, C., Robatmili, B.: A general constraint-centric scheduling framework for spatial architectures. SIGPLAN Not. **48**(6), 495–506 (2013). http://doi.acm.org/10.1145/2499370.2462163, (Proceedings PLDI 2013)
14. Tendulkar, P., Poplavko, P., Maler, O.: Symmetry breaking for multi-criteria mapping and scheduling on multicores. In: Braberman, V., Fribourg, L. (eds.) FORMATS 2013. LNCS, vol. 8053, pp. 228–242. Springer, Heidelberg (2013)
15. Topcuoglu, H., Hariri, S., Wu, M.Y.: Performance-effective and low-complexity task scheduling for heterogeneous computing. IEEE Transactions on Parallel and Distributed Systems **13**(3), 260–274 (2002)

Improving Search Order for Reachability Testing in Timed Automata

Frédéric Herbreteau[✉] and Thanh-Tung Tran

Université de Bordeaux, Bordeaux INP, CNRS, LaBRI UMR5800 LaBRI Bât A30,
351 Crs Libération, 33405 Talence, France
fh@labri.fr

Abstract. Standard algorithms for reachability analysis of timed automata are sensitive to the order in which the transitions of the automata are taken. To tackle this problem, we propose a *ranking system* and a *waiting strategy*. This paper discusses the reason why the search order matters and shows how a ranking system and a waiting strategy can be integrated into the standard reachability algorithm to alleviate and prevent the problem respectively. Experiments show that the combination of the two approaches gives optimal search order on standard benchmarks except for one example. This suggests that it should be used instead of the standard BFS algorithm for reachability analysis of timed automata.

1 Introduction

Reachability analysis for timed automata asks if there is an execution of an automaton reaching a given state. This analysis can be used to verify all kinds of safety properties of timed systems. The standard approach to reachability analysis of timed automata uses sets of clock valuations, called *zones*, to reduce the reachability problem in the infinite state space of a timed automaton to the reachability problem in a finite graph. We present two heuristics to improve the efficiency of the zone based reachability algorithm.

The algorithm for reachability analysis of timed automata is a depth-first search, or a breadth-first search on a graph whose nodes are pairs consisting of a state of the automaton and a zone describing the set of possible clock valuations in this state. The use of zone inclusion is crucial for efficiency of this algorithm. It permits to stop exploration from a smaller zone if a bigger zone with the same state has been already explored.

Due to the use of zone inclusion the algorithm is sometimes very sensitive to exploration order. Indeed, it may happen that a small zone is reached and explored first, but then it is removed when a bigger zone is reached later. We will refer to such a situation as a *mistake*. A mistake can often be avoided by taking a different exploration order that reaches the bigger zone first.

In this paper we propose two heuristics to reduce the number of mistakes in the reachability analysis. In the example below we explain the mistake phenomenon in more details, and point out that it can cause an exponential blowup

© Springer International Publishing Switzerland 2015
S. Sankaranarayanan and E. Vicario (Eds.): FORMATS 2015, LNCS 9268, pp. 124–139, 2015.
DOI: 10.1007/978-3-319-22975-1_9

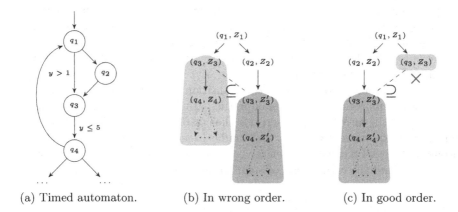

(a) Timed automaton.   (b) In wrong order.   (c) In good order.

Fig. 1. A timed automaton and two exploration graphs of its state-space. On the left, the transition to q_3 is explored first, which results in exploring the subtree of q_3 twice. On the right, the transition to q_2 is explored first and subsumption stops the second exploration as Z_3 is included in Z_3'.

in the search space; this happens in the FDDI standard benchmark. The two heuristics are quite different in nature, so we evaluate their performance on the standard examples. Based on these experimental results we propose a simple modification to the standard exploration algorithm that significantly improves the exploration order.

We now give a concrete example showing why exploration order matters. Consider the timed automaton shown in Figure 1a, and assume we perform a depth-first search (DFS) exploration of its state space. The algorithm starts in (q_1, Z_1) where $Z_1 = (y \geq 0)$ is the set of all clock values. Assume that the transition to q_3 is taken first as in Figure 1b. The algorithm reaches the node (q_3, Z_3) with $Z_3 = (y > 1)$ and explores its entire subtree. Then, the algorithm backtracks to (q_1, Z_1) and proceeds with the transition to q_2 reaching (q_2, Z_2), and then (q_3, Z_3') with $Z_2 = Z_3' = (y \geq 0)$. It happens that $Z_3 \subseteq Z_3'$: the node (q_3, Z_3') is *bigger* than the node (q_3, Z_3) which has been previously visited. At this point, the algorithm has to visit the entire subtree of (q_3, Z_3') since the clock valuations in $Z_3' \setminus Z_3$ have not been explored. The net result is that the earlier exploration from (q_3, Z_3) turns out to be useless since we need to explore from (q_3, Z_3') anyway. If, by chance, our DFS exploration had taken different order of transitions, and first considered the one from q_1 to q_2 as in Figure 1c, the exploration would stop at (q_3, Z_3) since the bigger node (q_3, Z_3') has already been visited and $Z_3 \subseteq Z_3'$. To sum up, in some cases DFS exploration is very sensible to the search order.

Several authors [3,6] have observed that BFS exploration is often much more efficient than DFS for reachability testing in timed automata. This can be attributed to an empirical observation that often a zone obtained by a short path is bigger than the one obtained by a longer path. This is the opposite in our example from Figure 1a. In consequence, a BFS algorithm will also do unnecessary explorations. When (q_3, Z_3') is visited, the node (q_4, Z_4) is already in the queue. Hence, while the algorithm has a chance to realise that exploring (q_3, Z_3) is useless due to the bigger node (q_3, Z_3'), it will keep visiting (q_4, Z_4) and all the subtree of (q_3, Z_3). Indeed, in the standard BFS algorithm, there is no mechanism to remove (q_4, Z_4) from the queue when (q_3, Z_3') is reached. Again, considering the transition from q_1 to q_2 before the transition to q_3 as in Figure 1c, avoids unnecessary exploration. Yet, by making the path $q_1 \rightarrow q_2 \rightarrow q_3$ one step longer we would obtain an example where all choices of search order would lead to unnecessary exploration. Overall, the standard reachability algorithm for timed automata, be it DFS or BFS, is sensitive to the alignment between the discovery of big nodes and the exploration of small nodes.

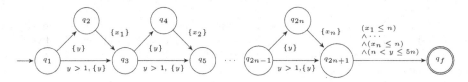

Fig. 2. Timed automaton with a racing situation.

One could ask what can be the impact of a pattern from Figure 1a, and does it really occur. The blowup of the exploration space can be exponential. One example is presented in Figure 2. It is obtained by iterating n times the pattern we have discussed above. The final state q_f is not reachable. By a similar analysis we can show that both the BFS and DFS algorithms with wrong exploration order explore and store exponentially more nodes than needed. In the automaton there are 2^n different paths to q_{2n+1}. The longest path $q_1, q_2, q_3, \ldots, q_{2n+1}$ generates the biggest zone, while there are about 2^n different zones that can be generated by taking different paths. If the DFS takes the worst exploration order, all these zones will be generated. If it takes the wrong order half of the times, then about $2^{n/2}$ zones will be generated. Similarly for BFS.

In the experiments section we show that, this far from optimal behaviour of BFS and DFS exploration indeed happens in the FDDI model, a standard benchmark model for timed automata.

In this paper we propose simple modifications of the exploration strategy to counter the problem as presented in the above examples. We will first describe a *ranking system* that mitigates the problem by assigning ranks to states, and using ranks to chose the transitions to explore. It will be rather clear that this system addresses the problem from our examples. Then we will propose *waiting strategy* that starts from a different point of view and is simpler to implement. The experiments on standard benchmarks show that the two approaches are incomparable but they can be combined to give optimal results in most of the cases. Since this combination is easy to implement, we propose to use it instead of standard BFS for reachability checking.

Related work: The influence of the search order has been discussed in the literature in the context of state-caching [7,11–13], and state-space fragmentation [3,6,8]. State-caching focuses on limiting the number of stored nodes at the cost of exploring more nodes. We propose a strategy that improves the number of visited nodes as well as the number of stored nodes. In [3,6,8], it is suggested that BFS is the best search order to avoid state-space fragmentation in distributed model checking. We have not yet experimented our approach for distributed state-space exploration.

In terms of implementation, our approaches add a metric to states. In a different context a metric mechanism has been used by Behrmann *et al.* to guide the exploration in priced timed automata in [5].

Organisation of the paper: In the next section we present preliminaries for this paper: timed automata, the reachability problem and the standard reachability algorithm for timed automata. In Section 3, we propose a ranking system to limit the impact of mistakes during exploration. Section 4 presents another strategy that aims at limiting the number of mistakes. Finally, Section 5 gives some experimental results on the standard benchmarks.

2   Preliminaries

We introduce preliminary notions about timed automata and the reachability problem. Then, we introduce the classical zone-based algorithm used to solve this problem.

2.1   Timed Automata and the Reachability Problem

Let $X = \{x_1, \ldots, x_n\}$ be a set of clocks, i.e. variables that range over the non-negative real numbers $\mathbb{R}_{\geq 0}$. A *clock constraint* ϕ is a conjunction of constraints $x \# c$ for $x \in X$, $\# \in \{<, \leq, =, \geq, >\}$ and $c \in \mathbb{N}$. Let $\Phi(X)$ be the set of clock constraints over the set of clocks X. A *valuation* over X is a function $v : X \to \mathbb{R}_{\geq 0}$. We denote by $\mathbf{0}$ the valuation that maps each clock in X to 0, and by $\mathbb{R}_{\geq 0}^X$ the set of valuations over X. A valuation v satisfies a clock constraint $\phi \in \Phi(X)$, denoted $v \models \phi$, when all the constraints in ϕ hold after replacing every clock x by its value $v(x)$. For $\delta \in \mathbb{R}_{\geq 0}$, we denote $v + \delta$ the valuation that maps every clock x to $v(x) + \delta$. For $R \subseteq X$, $R[v]$ is the valuation that sets x to 0 if $x \in R$, and that sets x to $v(x)$ otherwise.

A *timed automaton (TA)* is a tuple $\mathcal{A} = (Q, q_0, F, X, Act, T)$ where Q is a finite set of states with initial state $q_0 \in Q$ and accepting states $F \subseteq Q$, X is a finite set of clocks, Act is a finite alphabet of actions, $T \subseteq Q \times \Phi(X) \times 2^X \times Act \times Q$ is a finite set of transitions (q, g, R, a, q') where g is a *guard*, R is the set of clocks that are *reset* and a is the *action* of the transition.

The semantics of a TA $\mathcal{A}$ is given by a transition system whose states are *configurations* $(q, v) \in Q \times \mathbb{R}_{\geq 0}^X$. The *initial configuration* is $(q_0, \mathbf{0})$. We have delay transitions: $(q, v) \xrightarrow{\delta} (q, v + \delta)$ for $\delta \in \mathbb{R}_{\geq 0}$, and action transitions: $(q, v) \xrightarrow{a} (q', v')$

if there exists a transition $(q, g, R, a, q') \in T$ such that $v \models g$ and $v' = [R]v$. A *run* is a finite sequence of transitions starting from the initial configuration $(q_0, \mathbf{0})$. A run is *accepting* is it ends in a configuration (q, v) with an accepting state $q \in F$.

The *reachability problem* consists in deciding if a given TA $\mathcal{A}$ has an accepting run. This problem is known to be PSPACE-complete [1].

2.2 Symbolic Semantics

The reachability problem cannot be solved directly from $\mathcal{A}$ due to the uncountable number of configurations. The standard solution is to use symbolic semantics of timed automata by grouping valuations together. A *zone* is a set of valuations described by a conjunction of two kinds of constraints: $x_i \# c$ and $x_i - x_j \# c$ where $x_i, x_j \in X$, $c \in \mathbb{Z}$ and $\# \in \{<, \leq, =, \geq, >\}$.

The *zone graph* $\mathsf{ZG}(\mathcal{A})$ of a timed automaton $\mathcal{A} = (Q, q_0, F, X, Act, T)$ is a transition system with nodes of the form (q, Z) where $q \in Q$ and Z is a zone. The initial node is (q_0, Z_0) where $Z_0 = \{\mathbf{0} + \delta \mid \delta \in \mathbb{R}_{\geq 0}\}$. The nodes (q, Z) with $q \in F$ are accepting. There is a transition $(q, Z) \Rightarrow (q', Z')$ if there exists a transition $(q, g, R, a, q') \in T$ such that $Z' = \{v' \in \mathbb{R}_{\geq 0} \mid \exists v \in Z \exists \delta \in \mathbb{R}_{\geq 0} \ (q, v) \xrightarrow{a} \xrightarrow{\delta} (q', v')\}$ and $Z' \neq \emptyset$. The relation $\Rightarrow$ is well-defined as it can be shown that if Z is a zone, then Z' is a zone. Zones can be efficiently represented by Difference Bound Matrices (DBMs) [10] and the successor Z' of a zone Z can be efficiently computed using this representation.

The zone graph $\mathsf{ZG}(\mathcal{A})$ is still infinite [9], and an additional abstraction step is needed to obtain a finite transition system. An *abstraction operator* is a function $\mathfrak{a} : \mathcal{P}(\mathbb{R}_{\geq 0}^X) \to \mathcal{P}(\mathbb{R}_{\geq 0}^X)$ such that $W \subseteq \mathfrak{a}(W)$ and $\mathfrak{a}(\mathfrak{a}(W)) = \mathfrak{a}(W)$ for every set W of valuations. An abstraction operator defines an abstract symbolic semantics. Similarly to the zone graph, we define the *abstract zone graph* $\mathsf{ZG}^{\mathfrak{a}}(\mathcal{A})$. Its initial node is $(q_0, \mathfrak{a}(Z_0))$ and we have a transition $(q, Z) \Rightarrow_{\mathfrak{a}} (q', \mathfrak{a}(Z'))$ if $\mathfrak{a}(Z) = Z$ and $(q, Z) \Rightarrow (q', Z')$.

In order to solve the reachability problem for $\mathcal{A}$ from $\mathsf{ZG}^{\mathfrak{a}}(\mathcal{A})$, the abstraction operator $\mathfrak{a}$ should have the property that every run of $\mathcal{A}$ has a corresponding path in $\mathsf{ZG}^{\mathfrak{a}}(\mathcal{A})$ (completeness) and conversely, every path in $\mathsf{ZG}^{\mathfrak{a}}(\mathcal{A})$ should correspond to a run in $\mathcal{A}$ (soundness). Furthermore, $\mathsf{ZG}^{\mathfrak{a}}(\mathcal{A})$ should be finite. Several abstraction operators have been introduced in the literature [4,9]. The abstraction operator $\mathsf{Extra}_{\mathsf{LU}}^{+}$ [4] has all the required properties above. Moreover, the $\mathsf{Extra}_{\mathsf{LU}}^{+}$ abstraction of a zone is itself a zone. It can be computed from the DBM representation of the zone. This allows to compute the abstract zone graph efficiently using DBMs as a symbolic representation for zones. The $\mathsf{Extra}_{\mathsf{LU}}^{+}$ abstraction is used by most implementation including the state-of-the-art tool UPPAAL [2]. The theorem below reduces the reachability problem for $\mathcal{A}$ to the reachability problem in the finite graph $\mathsf{ZG}^{\mathsf{Extra}_{\mathsf{LU}}^{+}}(\mathcal{A})$.

Theorem 1 ([4]). *There is an accepting run in $\mathcal{A}$ iff there exists a path in $\mathsf{ZG}^{\mathsf{Extra}_{\mathsf{LU}}^{+}}(\mathcal{A})$ from $(q_0, \mathsf{Extra}_{\mathsf{LU}}^{+}(Z_0))$ to some state (q, Z) with $q \in F$. Furthermore $\mathsf{ZG}^{\mathsf{Extra}_{\mathsf{LU}}^{+}}(\mathcal{A})$ is finite.*

Algorithm 1.1. Standard reachability algorithm for timed automaton $\mathcal{A}$.

```
1   function reachability_check(A)
2       W := {(q₀, ExtraLU⁺(Z₀))};  P := W  // Invariant: W ⊆ P
3
4       while (W ≠ ∅) do
5           take and remove a node (q, Z) from W
6           if (q is accepting)
7               return Yes
8           else
9               for each (q, Z) ⇒ExtraLU⁺ (q', Z')
10                  if there is no (q_B, Z_B) ∈ P s.t. (q', Z') ⊆ (q_B, Z_B)
11                      for each (q_S, Z_S) ∈ P such that (q_S, Z_S) ⊆ (q', Z')
12                          remove (q_S, Z_S) from W and P
13                      add (q', Z') to W and to P
14
15      return No
```

2.3   Reachability Algorithm

Algorithm 1.1 is the standard reachability algorithm for timed automata. It explores the finite abstract zone graph $\mathsf{ZG}^{\mathsf{Extra_{LU}}^+}(\mathcal{A})$ of an automaton $\mathcal{A}$ from the initial node until it finds an accepting node, or it has visited the entire state-space of $\mathsf{ZG}^{\mathsf{Extra_{LU}}^+}(\mathcal{A})$. It maintains a set of *waiting nodes* W and a set of *visited nodes* P such that $W \subseteq P$.

Algorithm 1.1 uses zone inclusion to stop exploration, and this is essential for its efficiency. We have $(q, Z) \subseteq (q', Z')$ when $q = q'$ and $Z \subseteq Z'$. Notice that zone inclusion is a simulation relation over nodes since zones are sets of valuations. Zone inclusion is first used in line 10 to stop the exploration in (q, Z) if there is a bigger node (q_B, Z_B) in P. It is also used in line 12 to only keep the maximal nodes w.r.t. $\subseteq$ in P and W.

Algorithm 1.1 does not specify any exploration strategy. As we have stressed in the introduction, the search order greatly influences the number of nodes visited by the algorithm and stored in the sets W and P. At first sight it may seem strange why there should be a big difference between, say, BFS and DFS search orders. The cause is the optimisation due to subsumption w.r.t. $\subseteq$ in lines 10 and 12. When equality on nodes is used instead of zone inclusion, every node is visited. Hence, BFS and DFS coincide in the sense that they will visit the same nodes, while not in the same order. The situation is very different with zone inclusion. Consider again the two nodes $(q_2, Z_2) \subseteq (q_2, Z_2')$ in Figure 1b. Since the smaller node (q_2, Z_2) is reached first, the entire subtrees of both nodes are visited whereas it would be sufficient to explore the subtree of the bigger node (q_2, Z_2') to solve the reachability problem. Indeed, every node below (q_2, Z_2) is simulated by the corresponding node below (q_2, Z_2'). Notice that the problem occurs both with a DFS and with a BFS strategy since the bigger node (q_2, Z_2')

is further from the root node than the smaller node (q_2, Z_2). When the bigger node is found before the smaller one, as in Figure 1c, only the subtree of the bigger node is visited. An optimal search strategy would guarantee that big nodes are visited before small ones. In the remaining of the paper we propose two heuristics to optimise the search order.

3 Ranking System

In this section we propose an exploration strategy to address the phenomenon we have presented in the introduction: we propose a solution to stop the exploration of the subtree of a small node when a bigger node is reached. As we have seen, the late discovery of big nodes causes unnecessary explorations of small nodes and their subtrees. In the worst case, the number of needlessly visited nodes may be exponential (cf. Figure 2).

Our goal is to minimise the number of visited nodes as well as the number of stored nodes (i.e. the size of P in Algorithm 1.1). Consider again the situation in Figure 1b where $(q_3, Z_3) \subseteq (q_3, Z_3')$. When the big node (q_3, Z_3') is reached, we learn that exploring the small node (q_3, Z_3) is unnecessary. In such a situation, Algorithm 1.1 erases the small node (q_3, Z_3) (line 10), but all its descendants that are in the waiting list W will be still explored.

A first and straightforward solution would be to erase the whole subtree of the small node (q_3, Z_3). Algorithm 1.1 would then proceed with the waiting nodes in the subtree of (q_3, Z_3'). This approach is however too rudimentary. Indeed, it may happen that the two nodes (q_4, Z_4) and (q_4, Z_4') in Figure 1b are identical. Then, erasing the whole subtree of (q_3, Z_3) will lead to exploring (q_4, Z_4) and all its subtree twice. We have observed on classical benchmarks (see Section 5) that identical nodes are frequently found. While this approach is correct, it would result in visiting more nodes than the classical algorithm.

We propose a more subtle approach based on an interesting property of Algorithm 1.1. Consider the two nodes (q_4, Z_4) and (q_4, Z_4') in Figure 1b again, and assume that (q_4, Z_4') is reached after (q_4, Z_4). If the two nodes are identical, then (q_4, Z_4') is erased by Algorithm 1.1 in line 10, but (q_4, Z_4) is kept since it has been visited first. Conversely, if the two nodes are different, we still have $(q_4, Z_4) \subseteq (q_4, Z_4')$, then (q_4, Z_4) is erased by Algorithm 1.1 in line 10. Hence, as the algorithm explores the subtree of (q_3, Z_3'), it progressively erases all the nodes in the subtree of (q_3, Z_3) that are smaller than some node in the subtree of (q_3, Z_3'). At the same time, it keeps the nodes that are identical to some node below (q_3, Z_3'), hence avoiding several explorations of the same node.

Now, it remains to make all this happen before the subtree of (q_3, Z_3) is developed any further. This is achieved by giving a higher priority to (q_3, Z_3') than all the waiting nodes below (q_3, Z_3). This priority mechanism is implemented by assigning a *rank* to every node.

Algorithm 1.2 below is a modified version of Algorithm 1.1 that implements the ranking of nodes (the modifications are highlighted). Nodes are initialised with rank 0. The rank of a node (q', Z') is updated with respect to the ranks of the nodes (q_S, Z_S) that are simulated by (q', Z') (line 15). For each node (q_S, Z_S), we compute the maximum rank r of the waiting nodes below (q_S, Z_S). Then, $\mathsf{rank}(q', Z')$ is set to $\max(\mathsf{rank}(q', Z'), r+1)$ giving priority to (q', Z') over the waiting nodes below (q_S, Z_S).

Algorithm 1.2. Reachability algorithm with ranking of nodes for timed automaton $\mathcal{A}$. The set P is stored as a tree $\rightarrow$.

```
1   function reachability_check(A)
2       W := {(q_0, Extra_LU^+(Z_0))};  P := W
3       init_rank(q_0, Extra_LU^+(Z_0))
4
5       while (W ≠ ∅) do
6           take and remove a node (q, Z) with highest rank from W
7           if (q is accepting) then
8               return Yes
9           else
10              for each (q, Z) ⇒_Extra_LU+ (q', Z')
11                  init_rank(q', Z')
12                  if there is no (q_B, Z_B) ∈ P s.t. (q', Z') ⊆ (q_B, Z_B) then
13                      for each (q_S, Z_S) ∈ P s.t. (q_S, Z_S) ⊆ (q', Z')
14                          if (q_S, Z_S) ∉ W then // implies not a leaf node in P
15                              rank(q', Z') := max(rank(q', Z'), 1 + max_rank_waiting(q_S, Z_S))
16                          remove (q_S, Z_S) from W and P
17                      add (q', Z') to W and to P
18      return No
19
20  function max_rank_waiting(q, Z)
21      if (q, Z) is in W then // implies leaf node in P
22          return rank(q, Z)
23      else
24          r := 0;
25          for each edge (q, Z) → (q', Z') in P
26              r := max(r, max_rank_waiting(q', Z'))
27          return r
28
29  function init_rank(q, Z)
30      if Z is the true zone then
31          rank(q, Z) := ∞
32      else
33          rank(q, Z) := 0
```

The function max_rank_waiting determines the maximal rank among waiting nodes below (q_S, Z_S). To that purpose, the set of visited nodes P is stored as a reachability tree. When a node (q_S, Z_S) is removed in line 16, its parent node is connected to its child nodes to maintain reachability of waiting nodes. Observe that the node (q', Z') is added to the tree P in line 17 after its rank has been updated in line 15. This is needed in the particular case where (q_S, Z_S) is an ancestor of node (q', Z') in line 15. The rank of (q', Z') will be updated taking into account the waiting nodes below (q_S, Z_S). Obviously, (q', Z') should not be considered among those waiting nodes, which is guaranteed since (q', Z') does not belong to the tree yet.

The intuition behind the use of ranks suggest one more useful heuristic. Ranks are used to give priority to exploration from some nodes over the others. Nodes with true zones are a special case in this context, since they can never be covered, and in consequence it is always better to explore them first.

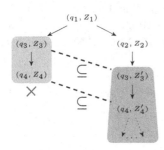

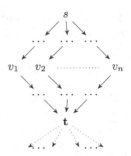

Fig. 3. Reachability tree for Algorithm 1.2 on the automaton in Figure 1a.

Fig. 4. Waiting strategy starts exploring from t only after all paths leading to t are explored.

We implement this observation by simply assigning the biggest possible rank (∞) to such nodes (line 31 in the Algorithm).

Let us explain how the Algorithm 1.2 works on an example. Consider again the automaton in Figure 1a. The final exploration graph is depicted in Figure 3. When (q_1, Z_1) is visited, both (q_3, Z_3) and (q_2, Z_2) are put into the waiting list W with rank 0. Recall that exploring (q_3, Z_3) first is the worst exploration order. This adds (q_4, Z_4) to the waiting list with rank 0. The exploration of (q_2, Z_2) adds (q_3, Z_3') to the waiting list. At this stage, the rank of (q_3, Z_3') is set to 1 since it is bigger than (q_3, Z_3) which is erased. The node (q_3, Z_3') has the highest priority among all waiting nodes and is explored next. This generates the node (q_4, Z_4') that is bigger than (q_4, Z_4). Hence (q_4, Z_4) is erased, (q_4, Z_4') gets rank 1 and the exploration proceeds from (q_4, Z_4'). One can see that, when a big node is reached, the algorithm not only stops the exploration of the smaller node but also of the nodes in its subtree. Figure 3 shows a clear improvement over Figure 1b.

4   Waiting Strategy

We present an exploration strategy that will aim at reducing the number of exploration mistakes: situations when a bigger node is discovered later than a smaller one. The ranking strategy from the previous section reduced the cost of a mistake by stopping the exploration from descendants of a small node when it found a bigger node. By contrast, the waiting strategy of this section will not develop a node if it is aware of some other parts of exploration that may lead to a bigger node.

The waiting strategy is based on topological-like order on states of automata. We first present this strategy on a single automaton. Then we consider networks of timed automata, and derive a topological-like ordering from orderings on the components. Before we start we explain what kind of phenomenon our strategy is capturing.

To see what we aim at, consider the part of a timed automaton depicted in Figure 4. There is a number of paths form state s to state t, not necessary of the same length. Suppose the search strategy from (s, Z) has reached (t, Z_1) by following the path through v_1. At this point it is reasonable to delay exploration from (t, Z_1) until all explorations of paths through $v_2, \ldots, v_k$ finish. This is because some of these explorations may result in a bigger zone than Z_1, and in consequence make an exploration from (t, Z_1) redundant.

The effect of such a waiting heuristic is clearly visible on our example from Figure 2. The automaton consists of segments: from q_1 to q_3, from q_3 to q_5, etc. Every segment is a very simple instance of the situation from Figure 4 that we have discussed in the last paragraph. There are two paths that lead from state q_1 to state q_3. These two paths have different lengths, so with a BFS exploration one of the paths will reach q_3 faster than the other. The longest path (that one going through q_2) gives the biggest zone in q_3; but BFS will no be able to use this information; and in consequence it will generate exponentially many nodes on this example. The waiting heuristic will collect all the search paths at states $q_3, q_5, \ldots$ and will explore only the best ones, so its search space will be linear.

We propose to implement these ideas via a simple modification of the standard algorithm. The waiting strategy will be based on a partial order $\sqsubseteq_{topo}$ of sates of $\mathcal{A}$. We will think of it as a topological order of the graph of the automaton (after removing cycles in some way). This order is then used to determine the exploration order.

Algorithm 1.3. Reachability algorithm with waiting strategy

This algorithm is obtained from the standard Algorithm 1.1 by changing line 5 to
take and **remove** (q, Z) minimal w.r.t. $\sqsubseteq_{topo}$ from W

In the remaining of the section we will propose some simple ways of finding a suitable $\sqsubseteq_{topo}$ order.

4.1 Topological-Like Ordering for a Timed Automaton

It is helpful to think of the order $\sqsubseteq_{topo}$ on states as some sort of topological ordering, but we cannot really assume this since the graphs of our automata may have loops. Given a timed automaton $\mathcal{A}$, we find a linear order on the states of $\mathcal{A}$ in two steps:

1. we find a maximal subset of transitions of $\mathcal{A}$ that gives a graph $\mathcal{A}_{DAG}$ without cycles;
2. then we compute a topological ordering of this graph.

Given an automaton $\mathcal{A}$, the graph $\mathcal{A}_{DAG}$ can be computed by running a depth-first search (DFS) from the initial state of $\mathcal{A}$. While traversing $\mathcal{A}$, we only consider the transitions that point downwards or sideways; in other words we ignore all the transitions that lead to a state that is on the current search stack. At the end of the search, when all the states have been visited, the transitions that have not been ignored form a graph $\mathcal{A}_{DAG}$.

As an example, consider the timed automaton $\mathcal{A}$ in Figure 1a. The transition from q_4 to q_1 is ignored when computing $\mathcal{A}_{DAG}$ starting from q_1. A topological-like ordering is computed from the resulting graph: $q_1 \sqsubseteq_{topo} q_2 \sqsubseteq_{topo} q_3 \sqsubseteq_{topo} q_4$. Let us see how $\sqsubseteq_{topo}$ helps Algorithm 1.1 to explore bigger nodes first. Starting from node $(q_1, true)$, Algorithm 1.1 adds $(q_2, true)$ and $(q_3, y > 1)$ to the waiting list. Since $q_2 \sqsubseteq_{topo} q_3$, the algorithm then explores node $(q_2, true)$, hence adding node $(q_3, true)$ to the waiting list. The small node $(q_3, y > 1)$ is then automatically erased, and the exploration proceeds from the big node $(q_3, true)$. Observe that the exploration of the node $(q_3, y > 1)$ is postponed until the second path reaches q_3. Upon this stage, the zone inclusion relation will help to stop all explorations of smaller nodes; in our case it is $(q_3, y > 1)$. Thus, the algorithm performs optimally on this example, no exploration step can be avoided.

4.2 Topological-Like Ordering for Networks of Timed Automata

Real-time systems often consist of several components that interact with each other. In order to apply the same approach we need to find an ordering on a set of global states of the system. For this we will find an ordering for each component and then extend it to the whole system without calculating the set of global states.

We suppose that each component of a system is modelled by a timed automaton $\mathcal{A}_i = (Q_i, q_{0i}, F_i, X_i, Act_i, T_i)$. The system is modelled as the product $\mathcal{A} = (Q, q_0, F, X, Act, T)$ of the components $(\mathcal{A}_i)_{1 \leq i \leq k}$. The states of $\mathcal{A}$ are the tuples of states of $\mathcal{A}_1, \ldots, \mathcal{A}_k$: $Q = Q_1 \times \cdots \times Q_k$ with initial state $q_0 = \langle q_{01}, \ldots, q_{0k} \rangle$ and final states $F = F_1 \times \cdots \times F_k$. Clocks and actions are shared among the processes: $X = \bigcup_{1 \leq i \leq k} X_i$ and $Act = \bigcup_{1 \leq i \leq k} Act_i$. Interactions are modelled by the synchronisation of processes over the same action. There is a transition $(\langle q_1, \ldots, q_n \rangle, g, R, a, \langle q'_1, \ldots, q'_n \rangle) \in T$ if

- either, there are two processes i and j with transitions $(q_i, g_i, R_i, \mathbf{a}, q'_i) \in T_i$ and $(q_j, g_j, R_j, \mathbf{a}, q'_j) \in T_j$ such that $g = g_i \wedge g_j$ and $R = R_i \cup R_j$, and $q'_l = q_l$ for every process $l \neq i, j$ (synchronised action)
- or there is a process i with transition $(q_i, g, R, a, q'_i) \in T_i$ such that for every process $l \neq i$, $a \notin Act_l$ and $q'_l = q_l$ (local action).

The product above allows synchronisation of 2 processes at a time. Our work does not rely on a specific synchronisation policy, hence other models of interactions (broadcast communications, n-ary synchronisation, etc.) could be considered as well. Notice that the product automaton $\mathcal{A}$ is, in general, exponentially bigger than each component $\mathcal{A}_i$.

The semantics of a network of timed automata $(\mathcal{A}_i)_{1 \leq i \leq k}$ is defined as the semantics of the corresponding product automaton $\mathcal{A}$. As a result, the reachability problem for $(\mathcal{A}_i)_{1 \leq i \leq k}$ reduces to the reachability problem in $\mathcal{A}$.

In order to apply the same approach as above, an ordering must be defined on the states of $\mathcal{A}$ which are tuples $\boldsymbol{q} = \langle q_1, \ldots, q_k \rangle$ of states of the component automata $\mathcal{A}_i$. It would not be reasonable to compute the product automaton $\mathcal{A}$

as its size grows exponentially with the number of its components. We propose an alternative solution that consists in computing a topological-like ordering $\sqsubseteq_{topo}^i$ for each component $\mathcal{A}_i$. To that purpose, we can apply the algorithm introduced in the previous section. Then, the ordering of tuples of states is defined pointwise:

Definition 1 (Joint ordering). *For $q, q' \in Q_1 \times \cdots \times Q_k$, we have $q \sqsubseteq_{topo} q'$ if $q_i \sqsubseteq_{topo}^i q'_i$ for all $1 \leq i \leq k$.*

Thus for networks of timed automata we consider the joint ordering in our waiting strategy.

5 Experimental Evaluation

We present and comment the experimental results that we have performed. The results indicate that a mix of a ranking and waiting strategies avoids mistakes in most the examples.

We have evaluated the ranking system (Section 3) and the waiting strategy (Section 4) on classical benchmarks from the literature[1]: CRITICAL REGION (CR), CSMA/CD (C), FDDI (FD), FISCHER (FI), FLEXRAY (FL-PL) and LYNCH (L), and on the BLOWUP (B) example in Figure 2. These automata have no reachable accepting state, hence forcing algorithms to visit the entire state-space of the automata to prove unreachability.

Our objective is to avoid mistakes during exploration of the state-space of timed automata. At the end of the run of the algorithm, the set of visited nodes P forms an invariant showing that accepting nodes are unreachable. Every node that is visited by the algorithm and that does not belong to P at the end of the run is useless to prove unreachability. This happens when the algorithm does a mistake: it first visits a small node before reaching a bigger node later. We aim at finding a search order that visits bigger nodes first, hence doing as few mistakes as possible. Notice that it is not always possible to completely avoid mistakes since the only paths to a big node may have to visit a small node first.

We compare three algorithms in Table 1: BFS the standard breadth-first search algorithm[2] (i.e. Algorithm 1.1), R-BFS which implements a breadth-first search with priority to the highest ranked nodes (i.e. Algorithm 1.2) and TW-BFS which combines giving highest priority to true-zone nodes and the waiting strategy. We report on the number of visited nodes, the number of mistakes, the maximum number of stored nodes, and the final number of stored nodes. We also mention in column "visited ranking" the number of nodes that are re-visited to update the rank of the nodes by algorithm R-BFS (line 15 in Algorithm 1.2). The number of visited nodes gives a good estimate of the running time of the algorithm, while the maximal number of stored nodes gives a precise indication of the memory used for the set P.

The ranking system gives very good results on all models except CSMA/CD. It makes no mistakes on FISCHER and LYNCH. This is due to the highest priority

---

[1] The models are available from http://www.labri.fr/perso/herbrete/tchecker.

[2] Algorithm 1.1 is essentially the algorithm that is implemented in UPPAAL [2].

given to true-zone nodes. Indeed, column "visited ranking" shows that ranks are never updated, hence the nodes keep their initial rank. It also performs impressively well on BLOWUP, FDDI and FLEXRAY, gaining several orders of magnitude in the number of mistakes. However, it makes more mistakes than BFS on CSMA/CD. Indeed, the ranking system is efficient when big nodes are reached quickly, as the example in Figure 3 shows. When the big node (q_3, Z'_3) is reached, the ranking system stops the exploration of the subtree of the small node (q_3, Z_3) at (q_4, Z_4). However, making the path $q_1 \rightarrow q_2 \rightarrow q_3$ longer in the automaton in Figure 1a leads to explore a bigger part of the subtree of (q_3, Z_3). If this path is long enough, the entire subtree of (q_3, Z_3) may be visited before (q_3, Z'_3) is reached. The ranking system does not provide any help in this situation. This bad scenario occurs in the CSMA/CD example.

We have experimented the waiting strategy separately (not reported in Table 1). While the results are good on some models (BLOWUP, FDDI, CSMA/CD), the waiting strategy makes a lot more mistakes than the standard BFS on LYNCH and FLEXRAY. Indeed, the waiting strategy is sensitive to the topological ordering. Consider the automaton in Figure 1a with an extra transition $q_3 \rightarrow q_2$. The loop on q_2 and q_3 may lead to different topological orderings, for instance $q_1 \sqsubseteq_{topo} q_2 \sqsubseteq_{topo} q_3 \sqsubseteq_{topo} q_4$ and $q_1 \sqsubseteq_{topo} q_3 \sqsubseteq_{topo} q_2 \sqsubseteq_{topo} q_4$. These two choices lead to very different behaviours of the algorithm. Once the initial node has been explored, the two nodes $(q_3, y > 1)$ and $(q_2, true)$ are in the waiting queue. With the first ordering, $(q_2, true)$ is selected first and generates $(q_3, true)$ that cuts the exploration of the smaller node $(q_3, y > 1)$. However, with the second ordering $(q_3, y > 1)$ is visited first. As a result, $(q_3, true)$ is reached too late, and the entire subtree of $(q_3, y > 1)$ is explored unnecessarily. We have investigated the robustness of the waiting strategy w.r.t. random topological orderings for the models in Table 1. The experiments confirm that the waiting strategy is sensitive to topological ordering. For most models, the best results are achieved using the topological ordering that comes from running a DFS on the automaton as suggested in Section 4.1.

The two heuristics perform well on different models. This suggests to combine their strengths. Consider again the automaton in Figure 1a with an extra transition $q_3 \rightarrow q_2$. As explained above, due to the cycle on q_2 and q_3, several topological orderings are possible for the waiting strategy. The choice of $q_1 \sqsubseteq_{topo} q_3 \sqsubseteq_{topo} q_2 \sqsubseteq_{topo} q_4$ leads to a bad situation where $(q_3, y > 1)$ is taken first when the two nodes $(q_3, y > 1)$ and $(q_2, true)$ are in the waiting queue. As a result, the node $(q_3, y > 1)$ is visited without waiting the bigger node $(q_3, true)$. In such a situation, combining ranking and the waiting strategies helps. Indeed, after $(q_3, y > 1)$ has been explored, the waiting queue contains two nodes $(q_2, true)$ and $(q_4, 1 < y \leq 5)$. Since $q_2 \sqsubseteq_{topo} q_4$, the algorithm picks $(q_2, true)$, hence generating $(q_3, true)$. As a true-zone node, $(q_3, true)$ immediately gets a higher rank than every waiting node. Exploring $(q_3, true)$ generates $(q_4, y \leq 5)$ that cuts the exploration from the small node $(q_4, 1 < y \leq 5)$.

We have tried several combinations of the two heuristics. The best one consists in using the waiting strategy with priority to true zones. More precisely, the resulting algorithm TW-BFS selects a waiting node as follows:

- True-zone nodes are taken in priority,
- If there is no true-zone node, the nodes are taken according to the waiting strategy, and in BFS order.

As Table 1 shows, TW-BFS makes no mistake on all models but three. CRITICAL REGION has unavoidable mistakes: big nodes that can only be reached after visiting a smaller node. The topological ordering used for FDDI is not optimal. Indeed, there exists an optimal topological search order for which TW-BFS makes no mistake, but it is not the one obtained by the algorithm presented in Section 4.1. Finally, the algorithm makes a lot of mistakes on FLEXRAY, but the memory usage is almost optimal: the mistakes are quickly eliminated. This example is the only one where applying the ranking heuristic clearly outperforms TW-BFS.

We have also evaluated TW-BFS using randomised versions of the models in Table 1. Randomisation consists in taking the transitions in a non-fixed order, hence increasing the possibility of racing situations like in Figure 1. The experiments show that the strategies are robust to such randomisation, and the results on random instances are very close to the ones reported in the table.

The ranking strategy R-BFS requires to keep a tree structure over the passed nodes. Using the classical left child-right sibling encoding, the tree can be represented with only two pointers per node. This tree is explored when the rank of a node is updated (line 15 in Algorithm 1.2). Column "visited ranking" in Table 1 shows that these explorations do not inflict any significant overhead in terms of explored nodes, except for CSMA/CD and CRITICAL REGION for which it has been noticed above that algorithm R-BFS does not perform well. Furthermore, exploring the tree is inexpensive since the visited nodes, in particular the zones, have already been computed. Both the ranking strategy and the waiting strategy require to sort the list of waiting nodes. Our prototype implementation based on insertion sort is slow. However, preliminary experiments show that implementing the list of waiting nodes as a heap turns out to be very efficient.

To summarise we can consider our findings from a practical point of view of an implementation. The simplest to implement strategy would be to give priority to true zones. This would already give some improvements, but for example for FDDI there would be no improvement since there are no true zones. R-BFS gives very good results on FLEXRAY model its implementation is more complex than TW-BFS strategy is relatively easy to implement and has very good performance on all but one model, where it is comparable to standard BFS. This suggests that TW-BFS could be used as a replacement for BFS.

Table 1. Experimental results: BFS corresponds to Algorithm 1.1 with a BFS order on the waiting nodes, R-BFS implements the ranking system on top of the BFS algorithm (i.e. Algorithm 1.2), and TW-BFS implements the waiting strategy with a priority to true-zone nodes.

	BFS				R-BFS					TW-BFS			
	visited	mist.	stored final	max	visited	mist.	stored final	max	visited ranking	visited	mist.	stored final	max
B-5	63	52	11	22	16	5	11	11	13	11	0	11	11
B-10	1254	1233	21	250	31	10	21	21	28	21	0	21	21
B-15	37091	37060	31	6125	46	15	31	31	43	31	0	31	31
FD-8	2635	2294	341	439	437	96	341	341	579	349	8	341	341
FD-10	10219	9694	525	999	684	159	525	525	1168	535	10	525	525
FD-15	320068	318908	1160	18707	1586	426	1160	1160	4543	1175	15	1160	1160
C-10	39698	5404	34294	48286	59371	25077	34294	52210	54319	34294	0	34294	34302
C-11	98118	17233	80885	124220	153042	72157	80885	130557	160822	80885	0	80885	80894
C-12	239128	50724	188404	311879	378493	190089	188404	320181	430125	188404	0	188404	188414
Fi-7	11951	4214	7737	7738	7737	0	7737	7737	0	7737	0	7737	7737
Fi-8	40536	15456	25080	25082	25080	0	25080	25080	0	25080	0	25080	25080
Fi-9	135485	54450	81035	81038	81035	0	81035	81035	0	81035	0	81035	81035
L-8	45656	15456	30200	30202	30200	0	30200	30200	0	30200	0	30200	30200
L-9	147005	54450	92555	92558	92555	0	92555	92555	0	92555	0	92555	92555
L-10	473198	186600	286598	286602	286598	0	286598	286598	0	286598	0	286598	286598
CR-3	1670	447	1223	1223	1532	309	1223	1223	1837	1563	340	1223	1223
CR-4	21180	7440	13740	13740	17694	3954	13740	13740	24295	19489	5749	13740	13740
CR-5	285094	113727	171367	171367	216957	45590	171367	171367	307010	257137	85770	171367	171367
FI-PL	881214	228265	652949	652949	655653	2704	652949	652949	6977	12660557	11997402	663155	684467

6   Conclusion

We have analysed the phenomenon of mistakes in the zone based reachability algorithm for timed automata. This situation occurs when the exploration algorithm visits a node that is later removed due to a discovery of a bigger node. It is well known that DFS exploration may suffer from an important number of mistakes. We have exhibited examples where BFS makes an important number of mistakes that can be avoided.

To limit the number of mistakes in exploration we have proposed two heuristics: *ranking system* and the *waiting strategy*. The experiments on standard models show that, compared with the standard BFS reachability algorithm the strategies using our heuristics give not only a smaller number of visited nodes, but also a smaller number of stored nodes. Actually, on most examples our strategies are optimal as they do not make any mistakes. In addition, the experiments indicate that the TW-BFS strategy works often as good as the combination of both waiting and ranking strategies, while its implementation is much simpler. Therefore, we suggest to use the TW-BFS algorithm instead of standard BFS for reachability checking.

Acknowledgements. The authors wish to thank Igor Walukiewicz for the many helpful discussions.

References

1. Alur, R., Dill, D.L.: A theory of timed automata. Theoretical Computer Science **126**(2), 183–235 (1994)
2. Behrmann, G., David, A., Larsen, K., Haakansson, J., Pettersson, P., Yi, W., Hendriks, M.: Uppaal 4.0. In: QEST, pp. 125–126. IEEE Computer Society (2006)
3. Behrmann, G.: Distributed reachability analysis in timed automata. International Journal on Software Tools for Technology Transfer **7**(1), 19–30 (2005)
4. Behrmann, G., Bouyer, P., Larsen, K.G., Pelánek, R.: Lower and upper bounds in zone-based abstractions of timed automata. International Journal on Software Tools for Technology Transfer **8**(3), 204–215 (2006)
5. Behrmann, G., Fehnker, A., Hune, T., Larsen, K.G., Pettersson, P., Romijn, J.M.T.: Efficient guiding towards cost-optimality in UPPAAL. In: Margaria, T., Yi, W. (eds.) TACAS 2001. LNCS, vol. 2031, pp. 174–188. Springer, Heidelberg (2001)
6. Behrmann, G., Hune, T., Vaandrager, F.W.: Distributing timed model checking - how the search order matters. In: CAV, pp. 216–231 (2000)
7. Behrmann, G., Larsen, K.G., Pelánek, R.: To store or not to store. In: Hunt Jr., W.A., Somenzi, F. (eds.) CAV 2003. LNCS, vol. 2725, pp. 433–445. Springer, Heidelberg (2003)
8. Braberman, V., Olivero, A., Schapachnik, F.: Zeus: A distributed timed model-checker based on Kronos. Electronic Notes in Theoretical Computer Science **68**(4), 503–522 (2002)
9. Daws, C., Tripakis, S.: Model checking of real-time reachability properties using abstractions. In: Steffen, B. (ed.) TACAS 1998. LNCS, vol. 1384, pp. 313–329. Springer, Heidelberg (1998)
10. Dill, D.L.: Timing assumptions and verification of finite-state concurrent systems. In: Sifakis, J. (ed.) Automatic Verification Methods for Finite State Systems. LNCS, vol. 407, pp. 197–212. Springer, Heidelberg (1989)
11. Evangelista, S., Kristensen, L.: Search-order independent state caching. T. Petri Nets and Other Models of Concurrency **4**, 21–41 (2010)
12. Godefroid, P., Holzmann, G.J., Pirottin, D.: State-space caching revisited. Formal Methods in System Design **7**(3), 227–241 (1995)
13. Pleánek, R., Rosecký, V., Sedenka, J.: Evaluation of state caching and state compression techniques. Tech. rep., Masaryk University, Brno (2008)

Symbolic Minimum Expected Time Controller Synthesis for Probabilistic Timed Automata

Aleksandra Jovanović[1], Marta Kwiatkowska[1], and Gethin Norman[2]([⊠])

[1] Department of Computer Science, University of Oxford, Oxford OX1 3QD, UK
[2] School of Computing Science, University of Glasgow, Glasgow G12 8RZ, UK
gethin.norman@glasgow.ac.uk

Abstract. In this paper we consider the problem of computing the minimum expected time to reach a target and the synthesis of the corresponding optimal controller for a probabilistic timed automaton (PTA). Although this problem admits solutions that employ the digital clocks abstraction or statistical model checking, symbolic methods based on zones and priced zones fail due to the difficulty of incorporating probabilistic branching in the context of dense time. We work in a generalisation of the setting introduced by Asarin and Maler for the corresponding problem for timed automata, where simple and nice functions are introduced to ensure finiteness of the dense-time representation. We find restrictions sufficient for value iteration to converge to the minimum expected time on the uncountable Markov decision process representing the semantics of a PTA. We formulate a Bellman operator on the backwards zone graph of a PTA and prove that value iteration using this operator equals that computed over the PTA's semantics. This enables us to extract an ε-optimal controller from value iteration in the standard way.

1 Introduction

Systems which exhibit real-time, probabilistic and nondeterministic behaviour are widespread and ubiquitous in many areas such as medicine, telecommunications, robotics and transport. Timing constraints are often vital to the correctness of embedded devices and stochasticity is needed due to unreliable channels, randomisations and component failure. Finally, nondeterminism is an important concept which allows us to model and analyse systems operating in a distributed environment and/or exhibiting concurrency. A natural model for such systems, *probabilistic timed automata* (PTAs), a probabilistic extension of timed automata (TAs) [1], was proposed in [20]. They are finite-state automata equipped with real-valued clocks which measure the passage of time and whose transitions are probabilistic. Transitions are expressed as discrete probability distributions over the set of edges, namely a successor location and a set of clocks to reset.

An important class of properties on PTAs are *probabilistic reachability* properties. They allow us to check statements such as: "with probability 0.05 or less the system aborts" or "the data packet will be delivered within 1 second

---

This research is supported by ERC AdG VERIWARE.

S. Sankaranarayanan and E. Vicario (Eds.): FORMATS 2015, LNCS 9268, pp. 140–155, 2015.
DOI: 10.1007/978-3-319-22975-1_10

with minimum 0.95 probability". Model checking algorithms for these properties are well studied. Forwards reachability [20] yields only approximate probability values (upper bounds on maximum reachability probabilities). An abstraction refinement method, based on stochastic games, has subsequently been proposed in [17] for the computation of exact values and implemented in PRISM [18]. An alternative method is backward reachability [21], also giving exact values. These are all symbolic algorithms based on *zones*, a structure that represents in a concise way sets of the automaton states with equivalent behaviour.

Another important class of properties, which is the focus of this paper, is *expected reachability*. They can express statements such as "the expected number of packets sent before failure is at least 100" or "the expected time until a message is delivered is at most 20ms". These properties turned out to be more difficult to verify on PTAs and currently no symbolic approach exists. Even for TAs, the research first concentrated on checking whether there exist system behaviours that satisfy a certain property ϕ (for example, reaching the target set of states). In many situations this is not sufficient, as we often want to distinguish between behaviours that reach target states in 10 or in 1000 seconds. In [2], a backward fixed-point algorithm was proposed for controller synthesis for TAs, which generates a controller that reaches the target in minimum time. The analogous problem for priced timed automata, a model comprising more general reward (or cost) structures, was also considered. The minimum reward reachability for this model has been solved using the region graph method [4], and later extended for more efficient *priced zones* [22] and implemented in UPPAAL [23].

Contributions. We propose the first zone-based algorithm to compute the minimum expected time to reach a target set and synthesise the ε-optimal controller for PTAs. The semantics of a PTA is an uncountable Markov decision process (MDP). Under suitable restrictions, we are able to prove that value iteration converges to the minimum expected time on this MDP. We formulate a Bellman operator on the backwards zone graph of a PTA and show that value iteration using this operator yields the same value as that computed on the MDP. This enables us to extract an ε-optimal controller from value iteration in the standard way. This problem has been open for several years, with previous symbolic zone-based methods, including priced zones, being unsuitable for computing expected values since accumulated rewards are *unbounded*. In order to represent the value functions we introduce rational k-simple and rational k-nice functions, a generalisation of Asarin and Maler's classes of functions [2].

Related Work. Expected reachability properties of PTAs can be verified using the *digital clocks* method [19], which assumes an integral model of time as opposed to a dense model of time. This method, however, suffers from state-space explosion. In [12], the minimum expected reward for priced timed games has been solved using *statistical model checking* and UPPAAL-SMC [11]. This is orthogonal to numerical model checking, based on simulation and hypothesis testing, giving only approximate results which are not guaranteed to be correct.

In [7] the authors consider priced probabilistic timed automata and study reward-bounded probabilistic reachability, which determines whether the maximal probability to reach a set of target locations, within given bounds on the accumulated reward and elapsed time, exceeds a threshold. Although this problem is shown to be undecidable [6], a semi-decidable backwards algorithm using priced zones, which terminates if the problem is affirmative, is implemented in FORTUNA [8].

Outline. In Section 2 we define MDPs and give existing results concerning optimal reward computation for uncountable MDPs. Section 3 defines PTAs and introduces the assumptions needed for the adoption of the results of Section 2. In Section 4, we present our algorithm for computing the minimum expected time and synthesis of an ε-optimal controller using the backwards zone graph of a PTA. Section 4 also introduces a representation of the value functions that generalise the simple and rational nice functions of [2] and gives an example demonstrating the approach. We conclude with Section 5.

An extended version of this paper, with proofs, is available as [15].

2   Background

Let $\mathbb{R}$ be the set of non-negative reals, $\mathbb{N}$ the integers, $\mathbb{Q}$ the rationals and $\mathbb{Q}_+$ the non-negative rationals. A discrete probability distribution over a set S is a function $\mu : S \to [0,1]$ such that $\sum_{s \in S} \mu(s) = 1$ and the set $\{s \in S \mid \mu(s) > 0\}$ is finite. We denote by $\mathsf{Dist}(S)$ the set of distributions over S.

Markov Decision Processes (MDPs) is a widely used formalism for modelling systems which exhibit both nondeterministic and probabilistic behaviour.

Definition 1. *An MDP is a tuple $\mathcal{M} = (S, s_0, A, P_{\mathcal{M}}, R_{\mathcal{M}})$, where S is a (possibly uncountable) set of states, $s_0 \in S$ is an initial state, A is a (possibly uncountable) set of actions, $P_{\mathcal{M}} : (S \times A) \to \mathsf{Dist}(S)$ is a (partial) probabilistic transition function and $R_{\mathcal{M}} : (S \times A) \to \mathbb{R}$ is a reward function.*

A state s of an MDP $\mathcal{M}$ has a set of enabled actions, denoted $A(s)$, given by the set of actions for which $P_{\mathcal{M}}(s, a)$ is defined. A transition in $\mathcal{M}$ from state s is first made by nondeterministically selecting an available action $a \in A(s)$. After the choice is made, a successor state s' is selected randomly according to the probability distribution $P_{\mathcal{M}}(s, a)$, i.e. the probability that a transition to s' occurs is equal to $P_{\mathcal{M}}(s, a)(s')$, and the reward $R_{\mathcal{M}}(s, a)$ is accumulated when making this transition.

An infinite *path* is a sequence $\omega = s_0 \xrightarrow{a_0} s_1 \xrightarrow{a_1} s_2 \xrightarrow{a_2} \cdots$ of transitions such that $P_{\mathcal{M}}(s_i, a)(s_{i+1}) > 0$ for all $i \geqslant 0$, and it represents a particular resolution of both nondeterminism and probability. A finite path is a prefix of an infinite path ending in a state. The $(i+1)$th state of a path ω is denoted by $\omega(i)$ and the action associated with the $(i+1)$th transition by $step(\omega, i)$. We denote the set of all infinite (finite) paths of $\mathcal{M}$ by *IPaths*$_{\mathcal{M}}$ (*FPaths*$_{\mathcal{M}}$) and the last state of a finite path ω by $last(\omega)$.

A *strategy* (also called an *adversary* or *policy*) of $\mathcal{M}$ resolves the choice between actions in each state, based on the execution so far.

Definition 2. *A strategy of an MDP $\mathcal{M}$ is a function $\sigma : FPaths_{\mathcal{M}} \rightarrow Dist(A)$ such that $\sigma(\omega)(a) > 0$ only if $a \in A(last(\omega))$.*

For a fixed strategy σ and state s, we can define a probability measure $\mathcal{P}_s^\sigma$ over the set of infinite paths starting in s [16]. A strategy σ is memoryless if its choices only depend on the current state, and deterministic if $\sigma(\omega)$ is a point distribution for all $\omega \in FPaths_{\mathcal{M}}$. The set of strategies of $\mathcal{M}$ is denoted by $\Sigma_{\mathcal{M}}$.

Two fundamental quantitative properties of MDPs are the probability of reaching a set of target states and the expected reward accumulated before reaching a target. For a strategy σ, state s and set of target states F, the probability of reaching F and expected reward accumulated before reaching F from s under σ are given by:

$$\mathbb{P}_{\mathcal{M}}^\sigma(s, F) \stackrel{\text{def}}{=} \mathcal{P}_s^\sigma\{\omega \in IPaths_{\mathcal{M}} \mid \omega(i) \in F \text{ for some } i \in \mathbb{N}\}$$
$$\mathbb{E}_{\mathcal{M}}^\sigma(s, F) \stackrel{\text{def}}{=} \int_{\omega \in IPaths_{\mathcal{M}}} rew(\omega, F) \, d\mathcal{P}_s^\sigma$$

where for any infinite path ω:

$$rew(\omega, F) \stackrel{\text{def}}{=} \begin{cases} \sum_{i=0}^{\min\{k-1 \mid \omega(k) \in F\}} R_{\mathcal{M}}(\omega(i), step(\omega, i)) & \text{if } \omega(k) \in F \text{ for some } k \in \mathbb{N} \\ \infty & \text{otherwise.} \end{cases}$$

The standard approach is to analyse the optimal values of these measures, i.e. the minimum and maximum values over all strategies. In this paper, we are concerned with the maximum probability of reaching a target and minimum expected accumulated reward before reaching a target:

$$\mathbb{P}_{\mathcal{M}}^{\max}(s, F) \stackrel{\text{def}}{=} \sup_{\sigma \in \Sigma_{\mathcal{M}}} \mathbb{P}_{\mathcal{M}}^\sigma(s, F) \quad \text{and} \quad \mathbb{E}_{\mathcal{M}}^{\min}(s, F) \stackrel{\text{def}}{=} \inf_{\sigma \in \Sigma_{\mathcal{M}}} \mathbb{E}_{\mathcal{M}}^\sigma(s, F).$$

The optimal values can be computed using a *Bellman operator* [5]. More precisely, under certain conditions on the MDP and target set under study, using a Bellman operator the optimal values can be obtained through a number of techniques, including *value iteration* and *policy iteration*, see for example [9,10]. Concerning minimum expected reachability we have the following definition.

Definition 3. *Given an MDP $\mathcal{M}$ and target set F, the Bellman operator $T_{\mathcal{M}} : (S \rightarrow \mathbb{R}) \rightarrow (S \rightarrow \mathbb{R})$ for minimum expected reachability is defined as follows. For any $f : S \rightarrow \mathbb{R}$ and $s \in S$:*

$$T_{\mathcal{M}}(f)(s) = \begin{cases} 0 & \text{if } s \in F \\ \inf_{a \in A(s)} \{R_{\mathcal{M}}(s, a) + \sum_{s' \in S} P_{\mathcal{M}}(s, a)(s') \cdot f(s')\} & \text{otherwise.} \end{cases}$$

Value iteration for $T_{\mathcal{M}}$ corresponds to repeatedly applying the operator when starting from some initial approximation f_0 until some convergence criterion is met, e.g. computing $T^{n+1}(f_0) = T(T^n(f_0))$ until $\|T^{n+1}(f_0) - T^n(f_0)\| \leqslant \varepsilon$ for some threshold ε. On the other hand, policy iteration starts with an arbitrary, deterministic and memoryless strategy, and then tries repeatedly to construct an improved (deterministic and memoryless) strategy. This is achieved by computing the expected reachability values for the current strategy and, if possible, updating the actions choices so that the expected reachability values decrease.

We now adapt the results of [14] for the total expected reward for possibly uncountable-state and uncountable-action set MDPs. The conditions imposed by [14] correspond, in our setting, to those given below (since we restrict to discrete distributions and non-negative reward values, the assumptions we require are weaker).

Assumption 1. *For an MDP $\mathcal{M}$ and target set F:*

(a) *$A(s)$ is compact for all $s \in S$;*
(b) *$R_\mathcal{M}$ is bounded and $a \mapsto R_\mathcal{M}(s, a)$ is lower semi-continuous for all $s \in S$;*
(c) *if σ is a memoryless, deterministic strategy which is not proper, then $\mathbb{E}^\sigma_\mathcal{M}(s, F)$ is unbounded for some $s \in S$;*
(d) *there exists a proper, memoryless, deterministic strategy;*

where a strategy σ is called proper if $\mathbb{P}^\sigma_\mathcal{M}(s, F){=}1$ for all $s \in S$.

Using these assumptions we have the following result.

Theorem 1 ([14]). *If $\mathcal{M}$ and F are an MDP and target set for which Assumption 1 holds, then:*

- *there exists a memoryless, deterministic strategy that achieves the minimum expected reward of reaching F;*
- *the minimum expected reward values are the unique solutions to $T_\mathcal{M}$;*
- *value iteration over $T_\mathcal{M}$ converges to the minimum expected reward values when starting from any bounded function;*
- *policy iteration converges to the minimum expected reward values when starting from any proper, memoryless, deterministic strategy.*

3   Probabilistic Timed Automata

We now introduce Probabilistic Timed Automata, a modelling framework for systems which incorporate probabilistic, nondeterministic and real-time behaviour.

Clocks, Clock Valuations and Zones. Let $\mathcal{X}$ be a set of real-valued variables called clocks, which increase at the same, constant rate. A function $v : \mathcal{X} \to \mathbb{R}$ is called clock valuation function and the set of all clock valuations is denoted as $\mathbb{R}^\mathcal{X}$. Let $\mathbf{0}$ be a valuation that assigns 0 to all clocks in $\mathcal{X}$. For any $R \subseteq \mathcal{X}$ and any valuation v on $\mathcal{X}$, we write $v[R]$ for the valuation on $\mathcal{X}$ such that $v[R](x){=}0$ if $x \in R$ and $v[R](x){=}v(x)$ otherwise. For $t \in \mathbb{R}$, $v{+}t$ denotes the valuation which assigns $(v{+}t)(x){=}v(x){+}t$ to all $x \in \mathcal{X}$. A zone is an expression of the form: $\zeta := x{\sim}c \mid x{-}y{\sim}c \mid \zeta \wedge \zeta$, where $x, y \in \mathcal{X}$, ${\sim} \in \{<, \leqslant, >, \geqslant\}$ and $c \in \mathbb{N}$. The set of zones on $\mathcal{X}$ is denoted $Zones(\mathcal{X})$. A clock valuation v satisfies a zone ζ, denoted $v \models \zeta$, if ζ resolves to true after substituting each occurrence of clock x with $v(x)$. A zone ζ represents the set of clock valuations v which satisfy it.

We require a number of classical operations on zones [24]. Zone $\nearrow \zeta$ contains all valuations reachable from a valuation in ζ by letting time pass. Conversely, $\swarrow \zeta$ contains all valuations that can reach ζ by letting time pass. Furthermore, for a set of clocks R, $\zeta[R]$ includes the valuations obtained by those in ζ by resetting the clocks R and $[R]\zeta$ the valuations which result in a valuation in ζ when the clocks in R are reset to 0.

Definition 4. *A PTA $\mathcal{P}$ is a tuple $(L, l_0, \mathcal{X}, Act, \mathsf{enab}, \mathsf{prob}, \mathsf{inv})$ where: L is a finite set of locations; $l_0 \in L$ is an initial location; $\mathcal{X}$ is a finite set of clocks; Act is a finite set of actions; $\mathsf{enab} : (L \times Act) \rightarrow Zones(\mathcal{X})$ is an enabling condition; $\mathsf{prob} : (L \times Act) \rightarrow \mathsf{Dist}(2^{\mathcal{X}} \times L)$ is a probabilistic transition function; $\mathsf{inv} : L \rightarrow Zones(\mathcal{X})$ is an invariant condition.*

A state of $\mathcal{P}$ is a pair $(l, v) \in L \times \mathbb{R}^{\mathcal{X}}$ such that the clock valuation v satisfies the invariant $\mathsf{inv}(l)$. A transition is a time-action pair (t, a) corresponding to letting time t elapse and then performing the action a. In a state (l, v), time can elapse as long as the invariant $\mathsf{inv}(l)$ remains continuously satisfied and action a can be performed only if the enabling condition $\mathsf{enab}(l, a)$ is then satisfied. If transition (t, a) is performed, then the set of clocks to reset and successor location are selected randomly according to the probability distribution $\mathsf{prob}(l, a)$.

For $(l, a) \in L \times Act$, an element $(R, l') \in 2^{\mathcal{X}} \times L$ such that $\mathsf{prob}(l, a)(R, l') > 0$ is called an *edge* of (l, a) and the set of all edges of (l, a) is denoted $\mathsf{edges}(l, a)$.

Definition 5. *For PTA $\mathcal{P} = (L, l_0, \mathcal{X}, Act, \mathsf{prob}, \mathsf{inv})$ its semantics is given by the (infinite-state) MDP $[\![\mathcal{P}]\!] = (S, s_0, \mathbb{R} \times Act, P_{[\![\mathcal{P}]\!]}, R_{[\![\mathcal{P}]\!]})$ where:*

- $S = \{(l, v) \in L \times \mathbb{R}^{\mathcal{X}} \mid v \models \mathsf{inv}(l)\}$ and $s_0 = (l_0, \mathbf{0})$;
- $P_{[\![\mathcal{P}]\!]}((l, v), (t, a)) = \mu$ if and only if $v + t' \models \mathsf{inv}(l)$ for all $0 \leqslant t' \leqslant t$, $v + t \models \mathsf{enab}(l, a)$ and for any $(l', v') \in S$:

$$\mu(l', v') = \sum \{\!| \mathsf{prob}(l, a)(R, l') \mid R \subseteq \mathcal{X} \wedge v' = (v + t)[R] |\!\}$$

- $R_{[\![\mathcal{P}]\!]}(t, a) = t$ for all $(t, a) \in \mathbb{R} \times Act$.

For Theorem 1 to be applicable to semantics of a PTA, we need to ensure Assumption 1 holds. To this end, we introduce the following assumptions.

Assumption 2. *For any PTA $\mathcal{P}$ we have:*

(a) *all invariants and enabling conditions of $\mathcal{P}$ are bounded;*
(b) *only non-strict inequalities are allowed in clock constraints ($\mathcal{P}$ is closed);*
(c) *$\mathcal{P}$ is structurally non-zeno [25] (this can be identified syntactically and in a compositional fashion [26] and guarantees time-divergent behaviour).*

Conditions (a) and (b) are necessary and sufficient to ensure $A(s)$ is compact for all states $s \in S$, i.e. Assumption 1(a) holds. Assumption 1(b) follows from Definition 5 as, for any $(t, a) \in \mathbb{R} \times Act$, we have $R_{[\![\mathcal{P}]\!]}(s, (t, a)) = t$ for all $s \in S$.

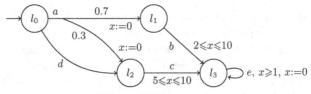

Fig. 1. PTA example

Structurally non-zeno is sufficient for ensuring Assumption 1(c) holds. More precisely, if for strategy σ the probability of reaching the target is less than 1, there is a non-negligible set of paths under σ which never reach the target and, since σ is non-zeno, elapsed time (and hence the accumulated reward) must diverge on the paths in this set.

The remaining assumption, Assumption 1(d), holds if we restrict attention to the sub-MDP of $[\![\mathcal{P}]\!]$ which contains only states s for which $\mathbb{P}_{[\![\mathcal{P}]\!]}^{\max}(s,F)=1$ [13]. More precisely, if $\mathbb{P}_{[\![\mathcal{P}]\!]}^{\max}(s,F)=1$, then, using the region graph construction [20], there exists a memoryless, deterministic strategy that reaches the target with probability 1, and hence this strategy will also be proper.

We have imposed several restrictions on PTAs we analyse. First, boundedness is not actually a restriction since bounded TAs are as expressive as standard TAs [4] and the result carries over to PTAs. The fact that PTAs must be closed is not a severe restriction in practice, as any PTA can be infinitesimally approximated by one with closed constraints. Non-zenoness is a standard assumption for both TAs and PTAs, as it discards unrealistic behaviours, i.e. executions for which time does not diverge.

Example 1. Consider the PTA shown in Figure 1 where the target is l_3. We assume the invariant in each location equals $x \leqslant 10$ and the enabling conditions for transitions labelled a and d equal $x \leqslant 10$. From the state (l_0, v), if action a is chosen, then the minimum expected time equals $0.3 \cdot 5 + 0.7 \cdot 2 = 2.9$. On the other hand, if action d is selected, then the minimum expected time equals $5 - v(x)$ if $v(x) \leqslant 5$ and 0 otherwise. Therefore, in the initial state, i.e. when $v(x)=0$, the minimum expected time equals $\min\{2.9, 5-0\} = 2.9$.

In this example, the optimal choices are to take transitions as soon as they are available. However, as we will see, this does not hold in general since we might need to wait longer in a location in order for an enabling condition to be satisfied later.

4   Minimum Expected Time Algorithm for PTAs

In this section we present our algorithm for the minimum expected time computation for PTAs. It is based on a backwards exploration of the state space. We adopt backwards as opposed to forwards search since, although forwards has proven successful in the context of TAs, for PTAs it yields only upper bounds for maximum probabilistic reachability [20]. For the remainder of the section we fix a PTA $\mathcal{P} = (L, l_0, \mathcal{X}, Act, \mathsf{enab}, \mathsf{prob}, \mathsf{inv})$, target set of locations F and suppose $[\![\mathcal{P}]\!] = (S, S_0, \mathbb{R} \times Act, P_{[\![\mathcal{P}]\!]}, R_{[\![\mathcal{P}]\!]})$ and $S_F = \{(l, v) \mid l \in F \wedge v \models \mathsf{inv}(l)\}$.

BackwardsReach($\mathcal{P}, F$)

---

1 Z := ∅
2 E := ∅
3 Y := $\{(l, \text{inv}(l)) \mid l \in F\}$
4 **while** (Y ≠ ∅)
5   **choose** y ∈ Y
6   Y := Y \ {y}
7   Z := Z ∪ {y}
8   **for** $(l, a) \in (L \backslash F) \times Act$ **and** $(R, l') \in \text{edges}(l, a)$
9   z := $\text{dpre}(l, a, R, l')(\text{tpre}(y))$
10   **if** (z ≠ ∅)
11   **if** (z ∉ Z) **then** Y := Y ∪ {z}
12   E := E ∪ $\{(z, a, (R, l'), y)\}$
13   **for** $(\tilde{z}, a, (\tilde{R}, \tilde{l}'), \tilde{y}) \in$ E such that $(\tilde{R}, \tilde{l}') \neq (R, l')$
14   **if** (z ∧ $\tilde{z}$ ≠ ∅) **and** z ∧ $\tilde{z}$ ∉ Z **then** Y := Y ∪ {z ∧ $\tilde{z}$}
15   **for** z ∈ Z **and** $(z', a, (R, l'), z'') \in$ E **do**
16   **if** z ⊆ z' **then**
17   E := $\{(z, a, (R, l'), z'')\}$ ∪ E
18   **return** (Z, E)

Fig. 2. Backward reachability algorithm

Symbolic States. A symbolic state z of $\mathcal{P}$ is a pair $(l, \zeta) \in L \times Zones(\mathcal{X})$ representing the set of PTA states $\{(l, v) \mid v \models \zeta\}$. Let $Z_F = \{(l, \text{inv}(l)) \mid l \in F\}$, i.e. the target set of symbolic states. For any symbolic states z = (l, ζ) and z' = (l, ζ') let z ∧ z' = $(l, \zeta \wedge \zeta')$, z ⊆ z' if and only if $\zeta \subseteq \zeta'$ and z = ∅ if and only if $\zeta = \text{false}$. The time and discrete predecessor operations for z = (l, ζ) are defined as follows:

$$\text{tpre}(z) = (l, \nearrow \zeta \wedge \text{inv}(l))$$

$$\text{dpre}(l'', a, (R, l'))(z) = \begin{cases} (l'', \text{false}) & \text{if } l \neq l' \\ (l'', [R]\zeta \wedge \text{enab}(l'', a)) & \text{otherwise} \end{cases}$$

where $(R, l') \in \text{edges}(l'', a)$, $l'' \in L$ and $a \in Act$.

Backward Reachability Algorithm. We use a slightly modified version of the backward reachability algorithm on symbolic states taken from [21] (the same operations are performed, we just add action labels to the edge tuples). The modified version is given in Figure 2.

The backwards algorithm returns a zone graph (Z, E) with symbolic states as vertices. Termination of the algorithm is guaranteed by the fact that only finitely many zones can be generated. As demonstrated in [21], from this graph one can build a finite state MDP for computing the exact maximum reachability probabilities of $[\![\mathcal{P}]\!]$. The MDP $\mathcal{M}_{(Z,E)}$ has state space Z, action set 2^E and if z ∈ Z and $E \in 2^E$, then $P_{\mathcal{M}_{(Z,E)}}(z, E)$ is defined if and only if there exists $a \in Act$ such that

- $(z'', a', (R, l'), z') \in E$ implies z'' = z and a' = a;
- $(z, a, (R, l'), z') \neq (z, a, (\tilde{R}, \tilde{l}'), \tilde{z}') \in E$ implies $(R, l') \neq (\tilde{R}, \tilde{l}')$;

where $P_{\mathcal{M}_{(Z,E)}}(\mathbf{z}, E)(\mathbf{z}') = \sum \{\mathsf{prob}(l, a)(R, l') \mid (\mathbf{z}, a, (R, l'), \mathbf{z}') \in E\}$ for $\mathbf{z}' \in Z$.

The following theorem shows the correspondence between the maximum reachability probabilities for $[\![\mathcal{P}]\!]$ and $\mathcal{M}_{(Z,E)}$.

Theorem 2 ([21]). *Let* (Z, E) *be the zone graph returned by* BackwardsReach$(\mathcal{P}, F)$, *then for any state* s *of* $[\![\mathcal{P}]\!]$ *we have:*

- $\mathbb{P}^{\max}_{[\![\mathcal{P}]\!]}(s, S_F) > 0$ *if and only if there exists* $\mathbf{z} \in Z$ *such that* $s \in \mathsf{tpre}(\mathbf{z})$;
- *if* $\mathbb{P}^{\max}_{[\![\mathcal{P}]\!]}(s, S_F) > 0$, *then* $\mathbb{P}^{\max}_{[\![\mathcal{P}]\!]}(s, S_F) = \max\left\{ \mathbb{P}^{\max}_{\mathcal{M}_{(Z,E)}}(\mathbf{z}, Z_F) \mid \mathbf{z} \in Z \wedge s \in \mathsf{tpre}(\mathbf{z}) \right\}$.

Using Theorem 2 we can find the states s of $[\![\mathcal{P}]\!]$ for which $\mathbb{P}^{\max}_{[\![\mathcal{P}]\!]}(s, S_F) = 1$ by computing the symbolic states $\mathbf{z}$ for which $\mathbb{P}^{\max}_{\mathcal{M}_{(Z,E)}}(\mathbf{z}, Z_F) = 1$. Finding these symbolic states does not require numerical computation [13], and hence we do not need to build $\mathcal{M}_{(Z,E)}$, but can use (Z, E) directly in the computation.

For the remainder of this section we assume we have computed the states of $\mathcal{M}_{(Z,E)}$, and hence of $[\![\mathcal{P}]\!]$, for which the maximum reachability probability is 1, and $[\![\mathcal{P}]\!]$ and (Z, E) are the sub-MDP and sub-graph restricted to these states. Using Theorem 2, $s \in S$ if and only if there exists $\mathbf{z} \in Z$ such that $s \in \mathsf{tpre}(\mathbf{z})$.

For states not considered, i.e. states for which the maximum reachability probability is less than 1, since we assume $\mathcal{P}$ is non-zeno (Assumption 2(c)) their minimum expected time equals infinity. Therefore, if we compute the minimum expected time for the states of the constructed sub-MDP, we will have found the minimum expected time for all states of the PTA.

Following the discussion in Section 3, $[\![\mathcal{P}]\!]$ now satisfies Assumption 1 and therefore we can use Theorem 1. In particular, value iteration for the Bellman operator of Definition 3 for $[\![\mathcal{P}]\!]$ and S_F converges to the minimum expected time when starting from any bounded function. Below we will present a value iteration method over (Z, E) and prove that it corresponds to that for $[\![\mathcal{P}]\!]$ and S_F, and hence will also converge to the minimum expected time values for $[\![\mathcal{P}]\!]$.

Value Iteration Over the Zone Graph. To present the value iteration operator for (Z, E), we require the following notation. For $(l, \zeta) \in Z$, the set of edges $E \subseteq \mathsf{E}$ is an element of $\mathsf{E}(l, \zeta)$ if and only if there exists $a \in Act$ such that $\mathsf{edges}(l, a) = \{(R_1, l_1), \dots, (R_n, l_n)\}$ and $E = \{(\mathbf{z}, a, (R_1, l_1), \mathbf{z}_1), \dots, (\mathbf{z}, a, (R_n, l_n), \mathbf{z}_n)\}$ for some $\mathbf{z}_1, \dots, \mathbf{z}_n \in Z$.

Definition 6. *The operator* $T_{(Z,E)} : (Z \to (S \to \mathbb{R})) \to (Z \to (S \to \mathbb{R}))$ *on the zone graph* (Z, E) *is such that for* $g : Z \to (S \to \mathbb{R})$, $(l, \zeta) \in Z$ *and* $(l, v) \in S$ *where* $(l, v) \in \mathsf{tpre}(l, \zeta)$ *we have* $T_{(Z,E)}(g)(l, \zeta)(l, v)$ *equals* 0 *if* $l \in F$ *and otherwise equals*

$$\inf_{t \in \mathbb{R} \wedge v + t \in \zeta} \min_{E \in \mathsf{E}(l, \zeta)} \left\{ t + \sum_{((l,\zeta),a,(R,l'),(l',\zeta')) \in E} \mathsf{prob}(l, a)(R, l') \cdot g(l', \zeta')(l', (v+t)[R]) \right\}.$$

We now demonstrate the correspondence between value iteration using this operator over (Z, E) and that given by Definition 3 over $[\![\mathcal{P}]\!]$.

Proposition 1. *If* $f : S \to \mathbb{R}$ *and* $g : Z \to (S \to \mathbb{R})$ *are functions such that* $f(s) = g(\mathbf{z})(s)$ *for all* $\mathbf{z} \in Z$ *and* $s \in \mathsf{tpre}(\mathbf{z})$, *then for any* $s \in S$ *and* $n \in \mathbb{N}$ *we have:* $T^n_{\llbracket \mathcal{P} \rrbracket}(f)(s) = \min\{\, T^n_{(Z,E)}(g)(\mathbf{z})(s) \mid \mathbf{z} \in Z \wedge s \in \mathsf{tpre}(\mathbf{z}) \,\}$.

Proof. Consider any $f : S \to \mathbb{R}$ and $g : Z \to (S \to \mathbb{R})$ such that $f(s) = g(\mathbf{z})(s)$ for all $\mathbf{z} \in Z$ and $s \in \mathbf{z}$. The proof is by induction on $n \in \mathbb{N}$. If $n=0$, then the result follows by construction of f and g and since $T^0_{\llbracket \mathcal{P} \rrbracket}(f) = f$ and $T^0_{(Z,E)}(g) = g$.

Next we assume the proposition holds for some $n \in \mathbb{N}$. For any $s=(l,v) \in S$, if $l \in F$, then by the construction of the zone graph (see Figure 2), Definition 3 and Definition 6 we have: $T^{n+1}_{\llbracket \mathcal{P} \rrbracket}(f)(s) = 0 = \min\left\{ T^{n+1}_{(Z,E)}(g)(\mathbf{z})(s) \mid \mathbf{z} \in Z \wedge s \in \mathsf{tpre}(\mathbf{z}) \right\}$.

It therefore remains to consider the case when $s=(l,v) \in S$ and $l \notin F$. For any $(t', a') \in A(s)$ and $(R, l') \in \mathsf{edges}(l, a)$ by the induction hypothesis there exists $(l', \zeta_{(R,l')}) \in Z$ with $(l', (v+t')[R]) \in \mathsf{tpre}(l', \zeta_{(R,l')})$ such that:

$$T^n_{(Z,E)}(g)(l', \zeta_{(R,l')})(l', (v+t')[R]) = T^n_{\llbracket \mathcal{P} \rrbracket}(f)(l', (v+t')[R]). \tag{1}$$

Now since $(t', a') \in A(s)$ and $(l', (v+t')[R]) \in \mathsf{tpre}(l', \zeta_{(R,l')})$ it follows from Definition 5 that $(l, v+t) \in \mathsf{dpre}(l, a', (R, l'))(\mathsf{tpre}(l', \zeta_{(R,l')}))$.

Since the edge $(R, l') \in \mathsf{edges}(l, a)$ was arbitrary, by the construction of the zone graph (see Figure 2), there exists $(l, \zeta) \in Z$ such that $v+t' \in \zeta$ and edge set:

$$E' = \{(l, \zeta), a', (R, l'), (l', \zeta_{(R,l')})) \mid (R, l') \in \mathsf{edges}(l, a)\} \in \mathsf{E}(l, \zeta). \tag{2}$$

Furthermore, by definition of tpre we have $(l, v) \in \mathsf{tpre}(l, \zeta)$. Now, by Definition 6, $T^{n+1}_{(Z,E)}(g)(l, \zeta)(l, v)$ equals:

$$\inf_{t \in \mathbb{R} \wedge v+t \in \zeta} \min_{E \in \mathsf{E}(l,\zeta)} \left\{ t + \sum_{((l,\zeta),a,(R,l'),(l',\zeta')) \in E} \mathsf{prob}(l, a)(R, l') \cdot T^n_{(Z,E)}(g)(l', \zeta')(l', (v+t)[R]) \right\}$$

$$\leqslant \min_{E \in \mathsf{E}(l,\zeta)} \left\{ t' + \sum_{((l,\zeta),a',(R,l'),(l',\zeta')) \in E} \mathsf{prob}(l, a')(R, l') \cdot T^n_{(Z,E)}(g)(l', \zeta')(l', (v+t')[R]) \right\}$$
$$\text{(since } v+t' \in \zeta)$$

$$\leqslant t' + \sum_{((l,\zeta),a,(R,l'),(l',\zeta')) \in E'} \mathsf{prob}(l, a')(R, l') \cdot T^n_{(Z,E)}(g)(l', \zeta')(l', (v+t')[R])$$
$$\text{(since } E' \in \mathsf{E}(l,\zeta))$$

$$= t' + \sum_{(R,l') \in \mathsf{edges}(l,a')} \mathsf{prob}(l, a')(R, l') \cdot T^n_{\llbracket \mathcal{P} \rrbracket}(f)(l', (v+t')[R]) \qquad \text{(by (1) and (2))}$$

$$= R_{\llbracket \mathcal{P} \rrbracket}(s, (t', a')) + \sum_{s' \in S} P_{\llbracket \mathcal{P} \rrbracket}(s, (t', a'))(s') \cdot T^n_{\llbracket \mathcal{P} \rrbracket}(f)(s') \qquad \text{(by Definition 5)}$$

Therefore, since $(t', a') \in A(s)$ was arbitrary it follows from Definition 3 that:

$$T^{n+1}_{\llbracket \mathcal{P} \rrbracket}(f)(s) \geqslant \min\left\{ T^{n+1}_{(Z,E)}(g)(\mathbf{z})(s) \mid \mathbf{z} \in Z \wedge s \in \mathsf{tpre}(\mathbf{z}) \right\}. \tag{3}$$

Next we consider any $\mathbf{z}=(l, \zeta) \in Z$ such that $v+t \in \zeta$ for some $t \in \mathbb{R}$ (i.e. $\mathbf{z} \in Z$ such that $s \in \mathsf{tpre}(\mathbf{z})$). For any $t' \in \mathbb{R}$ such that $v+t' \in \zeta$ and $E' \in \mathsf{E}(l, \zeta)$ by construction of the zone graph there exists $a' \in Act$ where:

$$E' = \{(l, \zeta), a', (R, l'), (l', \zeta_{(R,l')})) \mid (R, l') \in \mathsf{edges}(l, a')\} \tag{4}$$

and $(l', (v+t')[R]) \in \mathsf{tpre}(l', \zeta_{(R,l')})$ for all $(R, l') \in \mathsf{edges}(l, a)$. Now by the induction hypothesis for any $(R, l') \in \mathsf{edges}(l, a)$:

$$T^n_{[\![\mathcal{P}]\!]}(f)(l', (v+t')[R]) \leqslant T^n_{(Z,E)}(g)(l', \zeta_{(R,l')})(l', (v+t')[R]). \tag{5}$$

Furthermore, by Definition 5 we have $(t', a') \in A(s)$. Now by Definition 3:

$$
\begin{aligned}
T^{n+1}_{[\![\mathcal{P}]\!]}(f)(l, v) &= \inf_{(t,a)\in A(l,v)} \left\{ R_{[\![\mathcal{P}]\!]}(s, (t, a)) + \sum_{s'\in S} P_{[\![\mathcal{P}]\!]}(s, (t, a))(s') \cdot T^n_{[\![\mathcal{P}]\!]}(f)(s') \right\} \\
&\leqslant R_{[\![\mathcal{P}]\!]}(s, (t', a')) + \sum_{s'\in S} P_{[\![\mathcal{P}]\!]}(s, (t', a'))(s') \cdot T^n_{[\![\mathcal{P}]\!]}(f)(s') \quad \text{(since } (t', a') \in A(s)) \\
&= t' + \sum_{(R,l')\in \mathsf{edges}(l,a)} \mathsf{prob}(l, a')(R, l') \cdot T^n_{[\![\mathcal{P}]\!]}(f)(l', (v+t')[R]) \quad \text{(by Definition 5)} \\
&\leqslant t' + \sum_{(R,l')\in \mathsf{edges}(l,a)} \mathsf{prob}(l, a')(R, l') \cdot T^n_{(Z,E)}(g)(l', \zeta_{(R,l')})(l', (v+t')[R]) \quad \text{(by (5))} \\
&= t' + \sum_{((l,\zeta),a,(R,l'),(l',\zeta'))\in E'} \mathsf{prob}(l, a')(R, l') \cdot T^n_{(Z,E)}(g)(l', \zeta_{(R,l')})(l', (v+t')[R]) \\
&\qquad\qquad\qquad\qquad\qquad\qquad\qquad\qquad\qquad\qquad\qquad\qquad\qquad \text{(by (4))}
\end{aligned}
$$

Since $z=(l, \zeta) \in Z$ such that $v+t \in \zeta$ for some $t \in \mathbb{R}$, $t' \in \mathbb{R}$ such that $v+t' \in \zeta$ and $E' \in E(l, \zeta)$ were arbitrary, by Definition 6 it follows that:

$$T^{n+1}_{[\![\mathcal{P}]\!]}(f)(s) \leqslant \min \left\{ T^{n+1}_{(Z,E)}(g)(z)(s) \mid z \in Z \wedge s \in \mathsf{tpre}(z) \right\}. \tag{6}$$

Combining (3) and (6) we have:

$$T^{n+1}_{[\![\mathcal{P}]\!]}(f)(s) = \min \left\{ T^{n+1}_{(Z,E)}(g)(z)(s) \mid z \in Z \wedge s \in \mathsf{tpre}(z) \right\}.$$

and hence, since $s \in S$ was arbitrary, the proposition holds by induction. □

Rational Simple Functions and Rational Nice Functions. In [2], the authors introduce simple functions and show that all value functions encountered during the iterative procedure for computing the minimum time reachability for TAs belong to this special class. For a zone ζ, a function $f : \zeta \rightarrow \mathbb{R}$ is *simple* if and only if it can be represented as:

$$
f(v) = \begin{cases} c_j & \text{if } v \in C_j \\ d_l - v(x_l) & \text{if } v \in D_l \end{cases}
$$

where $c_j, d_l \in \mathbb{N}$, $x_l \in \mathcal{X}$, C_j and D_l are zones for $1 \leqslant j \leqslant M$ and $1 \leqslant l \leqslant N$.

When it comes to PTAs, due to the presence of probabilistic branching, simple functions are not sufficient, as shown by the example below. Moreover, the domain of clocks cannot be represented by zones, as we now need to allow more general linear constraints on clocks with rational coefficients.

Example 2. We return to the PTA of Example 1 (see Figure 1). Expressing the minimum expected time in the initial location as a function $f : \mathbb{R}^{\mathcal{X}} \rightarrow \mathbb{R}$ we have:

$$
f(v) = \begin{cases} 2.9 & \text{if } x \leqslant 2.1 \\ 5 - v(x) & \text{if } 2.1 \leqslant x \leqslant 5 \\ 0 & \text{if } 5 \leqslant x \leqslant 10 \end{cases}
$$

and hence it cannot be represented using simple functions.

We introduce *rational simple functions* to represent the functions encountered during value iteration. Let $\mathcal{X} = \{x_1, \ldots, x_n\}$ and k be the maximum constant appearing in $\mathcal{P}$. By Assumption 2(a) $\mathcal{P}$ is bounded, and hence all clock values in $\mathcal{P}$ are bounded by k.

Definition 7. *A (convex) k-polyhedron $C \subseteq \{v \in \mathbb{R}^{\mathcal{X}} \mid v(x) \leqslant k \text{ for } x \in \mathcal{X}\}$ is defined by finitely many linear inequalities; formally, it is of the form:*

$$C = \left\{ v \in \mathbb{R}^{\mathcal{X}} \mid \textstyle\sum_{i=1}^{n} q_{ij} \cdot v(x_i) \leqslant f_j \text{ for } 1 \leqslant j \leqslant M \right\}$$

where $q_{ij}, f_j \in \mathbb{Q}$ and $f_j \leqslant k$ for all $1 \leqslant i \leqslant n$ and $1 \leqslant j \leqslant M$ for some $M \in \mathbb{N}$.

Definition 8. *For zone ζ, a function $f : \zeta \to \mathbb{R}$ is rational k-simple if and only if it can be represented as:*

$$f(v) = \begin{cases} c_j & \text{if } v \in C_j \\ d_l - \sum_{i=1}^{n} p_{il} \cdot v(x_i) & \text{if } v \in D_l \end{cases}$$

where $c_j, d_l \in \mathbb{Q}_+$, $p_{il} \in \mathbb{Q}_+ \cap [0,1]$ such that $\sum_{i=1}^{n} p_{il} \leqslant 1$ and C_j, D_l are k-polyhedra for all $1 \leqslant i \leqslant n$, $1 \leqslant j \leqslant M$ and $1 \leqslant l \leqslant N$.

Furthermore, a function $f : Z \to (S \to \mathbb{R})$ is rational k-simple if $f(l, \zeta)(l, \cdot) : \swarrow \zeta \to \mathbb{R}$ is rational k-simple for all $(l, \zeta) \in Z$.

We require the following definition and lemma for rational k-simple functions.

Definition 9. *If $f : \zeta \to \mathbb{R}$ is a rational k-simple function and $R \subseteq \mathcal{X}$, let $f[R] : [R]\zeta \to \mathbb{R}$ be the function where $f[R](v) = f(v[R])$ for all $v \in \zeta$.*

Lemma 1. *If $f : \zeta \to \mathbb{R}$ is rational k-simple and $R \subseteq \mathcal{X}$, then $f[R] : [R]\zeta \to \mathbb{R}$ is rational k-simple. (The proof can be found in [15].)*

During value iteration we obtain functions of the form $v \mapsto t + f(l, \zeta)(l, v+t)$ where f is rational k-simple. This motivates the introduction of rational k-nice functions, based on Asarin and Maler's k-nice functions [2].

Definition 10. *A k-bipolyhedron is a set of the form $\{(v, t) \mid v \in C \wedge v+t \in D\}$ where C and D are k-polyhedra. For a zone ζ, a function $g : (\zeta \times \mathbb{R}) \to \mathbb{R}$ is rational k-nice if and only if it can be represented as:*

$$g(v, t) = \begin{cases} c_j + t & \text{if } (v, t) \in F_j \\ d_l - \sum_{i=1}^{n} p_{il} \cdot v(x_i) + (1 - \sum_{i=1}^{n} p_{il}) \cdot t & \text{if } (v, t) \in G_l \end{cases}$$

where $c_j, d_l \in \mathbb{Q}_+$, $p_{il} \in \mathbb{Q}_+ \cap [0,1]$ such that $\sum_{i=1}^{n} p_{il} \leqslant 1$ and F_j, G_l are rational k-bipolyhedra for all $1 \leqslant i \leqslant n$, $1 \leqslant j \leqslant M$ and $1 \leqslant l \leqslant N$.

We require the following properties of k-nice functions (proofs are available in [15]).

Lemma 2. *A convex combination of rational k-nice functions is rational k-nice.*

Lemma 3. *The minimum of rational k-nice functions is rational k-nice.*

Lemma 4. *For any zone ζ, if $g : (\zeta \times \mathbb{R}) \to \mathbb{R}$ is rational k-nice, then the function $f : \zeta \to \mathbb{R}$ where $f(v) = \inf_{t \in \mathbb{R}} g(v, t)$ for $v \in \zeta$ is rational k-simple.*

We are now in a position to show that that rational k-simple functions are a suitable representation for value functions.

Proposition 2. *If $f : \mathrm{Z} \to (S \to \mathbb{R})$ is a rational k-simple function, then $T_{(\mathrm{Z,E})}(f)$ is rational k-simple.*

Proof. Consider any rational k-simple function, $\mathbf{z} \in \mathrm{Z}$ and $E \in \mathrm{E}(\mathbf{z})$. For any $v \in \mathbb{R}^{\mathcal{X}}$ and $t \in \mathbb{R}$ we have:

$$t + \sum\nolimits_{((l,\zeta),a,(R,l'),(l',\zeta')) \in E} \mathsf{prob}(l,a)(R,l') \cdot f(l',\zeta')(l',(v+t)[R])$$

$$= t + \sum\nolimits_{((l,\zeta),a,(R,l'),(l',\zeta')) \in E} \mathsf{prob}(l,a)(R,l') \cdot f[R](l',\zeta')(l',v+t)$$
$$\text{(by Definition 9)}$$

$$= \sum\nolimits_{((l,\zeta),a,(R,l'),(l',\zeta')) \in E} \mathsf{prob}(l,a)(R,l') \cdot (t + f[R](l',\zeta')(l',v+t)) \qquad (7)$$

since $\mathsf{prob}(l,a)$ is a distribution. By construction f is rational k-simple, and hence for any $(\mathbf{z}, a, (R, l'), \mathbf{z}) \in E$ using Lemma 1 we have $f[R]$ is also rational k-simple. Therefore, it follows from Definition 10 that:

$$(v, t) \mapsto t + f[R](l', \zeta')(l', v+t)$$

is rational k-nice. Thus, since $(\mathbf{z}, a, (R, l'), \mathbf{z}) \in E$ was arbitrary, using Lemma 2 and (7) we have that:

$$(v, t) \mapsto t + \sum\nolimits_{((l,\zeta),a,(R,l'),(l',\zeta')) \in E} \mathsf{prob}(l,a)(R,l') \cdot f(l',\zeta')(l',(v+t)[R])$$

is also rational k-nice. Since $E \in \mathrm{E}(\mathbf{z})$ was arbitrary and $\mathrm{E}(\mathbf{z})$ is finite, Lemma 3 tells us:

$$(v, t) \mapsto \min_{E \in \mathrm{E}(\mathbf{z})} \left\{ t + \sum\nolimits_{((l,\zeta),a,(R,l'),(l',\zeta')) \in E} \mathsf{prob}(l,a)(R,l') \cdot f(l',\zeta')(l',(v+t)[R]) \right\}$$

is again rational k-nice. Finally, using Definition 6 and Lemma 4, it follows that $T_{(\mathrm{Z,E})}(f)(\mathbf{z})$ is rational k-simple as required.   □

Controller Synthesis. We now give an approach for computing the minimum expected time of reaching a target in a PTA and synthesising ε-optimal strategy when starting from the initial state. We first build the backwards zone graph $(\mathrm{Z, E})$ (see Figure 2), then, using Theorem 2 and graph-based algorithms [13], we can find the states of $[\mathcal{P}]$ for which the maximum probability of reaching the target is less than 1 and remove these from the zone graph. Next, using Definition 6, we apply value iteration to the zone graph which, by Proposition 2, can be performed using rational k-simple functions (and rational k-nice functions). Convergence to the minimum expected reachability values of $\mathcal{P}$ is guaranteed by

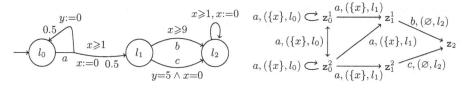

Fig. 3. PTA   **Fig. 4.** Backwards Zone graph

Proposition 1 and Theorem 1. An ε-optimal deterministic, memoryless strategy can be synthesised once value iteration has converged by starting from the initial state and stepping through the backwards graph, in each state choosing the time and action that achieve the values returned by value iteration.

Example 3. The PTA in Figure 3 presents an example where waiting longer than necessary in a location can reduce the time to reach the target. Again we suppose the invariant in all locations is $x \leqslant 10$. The target is location l_2 and the zone graph is given in Figure 4, where $z_0^1 = (l_0, x \geqslant 1)$, $z_0^2 = (l_0, y = 5 \wedge x \geqslant 1)$, $z_1^1 = (l_1, x \geqslant 9)$, $z_1^2 = (l_1, y = 5 \wedge x = 0)$ and $z_2 = (l_2, x \geqslant 1)$. Starting from the constant 0 function f_0 and performing value iteration gives for $n \geqslant 2$:

$$T_{(Z,E)}^n(f_0)(z_0^1) = \begin{cases} (1 - v(x)) + \sum_{i=1}^{n-1} 0.5^n \cdot 9 & \text{if } x \leqslant 1 \\ \sum_{i=1}^n 0.5^{n-1} \cdot 9 & \text{if } 1 \leqslant x \leqslant 10 \end{cases}$$

$$T_{(Z,E)}^n(f_0)(z_0^2) = \begin{cases} (5 - v(y)) + 0.5 \cdot (\sum_{i=1}^n 0.5^{n-1} \cdot 9) & \text{if } y \leqslant 5 \\ 0.5 \cdot (\sum_{i=1}^{n-1} 0.5^{n-1} \cdot 9) & \text{if } 5 \leqslant y \leqslant 10 \end{cases}$$

$$T_{(Z,E)}^n(f_0)(z_1^1) = \begin{cases} 9 - v(x) & \text{if } x \leqslant 9 \\ 0 & \text{if } 9 \leqslant y \leqslant 10 \end{cases}$$

and $T_{(Z,E)}^n(f_0)(z_1^2) = T_{(Z,E)}^n(f_0)(z_2) = 0$. Therefore, value iteration converges to:

$$f(z_0^1) = \begin{cases} (1 - v(x)) + 9 & \text{if } x \leqslant 1 \\ 9 & \text{if } 1 \leqslant x \leqslant 10 \end{cases} \quad \text{and} \quad f(z_0^2) = \begin{cases} (5 - v(y)) + 0.5 \cdot 9 & \text{if } y \leqslant 5 \\ 0.5 \cdot 9 & \text{if } 5 \leqslant y \leqslant 10 \end{cases}$$

and hence the minimum expected time for the initial state equals the minimum of $(1-0)+9$ and $(5-0)+0.5 \cdot 9$, yielding 9.5. Performing controller synthesis we find this corresponds to waiting until $y=5$, then performing the action a. If l_1 is reached, we immediately perform the action c and reach the target. On the other hand, if l_0 is reached, we repeatedly immediately perform a and, if l_1 is reached, wait until $x=9$ and then perform the action b reaching the target.

5   Conclusion

We have proposed an algorithm to compute the minimum expected time to reach a target set in a PTA. The algorithm is formulated as value iteration over the backwards zone graph of the PTA. We also demonstrate that there is an effective representation of the value functions in terms of rational simple and rational nice functions. However, zones are not sufficient and convex polyhedra are required. Nevertheless, the Parma Polyhedra Library [3] offers efficient ways to manipulate convex polyhedra and is commonly used in a variety of real-time verification problems. For example, methods based on priced zones for TAs and PTAs, such as [7] and [22], also use convex polyhedra, where similarly zones do not suffice.

Regarding future work, as well as working on an implementation, we note that optimisations to the backwards algorithm presented in [8], including first performing forwards reachability to restrict analysis to the reachable state space, could be considered here as well. Since policy iteration also converges (see Theorem 1), we plan to investigate this approach and compare with value iteration. Extending to linearly-priced PTAs does not appear straightforward, as rational simple functions are not sufficient. Likewise, the case of maximum expected values raises additional issues, since here one relies on minimum probabilistic reachability, which is more complex to compute using zones and convexity is lost [21].

References

1. Alur, R., Dill, D.L.: A theory of timed automata. TCS **126**, 183–235 (1994)
2. Asarin, E., Maler, O.: As soon as possible: time optimal control for timed automata. In: Vaandrager, F.W., van Schuppen, J.H. (eds.) HSCC 1999. LNCS, vol. 1569, pp. 19–30. Springer, Heidelberg (1999)
3. Bagnara, R., Hill, P.M., Zaffanella, E.: The Parma Polyhedra Library: Toward a complete set of numerical abstractions for the analysis and verification of hardware and software systems. Science of Computer Programming **72**(1–2), 3–21 (2008)
4. Behrmann, G., Fehnker, A., Hune, T., Larsen, K.G., Pettersson, P., Romijn, J.M.T., Vaandrager, F.W.: Minimum-cost reachability for priced timed automata. In: Di Benedetto, M.D., Sangiovanni-Vincentelli, A.L. (eds.) HSCC 2001. LNCS, vol. 2034, pp. 147–161. Springer, Heidelberg (2001)
5. Bellman, R.: Dynamic Programming. Princeton University Press (1957)
6. Berendsen, J., Chen, T., Jansen, D.N.: Undecidability of cost-bounded reachability in priced probabilistic timed automata. In: Chen, J., Cooper, S.B. (eds.) TAMC 2009. LNCS, vol. 5532, pp. 128–137. Springer, Heidelberg (2009)
7. Berendsen, J., Jansen, D., Katoen, J.-P.: Probably on time and within budget - on reachability in priced probabilistic timed automata. In: Proc. QEST 2006. IEEE Press (2006)
8. Berendsen, J., Jansen, D., Vaandrager, F.: Fortuna: Model checking priced probabilistic timed automata. In: Proc. QEST 2010. IEEE Press (2010)
9. Bertsekas, D.: Dynamic Programming and Optimal Control, vol. 1 and 2. Athena Scientific (1995)
10. Bertsekas, D., Tsitsiklis, J.: An analysis of stochastic shortest path problems. Mathematics of Operations Research **16**(3), 580–595 (1991)
11. Bulychev, P., David, A., Larsen, K., Mikučionis, M., Poulsen, D.B., Legay, A., Wang, Z.: UPPAAL-SMC: statistical model checking for priced timed automata. In: Proc. QAPL 2012, vol. 85 of EPTCS. Open Publishing Association (2012)
12. David, A., Jensen, P.G., Larsen, K.G., Legay, A., Lime, D., Sørensen, M.G., Taankvist, J.H.: On time with minimal expected cost!. In: Cassez, F., Raskin, J.-F. (eds.) ATVA 2014. LNCS, vol. 8837, pp. 129–145. Springer, Heidelberg (2014)

13. de Alfaro, L.: Computing minimum and maximum reachability times in probabilistic systems. In: Baeten, J.C.M., Mauw, S. (eds.) CONCUR 1999. LNCS, vol. 1664, pp. 66–81. Springer, Heidelberg (1999)

14. James, H., Collins, E.: An analysis of transient Markov decision processes. Journal of Applied Probability **43**(3), 603–621 (2006)

15. Jovanović, A., Kwiatkowska, M., Norman, G.: Symbolic minimum expected time controller synthesis for probabilistic timed automata. Technical Report CS-RR-15-04, Oxford University (2015)

16. Kemeny, J., Snell, J., Knapp, A.: Denumerable Markov Chains. Springer (1976)

17. Kwiatkowska, M., Norman, G., Parker, D.: Stochastic games for verification of probabilistic timed automata. In: Ouaknine, J., Vaandrager, F.W. (eds.) FORMATS 2009. LNCS, vol. 5813, pp. 212–227. Springer, Heidelberg (2009)

18. Kwiatkowska, M., Norman, G., Parker, D.: PRISM 4.0: verification of probabilistic real-time systems. In: Gopalakrishnan, G., Qadeer, S. (eds.) CAV 2011. LNCS, vol. 6806, pp. 585–591. Springer, Heidelberg (2011)

19. Kwiatkowska, M., Norman, G., Parker, D., Sproston, J.: Performance analysis of probabilistic timed automata using digital clocks. FMSD **29**, 33–78 (2006)

20. Kwiatkowska, M., Norman, G., Segala, R., Sproston, J.: Automatic verification of real-time systems with discrete probability distributions. TCS **282**, 101–150 (2002)

21. Kwiatkowska, M., Norman, G., Sproston, J., Wang, F.: Symbolic model checking for probabilistic timed automata. Information and Computation **205**(7), 1027–1077 (2007)

22. Larsen, K.G., Behrmann, G., Brinksma, E., Fehnker, A., Hune, T., Pettersson, P., Romijn, J.M.T.: As cheap as possible: efficient cost-optimal reachability for priced timed automata. In: Berry, G., Comon, H., Finkel, A. (eds.) CAV 2001. LNCS, vol. 2102, pp. 493–505. Springer, Heidelberg (2001)

23. Larsen, K.G., Pettersson, P., Yi, W.: UPPAAL in a Nutshell. Int. Journal on Software Tools for Technology Transfer **1**, 134–152 (1997)

24. Tripakis, S.: The analysis of timed systems in practice. PhD thesis, Université Joseph Fourier, Grenoble (1998)

25. Tripakis, S.: Verifying progress in timed systems. In: Katoen, J.-P. (ed.) AMAST-ARTS 1999, ARTS 1999, and AMAST-WS 1999. LNCS, vol. 1601, pp. 299–314. Springer, Heidelberg (1999)

26. Tripakis, S., Yovine, S., Bouajjan, A.: Checking timed Büchi automata emptiness efficiently. Formal Methods in System Design **26**(3), 267–292 (2005)

Quantitative Attack Tree Analysis via Priced Timed Automata

Rajesh Kumar[✉], Enno Ruijters, and Mariëlle Stoelinga

Formal Methods and Tools, University of Twente, Enschede, The Netherlands
r.Kumar@utwente.nl

Abstract. The success of a security attack crucially depends on the resources available to an attacker: time, budget, skill level, and risk appetite. Insight in these dependencies and the most vulnerable system parts is key to providing effective counter measures.

This paper considers attack trees, one of the most prominent security formalisms for threat analysis. We provide an effective way to compute the resources needed for a successful attack, as well as the associated attack paths. These paths provide the optimal ways, from the perspective of the attacker, to attack the system, and provide a ranking of the most vulnerable system parts.

By exploiting the priced timed automaton model checker Uppaal CORA, we realize important advantages over earlier attack tree analysis methods: we can handle more complex gates, temporal dependencies between attack steps, shared subtrees, and realistic, multi-parametric cost structures. Furthermore, due to its compositionality, our approach is flexible and easy to extend.

We illustrate our approach with several standard case studies from the literature, showing that our method agrees with existing analyses of these cases, and can incorporate additional data, leading to more informative results.

1 Introduction

Security attacks are a primary concern for business and government organizations, as they are a threat to vital infrastructure, such as internet banking, power grids, health care and transportation systems. The challenge for security engineers is to protect such systems, by providing countermeasures for the most damaging and most likely attacks. Thus, defense against cyberattacks is an optimization problem: given the available budget, what are the most effective countermeasures.

Often security decisions are made informally, e.g. by brainstorming. More structured approaches are based on spreadsheets and technical standards, like FMEA [11], the AS/NZS 4360 standard [5], and Factor Analysis of Information Risks (FAIR) [6]. Model-based approaches are gaining popularity, such as the UML-based extension CORAS [1], the ADVISE method [21], and security extension of the SAE standardized language AADL [17].

© Springer International Publishing Switzerland 2015
S. Sankaranarayanan and E. Vicario (Eds.): FORMATS 2015, LNCS 9268, pp. 156–171, 2015.
DOI: 10.1007/978-3-319-22975-1_11

One of the most prominent model-based security formalisms is attack trees (ATs), see Figure 1. Much of its popularity comes from its hierarchical, intuitive representation of multi-step attack scenarios. A wide range of qualitative and quantitative analysis methods for attack trees are available, see [20] for an overview. The most well-known follow a bottom-up approach and propagate values from the leaves to the top of the tree. Although they are very efficient and flexible, most current approaches cannot handle temporal and causal dependencies, or shared subtrees. Also, existing approaches do not support realistic cost structures. Finally, little attention is given to the important issue of attack path generation and ranking: which steps are taken in the most dangerous attacks?

This paper provides a multi-objective optimization framework for attack trees. We augment AT leaves with a rich cost structure that consists of various components, such as time, skill, and resources. These components can be dependent, e.g. time can depend on skill level. Our framework supports the computation of a wide range of security metrics: (1) *Attack values.* Given an attack tree, and a quantity of interest, we can compute its value: What is the minimal time, resources, or skill level needed to complete a successful attack? What is the maximal damage an attacker can do? (2) *Attack paths.* Apart from the value of an attack, it is very useful to know the attack path leading to the optimal attack. Note that the path is in fact a subtree, since optimal attacks often carry out several steps need in parallel. (3) *Ranking.* Apart from computing the optimal attack values and path, we can also determine the top-10 of worst attacks, which is very important to determine appropriate counter measures. (4) *Pareto-optimal curves* that show trade-offs when multiple objectives conflict. For instance, what is the minimal time needed to complete a successful attack within a given budget? What is the maximal damage that can be incurred in one year?

Technically, our framework is realized via Uppaal CORA: we translate each attack tree gate and leaf into a priced timed automata (PTA). Together these form a network of PTAs representing the entire attack tree. This modular approach yields a flexible framework that can easily be extended with future needs, such as countermeasures. We express our security queries in weighted CTL, and use the model checker Uppaal CORA [8] to obtain the cost optimal traces that correspond to optimal attack paths in the AT.

We illustrate our approach with several well-known examples in attack tree analysis, namely the forestalling release of software [18], obtaining administrator privileges [19] and a password protected file [25]. We provide the results from two perspectives: For the attacker, we consider cost and time, and for the attackee, the incurred damage. Also, we have considered several attacker profiles into consideration. Our analysis shows that the vulnerable paths in the system are strongly linked to the skills and risk appetite of attacker. Hence, any security risk analysis should be multifaceted, taking the potential attackers into consideration.

Related Work. Attack trees; as popularized by Schneier [27], were introduced by Weiss as threat logic trees [30] and by Amoroso as threat trees [3]. Amid several variants studied in literature, they can broadly be classified as *static* [19, 23, 26] or *dynamic* [15, 24] based on evolution of time. Classically, an attack tree takes a single parameter such as time or cost [23, 27]. Buldas [14] et al. introduces a multiparameter attack tree consisting of interdependent parameters. In [22], Lenin et al., while making a clear distinction between threat and vulnerability landscape, improve the parallel model [18] by integrating attacker profiles. A comprehensive overview of attack trees can be found in [20]. Some other approaches to model the system description and attacker behaviour are via attack graphs [28] or adversary based security analysis [13, 16].

2   Graphical Security Modeling

2.1   Attack Trees

Attack trees (ATs) are an important formalism to model and analyze the security of complex systems. An attack tree consists of a *root*, representing the attacker's goal. The root is further refined into subgoals via *gates*, until the subgoals cannot be refined further and the *basic attack steps (BASs)* are reached, constituting the leaves of the attack tree. When subtrees can be shared, ATs can be directed acyclic graphs, rather than trees.

Gates. Classical attack trees model the propagation of success through AND- and OR-gates: an AND-gate is a conjunctive composition of child nodes, indicating that all children need to be successfully attacked for an attacker to successfully execute the subgoal at hand. Similarly, the OR-gate is a disjunctive union of child nodes, where an attacker has to execute at least one child node successfully.

It has been widely recognized that temporal order is crucial in security. Therefore, the sequential versions of the AND and OR gates, named SAND and SOR, have been proposed [4, 25]. Both represent attacks executed from left to right: Starting with the the leftmost child, the attacker will only start executing the next subgoal (i.e., the subsequent child node) after all previous subgoals have been executed successfully. The SAND gate is successful if all steps are executed successfully; the SOR-gate is successful if any of its children is executed successfully.

Example 1. The attack tree in Figure 1, combined with the values in Table 1, models the forestalling of the release of some software, adopted from [14]. Here, a competitor steals a piece of software code and then builds it into his own product, as modeled by the top-level SAND gate. The OR gate at node *Steal code* shows that the code can be stolen in three different ways: via *Bribing*, a *Network Attack* or *Physical robbery*. Bribing is modeled as a two-step sequential process of first successfully bribing a programmer and then obtaining the code, represented by a SAND-gate. Similarly, one can employ a robber who has networking knowledge. This can lead to two different attack paths modeled through a shared node. One in which the hired person finds a bug and exploits it to obtain the code via a network attack, and another path in which he is physically involved in a robbery after being hired to steal the code. This dependency is again modeled through a SAND gate.

Basic Attack Steps. Basic attack steps (BASs) represent individual atomic steps within a composite attack, and appear as leaves of the AT.

We consider a fixed set of attribute variables $\mathsf{Attr} = \{T, a_1, \ldots a_n\}$. Here, T is a special attribute, namely the time since the BAS was started. Other attributes can be skill level, monetary costs, damage, difficulty, etc. We denote by $Val = (\mathbb{R}_{\geq 0}^{\infty})^{n+1}$ the set of complete valuations of the attributes, and by $Val_{\backslash t} = (\mathbb{R}_{\geq 0}^{\infty})^n$ the set of valuations excluding time. For simplicity, we assume that attribute variables take values in $\mathbb{R}_{\geq 0}^{\infty}$; handling other domains is technically no more complex, but syntactically more cumbersome.

Each BAS is equipped with two preconditions $Enable : Val_{\backslash t} \to \{0, 1\}$ and $CanSucceed : Val \to \{0, 1\}$ that indicate when the BAS is enabled, and when it can succeed. Each BAS also has an effect Eff that updates the attribute values when the BAS is successfully executed. Preconditions are Boolean combinations over linear equations over Attr. In this way, an attack step that requires (at least) medium skill level is equipped with the enabling precondition $Skill \geq med$ (where med is a suitable constant); and an attack step that takes between 90 and 100 time units for medium-skilled attackers gets a success precondition ($Skill = med$) $\to (90 \leq T \leq 100)$.

The effect $Eff : \mathsf{Attr} \times Val_{\backslash t} \to \mathbb{R}_{\geq 0} \to \mathbb{R}_{\geq 0}$ is a function that updates the values for the attributes when this BAS is started. For example, costs are incurred by the attacker, and damage is incurred by the attacked entity. These effects are typically time dependent: the longer an attack takes, the higher the costs and damage. We assume that time dependence is linear, i.e., is incurred with a fixed rate v_i per time unit. Thus, the effect function is given by $Eff(a_i, (p_1, \ldots, p_n))(t) = f_i + v_i \cdot t$, where $f_i = f_i(p_1, \ldots p_n)$ and $v_i = v_i(p_1, \ldots p_n)$ are parameters that depend on the attribute values. The effects are summed to the existing value of the variable, to obtain the cumulative effect.

Attacker Profiles. An attacker profile is an assignment $R : \{a_1, \ldots a_n\} \to \mathbb{R}_{\geq 0}$ of the non-time attribute variables to concrete values. Thus, we obtain an initial valuation of the attributes as $(0, R(a_1), \ldots, R(a_n))$.

Example. Consider an burglary that takes between 5 and 10 minutes to execute for a medium-skilled attacker, between 1 and 2 minutes for a highly

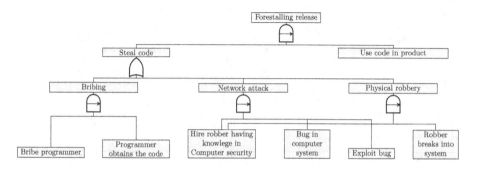

Fig. 1. Attack tree modeling the forestalling of software.

skilled attacker, and cannot be performed by a low-skilled attacker. All attackers steal 1000 dollars worth of goods if they are successful, but the medium-skilled attacker also inflicts 500 dollars of property damage in the process. This BAS can be described using the attribute set $\mathsf{Attr} = \{T, Skill, Damage\}$. It has enabling precondition $Enable(s, d) = s \geq med$ and success condition $CanSucceed(t, s, d) = (s = med \wedge 5 \leq t \leq 10) \vee (s = hi \wedge 1 \leq t \leq 2)$. The effect is $Eff(Damage, (s, d))(t) = 1000$ if $s = hi, 1500$ otherwise and $Eff(a, V)(t) = 0$ for all $a \neq Damage$ (here med and hi are appropriate constants).

Based on the explanation above, attack trees can be defined as follows.

Definition 1 (AT elements). *We define the set of AT gate types as* $\mathsf{Gates} = \{AND, SAND, OR, SOR\}$, *the set of BAS information as* BAI, *where each element of* BAI *is a triple* $(Enable, CanSucceed, Eff)$ *of the functions described above. We denote* $\mathsf{Elements} = \mathsf{Gates} \cup \mathsf{BAI}$.

Definition 2 (Attack tree). *An attack tree A is a tuple* $(V, \mathsf{Child}, \mathsf{Top}, \mathsf{Attr}, R, L)$, *where*

- *V is a finite set of nodes.*
- *$\mathsf{Child} : V \to V^*$ maps each node to its child nodes.*
- *$\mathsf{Top} \in V$ is the unique top level element, representing the goal of the attacker.*
- *Attr is the set of attributes.*
- *R is the attacker profile.*
- *$L : V \to \mathsf{Elements}$ is a labelling function that assigns an AT element to each node in V.*

ATs must be well-formed. We define the set of *edges* of A by $E = \{(v, w) \in V^2 \mid \exists i . w = (\mathsf{Child}(v))_i\}$ and $\mathsf{Leaves} = \{v \in V \mid \mathsf{Child}(v) = \epsilon\}$. We require for each AT that (a) the graph (V, E) is a directed acyclic graph with a unique root $\mathsf{Top} \in V$ from which all other nodes are reachable; (b) the labelling function assigns to each leaf in the tree a value in BAI and to each non-leaf an element in Gates, i.e., $L(v) \in \mathsf{BAI}$ iff $v \in \mathsf{Leaves}$.

Table 1. Values used for annotating leaves of Figure 1

BAS	Attacker		Values		
	Profile	Skill	Time (in days)	Cost (in US $)	Cost to company (in US $)
Bribe a programmer	Generic attacker	Low	15-20	1500 + 50t	500.000
	Generic attacker	Med	10-20	1000 + 150t	500.000
	Generic attacker	High	0-10	500	500.000
	Software Engineer	Any	0-5	5000 + 100t	500.000
Programmer obtains the code	Generic attacker	Any	5-15	1000 + 100t	1.000.000
	Software Engineer	Any	0-5	2000 + 50t	1.000.000
Hire robber with knowledge of computer security	Any	Any	5-15	4000 + 50t	0
Bug in Computer system	Any	Low	15-20	1000 + 50t	0
	Any	Med	5-10	1000 + 50t	0
	Any	High	0-5	1000 + 50t	0
Person exploits the bug	Any	Any	0-5	1000 + 50t	1.000.000
Person breaks into the system	Any	Any	0-5	2000 + 100t	400.000
Code is completed into product	Any	Any	5-15	2000 + 50t	100.000

2.2 Metrics on ATs

Our framework can be used to determine several important security metrics. (1) *(Constrained) attack values.* For any of the attributes a_i, we can compute the minimum value along the tree. These values can be affected by constraints on other attributes. For instance, we can compute the minimum time needed to complete an attack within a maximum budget and skill level. (2) *Pareto optimal curves.* For any pair of attributes, we can compute the minimum value needed of one attribute given a value of the other. By varying the bound of one attribute, we can generate curves indicating the relation between these minima. For instance, there is typically a trade-off between spending more time or more money; a Pareto curve shows for every budget how much time is needed for the attack. (3) *Attack paths.* When computing the minimal value of an attribute that can complete an attack, we generate a concrete attack path showing the steps an attacker can take to perform the attack incurring as little of the attribute as possible. For instance, considering Figure 1, to reach the goal in the minimum time, we can obtain the attack trace which consists of *Hire a robberer, Robberer breaks into system* and *Use code in product.* (4) *Ranking.* In addition to the single minimum of an attribute and a corresponding attack path, we can enumerate further attacks in increasing value of the attribute. We can, for example, list the ten cheapest attacks on a given system, or all attack paths that meet a given time constraint. For example, in Figure 1, with the attributes in Table 1, the optimal cost is 6000 units and the second best cost is 8500 units.

3   Priced Timed Automata

The Priced Timed Automata Model. Priced timed automata (PTA) [8] extend timed automata [2], by adding costs to locations and actions. In the following definition, we denote by $\Phi(X)$ the set of all possible boolean predicates over a set X of clocks.

Definition 3. *A priced timed automaton* P *is a tuple* $\langle L, l_0, X, Act, E, I, C \rangle$ *where:*

- L *is a finite set of* locations,
- $l_0 \in L$ *is the initial state,*
- X *is a set of clock variables,*
- Act *is a set of actions, also called signals or labels,*
- $E \subseteq L \times \Phi(X) \times Act \times 2^X \times L$ *gives the set of transitions. Here an edge* $\langle l, \phi, a, \lambda, l' \rangle$ *represents a transition from state* l *to state* l' *taking an action* a. *This transition can only be taken when the clock constraint* ϕ *over* X *is true, and the set* $\lambda \subseteq X$ *gives the set of clocks to be reset with this transition,*
- $I : L \to \Phi(X)$ *assigns invariants to locations,*
- $C : L \cup E \to \mathbb{N}^n_{\geq 0}$ *assigns cost rates to locations and costs to edges.*

Definition 4. *A trace of a PTA* $P = \langle L, l_0, X, Act, E, I, C \rangle$ *is a sequence of states and transitions* $\rho = l_0 \xrightarrow[\lambda_0]{a_0, t_0}_{c_0} l_1 \xrightarrow[\lambda_1]{a_1, t_1}_{c_1} l_2 \ldots$ *where:*

- For every i, there is some transition $T_i = (l_i, \phi_i, a_i, \lambda_i, l_{i+1}) \in E$.
- For every i, $c_i = C(T_i) + t_i \cdot C(l_i)$ is the cost incurred in the transition.
- There is an initial clock valuation $X_0 = 0$.
- After every transition, there is a new clock valuation $X_{i+1} = (X_i + t_i)[\lambda_i = 0]$ obtained by increasing every clock variable in X_i by t_i and resetting all clocks in λ_i to 0.
- Every clock valuation $X_i + t$ for $t < t_i$ satisfies the invariant $I(l_i)$.
- The clock valuation $X_i + t_i$ satisfies ϕ_i for every i.

Parallel Composition. The parallel composition operator $\parallel$ allows one to construct a large PTA from several smaller ones. The component PTAs synchronize their transitions via joint signals. For example, a basic attack step can send a 'success' signal to its parent gate, based on which this gate may itself succeed or wait for signals from its other children. Our models use broadcast signals, which can be either output, denoted with an exclamation mark (e.g. 'succ!'), or input, denoted with a question mark (e.g. 'succ?'). We require PTAs to be input-enabled, that is, all input actions of a PTA are enabled at any location, at any time. Thus, if some PTA performs a transition labeled with an output action $a!$, then all receiving PTAs synchronize by taking an $a?$-labeled transition. The formal definition can be found in the Uppaal CORA documentation [29], or in [9].

Queries. We express our security questions in an extension of the *Weighted CTL* logic [12], over a PTA whose locations l are decorated with a set of atomic propositions $Prop(l) \subseteq AP$. We slightly extend the syntax given by [10]: Rather than providing a single constraint $v \sim c$ asking that value v meets bound c, we need a vector of constraints $x_i \sim c_i$, asking that all values v_i meets their bounds c_i.

Definition 5. *The syntax of the WCTL logic is given by the following grammar:*

$$WCTL \ni \phi, \psi ::= p \mid \neg\phi \mid \phi \wedge \psi \mid \exists(\phi \ U_{\sim \mathbf{c}} \ \psi) \mid \forall(\phi \ U_{\sim \mathbf{c}} \ \psi)$$

Where $p \in AP$, $\mathbf{c} \in \mathbb{R}_{\geq 0}^n$, and $\sim \in \{<, \leq, =, \geq, >\}^n$.

The semantics of the boolean operators follows the usual conventions. The existential until operator $\exists(\phi U_{\sim \mathbf{c}} \psi)$ is true if there exists a trace of the PTA in which some state s_f satisfies ψ, all states before s_f satisfy ϕ, and the total costs incurred before reaching s_f satisfy the relation $\sim \mathbf{c}$. Note that time is considered a cost in this notation. The universal until operator is similar, except that the conditions must hold for every trace. As usual, $\exists\Diamond_{\sim \mathbf{c}}\phi$ is shorthand for $\exists(\text{true } U_{\sim \mathbf{c}}\phi)$.

Uppaal CORA. Uppaal CORA is an extension of Uppaal with an additional variable *Cost* used for optimal scheduling and cost optimal reachability analysis. With the inbuilt *Best trace option*; it can be used to it find an optimal trace [7]. The rate of change of cost is specified as *Cost'*. Here, the optimal path refers to the trace with the lowest accumulated costs.

4   Analyzing Attack Trees via Price Timed Automata

To analyze an attack tree, we provide a compositional semantics in terms of priced timed automata. That is, we translate each AT element into a PTA and obtain the PTA for the entire AT by putting together all element PTAs via the parallel composition operator $\|$. Then, we analyze ATs by formulating the security measures as queries in the logic mWCTL, which is a slightly extended version of standard weighted computational tree logic that allows us to perform multi-criterion optimization.

In this way, we obtain a versatile and flexible framework for AT analysis. Indeed, if one wants to add a new AT element to the framework, one can simply provide the AT translation, while leaving the rest of the framework unchanged.

4.1   From Attack Trees to Price Timed Automata

Basic Attack Steps. The PTA for a basic attack step v is shown in Figure 2. This PTA models the attacker's choice of whether and when to execute basic attack step, and tracks the time and costs used to do so.

Formally, we convert a BAS S with BAI $(Enable, CanSucceed, Eff)$, given attacker profile R, into a PTA $P(S) = \langle L, l_0, X, Act, E, I, C \rangle$ with elements:

- $L = \{I, A, B, F, D\}$
- $l_0 = I$
- $X = \{x\}$
- $Act = \{Act_S?, succ_S!, fail_S!, \tau\}$
- $E = \{\langle I, \top, Act_S?, \emptyset, A \rangle, \langle A, Enable(R), \tau, \{x\}, B \rangle,$
   $\langle B, \top, fail_S!, \emptyset, F \rangle, \langle B, CanSucceed(R), succ_S!, \emptyset, D \rangle\}$
- $I(l) = \top$

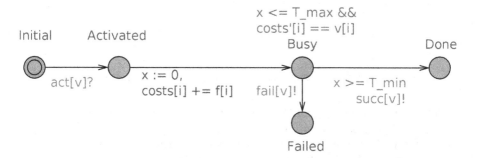

Fig. 2. PTA for a basic attack step. Here v is a unique identifier for the BAS, x is a clock to track the duration of BAS$[v]$, T_min and T_max are the minimum and maximum times, *costs* is an array keeping track of all accumulated costs, and *costs'* is an array for variable costs.

– $C(e) =$
$$\begin{cases} \bigoplus_{i=1}^{n} \mathit{Eff}(a_i, R)(0) & \text{if } e = \langle A, \mathit{Enable}(R), \tau, \{x\}, B\rangle \\ \bigoplus_{i=1}^{n}(\mathit{Eff}(a_i, R)(1) - \mathit{Eff}(a_i, R)(0)) & \text{if } e = B \\ 0 & \text{otherwise} \end{cases}$$

Here we slightly abuse the notation so that $f(R)$ denotes the result of applying f to the valuation obtained from R of all the attributes, and $\bigoplus$ denotes the combination of elements into a vector.

Initially, the BAS waits for an activation signal. As it is received from the parent, the attacker may begin executing the step by incurring the fixed costs. The execution of a BAS is bounded by the minimum and maximum time to complete the attack. While the step is being performed, the variable costs are incurred. The attack may fail at any time, stop incurring further costs and send a failure signal to its parents. Otherwise, it succeeds between the minimum and maximum time constraint for the step and transmits a success signal.

Gates. To model attacker preferences and behavior as illustrated in example 1, we distinguish between sequential and parallel gates. The automata for the parallel AND gate is shown in Figure 3 while the automata for sequential AND gate is shown in Figure 4.

The gates depicted here have only two children. We can construct PTAs having more than two children, however this is cumbersome and requires many more states. Hence, we express AT gates with multiple children by simply chaining two-input gates: For example, an AND-gate with inputs A, B, and C can also be expressed as $A \wedge (B \wedge C)$.

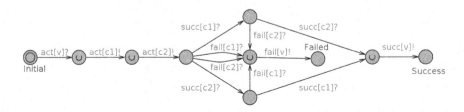

Fig. 3. PTA for parallel AND gate of node v, when $child(v) = c_1 c_2$.

Note that the semantics of OR and AND gates are identical except that the behaviours of success and failure are inverted.

The PTAs for these gates begin by waiting for their activation signal, and activating their children. After this, they wait for one of their children to send a signal. For an AND gate, receiving a failure signal always leads the gate to emit its own failure signal, since it is no longer possible for both children to succeed. Conversely, when an OR gate receives one success signal, it always emits its own success. When both children of an AND or OR gate have succeeded or resp. failed, the gate also succeeds or fails.

The sequential gates operate similarly, but they enforce an ordering on their children. First the leftmost child is activated, and the gate waits for a signal from this child. In case of an SAND gate, success of the first child leads to an activation of the second child, and the success of this child cause the success of the gate. Failure of either child leads to failure of the gate, possibly before even activating the second child. The behavior of SOR is similar to sequential AND with success and failure signals swapped.

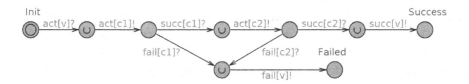

Fig. 4. PTA for sequential AND gate of node v, when $child(v) = c_1 c_2$.

Combining the Nodes. For an attack tree A, the PTA associated with A is obtained as the parallel composition of the PTAs for all the nodes, and an additional PTA A_{Top}. If we denote by $P(v, A)$ the PTA corresponding to node v of attack tree A, the total PTA consists of $P_A = P(v_1, A)||P(v_2, A)|| \ldots ||P(v_n, A)||A_{\mathsf{Top}}$.

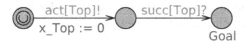

Fig. 5. Automaton for the attack goal Top

The top-level gate Top is associated with a second PTA A_{Top}, shown in Figure 5 that initializes the attack by generating an activation signal for Top. Moreover, it has a clock x_{Top} that tracks the global time, and observes successful completion of an attack via its input $succ[\mathsf{Top}]?$. Thus, the location 'Goal' indicates that an attacker has reached the goal.

4.2   Quantitative Analysis of Attack Trees

Given the PTA for an attack tree, we can compute the security metrics as enumerated in Section 2.2 as follows:

(Unconstrained) Attack Values and Attack Paths: The Uppaal CORA program has a built-in method to find an optimum if only one cost needs to be tracked. Here, we obtain the *Optimal accumulated costs* through the 'Best first' function built-in Uppaal CORA.

(Constrained) Attack Values and Attack Paths: Optimal attack values can be obtained by repeatedly querying for the existence of traces reaching the attack goal with increasingly tight constraints. When the tightest possible bound has been obtained, this corresponds to an optimum. Since a positive result for the query also produces a trace that satisfies it, this procedure also yields an optimal attack path.

For example, to obtain the minimum time to succeed in the AT in Figure 1 given a cost limit of 10000 (assuming this is the only cost variable), we first query $\exists \Diamond_{x_{\mathsf{Top}} \geq 0, C \leq 10000}(P_{\mathsf{Top}}.Goal)$ to obtain some successful attack and its corresponding time, e.g. Suppose this yields an attack that takes 10 days to complete, then we perform a new query $\exists \Diamond_{x_{\mathsf{Top}} < 10, C \leq 10000}(P_{\mathsf{Top}}.Goal)$ to try to find a faster attack. If no such attack exists, we know that the minimal time to complete an attack given the budget is 10 days, and we have obtained an attack path that succeeds in this time and budget.

Ranking: To find different attacks ranked according to their cost, we repeat the procedure above, each time excluding the attack paths we have already found. For example, if the attack consisting of BASs 1 and 3 is the fastest possible attack, the second-fastest is found using the query $\exists \Diamond_{x_{\mathsf{Top}} \leq T}(P_{\mathsf{Top}}.Goal \wedge \neg(P(v_1, A).Success \wedge P(v_3, A).Success))$ and finding the smallest value for T to obtain the second-fastest attack. This process can be repeated until the desired number of optimal attacks has been found.

Pareto Optimal Curves: Pareto optimal curves can be obtained by finding the optimal attacks subject to an increasing constraint. For example, to find the curve of minimal time vs. cost, we begin by finding the minimal time to attack, and computing the lowest-cost attack that meets this time bound. Then, we compute the minimal time to attack with a smaller budget, and again find the lowest-cost attack that meets the new time bound. This process is repeated until no attacks exist that meet the latest budget.

To illustrate, consider again the attack tree in Figure 1. The minimal time to complete an attack is 5 days, and the lowest-cost attack that meets this time limits costs $9250. The fastest attack that costs less than $9250 takes 10 days, and the lowest cost attack that can be performed within 10 days costs $8500. There is no attack that costs less than $8500. Thus we obtain the pareto curve shown in Figure 7.

5   Case Studies

We demonstrate our approach through three well-known case studies taken from the literature. For each case, we analyze optimal attack values such as time and cost for the attacker, and the minimal damage borne by the company by taking different attacker profiles. Here, we consider the attacker's resources (time and budget), skills, motivation, access to infrastructure, risk appetite, and preferences as attributes of a rational attacker.

As is often the case in security analysis, it is difficult to obtain precise data, and our guesses are not intended to reflect reality, but rather to illustrate the analysis method.

Table 2. Analysis results for the cracking password protected file.

Profile	Criterion	Attack value	Attack Path		
			BAS	Time	Cost
Generic attacker	Minimum cost	7250	Dictionary	0 - 15	7250
	2nd best min. cost	7250	Brute force	0 - 15	7250
	Minimum time	15	Bruteforce	0 - 15	7250
	Min. cost to company	0	Guessing	0 - 15	7250
Social Worker	Minimum cost	4000	Generic reconnaissance	0 - 0	50
			Phone trap Execution	0 - 15	3500
	2nd best min. cost	4500	Generic reconnaissance (*fails*)	0 - 0	500
			Physical reconnaissance	0 - 0	500
			Key logger local installation	0 - 5	1750
			Password intercept	5 - 10	1750
	Minimum time	10	Generic reconnaissance (*fails*)	0 - 0	500
			Physical reconnaissance	0 - 0	500
			Key logger local installation	0 - 5	1750
			Password intercept	5 - 10	1750
	Min. cost to company	0	Dictionary	0 - 15	7250

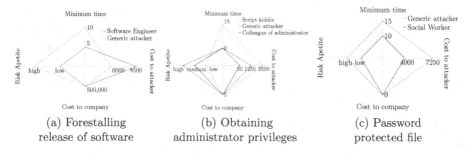

(a) Forestalling release of software

(b) Obtaining administrator privileges

(c) Password protected file

Fig. 6. Analysis of attacker attributes in all three case studies.

The attack steps are decorated with the time required to successfully execute the step, as well as fixed and variable costs incurred by the attacker. These values are specified for the different attacked roles and skills levels. A cost for the attacked company is also included, but this is independent of the attacker profile.

Our analysis can provides insightful information about vulnerable paths and values relevant to risk managers. An input table is provided as Table 1 for Case study 1 to illustrate our methodology and we use similar

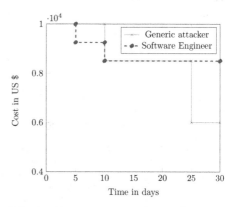

Fig. 7. Pareto curve of attack tree in Figure 1

scale to perform other case studies provided in the paper. The exact values for other case studies will be provided in a detailed report.

Forestalling release of software. As elaborated in Example 1, the AT in Figure 1 models the forestalling of software from [18]. We consider two attacker profiles:

A generic attacker and a software engineer. The generic attacker is profit-motivated and has a high risk appetite, but is not particularly skilled in this type of attack. The software engineer has better access, skills, equipment, but low risk appetite. The role of the attacker and the skill level are explicitly included in the attacker profile, while the other attributes are reflected in the values of time and cost to perform the step.

Formally, the profile of the generic attacker is defined by $R_{GA}(Role) =$ '*Generic Attacker*' and $R_{GA}(Skill) = $ '*Low*'. Similarly, the profile for the software engineer is $R_{SE}(Role) = $ '*Software Engineer*' and $R_{SE}(Skill) = $ '*High*'.

Table 1 shows the input parameters. The analysis results are presented as a Pareto curve in Figure 7, where the generic attacker requires 10 days incurring a minimum cost of $9250 while a software engineer incurs a cost of $8500, but can complete the attack in 5 days.

Here, we see that both attack values and the choice of attack path heavily depend on the attacker profile. In contrast to the generic attacker whose cost optimal attack trace is to bribe a programmer, a better skilled software engineer exploits a bug in the computer system to steal the code. The minimum time required to accomplish the attack also heavily depends on which attack steps are executed and when. While a generic attacker takes 10 days to successfully execute the attack by physical robbery, a software engineer with insider benefits takes only 5 days to accomplish his goal. Also, there is an attack trace i.e *Hire a robber, Robber breaks into system, Code is completed into product* which results in an *optimum Cost to company* as $500,000 irrespective of the considered attacker profiles.

Cracking a password protected file. The attack tree depicted in Figure 8 models an attack on a password protected file. It is taken from [25] and modified to add SAND and SOR gates. The goal of the attack is to obtain a password. This, can be done by either performing a *brute force attack* or taking a multistep approach

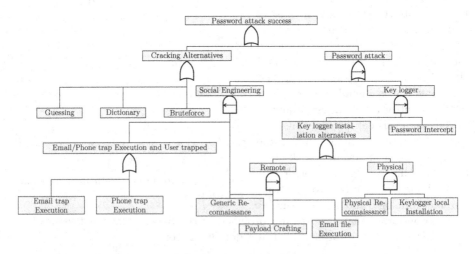

Fig. 8. Dynamic Attack Tree modelling the attack on password protected file.

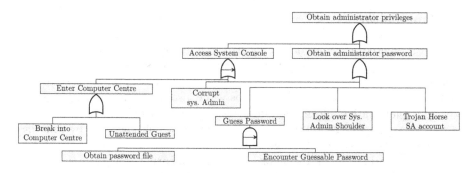

Fig. 9. To obtain administrator privileges.

of trying a *password attack*. To model different attacker behavior, we take two attackers profiles into account.

A generic attacker who is a profit-motivated, skilled professional willing to bear penalties; and a social worker, a popular public figure who is also profit-motivated, but has a low risk appetite. Table 2 tabulates the optimum attack values and traces which illustrate that adversarial behavior greatly depends on his possessed attributes and his perceived goal. While a social worker; being good in social engineering can crack the password in minimum 10 days through *Physical reconnaissance*, he prefers *Generic reconnaissance* for achieving his goal, incurring the minimum cost of $4000 US. In contrast, a generic attacker prefers more technical approaches like *Bruteforce* in achieving his goal in a minimum time of 15 days and *Dictionary attack* by incurring the minimum cost of $7250.

Obtaining administrator privileges. The goal of the attack tree in Figure 9 is to obtain administrator privileges and has been adopted from [19]. We consider three different attacker profiles for our analysis.

A generic attacker who is a professional hacker, with high risk appetite and malicious intentions to disrupt the availability of the system; a script kiddie fearful by conscience trying to hack just for fun and who has low risk taking ability; and an insider: a colleague of a system administrator with better access to the computer center. The insider, knowing system details expects a huge profit from the attack and is this willing to bear risk to a greater extent. The results in Figure 6(b) show that the colleague of the system administrator, knowing the vulnerabilities of the system, can reach the goal with minimal investments. Having less resources, a juvenile attacker's optimal cost and time are both higher than professional generic attacker and the malicious insider. Note that the fastest attack may not be the cheapest one due to several attack steps being performed concurrently under different constraints of time and base costs.

Figure 6 provides a succinct representation of these different attack scenarios. We put the attacker objectives as vertices (i.e Minimum cost, Minimal time, Risk appetite, Cost to company) and the connecting lines are the attacker profiles (discussed is the case descriptions). The figure shows a trade-off among different attack values for the considered attacker profiles which an enterprise risk manager can use to effectively plan countermeasures.

6 Conclusion

We have presented a framework of security risk analysis by reducing a multi-parameter attack tree into priced timed automata. By slightly deviating from the strict formalism of attack trees by allowing shared subtrees, we preserve the intuitive representation of attack scenarios while also providing insightful qualitative and quantitative information in terms of optimal attack paths and values. Furthermore, our analysis takes temporal dependencies into account by defining the semantics of SAND and SOR gates.

As future work, we plan to analyze case studies incorporating realistic values, and to extend our framework by including success probabilities of basic attack steps. We see clear parallels between our approach and stochastic games and in the future we would like to integrate the best of both.

Acknowledgement. This work has been supported by the EU FP7 project TREsPASS (318003) and by the STW-ProRail partnership program ExploRail under the project ArRangeer (12238).

References

1. Aagedal, J., Braber, F., Dimitrakos, T., Gran, B.A., Raptis, D., Stølen, K.: Model-based risk assessment to improve enterprise security. In: Proc. 6th Int. Enterprise Distributed Object Computing Conf. (EDOC 2002), p. 51 (2002)
2. Alur, R., Dill, D.L.: A theory of timed automata. Theoretical Computer Science 126(2), 183–235 (1994)
3. Amoroso, E.: Fundamentals of computer security technology. Prentice-Hall Inc., Upper Saddle River (1994)
4. Arnold, F., Hermanns, H., Pulungan, R., Stoelinga, M.: Time-dependent analysis of attacks. In: Abadi, M., Kremer, S. (eds.) POST 2014 (ETAPS 2014). LNCS, vol. 8414, pp. 285–305. Springer, Heidelberg (2014)
5. Risk Management. Australian/New Zealand Standard, AS/NZS 4360:2004 14443 (2004)
6. Technical standard to Risk Taxonomy, The Open Group, C081 (2009)
7. Behrmann, G., Larsen, K.G., Rasmussen, J.I.: Optimal scheduling using priced timed automata. SIGMETRICS Performance Evaluation Review 32(4) (2005)
8. Behrmann, G., Larsen, K.G., Rasmussen, J.I.: Priced timed automata: algorithms and applications. In: de Boer, F.S., Bonsangue, M.M., Graf, S., de Roever, W.-P. (eds.) FMCO 2004. LNCS, vol. 3657, pp. 162–182. Springer, Heidelberg (2005)
9. Bengtsson, J.E., Yi, W.: Timed automata: semantics, algorithms and tools. In: Desel, J., Reisig, W., Rozenberg, G. (eds.) Lectures on Concurrency and Petri Nets. LNCS, vol. 3098, pp. 87–124. Springer, Heidelberg (2004)
10. Bouyer, P.: Weighted timed automata: Model-checking and games. Electronic Notes in Theoretical Computer Science 158, 3–17 (2006)
11. Bowles, J.B., Hanczaryk, W.: Threat effects analysis: Applying FMEA to model computer system threats. In: 2008 Annual Reliability and Maintainability Symp., pp. 463–468. IEEE, January 2008
12. Brihaye, T., Bruyère, V., Raskin, J.-F.: Model-checking for weighted timed automata. In: Lakhnech, Y., Yovine, S. (eds.) FORMATS 2004 and FTRTFT 2004. LNCS, vol. 3253, pp. 277–292. Springer, Heidelberg (2004)

13. Buckshaw, D.L.: Use of Decision Support Techniques for Information System Risk Management. John Wiley Sons, Ltd. (2014)
14. Buldas, A., Laud, P., Priisalu, J., Saarepera, M., Willemson, J.: Rational choice of security measures via multi-parameter attack trees. In: López, J. (ed.) CRITIS 2006. LNCS, vol. 4347, pp. 235–248. Springer, Heidelberg (2006)
15. Dacier, M., Deswarte, Y.: Privilege graph: an extension to the typed access matrix model. In: Proc. Third European Symp. on Research in Computer Security (ESORICS), Brighton, UK, November 7–9. pp. 319–334 (1994)
16. Ford, M.D., Keefe, K., LeMay, E., Sanders, W.H., Muehrcke, C.: Implementing the ADVISE security modeling formalism in Möbius. In: Proc. 43rd Int. Conf. on Dependable Systems and Networks (DSN), pp. 1–8 (2013)
17. Hansson, J., Wrage, L., Feiler, P.H., Morley, J., Lewis, B.A., Hugues, J.: Architectural modeling to verify security and nonfunctional behavior. IEEE Security & Privacy 8(1), 43–49 (2010)
18. Jürgenson, A., Willemson, J.: Processing multi-parameter attacktrees with estimated parameter values. In: Miyaji, A., Kikuchi, H., Rannenberg, K. (eds.) IWSEC 2007. LNCS, vol. 4752, pp. 308–319. Springer, Heidelberg (2007)
19. Jürgenson, A., Willemson, J.: Computing exact outcomes of multi-parameter attack trees. In: Meersman, R., Tari, Z. (eds.) OTM 2008, Part II. LNCS, vol. 5332, pp. 1036–1051. Springer, Heidelberg (2008)
20. Kordy, B., Piètre-Cambacédès, L., Schweitzer, P.: DAG-based attack and defense modeling: Don't miss the forest for the attack trees. Computer Science Review 13–14, 1–38 (2014)
21. LeMay, E., Ford, M.D., Keefe, K., Sanders, W.H.: Model-based security metrics using adversary view security evaluation (ADVISE). In: 2011 Eigth Int. Conf. on Quantitative Eval. of Systems (QEST). IEEE (2011)
22. Lenin, A., Willemson, J., Sari, D.P.: Attacker profiling in quantitative security assessment based on attack trees. In: Bernsmed, K., Fischer-Hübner, S. (eds.) NordSec 2014. LNCS, vol. 8788, pp. 199–212. Springer, Heidelberg (2014)
23. Mauw, S., Oostdijk, M.: Foundations of attack trees. In: Won, D.H., Kim, S. (eds.) ICISC 2005. LNCS, vol. 3935, pp. 186–198. Springer, Heidelberg (2006)
24. McQueen, M., Boyer, W., Flynn, M., Beitel, G.: Quantitative cyber risk reduction estimation methodology for a small scada control system. In: Proc. 39th Annual Hawaii Int. Conf. on System Sciences (HICSS), vol. 9, p. 226, January 2006
25. Piètre-Cambacédès, L., Bouissou, M.: Beyond attack trees: Dynamic security modeling with boolean logic driven markov processes (BDMP). In: Dependable Computing Conf. (EDCC), pp. 199–208 (2010)
26. Ray, I., Poolsapassit, N.: Using attack trees to identify malicious attacks from authorized insiders. In: di Vimercati, S.C., Syverson, P.F., Gollmann, D. (eds.) ESORICS 2005. LNCS, vol. 3679, pp. 231–246. Springer, Heidelberg (2005)
27. Schneier, B.: Attack trees: modeling security threats. In: Dr. Dobb's journal, December 1999
28. Sheyner, O., Haines, J., Jha, S., Lippmann, R., Wing, J.: Automated generation and analysis of attack graphs. In: Security and Privacy, Proc. 2002 IEEE Symp., pp. 273–284 (2002)
29. Uppaal CORA. http://people.cs.aau.dk/adavid/cora/index.html
30. Weiss, J.: A system security engineering process. In: Proc. 14th National Computer Security Conference, vol. 249, October 1991

Fluid Model Checking of Timed Properties

Luca Bortolussi[1,2,3] and Roberta Lanciani[4(✉)]

[1] Modelling and Simulation Group, Saarland University, Saarbrücken, Germany
luca@dmi.units.it
[2] DMG, University of Trieste, Trieste, Italy
[3] CNR/ISTI, Pisa, Italy
[4] IMT Lucca, Lucca, Italy
roberta.lanciani@imtlucca.it

Abstract. We address the problem of verifying timed properties of Markovian models of large populations of interacting agents, modelled as finite state automata. In particular, we focus on time-bounded properties of (random) individual agents specified by Deterministic Timed Automata (DTA) endowed with a single clock. Exploiting ideas from fluid approximation, we estimate the satisfaction probability of the DTA properties by reducing it to the computation of the transient probability of a subclass of Time-Inhomogeneous Markov Renewal Processes with exponentially and deterministically-timed transitions, and a small state space. For this subclass of models, we show how to derive a set of Delay Differential Equations (DDE), whose numerical solution provides a fast and accurate estimate of the satisfaction probability. In the paper, we also prove the asymptotic convergence of the approach, and exemplify the method on a simple epidemic spreading model. Finally, we also show how to construct a system of DDEs to efficiently approximate the average number of agents that satisfy the DTA specification.

Keywords: Stochastic model checking · Fluid model checking · Deterministic timed automata · Time-inhomogeneous markov renewal processes · Fluid approximation · Delay differential equations

1 Introduction

One of the major technological challenges in computer science and engineering is the design and analysis of large-scale distributed systems, where many autonomous components interact in an open environment. Examples include the public and shared transportation in smart cities, the power distribution in smart grids, and the robust communication protocols of online multimedia services. In this context, the mathematical and computational modelling plays a crucial role in the management of such *Collective Adaptive Systems* (CAS), due to the need

This research has been partially funded by the EU-FET project QUANTICOL (nr. 600708) and by the German Research Council (DFG) as part of the Cluster of Excellence on Multimodal Computing and Interaction at Saarland University.

© Springer International Publishing Switzerland 2015
S. Sankaranarayanan and E. Vicario (Eds.): FORMATS 2015, LNCS 9268, pp. 172–188, 2015.
DOI: 10.1007/978-3-319-22975-1_12

of understanding and control of their emergent behaviours in open working conditions. The intrinsic uncertainty of CAS can be properly captured by *stochastic models*, but the large number of interacting entities always results in a severe *state space explosion*, introducing exceptional computational challenges. In particular, the scalability of the models and of their analysis techniques is a major issue in the development of *stochastic model checking* procedures for the verification of formal properties. In this context, up to now, the numerical approaches [24] are deeply hampered by the state space explosion of the large stochastic models, and the statistical methods based on simulation require a large computational effort.

A recent line of work tries to address the issue of scalability by exploiting stochastic approximation techniques [10,11], like the *Fluid Approximation* [8,9,18]. In this method, a stochastic discrete model is replaced by a simpler continuous one, whose dynamics is described by a set of differential equations. In [8], the authors exploit this limit construction to verify properties that asses the behaviour of a single individual in a collective system, and define a procedure called the *Fluid Model Checking* (FMC) [7,25]. This technique is based on the *Fast Simulation Theorem* [16], which ensures that in a large population, a single entity is influenced only by the mean behaviour of the rest of the agents.

In this work, we extend [8] to more complex *time-bounded properties* specified by *Deterministic Timed Automata* endowed with a single clock [1,3,17]. As in [8,10,13,23], we combine the agent and the DTA specification with a product construction, obtaining a *Time-Inhomogeneous Markov Renewal Process* [15]. We then exploit results [6,22], defining the Fluid Approximation of this type of models as the solution of a system of *Delay Differential Equations* (DDE) [16]. Other works dealing with the verification of DTA properties are [4,12,14,19].

Main Result. We introduce a new fast and efficient Fluid Model Checking procedure to accurately approximate the probability that a single agent satisfies a single-clock DTA specification up to time T. Similarly to [8], the technique is based of the Fast Simulation Theorem, and couples the Fluid Approximation of the collective system with a set of Delay Differential Equations for the transient probability of the Time-Inhomogeneous Markov Renewal Process obtained by the product construction between the single agent and the DTA specification.

In the paper, we discuss the *theoretical aspects* of our approach, proving the *convergence* of the estimated probability to the true one in the limit of an infinite population. We also show the procedure at work on a running example of a simple epidemic process, emphasising the quality of the approximation and the gain in terms of computational time. Finally, by exploiting the construction of [10,22], we also show how to define a set of DDEs approximating the mean number of agents satisfying a single-clock DTA specification up to time T.

Paper Structure. In Sec. 2, we introduce the modelling language, the Fluid Approximation, the Fast Simulation Theorem, and the DTA specification for the timed properties. In Sec. 3, we present our FMC procedure, defining the DDEs for the probability that the single agent satisfies the timed property. In Sec. 3.1, we adapt our verification technique to compute the mean number of agents that meet the DTA requirement. In Sec. 4, we discuss the quality of the approximation on the epidemic example. Finally, in Sec. 5, we draw the final conclusions. The proofs of the theoretical results are omitted and can be found in the extended version available at http://arxiv.org/abs/1506.05909.

2 Background and Modelling Language

Agent Classes and Population Models. A collective system is comprised of a large number of interacting *agents*. To describe its dynamics, we define a *population model* [10,11] in which the agents are divided into classes, called *agent classes*, according to their behaviour.

Definition 1 (Agent Class). *An agent class $\mathscr{A}$ is a pair (S, E) in which $S = \{1, \ldots, m\}$ is the (finite) state space and $E = \{\epsilon_1, \ldots, \epsilon_\eta\} \subseteq S \times \mathscr{L} \times S$ is the (finite) set of local transitions of the form $\epsilon_i = s_i \xrightarrow{\alpha_i} s_i'$, where $s_i, s_i' \in S$ are the initial and arrival states, and $\alpha_i \in \mathscr{L}$ is the unique label of ϵ_i, i.e. $\alpha_i \neq \alpha_j$ for $i \neq j$*[1].

Intuitively, an agent in class $\mathscr{A} = (S, E)$ is a finite state automaton that can change state by performing the actions in E. Then, assuming that agents in the same state are indistinguishable, to define the population model, we rely on the *counting abstraction*, counting how many agents are in each state at time t. Hence, for each agent class, we define the *collective* or *counting variables* $X_1^{(N)}(t), \ldots, X_m^{(N)}(t)$ given by $X_j^{(N)}(t) = \sum_k \mathbb{1}_{\{Y_k^{(N)}(t)=j\}}$, where $Y_k^{(N)}(t) \in \{1, \ldots, m\}$ is the random variable denoting the state of agent k at time t, and $N = \sum_{\mathscr{A}} \sum_j X_j^{(N)}$ is the *population size*, that we assume constant in time (cf. also [8]). Then, given $n = \sum_{\mathscr{A}} |S|$, the state of the population model is given by the vector $\mathbf{X}^{(N)}(t) \in (\mathbb{R}_{\geq 0})^n$ that enlists the counting variables of the agent classes.

Definition 2 (Population Model). *A population model $\mathcal{X}^{(N)}$ is a tuple $\mathcal{X}^{(N)} = (\mathbb{A}, \mathcal{T}^{(N)}, \mathbf{x}_0^{(N)})$, where $\mathbb{A} = \{\mathscr{A}_1, \ldots, \mathscr{A}_\nu\}$ is the set of agent classes, as in Definition 1; $\mathbf{x}_0^{(N)} = \mathbf{X}^{(N)}(0)$ is the initial state; and $\mathcal{T}^{(N)} = \{\tau_1, \ldots, \tau_\ell\}$ is the set of global transitions of the form $\tau_i = (\mathbb{S}_i, f_i^{(N)}, \mathbf{v}_i^{(N)})$, where:*

- $\mathbb{S}_i = \{s_1 \xrightarrow{\alpha_1} s_1', \ldots, s_p \xrightarrow{\alpha_p} s_p'\}$ *is the (finite) multi-set of local transitions synchronized by τ_i;*
- $f_i^{(N)} : (\mathbb{R}_{\geq 0})^n \longrightarrow \mathbb{R}_{\geq 0}$ *is the (Lipschitz continuous) global rate function;*
- $\mathbf{v}_i = \sum_{\alpha_j \in \mathbb{S}_i} |\{\alpha_j\}| (\mathbb{1}_{s_j} - \mathbb{1}_{s_j'})$ *is the update vector, where $|\{\alpha_j\}|$ is the multiplicity of α_i in $\mathbb{S}_i$, and $\mathbb{1}_{s_j}$ is the vector equal to 1 on s_j and 0 elsewhere.*

---

[1] The restriction on the uniqueness of the labels can be dropped (as in [10]) at the price of heavier notation and combinatorics in the definitions of the rest of the paper.

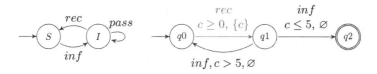

Fig. 1. The agent class $\mathscr{A}$ (left) and property $\mathbb{D}$ (right) of the running example.

When a global transition $\tau_i = (\mathbb{S}_i, f_i^{(N)}, \mathbf{v}_i)$ is taken, the transitions in $\mathbb{S}_i$ fire at the local level, meaning that, for each $s \xrightarrow{\alpha} s'$ in $\mathbb{S}_i$, an agent moves from s to s'. Hence, the update vector $\mathbf{v}_i$ encodes the net change in the state $\mathbf{X}^{(N)}(t)$ of $\mathcal{X}^{(N)}$ due to transition τ_i. Moreover, for the model to be meaningful, whenever at time t it is not possible to execute τ_i, because there are not enough agents available, i.e. $\left(\mathbf{X}^{(N)}(t) - \mathbf{v}_i\right)_j < 0$ for some $j \in \{1, \ldots, n\}$ with $n = |\mathbf{X}^{(N)}(t)|$, we require the rate function to be zero, i.e. $f_i^{(N)}(\mathbf{X}^{(N)}(t)) = 0$.

Example. The running example that we consider is a simple *SIS model*, describing the spreading of a disease inside a population. All agents belong to the same agent class $\mathscr{A}$, depicted in Fig. 1, and can be either *susceptible* (S) or *infected* (I). When they are *susceptible*, they can be infected (*inf*), and when they are *infected*, they can either pass the infection (*pass*) or recover (*rec*). Hence, the state $\mathbf{X}^{(N)}(t)$ of the population model is $\mathbf{X}^{(N)}(t) = (X_S^{(N)}(t), X_I^{(N)}(t))$, and we define 2 global transitions: $\tau_r = (\{I \xrightarrow{rec} S\}, f_r^{(N)})$ and $\tau_i = (\{S \xrightarrow{inf} I, I \xrightarrow{pass} I\}, f_i^{(N)})$. The former, τ_r, mimics the recovery of one entity inside the population, while τ_i synchronises two local actions, namely $S \xrightarrow{inf} I$ and $I \xrightarrow{pass} I$, and models the transmission of the virus from an infected agent to a susceptible one. Finally, the rate functions depend on the number of agents involved in the transitions and follow the classical *rule of mass action* [2]: $f_r^{(N)}(t) = k_r X_I^{(N)}(t)$ and $f_i^{(N)}(t) = \frac{1}{N} k_i X_S^{(N)}(t) X_I^{(N)}(t)$, where $k_r, k_i \in \mathbb{R}_{\geq 0}$.

Fluid Approximation. The *Fluid Approximation* [8,9,18] of a population model $\mathcal{X}^{(N)} = (\mathbb{A}, \mathcal{T}^{(N)}, \mathbf{x}_0^{(N)})$ is an estimate of the *mean* behaviour of its agents. To compute this approximation, we first *normalise* $\mathcal{X}^{(N)}$ by dividing the state vector $\mathbf{X}^{(N)}(t)$ and the initial state $\mathbf{x}_0^{(N)}$ by the population size N, i.e. we define $\widehat{\mathbf{X}}^{(N)}(t) = \mathbf{X}^{(N)}(t)/N$ and $\widehat{\boldsymbol{x}}_0^{(N)} = \mathbf{x}_0^{(N)}/N$. Then, for all transition $\tau_i \in \mathcal{T}^{(N)}$, we let $\widehat{f}_i^{(N)}(\widehat{\mathbf{X}})$ be the rate function, where we substitute the counting variables of $\mathbf{X}^{(N)}(t)$ with the new normalised counting variables of $\widehat{\mathbf{X}}(t)$. Moreover, we assume that for each $\widehat{f}_i^{(N)}(\widehat{\mathbf{X}})$, there exist a *Lipschitz function* $f_i(\widehat{\mathbf{X}})$ such that $\widehat{f}_i^{(N)}(\widehat{\mathbf{X}})/N \xrightarrow{N \to +\infty} f_i(\widehat{\mathbf{X}})$ uniformly. Finally, in terms of $f_i(\widehat{\mathbf{X}})$, we define the *drift* $\mathbf{F}(\widehat{\mathbf{X}})$ given by $\mathbf{F}(\widehat{\mathbf{X}}) = \sum_{\tau_i} \mathbf{v}_i f_i(\widehat{\mathbf{X}})$, whose components represent the instantaneous net flux of agents in each state of the model. Then, given a *time* *horizon* $T < +\infty$, the *Fluid Approximation* $\Phi(t)$ of $\mathcal{X}^{(N)}$ is the unique[2] solution of the system of *Ordinary Differential Equations* (ODEs) given by

$$\frac{d\Phi}{dt}(t) = \mathbf{F}(\Phi(t)), \qquad \text{for } 0 \le t \le T,$$

with $\Phi(0) = \mathbf{x}_0$. The accuracy of the approximation *improves* the larger is the ensemble of agents that we consider, i.e. *the larger is N*, and is exact in the limit of an infinite population. Indeed, the following theorem holds true [18].

Theorem 1 (Fluid Approximation). *For any $T < +\infty$ and $\epsilon > 0$,*

$$Prob\left\{ \sup_{0 \le t \le T} ||\widehat{\mathbf{X}}^{(N)}(t) - \Phi(t)|| > \epsilon \right\} \xrightarrow{N \to +\infty} 0.$$

Fast Simulation. In this paper, we are interested in the behaviour of a (random) *single agent* inside a population. As we have just seen, the dynamics of a large population can be accurately described by a *deterministic* limit, the Fluid Approximation. But when we focus on one single agent in a collective system, we need to keep in mind that its behaviour in time will always remain a *stochastic* process, even in large populations. Nevertheless, the *Fast Simulation Theorem* [5,16,20] guarantees that in the limit of an infinite population size, the stochastic process of the single agent senses only the *mean* behaviour of the rest of the agents (i.e. there is no need to keep track of all the states of all the other entities in the population). This means that, when the population size is large enough, to analyse the dynamics the single agent, we can define the Fluid Approximation of the population model, and then use its state (i.e. the mean state of the rest of the agents) to compute the rates of a *Time-Inhomogeneous CTMC* (ICTMC) [8] that describes the behaviour of the single agent.

Formally, let $Y^{(N)}(t)$ be the stochastic process that describes the state of the single agent in the population model $\mathcal{X}^{(N)} = (\mathbb{A}, \mathcal{T}^{(N)}, \mathbf{x}_0^{(N)})$ with state vector $\mathbf{X}^{(N)}(t)$. By definition, $Y^{(N)}(t)$ *is not independent of* $\mathbf{X}^{(N)}(t)$. Now consider the normalised model $\widehat{\mathcal{X}}^{(N)}$ described by $\widehat{\mathbf{X}}^{(N)}(t)$, and let $\Phi(t)$ be the Fluid Approximation of $\mathcal{X}^{(N)}$. Define the *generator matrix* $\mathbf{Q}^{(N)}(\mathbf{x}) = (q_{ij}^{(N)}(\mathbf{x}))$ of $Y^{(N)}(t)$ as a function of the normalised counting variables, i.e. $\forall\, q_{ij}^{(N)}(\mathbf{x})$,

$$Prob\left\{ Y^{(N)}(t + dt) = j \mid Y^{(N)}(t) = i, \widehat{\mathbf{X}}^{(N)}(t) = \mathbf{x} \right\} = q_{ij}^{(N)}(\mathbf{x})dt.$$

Notice that $\mathbf{Q}^{(N)}(\mathbf{x})$ can be computed from the rates in $\mathcal{X}^{(N)}$. Indeed, for $i \ne j$,

$$q_{ij}^{(N)}(\mathbf{x}) = \sum_{\tau \in \mathcal{T}} \left[\frac{|\{i \to j \in \mathbb{S}_\tau\}|}{X_i} \frac{\widehat{f}_\tau^{(N)}(\widehat{\mathbf{X}})}{N} \right],$$

where $|\{i \to j \in \mathbb{S}_\tau\}|$ is the multiplicity of $i \to j$ in the transition set $\mathbb{S}_\tau$ of τ, i.e. the number of agents that take such transition according to τ. Furthermore,

---

[2] Existence and uniqueness of $\Phi(t)$ are guaranteed by the Lipschitzianity of the $f_i(\widehat{\mathbf{X}})$.

as customary, let $q_{ii}^{(N)}(\boldsymbol{x}) = -\sum_{j \neq i} q_{ij}^{(N)}(\boldsymbol{x})$. Then, since $\hat{f}_i^{(N)}(\hat{\mathbf{X}})/N \xrightarrow{N \to +\infty} f_i(\hat{\mathbf{X}})$, we have that $\boldsymbol{Q}^{(N)}(\boldsymbol{x}) \to \boldsymbol{Q}(\boldsymbol{x})$, where $\boldsymbol{Q}(\boldsymbol{x})$ is computed in terms of the Lipschitz limits $f_i(\hat{\mathbf{X}})$. Now, define the stochastic processes:

1. $Z^{(N)}(t)$, that describes the state of the process $Y^{(N)}(t)$ for the single agent in class $\mathscr{A}$, when $Y^{(N)}(t)$ is marginalised from $\mathbf{X}^{(N)}(t)$;
2. $Z(t)$, that is the ICTMC, defined on the same state space of $Z^{(N)}(t)$, with *time-dependent* generator matrix $\boldsymbol{Q}(\boldsymbol{\Phi}(t))$, i.e. the generator matrix $\boldsymbol{Q}(t)$, where the Lipschitz limits $f_i(t)$ are computed over the components of $\boldsymbol{\Phi}(t)$.

Then, the following theorem can be proved [16].

Theorem 2 (Fast Simulation). *For any time horizon $T < +\infty$ and $\epsilon > 0$,*

$$Prob\left\{ \sup_{0 \leq t \leq T} ||Z^{(N)}(t) - Z(t)|| > \epsilon \right\} \xrightarrow{N \to +\infty} 0.$$

Example. For the running example, if we consider a population of 1000 agents, i.e $N = 1000$, and an initial state $\mathbf{x}_0^{(N)} = (900, 100)$, then the Fluid Approximation $\boldsymbol{\Phi}(t)$ of the population model is the unique solution of the following ODEs:

$$\begin{cases} \frac{d\Phi_S}{dt}(t) = -k_i \Phi_I(t) \Phi_S(t) + k_r \Phi_I(t); \\ \frac{d\Phi_I}{dt}(t) = +k_i \Phi_I(t) \Phi_S(t) - k_r \Phi_I(t); \end{cases} \quad \text{with} \quad \begin{cases} \Phi_S(0) = 0.9; \\ \Phi_I(0) = 0.1. \end{cases} \quad (1)$$

The generator $\boldsymbol{Q}(\boldsymbol{\Phi}(t))$ of the ICTMC $Z(t)$ for the single agent, instead, is:

$$q_{S,S}(t) = -q_{S,I}(t); \quad q_{S,I}(t) = k_i \Phi_I(t); \quad q_{I,S}(t) = k_r; \quad q_{I,I}(t) = -q_{I,S}(t). \quad (2)$$

2.1 Timed Properties

We are interested in properties specifying how a single agent behaves in *time*. In order to monitor such requirements, we assign to it a unique *personal clock*, which starts at time 0 and can be reset whenever the agent undergoes specific transitions. In this way, the properties that we consider can be specified by a *single-clock Deterministic Timed Automata* (DTA)[1,13], which keeps track of the behaviour of the single agent with respect to its personal clock. Moreover, since we want to exploit the Fast Simulation Theorem, we restrict ourselves to *time bounded* properties and, hence, we assign to the DTA a finite *time horizon* $T < +\infty$, within which the requirement must be true.

Definition 3 (Timed Properties). *A timed property for a single agent in agent class $\mathscr{A}$ is specified as a single-clock DTA of the form $\mathbb{D} = \mathbb{D}(T) = (T, \mathscr{L}, c, \mathcal{CC}, Q, q_0, F, \to)$, where $T < +\infty$ is the finite time horizon; $\mathscr{L}$ is the label set of $\mathscr{A}$; c is the personal clock; $\mathcal{CC}$ is the set of clock constraints, which are conjunctions of atoms of the form $c < \lambda$, $c \leq \lambda$, $c \geq \lambda$ or $c > \lambda$ for $\lambda \in \mathbb{Q}$; Q is the (finite) set of states; $q_0 \in Q$ is the initial state; $F \subseteq Q$ is the set of final (or accepting) states; and $\to \subseteq Q \times \mathscr{L} \times \mathcal{CC} \times \{\varnothing, \{c\}\} \times Q$ is the edge relation. Moreover, $\mathbb{D}$ has to satisfy:*

- *(determinism) for each initial state $q \in Q$, label $\alpha \in \mathcal{L}$, clock constraint $c_{\bowtie} \in CC$, and clock valuation $\eta(c) \in \mathbb{R}_{\geq 0}$, there exists exactly one edge $q \xrightarrow{\alpha, c_{\bowtie}, r} q'$ such that $\eta(c) \models_{CC} c_{\bowtie}$[3];*
- *(absorption) the final states are all absorbing.*

A timed property $\mathbb{D}$ is assessed over the time-bounded paths (of total duration T) of the agent class $\mathscr{A}$ sampled from the stochastic processes $Z^{(N)}(t)$ and $Z(t)$ defined for the Fast Simulation in Sec. 2. The labels of the transitions of $\mathscr{A}$ act as inputs for the DTA $\mathbb{D}$, and the latter is defined in such a way that it *accepts* a time-bounded path σ if and only if the behaviour of the single agent encoded in σ satisfies the property represented by $\mathbb{D}$. Formally, a time-bounded path $\sigma = s_0 \xrightarrow{\alpha_0, t_0} s_1 \xrightarrow{\alpha_1, t_1} \ldots \xrightarrow{\alpha_n, t_n} s_{n+1}$ of $\mathscr{A}$ sampled from $Z^{(N)}(t)$ (resp. $Z(t)$), with $\sum_{j=0}^{n} t_j \leq T$, is *accepted* by $\mathbb{D}$ if and only if there exists a path $q_0 \xrightarrow{\alpha_0} q^{(1)} \xrightarrow{\alpha_1} q^{(2)} \xrightarrow{\alpha_2} \ldots \xrightarrow{\alpha_n} q^{(n+1)}$ of $\mathbb{D}$ such that $q^{(n+1)} \in F$. In the path of $\mathbb{D}$, $q^{(i+1)} \in Q$ denotes the (unique) state that can be reached form $q^{(i)} \in Q$ taking the action $q^{(i)} \xrightarrow{\alpha_i, c_{\bowtie}, r} q^{(i+1)}$ whose clock constraint $c_{\bowtie}$ is satisfied by the clock valuation $\eta(c)$ updated according to time t_i. In the following, we will denote by $\Sigma_{\mathscr{A}, \mathbb{D}, T}$ the *set of time-bounded paths of $\mathscr{A}$ accepted by $\mathbb{D}$*.

Example. We consider the following property for the running example: *within time T, the agent gets infected at least once during the $\Delta = 5$ time units that follow a recovery.* To verify such requirement, we use the DTA $\mathbb{D} = \mathbb{D}(T)$ represented in Fig. 1. If we record the actions of the single agent on $\mathbb{D}$, i.e. we synchronise $\mathscr{A}$ and $\mathbb{D}$, when the agent recovers (*rec*), $\mathbb{D}$ passes from state $q0$ to $q1$, resetting the personal clock c. After that, if the agent gets infected (*inf*) within 5 time units, the property is satisfied, and $\mathbb{D}$ passes from state $q1$ to $q2$, which is accepting. If instead the agent is infected (*inf*) after 5 units of time, $\mathbb{D}$ moves back to state $q0$, and we start monitoring the behaviour of the agent again. In red we highlight the transition that resets the personal clock c in $\mathbb{D}$.

3   Fluid Model Checking of Timed Properties

Consider a single agent of class $\mathscr{A} = (S, E)$ in a population model $\mathcal{X}^{(N)} = (\mathscr{A}, T^{(N)}, \mathbf{x}_0^{(N)})$, and a timed property $\mathbb{D} = \mathbb{D}(T) = (T, \mathcal{L}, \Gamma_S, CC, Q, q_0, F, \rightarrow)$. Let $\Sigma_{\mathscr{A}, \mathbb{D}, T}$ be the set of time-bounded paths of $\mathscr{A}$ accepted by $\mathbb{D}$. Moreover, let $Z^{(N)}(t)$ and $Z(t)$ be the two stochastic processes defined for the Fast Simulation in Sec. 2. The following result holds true.

Proposition 1. *The set $\Sigma_{\mathscr{A}, \mathbb{D}, T}$ is measurable for the probability measures $Prob_{Z^{(N)}}$ and $Prob_Z$ defined over the paths of $Z^{(N)}(t)$ and $Z(t)$, respectively.* □

Let $P^{(N)}(T) = Prob_{Z^{(N)}}\{\Sigma_{\mathscr{A}, \mathbb{D}, T}\}$ and $P(T) = Prob_Z\{\Sigma_{\mathscr{A}, \mathbb{D}, T}\}$. In this paper, we are interested in the *satisfaction probability* $P^{(N)}(T)$, i.e. the probability

---

[3] The notation $\eta(c) \models_{CC} c_{\bowtie}$ stands for the fact that the value of the valuation $\eta(c)$ of c satisfies the clock constraint $c_{\bowtie}$.

that the single agent satisfies property $\mathbb{D}$ within time T in $\mathcal{X}^{(N)}$. Then, the main result that we exploit in our Fluid Model Checking procedure is that, when the population is large enough (i.e N is large enough), $P^{(N)}(T)$ can be accurately approximated by $P(T)$, which is computed over the ICTMC $Z(t)$, whose rates are defined in terms of the Fluid Approximation $\Phi(t)$ of $\mathcal{X}^{(N)}$. The correctness of the approximation relies on the Fast Simulation Theorem and is guaranteed by the following result.

Theorem 3. *For any $T < +\infty$,* $\lim_{N \to \infty} P^{(N)}(T) = P(T)$. $\square$

Moreover, to compute $P(T)$, we consider a suitable product construction $\mathscr{A}_\mathbb{D} = \mathscr{A} \otimes \mathbb{D}$, whose state is described by a *Time-Inhomogeneous Markov Renewal Process* (IMRP) [15] that we denote by $Z_{\mathscr{A}_\mathbb{D}}(t)$. In the rest of this section, we define $\mathscr{A}_\mathbb{D}$ and $Z_{\mathscr{A}_\mathbb{D}}(t)$, and we show how to compute the *satisfaction probability* $P(T)$ in terms of the *transient probability* $\boldsymbol{P}(T)$ of $Z_{\mathscr{A}_\mathbb{D}}(t)$.

The Product $\mathscr{A}_\mathbb{D}$. We now introduce the product $\mathscr{A}_\mathbb{D}$ between $\mathscr{A}$ and $\mathbb{D}$, whose state is described by a *Time-Inhomogeneous Markov Renewal Process* (IMRP) $Z_{\mathscr{A}_\mathbb{D}}(t)$ that has rates computed over the Fluid Approximation $\Phi(t)$ of $\mathcal{X}^{(N)}$.

A *Markov Renewal Process* (MRP) [15] is a jump-process, where the sojourn times in the states can have a general probability distribution. In particular, in the MRP $Z_{\mathscr{A}_\mathbb{D}}(t)$, we will allow both *exponentially* and *deterministically-timed* transitions, and in the following, we will refer to them as the *Markovian* and *deterministic transitions*, respectively. Since the transition rates of $Z_{\mathscr{A}_\mathbb{D}}(t)$ will be time-dependent, $Z_{\mathscr{A}_\mathbb{D}}(t)$ will be a *Time-Inhomogeneous MRP*.

To define the product $\mathscr{A}_\mathbb{D} = (\mathscr{A}, S_\mathbb{D}, \{\mathcal{M}, \mathcal{E}\}, s_{0,\mathbb{D}}, F_\mathbb{D})$, let $\delta_1 < \ldots < \delta_k$ be the (ordered) constants that appear in the clock constraints of $\mathbb{D}$, and extend the sequence with $\delta_0 = 0$ and $\delta_{k+1} = T$. The *state space* $S_\mathbb{D}$ of $\mathscr{A}_\mathbb{D}$ is given by $\{1, \ldots, k+1\} \times S \times Q$. The first element of $S_\mathbb{D}$ identifies a time region of the clock c, and we refer to $S_{\mathbb{D}_i} = \{(i, s, q) \mid s \in S, q \in Q\}$ as the *i-th Time Region* of $S_\mathbb{D}$. The rest of $\mathscr{A}_\mathbb{D}$ will be defined in such a way that the agent is in $S_{\mathbb{D}_i}$ if and only if c satisfies $\delta_{i-1} \leq \eta(c) \leq \delta_i$, where η is the valuation of c.

The *set $\mathcal{M}$ of Markovian transitions* of $\mathscr{A}_\mathbb{D}$ is the smallest relation such that

$$\forall\, i \in 1, \ldots, k+1, \qquad \frac{s \xrightarrow{\alpha} s' \in E \;\wedge\; q \xrightarrow{\alpha, c_{\bowtie}, \varnothing} q' \in\to \;\wedge\; [\delta_{i-1}, \delta_i] \models c_\bowtie}{(i, s, q) \xrightarrow{\alpha} (i, s', q') \in \mathcal{M}}, \qquad (3)$$

$$\forall\, i \in 1, \ldots, k+1, \qquad \frac{s \xrightarrow{\alpha} s' \in E \;\wedge\; q \xrightarrow{\alpha, c_{\bowtie}, \{c\}} q' \in\to \;\wedge\; [\delta_{i-1}, \delta_i] \models c_\bowtie}{(i, s, q) \xrightarrow{\alpha} (1, s', q') \in \mathcal{M}}. \qquad (4)$$

Intuitively, rule (3) synchronises the local transitions $s \xrightarrow{\alpha} s' \in E$ of the agent class $\mathscr{A} = (S, E)$ with the transition $q \xrightarrow{\alpha, c_{\bowtie}, \varnothing} q' \in\to$ that has the same label in $\mathbb{D}$, obtaining a local transition $(i, s, q) \xrightarrow{\alpha} (i, s', q') \in \mathcal{M}$ in $\mathscr{A}_\mathbb{D}$ for each time region i whose time interval $[\delta_{i-1}, \delta_i] \subseteq [0, T]$ satisfies the clock constraint $c_\bowtie$, meaning that $\forall t \in [\delta_{i-1}, \delta_i], \ t \models c_\bowtie$. Rule (4), instead, defines the *reset transitions* $(i, s, q) \xrightarrow{\alpha} (1, s', q') \in \mathcal{M}$ that reset the personal clock c either within the 1st Time Region (when $i = 1$), or by bringing the agent *back to* the 1st Time Region. In the following, we denote by $\mathcal{R} \subset \mathcal{M}$ the *set of the reset transitions*.

To describe the deterministic transitions of $\mathscr{A}_\mathbb{D}$, instead, we define a set $\mathcal{E}$ of *clock events*. Each clock event has the form $e = (\mathcal{A}_e, \Delta, p_e)$, where $\mathcal{A}_e \subset S_{\mathbb{D}_i}$ is the *active set*, Δ is the *duration*, and $p_e : \mathcal{A}_e \times S_\mathbb{D} \longrightarrow [0,1]$ is the *probability distribution*. If the agent enters $\mathcal{A}_e$, that is the sets of states in which e can be active, a countdown starts from Δ. When this elapses, e_i is deactivated and the agent is immediately moved to a new state sampled from $p_e((i, s, q), \cdot) : S_\mathbb{D} \longrightarrow [0,1]$, where $(i, s, q) \in \mathcal{A}_e$ is the state in which the agent is when the countdown hits zero. Moreover, e_i is deactivated also when the agent takes a reset transition. In $\mathscr{A}_\mathbb{D}$, we define:

- one clock event $e_i \in \mathcal{E}$ for each time region $S_{\mathbb{D}i}$, $i = 2, \ldots, k$;
- $\ell + 1$ clock events $e_1^0, e_1^1, \ldots, e_1^\ell \in \mathcal{E}$ for the 1st Time Region, where ℓ is the number of reset events $(1, s, q) \xrightarrow{\alpha} (1, s', q') \in \mathcal{R}$ defined by (4) with $i = 1$.

For $i > 1$, $\mathcal{A}_i = S_{\mathbb{D}i}$, $\Delta_i = \delta_i - \delta_{i-1}$, and the probability distribution is

$$p_i((i, s, q), (i', s', q')) = \begin{cases} 1 & \text{if } i' = i + 1, s' = s, q' = q, \\ 0 & \text{otherwise.} \end{cases} \tag{5}$$

As it is defined, each clock event e_i with $i > 1$ connects each state $(i, s, q) \in \mathcal{A}_i$ with $(i + 1, s, q) \in S_{\mathbb{D}i+1}$, hence, when the duration Δ_i of e_i elapses, the clock event moves the agent from its state to the equivalent one in the next time region. When $i = 1$, instead, the duration and the probability distribution of each clock event e_1^j, $j = 1, \ldots, \ell$, are defined in the same way as before (i.e. $\Delta_1^j = \delta_1 - \delta_0 = \delta_1$, and p_1^j is given by (5)), but the activation sets are now subsets of $S_{\mathbb{D}_1}$. Indeed, since each reset transition $(1, s, q) \xrightarrow{\alpha_j} (1, s', q') \in \mathcal{R}$ initiates the clock, for each of them, we need to define a clock event e_1^j, whose activation set $\mathcal{A}_i^j$ is the set of states in $S_{\mathbb{D}_1}$ that can be reached by the agent *after* it has taken the reset transition $(1, s, q) \xrightarrow{\alpha_j} (1, s', q')$. Furthermore, we have to define an extra clock event e_1^0, with $\mathcal{A}_1^0 = S_{\mathbb{D}_1}$, $\Delta_1^0 = \delta_1$, and p_1^0 given by (5), that is the only clock event initiated at time $t = 0$ (and not by the agent entering $\mathcal{A}_1^0$). Indeed, we require for the *initial state* $s_{0,\mathbb{D}}$ of $\mathscr{A}_\mathbb{D}$ to be one of the states of the form $(1, s, q_0)$, where $s \in S$ and q_0 is the initial state of $\mathbb{D}$ (hence, $s_{0,\mathbb{D}}$ belongs to $\mathcal{A}_1^0$). Finally, since the probability distributions p_1^j, $\forall j$, are all defined as in (5), also the clock events of the 1st Time Region move the agent from a state to the equivalent one in the next time region (the 2nd), when the countdown from $\Delta_1^j = \delta_1$ elapses. In the following, we denote by $(i, s, q) \dashrightarrow_e (i + 1, s, q)$ the deterministic transition from $(i, s, q) \in S_{\mathbb{D}i}$ to $(i + 1, s, q) \in S_{\mathbb{D}i+1}$ encoded by $e \in \mathcal{E}$, and by $\nu_{e,s,q} = \mathbb{1}_{(i+1,s,q)} - \mathbb{1}_{(i,s,q)}$ its update vector. The last component of $\mathscr{A}_\mathbb{D}$ that we define is the *set of final states* $F_\mathbb{D}$, which is given by $F_\mathbb{D} = \{(i, s, q) \in S_\mathbb{D} \mid q \in F\}$.

Example. Fig. 2 represents the product $\mathscr{A}_\mathbb{D}$ between the agent class $\mathscr{A}$ and the property $\mathbb{D}$ of the running example (Fig. 1). The state $(1, I, q1)$ that cannot be

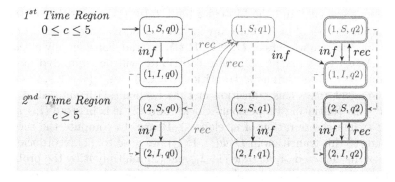

Fig. 2. The agent class $\mathscr{A}_{\mathbb{D}}$ associated with the DTA $\mathbb{D}$ of the running example.

reached by the single agent is omitted. The black transitions are the Markovian transitions without reset; the red transitions are the Markovian transitions that reset the clock; finally, we define 2 clock events, e_1^0 and e_1^1, with duration $\Delta = 5$ for the 1st Time Region, and the dashed green (resp. blue) transitions are the deterministic transitions encoded by e_1^0 (resp. e_1^1). In blue, we also highlight the states that belong to the activation set $\mathcal{A}_{e_1^1}$ (while $\mathcal{A}_{e_1^0}$ is the whole 1st Time Region). Intuitively, the agent can be found in one of the states belonging to the 1st Time Region whenever its personal clock c is between 0 and 5, i.e. less that 5 time units have passed since $t = 0$ or since a recovery rec. In a similar way, the agent is in the 2nd Time Region when the valuation of c is above 5. Moreover, when the the duration of the clock events elapses (i.e. the countdown from 5 hits 0), the agent is moved from the 1st Time Region to the 2nd Time Region by the deterministic green and blue transitions, that indeed have duration $\Delta = 5$ and are initiated at $t = 0$ or by the reset actions rec, respectively. At the end, the agent is in one of the final states ($(1, S, q2)$, $(1, I, q2)$, $(2, S, q2)$ or $(2, I, q2)$) at time T, if it meets property $\mathbb{D}$ within time T, i.e. within T, the agent has been infected during the 5 time units that follow a recovery. Hence, to verify $\mathbb{D}$, we will compute the probability of being in one of the final states of $\mathscr{A}_{\mathbb{D}}$ at time T.

The IMRP $Z_{\mathscr{A}_{\mathbb{D}}}(t)$ and the Satisfaction Probability $P(T)$. Now we show how to formally define the IMRP $Z_{\mathscr{A}_{\mathbb{D}}}(t)$ that describes the state of the product $\mathscr{A}_{\mathbb{D}}$ in the mean field regime. In particular, we derive the *Delay Differential Equations* (DDE) [15] for the *transient probability* $\boldsymbol{P}(t)$ of $Z_{\mathscr{A}_{\mathbb{D}}}(t)$, in terms of which we compute the *satisfaction probability* $P(T)$.

Let $\boldsymbol{\Phi}(t)$ be the Fluid Approximation of the population model $\mathcal{X}^{(N)}$. To define the transient probability $\boldsymbol{P}(t)$ of $Z_{\mathscr{A}_{\mathbb{D}}}(t)$, we exploit the fact that, in the case of an IMRP, we have: $\frac{d\boldsymbol{P}}{dt}(t) = \boldsymbol{M}(\boldsymbol{\Phi}(t))\boldsymbol{P}(t) + \boldsymbol{D}(\boldsymbol{\Phi}(t), \boldsymbol{P}(t))$ (cf. [15]). In this equation, $\boldsymbol{M}(\boldsymbol{\Phi}(t))$ is the *generator matrix* for the Markovian transitions, and $\boldsymbol{D}(\boldsymbol{\Phi}(t), \boldsymbol{P}(t))$ accounts for the deterministic events. The elements of $\boldsymbol{M}(\boldsymbol{\Phi}(t))$ are computed following the same procedure that was described in Sec. 2, where the multiplicity of each transition $(i, s, q) \xrightarrow{\alpha} (i, s', q') \in \mathcal{M}$ in $\mathscr{A}_{\mathbb{D}}$ is always equal to 1 (one single agent) and the Lipschitz limit $f_\alpha(\boldsymbol{\Phi}(t))$ of α is that of the rate of the transition $s \xrightarrow{\alpha} s'$ in $\mathcal{X}^{(N)}$ from which α was derived (by rules (3) or (4)).

To define the components of $\boldsymbol{D}(\boldsymbol{\Phi}(t), \boldsymbol{P}(t))$, instead, consider any clock event $e = (\mathcal{A}_i, \Delta_i, p_i) \in \mathcal{E}$, *except* e_1^0, whose contribute will be computed later on[4]. Choose one of the deterministic transitions $(i, s, q) \dashrightarrow_{e_i} (i + 1, s, q)$ encoded by e_i. The agent takes this transition at time t when: (1) it entered $\mathcal{A}_i \subseteq S_{\mathbb{D}_i}$ at time $t - \Delta_i$ (initiating its personal clock), and (2) it is in state $(i, s, q) \in \mathcal{A}_i$ at time t (when the duration of e_i elapses). Hence, to compute the term that corresponds to this transition in $\boldsymbol{D}(\boldsymbol{\Phi}(t), \boldsymbol{P}(t))$, we need to: (1) record the flux of probability that entered $\mathcal{A}_i$ at time $t - \Delta_i$, and (2) multiply it by the probability that the agent reaches $(i, s, q) \in \mathcal{A}_i$ at time t, conditional on the state at which it entered $\mathcal{A}_i$ at $t - \Delta_i$.

To compute the probability of step (2), we need to keep track of the dynamics of the agent while the clock event e_i is active. For this purpose, let $\bar{\mathcal{A}}_i$ be the activation set $\mathcal{A}_i$ of e_i extended to contain an extra state $s_{out} = (i, s_{out}, q_{out})$, and let $\bar{\mathcal{M}}$ be the set $\mathcal{M}$ of Markovian transitions in $\mathscr{A}_{\mathbb{D}}$ modified in order to make the reset transitions that start in $\mathcal{A}_i$ finish into s_{out} (i.e. for every $(i, s, q) \xrightarrow{\alpha} (i', s', q') \in \mathcal{R} \subset \mathcal{M}$, we define $(i, s, q) \xrightarrow{\alpha} s_{out} \in \bar{\mathcal{M}}$), and to have s_{out} absorbing[5]. Let $\mathbf{G}_i(\boldsymbol{\Phi}(t)) \in \mathrm{Matr}(|\bar{A}_i| \times |\bar{A}_i|)$ be the time-dependent matrix s.t.

$$(\mathbf{G}_i(\boldsymbol{\Phi}(t)))_{(i,s,q),(i,s',q')} = \sum_{(i,s,q) \xrightarrow{\alpha} (i,s',q') \in \bar{\mathcal{M}}} \left[\frac{1}{\Phi_s(t)} f_\alpha(\boldsymbol{\Phi}(t)) \right], \qquad (6)$$

where again the Lipschitz limit $f_\alpha(t)$ of each $\alpha \in \bar{\mathcal{M}}$ is that of the transition $s \xrightarrow{\alpha} s'$ in $\mathcal{X}^{(N)}$ from which its copy $\alpha \in \mathcal{M}$ was derived (by (3) and (4)). Moreover, let the diagonal elements of $\mathbf{G}_i(\boldsymbol{\Phi}(t))$ to be defined so that the rows sum up to zero. Then, we introduce the *probability matrix* $\boldsymbol{Y}_i(t)$, which is computed in terms of the *generator* $\mathbf{G}_i(\boldsymbol{\Phi}(t))$ according to the following ODEs (see also [8]):

$$\begin{cases} \frac{d\boldsymbol{Y}_i}{dt}(t) = \boldsymbol{Y}_i(t)\mathbf{G}_i(\boldsymbol{\Phi}(t)) - \mathbf{G}(\boldsymbol{\Phi}(t - \Delta_i))\boldsymbol{Y}_i(t), & \Delta_i \leq t \leq T, \\ \frac{d\boldsymbol{Y}_i}{dt}(t) = \boldsymbol{Y}_i(t)\mathbf{G}_i(\boldsymbol{\Phi}(t)), & 0 \leq t \leq \Delta_i, \end{cases} \qquad (7)$$

with $\boldsymbol{Y}_i(0) = \mathbf{I}$. By definition, $(\boldsymbol{Y}_i(t))_{(i,s',q'),(i,s,q)}$ is the Fluid Approximation of the probability of step (2), i.e. the probability that the agent, which has entered $\mathcal{A}_i$ in state (i, s', q') at time $t - \Delta_i$, moves (Markovianly) within $\mathcal{A}_i$ for Δ_i units of time, and reaches $(i, s, q) \in \mathcal{A}_i$ at time t (exactly when e_i elapses).

In terms of the probability matrix $\boldsymbol{Y}_i(t)$, we can now define the component of $\boldsymbol{D}(\boldsymbol{\Phi}(t), \boldsymbol{P}(t))$ that corresponds to the deterministic transition $(i, s, q) \dashrightarrow_{e_i} (i + 1, s, q)$ of the clock event $e_i \in \mathcal{E}$. This component is the element in position $((i, s, q), (i + 1, s, q))$ in $\boldsymbol{D}(\boldsymbol{\Phi}(t), \boldsymbol{P}(t))$, we call it $D_{e_i,s,q}(\boldsymbol{\Phi}(t), \boldsymbol{P}(t))$, and is given by

---

[4] If e is one of events of the 1st Time Region, i.e. $e = e_1^j$, for some $j = 1, \ldots, \ell$, in this section, we drop the index j to ease the notation, i.e. we write $e_1^j = e_1 = (\mathcal{A}_1, \Delta_1, p_1)$.

[5] The absorbing state s_{out} is needed for the probability $\boldsymbol{Y}_i(t)$ of step (2) to be well defined. Indeed, the agent can deactivate e_i by taking a reset transition.

$$D_{e_i,s,q}(\boldsymbol{\Phi}(t), \boldsymbol{P}(t)) = \sum_{(i,\bar{s},\bar{q})\in\mathcal{A}_i} \Bigg[1_{\{i>1\}} D_{e_{i-1},\bar{s},\bar{q}}(\boldsymbol{\Phi}(t-\Delta_i), \boldsymbol{P}(t-\Delta_i)) + 1_{\{i=1\}} \times$$

$$\times \sum_{(i',s',q')\xrightarrow{\alpha}(1,\bar{s},\bar{q})\in\mathcal{R}} \frac{1}{\Phi_{s'}(t)} f_\alpha(\boldsymbol{\Phi}(t-\Delta_1))(\boldsymbol{P}(t-\Delta_1))_{(i',s',q')} \Bigg] (\boldsymbol{Y}_i(t))_{(i,\bar{s},\bar{q}),(i,s,q)},$$

(8)

where $(\boldsymbol{P}(t-\Delta_1))_{(i',s',q')}$ is the component in position $(i',s',q') \in S_{\mathbb{D}_{i'}}$ in the vector of the transient probability $\boldsymbol{P}(t-\Delta_1)$ of $Z_{\mathscr{A}_\mathbb{D}}$ at time $t-\Delta_1$. In (8), for each state $(i,\bar{s},\bar{q})$ in the activation set $\mathcal{A}_i$, the quantity inside the squared brackets is the probability flux that entered $(i,\bar{s},\bar{q})$ at time $t-\Delta_i$. In particular, when $i > 1$, $D_{e_{i-1},\bar{s},\bar{q}}(\boldsymbol{\Phi}(t-\Delta_i), \boldsymbol{P}(t-\Delta_i))$ accounts for the termination of clock event e_{i-1} (i.e. the deterministic transition $(i-1,\bar{s},\bar{q}) \dashrightarrow_{e_i} (i,\bar{s},\bar{q})$ fired at time $t-\Delta_i$). When we consider the 1st Time Region, i.e. $i = 1$, instead, each term in the sum over the reset transitions is the flux of probability entering $(1,\bar{s},\bar{q})$ at time $t-\Delta_1$ due to a clock reset. Finally, $(\boldsymbol{Y}_i(t))_{(i,\bar{s},\bar{q}),(i,s,q)}$ is again the probability of reaching $(i,s,q) \in \mathcal{A}_i$ from $(i,\bar{s},\bar{q}) \in \mathcal{A}_i$ in Δ_i units of time.

All the other off-diagonal elements of $\boldsymbol{D}(\boldsymbol{\Phi}(t), \boldsymbol{P}(t))$ can be computed in a similar way, while the diagonal ones are defined so that the rows sum up to zero. Moreover, since at the end $\boldsymbol{D}(\boldsymbol{\Phi}(t), \boldsymbol{P}(t))$ depends on the state of the system at times $t-\Delta_1, \ldots, t-\Delta_k$ (through the probabilities $\boldsymbol{Y}_i(t)$, $i = 1, \ldots, k$), we write $\boldsymbol{D}(\boldsymbol{\Phi}(t)) = \boldsymbol{D}(\boldsymbol{\Phi}, \boldsymbol{P}, \Delta_1, \ldots, \Delta_k, t)$. Then, we define the *transient probability* $\boldsymbol{P}(t)$ of the IMRP $Z_{\mathscr{A}_\mathbb{D}}(t)$ as the solution of the following system of DDEs:

$$\boldsymbol{P}(t) = \int_0^t \boldsymbol{M}(s)\boldsymbol{P}(t)ds + \int_0^t \boldsymbol{D}(\boldsymbol{\Phi}, \boldsymbol{P}, \Delta_1, \ldots, \Delta_k, s)ds + 1_{t\geq\Delta_1} \sum_{(s,q)\in S\times Q} y_{e_1^0}\boldsymbol{\nu}_{e_1^0,s,q}.$$

(9)

In (9), the third term is a deterministic jump in the value of $\boldsymbol{P}(t)$ at time $t = \Delta_1$, and represents the contribute of the clock event e_1^0. In such term, the vectors $\boldsymbol{\nu}_{e_1^0,s,q}$ are the update vectors of the deterministic transitions encoded by e_0^1 (hence, the sum is computed over all such transitions), and the probability $y_{e_1^0}$ is the value at time $t = \Delta_1$ of the component in position $(s_{0,\mathbb{D}}, (1,s,q))$ (where $s_{0,\mathbb{D}}$ is the initial state of $\mathscr{A}_\mathbb{D}$) in the matrix $\boldsymbol{Y}_{e_1^0}(t)$ defined by:

$$\frac{d\boldsymbol{Y}_{e_1^0}}{dt}(t) = \boldsymbol{Y}_{e_1^0}(t)\boldsymbol{G}_1(\boldsymbol{\Phi}(t)), \quad 0 \leq t \leq \Delta_1,$$

with $\boldsymbol{G}_1(\boldsymbol{\Phi}(t))$ defined as in (6), and $\boldsymbol{Y}_{e_1^0}(0) = \boldsymbol{I}$. Hence, $y_{e_1^0} = (\boldsymbol{Y}_{e_1^0}(\Delta_1))_{s_{0,\mathbb{D}},(1,s,q)}$ is the probability that, starting form $s_{0,\mathbb{D}}$, the agents reaches $(1,s,q) \in S_{\mathbb{D}_1}$ at time $t = \Delta_1$ (exactly when the deterministic event $(1,s,q) \dashrightarrow_{e_1^0} (2,s,q)$ fires).

Given the product $\mathscr{A}_{\mathbb{D}}$, the IMRP $Z_{\mathscr{A}_{\mathbb{D}}}(t)$, and its transient probability $\boldsymbol{P}(t)$, the following result holds true.

Proposition 2. *There is a 1:1 correspondence between $\Sigma_{\mathscr{A},\mathbb{D},T}$ and the set $AccPath(\mathscr{A}_{\mathbb{D}}, T)$ of accepted paths of duration T of $\mathscr{A}_{\mathbb{D}}$. Hence,*

$$P(T) = Prob_Z\{\Sigma_{\mathscr{A},\mathbb{D},T}\} = Prob_{Z_{\mathscr{A}_{\mathbb{D}}}}\{AccPath(\mathscr{A}_{\mathbb{D}}, T)\} = P_{F_{\mathbb{D}}}(T),$$

where $Prob_{Z_{\mathscr{A}_{\mathbb{D}}}}$ is the probability measure defined by $Z_{\mathscr{A}_{\mathbb{D}}}$, and $P_{F_{\mathbb{D}}}(T)$ is the sum of the components of $\boldsymbol{P}(T)$ corresponding to the final states $F_{\mathbb{D}}$ of $\mathscr{A}_{\mathbb{D}}$.   □

In other words, according to Proposition 2, when the population of $\mathcal{X}^{(N)}$ is large enough, $P_{F_{\mathbb{D}}}(T)$ is an accurate approximation of the probability that a (random) single agent in $\mathcal{X}^{(N)}$ satisfies property $\mathbb{D}$ within time T.

Example. For the product $\mathscr{A}_{\mathbb{D}}$ in Fig. 2, the non-zero off-diagonal entries of the generator matrix $\boldsymbol{G}_{e_1^1}(\boldsymbol{\Phi}(t))$ of the clock event e_1^1 are: $G_{(S,q1)(I,q2)}(t) = k_i\Phi_I(t)$; $G_{(S,q2)(I,q2)}(t) = k_i\Phi_I(t)$; and $G_{(I,q2)(S,q2)}(t) = k_r$. In terms of $\boldsymbol{G}_{e_1^1}(\boldsymbol{\Phi}(t))$, we can define $\boldsymbol{Y}_{e_1^1}(t)$, as in (7), that is then used in the DDEs (9) for the probability $\boldsymbol{P}(t)$. In this latter set of 9 DDEs (one for each state of $\mathscr{A}_{\mathbb{D}}$), we have:

$$\boldsymbol{P}_{(1,S,q1)}(t) = \int_0^t k_r \boldsymbol{P}_{(1,S,q1)}(s)ds - \int_0^t k_i\Phi_I(s)\boldsymbol{P}_{(1,S,q1)}(s)ds +$$

$$- \int_0^t k_r \boldsymbol{Y}_{(1,S,q1),(1,S,q1)}(s-5,s)\boldsymbol{P}_{(1,S,q1)}(s)ds.$$

Remark. The presence of *only one clock* in $\mathbb{D}$ enables us to define $\mathscr{A}_{\mathbb{D}}$ in such a way that $Z_{\mathscr{A}_{\mathbb{D}}}(t)$ is an IMRP. This cannot be done when we consider *multiple clocks* in $\mathbb{D}$. Indeed, in the latter case, the definition of the stochastic process which describes the state of the product $\mathscr{A}_{\mathbb{D}}$ is much more complicated, since, when a reset event occurs, we still need to keep track of the valuations of all the other clocks in the model (hence, the dynamics between the time regions of $\mathscr{A}_{\mathbb{D}}$ is not as simple as in the case of one single clock). In the future, we plan to investigate possible extensions of our model checking procedure to timed properties with multiple clocks, also taking into account the results of [19] and [4].

3.1   The Mean Behaviour of the Population Model

It is possible to modify our FMC procedure in order to compute the *mean* number of agents that satisfy $\mathbb{D}$. This can be done by assigning a personal clock to each agent, and monitoring all of them using as agent class the product $\mathscr{A}_{\mathbb{D}}$ defined in Sec. 3. In terms of $\mathscr{A}_{\mathbb{D}}$, we can build the population model $\mathcal{X}_{\mathbb{D}}$, with $\mathscr{A}_{\mathbb{D}}$ as the only agent class, and the sum $P_{F_{\mathbb{D}}}(T)$ of the components corresponding to the final states of $\mathscr{A}_{\mathbb{D}}$ in the Fluid Approximation $\boldsymbol{\Phi}(t)$ of $\mathcal{X}_{\mathbb{D}}$ computed at $t = T$ is indeed the mean number of agents satisfying property $\mathbb{D}$ within time T. The construction of $\mathcal{X}_{\mathbb{D}}$ is not difficult: it follows the procedure of [10],

Table 1. Mean Relative Error (MeanRelErr), Maximum Relative Error (MaxRelErr), and Relative Error at final time (RelErr(T)) of the FMC (top) and the Fluid Approximation of the mean behaviour (bottom) for different values of N. The table enlists also the execution times (in seconds) of the DES (TimeDES) and the approximations (TimeFMC and TimeFluid), and the speedups (TimeDES divided by the other times).

Fluid Model Checking

N	MeanRelErr	MaxRelErr	RelErr(T)	TimeDES	TimeFMC	Speedup
250	0.0927	6.4512	0.1043	11.0273	0.4731	23.3086
500	0.0204	1.7191	0.0048	44.0631	0.3980	110.7113
1000	0.0118	0.7846	0.0003	170.9154	0.3998	427.5022

Fluid Approximation of the mean behaviour

N	MeanRelErr	MaxRelErr	RelErr(T)	TimeDES	TimeFluid	Speedup
250	0.1127	0.2316	0.0921	105.5647	0.4432	339.7217
500	0.0289	0.3177	0.0289	415.0635	0.4237	979.6165
1000	0.0117	0.2216	0.0117	1547.0340	0.4213	3672.0484

where a little extra care has to be taken just in the definition of the global transitions of $\mathcal{X}_{\mathbb{D}}$. Indeed, if we build for instance the population model $\mathcal{X}_{\mathbb{D}}$ of the running example, we need to consider that the infected individual that passes the virus to an agent in state $(1, S, q0)$ can be now in one of *five* states: $(1, I, q0), (1, I, q2), (2, I, q0), (2, I, q1)$ or $(2, I, q2)$. For this reason, we have to define *five* Markovian global transition in $\mathcal{X}_{\mathbb{D}}$, each of which moves an agent from $(1, S, q0)$ to $(1, I, q0)$ at a rate that is influenced by the number of individuals that are in the infected states of $\mathscr{A}_{\mathbb{D}}$, recorded in the counting variables $X_{(1,I,q0)}(t), X_{(1,I,q2)}(t), X_{(2,I,q0)}(t), X_{(2,I,q1)}(t)$ or $X_{(2,I,q2)}(t)$. The same reasoning has to be followed for the definition of the infections of the agents in states $(1, S, q1), (1, S, q2), (2, S, q0), (2, S, q1)$ and $(2, S, q2)$. At the end, as for the single agent, due to the deterministic events, the Fluid Approximation $\boldsymbol{\Phi}(t)$ of $\mathcal{X}_{\mathbb{D}}$ is the solution of a system of DDEs similar to (9). The definition of such approximating equations for a population model with exponential and deterministic transitions is not new [22], but, even if the results are promising (see Sec. 4), to our knowledge, nobody has yet proven the convergence of the estimation in the limit $N \to +\infty$. We save the investigation of this result for future work.

4   Experimental Results

To validate the procedures of Sec. 3, we performed a set of experiments on the running example, where we fixed: $k_i = 1.2$, $k_r = 1$, $\Delta = 5$, and an initial state of the population model with a susceptible-infected ratio of 9:1. As in Fig. 2, we let the single agent start in the susceptible state, and we considered three different values of the population size: $N = 250, 500, 1000$. For each N, we compared our procedures with a statistical estimate from 10000 runs, obtained by a dedicated Java implementation of a Discrete Event Simulator (DES). The errors and the execution times obtained by our FMC procedure (top) and the

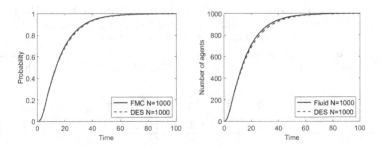

Fig. 3. The satisfaction probability $P(T) = P_{F_\mathbb{D}}(T)$ obtained by the Fluid Model Checking (left) and the Fluid Approximation of the mean behaviour (right) in the case $N = 1000$. The results are compared with those obtained by the DES.

Fluid Approximation of the mean behaviour (bottom) are reported in Tab. 1. Regarding the errors, we would like to remark that the Relative Errors (RE) of both the FMC and the Fluid Approximation reach their maximum in the very first instants of time, when the true satisfaction probability (i.e. the denominator of the REs) is indeed really small, but then they decay really fast as the values of $P_{F_\mathbb{D}}(t)$ increase (this can be easily deduced from the values of the mean REs and the REs at final time). As expected, the accuracy of the approximations increases with the population size, and is already reasonably good for $N = 500$. Moreover, the resolution of the DDEs is computationally independent of N, and also much faster (approximatively 3 orders of magnitude in the case of the Fluid for $N = 1000$) than the simulation based method. Fig. 3 shows the results of the FMC and the Fluid Approximation in the case N=1000.

5   Conclusions

We defined a fast and efficient FMC procedure that accurately estimates the probability that a single agent inside a large collective system satisfies a time-bounded property specified by a single-clock DTA. The method requires the integration of a system of DDEs for the transient probability of an IMRP, and the exactness of the estimation is guaranteed in the limit of an infinite population.

Future Work. During the experimental analysis, we realised that, on certain models and properties, the DDEs (7) can be *stiff*, and their numerical integration in MATLAB is unstable (see also [8]). In the future, we want to address this issue by considering alternative integration methods [21], investigating also numerical techniques for MRP with time-dependent rates[26]. Furthermore, we plan to prove the convergence of the Fluid Approximation of Sec. 3.1, and to investigate higher-order estimates as in [10,11]. Finally, we want to extend the FMC procedure of this paper to validate requirements specified in the logic CSL^{TA} [17] and DTA properties endowed with multiple clocks (possibly considering the approximation techniques defined in [19] and [4]).

References

1. Alur, R., Dill, D.L.: A Theory of Timed Automata. Theor. Comput. Sci. (1994)
2. Andersson, H., Britton, T.: Stochastic Epidemic Models and their Statistical Analysis. Springer, New York (2000)
3. Baier, C., Katoen, J.P.: Principles of Model Checking. MIT press (2008)
4. Barbot, B., Chen, T., Han, T., Katoen, J.-P., Mereacre, A.: Efficient CTMC model checking of linear real-time objectives. In: Abdulla, P.A., Leino, K.R.M. (eds.) TACAS 2011. LNCS, vol. 6605, pp. 128–142. Springer, Heidelberg (2011)
5. Benaim, M., Le Boudec, J.-Y.: A class of mean field interaction models for computer and communication systems. Perform. Evaluation (2008)
6. Bortolussi, L., Hillston, J.: Fluid approximation of CTMC with deterministic delays. In: Proceedings of QEST (2012)
7. Bortolussi, L., Hillston, J.: Efficient checking of individual rewards properties in Markov population models. In: Proceedings of QAPL (2015)
8. Bortolussi, L., Hillston, J.: Model Checking Single Agent Behaviours by Fluid Approximation. Inform. Comput. (2015)
9. Bortolussi, L., Hillston, J., Latella, D., Massink, M.: Continuous Approximation of Collective Systems Behaviour: a Tutorial. Perform. Evaluation (2013)
10. Bortolussi, L., Lanciani, R.: Model checking Markov population models by central limit approximation. In: Joshi, K., Siegle, M., Stoelinga, M., D'Argenio, P.R. (eds.) QEST 2013. LNCS, vol. 8054, pp. 123–138. Springer, Heidelberg (2013)
11. Bortolussi, L., Lanciani, R.: Stochastic approximation of global reachability probabilities of Markov population models. In: Horváth, A., Wolter, K. (eds.) EPEW 2014. LNCS, vol. 8721, pp. 224–239. Springer, Heidelberg (2014)
12. Chen, T., Diciolla, M., Kwiatkowska, M., Mereacre, A.: Verification of linear duration properties over CTMCs. Proceedings of TOCL (2013)
13. Chen, T., Han, T., Katoen, J.-P., Mereacre, A.: Model Checking of Continuous-Time Markov Chains Against Timed Automata Specifications. Logical Methods in Computer Science (2011)
14. Chen, T., Han, T., Katoen, J.-P., Mereacre, A.: Observing continuous-time MDPs by 1-clock timed automata. In: Delzanno, G., Potapov, I. (eds.) RP 2011. LNCS, vol. 6945, pp. 2–25. Springer, Heidelberg (2011)
15. Cinlar, E.: Introduction to Stochastic Processes. Courier Corporation (2013)
16. Darling, R., Norris, J., et al.: Differential Equation Approximations for Markov Chains. Probability Surveys (2008)
17. Donatelli, S., Haddad, S., Sproston, J.: Model Checking Timed and Stochastic Properties with CSL^{TA}. IEEE Trans. Software Eng. (2009)
18. Ethier, S.N., Kurtz, T.G.: Markov Processes: Characterization and Convergence. Wiley (2005)
19. Fu, H.: Approximating acceptance probabilities of ctmc-paths on multi-clock deterministic timed automata. In: Proceedings of HSCC (2013)
20. Gast, N., Bruno, G.: A Mean Field Model of Work Stealing in Large-Scale Systems. ACM SIGMETRICS Performance Evaluation Review (2010)
21. Guglielmi, N., Hairer, E.: Implementing Radau IIA Methods for Stiff Delay Differential Equations. Computing (2001)
22. Hayden, R.A.: Mean field for performance models with deterministically-timed transitions. In: Proceedings of QEST (2012)
23. Hayden, R.A., Bradley, J.T., Clark, A.: Performance Specification and Evaluation with Unified Stochastic Probes and Fluid Analysis. IEEE Trans. Software Eng. (2013)

24. Kwiatkowska, M., Norman, G., Parker, D.: PRISM 4.0: verification of probabilistic real-time systems. In: Gopalakrishnan, G., Qadeer, S. (eds.) CAV 2011. LNCS, vol. 6806, pp. 585–591. Springer, Heidelberg (2011)
25. Latella, D., Loreti, M., Massink, M.: On-the-fly fast mean-field model-checking. In: Abadi, M., Lluch Lafuente, A. (eds.) TGC 2013. LNCS, vol. 8358, pp. 297–314. Springer, Heidelberg (2014)
26. Zimmermann, A., Freiheit, J., German, R., Hommel, G.: Petri net modelling and performability evaluation with timeNET 3.0. In: Haverkort, B.R., Bohnenkamp, H.C., Smith, C.U. (eds.) TOOLS 2000. LNCS, vol. 1786, p. 188. Springer, Heidelberg (2000)

Nested Timed Automata with Frozen Clocks

Guoqiang Li[1]([✉]), Mizuhito Ogawa[2], and Shoji Yuen[3]

[1] BASICS, School of Software, Shanghai Jiao Tong University, Shanghai, China
li.g@sjtu.edu.cn
[2] Japan Advanced Institute of Science and Technology, Nomi, Japan
mizuhito@jaist.ac.jp
[3] Graduate School of Information Science, Nagoya University, Nagoya, Japan
yuen@is.nagoya-u.ac.jp

Abstract. A nested timed automaton (NeTA) is a pushdown system whose control locations and stack alphabet are *timed automata (TAs)*. A control location describes a working TA, and the stack presents a pile of interrupted TAs. In NeTAs, all local clocks of TAs proceed uniformly also in the stack. This paper extends NeTAs with frozen local clocks (NeTA-Fs). All clocks of a TA in the stack can be either frozen or proceeding when it is pushed. A NeTA-F also allows global clocks adding to local clocks in the working TA, which can be referred and/or updated from the working TA. We investigate the reachability of NeTA-Fs showing that (1) the reachability with a single global clock is *decidable*, and (2) the reachability with multiple global clocks is *undecidable*.

1 Introduction

Recently, modeling and analyzing complex real-time systems with recursive context switches have attracted attention. Difficulty on decidability of crucial properties, e.g. safety, comes from two dimensions of infinity, an unboundedly large stack and various types of clocks that record dense time.

Timed automata (TAs) [1] are finite automata with a finite set of *clocks*, of which the constant slope is always 1. A special type of a clock is a stopwatch, which has either 1 or 0 as the constant slope. A *stopwatch automaton* is a TA with stopwatches, and surprisingly its reachability becomes undecidable [5].

For a component-based recursive timed system, clocks are naturally classified into *global clocks*, which can be updated and observed by all contexts, and *local clocks*, which belong to the context of a component and will be stored in the stack when the component is interrupted. Similar to stopwatches, we introduce a special type of local clocks, named *frozen clocks*, whose values are not updated while their context is preempted and restart update when resumed. Other local clocks are *proceeding*. The reachability of a recursive timed systems are investigated in various models, such as *recursive timed automata (RTAs)* [2], *timed recursive state machines (TRSMs)* [3], and *nested timed automata (NeTAs)* [4]. Recently, RTAs are extended to *recursive hybrid automata (RHA)* [7].

Both RTAs [2] and TRSMs [3] adopt timed state machines as a formalization, which is regarded as a TA with explicit entry and exit states. In both models,

© Springer International Publishing Switzerland 2015
S. Sankaranarayanan and E. Vicario (Eds.): FORMATS 2015, LNCS 9268, pp. 189–205, 2015.
DOI: 10.1007/978-3-319-22975-1_13

each timed state machine (TSM) shares the same set of clocks. To guarantee the decidability of the reachability, RTAs restrict all clocks to be either call-by-value or call-by-reference, in our terminology frozen or global clocks, respectively. TRSMs are restricted to be either local or initialized. Local TRSMs restore the values of all clocks when a pop occurs. Initialized TRSMs reset all clocks to zero when a push occurs. The clocks in local-TRSMs are regarded as frozen clocks, while those in initialized-TRSMs are special cases of global clocks.

Similar to stopwatches, frozen clocks significantly affect the decidability of the reachability, observed by encoding counters with the N-wrapping technique (Fig. 1 in Section 4.2). The recursive timed systems above either prohibit to pass values between clocks and stopwatches, or have no stopwatches. Thus, they avoid the wrapping technique and the reachability remains decidable. Note that the wrapping technique is avoided if a TA has a single stopwatch (without other clocks). *Interrupt timed automata* [6] push such a stopwatch automaton into the stack, and the single stopwatch restriction preserves the decidable reachability.

This paper investigates the decidability of the reachability of *NeTAs with frozen clocks* (NeTA-Fs), which have all three types of clocks. All local clocks of a TA in a NeTA-F are either frozen or proceeding when the TA is pushed to the stack. Moreover, global clocks may exchange values with local clocks in the working TA. We show that (1) the reachability with a single global clock is *decidable*, and (2) the reachability with multiple global clocks is *undecidable*.

NeTA-Fs naturally express interrupt behavior with time as follows. At the moment of interrupt, the current working component is pushed to the stack (its local clocks are either proceeding or frozen), and a handler component starts with the initial setting. When the handler component is finished, the suspended component is popped from the stack to be resumed. Global clocks together with local clocks in the working TA work as proceeding clocks to specify time constraints as well as channels by value passing among components.

The decidability for a NeTA-F with a single global clock is shown by two steps encoding: (1) to an extension of a *dense timed pushdown automaton (DTPDA)* [8, 9] with frozen ages (DTPDA-F), and (2) its digitization a *snapshot pushdown systems* (snapshot PDS), which is a *well-structured pushdown system* [10,11] with a *well-formed constraint* [9]. Both encoding steps preserve the reachability. The undecidability of the reachability follows from simulating a Minsky machine by a NeTA-F with two global clocks, applying the N-wrapping technique [17].

The rest of the paper is organized as follows. Section 2 recalls TAs and DTPDAs, and then introduces DTPDA-Fs. Section 3 proves the decidability of the reachability of DTPDA-F with a single global clock. Section 4 presents NeTA-F, and proves its decidability and undecidability results depending on the number of global clocks. Section 5 concludes the paper.

2   Dense Timed Pushdown Automata with Frozen Ages

For finite words $w = aw'$, we denote $a = head(w)$ and $w' = tail(w)$. The concatenation of two words w, v is denoted by $w.v$, and ϵ is the empty word.

Let $\mathbb{R}^{\geq 0}$ and $\mathbb{N}$ be the sets of non-negative real and natural numbers, respectively. Let $\mathbb{N}_\omega := \mathbb{N} \cup \{\omega\}$, where ω is the least limit ordinal. $\mathcal{I}$ denotes the set of *intervals*, which are (a, b), $[a, b]$, $[a, b)$ or $(a, b]$ for $a \in \mathbb{N}$ and $b \in \mathbb{N}_\omega$.

Let $X = \{x_1, \ldots, x_n\}$ be a finite set of *clocks*. A *clock valuation* $\nu : X \to \mathbb{R}^{\geq 0}$, assigns a value to each clock $x \in X$. ν_0 represents all clocks in X assigned to 0. Given a clock valuation ν and a time $t \in \mathbb{R}^{\geq 0}$, $(\nu + t)(x) = \nu(x) + t$, for $x \in X$. A clock assignment function $\nu[y \leftarrow b]$ is defined by $\nu[y \leftarrow b](x) = b$ if $x = y$, and $\nu(x)$ otherwise. $\mathcal{V}al(X)$ is used to denote the set of clock valuation of X.

2.1 Dense Timed Pushdown Automata

Dense timed pushdown automata [8] extend timed pushdown automata with time update in the stack. Each symbol in the stack is equipped with a local clock named an *age*, and all ages in the stack proceed uniformly. An age in each context is assigned to the value of a clock when a push action occurs. A pop action pops the top symbol to assign the value of its age to a specified clock.

Note that, by deleting **push** and **pop** actions (as well as Γ) from a DTPDA, we obtain a timed automaton (TA) [1,12].

Definition 1 (Dense Timed Pushdown Automata). *A dense timed pushdown automaton is a tuple $\mathcal{A} = \langle Q, q_0, \Gamma, X, \Delta \rangle \in \mathscr{A}$, where*

- *Q is a finite set of control states with the initial state $q_0 \in Q$,*
- *Γ is finite stack alphabet,*
- *X is a finite set of clocks, and*
- *$\Delta \subseteq Q \times Actions \times Q$ is a finite set of actions.*

A (discrete) transition $\delta \in \Delta$ is a sequence of actions $(q_1, \varphi_1, q_2), \cdots, (q_i, \varphi_i, q_{i+1})$ written as $q_1 \xrightarrow{\varphi_1; \cdots; \varphi_i} q_{i+1}$, in which φ_j (for $1 \leq j \leq i$) is one of the followings,

- **Local** *ϵ, an empty operation,*
- **Test** *$x \in I?$, where $x \in X$ is a clock and $I \in \mathcal{I}$ is an interval,*
- **Assign** *$x \leftarrow I$ where $x \in X$ and $I \in \mathcal{I}$,*
- **Value passing** *$x \leftarrow x'$ where $x, x' \in X$.*
- **Push** *$push(\gamma, x)$, where $\gamma \in \Gamma$ is a stack symbol and $x \in X$, and*
- **Pop** *$pop(\gamma, x)$, where $\gamma \in \Gamma$ is a stack symbol and $x \in X$.*

A transition as a sequence of actions $q_1 \xrightarrow{\varphi_1; \cdots; \varphi_i} q_{i+1}$ prohibits interleaving time progress. This can be encoded with an extra clock by resetting it to 0 and checking it still 0 after transitions, and introducing fresh control states.

Given a DTPDA $\mathcal{A} \in \mathscr{A}$, we use $Q(\mathcal{A})$, $q_0(\mathcal{A})$, $X(\mathcal{A})$ and $\Delta(\mathcal{A})$ to represent the set of control states, the initial state, the set of clocks and the set of transitions, respectively. We will use similar notations throughout the paper.

Definition 2 (Semantics of DTPDA). *For a dense timed pushdown automaton $\langle Q, q_0, \Gamma, X, \Delta \rangle$, a configuration is a triplet (q, w, ν) with $q \in Q$, $w \in (\Gamma \times \mathbb{R}^{\geq 0})^*$, and a clock valuation ν on X. Time passage of the stack $w + t = (\gamma_1, t_1 + t). \cdots . (\gamma_n, t_n + t)$ for $w = (\gamma_1, t_1). \cdots . (\gamma_n, t_n)$.*

The transition relation of a DTPDA consists of time progress and a discrete transition which is defined by that of actions below.

- Time progress: $(q, w, \nu) \xrightarrow{t}_{\mathscr{A}} (q, w + t, \nu + t)$, where $t \in \mathbb{R}^{\geq 0}$.
- Discrete transition: $(q_1, w_1, \nu_1) \xrightarrow{\varphi}_{\mathscr{A}} (q_2, w_2, \nu_2)$, if $q_1 \xrightarrow{\varphi} q_2$, and one of the following holds,
  - **Local** $\varphi = \epsilon$, then $w_1 = w_2$, and $\nu_1 = \nu_2$.
  - **Test** $\varphi = x \in I?$, then $w_1 = w_2$, $\nu_1 = \nu_2$ and $\nu_1(x) \in I$ holds.
  - **Assign** $\varphi = x \leftarrow I$, then $w_1 = w_2$, $\nu_2 = \nu_1[x \leftarrow r]$ where $r \in I$.
  - **Value passing** $\varphi = x \leftarrow x'$, then $w_1 = w_2$, $\nu_2 = \nu_1[x \leftarrow \nu_1(x')]$.
  - **Push** $\varphi = push(\gamma, x)$, then $\nu_1 = \nu_2$, $w_2 = (\gamma, \nu_1(x)).w_1$.
  - **Pop** $\varphi = pop(\gamma, x)$, then $\nu_2 = \nu_1[x \leftarrow t]$, $w_1 = (\gamma, t).w_2$.

The initial configuration $\varrho_0 = (q_0, \epsilon, \nu_0)$.

Remark 1. For simplicity of the later proofs, the definition of DTPDAs is slightly modified from the original [8]. **Value-passing** is introduced; instead $push(\gamma, I)$ and $pop(\gamma, I)$ are dropped, since they are described by $(x \leftarrow I; push(\gamma, x))$ and $(pop(\gamma, x); x \in I?)$, respectively.

2.2 DTPDAs with Frozen Ages

A DTPDA with frozen ages (DTPDA-F) is different from Definition 1 at:

- clocks are partitioned into the set X of local clocks (of the fixed number k) and the set C of global clocks,
- a tuple of ages (for simplicity, we fix the length of a tuple to be k) is pushed on the stack and/or popped from the stack, and
- each tuple of ages is either *proceeding* (as in Definition 1) or *frozen*. After pushing the tuple, all local clocks are reset to zero.

Definition 3 (DTPDAs with Frozen Ages). *A DTPDA with frozen ages (DTPDA-F) is a tuple* $\mathcal{D} = \langle S, s_0, \Gamma, X, C, \Delta \rangle \in \mathscr{D}$, *where*

- *S is a finite set of states with the initial state $s_0 \in S$,*
- *Γ is finite stack alphabet,*
- *X is a finite set of local clocks (with $|X| = k$),*
- *C is a finite set of global clocks, and*
- *$\Delta \subseteq S \times Action^F \times S$ is a finite set of actions.*

A (discrete) transition $\delta \in \Delta$ is a sequence of actions $(s_1, \varphi_1, s_2), \cdots, (s_i, \varphi_i, s_{i+1})$ *written as* $s_1 \xrightarrow{\varphi_1; \cdots; \varphi_i} s_{i+1}$, *in which φ_j (for $1 \leq j \leq i$) is one of the followings,*

- **Local** ϵ, *an empty operation,*
- **Test** $x \in I?$, *where $x \in X \cup C$ is a clock and $I \in \mathcal{I}$ is an interval,*
- **Assign** $x \leftarrow I$ *where $x \in X \cup C$ and $I \in \mathcal{I}$,*
- **Value passing** $x \leftarrow x'$ *where $x, x' \in X \cup C$.*
- **Push** $push(\gamma)$, *where $\gamma \in \Gamma$,*
- **Freeze-Push (F-Push)** $fpush(\gamma)$, *where $\gamma \in \Gamma$, and*
- **Pop** $pop(\gamma)$, *where $\gamma \in \Gamma$.*

Definition 4 (Semantics of DTPDA-F). *For a DTPDA-F $\langle S, s_0, \Gamma, X, C, \Delta \rangle$, a configuration is a triplet (s, w, ν) with $s \in S$, $w \in (\Gamma \times (\mathbb{R}^{\geq 0})^k \times \{0,1\})^*$, and a clock valuation ν on $X \cup C$. For $w = (\gamma_1, \bar{t}_1, flag_1). \cdots .(\gamma_n, \bar{t}_n, flag_n)$, t-time passage on the stack, written as $w + t$, is $(\gamma_1, progress(\bar{t}_1, t, flag_1), flag_1). \cdots .(\gamma_n, progress(\bar{t}_n, t, flag_n), flag_n)$ where*

$$progress(\bar{t}, t, flag) = \begin{cases} (t_1 + t, \cdots, t_k + t) & \text{if } flag = 1 \text{ and } \bar{t} = (t_1, \cdots, t_k) \\ \bar{t} & \text{if } flag = 0 \end{cases}$$

The transition relation consists of time progress and a discrete transition.

- Time progress: $(s, w, \nu) \xrightarrow{t}_{\mathscr{D}} (s, w + t, \nu + t)$, where $t \in \mathbb{R}^{\geq 0}$.
- Discrete transition: $(s_1, w_1, \nu_1) \xrightarrow{\varphi}_{\mathscr{D}} (s_2, w_2, \nu_2)$, if $s_1 \xrightarrow{\varphi} s_2$, and one of the following holds,
  - **Local** $\varphi = \epsilon$, then $w_1 = w_2$, and $\nu_1 = \nu_2$.
  - **Test** $\varphi = x \in I?$, then $w_1 = w_2$, $\nu_1 = \nu_2$, and $\nu_1(x) \in I$ holds.
  - **Assign** $\varphi = x \leftarrow I$, then $w_1 = w_2$, $\nu_2 = \nu_1[x \leftarrow r]$ where $r \in I$.
  - **Value passing** $\varphi = x \leftarrow x'$, then $w_1 = w_2$, $\nu_2 = \nu_1[x \leftarrow \nu_1(x')]$.
  - **Push** $\varphi = push(\gamma)$, then $\nu_2 = \nu_0$, $w_2 = (\gamma, (\nu_1(x_1), \cdots, \nu_k(x_k)), 1).w_1$ for $X = \{x_1, \cdots, x_k\}$.
  - **F-Push** $\varphi = fpush(\gamma)$, then $\nu_2 = \nu_0$, $w_2 = (\gamma, (\nu_1(x_1), \cdots, \nu_k(x_k)), 0).w_1$ for $X = \{x_1, \cdots, x_k\}$.
  - **Pop** $\varphi = pop(\gamma)$, then $\nu_2 = \nu_1[\bar{x} \leftarrow (t_1, \cdots, t_k)]$, $w_1 = (\gamma, (t_1, \cdots, t_k), flag).w_2$.

The initial configuration $\varrho_0 = (s_0, \epsilon, \nu_0)$. We use $\hookrightarrow$ to range over these transitions, and $\hookrightarrow^*$ is the reflexive and transitive closure of $\hookrightarrow$.

Example 1. The figure shows transitions $\varrho_1 \hookrightarrow \varrho_2 \hookrightarrow \varrho_3 \hookrightarrow \varrho_4$ of a DTPDA-F with $S = \{\bullet\}$ (omitted in the figure), $X = \{x_1, x_2\}$, $C = \{c_1\}$, and $\Gamma = \{a, b, d\}$. At $\varrho_1 \hookrightarrow \varrho_2$, the values of x_1 and x_2 (0.5 and 3.9) are pushed with d, and frozen. After pushing, value of x_1 and x_2 will be reset to zero, Then, x_2 is set a value in $(1, 2]$, say 1.7. At $\varrho_2 \hookrightarrow \varrho_3$, time elapses 2.6, but frozen ages in the top and third stack frames do not change. The rest (in **bold**) proceed. At $\varrho_3 \hookrightarrow \varrho_4$, test whether the value of x_2 is in $(4, 6)$. Yes, then pop the stack and x_1, x_2 are set to the popped ages. Last, the value of x_1 is set to c_1.

	$(d, (0.5, 3.9), 0)$	$(d, (0.5, 3.9), 0)$	
$(a, (1.9, 4.5), 1)$	$(a, (1.9, 4.5), 1)$	$(a, (\mathbf{4.5}, \mathbf{7.1}), 1)$	$(a, (4.5, 7.1), 1)$
$(b, (6.7, 2.9), 0)$	$(b, (6.7, 2.9), 0)$	$(b, (6.7, 2.9), 0)$	$(b, (6.7, 2.9), 0)$
$(a, (3.1, 5.2), 1)$	$(a, (3.1, 5.2), 1)$	$(a, (\mathbf{5.7}, \mathbf{7.8}), 1)$	$(a, (5.7, 7.8), 1)$
$(d, (4.2, 3.3), 1)$	$(d, (4.2, 3.3), 1)$	$(d, (\mathbf{6.8}, \mathbf{5.9}), 1)$	$(d, (6.8, 5.9), 1)$

$x_1 \leftarrow 0.5$	$x_1 \leftarrow 0$	$x_1 \leftarrow \mathbf{2.6}$	$x_1 \leftarrow \mathbf{4.9}$
$x_2 \leftarrow 3.9$	$x_2 \leftarrow 1.7$	$x_2 \leftarrow \mathbf{4.3}$	$x_2 \leftarrow \mathbf{3.9}$
$c_1 \leftarrow 2.3$	$c_1 \leftarrow 2.3$	$c_1 \leftarrow \mathbf{4.9}$	$c_1 \leftarrow 4.9$

$$\varrho_1 \xrightarrow{fpush(d); x_2 \leftarrow (1,2]}_{\mathscr{D}} \varrho_2 \xrightarrow{2.6}_{\mathscr{D}} \varrho_3 \xrightarrow{x_2 \in (4,6)?; pop(d); x_1 \leftarrow c_1}_{\mathscr{D}} \varrho_4$$

3   Reachability of DTPDAs with Frozen Ages

In this section, we assume $|C| = 1$, i.e., a DTPDA-F has a single global clock. We denote the set of finite multisets over D by $\mathcal{MP}(D)$, and the union of two multisets M, M' by $M \uplus M'$. We regard a finite set as a multiset with the multiplicity 1, and a finite word as a multiset by ignoring the ordering.

3.1   Digiword and Its Operations

Let $\langle S, s_0, \Gamma, X, C, \Delta \rangle$ be a DTPDA-F, and let n be the largest integer (except for ω) appearing in Δ. For $v \in \mathbb{R}^{\geq 0}$, $proj(v) = \mathbf{r}_i$ if $v \in \mathbf{r}_i \in Intv(n)$, where

$$Intv(n) = \{\mathbf{r}_{2i} = [i,i] \mid 0 \leq i \leq n\} \cup \{\mathbf{r}_{2i+1} = (i, i+1) \mid 0 \leq i < n\} \cup \{\mathbf{r}_{2n+1} = (n, \omega)\}$$

The idea of the next digitization is inspired by [13–15].

Definition 5. *Let* $frac(x,t) = t - floor(t)$ *for* $(x,t) \in (C \cup X \cup \Gamma) \times \mathbb{R}^{\geq 0}$. *A* digitization digi $: \mathcal{MP}((C \cup X \cup \Gamma) \times \mathbb{R}^{\geq 0} \times \{0,1\}) \to \mathcal{MP}((C \cup X \cup \Gamma) \times Intv(n) \times \{0,1\})^*$ *is defined as follows.*

For $\bar{y} \in \mathcal{MP}((C \cup X \cup \Gamma) \times \mathbb{R}_{\geq 0} \times \{0,1\})$, *let* $Y_0, Y_1, \cdots, Y_m$ *be multisets that collect* $(x, proj(t), flag)$'s *having the same* $frac(x,t)$ *for* $(x,t,flag) \in \bar{y}$. *Among them,* Y_0 *(which is possibly empty) is reserved for the collection of* $(x, proj(t), flag)$ *with* $frac(t) = 0$ *and* $t \leq n$ *(i.e.,* $proj(t) = \mathbf{r}_{2i}$ *for* $0 \leq i \leq n$). *We assume that* Y_i's *except for* Y_0 *is non-empty (i.e.,* $Y_i = \emptyset$ *with* $i > 0$ *is omitted), and* Y_i's *are sorted by the increasing order of* $frac(x,t)$ *(i.e.,* $frac(x,t) < frac(x',t')$ *for* $(x, proj(t), flag) \in Y_m$ *and* $(x', proj(t'), flag') \in Y_{i+1}$).

Note that $flag$ in $(x, proj(t), flag)$ is always 1 for $x \in C \cup X$. For $Y \in \mathcal{MP}((C \cup X \cup \Gamma) \times Intv(n) \times \{0,1\})$, we define the projections by $prc(Y) = \{(x, proj(t), 1) \in Y\}$ and $frz(Y) = \{(x, proj(t), 0) \in Y\}$. We overload the projections on $\bar{Y} = Y_0 Y_1 \cdots Y_m \in (\mathcal{MP}((C \cup X \cup \Gamma) \times Intv(n) \times \{0,1\}))^*$ such that $frz(\bar{Y}) = frz(Y_0) frz(Y_1) \cdots frz(Y_m)$ and $prc(\bar{Y}) = prc(Y_0) prc(Y_1) \cdots prc(Y_m)$.

For a stack frame $v = (\gamma, (t_1, \cdots, t_k), flag)$ of a DTPDA-F, we denote a word $(\gamma, t_1, flag) \cdots (\gamma, t_k, flag)$ by $dist(v)$. Given a clock valuation ν, we denote a clock word $(x_1, \nu(x_1), flag) \ldots (x_n, \nu(x_n), flag)$ where $x_1 \ldots x_n \in X \cup C$.

Example 2. In Example 1, $n = 6$ and we have 13 intervals illustrated below.

0 $\mathbf{r}_1$ 1 $\mathbf{r}_3$ 2 $\mathbf{r}_5$ 3 $\mathbf{r}_7$ 4 $\mathbf{r}_9$ 5 $\mathbf{r}_{11}$ 6 $\mathbf{r}_{13}$

$\mathbf{r}_0$ $\mathbf{r}_2$ $\mathbf{r}_4$ $\mathbf{r}_6$ $\mathbf{r}_8$ $\mathbf{r}_{10}$ $\mathbf{r}_{12}$

For the configuration $\varrho_1 = (\bullet, v_4 \cdots v_1, \nu)$ in Example 1, let $\bar{y} = dist(v_4) \uplus \ldots \uplus dist(v_1) \uplus time(\nu)$ be a word, and $\bar{Y} = \text{digi}(\bar{y})$, i.e.,

$$\begin{aligned}
\bar{y} = &\{(a, 1.9, 1), (a, 4.5, 1), (b, 6.7, 0), (b, 2.9, 0), (a, 3.1, 1), (a, 5.2, 1), (d, 4.2, 1), \\
&(d, 3.3, 1), (x_1, 0.5, 1), (x_2, 3.9, 1), (c_1, 2.3, 1)\} \\
\bar{Y} = &\{(a, \mathbf{r}_7, 1)\}\{(a, \mathbf{r}_{11}, 1), (d, \mathbf{r}_9, 1)\}\{(c_1, \mathbf{r}_5, 1), (d, \mathbf{r}_7, 1)\}\{(x_1, \mathbf{r}_1, 1), (a, \mathbf{r}_9, 1)\} \\
&\{(b, \mathbf{r}_{13}, 0)\}\{(x_2, \mathbf{r}_7, 1), (a, \mathbf{r}_3, 1), (b, \mathbf{r}_5, 0)\} \\
prc(\bar{Y}) = &\{(a, \mathbf{r}_7, 1)\}\{(a, \mathbf{r}_{11}, 1), (d, \mathbf{r}_9, 1)\}\{(c_1, \mathbf{r}_5, 1), (d, \mathbf{r}_7, 1)\}\{(x_1, \mathbf{r}_1, 1), (a, \mathbf{r}_9, 1)\} \\
&\{(x_2, \mathbf{r}_7, 1), (a, \mathbf{r}_3, 1)\} \\
frz(\bar{Y}) = &\{(b, \mathbf{r}_{13}, 0)\}\{(b, \mathbf{r}_5, 0)\}
\end{aligned}$$

A word in $(\mathcal{MP}((C \cup X \cup \Gamma) \times Intv(n) \times \{0,1\}))^*$ is called a *digiword*. We denote $\bar{Y}|_\Lambda$ for $\Lambda \subseteq \Gamma \cup C \cup X$, by removing $(x, \mathbf{r}_i, flag)$ with $x \notin \Lambda$. A *k-pointer* $\bar{\rho}$ of $\bar{Y}$ is a tuple of k pointers to mutually different k elements in $\bar{Y}|_\Gamma$. We refer the element pointed by the i-th pointer by $\bar{\rho}[i]$. From now on, we assume that

- the occurrence of $(x, \mathbf{r}_i, 1)$ with $x \in C \cup X$ in $\bar{Y}$ is exactly once, and
- a digiword has two pairs of k-pointers $(\bar{\rho}_1, \bar{\rho}_2)$ and $(\bar{\tau}_1, \bar{\tau}_2)$ that point to only proceeding and frozen ages, respectively. We call $(\bar{\rho}_1, \bar{\rho}_2)$ *proceeding k-pointers* and $(\bar{\tau}_1, \bar{\tau}_2)$ *frozen k-pointers*. We assume that they do not overlap each other, i.e., there are no i, j, such that $\bar{\rho}_1[i] = \bar{\rho}_2[j]$ or $\bar{\tau}_1[i] = \bar{\tau}_2[j]$.

$\bar{\rho}_1$ and $\bar{\rho}_2$ intend the store of values of the local clocks at the last and one before the last **Push**, respectively. $\bar{\tau}_1$ and $\bar{\tau}_2$ intend similar for **F-Push**.

Example 3. $\bar{Y}$ in Example 2 have proceeding 2-pointers $(\bar{\rho}_1, \bar{\rho}_2)$ (marked with the numbered overlines and underlines) frozen 2-pointers 2-pointers $(\bar{\tau}_1, \bar{\tau}_2)$ (marked with the numbered double overlines and double underlines).

$$\bar{Y} = \{\underline{(a, \mathbf{r}_7, 1)}_1\}\{\underline{(a, \mathbf{r}_{11}, 1)}_2, (d, \mathbf{r}_9, 1)\}\{(c_1, \mathbf{r}_5, 1), (d, \mathbf{r}_7, 1)\}\{(x_1, \mathbf{r}_1, 1), \overline{\overline{(a, \mathbf{r}_9, 1)}}^2\}$$
$$\{\underline{\underline{(b, \mathbf{r}_{13}, 0)}}_1\}\{(x_2, \mathbf{r}_7, 1), \overline{(a, \mathbf{r}_3, 1)}^1, \underline{\underline{(b, \mathbf{r}_5, 0)}}^2\}$$

$$\bar{Y}|_\Gamma = \{\underline{(a, \mathbf{r}_7, 1)}_1\}\{\underline{(a, \mathbf{r}_{11}, 1)}_2, (d, \mathbf{r}_9, 1)\}\{(d, \mathbf{r}_7, 1)\}\{\overline{\overline{(a, \mathbf{r}_9, 1)}}^2\}$$
$$\{\underline{\underline{(b, \mathbf{r}_{13}, 0)}}_1\}\{\overline{(a, \mathbf{r}_3, 1)}^1, \underline{\underline{(b, \mathbf{r}_5, 0)}}^2\}$$

Definition 6. *For digiwords $\bar{Y} = Y_1 \cdots Y_m$ and $\bar{Z} = Z_1 \cdots Z_{m'}$ with pairs of k-pointers $(\bar{\rho}_1, \bar{\rho}_2), (\bar{\tau}_1, \bar{\tau}_2)$, and $(\bar{\rho}_1', \bar{\rho}_2'), (\bar{\tau}_1', \bar{\tau}_2')$, respectively. We define an embedding $\bar{Y} \sqsubseteq \bar{Z}$, if there exists a monotonic injection $f : [1..m] \to [1..m']$ such that $Y_i \subseteq Z_{f(i)}$ for each $i \in [1..m]$, $f \circ \bar{\rho}_i = \bar{\rho}_i'$ and $f \circ \bar{\tau}_i = \bar{\tau}_i'$ for $i = 1, 2$.*

Definition 7. *Let $\bar{Y} = Y_0 \cdots Y_m, \bar{Y}' = Y_0' \cdots Y_{m'}' \in (\mathcal{MP}((\Gamma \cup C \cup X) \times Intv(n) \times \{0,1\}))^*$ such that $\bar{Y}$ (resp. $\bar{Y}'$) has two pairs of proceeding and frozen k-pointers $(\bar{\rho}_1, \bar{\rho}_2)$ and $(\bar{\tau}_1, \bar{\tau}_2)$ (resp. $(\bar{\rho}_1', \bar{\rho}_2')$ and $(\bar{\tau}_1', \bar{\tau}_2')$). We define digiword operations as follows. Note that except for $\mathbf{Map}^{flag}_\to$, $\mathbf{Map}^{flag}_\leftarrow$, and **Permutation**, k-pointers do not change.*

- **Decomposition** *Let $Z \in \mathcal{MP}((C \cup X \cup \Gamma) \times Intv(n) \times \{0,1\})$. If $Z \subseteq Y_j$, $decomp(\bar{Y}, Z) = (Y_0 \cdots Y_{j-1}, Y_j, Y_{j+1} \cdots Y_m)$.*
- **Insert$_I$** *Let $Z \in \mathcal{MP}((\Gamma \cup C \cup X) \times Intv(n) \times \{0,1\})$ with $(x, \mathbf{r}_i, flag) \in Z$ for $x \in C \cup X \cup \Gamma$. $insert_I(\bar{Y}, Z)$ inserts Z to $\bar{Y}$ such that*

$$\begin{cases} \text{either take the union of } Z \text{ and } Y_j \text{ for } j > 0, \text{ or put } Z \text{ at any place after } Y_0 \\ \qquad\qquad\qquad\qquad \text{if } i \text{ is odd} \\ \text{take the union of } Z \text{ and } Y_0 \qquad \text{if } i \text{ is even} \end{cases}$$

- **Insert$_x$** *$insert_x(\bar{Y}, x, y)$ adds $(x, \mathbf{r}_i, 1)$ to X_j for $(y, \mathbf{r}_i, 1) \in X_j$, $x, y \in C \cup X$.*
- **Init** *For $\bar{Y} = Y_0 \cdots Y_m$, $init(\bar{Y})$ is obtained by removing all elements $(x, \mathbf{r}_i)$ for $x \in X$ and updating Y_0 with $Y_0 \uplus \{(x_i, \mathbf{r}_0) \mid x_i \in X\}$.*
- **Delete** *$delete(\bar{Y}, x)$ for $x \in C \cup X$ is obtained from $\bar{Y}$ by deleting the element $(x, \mathbf{r})$ indexed by x.*

- **Permutation.** *Let* $\bar{V} = prc(\bar{Y}) = V_0 V_1 \cdots V_k$ *and* $\bar{U} = frz(\bar{Y}) = U_0 U_1 \cdots U_{k'}$. *A one-step permutation* $\bar{Y} \Rightarrow \bar{Y}'$ *is given by* $\Rightarrow = \Rightarrow_s \cup \Rightarrow_c$, *defined below.*

  $(\Rightarrow_s)$ *Let*
  $$\begin{cases} decomp(\bar{Y}, V_k) = (\bar{Y}_\dashv^k, \hat{Y}^k, \bar{Y}_\vdash^k) \\ decomp(insert_I((\hat{Y}^k \setminus V_k).\bar{Y}_\vdash^k, V_k), V_k) = (\bar{Z}_\dashv^k, \hat{Z}^k, \bar{Z}_\vdash^k). \end{cases}$$
  For j *with* $0 \le j < k$, *we repeat to set*
  $$\begin{cases} decomp(\bar{Y}_\dashv^{j+1}.\bar{Z}_\dashv^{j+1}, V_j) = (\bar{Y}_\dashv^j, \hat{Y}^j, \bar{Y}_\vdash^j) \\ decomp(insert_I((\hat{Y}^j \setminus V_j).\bar{Y}_\vdash^j, V_j), V_j) = (\bar{Z}_\dashv^j, \hat{Z}^j, \bar{Z}_\vdash^j). \end{cases}$$
  Then, $\bar{Y} \Rightarrow_s \bar{Y}' = \bar{Z}_\dashv^0 \hat{Z}^0 \bar{Z}_\dashv^1 \hat{Z}^1 \cdots \bar{Z}_\dashv^k \hat{Z}^k \bar{Z}_\vdash^k$.

  $(\Rightarrow_c)$ *Assume* $V_k \subseteq Y_{i'}$. *For each* $(x, \mathbf{r}_{2i+1}, flag) \in V_k$ *with* $x \in C \cup X \cup \Gamma$ *and* $i < k$, *we obtain* V_k' *by replacing* $\mathbf{r}_{2i+1}$ *with* $\mathbf{r}_{2i+2}$.
  $$\begin{cases} decomp((Y_0 \cup V_k') Y_1 \cdots (Y_{i'} \setminus V_k) \cdots Y_m, V_{k-1}) = (\bar{Y}_\dashv^{k-1}, \hat{Y}^{k-1}, \bar{Y}_\vdash^{k-1}) \\ decomp(insert_I(\bar{Y}_\vdash^{k-1}.(\hat{Y}^{k-1} \setminus V_{k-1}), V_{k-1}), V_{k-1}) = (\bar{Z}_\dashv^{k-1}, \hat{Z}^{k-1}, \bar{Z}_\vdash^{k-1}). \end{cases}$$
  For j *with* $0 \le j < k - 1$, *we repeat to set*
  $$\begin{cases} decomp(\bar{Y}_\dashv^{j+1}.\bar{Z}_\dashv^{j+1}, V_j) = (\bar{Y}_\dashv^j, \hat{Y}^j, \bar{Y}_\vdash^j) \\ decomp(insert_I(\bar{Y}_\vdash^j.(\hat{Y}^j \setminus V_j), V_j), V_j) = (\bar{Z}_\dashv^j, \hat{Z}^j, \bar{Z}_\vdash^j). \end{cases}$$
  Then, $\bar{Y} \Rightarrow_c \bar{Y}' = \bar{Z}_\dashv^0 \hat{Z}^0 \bar{Z}_\dashv^1 \hat{Z}^1 \cdots \bar{Z}_\dashv^{k-1} \hat{Z}^{k-1} \bar{Z}_\vdash^{k-1}$.
  $(\bar{\rho}_1, \bar{\rho}_2)$ *is updated to correspond to the permutation accordingly, and* $(\bar{\tau}_1, \bar{\tau}_2)$ *is kept unchanged.*

- **Rotate** *For proceeding k-pointers* $(\bar{\rho}_1, \bar{\rho}_2)$ *of* $\bar{Y}$ *and* $\bar{\rho}'$ *of* $\bar{Z}$, *let* $\bar{Y}|_\Gamma \Rightarrow^* \bar{Z}|_\Gamma$ *such that the permutation makes* $\bar{\rho}_1$ *match with* $\bar{\rho}$. *Then,* $rotate_{\bar{\rho}_1 \mapsto \bar{\rho}}(\bar{\rho}_2)$ *is the corresponding k-pointer of* $\bar{Z}$ *to* $\bar{\rho}_2$.

- **Map**$_\rightarrow^{flag}$ $map_\rightarrow^{fl}(\bar{Y}, \gamma)$ *for* $\gamma \in \Gamma$ *is obtained from* $\bar{Y}$ *by, for each* $x_i \in X$, *replacing* $(x_i, \mathbf{r}_j, 1)$ *with* $(\gamma, \mathbf{r}_j, fl)$. *Accordingly, if* $fl = 1$, $\bar{\rho}_1[i]$ *is updated to point to* $(\gamma, \mathbf{r}_j, 1)$, *and* $\bar{\rho}_2$ *is set to the original* $\bar{\rho}_1$. *If* $fl = 0$, $\bar{\tau}_1[i]$ *is updated to point to* $(\gamma, \mathbf{r}_j, 0)$, *and* $\bar{\tau}_2$ *is set to the original* $\bar{\tau}_1$.

- **Map**$_\leftarrow^{flag}$ $map_\leftarrow^{fl}(\bar{Y}, \bar{Y}', \gamma,)$ *for* $\gamma \in \Gamma$ *is obtained,*
  (if $fl = 1$**)** *by replacing each* $\bar{\rho}_1[i] = (\gamma, \mathbf{r}_j, 1)$ *in* $\bar{Y}|_{C \cup \Gamma}$ *with* $(x_i, \mathbf{r}_j, 1)$ *for* $x_i \in X$. *Accordingly, new* $\bar{\rho}_1$ *is set to the original* $\bar{\rho}_2$, *and new* $\bar{\rho}_2$ *is set to* $rotate_{\bar{\rho}_1' \mapsto \bar{\rho}_2}(\bar{\rho}_2')$. $\bar{\tau}_1$ *and* $\bar{\tau}_2$ *are kept unchanged.*
  (if $fl = 0$**)** *by replacing each* $\bar{\tau}_1[i] = (\gamma, \mathbf{r}_j, 0)$ *in* $\bar{Y}|_{C \cup \Gamma}$ *with* $(x_i, \mathbf{r}_j, 1)$ *for* $x_i \in X$. *Accordingly, new* $\bar{\tau}_1$ *is set to the original* $\bar{\tau}_2$, *and new* $\bar{\tau}_2$ *is set to* $\bar{\rho}_2'$. $\bar{\rho}_1$ *and* $\bar{\rho}_2$ *are kept unchanged.*

Remark 2. **Permutation** intends to describe (nondeterministic) time progress. The figure shows that, after where V_{j+1} shifts is decided, $\bar{Y}_\dashv^{j+1}.\bar{Z}_\dashv^{j+1}$ describes the prefix of the destination of V_{j+1}. Then, the possible destination of V_j is in $\bar{Y}_\dashv^{j+1}.\bar{Z}_\dashv^{j+1}$ after the current occurrence of V_j. This range is denoted by $\bar{Z}_\vdash^j$. Note that U_i's do not change their positions.

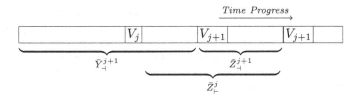

Example 4. We begin with the digiword $\bar{Y}$ in Example 3, to simulate transitions $\varrho_1 \hookrightarrow^* \varrho_3$ in Example 1.

– $fpush(d)$ is simulated by $\bar{Y}_1 = init(map^1_\rightarrow(\bar{Y}, \gamma))$.
  $\bar{Y}_1 = \{(x_1, \mathbf{r}_0, 1), (x_2, \mathbf{r}_0, 1)\}\{\overline{(a, \mathbf{r}_7, 1)}_1\}\{\overline{(a, \mathbf{r}_{11}, 1)}_2, (d, \mathbf{r}_9, 1)\}\{(c_1, \mathbf{r}_5, 1), (d, \mathbf{r}_7, 1)\}$
  $\{\overline{(a, \mathbf{r}_9, 1)}^2, \overline{(d, \mathbf{r}_1, 0)}^1\}\{\overline{(b, \mathbf{r}_{13}, 0)}_1\}\{\overline{(a, \mathbf{r}_3, 1)}^1, \overline{(b, \mathbf{r}_5, 0)}_2, \overline{(d, \mathbf{r}_7, 0)}^1\}$

– $x_2 \leftarrow (1, 2]$ is simulated by $\bar{Y}_2 = insert_I(delete(\bar{Y}_1, x_2), (x_2, \mathbf{r}_i)$.
  $\bar{Y}_2 = \{(x_1, \mathbf{r}_0, 1)\}\{\overline{(a, \mathbf{r}_7, 1)}_1\}\{\overline{(a, \mathbf{r}_{11}, 1)}_2, (d, \mathbf{r}_9, 1)\}\{(c_1, \mathbf{r}_5, 1), (d, \mathbf{r}_7, 1)\}$
  $\{\overline{(a, \mathbf{r}_9, 1)}^2, \overline{(d, \mathbf{r}_1, 0)}^1\}\{(x_2, \mathbf{r}_3, 1), \overline{(b, \mathbf{r}_{13}, 0)}_1\}\{\overline{(a, \mathbf{r}_3, 1)}^1, \overline{(b, \mathbf{r}_5, 0)}_2, \overline{(d, \mathbf{r}_7, 0)}^1\}$

– Time elapse of 2.6 time units is simulated by $\bar{Y}_2 \Rightarrow^* \bar{Y}_3$
  $\bar{Y}_3 = \{\overline{(a, \mathbf{r}_{13}, 1)}^2\}\{(x_2, \mathbf{r}_9, 1)\}\{\overline{(a, \mathbf{r}_9, 1)}^1, \overline{(d, \mathbf{r}_1, 0)}^1\}\{(x_1, \mathbf{r}_5, 1)\}\{\overline{(a, \mathbf{r}_{11}, 1)}_1,$
  $\overline{(b, \mathbf{r}_{13}, 0)}_1\}\{\overline{(a, \mathbf{r}_{13}, 1)}_2, (d, \mathbf{r}_{13}, 1)\}\{(c_1, \mathbf{r}_9, 1), (d, \mathbf{r}_{11}, 1), \overline{(b, \mathbf{r}_5, 0)}_2, \overline{(d, \mathbf{r}_7, 0)}^1\}$

3.2 Snapshot Pushdown System

A *snapshot pushdown system* (snapshot PDS) keeps the digitization of all values of (global and local) clocks and ages in the top stack frame, as a *digiword*. It is associated with a flag, which shows that the last push is either **Push** ($flag = 1$) or **F-Push** ($flag = 0$). It contains both proceeding and frozen ages, and only proceeding ages proceed synchronously to global and local clocks.

We show that a DTPDA-F with a single global clock is encoded into its digitization, called a *snapshot PDS*. The keys of the encoding are, (1) when a pop occurs, the time progress recorded at the top stack symbol is propagated to the next stack symbol after finding a permutation by matching between proceeding k-pointers $\bar{\rho}_2$ and $\bar{\rho}'_1$, and (2) the single global clock assumption allows us to compare current local clock values with a past one (which is stored in the global clock), but unable to compare past local clock values.

Definition 8. *Let $\pi : \varrho_0 = (q_0, \epsilon, \nu_0) \hookrightarrow^* \varrho = (s, w, \nu)$ be a transition sequence of a DTPDA-F from the initial configuration. If π is not empty, we refer the last step as $\lambda : \varrho' \hookrightarrow \varrho$, and the preceding sequence by $\pi' : \varrho_0 \hookrightarrow^* \varrho'$. Let $w = v_m \cdots v_1$. A snapshot is $snap(\pi) = (\bar{Y}, flag(v_m))$, where*
$$\bar{Y} = \mathtt{digi}(\uplus_i dist(v_i) \uplus \{(x, \nu(x), 1) \mid x \in C \cup X\})$$

Let a k-pointer $\bar\xi(\pi)$ be $\bar\xi(\pi)[i] = (\gamma, proj(t_i), flag(v_m))$ for $(\gamma, t_i) \in dist(v_m)$. A snapshot configuration $Snap(\pi)$ is inductively defined from $Snap(\pi')$.

$$\begin{cases} (q_0, snap(\epsilon)) & \text{if } \pi = \epsilon. \ (\bar\rho_1, \bar\rho_2) \text{ and } (\bar\tau_1, \bar\tau_2) \text{ are undefined.} \\ (s', snap(\pi)\ tail(Snap(\pi'))) & \text{if } \lambda \text{ is } \textbf{Time progress } with \ \bar Y' \Rightarrow^* \bar Y. \\ \qquad \text{Then, the permutation } \bar Y' \Rightarrow^* \bar Y \text{ updates } (\bar\rho'_1, \bar\rho'_2) \text{ to } (\bar\rho_1, \bar\rho_2). \\ (s', snap(\pi)\ tail(Snap(\pi'))) & \text{if } \lambda \text{ is } \textbf{Local, Test, Assign, Value-passing.} \\ (s, snap(\pi)\ Snap(\pi')) & \text{if } \lambda \text{ is } \textbf{Push.} \text{ Then, } (\bar\rho_1, \bar\rho_2) = (\bar\xi(\pi), \bar\rho'_1). \\ (s, snap(\pi)\ Snap(\pi')) & \text{if } \lambda \text{ is } \textbf{F-Push.} \text{ Then, } (\bar\tau_1, \bar\tau_2) = (\bar\xi(\pi), \bar\tau'_1). \\ (s, snap(\pi)\ tail(tail(Snap(\pi')))) & \text{if } \lambda \text{ is } \textbf{Pop.} \\ \qquad \text{If } flag = 1, (\bar\rho_1, \bar\rho_2) = (\bar\rho'_2, rotate_{\bar\rho''_1 \mapsto \bar\rho'_2}(\bar\rho''_2)); \text{ otherwise, } (\bar\tau_1, \bar\tau_2) = (\bar\tau'_2, \bar\tau''_2). \end{cases}$$

We refer $head(Snap(\pi'))$ by $(\bar Y', flag')$, $head(tail(Snap(\pi'))$ by $(\bar Y'', flag'')$. Pairs of proceeding k-pointers of $\bar Y$, $\bar Y'$, and $\bar Y''$ are denoted by $(\bar\rho_1, \bar\rho_2)$, $(\bar\rho'_1, \bar\rho'_2)$, and $(\bar\rho''_1, \bar\rho''_2)$, respectively. Similarly, pairs of frozen ones are denoted by $(\bar\tau_1, \bar\tau_2)$, $(\bar\tau'_1, \bar\tau'_2)$, and $(\bar\tau''_1, \bar\tau''_2)$, respectively. If not mentioned, k-pointers are kept as is.

Example 5. In Example 1, ϱ_3 is described by $Snap(\pi)$ below for an execution path $\pi = \cdots \hookrightarrow \varrho_1 \hookrightarrow \varrho_2 \hookrightarrow \varrho_3$ from the initial configuration to ϱ_3.

$(\ \{\overline{(a, r_{13}, 1)}^2\}\{(x_2, r_9, 1)\}\{\overline{(a, r_9, 1)}^1, \overline{(d, r_1, 0)}^1\}\{(x_1, r_5, 1)\}\{\overline{(a, r_{11}, 1)}_1, \overline{(b, r_{13}, 0)}_1\}$ $\{\overline{(a, r_{13}, 1)}_2, (d, r_{13}, 1)\}\{(c_1, r_9, 1), (d, r_{11}, 1), \underline{(b, r_5, 0)}_2, \overline{(d, r_7, 0)}\}, \quad fl = 0 \ )$
$(\ \{\overline{(a, r_7, 1)}_1\}\{\overline{(a, r_{11}, 1)}_2, (d, r_9, 1)\}\{(c_1, r_5, 1), (d, r_7, 1)\}\{(x_1, r_1, 1), \overline{(a, r_9, 1)}^2\}$ $\{\overline{(b, r_{13}, 0)}_1\}\{(x_2, r_7, 1), \overline{(a, r_3, 1)}^1, \overline{(b, r_5, 0)}^2\}, \quad fl = 1 \ )$
$(\ \{\overline{(a, r_7, 1)}^1\}\{\overline{(a, r_{11}, 1)}^2, \underline{(d, r_9, 1)}_1\}\{(c_1, r_5, 1), \underline{(d, r_7, 1)}_2\}\{(x_1, r_1, 1)\}$ $\{\overline{(b, r_{13}, 0)}_1\}\{(x_2, r_7, 1), \overline{(b, r_5, 0)}^2\}, \quad fl = 0 \ )$
$(\ \{\overline{(a, r_7, 1)}^1\}\{\overline{(a, r_{11}, 1)}^2, \underline{(d, r_9, 1)}_1\}\{(c_1, r_5, 1), \underline{(d, r_7, 1)}_2\}\{(x_1, r_1, 1)\}\{(x_2, r_7, 1)\}, $ $fl = 1 \ )$
$(\ \{\overline{(d, r_9, 1)}^1\}\{(c_1, r_5, 1), \overline{(d, r_7, 1)}^2\}\{(x_1, r_1, 1)\}\{(x_2, r_7, 1)\}, \quad fl = 1 \ )$

Definition 9. For a *DTPDA-F* $\langle S, s_0, \Gamma, X, C, \Delta \rangle$ with $|C| = 1$, a snapshot PDS $\mathcal{S}$ is a PDS (ith possibly infinite stack alphabet)

$$\langle S, s_0, (\mathcal{MP}((C \cup X \cup \Gamma) \times Intv(n) \times \{0, 1\}))^*, \Delta_d \rangle.$$

with the initial configuration $\langle s_{init}, \{(x, r_0) \mid x \in C \cup X\}\rangle$. Then Δ_d consists of:

Time progress $\langle s, (\bar Y, flag)\rangle \hookrightarrow_{\mathcal{S}} \langle s, (\bar Y',, flag)\rangle$ for $\bar Y \Rightarrow^* \bar Y'$.
Local $(s \xrightarrow{\epsilon} s' \in \Delta)$ $\langle s, (\bar Y, flag)\rangle \hookrightarrow_{\mathcal{S}} \langle s', (\bar Y, flag)\rangle$.
Test $(s \xrightarrow{x \in I?} s' \in \Delta)$ If $r_i \subseteq I$ and $(x, r_i, 1) \in \bar Y$,
$\quad \langle s, (\bar Y, flag)\rangle \hookrightarrow_{\mathcal{S}} \langle s', (\bar Y, flag)\rangle$.
Assign $(s \xrightarrow{x \leftarrow I} s' \in \Delta$ with $x \in X)$ For $r_i \subseteq I$,
$\quad \langle s, (\bar Y, flag)\rangle \hookrightarrow_{\mathcal{S}} \langle s', (insert_I(delete(\bar Y, x), \{(x, r_i, 1)\}), flag)\rangle$.
Assign $(s \xrightarrow{c \leftarrow I} s' \in \Delta$ with $c \in C)$ For $r_i \subseteq I$,
$\quad \langle s, (\bar Y, flag)\rangle \hookrightarrow_{\mathcal{S}} \langle s', (insert_I(delete(\bar Y, c), \{(c, r_i, 1)\}), flag)\rangle$.

Value-passing *(s $\xrightarrow{x \leftarrow y}$ s' $\in \Delta$ with $x \in X$)*
$\langle s, (\bar{Y}, flag) \rangle \hookrightarrow_S \langle s', (insert_x(delete(\bar{Y}, c), x, y), flag) \rangle$.

Value-passing *(s $\xrightarrow{c \leftarrow y}$ s' $\in \Delta$ with $c \in C$)*
$\langle s, (\bar{Y}, flag) \rangle \hookrightarrow_S \langle s', (insert_x(delete(\bar{Y}, c), c, y), flag) \rangle$.

Push *(s $\xrightarrow{push(\gamma)}$ s' $\in \Delta$; fl = 1)* and **F-Push** *(s $\xrightarrow{fpush(\gamma)}$ s' $\in \Delta$; fl = 0)*
$\langle s, (\bar{Y}, flag) \rangle \hookrightarrow_S \langle s', (init(map^{fl}_{\rightarrow}(\bar{Y}, \gamma)), fl)(\bar{Y}, flag) \rangle$.

Pop *(s $\xrightarrow{pop(\gamma)}$ s' $\in \Delta$)*
$\langle s, (\bar{Y}, flag)(\bar{Y}', flag') \rangle \hookrightarrow_S \langle s', (map^{flag}_{\leftarrow}(\bar{Y}, \bar{Y}', \gamma), flag') \rangle$.

Example 6. Following to Example 5, $\varrho_3 \hookrightarrow \varrho_4$ in Example 1 is described by $Snap(\pi) \hookrightarrow_S Snap(\pi')$ with $Snap(\pi')$ below for $\pi' = \pi \hookrightarrow \varrho_4$.

($\{\overline{(a, \mathbf{r}_{13}, 1)}^2\}\{(x_2, \mathbf{r}_9, 1)\}\{\overline{(a, \mathbf{r}_9, 1)}^1\}\{(x_1, \mathbf{r}_5, 1)\}\{\overline{(a, \mathbf{r}_{11}, 1)}_1, \overline{\overline{(b, \mathbf{r}_{13}, 0)}}^1\}$
$\{\overline{(a, \mathbf{r}_{13}, 1)}_2, (d, \mathbf{r}_{13}, 1)\}\{(c_1, \mathbf{r}_9, 1), (d, \mathbf{r}_{11}, 1), \overline{(b, \mathbf{r}_5, 0)}^2\}$, $fl = 1$)
($\{\overline{(a, \mathbf{r}_7, 1)}^1\}\{\overline{(a, \mathbf{r}_{11}, 1)}^2, (d, \mathbf{r}_9, 1)\}\{(c_1, \mathbf{r}_5, 1), \underline{(d, \mathbf{r}_7, 1)}_2\}\{(x_1, \mathbf{r}_1, 1)\}$
$\{\overline{(b, \mathbf{r}_{13}, 0)}^1\}\{(x_2, \mathbf{r}_7, 1), \overline{(b, \mathbf{r}_5, 0)}^2\}$, $fl = 0$)
($\{\overline{(a, \mathbf{r}_7, 1)}^1\}\{\overline{(a, \mathbf{r}_{11}, 1)}^2, \underline{(d, \mathbf{r}_9, 1)}_1\}\{(c_1, \mathbf{r}_5, 1), \underline{(d, \mathbf{r}_7, 1)}_2\}\{(x_1, \mathbf{r}_1, 1)\}\{(x_2, \mathbf{r}_7, 1)\}$,
$fl = 1$)
($\{\overline{(d, \mathbf{r}_9, 1)}^1\}\{(c_1, \mathbf{r}_5, 1), \overline{(d, \mathbf{r}_7, 1)}^2\}\{(x_1, \mathbf{r}_1, 1)\}\{(x_2, \mathbf{r}_7, 1)\}$, $fl = 1$)

By induction on the number of steps of transitions, the encoding relation between a DTPDA-F with a single global clock and a snapshot PDS is observed. Note that the initial clock valuation of the DTPDA-F to be set ν_0 is essential.

Lemma 1. *Let us denote ϱ_0 and ϱ (resp. $\langle q_0, \tilde{w}_0 \rangle$ and $\langle s, \tilde{w} \rangle$) for the initial configuration and a configuration of a DTPDA-F (resp. its snapshot PDS $\mathcal{S}$).*

(Preservation) *If $\pi : \varrho_0 \hookrightarrow^* \varrho$, there exists $\langle s, \tilde{w} \rangle$ such that $\langle q_0, \tilde{w}_0 \rangle \hookrightarrow^*_\mathcal{S} \langle s, \tilde{w} \rangle$ and $Snap(\pi) = \langle s, \tilde{w} \rangle$.*

(Reflection) *If $\langle q_0, \tilde{w}_0 \rangle \hookrightarrow^*_\mathcal{S} \langle s, \tilde{w} \rangle$, there exists $\pi : \varrho_0 \hookrightarrow^* \varrho$ with $Snap(\pi) = \langle s, \tilde{w} \rangle$.*

3.3 Well-Formed Constraint

A snapshot PDS is *a growing WSPDS* (Definition 6 in [9]) and $\Downarrow_\Upsilon$ gives a *well-formed constraint* (Definition 8 in [9]). Let us recall the definitions.

Let P be a set of control locations and let Γ be a stack alphabet. Different from an ordinary definition of PDSs, we do not assume that P and Γ are finite, but associated with well-quasi-orderings (WQOs) $\preceq$ and $\leq$, respectively. Note that the embedding $\sqsubseteq$ over digiwords is a WQO by Higman's lemma.

For $w = \alpha_1 \alpha_2 \cdots \alpha_n, v = \beta_1 \beta_2 \cdots \beta_m \in \Gamma^*$, let $w \ll v$ if $m = n$ and $\forall i \in [1..n].\alpha_i \leq \beta_i$. We extend $\ll$ on configurations such that $(p, w) \ll (q, v)$ if $p \preceq q$ and $w \ll v$ for $p, q \in P$ and $w, v \in \Gamma^*$. A partial function $\psi \in \mathcal{PF}un(X, Y)$ is *monotonic* if $\gamma \leq \gamma'$ with $\gamma \in dom(\psi)$ implies $\psi(\gamma) \ll \psi(\gamma')$ and $\gamma' \in dom(\psi)$.

A *a well-structured PDS* (WSPDS) is a triplet $\langle (P, \preceq), (\Gamma, \leq), \Delta \rangle$ of a set $(P, \preceq)$ of WQO states, a WQO stack alphabet $(\Gamma, \leq)$, and a finite set $\Delta \subseteq \mathcal{P}Fun(P \times \Gamma, P \times \Gamma^{\leq 2})$ of monotonic partial functions. A WSPDS is *growing* if, for each $\psi(p, \gamma) = (q, w)$ with $\psi \in \Delta$ and $(q', w') \geqslant (q, w)$, there exists (p', γ') with $(p', \gamma') \geqslant (p, \gamma)$ such that $\psi(p', \gamma') \geqslant (q', w')$.

Definition 10. *For a WSPDS* $\langle (P, \preceq), (\Gamma, \leq), \Delta \rangle$, *a pair* $(\Upsilon, \Downarrow_\Upsilon)$ *of a set* $\Upsilon \subseteq P \times \Gamma^*$ *and a projection function* $\Downarrow_\Upsilon : P \times \Gamma^* \to (P \times \Gamma^*) \cup \{\#\}$ *is a* well-formed constraint *if, for configurations* c, c',

- $c \hookrightarrow c'$ *implies that* $c \in \Upsilon$ *if, and only if* $c' \in \Upsilon$,
- $c \hookrightarrow c'$ *implies* $\Downarrow_\Upsilon (c) \hookrightarrow \Downarrow_\Upsilon (c')$,
- $\Downarrow_\Upsilon (c) \lll c$, *and*
- $c \lll c'$ *implies either* $\Downarrow_\Upsilon (c) = \Downarrow_\Upsilon (c')$ *or* $\Downarrow_\Upsilon (c) = \#$,

where $\#$ *is added to* $P \times \Gamma^*$ *as the least element (wrt* $\lll$*) and* $\Upsilon = \{c \in P \times \Gamma^* \mid c = \Downarrow_\Upsilon (c)\}$. *(*$\#$ *represents failures of* $\Downarrow_\Upsilon$*.)*

A well-formed constraint describes a syntactical feature that is preserved under transitions. Theorem 3 in [9] ensures the decidability the quasi-coverability of a growing WSPDS, and Theorem 5 in [9] lifts it to the reachability when a growing WSPDS has a well-formed constraint. Theorem 4 in [9] shows the finite convergence of a P-automaton for the quasi-coverability, which concludes that a WSPDS with a well-formed constraint holds the decidability of the reachability.

Definition 11. *Let a configuration* $(s, \tilde{w})$ *of a snapshot PDS* $\mathcal{S}$. *An element in a stack frame of* $\tilde{w}$ *has a* parent *if it has a corresponding element in the next stack frame. The transitive closure of the parent relation is an* ancestor. *An element in* $\tilde{w}$ *is* marked, *if its ancestor is pointed by a k-pointer in some stack frame. We define a* projection $\Downarrow_\Upsilon (\tilde{w})$ *by removing unmarked elements in* $\tilde{w}$. *We say that* $\tilde{w}$ *is* well-formed *if* $\Downarrow_\Upsilon (\tilde{w}) = \tilde{w}$.

The idea of $\Downarrow_\Upsilon$ is, to remove unnecessary elements (i.e., elements not related to previous actions) from the stack content. Note that a configuration reachable from the initial configuration by $\hookrightarrow^*_{\mathcal{S}}$ is always well-formed. Since a snapshot PDS is a growing WSPDS with $\Downarrow_\Upsilon$, we conclude our first theorem from Lemma 1.

Theorem 1. *The reachability of a DTPDA-F* $\langle S, s_0, \Gamma, X, C, \Delta \rangle$ *is decidable, if* $|C| = 1$.

4   Nested Timed Automata with Frozen Clocks

4.1   Nested Timed Automata with Frozen Clocks

Definition 12 extends Definition 5 in [4] with the choice that all clocks of an interrupted TA are either proceeding or frozen. In [4], only the former is allowed. For simplicity, we assume that each $\mathcal{A}_i$ in T shares the same set of local clocks.

Definition 12 (Nested Timed Automata with Frozen Clocks). *A NeTA-F is a quadruplet* $\mathcal{N} = (T, \mathcal{A}_0, X, C, \Delta)$, *where*

- *T is a finite set $\{\mathcal{A}_0, \mathcal{A}_1, \cdots, \mathcal{A}_k\}$ of TAs, with the initial TA $\mathcal{A}_0 \in T$. We assume the sets of states of $\mathcal{A}_i$, denoted by $S(\mathcal{A}_i)$, are mutually disjoint, i.e., $S(\mathcal{A}_i) \cap S(\mathcal{A}_j) = \emptyset$ for $i \neq j$. We denote the initial state of $\mathcal{A}_i$ by $q_0(\mathcal{A}_i)$.*
- *C is a finite set of global clocks, and X is the finite set of k local clocks.*
- *$\Delta \subseteq Q \times (Q \cup \{\varepsilon\}) \times Actions^+ \times Q \times (Q \cup \{\varepsilon\})$ describes transition rules below, where $Q = \cup_{\mathcal{A}_i \in T} S(\mathcal{A}_i)$.*

A transition rule is described by a sequence of Actions = {internal, push, fpush, pop, $c \in I, c \leftarrow I, x \leftarrow c, c \leftarrow x$} where $c \in C$, $x \in X$, and $I \in \mathcal{I}$. The internal actions are **Local**, **Test**, **Assign**, *and* **Value-passing** *in Definition 1.*

Internal *$(q, \varepsilon, internal, q', \varepsilon)$, which describes an internal transition in the working TA (placed at a control location) with $q, q' \in \mathcal{A}_i$.*

Push *$(q, \varepsilon, push, q_0(\mathcal{A}_{i'}), q)$, which interrupts the currently working TA $\mathcal{A}_i$ at $q \in S(\mathcal{A}_i)$. Then, a TA $\mathcal{A}_{i'}$ newly starts. Note that all local clocks of $\mathcal{A}_i$ pushed onto the stack simultaneously proceed to global clocks.*

F-Push *$(q, \varepsilon, fpush, q_0(\mathcal{A}_{i'}), q)$, which is the same as* **Push** *except that all local clocks of $\mathcal{A}_i$ are frozen.*

Pop *$(q, q', pop, q', \varepsilon)$, which restarts $\mathcal{A}_{i'}$ in the stack from $q' \in S(\mathcal{A}_{i'})$ after $\mathcal{A}_i$ has finished at $q \in S(\mathcal{A}_i)$.*

Global-test *$(q, \varepsilon, c \in I?, q, \varepsilon)$, which tests whether the value of a global clock c is in I.*

Global-assign *$(q, \varepsilon, c \leftarrow I, q, \varepsilon)$, which assigns a value in $r \in I$ to a global clock c.*

Global-load *$(q, \varepsilon, x \leftarrow c, q, \varepsilon)$, which assign the value of a global clock c to a local clock $x \in X$ in the working TA.*

Global-store *$(q, \varepsilon, c \leftarrow x, q, \varepsilon)$, which assign the value of a local clock $x \in X$ of the working TA to a global clock c.*

Definition 13 (Semantics of NeTA-F). *Given a NeTA-F $(T, \mathcal{A}_0, X, C, \Delta)$, the current control state is referred by q. Let $Val_X = \{\nu : X \to \mathbb{R}^{\geq 0}\}$ and $Val_C = \{\mu : C \to \mathbb{R}^{\geq 0}\}$. A configuration of a NeTA-F is an element in $(Q \times Val_X \times Val_C, (Q \times \{0, 1\} \times Val_X)^*)$.*

- *Time progress transitions: $(\langle q, \nu, \mu \rangle, v) \xrightarrow{t} (\langle q, \nu+t, \mu+t \rangle, v+t)$ for $t \in \mathbb{R}^{\geq 0}$, where $v + t$ set $\nu' := progress(\nu', t, flag)$ of each $\langle q', flag, \nu' \rangle$ in the stack.*
- *Discrete transitions: $\kappa \xrightarrow{\varphi} \kappa'$ is defined as follows.*
    - **Internal** *$(\langle q, \nu, \mu \rangle, v) \xrightarrow{\varphi} (\langle q', \nu', \mu \rangle, v)$, if $\langle q, \nu \rangle \xrightarrow{\varphi} \langle q', \nu' \rangle$ is in Definition 2, except for* **push** *or* **pop***.*
    - **Push** *$(\langle q, \nu', \mu \rangle, v) \xrightarrow{push} (\langle q_0(\mathcal{A}_{i'}), \nu_0, \mu \rangle, \langle q, 1, \nu \rangle.v)$.*
    - **F-Push** *$(\langle q, \nu', \mu \rangle, v) \xrightarrow{f\text{-}push} (\langle q_0(\mathcal{A}_{i'}), \nu_0, \mu \rangle, \langle q, 0, \nu \rangle.v)$.*
    - **Pop** *$(\langle q, \nu, \mu \rangle, \langle q', flag, \nu' \rangle.w) \xrightarrow{pop} (\langle q', \nu', \mu \rangle, w)$.*
    - **Global-test** *$(\langle q, \nu, \mu \rangle, v) \xrightarrow{c \in I?} (\langle q, \nu, \mu \rangle, v)$, if $\mu(c) \in I$.*

- **Global-assign** $(\langle q, \nu, \mu \rangle, v) \xrightarrow{c \leftarrow I} (\langle q, \nu, \mu[c \leftarrow r] \rangle, v)$ *for* $r \in I$.
- **Global-load** $(\langle q, \nu, \mu \rangle, v) \xrightarrow{x \leftarrow c} (\langle q, \nu[x \leftarrow \mu(c)], \mu \rangle, v)$.
- **Global-store** $(\langle q, \nu, \mu \rangle, v) \xrightarrow{c \leftarrow x} (\langle q, \nu, \mu[c \leftarrow \nu(x)] \rangle, v)$.

The initial configuration of NeTA-F is $(\langle q_0(\mathcal{A}_0), \nu_0, \mu_0 \rangle, \varepsilon)$, *where* $\nu_0(x) = 0$ *for* $x \in X$ *and* $\mu_0(c) = 0$ *for* $c \in C$. *We use* $\longrightarrow$ *to range over these transitions.*

4.2   Reachability of NeTA-Fs with Multiple Global Clocks

For showing the undecidability, we encode the halting problem of Minsky machines [16] in a NeTA-F. A Minsky machine $\mathcal{M}$ is a tuple (L, C, D) where:

- L is a finite set of states, and $l_f \in L$ is the terminal state,
- $C = \{ct_1, ct_2\}$ is the set of two counters, and
- D is the finite set of transition rules of the following types,
  - **increment counter** $d_i : ct := ct + 1$, goto l_k,
  - **test-and-decrement counter** $d_i :$ if $(ct > 0)$ then $(ct := ct - 1$, goto $l_k)$ else goto l_m,

  where $ct \in C$, $d_i \in D$ and $l_k, l_m \in L$.

Example 7. By the N-wrapping technique [17], a Minsky machine can be encoded into a NeTA-F $\mathcal{N} = (T, \mathcal{A}_0, C, \Delta)$, with $T = \{\mathcal{A}_0, \mathcal{A}_1, \mathcal{A}_2\}$ where

- $S(\mathcal{A}_0) = \{q_0\}$ and $X(\mathcal{A}_0) = \{x_f, x_p\}$, $S(\mathcal{A}_1) = \{q_1\}$ and $X(\mathcal{A}_0) = \{x_1, dum_1\}$, and $S(\mathcal{A}_2) = \{q_2\}$ and $X(\mathcal{A}_0) = \{dum_2, dum_3\}$, where the dummy clocks dum_i's are introduced to set $k = 2$. We introduce different names of 2 local clocks to clarify the context.
- $C = \{c_{sys}, c_v\}$ where c_{sys} is a system clock that will be reset to zero when its value becomes equal to N; c_v is a clock to encode values of two counters such that $\mu(c_v) = 2^{-ct_1} \cdot 3^{-ct_2}$.

Decrementing and incrementing the counter ct_1 are simulated by doubling and halving of the value of the clock c_v, respectively, while those for ct_2 are simulated by tripling and thirding the value of clock c_v. Zero-test of ct_1 is simulated by (1) multiplying the value of c_v by a power of 3, and (2) comparing it with 3. Similar for ct_2. These operations are illustrated in Fig. 1, and formally described below.

Doubling: Initially $\nu(c_{sys}) = 0$ and $\nu(c_v) = d$ with $0 < d < 1$. Then the doubling the value of c_v is obtained at the end, as $\nu(c_{sys}) = 0$ and $\nu(c_v) = 2d$.

$q_0 \xrightarrow{c_v \in [N,N]?} \xrightarrow{c_v \leftarrow [0,0]} q_0 \xrightarrow{c_{sys} \in [N,N]?} \xrightarrow{c_{sys} \leftarrow [0,0]} \xrightarrow{x_f \leftarrow c_v} \xrightarrow{f\text{-}push}$

$q_1 \, q_0 \xrightarrow{c_v \in [N,N]?} \xrightarrow{pop} \xrightarrow{c_v \leftarrow x_f} q_0 \xrightarrow{c_{sys} \in [N,N]?} \xrightarrow{c_{sys} \leftarrow [0,0]} q_0$

Halving: During the halving the value of c_v, it will be nondeterministically stored to x_f in a frozen TA. When c_{sys} is reset to zero, x_f will be popped to restart. Only if the values of x_f and c_v coincide (i.e., they reach to N together), the value of c_v becomes $d/2$ when c_{sys} is wrapped twice.

$$q_0 \xrightarrow{c_v \in [N,N]?} \xrightarrow{c_v \leftarrow [0,0]} q_0 \xrightarrow{x_f \leftarrow c_v} \xrightarrow{c_v \leftarrow [0,0]} \xrightarrow{f\text{-}push}$$

$$q_1 \ q_0 \xrightarrow{c_{sys} \in [N,N]?} \xrightarrow{c_{sys} \leftarrow [0,0]} \xrightarrow{pop} q_0 \xrightarrow{c_v \in [N,N]?} \xrightarrow{x_f \in [N,N]?} \xrightarrow{c_v \leftarrow [0,0]}$$

$$q_0 \xrightarrow{c_{sys} \in [N,N]?} \xrightarrow{c_{sys} \leftarrow [0,0]} q_0$$

Tripling: Tripling requires an extra local clock x_p in $\mathcal{A}_0$.

$$q_0 \xrightarrow{c_v \in [N,N]?} \xrightarrow{c_v \leftarrow [0,0]} q_0 \xrightarrow{c_{sys} \in [N,N]?} \xrightarrow{c_{sys} \leftarrow [0,0]} \xrightarrow{x_f \leftarrow c_v} \xrightarrow{f\text{-}push}$$

$$q_1 \ q_0 \xrightarrow{c_v \in [N,N]?} \xrightarrow{pop} \xrightarrow{c_v \leftarrow x_f} \xrightarrow{x_p \leftarrow [0,0]} q_0 \xrightarrow{c_{sys} \in [N,N]?} \xrightarrow{c_{sys} \leftarrow [0,0]} \xrightarrow{x_f \leftarrow c_v}$$

$$\xrightarrow{c_v \leftarrow x_p} \xrightarrow{f\text{-}push} q_1 \ q_0 \xrightarrow{c_v \in [N,N]?} \xrightarrow{pop} \xrightarrow{c_v \leftarrow x_f} q_0 \xrightarrow{c_{sys} \in [N,N]?} \xrightarrow{c_{sys} \leftarrow [0,0]} q_0$$

Thirding: Thirding requires an extra TA $\mathcal{A}_2$ with a local clock x_1 .

$$q_0 \xrightarrow{c_v \in [N,N]?} \xrightarrow{c_v \leftarrow [0,0]} q_0 \xrightarrow{x_f \leftarrow c_v} \xrightarrow{c_v \leftarrow [0,0]} \xrightarrow{f\text{-}push}$$

$$q_1 \ q_0 \xrightarrow{x_1 \leftarrow c_v} \xrightarrow{c_v \leftarrow [0,0]} \xrightarrow{f\text{-}push} q_2 \ q_1 \ q_0 \xrightarrow{c_{sys} \in [N,N]?} \xrightarrow{c_{sys} \leftarrow [0,0]} \xrightarrow{pop}$$

$$q_1 \ q_0 \xrightarrow{c_v \in [N,N]?} \xrightarrow{x_1 \in [N,N]?} \xrightarrow{c_v \leftarrow [0,0]} q_1 \ q_0 \xrightarrow{c_{sys} \in [N,N]?} \xrightarrow{c_{sys} \leftarrow [0,0]} \xrightarrow{pop}$$

$$q_0 \xrightarrow{c_v \in [N,N]?} \xrightarrow{x_f \in [N,N]?} \xrightarrow{c_v \leftarrow [0,0]} q_0 \xrightarrow{c_{sys} \in [N,N]?} \xrightarrow{c_{sys} \leftarrow [0,0]} q_0$$

Theorem 2. *The reachability of a NeTA-F* $(T, \mathcal{A}_0, C, \Delta)$ *is undecidable, if* $|C| > 1$.

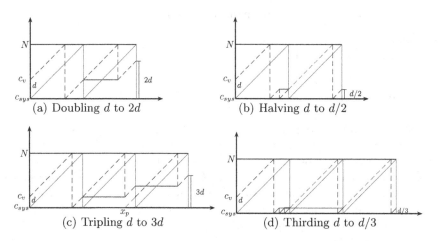

Fig. 1. Doubling, Halving, Tripling and Thirding the Value of c_v

4.3   Reachability of NeTA-F with a Single Global Clock

Let $\mathcal{N} = (T, \mathcal{A}_0, X, C, \Delta)$ be a NeTA-F. We define a corresponding DTPDA-F $\mathcal{E}(\mathcal{N}) = \langle S, s_0, \Gamma, X, C, \nabla \rangle$, such that

- $S = \Gamma = \bigcup_{\mathcal{A}_i \in T} S(\mathcal{A}_i)$ is the set of all locations of TAs in T, with
- $s_0 = q_0(\mathcal{A}_0)$ is the initial location of the initial TA $\mathcal{A}_0$ of $\mathcal{N}$.

- $X = \{x_1, \ldots, x_k\}$ is the set of k local clocks, and C is the singleton set $\{c\}$.
- ∇ is the union $\bigcup_{\mathcal{A}_i \in T} \Delta(\mathcal{A}_i) \bigcup \mathcal{G}(\mathcal{N}) \bigcup \mathcal{H}(\mathcal{N})$ where

$$\begin{cases} \Delta(\mathcal{A}_i) = \{\textbf{Local}, \textbf{Test}, \textbf{Assign}, \textbf{Value-passing}\}, \\ \mathcal{G}(\mathcal{N}) = \{\textbf{Global-test}, \textbf{Global-assign}, \textbf{Global-load}, \textbf{Global-store}\}, \\ \mathcal{H}(\mathcal{N}) \text{ consists of rules below.} \end{cases}$$

Push	$q \xrightarrow{push(q)} q_0(\mathcal{A}_{i'})$	if $(q, \varepsilon, push, q_0(\mathcal{A}_{i'}), q) \in \Delta(\mathcal{N})$
F-Push	$q \xrightarrow{fpush(q)} q_0(\mathcal{A}_{i'})$	if $(q, \varepsilon, f\text{-}push, q_0(\mathcal{A}_{i'}), q) \in \Delta(\mathcal{N})$
Pop	$q \xrightarrow{pop(q')} q'$	if $(q, q', pop, q', \varepsilon)) \in \Delta(\mathcal{N})$

Definition 14. *Let $\mathcal{N}$ be a NeTA-F $(T, \mathcal{A}_0, C, \Delta)$ and let $\mathcal{E}(\mathcal{N})$ be a DTPDA-F $\langle S, s_0, \Gamma, X, C, \nabla \rangle$. For a configuration $\kappa = (q, \nu, \mu), v)$ of $\mathcal{N}$ such that $v = (q_1, flag_1, \nu_1) \ldots (q_n, flag_n, \nu_n)$, $[\![\kappa]\!]$ denotes a configuration $(q, \overline{w}(\kappa), \nu \cup \mu)$ of $\mathcal{E}(\mathcal{N})$ where $q_i \in S(\mathcal{A}_i)$ and $\overline{w}(\kappa) = w_1 \cdots w_n$ with $w_i = (q_i, \nu_i, flag_i)$.*

Lemma 2.
For a NeTA-F $\mathcal{N}$, a DTPDA-F $\mathcal{E}(\mathcal{N})$, and configurations κ, κ' of $\mathcal{N}$,

(Preservation) *if $\kappa \longrightarrow_{\mathcal{N}} \kappa'$, then $[\![\kappa]\!] \hookrightarrow^*_{\mathcal{E}(\mathcal{N})} [\![\kappa']\!]$, and*
(Reflection) *if $[\![\kappa]\!] \hookrightarrow^*_{\mathcal{N}} \varrho$, there exists κ' with $\varrho \hookrightarrow^*_{\mathcal{E}(\mathcal{N})} [\![\kappa']\!]$ and $\kappa \longrightarrow^*_{\mathcal{N}} \kappa'$.*

By this encoding, we have our main result from Theorem 1.

Theorem 3.
The reachability of a NeTA-F $(T, \mathcal{A}_0, C, \Delta)$ is decidable, if $|C| = 1$.

5   Conclusion

This paper extends nested timed automata (NeTAs) to NeTA-Fs with *frozen local clocks*. A NeTA(-F) has a stack whose alphabet consists of timed automata. By the frozen clocks combined with value passing between clocks, past local clock values are recorded. The reachability of NeTA-F with 2 global clocks was shown to be undecidable by simulating the Minsky machine. However, with a single global clock, the reachability was shown to be *decidable*, by encoding NeTA-F to a snapshot PDS, which is a WSPDS with a well-formed constraint [9].

Acknowledgments. This work is supported by the NSFC-JSPS bilateral joint research project (61511140100), NSFC(61472240, 91318301, 61261130589), and JSPS KAKENHI Grant-in-Aid for Scientific Research(B) (15H02684, 25280023) and Challenging Exploratory Research (26540026).

References

1. Alur, R., Dill, D.L.: A Theory of Timed Automata. Theoretical Computer Science **126**, 183–235 (1994)
2. Trivedi, A., Wojtczak, D.: Recursive timed automata. In: Bouajjani, A., Chin, W.-N. (eds.) ATVA 2010. LNCS, vol. 6252, pp. 306–324. Springer, Heidelberg (2010)
3. Benerecetti, M., Minopoli, S., Peron, A.: Analysis of timed recursive state machines. In: TIME 2010, pp. 61–68. IEEE (2010)
4. Li, G., Cai, X., Ogawa, M., Yuen, S.: Nested timed automata. In: Braberman, V., Fribourg, L. (eds.) FORMATS 2013. LNCS, vol. 8053, pp. 168–182. Springer, Heidelberg (2013)
5. Cassez, F., Larsen, K.G.: The impressive power of stopwatches. In: Palamidessi, C. (ed.) CONCUR 2000. LNCS, vol. 1877, pp. 138–152. Springer, Heidelberg (2000)
6. Berard, B., Haddad, S., Sassolas, M.: Real time properties for interrupt timed automata. In: TIME 2010, pp. 69–76. IEEE (2010)
7. Krishna, S.N., Manasa L., Trivedi, A.: What's decidable about recursive hybrid automata? In: HSCC 2015, pp. 31–40. ACM (2015)
8. Abdulla, P.A., Atig, M.F., Stenman, J.: Dense-timed pushdown automata. In: LICS 2012, pp. 35–44. IEEE (2012)
9. Cai, X., Ogawa, M.: Well-structured pushdown system: case of dense timed pushdown automata. In: Codish, M., Sumii, E. (eds.) FLOPS 2014. LNCS, vol. 8475, pp. 336–352. Springer, Heidelberg (2014)
10. Cai, X., Ogawa, M.: Well-structured pushdown systems. In: D'Argenio, P.R., Melgratti, H. (eds.) CONCUR 2013 – Concurrency Theory. LNCS, vol. 8052, pp. 121–136. Springer, Heidelberg (2013)
11. Leroux, J., Praveen, M., Sutre, G.: Hyper-ackermannian bounds for pushdown vector addition systems. In: CSL-LICS 2014, pp. 63:1–63:10. IEEE (2014)
12. Henzinger, T.A., Nicollin, X., Sifakis, J., Yovine, S.: Symbolic Model Checking for Real-Time Systems. Information and Computation **111**, 193–244 (1994)
13. Ouaknine, J., Worrell, J.: On the language inclusion problem for timed automata: closing a decidability gap. In: LICS 2004, pp. 54–63. IEEE (2004)
14. Abdulla, P.A., Jonsson, B.: Verifying networks of timed processes (extended abstract). In: Steffen, B. (ed.) TACAS 1998. LNCS, vol. 1384, pp. 298–312. Springer, Heidelberg (1998)
15. Abdulla, P., Jonsson, B.: Model Checking of Systems with Many Identical Time Processes. Theoretical Computer Science **290**, 241–264 (2003)
16. Minsky, M.L.: Computation: Finite and Infinite Machines. Prentice-Hall (1967)
17. Henzinger, T., Kopke, P., Puri, A., Varaiya, P.: What's Decidable about Hybrid Automata? Journal of Computer and System Sciences **57**, 94–124 (1998)

Quantitative Analysis of Concurrent Reversible Computations

Andrea Marin and Sabina Rossi[(✉)]

DAIS, Università Ca' Foscari Venezia, Via Torino, 155, Venezia, Italy
{marin,srossi}@dais.unive.it

Abstract. Reversible computing is a paradigm of computation that extends the standard forward-only programming to reversible programming, so that programs can be executed both in the standard, forward direction, and backward, going back to past states. In this paper we present novel quantitative stochastic model for concurrent and cooperatsible computations. More precisely, we introduce the class of ρ-reversible stochastic automata and define a semantics for the synchronization ensuring that this class of models is closed under composition. For this class of automata we give an efficient way of deriving the equilibrium distribution. Moreover, we prove that the equilibrium distribution of the composition of reversible automata can be derived as the product of the equilibrium distributions of each automaton in isolation.

1 Introduction

Reversible computing is a paradigm of computation which relies on the idea that programs can be executed both in the standard, forward direction, and backward. In contrast to traditional forward-only computations, reversible executions may restore a past state by undoing, one by one, all the previously performed operations. According to [26] a *bi-directional* execution is any program execution that carries with it the notion of a runtime choice between forward and backward execution, regardless of the granularity of the execution unit. Although still not widely used, reversible computing has a growing number of promising applications. For instance, it has been shown in [4,5] that ideally reversible computations can be performed without loss of energy. Another application scenario is the improvement of the performance in parallel computations. Indeed, by assuming the reversibility of the computations we may increase the concurrency of the systems by allowing the local processors to execute their jobs asynchronously. In case of data dependence violations, the backward execution rolls back the processor to the execution point where the dependency violation occurred. A practical application of this idea is the popular "time warp" mechanism proposed by Jefferson in [17,18]. Other applications include processors with speculative executions [11], debugging [8,22], fault detection [7] and tolerance [27], database transaction rollbacks and quantum computing [25,30] (see [26] for a survey of these application scenarios). Reversible computing can be implemented in essentially two ways: the first consists in recording a set of

© Springer International Publishing Switzerland 2015
S. Sankaranarayanan and E. Vicario (Eds.): FORMATS 2015, LNCS 9268, pp. 206–221, 2015.
DOI: 10.1007/978-3-319-22975-1_14

checkpoints that store the state of the processor at some epochs of the computation, the second in implementing fully reversible programs where each step of the computation may be inverted. *Janus* [33,34] is an example of a time-reversible programming language and many research efforts have been devoted to the construction of reversible hardware components.

While the functional analysis of reversible computations has been widely explored in previous works (see [4,9,20,28]), the quantitative analysis is a topic that has still to be addressed. For forward-only computations, time-based quantitative analysis has been deeply studied especially in the context of systems in which some aspects are abstracted out and assumed to have a probabilistic nature (see, e.g.,[2]).

In this paper we focus on the problem of defining quantitative stochastic models for concurrent and cooperating reversible computations. The stochastic processes underlying our models are continuous-time Markov processes with a discrete-state space (i.e., Continuous Time Markov Chains, CTMCs) which is a common framework for the formal specification and evaluation of quantitative properties of systems [13,15,29]. We focus on the derivation of the equilibrium (or steady-state) performance indices, i.e., we aim at computing the probability of observing the system in a certain state when the time elapsed since the beginning of the computation is long enough (ideally infinite). Indeed, we can imagine to repeat the computation infinite times, and the equilibrium distribution represents the probability of observing a certain state under this assumption. For models with an underlying CTMC the necessary and sufficient condition for the existence of a unique equilibrium distribution is that the chain is ergodic, i.e., its reachability graph is irreducible and the expected time elapsed from a visit to any state until the next visit to the same state is finite.

Contribution. In this paper we use stochastic automata in the style of [29] to model reversible processes. We introduce the class of *ρ-reversible stochastic automata* and define a semantics for the synchronisation of reversible automata that ensures that this class of models is closed under composition. For simplicity, we introduce the synchronisation semantics for pairs of automata and then we discuss how it is possible to extend it to an arbitrary number of automata. We also address the problem of the computation of the equilibrium distribution. Indeed, for general Markovian models, the derivation of the equilibrium distribution is known to be time expensive ($\mathcal{O}(n^3)$ with n being the number of model states) and prone to numerical stability problems [31] since it requires the numerical solution of a linear system of equations. For the class of reversible automata we give an efficient way of deriving the steady-state distribution which is also numerically stable since it involves only the product of floating point numbers. Even more interestingly, we prove that the equilibrium distribution of the composition of reversible automata can be derived as the product of the equilibrium distributions of each automaton in isolation. In the literature, this property is known as *product-form* [3,19].

Related Work. Formalisms for the description and the analysis of reversible computations have been proposed in [10,21] and the references therein. The behavioural analysis of reversible computations has been studied in [9,20,28] where the authors address the problem of reachability and system equivalences via bisimulation. In [1] and subsequent papers, the authors propose a quantitative evaluation of the energy costs required to allow the system to reach a steady-state behaviour. Our contribution is more related to formal methods for the quantitative analysis of reversible computations and the computation of the equilibrium distribution that, to the best of our knowledge, has still to be explored. From a theoretical point of view, time-reversibility in CTMCs is mainly studied in [19] where the author introduces also a class of product-form models. In [23,24] the authors introduce novel reversibility-based definitions for Markov chains but, differently from the present work, there is not any notion of compositionality. With respect to the above mentioned works, here we consider interacting labelled automata representing reversible computations and define a synchronisation semantics that is closed with respect to this class of computations. Moreover, we study their equilibrium distribution which, surprisingly, is proved to exhibit an unconditional product-form. This is different from the well-known quasi-reversibility based product-forms studied in [12,19].

Plan of the paper. The paper is organized as follows. Section 2 introduces the fundamental notions of Markov chain and reversibility. In Section 3 we introduce the definition of stochastic automaton and provide the synchronization semantics. In Section 4 we present our main theoretical results about reversible automata, their closure under synchronization and their product-form solution. Section 5 concludes the paper.

2   Continuous-Time Markov Chains

Let $X(t)$ be a stochastic process taking values into a state space $\mathcal{S}$ for $t \in \mathbb{R}^+$. $X(t)$ is *stationary* if $(X(t_1), X(t_2), \ldots, X(t_n))$ has the same distribution as $(X(t_1 + \tau), X(t_2 + \tau), \ldots, X(t_n + \tau))$ for all $t_1, t_2, \ldots, t_n, \tau \in \mathbb{R}^+$. $X(t)$ satisfies the *Markov property* and is called *Markov process* if the conditional (on both past and present states) probability distribution of its future behaviour is independent of its past evolution until the present state.

A Continuous-Time Markov Chain (CTMC) is a Markov process with a discrete state space. A CTMC $X(t)$ is *time homogeneous* if the conditional probability $P(X(t + \tau) = s \mid X(t) = s')$ does not depend upon t, and is *irreducible* if every state in $\mathcal{S}$ can be reached from every other state. A state in a CTMC is called *recurrent* if the probability that the process will eventually return to the same state is one. A recurrent state is called *positive-recurrent* if the expected number of steps until the process returns to it is finite. A CTMC is *ergodic* if it is irreducible and all its states are positive-recurrent. We assume that any CTMC which we deal with is *ergodic*. A process satisfying all these assumptions possesses an *equilibrium* (or *steady-state*) *distribution*, that is the *unique* collection of positive numbers $\pi(s)$ with $s \in \mathcal{S}$ such that $lim_{t \to \infty} P(X(t) = s \mid X(0) = s') = \pi(s)$ for all $s' \in \mathcal{S}$.

The transition rate between two states s and s' is denoted by $q(s, s')$, with $s \neq s'$. The infinitesimal generator matrix $\mathbf{Q}$ of a Markov process is such that the $q(s, s')$'s are the off-diagonal elements while the diagonal elements are formed as the negative sum of the non-diagonal elements of each row. The equilibrium distribution π is the unique row vector of positive numbers $\pi(s)$ with $s \in \mathcal{S}$, summing to unit and satisfying the system of global balance equations (GBEs):

$$\pi \mathbf{Q} = \mathbf{0} \,. \tag{1}$$

The solution of system (1) is often unfeasible due to the large number of states of the CTMC. The analysis of an ergodic CTMC in equilibrium can be greatly simplified if it satisfies the property that when the direction of time is reversed the behaviour of the process remains the same.

Given a stationary CTMC, $X(t)$ with $t \in \mathbb{R}^+$, we call $X(\tau - t)$ its reversed process. We denote by $X^R(t)$ the reversed process of $X(t)$. It can be shown that $X^R(t)$ is also a stationary CTMC. We say that $X(t)$ is *reversible* if it is stochastically identical to $X^R(t)$, i.e., the process $(X(t_1), \ldots, X(t_n))$ has the same distribution as $(X(\tau - t_1), \ldots, X(\tau - t_n))$ for all $t_1, \ldots, t_n, \tau \in \mathbb{R}^+$ [19].

For a stationary Markov process there exists a necessary and sufficient condition for reversibility expressed in terms of the equilibrium distribution π and the transition rates.

Proposition 1. (Transition rates of reversible processes [19]) *A stationary CTMC with state space $\mathcal{S}$ and infinitesimal generator $\mathbf{Q}$ is reversible if and only if for all $s, s' \in \mathcal{S}$ with $s \neq s'$,*

$$\pi(s)q(s, s') = \pi(s')q(s', s) \,.$$

A reversible CTMC $X(t)$ and its dual $X^R(t)$ have the same equilibrium distribution.

The *reversed process* $X^R(t)$ of a Markov process $X(t)$ can always be defined even when $X(t)$ is not reversible. In [12] the author shows that $X^R(t)$ is a CTMC and its transition rates are defined according to the following proposition.

Proposition 2. (Transition rates of reversed process [12]) *Given the stationary CTMC $X(t)$ with state space $\mathcal{S}$ and infinitesimal generator $\mathbf{Q}$, the transition rates of the reversed process $X^R(t)$, forming its infinitesimal generator $\mathbf{Q}^R$, are defined as follows: for all $s, s' \in \mathcal{S}$,*

$$q^R(s', s) = \frac{\pi(s)}{\pi(s')} q(s, s') \,, \tag{2}$$

where $q^R(s', s)$ denotes the transition rate from s' to s in the reversed process.

The equilibrium distribution π is the same for both the forward and the reversed process.

3   Stochastic Automata

Many high-level specification languages for stochastic discrete-event systems are based on *Markovian process algebras* [6,14,15] that naturally supply powerful composition operators and timed actions whose delay is governed by independent random variables with a continuous-time exponential distribution. The expressivity of such languages allows the development of well-structured specifications and efficient analyses of both qualitative and quantitative properties in a single framework. Their semantics is given in terms of stochastic automata, an extension of labelled automata with clocks that are exponentially distributed random variables.

In this paper we consider stochastic concurrent automata with an underlying continuous-time Markov chain as common denominator of a wide class of Markovian stochastic process algebra. Stochastic automata are equipped with a *composition operator* which allows a complex automaton to be constructed from simpler components. Our model draws a distinction between *active* and *passive* action types, and in forming the composition of automata only active/passive synchronisations are permitted.

Definition 1. (Stochastic Automaton (SA)) *A stochastic automaton P is a tuple $(\mathcal{S}_P, \mathcal{A}_P, \mathcal{P}_P, \leadsto_P, q_P)$ where*

- *$\mathcal{S}_P$ is a denumerable set of states called* state space *of P*
- *$\mathcal{A}_P$ is a finite set of* active *types*
- *$\mathcal{P}_P$ is a finite set of* passive *types*
- *τ denotes the* unknown *type*
- *$\leadsto_P \subseteq (\mathcal{S}_P \times \mathcal{S}_P \times \mathcal{T}_P)$ is a transition relation where $\mathcal{T}_P = (\mathcal{A}_P \cup \mathcal{P}_P \cup \{\tau\})$ and for all $s \in \mathcal{S}_P$, $(s, s, \tau) \notin \leadsto_P$[1]*
- *q_P is a function from $\leadsto_P$ to $\mathbb{R}^+$ such that $\forall s_1 \in \mathcal{S}_P$ and $\forall a \in \mathcal{P}_P$, $\sum_{s_2:(s_1,s_2,a)\in\leadsto_P} q_P(s_1, s_2, a) \leq 1$.*

In the following we denote by $\rightarrow_P$ the relation containing all the tuples of the form (s_1, s_2, a, q) where $(s_1, s_2, a) \in \leadsto_P$ and $q = q_P(s_1, s_2, a)$. We say that $q_P(s, s', a) \in \mathbb{R}^+$ is the *rate* of the transition from state s to s' with type a if $a \in \mathcal{A}_P \cup \{\tau\}$. Notice that this is indeed the apparent transition rate from s to s' relative to a [15]. If a is passive then $q_P(s, s', a) \in (0, 1]$ denotes the *probability* that the automaton synchronises on type a with a transition from s to s'. Hereafter, we assume that $q_P(s, s', a) = 0$ whenever there are no transitions with type a from s to s'. If $s \in \mathcal{S}_P$, then for all $a \in \mathcal{T}_P$ we write $q_P(s, a) = \sum_{s' \in \mathcal{S}_P} q_P(s, s', a)$. We say that P is *closed* if $\mathcal{P}_P = \emptyset$. We use the notation $s_1 \overset{a}{\leadsto}_P s_2$ to denote the tuple $(s_1, s_2, a) \in \leadsto_P$; we denote by $s_1 \xrightarrow{(a,r)}_P s_2$ (resp., $s_1 \xrightarrow{(a,p)}_P s_2$) the tuple $(s_1, s_2, a, r) \in \rightarrow_P$ (resp., $(s_1, s_2, a, p) \in \rightarrow_P$).

---

[1] Notice that τ self-loops do not affect the equilibrium distribution of the CTMC underlying the automaton. Moreover, the choice of excluding τ self-loops will simplify the definition of automata synchronisation.

Table 1. Operational rules for SA synchronisation

$$\dfrac{s_{p_1} \xrightarrow{(a,r)}_P s_{p_2} \quad s_{q_1} \xrightarrow{(a,p)}_Q s_{q_2}}{(s_{p_1}, s_{q_1}) \xrightarrow{(a,pr)}_{P\otimes Q} (s_{p_2}, s_{q_2})} \ (a \in \mathcal{A}_P = \mathcal{P}_Q)$$

$$\dfrac{s_{p_1} \xrightarrow{(a,p)}_P s_{p_2} \quad s_{q_1} \xrightarrow{(a,r)}_Q s_{q_2}}{(s_{p_1}, s_{q_1}) \xrightarrow{(a,pr)}_{P\otimes Q} (s_{p_2}, s_{q_2})} \ (a \in \mathcal{P}_P = \mathcal{A}_Q)$$

$$\dfrac{s_{p_1} \xrightarrow{(\tau,r)}_P s_{p_2}}{(s_{p_1}, s_{q_1}) \xrightarrow{(\tau,r)}_{P\otimes Q} (s_{p_2}, s_{q_1})} \qquad \dfrac{s_{q_1} \xrightarrow{(\tau,r)}_Q s_{q_2}}{(s_{p_1}, s_{q_1}) \xrightarrow{(\tau,r)}_{P\otimes Q} (s_{p_1}, s_{q_2})}$$

Definition 2. (CTMC underlying a closed automaton) *The CTMC underlying a closed automaton P, denoted $X_P(t)$, is defined as the CTMC with state space $\mathcal{S}_P$ and infinitesimal generator matrix $\mathbf{Q}$ defined as: for all $s_1 \neq s_2 \in \mathcal{S}_P$,*

$$q(s_1, s_2) = \sum_{a,r:(s_1,s_2,a,r)\in\to_P} r .$$

We say that a closed automaton P is ergodic (irreducible) if its underlying CTMC is ergodic (irreducible). We denote the equilibrium distribution of the CTMC underlying P by $\boldsymbol{\pi}_P$.

The synchronisation operator between two stochastic automata P and Q is defined in the style of master/slave synchronisation of SANs [29] based on the Kronecker's algebra and the active/passive cooperation used in Markovian process algebra such as PEPA [15,16].

Definition 3. (SA synchronisation) *Given two automata P and Q such that $\mathcal{A}_P = \mathcal{P}_Q$ and $\mathcal{A}_Q = \mathcal{P}_P$ we define the automaton $P \otimes Q$ as follows:*

- *$\mathcal{S}_{P\otimes Q} = \mathcal{S}_P \times \mathcal{S}_Q$*
- *$\mathcal{A}_{P\otimes Q} = \mathcal{A}_P \cup \mathcal{A}_Q = \mathcal{P}_P \cup \mathcal{P}_Q$*
- *$\mathcal{P}_{P\otimes Q} = \emptyset$*
- *τ is the unknown type*
- *$\leadsto_{P\otimes Q}$ and $q_{P\otimes Q}$ are defined according to the rules for $\to_{P\otimes Q}$ depicted in Table 1 where $\to_{P\otimes Q}$ contains the tuples $((s_{p_1}, s_{q_1}),(s_{p_1}, s_{q_2}), a, q)$ with $((s_{p_1}, s_{q_1}),(s_{p_1}, s_{q_2}), a)\in\leadsto_{P\otimes Q}$ and $q = q_{P\otimes Q}((s_{p_1}, s_{q_1}),(s_{p_1}, s_{q_2}), a)$.*

Notice that although we define a semantics for pairwise SA synchronisations, this can be easily extended in order to include an arbitrary finite number of pairwise cooperating automata as discussed in Section 4.1. We point out that the assumption that an automaton obtained by a cooperation does not have passive types ensures that the resulting automaton has an underlying CTMC and then we can study its equilibrium distribution.

4   Reversible Stochastic Automata

In this section we introduce the notion of ρ-*reversibility* for stochastic automata. This is defined in the style of the Kolmogorov's criteria presented in [19]. We assume that for each forward action type a there is a corresponding backward type a with $\tau = \tau$. Formally $\cdot$ is a bijection (renaming) from $\mathcal{T}_P$ to $\mathcal{T}_P$. In most of practical cases, $\cdot$ is an involution, i.e., $a = a$ for all $a \in \mathcal{T}_P$, and hence the semantics becomes similar to the one proposed in [10]. We say that $\cdot$ respects the active/passive types of an automaton P if $\tau = \tau$ and for all $a \in \mathcal{T}_P \setminus \{\tau\}$ we have that $a \in \mathcal{A}_P \Leftrightarrow a \in \mathcal{A}_P$ (or equivalently $a \in \mathcal{P}_P \Leftrightarrow a \in \mathcal{P}_P$).

Definition 4. (*ρ-reversible automaton*) *Let P be an irreducible stochastic automaton, then P is ρ-reversible if $\rho : \mathcal{S}_P \rightarrow \mathcal{S}_P$ is a renaming (permutation) of the states and $\cdot$ is a bijection from $\mathcal{T}_P$ to $\mathcal{T}_P$ that respects the active/passive typing, such that:*

1. $q(s,a) = q(\rho(s),a)$, for each state $s \in \mathcal{S}_P$;
2. for each cycle $\Psi = (s_1 \overset{a_1}{\rightsquigarrow} s_2 \overset{a_2}{\rightsquigarrow} \ldots \overset{a_{n-1}}{\rightsquigarrow} s_n \overset{a_n}{\rightsquigarrow} s_1)$ in P there exists one cycle

$$\Psi = (\rho(s_1) \overset{a_n}{\rightsquigarrow} \rho(s_n) \overset{a_{n-1}}{\rightsquigarrow} \ldots \overset{a_2}{\rightsquigarrow} \rho(s_2) \overset{a_1}{\rightsquigarrow} \rho(s_1)) \text{ in } P \text{ such that:}$$

$$\prod_{i=1}^{n} q(s_i, s_{i+1}, a_i) = \prod_{i=1}^{n} q(\rho(s_{i+1}), \rho(s_i), a_i) \text{ with } s_{n+1} \equiv s_1.$$

We say that Ψ is the inverse *of cycle Ψ. If ρ is the identity function we simply say that P is reversible.*

Observe that the cycle Ψ is unique. This follows from the fact that, by Definition 1 of stochastic automaton, there exists at most one transition between any pair of states with a certain type $a \in \mathcal{T}_P$. We stress on the fact that this class of models does not belong to any well-known class of compositional reversible models including those studied in [12,19].

Example 1. (Reversible Random Number Generators) In the context of concurrent simulations, the Time Warp mechanism [17,18] is an optimistic synchronisation protocol which is used to synchronize parallel discrete event simulations allowing a process to roll back when an event occuring in another process invalidates part of its computation. The state of the process depends on a set of random numbers that are generated by a pseudo Random Number Generator (RNG). Reversible RNGs allow their state to move both forward and backward so that if the simulation process is itself reversible, the rollback can be performed without storing the process state in memory [26]. We can model a reversible RNG by a simple sequential reversible automaton as shown in Fig. 1 (a). The model consists of a denumerable set of states $s_1, s_2, \ldots$. From each state s_i a random number is generated causing a synchronising label a_i and a transition to state s_{i+1} with rate r_f. In the backward flow, the transition occurs from state s_{i+1} to s_i with type b_i. Although it must be the case that the pseudo random number

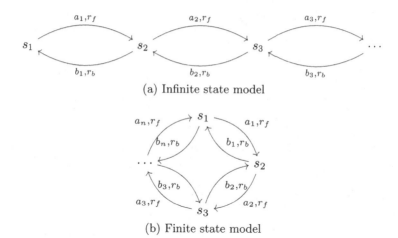

(a) Infinite state model

(b) Finite state model

Fig. 1. Models for RNGs

generated by type a_i is the same generated in the backward transition typed b_i, the use of two different types allows the synchronising process to drive the RNG in the forward or in the backward direction. Conversely, the use of the same type would have led to a situation in which the simulator process is executing in the forward direction while the RNG process draws pseudo random numbers in the backward direction, hence introducing an undesired behaviour. The automaton is ρ-reversible with ρ being the identity function and $a_i = b_i$, $b_i = a_i$.

Let us now consider a cyclic RNG in which, in the forward computation, the state that follows s_n is s_1 for a given $n > 2$ as depicted in Fig. 1 (b). In this case, we have also to consider the cycle $s_1 \xrightarrow{a_1, r_f} s_2 \cdots \xrightarrow{a_{n-1}, r_f} s_n \xrightarrow{a_n, r_f} s_1$ whose inverse is $s_1 \xrightarrow{b_n, r_b} s_n \cdots \xrightarrow{b_2, r_b} s_2 \xrightarrow{b_1, r_b} s_1$. In order for the rate condition of Definition 4 to be satisfied, equation $r_f^n = r_b^n$ must hold, i.e., $r_f = r_b$ is required. In other words, the automaton is reversible if the rate of generation of random numbers is the same in the forward and backward flow.

Example 2. (Reversible computations with checkpoints) Traditional means for restoring a computation to a previous state involve checkpoints, that are fixed conditions such that when a checkpoint is reached the computation may decide to proceed forward to the next checkpoint or backward to the previous one. In these cases, differently from the model studied in Example 1, the decision about moving forward or backward is not taken in each model state but only at the fixed checkpoints. Fig. 2 shows the stochastic automaton underlying such computations. From checkpoint CK_1 the computation proceeds forward to states $s_1, s_2, \ldots s_n$ and then reaches checkpoint CK_2. At checkpoint CK_2 the computation can move backward to $s_n', \ldots, s_2', s_1'$ and then to CK_1. We can show that the computation is ρ-reversible with $\rho(CK_i) = CK_i$, $\rho(s_i) = s_i'$, $\rho(s_i') = \rho(s_i)$ and $a_i = b_i$, $b_i = a_i$ for all i. In order for the rate condition of Definition 4 to

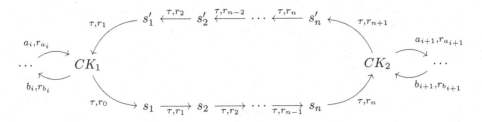

Fig. 2. Model for a reversible computation with checkpoint

be satisfied, the following cycle has to be considered:

$$\Psi = CK_1 \xrightarrow{\tau,r_0} s_1 \xrightarrow{\tau,r_1} s_2 \xrightarrow{\tau,r_2} \cdots s_n \xrightarrow{\tau,r_n} CK_2$$
$$\xrightarrow{\tau,r_{n+1}} s'_n \xrightarrow{\tau,r_n} \cdots s'_2 \xrightarrow{\tau,r_2} s'_1 \xrightarrow{\tau,r_1} CK_1 .$$

The condition is trivially satisfied since the inverse cycle Ψ, under the renaming function ρ, coincides with Ψ. Moreover, for all s_i we have $q(s_i, \tau) = q(s'_i, \tau)$.

The following theorem provides a necessary condition for ρ-reversibility expressed in terms of the equilibrium distribution π_P and the transition rates. It is worth of notice the analogies between Theorem 1 and Propositions 1 and 2.

Theorem 1. (Detailed balance equations) *If P is ergodic and ρ-reversible then for each pair of states $s, s' \in S_P$, and for each type $a \in T_P$, we have*

$$\pi_P(s)q(s, s', a) = \pi_P(s')q(\rho(s'), \rho(s), a) .$$

Notice that Theorem 1 differs from those proposed in [19,32] in the sense that in our theorem action types are taken into account.

The next proposition says that the states of an ergodic ρ-reversible automaton the same equilibrium probability of the corresponding image under ρ.

Proposition 3. (Equilibrium probability of the renaming of a state) *Let P be an ergodic ρ-reversible automaton. Then for all $s \in S_P$,*

$$\pi_P(s) = \pi_P(\rho(s)) .$$

The class of ρ-reversible automata satisfies the property that any ρ-reversible automaton can be rescaled allowing one to close the automaton by assigning the same rate to each passive action with a certain label weighted on its probability, while maintaining the equilibrium distribution.

Definition 5. (Scaled automaton) *Let P be an automaton, $a \in T_P$ and $k \in \mathbb{R}^+$. The automaton $S = P\{a \cdot k\}$ is defined as follows:*

- $S_S = S_P$
- $A_S = A_P$ *and* $P_S = P_P$ *if* $a \in A_P \cup \{\tau\}$

- $\mathcal{A}_S = \mathcal{A}_P \cup \{a\}$ *and* $\mathcal{P}_S = \mathcal{P}_P \setminus \{a\}$ *if* $a \in \mathcal{P}_P$
- $\leadsto_S = \leadsto_P$
- $q_S(s_1, s_2, b) = \begin{cases} q_P(s_1, s_2, b) & \text{if } b \neq a \\ q_P(s_1, s_2, b) \cdot k & \text{if } b = a \end{cases}$

Intuitively, the rescaling of a passive type a with a factor k_a should be interpreted as if the automaton is synchronising with an event that occurs according to an independent homogeneous Poisson process with rate k_a and hence can be seen as a way to close an open automaton. The rescaling of an active type b by a factor $k_b \leq 1$ should be interpreted as the reduction of the rates of the transitions with type b due to the fact that a cooperating automaton is ready to synchronise on b with a state independent probability k_b. If $k_b > 1$ we interpret this as a speed up of the active transitions, e.g., because the synchronising automaton models the fact that one component performs part of the work that is associated with the synchronising transition.

Since $\cdot$ is a permutation of the labels, we denote by $[a]$ the orbit of type a, i.e., $a \in [a]$, $a \in [a]$, $a \in [a]$ and so on. When $\cdot$ is an involution then for all a we have that $[a]$ is either a singleton or contains two types. Notice that if $\cdot$ respects the active/passive types of P, then for all a we have that the elements of $[a]$ are either all active or all passive. Notice that $[\tau] = \{\tau\}$.

Proposition 4. *(ρ-reversible scaled automaton) If P is an ergodic ρ-reversible automaton, then for all $a \in \mathcal{T}_P$, the automaton $P' = P\{b \cdot k, b \in [a]\}$ is also ρ-reversible. Moreover, $\pi_P(s) = \pi_{P'}(s)$ for all states $s \in \mathcal{S}_P$.*

According to Proposition 4 the ergodicity and the equilibrium distribution of a ρ-reversible automaton does not depend on the rescaling of all the types belonging to an orbit of $\cdot$. As a consequence, if the automaton is open and we close it by rescaling, its equilibrium distribution and ergodicity does not change with the rescaling factor. Henceforth, we will talk about equilibrium distribution and ergodicity of open automata in the sense that they are the same for any closure obtained by rescaling.

The following relationship states that ρ-reversibility for stochastic automata implies the reversibility of the underlying CTMC when the renaming function ρ is the identity.

Proposition 5. *(CTMC-reversibility) Let P be an ergodic automaton. If P is ρ-reversible and ρ is the identity function then its underlying CTMC is reversible.*

The opposite is, in general, not true.

Example 3. (Automaton ρ-reversibility and CTMC reversibility) Consider the automaton depicted in Fig. 3 (a). Since it has only one active type a (indeed, in this case, $a = a$), the underlying CTMC can be trivially derived and it is identical to the model in Fig. 3 (a) where the action type a is not present. Since the CTMC underling the automaton is ergodic, we may construct the time-reversed

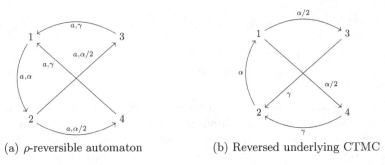

(a) ρ-reversible automaton   (b) Reversed underlying CTMC

Fig. 3. A ρ-reversible automaton with an underlying non-reversible CTMC.

CTMC displayed in Fig. 3 (b). We notice that the two CTMCs are different and hence the automaton is not reversible, however we can prove that under the renaming $\rho = \{1 \rightarrow 2, 2 \rightarrow 1, 3 \rightarrow 4, 4 \rightarrow 3\}$ the labelled automaton in Fig. 3 (a) satisfies the conditions of Definition 4, i.e., it is ρ-reversible.

The following theorems are important to tackle the state space explosion when studying a network of synchronising automata. Theorem 2 states that the synchronisation of ρ-reversible automata is still ρ-reversible and therefore networks of more than two automata can be defined by combining pairs of automata. Notice that operator $\otimes$ among ρ-reversible automata inherits the associativity from Kronecker's operator of the Stochastic Automata [29] or from the synchronisation operator of PEPA [15]. Theorem 3 states that the composition of two ρ-reversible automata has an equilibrium distribution that can be derived by the analysis of the isolated cooperating automata (i.e., without generating the joint state space and solving the system of global balance equations). Notice that this analysis, differently from those based on the concepts of quasi-reversibility [12,19] and reversibility, does not require a re-parameterisation of the cooperating automata, i.e., the expressions of the equilibrium distributions of the isolated automata are *as if* their behaviours are stochastically independent although they are clearly not.

Theorem 2. (Closure under ρ-reversibility) *Let P and Q be two ρ_P- and ρ_Q-reversible automata with respect to the same function $\cdot$ on the action types. Then, the automaton $P \otimes Q$ is $\rho_{P \otimes Q}$-reversible with respect to the same $\cdot$, where, for all $(s_1, s_2) \in \mathcal{S}_P \times \mathcal{S}_Q$,*

$$\rho_{P \otimes Q}(s_p, s_q) = (\rho_P(s_p), \rho_Q(s_q)). \tag{3}$$

Theorem 3 plays a pivotal role in the theory developed in this paper. Indeed, if we have a set of M cooperating automata the cardinality of the state space may have the size of the Cartesian product of the state space of each single automaton. Assuming that each automaton has a finite state space of cardinality N, the joint state space has, in the worst case, a cardinality of N^M. Since the computation of the equilibrium distribution of a CTMC requires the solution of the linear system of global balance equations, its complexity is $\mathcal{O}(N^{3M})$. In case of ρ-reversible automata, the steady-state distribution can be computed efficiently by means of Theorem 1 in linear time on the cardinality of the state space for each automaton, and hence by Theorem 3 the complexity of the computation of the joint equilibrium distribution is $\mathcal{O}(NM)$.

Theorem 3. (Product-form solution) *Let P and Q be two ergodic ρ_P- and ρ_Q-reversible automata with respect to the same function $\cdot$ on the action types, and let π_P and π_Q be the equilibrium distributions of the CTMCs underlying P and Q, respectively. If $S = P \otimes Q$ is ergodic on the state space given by the Cartesian product of the state spaces of P and Q, then for all $(s_p, s_q) \in \mathcal{S}_P \times \mathcal{S}_Q$,*

$$\pi_S(s_p, s_q) = \pi_P(s_p)\pi_Q(s_q). \tag{4}$$

In this case we say that the composed automaton S exhibits a product-form *solution.*

It is worth of stressing on the fact that the cooperating automata are *not* stochastically independent. Indeed Theorem 3 holds only for the equilibrium distribution of the joint model, i.e., when $t \to \infty$. This is coherent with the literature on product-forms of stochastic models, i.e., stochastic independence clearly implies product-form but the opposite in not true.

Example 4. We consider the model for a reversible computation shown in Fig. 4. P and Q communicate on an unreliable channel, i.e., a packet sent from P to Q is recevied by Q with probability p and lost with probability $1 - p$. P executes its computation in the forward $(s_0 \to s_1 \to s_2 \to s_3 \to s_4 \to s_5)$ or backward $(s_5 \to s_4 \to s_3' \to s_2' \to s_1 \to s_0)$ direction. It has two checkpoints modelled by states s_1 and s_4 and the synchronisations with Q occur on the transitions from s_0 to s_1 (and its dual from s_1 to s_0) and from s_4 to s_5 (and its dual from s_5 to s_4). Q moves from s_0 to s_1 or s_2 with a probabilistic choice upon the synchronisation with type a. Notice that when P is executing in the backward direction also Q is rolling back because of the synchronising type $\bar{a}$. Assume that the model encodes the result of the computation in state (s_5, s_4) or (s_5, s_5) (where the first component of the state is associated with P and the second with Q). We aim to compute the equilibrium probability of these two states that represents the fraction of time that the process spends in the states that encode the desired result. Notice that $a, b, \bar{a}, \bar{b} \in \mathcal{A}_P = \mathcal{P}_Q$.

Let us define the involution $\cdot$ as: $a = \bar{a}$, $b = \bar{b}$. Moreover, let $\rho_P(s_i) = s_i$ for $i = 0, 1, 4, 5$ and $\rho_P(s_i) = s_i'$ and $\rho_P(s_i') = s_i$ for $i = 2, 3$, while $\rho_Q(s_i)$ is the identity for all $i = 0, \ldots, 5$. We can prove that P and Q are ρ-reversible with respect to ρ_P and ρ_Q, respectively, and $\cdot$.

Now we use Theorem 1 to derive the equilibrium distribution of the isolated automata. Let us consider an abitrary state in P, say s_0. We can immediately derive $\pi_P(s_1)$ by using the detail balance equation and we obtain:

$$\pi_P(s_0)\lambda(1 - p) = \pi_P(s_1)\mu(1 - p),$$

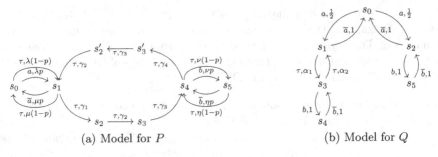

(a) Model for P (b) Model for Q

Fig. 4. A model for two communicating programs

which gives $\pi_P(s_1) = \pi_P(s_0)\lambda/\mu$. Then, we derive $\pi_P(s_2)$ using the detailed balance equation with s_1 and obtain: $\pi_P(s_2) = \pi_P(s_0)\lambda\gamma_1/(\mu\gamma_2)$. By Proposition 3 we immediately have $\pi_P(s_2') = \pi_P(s_2)$. Then we derive $\pi_P(s_3') = \pi_P(s_3) = \pi_P(s_0)\lambda\gamma_1/(\mu\gamma_3)$, $\pi_P(s_4) = \pi_P(s_0)\lambda\gamma_1/(\mu\gamma_4)$ and $\pi_P(s_5) = \pi_P(s_0)\lambda\gamma_1\beta/(\mu\gamma_4\eta)$. Notice that there may be more than one candidate detailed balance equation that can be applied to derive the equilibrium distribution of a state, but Theorem 1 ensures that this can be arbitrarly chosen. It remains to derive $\pi_P(s_0)$ that is computed by normalising the probabilities, i.e.:

$$\pi_P(s_0) = \frac{\gamma_2\gamma_3\gamma_4\eta\mu}{\beta\gamma_1\gamma_2\gamma_3\lambda + \gamma_1(\gamma_2\gamma_3 + 2(\gamma_2+\gamma_3)\gamma_4)\lambda\eta + \gamma_2\gamma_3\gamma_4\eta(\lambda+\mu)}.$$

We can apply the same approach to derive the equilibrium distribution of Q, obtaining:

$$\pi_Q(s_5) = \pi_Q(s_2) = \pi_Q(s_1) = \pi_Q(s_0)\frac{1}{2}, \quad \pi_Q(s_3) = \pi_Q(s_4) = \pi_Q(s_0)\frac{\alpha_1}{2\alpha_2}.$$

and by normalising the probabilities $\pi_Q(s_0) = 2\alpha_2/(2\alpha_1 + 5\alpha_2)$. By Theorem 3 we have:

$$\pi_{P\otimes Q}(s_5, s_4) + \pi_{P\otimes Q}(s_5, s_5) = \pi_P(s_5)\pi_Q(s_4) + \pi_P(s_5)\pi_Q(s_5).$$

Notice that we have not build the joint state space and also that the automata P and Q are not independent. For example, when Q is in state s_2 and P is in checkpoint s_4, Q moves to s_5 only if P decides not to roll back to checkpoint s_1 and the communication between P and Q is succesfull.

4.1   Synchronisation of an Arbitrary Number of Automata

Since Definition 3 considers only cooperations of two stochastic automata, in this section we discuss how it is possible to define networks with an arbitrary number of synchronising ρ-reversible automata. The semantics we refer to when we deal with multi-way synchronisations is an instance of that presented in [15,29]. Informally, the automata synchronise on a set of types L, i.e., the activities with type in L are carried out only jointly, while those outside are carried out independently. It is well-known that this synchronisation semantics is associative. It remains to prove that the results on ρ-reversible automata proposed here, are applicable also for this multi-way synchronisation semantics.

Let P be a ρ-reversible automaton, and $a \notin \mathcal{T}_P$, then also the automaton P^{+a} (P^{-a}) is ρ-reversible where P^{+a} (P^{-a}) is identical to P but has active (passive) type a as self-loop in each state with rate (probability) 1. Moreover, let $b \in \mathcal{A}_P$, and let P^{*b} be identical to P with the exception that label b is passive (we are assuming that for all $s_1 \in \mathcal{S}_P$ we have $\sum_{s_1 \in \mathcal{S}_P} q_P(s_1, s_2, b) \leq 1$). Then, assume we want to define a network of ρ_{P_i}−reversible automata $P_1, \ldots, P_M$. Let $\cdot$ be defined on all the types in $\cup_{i=1}^M \mathcal{T}_{P_i}$, then we can proceed as follows. Consider the automata P_1 and P_2 and define the automata $P_1^{+a_i - a_j}$ where $a_i \in \mathcal{P}_{P_2} \backslash \mathcal{A}_{P_1}$, $a_j \in \mathcal{A}_{P_2} \backslash \mathcal{P}_{P_1}$ and $P_2^{+a_k - a_h}$, where a_k and a_h are defined analogously. Then, the automaton $P_{12} = P_1^{+a_i - a_j} \otimes P_2^{+a_k - a_h}$ is well-defined according to Definition 3, is ρ-reversible and by Theorem 3 its steady-state probability is in product-form. In order to make P_{12} synchronise with P_3 we define P_{12}^{*b}, for all $b \in (\mathcal{P}_{P_1} \backslash \mathcal{A}_{P_2}) \cup (\mathcal{P}_{P_2} \backslash \mathcal{A}_{P_1})$ and repeat the procedure for the synchronisation of P_{12}^{*b} with P_3. Notice that this procedure gives the same semantics of the master/slave synchronisation of SAN. Here, the advantage of proceeding pairwise is that we can iteratively apply Theorem 3 to derive the equilibrium distribution of the joint process very efficiently.

5   Conclusion

In this paper we studied a class of stochastic models, named ρ-reversible automata, as a novel formalism for the quantitative analysis of reversible computations. Similarly to reversible processes [19], ρ-reversible automata satisfy a system of detailed balance equations which provide an efficient technique for the computation of their equilibrium distribution. ρ-reversible automata are equipped with a synchronisation operator similar to that of [15,29] which is associative and the class of ρ-reversible automata is closed under the synchronising operator. Moreover, ρ-reversible automata always exhibit a product-form solution (which is in general different from those known from the literature) allowing one to compute the joint equilibrium distribution as the product of the equilibrium distributions of the synchronising sub-components considered in isolation. We prove that the equilibrium distribution of any ρ-reversible stochastic automaton is insensitive to any ρ-reversible context. Therefore, our theory allows for the definition of system components whose equilibrium performance indices are independent of their context.

Acknowledgments. Work partially supported by the MIUR Project CINA: "Compositionality, Interaction, Negoziation, Autonomicity for the future ICT society".

References

1. Bacci, G., Danos, V., Kammar, O.: On the statistical thermodynamics of reversible communicating processes. In: Corradini, A., Klin, B., C'îrstea, C. (eds.) CALCO 2011. LNCS, vol. 6859, pp. 1–18. Springer, Heidelberg (2011)
2. Baier, C., Hahn, E.M., Haverkort, B.R., Hermanns, H., Katoen, J.-P.: Model checking for performability. Math. Structures in Comp. Sci. **23**(S.I. 04) (2013)
3. Balsamo, S., Marin, A.: Performance engineering with product-form models: efficient solutions and applications. In: Proc. of ICPE, pp. 437–448 (2011)
4. Bennett, C.: Logical reversibility of computations. IBM J. Res. Dev. **17**(6), 525–532 (1973)
5. Bennett, C.: Thermodynamics of computation. Int. J. of Physics **21**, 905–940 (1982)
6. Bernardo, M., Gorrieri, R.: A tutorial on EMPA: A theory of concurrent processes with nondeterminism, priorities, probabilities and time. Theoretical Computer Science **202**, 1–54 (1998)
7. Bishop, P.G.: Using reversible computing to achieve fail-safety. In: Proc. of 8th Int. Symp. on Soft. Reliability Eng., pp. 182–191 (1997)
8. Boothe, B.: Efficient algorithms for bidirectional debugging. SIGPLAN Not. **35**(5), 299–310 (2000)
9. Cardelli, L., Laneve, C.: Reversibility in massive concurrent systems. Scientific Annals of Computer Science **21**(2), 175–198 (2011)
10. Danos, V., Krivine, J.: Reversible communicating systems. In: Gardner, P., Yoshida, N. (eds.) CONCUR 2004. LNCS, vol. 3170, pp. 292–307. Springer, Heidelberg (2004)
11. Dubois, M., Annavaram, M., Stenstrom, P.: Parallel Computer Organization and Design. Cambridge Press (2012)
12. Harrison, P.G.: Turning back time in Markovian process algebra. Theoretical Computer Science **290**(3), 1947–1986 (2003)
13. Hermanns, H.: Interactive Markov Chains. Springer (2002)
14. Hermanns, H., Herzog, U., Katoen, J.P.: Process algebra for performance evaluation. Theor. Comput. Sci. **274**(1–2), 43–87 (2002)
15. Hillston, J.: A Compositional Approach to Performance Modelling. Cambridge Press (1996)
16. Hillston, J., Marin, A., Piazza, C., Rossi, S.: Contextual lumpability. In: Proc. of Valuetools 2013 Conf. ACM Press (2013)
17. Jefferson, D.R.: Virtual time. ACM Trans. on Programming Languages and Systems **7**(3), 404–425 (1985)
18. Jefferson, D.R., Reiher, P.: Supercritical speedup. In: Proc. of the 24th Annual Simulation Symp., pp. 159–168 (1991)
19. Kelly, F.: Reversibility and stochastic networks. Wiley, New York (1979)
20. Lanese, I., Lienhardt, M., Mezzina, C.A., Schmitt, A., Stefani, J.-B.: Concurrent flexible reversibility. In: Felleisen, M., Gardner, P. (eds.) ESOP 2013. LNCS, vol. 7792, pp. 370–390. Springer, Heidelberg (2013)
21. Lanese, I., Antares Mezzina, C., Tiezzi, F.: Causal-consistent reversibility. Bulletin of the EATCS **114** (2014)
22. Lee, J.: Dynamic reverse code generation for backward execution. Elect. notes in Theor. Comp. Sci. **174**(4), 37–54 (2007)
23. Marin, A., Rossi, S.: Autoreversibility: exploiting symmetries in Markov chains. In: Proc. of MASCOTS 2013, pp. 151–160. IEEE Computer Society (2013)

24. Marin, A., Rossi, S.: On the relations between lumpability and reversibility. In: Proc. of MASCOTS 2014, pp. 427–432 (2014)
25. Nielsen, M.A., Chuang, I.L.: Quantum Computation and Quantum Information. Cambridge University Press, New York (2000)
26. Perumalla, K.S.: Introduction to reversible computing. CRC Press (2013)
27. Perumalla, K.S., Park, A.J.: Reverse computation for rollback-based fault tolerance in large parallel systems. Cluster Computing **16**(2), 303–313 (2013)
28. Phillips, I., Ulidowski, I.: Reversing algebraic process calculi. Journal of Logic and Algebraic Programming **73**, 70–96 (2007)
29. Plateau, B.: On the stochastic structure of parallelism and synchronization models for distributed algorithms. SIGMETRICS Perf. Eval. Rev. **13**(2), 147–154 (1985)
30. Rieffel, E.G., Polak, W.H.: Quantum Computing: a Gentle Introduction. MIT Press (2011)
31. Stewart, W.J.: Introduction to the Numerical Solution of Markov Chains. Princeton University Press, UK (1994)
32. Whittle, P.: Systems in stochastic equilibrium. John Wiley & Sons Ltd. (1986)
33. Yokoyama, T.: Reversible computation and reversible programming languages. Elect. notes in Theor. Comp. Sci. **253**(6), 71–81 (2010)
34. Yokoyama, T., Glück, R.: A reversible programming language and its invertible self-interpreter. In: Proc. of the 2007 ACM SIGPLAN Symposium on Partial Evaluation and Semantics-based Program Manipulation, pp. 144–153. ACM, New York (2007)

Hybrid Tools for Hybrid Systems – Proving Stability and Safety at Once

Eike Möhlmann$^{(\boxtimes)}$, Willem Hagemann, and Oliver Theel

Carl von Ossietzky University of Oldenburg, 26111 Oldenburg, Germany
{eike.moehlmann,willem.hagemann,theel}@informatik.uni-oldenburg.de

Abstract. Industrial applications usually require safety and stability properties. The safety property guarantees that "something bad" never happens, and the stability property guarantees that "something good" eventually happens. The analyses of both properties are usually performed in isolation. In this work, we consider analyzing both properties by a single automatic approach for hybrid systems. We basically merge analyses of both properties to exploit the knowledge gained from the analysis of each of them in the analysis of the other. We show how both analyses can be divided into multiple steps and interlocked such that both benefit from each other. In fact, we compute single-mode Lyapunov functions, unroll the hybrid system's automaton via repeated reachability queries, and, finally, compute a global Lyapunov function. Each reachability query is simplified by exploiting the knowledge gained from the single-mode Lyapunov functions. The final computation of the global Lyapunov function is simplified by a precise characterization of the reachable states and reuses the single-mode Lyapunov functions.

We provide automated tools necessary to link the analyses and report on promising experiments we performed using our new prototype tool.

Keywords: Hybrid systems · Automatic verification · Stability · Safety · Reachability · Lyapunov theory · Geometry · Unrolling

1   Introduction

We present an approach to verify safety and stability properties of hybrid systems at once. The theory of hybrid systems provides a well-suited and natural framework for the analysis of interacting discrete and continuous behavior of a system. Examples are cyber-physical systems like vehicles or chemical processes. A hybrid system is called *safe* if some "bad states" cannot be reached, and it is called *(asymptotically) stable* if the system converges to some "good states".

Although there has been a lot of progress in recent time, verifying these types of properties is hard, especially in industrial applications where typical hybrid

---

This work has been partly supported by the German Research Foundation (DFG) as part of the Transregional Collaborative Research Center "Automatic Verification and Analysis of Complex Systems" (SFB/TR 14 AVACS, www.avacs.org).

© Springer International Publishing Switzerland 2015
S. Sankaranarayanan and E. Vicario (Eds.): FORMATS 2015, LNCS 9268, pp. 222–239, 2015.
DOI: 10.1007/978-3-319-22975-1_15

systems are often large. Consequently, abstractions or compositional frameworks are used to obtain simplified systems for which safety and stability can be proven and which are still powerful enough to establish the respective property of the original system. While the verification of safety and stability is usually done separately, we propose to integrate both analyses in a symbiotic fashion.

From the safety perspective, we use Lyapunov functions to detect regions that are guaranteed to be safe. Exploiting these regions helps us to shorten the reachability analysis. Indeed, if all trajectories eventually enter a safe region, then there is no need to compute infinite traces of the trajectories.

From the stability perspective, we obtain a more precise description of the feasible trajectories of a system. By discovering implicit knowledge and making it explicit, we lower the computational burden to obtain Lyapunov functions.

2   Related Work

Safety and Reachability analysis of hybrid systems has to deal with two problems: how to tackle the dynamics of the system, and how to represent the reachable states systematically. Both problems are related since the choice of the admissible dynamics has an impact on the required operations for post-image computation. For reachability analysis we will consider systems whose dynamics are given by linear differential inclusions [13,15,21]. Differential inclusions allows us to approximate systems with richer dynamics [3,4,11].

For state representation we focus on convex approaches where reachable states are usually represented by unions of convex sets. Different representations, like polyhedra [7], template polyhedra [37], zonotopes [15], ellipsoids [21], and support functions [22], are commonly used. The choice of the representation has wide influence on the approximations of the underlying sets and on the efficiency of operations required for reachability analysis. Depending on the choice of the representation, some operations may be difficult, e. g. zonotopes and support functions are challenging for intersections with guard sets [2,16].

Recently, the support function-based tool SPACEEX [13] has become popular for reachability analysis. With respect to reachability, this paper considers the same class of hybrid automata that SPACEEX can deal with.

Stability analysis of hybrid systems has – in contrast to safety analysis – not yet received that much attention wrt. automatic proving, and, therefore, only a few tools are available. A tool by Podelski and Wagner, presented in [31], proves region stability via the search for a decreasing sequence of snapshots. Oehlerking et al. [28] implemented a powerful state space partitioning scheme for linear hybrid systems. The RSOLVER by Ratschan and She [36] computes Lyapunov-like functions for continuous systems. Duggirala and Mitra [12] combined Lyapunov functions with searching for a well-foundedness relation for symmetric linear hybrid systems. Prabhakar and García [34] presented a technique for proving stability of hybrid systems with constant derivatives. YALMIP [23] and SOSTOOLS [30] are convenient MATLAB toolboxes assisting in the manual search for Lyapunov functions.

Related theoretical works are the decompositional technique by Oehlerking and Theel [29] and the work on pre-orders for reasoning about stability by Prabhakar et al. [32,33] whose aim is a precise characterization of the soundness of abstractions for stability properties.

Reach-Avoid problems are related to the investigated problem. In reach-avoid one is interested in finding a control strategy or initial condition to reach a certain set of desired states while avoiding another set of undesired states. In [25] Mitchell and Tomlin propose an exact algorithm for this problem which – like our algorithm – makes use of level sets. In [1] Abate et al. give a specification of the corresponding probabilistic problem. However, reach-avoid is an *existential problem*, while we ask *all* trajectories to converge and avoid undesired states.

3   Preliminaries

In this section we give definitions of the hybrid system model, global asymptotic stability, and Lyapunov functions. Furthermore, we briefly present two tools: 1. STABHYLI [26] which automatically computes Lyapunov functions and thereby certifies stability and 2. SOAPBOX [17] which automatically computes reachable state sets and, thus, allows us to check for (non-)reachable states.

Definition 1. $\mathcal{H} = (\mathcal{V}, \mathcal{M}, \mathcal{T}, Flow, Inv, Inits)$ *is a* Hybrid Automaton *where*
  – $\mathcal{V}$ *is a finite set of* variables *and* $\mathcal{S} = \mathbb{R}^{|\mathcal{V}|}$ *is the corr.* continuous state space,
  – $\mathcal{M}$ *is a finite set of* modes,
  – $\mathcal{T}$ *is a finite set of* transitions (m_1, G, U, m_2) *where*
    • $m_1, m_2 \in \mathcal{M}$ *are the* source *and* target mode *of the transition, resp.,*
    • $G \subseteq \mathcal{S}$ *is a* guard *which denotes whether a transition can be taken,*
    • $U : \mathcal{S} \to \mathcal{S}$ *is the* update function,
  – $Flow : \mathcal{M} \to [\mathcal{S} \to \mathcal{P}(\mathcal{S})]$ *is the* flow function *which assigns a flow to every mode. A flow* $f : \mathcal{S} \to \mathcal{P}(\mathcal{S})$ *assigns a closed subset of* $\mathcal{S}$ *to each* $\mathbf{x} \in \mathcal{S}$, *which can be seen as the right-hand side of a differential inclusion* $\dot{\mathbf{x}} \in f(\mathbf{x})$,
  – $Inv : \mathcal{M} \to \mathcal{P}(\mathcal{S})$ *is the* invariant function *which assigns a closed subset of the continuous state space to each mode* $m \in \mathcal{M}$, *and therefore restricts valuations of the variables for which this mode can be active.*
  – $(Init, m) \in Inits \subseteq \mathcal{S} \times \mathcal{M}$ *is a closed set of* initial (hybrid) states *where* m *is the* discrete state *and* $Init$ *is the* continuous state.
A trajectory *of* $\mathcal{H}$ *is an infinite solution in form of a function* $\tau(t) = (\mathbf{x}(t), m(t))$ *over time* t *where* $\mathbf{x}(\cdot)$ *describes the evolution of the continuous variables and* $m(\cdot)$ *the corresponding evolution of the modes [27, p.35].*

3.1   Checking Stability via Stabhyli

STABHYLI can be used to obtain Lyapunov functions which certify stability of hybrid systems whose behavior is expressible in forms of polynomials. STABHYLI can be used to obtain common Lyapunov functions, piecewise Lyapunov functions and performing the (de-)compositional proof schemes presented in [8,29].

These features are fully automatized and combined with pre- and postprocessing steps that simplify the design and counteract numerical problems. Furthermore, in case stability cannot be proven, STABHYLI returns a hint to the user. In the sequel we sketch the theoretical basis of STABHYLI.

Roughly speaking, stability is a property basically expressing that all trajectories of the system eventually reach an equilibrium point of the sub-state space and stay in that point forever. Usually, for technical reasons the equilibrium point is assumed to be the origin $\mathbf{0}$ of the continuous state space. This is not a restriction since a system can always be shifted such that the equilibrium point is $\mathbf{0}$ via a coordinate transformation. In the sequel we focus on *asymptotic stability* which does not require the origin to be reached in finite time, but only requires every trajectory to converge. This property is weaker than *exponential stability* where the existence of an exponential convergence rate is additionally required.

In the following we refer to $\mathbf{x}_{\downarrow \mathcal{V}'} \in \mathbb{R}^{|\mathcal{V}'|}$ as the sub-vector of a vector $\mathbf{x} \in \mathbb{R}^{|\mathcal{V}|}$ containing only values of variables in $\mathcal{V}' \subseteq \mathcal{V}$.

Definition 2 (Global Asymptotic Stability [27]). *Given a hybrid automaton $\mathcal{H} = (\mathcal{V}, \mathcal{M}, \mathcal{T}, Flow, Inv)$ and a set of variables $\mathcal{V}' \subseteq \mathcal{V}$ that are required to converge to the equilibrium point $\mathbf{0}$. A continuous-time dynamic system $\mathcal{H}$ is called Lyapunov stable (LS) with respect to $\mathcal{V}'$ if for all functions $\mathbf{x}_{\downarrow \mathcal{V}'}(\cdot)$ of $\mathcal{H}$,*

$$\forall \epsilon > 0 : \exists \delta > 0 : \forall t \geq 0 : ||\mathbf{x}(0)|| < \delta \Rightarrow ||\mathbf{x}_{\downarrow \mathcal{V}'}(t)|| < \epsilon.$$

$\mathcal{H}$ is called globally attractive (GA) wrt. $\mathcal{V}'$ if for all functions $\mathbf{x}_{\downarrow \mathcal{V}'}(\cdot)$ of $\mathcal{H}$,

$$\lim_{t \to \infty} \mathbf{x}_{\downarrow \mathcal{V}'}(t) = \mathbf{0}, \; i.\,e., \forall \epsilon > 0 : \exists t_0 \geq 0 : \forall t > t_0 : ||\mathbf{x}_{\downarrow \mathcal{V}'}(t)|| < \epsilon,$$

where $\mathbf{0}$ is the origin of $\mathbb{R}^{|\mathcal{V}'|}$. If a system is both Lyapunov stable with respect to $\mathcal{V}'$ and globally attractive with respect to $\mathcal{V}'$, then it is called globally asymptotically stable (GAS) with respect to $\mathcal{V}'$.

Intuitively, LS means that trajectories starting δ-close to the origin remains ϵ-close to the origin. GA means that for each ϵ-distance to the origin, there exists a point in time t_0 such that a trajectory always remains within this distance. It follows that each trajectory is eventually always approaching the origin. This property can be proven using Lyapunov theory [24]. Lyapunov theory was originally restricted to continuous systems, but has been lifted to hybrid systems.

Theorem 1 (Discontinuous Lyapunov Functions [27]). *Given a hybrid automaton $\mathcal{H} = (\mathcal{V}, \mathcal{M}, \mathcal{T}, Flow, Inv)$ and a set of variables $\mathcal{V}' \subseteq \mathcal{V}$ that are required to converge. If for each $m \in \mathcal{M}$, there exists a set of variables $\mathcal{V}_m$ with $\mathcal{V}' \subseteq \mathcal{V}_m \subseteq \mathcal{V}$ and a continuously differentiable function $V_m : \mathcal{S} \to \mathbb{R}$ such that*
1. for each $m \in \mathcal{M}$, there exist two class K^∞ functions α and β such that

$$\forall \mathbf{x} \in Inv(m) : \alpha(||\mathbf{x}_{\downarrow \mathcal{V}_m}||) \leq V_m(\mathbf{x}) \leq \beta(||\mathbf{x}_{\downarrow \mathcal{V}_m}||),$$

2. *for each $m \in \mathcal{M}$, there exists a class K^{∞} function γ such that*

$$\forall \mathbf{x} \in Inv(m) : \dot{V}_m(\mathbf{x}) \leq -\gamma(\|\mathbf{x}_{\downarrow \mathcal{V}_m}\|)$$

for each $\dot{V}_m(\mathbf{x}) \in \left\{ \left\langle \frac{dV_m(\mathbf{x})}{d\mathbf{x}} \,\middle|\, f(\mathbf{x}) \right\rangle \,\middle|\, f(\mathbf{x}) \in Flow(m) \right\}$,

3. *for each $(m_1, G, U, m_2) \in \mathcal{T}$,*

$$\forall \mathbf{x} \in G : V_{m_2}(U(\mathbf{x})) \leq V_{m_1}(\mathbf{x}),$$

then $\mathcal{H}$ is globally asymptotically stable with respect to $\mathcal{V}'$. Each V_m is called a Local Lyapunov Function (LLF) *of m, and the function $V(\mathbf{x}, m) = V_m(\mathbf{x})$ is called the* Global Lyapunov Function *(GLF).*

In Thm. 1, $\left\langle \frac{dV(\mathbf{x})}{d\mathbf{x}} \,\middle|\, f(\mathbf{x}) \right\rangle$ denotes the inner product of the gradient of V and a flow function $f(\mathbf{x})$. Please refer to [27, p.43] for the details of K^{∞} functions. Throughout the paper we denote by *mode constraints* the constraints of Type 1 and Type 2 and by *transition constraints* the constraints of Type 3.

Note 1. For each LF V (local or global), it holds that for any trajectory $\mathbf{x}(\cdot)$ the LF's value does not increase, i.e., $\forall t_0, t \geq 0 : V(\mathbf{x}(t_0 + t)) \leq V(\mathbf{x}(t_0))$ (or $\forall t_0, t \geq 0 : V(\mathbf{x}(t_0 + t), m(t_0 + t)) \leq V(\mathbf{x}(t_0), m(t_0))$ for the GLF).

STABHYLI generates constraint systems which – using the so called *sums-of-squares* method [35] and the S-Procedure [6] – are relaxed to a linear matrix inequality (LMI). The LMI can then be solved by a *semi-definite program (SDP)*. For this purpose, we use the numerical solver CSDP [5] is in charge. If the LMI is feasible, then each solution represents a valid Lyapunov function.

Note 2. Since STABHYLI employs the sums-of-squares method, every computed Lyapunov function is representable as a sum-of-squares. However, in the following we restrict ourselves to *quadratic* Lyapunov functions as they are sufficient for many applications.

3.2   Checking Reachability via SoapBox

SOAPBOX is a tool for reachability analysis of hybrid systems. It is implemented in MATLAB. SOAPBOX handles hybrid systems with continuous dynamics described by linear differential inclusions and arbitrary affine maps for discrete updates. The invariants, guards, and sets of reachable states are given as convex polyhedra. Internally, the reachability algorithm of SOAPBOX is based on symbolic orthogonal projections (sops) [17]. Sops extend the half-space representation of polyhedra ($\mathcal{H}$-polyhedra) such that the operations required for the post-image computation, including convex hulls, Minkowski sums, affine maps, and intersections, can be performed efficiently and exactly. Hence, using sops yields tighter overapproximation than support functions.

A drawback, which sops and support functions have in common, is that there is no efficient and exact method for deciding subset-relations in general.

Hence, an exact fix-point check is hard to achieve. However, at least the decision whether a given set – represented as a sop or by support functions – is contained in an $\mathcal{H}$-polyhedron or not can be done efficiently.

Although SOAPBOX is a fully functional model checker handling continuous and discrete updates of a hybrid system, for our approach it suffices to present the mode-specific continuous post-image computation provided by the method Reach($Init$, $Flow(m)$, $Inv(m)$, $Safe$, T). It expects as input an $\mathcal{H}$-polyhedron representing the initial states $Init$, a differential inclusion $Flow(m)$ describing the differential inclusion $\dot{\mathbf{x}} = A\mathbf{x} + \mathbf{E}$, where $\mathbf{E}$ is an $\mathcal{H}$-polytope modeling the bounded input, an $\mathcal{H}$-polyhedron representing the invariant $Inv(m)$, an $\mathcal{H}$-polyhedron representing the target set[1] T, and an $\mathcal{H}$-polyhedron $Safe$. The method computes a tight overapproximation of all reachable states on trajectories solving

$$\dot{\mathbf{x}}(t) = A\mathbf{x}(t) + \mathbf{E}, \ \mathbf{x}(0) \in Init, \ \forall t \geq 0 \colon \mathbf{x}(t) \in Inv(m),$$

until either all states leave the invariant or all states have entered the set $Safe$. Then, it returns a polyhedral set representing a tight polyhedral overapproximation of the intersection of the reachable states with the target set T.[2]

4   Hybrid Stability and Reachability Tool

We present our algorithm that combines safety and stability analysis. We show how the combination of both analyses mutually simplifies the verification task.

While GAS is defined over trajectories, Thm. 1 argues over states and searches for LLFs which have to be compatible wrt. the transition constraints. We observed that, often, we are able to find the LLFs but fail to establish the necessary compatibility wrt. the transition constraints. Among other reasons, this may be due to cyclic dependencies imposed by the transitions of the hybrid automaton.

Our approach is to unroll the hybrid automaton to an equivalent hybrid automaton for which we can verify GAS via Thm. 1. Here, "equivalence" denotes that both automata exhibit an identical continuous behavior, i.e., for each trajectory of either automaton there is a trajectory of the other automaton with the same continuous evolution. Hence, the original hybrid automaton is also GAS.

We define the following notion of the depth of a reachable state. The set $\mathcal{R}_0 = Inits$ is the set of all reachable states of depth 0. Given the set $\mathcal{R}_n$ of all reachable states at depth n, we recursively define $\mathcal{R}_{n+1}$ as the set of all tuples $(\mathbf{x}_{n+1}, m_{n+1})$ which are reachable from any tuple $(\mathbf{x}_n, m_n) \in \mathcal{R}_n$ by a combination of a continuous evolution and a subsequent discrete transition, i.e., there exists a flow $f \in Flow(m_n)$, an instant of time $t \geq 0$, and a transition $(m_n, G, U, m_{n+1}) \in T$ such that for $\mathbf{y}(t) = \int_0^t f(\mathbf{y}) \, d\tau$ it holds $\mathbf{y}(\tau) \in Inv(m_n)$

---

[1] Usually, Reach() handles finite unions of polyhedral target sets at once. For the sake of simplicity, our presentation is restricted to a single target set.

[2] As before, Reach() returns unions of polyhedra, each representing a single traversal of a target set.

for all $\tau \in [0,t]$, $\mathbf{y}(0) = \mathbf{x}_n$, $\mathbf{y}(t) \in G$, and $U(\mathbf{y}(t)) = \mathbf{x}_{n+1}$. Clearly, $(\mathbf{x}, m)$ is reachable if and only if there exists some n with $(\mathbf{x}, m) \in \mathcal{R}_n$.

Our idea is as follows: First we compute for each mode a Lyapunov function, called a "single-mode Lyapunov Function" (SMLF). Then, starting with $\mathcal{R}_0$, we successively compute the sets $\mathcal{R}_n$. For each mode this reduces to the reachability problem of computing the *reachset*, that is the set obtained by computing all reachable states in the transition guards and subsequent application of the respective discrete updates. During each reachset computation, we additionally assess safety, i.e., we decide whether *Unsafe* can be reached or not. Moreover, the SMLFs enable us to compute safe sets which substantially simplify the reachability analysis: An appropriate safe set has no intersection with neither the unsafe set nor any guard of an outgoing transition and it is invariant under the flow. Thus, we may stop the reachability analysis as soon as a safe set is entered.

If this approach successfully terminates, then it does not only help to ensure safety, but we also obtain an unrolled (or unfolded) version of the original hybrid automaton. The unrolled automaton is free of cyclic dependencies. Additionally, guards are restricted to their intersection with the reachable states. Both facts enormously simplify the task of establishing compatibility of the SMLFs with the transition constraints, which finally yields a global Lyapunov function.

4.1 Single-Mode Lyapunov Function Computation

As mentioned above, in the first step, we compute Lyapunov functions for each mode in isolation. We call a Lyapunov function *SMLF*, if it satisfies the mode constraints, but not necessarily the transition constraints of Thm. 1.

STABHYLI can compute Lyapunov functions automatically. To obtain the *single-mode Lyapunov functions*, we simply "feed" STABHYLI with a single-mode automaton $\mathcal{H}_m$ for every $m \in \mathcal{M}$, where the *single-mode hybrid automaton* is defined as $\mathcal{H}_m = (\mathcal{V}, \{m\}, \varnothing, \{m \mapsto Flow(m)\}, \{m \mapsto Inv(m)\}, \{(Inv(m), m)\})$.

Computing the single-mode Lyapunov functions certifies that each single-mode hybrid automaton is GAS. Note that this is not sufficient to conclude that the full hybrid automaton is GAS. However, we exploit single-mode Lyapunov function during the following reachability analysis. In a final step, we combine the single-mode Lyapunov functions with the results of the reachability analyses to verify GAS of the full hybrid automaton (see Sec. 4.5).

4.2 SafeSet Computation

As in the previous section, we restrict our attention to a single mode m of a hybrid automaton $\mathcal{H}$. Firstly, we introduce the notion of a level set.

Definition 3 (Level Set). *Let $V(\cdot)$ be a Lyapunov function of mode m. For any $s \geq 0$, we call $\mathcal{L}_{V,s} = \{\mathbf{x} \mid V(\mathbf{x}) \leq s\}$ a level set of mode m.*

A Lyapunov function assigns a value to any state of the state space, and its values along any trajectory does not increase. Hence, all trajectories starting in a level set will not leave the level set. In general, we call any subset of states which cannot be left by the continuous trajectories an *invariant set* (for the formal definition see Def. 4). This property allows a strong prediction on the future of the trajectory. However, the prediction does not suffice to establish safety if the intersection of the invariant set with *Unsafe* or some guards is not empty, since then the mode could be unsafe or it could be left by a discrete transition.

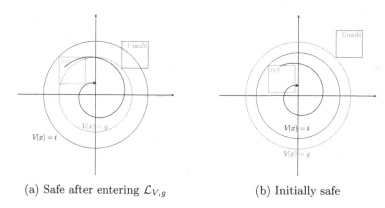

(a) Safe after entering $\mathcal{L}_{V,g}$ (b) Initially safe

Fig. 1. Sketch of safe sets

Definition 4 (Safe Set, Avoid Set, and Invariant Set). *Let $\mathcal{A}$ and $\mathcal{S}'$ be two subset of $\mathcal{S}$ such that $\mathcal{S}' \subset Inv(m)$. If for all trajectories $\mathbf{x}(\cdot)$ with $\mathbf{x}(0) \in \mathcal{S}'$ and for all $t \geq 0$ it holds*

$$\forall \tau \ (0 \leq \tau \leq t \rightarrow \mathbf{x}(\tau) \in Inv(m)) \quad \Longrightarrow \quad \forall \tau \ (0 \leq \tau \leq t \rightarrow \mathbf{x}(\tau) \in \mathcal{S}') \quad (1)$$
$$\forall \tau \ (0 \leq \tau \leq t \rightarrow \mathbf{x}(\tau) \in Inv(m)) \quad \Longrightarrow \quad \forall \tau \ (0 \leq \tau \leq t \rightarrow \mathbf{x}(\tau) \notin \mathcal{A}), \quad (2)$$

then $\mathcal{A}$ is called an avoid set *and $\mathcal{S}'$ is called a* safe set *for $\mathcal{A}$ of a mode m. A safe set for $\mathcal{A}$ is denoted by $Safe_{\mathcal{A}}$.*

The set $\mathcal{S}' \subseteq Inv(m)$ is an invariant set *if condition (1) holds.*

Clearly, any level set of a mode is also an invariant set of the mode. Furthermore, any invariant set which has an empty intersection with some avoid set $\mathcal{A}$ is obviously a safe set for $\mathcal{A}$.

Corollary 1. *Any level set which has an empty intersection with $\mathcal{A}$ is a safe set for the avoid set $\mathcal{A}$.*

Now, the alleviating argument for the reachability analysis is that a certain set, like *Unsafe* or a guard, cannot be reached as soon as a safe set for the respective set is entered.

Following Cor. 1 we aim for maximizing the extent of the level set $\mathcal{L}_{V,s} = \{\mathbf{x} \mid V(\mathbf{x}) \leq s\}$ for a given avoid set $\mathcal{A}$. Let $g < \inf_{\mathbf{x} \in \mathcal{A}} V(\mathbf{x})$ be a strict lower bound for the values of the Lyapunov function over $\mathcal{A}$. Since all states with a lower value are guaranteed not to be in $\mathcal{A}$, the set $Safe_{\mathcal{A}} = \mathcal{L}_{V,g}$ is a safe set for

---

Function 1. The Prepare Function

---

   input : A hybrid automaton $\mathcal{H}$, a set *Unsafe.*
   output: A set of LFs *LFs*, and a prepared version of $\mathcal{H}$.

1 *Inits′*, $\mathcal{T}'$, *LFs* ← ∅;
    // compute Lyapunov functions for each mode in isolation
2 **foreach** $m \in \mathcal{H}.\mathcal{M}$ **do** *LFs*(m) ← computeLF($Flow(m), Inv(m)$);
3 $\mathcal{T}'$ ← $\mathcal{H}.\mathcal{T}$;   // copy transitions
4 **foreach** $(Init, m) \in \mathcal{H}.Inits$ **do**   // separate each initial mode
5   m' ← copyMode($\mathcal{H}$, *Unsafe*, *LFs*, m);   // copy the mode
6   *Inits′* ← *Inits′* ∪ {$(Init, m')$} ;   // add the new init
       // copy each outgoing transition to the new mode
7   **foreach** $(m, G, U, m_2) \in \mathcal{T}'$ **do** $\mathcal{H}.\mathcal{T}$ ← $\mathcal{H}.\mathcal{T}$ ∪ {(m', G, U, m_2)};
8 $\mathcal{H}.Inits$ ← *Inits′* ;   // replace initial states

---

$\mathcal{A}$. Furthermore, if we find an upper bound $i \geq \sup_{\mathbf{x} \in Init} V(\mathbf{x})$ with $g \geq i$, then $\mathcal{A}$ is unreachable from all initial states, and we can omit the reachset computation entirely. Both cases are visualized in Fig. 1.

4.3 SafeBox Conversion

In order to use safe sets for trajectory truncation in a polyhedral-based tool like SOAPBOX, we generate polyhedral underapproximatons of safe sets. We shortly describe the idea of our method. STABHYLI generates quadratic Lyapunov functions. Hence, a level set in our context is a quadric $\left\{\mathbf{x} \mid \mathbf{x}^T V \mathbf{x} \leq c^2\right\}$ with $c > 0$ and a symmetric matrix V. Projectively principal axis transformation yields an invertible matrix L and a diagonal matrix E, whose coefficients are equal to -1, 1, or 0, and sorted in descending order such that $\tilde{V} = \begin{pmatrix} V & \mathbf{0} \\ \mathbf{0}^T & -c^2 \end{pmatrix} = L\tilde{E}L^T$. By Sylverster's law of inertia, the numbers of negative, positive, and zero coefficients are uniquely determined. Furthermore, since $\tilde{V}$ contains the block matrix $-c^2$, the last coefficient of $\tilde{E}$ is -1, i. e., $\tilde{E} = \begin{pmatrix} E & \mathbf{0} \\ \mathbf{0}^T & -1 \end{pmatrix}$. This yields the implication $\mathbf{y}^T E' \mathbf{y} \leq 1 \Rightarrow \mathbf{y}^T E \mathbf{y} \leq 1$, where E' is obtained from E by replacing all occurrences of -1 by 0. Hence, the cylinder $\left\{\mathbf{y} \mid \mathbf{y}^T E' \mathbf{y} \leq 1\right\}$ over a lower-dimensional unit sphere is the largest inscribed convex and cylindrical set of $\left\{\mathbf{y} \mid \mathbf{y}^T E \mathbf{y} \leq 1\right\}$. Now, given template $\mathcal{H}$-polyhedra with circumspheres of arbitrary dimension, it is easy to generate an inscribed $\mathcal{H}$-polyhedron of the spherical cylinder. For our experiments we used hypercubes and cross-polytopes. It remains to compute the image of the resulting polyhedra under the inverse transformation to $\begin{pmatrix} \mathbf{y} \\ \mu \end{pmatrix} = L^T \begin{pmatrix} \mathbf{x} \\ \lambda \end{pmatrix}$, which is computationally easy but involves non-trivial insights in projective geometry[3] which we had to omit here due to lack of space (for details see [18,20]).

---

[3] Actually, we use a projective generalization of polyhedra similar to the notion of *projective polyhedra* as it has been introduced in [14].

4.4 Unrolling Algorithm

Func. 1 and Alg. 2 show the unrolling algorithm. Func. 1 is a *preparation function* that creates copies of the modes as well as all outgoing edges for each initial state set. The function copyMode creates a fresh copy of a mode with the same flow, invariant, SMLF, and unsafe set as the original mode. Alg. 2 is the main *unrolling algorithm*. It is executed after the preparation function. It maintains a job queue which is initialized with the initial state sets. Until the job queue is empty, it selects a job, computes safe sets and reachsets wrt. *Unsafe* and the guards of the outgoing transition. An intersection of the reachset with *Unsafe* shows that the hybrid system is unsafe. Intersections with guards are used to tighten the guards of transitions and are enqueued for further exploration. This unrolls the hybrid automaton in a breath first manner. If the job queue is empty, then the unrolling is followed by a post-processing. The post-processing removes all nodes that are not connected to a mode of the initial set. The result is a forest of hybrid automata describing the trajectories abstractly. The unrolled hybrid automaton can be proven stable very efficiently according to Thm. 2. In fact, since the unrolled hybrid automaton is acyclic, the single-mode Lyapunov functions computed may be reused.

Algorithm 2. The Unrolling Algorithm

---

input : A hybrid automaton $\mathcal{H}$, a set *Unsafe*, and a set of LFs *LFs*.
output: An unrolled version of $\mathcal{H}$.

1 Jobs $\leftarrow \mathcal{H}.Inits$;   // start from each initial state set
2 **while** Jobs $\neq \varnothing$ **do**
3 $\quad (Init, m) \leftarrow$ pop(Jobs);   // select a job
$\quad$ // compute safe sets wrt. unsafe and convert them to safe boxes
4 $\quad Safe_{Unsafe} \leftarrow$ convertToBoxes(safeSets($LFs(m), Init, Unsafe(m)$));
$\quad$ // compute reachset wrt. unsafe
5 $\quad R \leftarrow$ Reach($Init, Flow(m), Inv(m), Safe_{Unsafe}, Unsafe(m)$);
6 $\quad$ **if** $R \neq \varnothing$ **then** markUnsafe(m, R);   // model is unsafe
7 $\quad T' \leftarrow \mathcal{H}.T$;   // copy transitions
$\quad$ // check reachability of each outgoing transition
8 $\quad$ **foreach** $(m, G, U, m_2) \in T'$ **do**
9 $\quad\quad \mathcal{H}.T \leftarrow \mathcal{H}.T \setminus \{(m, G, U, m_2)\}$;   // remove old transition
$\quad\quad$ // compute safe sets wrt. guard and convert them to safe boxes
10 $\quad\quad Safe_G \leftarrow$ convertToBoxes(safeSets($LFs(m), Init, G$));
$\quad\quad$ // compute reachset wrt. guard
11 $\quad\quad R \leftarrow$ Reach($Init, Flow(m), Inv(m), Safe_G, G$);
12 $\quad\quad$ **if** $R = \varnothing$ **then continue**;   // guard unreachable
13 $\quad\quad m' \leftarrow$ copyMode($\mathcal{H}, Unsafe, LFs, m_2$);   // copy the mode
14 $\quad\quad \mathcal{H}.T \leftarrow \mathcal{H}.T \cup \{(m, R, U, m')\}$; // add refined incoming transition
$\quad\quad$ // copy each outgoing transitions to the new mode
15 $\quad\quad$ **foreach** $(m_2, G_2, U_2, m_3) \in T'$ **do** $\mathcal{H}.T \leftarrow \mathcal{H}.T \cup \{(m', G_2, U_2, m_3)\}$;
16 $\quad\quad$ Jobs $\leftarrow$ Jobs $\cup \{(\text{apply}(R, U), m')\}$;   // append updated postset

4.5   Global Lyapunov Function Computation

Now that we have established safety, we verify GAS of the unrolled hybrid automaton reusing the single-mode Lyapunov functions. Since both automata are equivalent, this implies GAS of the original hybrid automaton.

Theorem 2 (GAS of an unrolled Hybrid Automaton). *Let $\mathcal{H}$ be an unrolled hybrid automaton. If all modes are globally attractive, then so is $\mathcal{H}$. If all modes are Lyapunov stable and for all transitions (m_1, G, U, m_2) it holds that*

$$\exists c > 0 : \forall \mathbf{x} \in G : V_{m_2}(U(\mathbf{x})) \leq c \cdot V_{m_1}(\mathbf{x}),$$

then $\mathcal{H}$ is Lyapunov stable. Consequently, $\mathcal{H}$ is GAS.

Proof. Follows directly from [27, Thm. 4.1, Remark 4.3]. $\qquad\blacksquare$

Since we already have single-mode Lyapunov functions, it remains to show that for each transition the factor c as used in Thm. 2 actually exists. If this is successful, then we can conclude that the hybrid automaton is GAS.

5   Benchmarking

In this section we present four benchmarks and compare the time needed for verification of their respective properties. The benchmark set contains one example where we verify stability and safety (actually, it is part of a case study on parallel composition of hybrid systems), two examples with more complex discrete behavior for which we only verify pure stability properties,[4] and one example for which it is impossible to prove stability without further reachability analysis.

Example 1: The Velocity Controller (VC) – visualized in Fig. 2 – is part of the Advanced Driver Assistance System (ADAS) presented and analyzed in [9,10,19]. The ADAS consists of two concurrent controllers (as well as helper components) that cooperatively achieve the following objectives: **(o1)** maintain a centrifugal force comfortable for a driver, **(o2)** bring and then keep the car on the center of its lane, **(o3)** control the speed whereby also considering driver requests for a certain speed value. The VC contributes to Objective (o1) and Objective (o3).

The model has three modes: one mode with a constant acceleration, one mode with a constant deceleration and one mode doing the fine tuning via a PI controller. The VC's task is to drive the current velocity of the vehicle vel_{cur} to a desired velocity vel_{goal}. This desired velocity is given by an external input that might be updated discretely. The verification task is to show that

- vel_{cur} converges to vel_{goal},
- if $vel_{cur} - vel_{goal} \leq -3$ initially holds then always holds $vel_{cur} - vel_{goal} \leq 3$,
- if $vel_{cur} - vel_{goal} \in [-3, -2]$ initially holds then always holds $vel_{cur} - vel_{goal} \leq 2$,

---

[4] Note that the unrolling algorithm performs a complete reachability analysis. Hence, extending the examples by an unsafe set is rather trivial.

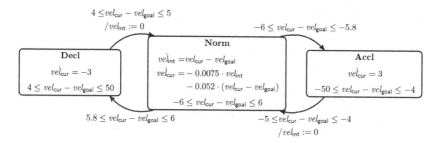

$$4 \leq vel_{cur} - vel_{goal} \leq 5$$
$$/vel_{int} := 0$$

$$-6 \leq vel_{cur} - vel_{goal} \leq -5.8$$

Norm

Decl

$$\dot{vel}_{cur} = -3$$

$$4 \leq vel_{cur} - vel_{goal} \leq 50$$

$$\dot{vel}_{int} = vel_{cur} - vel_{goal}$$
$$\dot{vel}_{cur} = -0.0075 \cdot vel_{int}$$
$$- 0.052 \cdot (vel_{cur} - vel_{goal})$$
$$-6 \leq vel_{cur} - vel_{goal} \leq 6$$

Accl

$$\dot{vel}_{cur} = 3$$

$$-50 \leq vel_{cur} - vel_{goal} \leq -4$$

$$5.8 \leq vel_{cur} - vel_{goal} \leq 6$$

$$-5 \leq vel_{cur} - vel_{goal} \leq -4$$
$$/vel_{int} := 0$$

Fig. 2. The Velocity Controller [9]

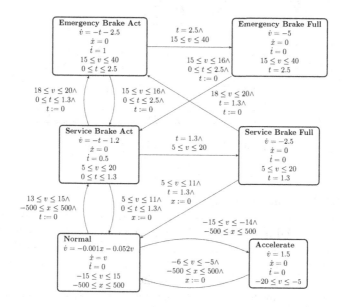

Fig. 3. The Automatic Cruise Controller [27]

– if $vel_{cur} - vel_{goal} \in [-2, 0]$ initially holds then always holds $vel_{cur} - vel_{goal} \leq 1$. The later three are safety properties and restrict the peak-overshoot. For the verification, all properties are considered under the assumption that vel_{goal} remains constant once set.

Example 2: The Automatic Cruise Controller (ACC) regulates the velocity of a vehicle. Fig. 3 shows the controller as an automaton. The task of the controller is to approach a user-chosen velocity – here the variable v represents the velocity relative to the desired velocity. The ACC is a bit more complex than the VC as it has two different brakes: a service break for minor corrections and an emergency break for huge differences. Both brakes have an activation phase, in which the deceleration is continuously increased.

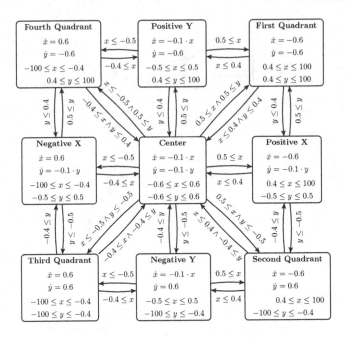

Fig. 4. The Simple Planar Spidercam

Example 3: The Spidercam is a movable robot equipped with a camera used at sport events. The robot is connected to four cables. Each cable is attached to a motor that is placed in a corner high above the playing field of a sports arena. By winding and unwinding the cables, the spidercam is able to reach nearly any position in the three-dimensional space above the playing field. Fig. 4 shows a very simple model of such a spidercam in the plane. The target is to stabilize the camera at a certain position. The continuous variables x and y denote the distance relative to the desired position on the axis induced by the cables. In the model, we assume a high-level control of the motor engines, i. e., the movement is on x and y axes instead of a low-level control of each individual motor.

Example 4: The Artificial Example is a model (see Fig. 5a) which cannot be proven stable without further reachability information. The reason is that the guard of the transition from mode Turbo Fast to Wait does not restrict values of x. Thus, naïvely generating constraints due to Thm. 1 leads to the following snippet of constraints

$$\forall x, t : x \in [-100, 100] \wedge t \in [0, 5] \Rightarrow 0 < V_{\texttt{Wait}}(x, t)$$
$$\forall t : t \in [0, 5] \Rightarrow V_{\texttt{Turbo Fast}}(0, t) = 0$$
$$\forall x : V_{\texttt{Wait}}(0.9x + 0.1, 0) \leq V_{\texttt{Turbo Fast}}(x, 5).$$

Obviously, no such $V_{\text{Wait}}, V_{\text{Turbo Wait}}$ exist. On the other hand, due to the unrolling, we can conclude that the transition may only be taken with $x \in [10.1, 38.9]$ which allows us to replace the last constraint by

$$\forall x : x \in [10.1, 38.9] \Rightarrow V_{\text{Wait}}(0.9x + 0.1, 0) \leq V_{\text{Turbo Fast}}(x, 5),$$

and, indeed, for $x \geq 10$ the Lyapunov function value may not increase.[5] The unrolled automaton is sketched in Fig. 5b.

Results

Tab. 1 shows, in order, the depth of the unrolled hybrid automaton and the time needed to compute the SMLFs, the safe sets, the inscribed polygon (hypercube and cross-polytope), the reachability information, and, in the last column, the total runtime.[6] Since SOAPBOX is written in MATLAB and our current prototype tool runs SOAPBOX for each reachset computation, we have included two times: with and without the time for the MATLAB reinitialization (once for each computation).

Table 1. Detailed Computation Times

	Depth	STABHYLI	SafeSet	BoxConvert	SOAPBOX	Total Time w/o MATLAB	w/ MATLAB
Exm. 1	3	0.39s	0.16s	2.4s	14.6s	17.55s	41.55s
Exm. 2	6	0.82s	1s	57.2s	39.6s	98.62s	350.62s
Exm. 3	5	2.14s	580.3s	11s	1098.7s	1692.14s	4408.14s
Exm. 4	8	1.65s	5.67s	0.06s	10.04s	17.42s	65.42s

In Tab. 2 we compare the runtime of the proposed approach with the runtime of STABHYLI searching for a common Lyapunov function, STABHYLI searching for a piecewise Lyapunov function, and STABHYLI using the decompositional approach. We can conclude that although the proposed unrolling technique is not the fastest, its runtime is comparable to the runtime of the decompositional approach and may handle examples that other approaches cannot handle. Furthermore, if a benchmark exposes a safety property, too (like the VC), then additional time is required to verify the safety properties which nullifies the advantage of the shorter runtime.

---

[5] Note that the update increases x in case the transition is taken with $x < 10$. This would render the system non-LS (cf. Def. 2). However, reachability information reveals that no such trajectory exists.

[6] An Intel© Core™ i7-3770T CPU with 2.50GHz and 8GB of RAM (in single-core mode) was used to run the benchmarks.

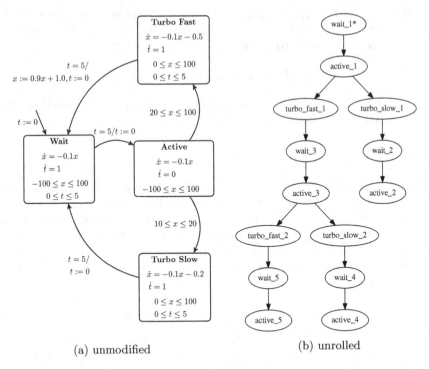

(a) unmodified   (b) unrolled

Fig. 5. An Artificial Example

6   Summary

We have presented an approach to verify both, safety and stability properties of hybrid systems. In contrast to the simple approach of verifying the properties separately, we merge the verification procedures such that it makes either verification task simpler. Our approach allows

Table 2. Comparison of Computation Times

	STABHYLI (common)	STABHYLI (piecewise)	STABHYLI (decomp.)	Unrolling
Exm. 1	X	0.21s	22.29s	17.55
Exm. 2	X	1.70s	112.99s	98.62
Exm. 3	1.37s	6.97s	X	1692.14
Exm. 4	X	X	X	17.42

us to exploit the knowledge that is gained during the verification of one problem in the verification of the other one. From the safety perspective, we use the fact that level sets – which are obtained from Lyapunov functions – reveal subsets of the state space which are known to be safe. We stop the reachability analysis as soon as the safe set is entered. From the stability perspective, we use an unrolled version of the hybrid system's automaton – which is obtained by repeated reachset computations – to have a more precise characterization of the feasible trajectories. Obtaining Lyapunov functions for this unrolled hybrid automaton reduces the computational effort. It allows us to find LFs for systems where the system's representation contains implicit information that is needed to successfully prove stability.

In the future we plan to investigate sufficient and necessary termination criteria for the unrolling algorithm. Even if it turns out that termination of the unrolling algorithm will fail on a particular automaton, we believe that the presented techniques still can fruitfully be applied to parts of the automaton. Reachability analysis profits from safe sets even when the stability of the overall automaton cannot be established. Additionally, knowledge gained by partial reachability computations on sub-components of the automaton helps us to relax the transition constraints for the computation of the GLF. However, the usefulness of our approach has already been shown by some promising experiments (see Sec. 5).

References

1. Abate, A., Prandini, M., Lygeros, J., Sastry, S.: Probabilistic reachability and safety for controlled discrete time stochastic hybrid systems. Automatica **44**(11), 2724–2734 (2008)
2. Althoff, M., Krogh, B.H.: Avoiding geometric intersection operations in reachability analysis of hybrid systems. In: HSCC, pp. 45–54. ACM (2012)
3. Asarin, E., Dang, T., Girard, A.: Reachability analysis of nonlinear systems using conservative approximation. In: Maler, O., Pnueli, A. (eds.) HSCC 2003. LNCS, vol. 2623, pp. 20–35. Springer, Heidelberg (2003)
4. Asarin, E., Dang, T., Girard, A.: Hybridization methods for the analysis of nonlinear systems. Acta Informatica **43**(7), 451–476 (2007)
5. Borchers, B.: CSDP, a c library for semidefinite programming. Optim. Met. Softw. **10**, 613–623 (1999)
6. Boyd, S., Vandenberghe, L.: Convex Optimization. Cambridge Uni. Press (2004)
7. Chutinan, A., Krogh, B.: Computational techniques for hybrid system verification. IEEE Transactions on Automatic Control **48**(1), 64–75 (2003)
8. Damm, W., Dierks, H., Oehlerking, J., Pnueli, A.: Towards component based design of hybrid systems: safety and stability. In: Manna, Z., Peled, D.A. (eds.) Time for Verification. LNCS, vol. 6200, pp. 96–143. Springer, Heidelberg (2010)
9. Damm, W., Hagemann, W., Möhlmann, E., Rakow, A.: Component based design of hybrid systems: A case study on concurrency and coupling. Technical Report 95, SFB/TR 14 AVACS (2014)
10. Damm, W., Möhlmann, E., Rakow, A.: Component based design of hybrid systems: a case study on concurrency and coupling. In: HSCC, pp. 145–150. ACM (2014)
11. Dang, T., Maler, O., Testylier, R.: Accurate hybridization of nonlinear systems. In: HSCC, pp. 11–20. ACM (2010)
12. Duggirala, P.S., Mitra, S.: Lyapunov abstractions for inevitability of hybrid systems. In: HSCC, pp. 115–124. ACM (2012)
13. Frehse, G., et al.: SpaceEx: scalable verification of hybrid systems. In: Gopalakrishnan, G., Qadeer, S. (eds.) CAV 2011. LNCS, vol. 6806, pp. 379–395. Springer, Heidelberg (2011)
14. Gallier, J.: Notes on convex sets, polytopes, polyhedra, combinatorial topology, Voronoi diagrams and Delaunay triangulations. Technical Report 650, University of Pennsylvania Department of Computer and Information Science (2009)

15. Girard, A.: Reachability of uncertain linear systems using zonotopes. In: Morari, M., Thiele, L. (eds.) HSCC 2005. LNCS, vol. 3414, pp. 291–305. Springer, Heidelberg (2005)
16. Girard, A., Le Guernic, C.: Zonotope/hyperplane intersection for hybrid systems reachability analysis. In: Egerstedt, M., Mishra, B. (eds.) HSCC 2008. LNCS, vol. 4981, pp. 215–228. Springer, Heidelberg (2008)
17. Hagemann, W.: Reachability analysis of hybrid systems using symbolic orthogonal projections. In: Biere, A., Bloem, R. (eds.) CAV 2014. LNCS, vol. 8559, pp. 407–423. Springer, Heidelberg (2014)
18. Hagemann, W., Möhlmann, E.: Inscribing $\mathcal{H}$-polyhedra in quadrics using a projective generalization of closed sets. In: CCCG (2015, to appear)
19. Hagemann, W., Möhlmann, E., Rakow, A.: Verifying a PI controller using SoapBox and Stabhyli: experiences on establishing properties for a steering controller. In: ARCH (2014)
20. Hagemann, W., Möhlmann, E., Theel, O.E.: Hybrid tools for hybrid systems: Proving stability and safety at once. Technical Report 108, SFB/TR 14 AVACS (2015)
21. Kurzhanski, A.B., Varaiya, P.: Ellipsoidal techniques for reachability analysis. In: Lynch, N.A., Krogh, B.H. (eds.) HSCC 2000. LNCS, vol. 1790, pp. 202–214. Springer, Heidelberg (2000)
22. Le Guernic, C., Girard, A.: Reachability analysis of hybrid systems using support functions. In: Bouajjani, A., Maler, O. (eds.) CAV 2009. LNCS, vol. 5643, pp. 540–554. Springer, Heidelberg (2009)
23. Löfberg, J.: YALMIP: A toolbox for modeling and optimization in MATLAB. In: CACSD, Taipei, Taiwan (2004)
24. Lyapunov, A.M.: Problème général de la stabilité du movement. In: Ann. Fac. Sci. Toulouse, 9, pp. 203–474. Université Paul Sabatier (1907)
25. Mitchell, I., Tomlin, C.J.: Level set methods for computation in hybrid systems. In: Lynch, N.A., Krogh, B.H. (eds.) HSCC 2000. LNCS, vol. 1790, pp. 310–323. Springer, Heidelberg (2000)
26. Möhlmann, E., Theel, O.E.: Stabhyli: a tool for automatic stability verification of non-linear hybrid systems. In: HSCC, pp. 107–112. ACM (2013)
27. Oehlerking, J.: Decomposition of Stability Proofs for Hybrid Systems. PhD thesis, University of Oldenburg, Dept. of Computer Science, Oldenburg, Germany (2011)
28. Oehlerking, J., Burchardt, H., Theel, O.: Fully automated stability verification for piecewise affine systems. In: Bemporad, A., Bicchi, A., Buttazzo, G. (eds.) HSCC 2007. LNCS, vol. 4416, pp. 741–745. Springer, Heidelberg (2007)
29. Oehlerking, J., Theel, O.: Decompositional construction of lyapunov functions for hybrid systems. In: Majumdar, R., Tabuada, P. (eds.) HSCC 2009. LNCS, vol. 5469, pp. 276–290. Springer, Heidelberg (2009)
30. Papachristodoulou, A., Anderson, J., Valmorbida, G., Prajna, S., Seiler, P., Parrilo, P.A.: SOSTOOLS: Sum-of-Squares Optimization Toolbox for MATLAB. http://arxiv.org/abs/1310.4716 (2013)
31. Podelski, A., Wagner, S.: Region stability proofs for hybrid systems. In: Raskin, J.-F., Thiagarajan, P.S. (eds.) FORMATS 2007. LNCS, vol. 4763, pp. 320–335. Springer, Heidelberg (2007)
32. Prabhakar, P., Dullerud, G.E., Viswanathan, M.: Pre-orders for reasoning about stability. In: HSCC, pp. 197–206 (2012)
33. Prabhakar, P., Liu, J., Murray, R.M.: Pre-orders for reasoning about stability properties with respect to input of hybrid systems. In: EMSOFT, pp. 1–10 (2013)

34. Prabhakar, P., Garcia Soto, M.: Abstraction based model-checking of stability of hybrid systems. In: Sharygina, N., Veith, H. (eds.) CAV 2013. LNCS, vol. 8044, pp. 280–295. Springer, Heidelberg (2013)
35. Prajna, S., Papachristodoulou, A.: Analysis of switched and hybrid systems - beyond piecewise quadraticmethods.In: ACC, vol. 4, pp. 2779–2784 (2003)
36. Ratschan, S., She, Z.: Providing a basin of attraction to a target region of polynomial systems by computation of Lyapunov-like functions. SIAM J. Control and Optimization **48**(7), 4377–4394 (2010)
37. Sankaranarayanan, S., Dang, T., Ivančić, F.: Symbolic model checking of hybrid systems using template polyhedra. In: Ramakrishnan, C.R., Rehof, J. (eds.) TACAS 2008. LNCS, vol. 4963, pp. 188–202. Springer, Heidelberg (2008)

Verification and Control of Partially Observable Probabilistic Real-Time Systems

Gethin Norman[1]([✉]), David Parker[2], and Xueyi Zou[3]

[1] School of Computing Science, University of Glasgow, Glasgow, UK
gethin.norman@glasgow.ac.uk
[2] School of Computer Science, University of Birmingham, Birmingham, UK
[3] Department of Computer Science, University of York, York, UK

Abstract. We propose automated techniques for the verification and control of probabilistic real-time systems that are only partially observable. To formally model such systems, we define an extension of probabilistic timed automata in which local states are partially visible to an observer or controller. We give a probabilistic temporal logic that can express a range of quantitative properties of these models, relating to the probability of an event's occurrence or the expected value of a reward measure. We then propose techniques to either verify that such a property holds or to synthesise a controller for the model which makes it true. Our approach is based on an integer discretisation of the model's dense-time behaviour and a grid-based abstraction of the uncountable belief space induced by partial observability. The latter is necessarily approximate since the underlying problem is undecidable, however we show how both lower and upper bounds on numerical results can be generated. We illustrate the effectiveness of the approach by implementing it in the PRISM model checker and applying it to several case studies, from the domains of computer security and task scheduling.

1 Introduction

Guaranteeing the correctness of complex computerised systems often needs to take into account quantitative aspects of system behaviour. This includes the modelling of *probabilistic* phenomena, such as failure rates for physical components, uncertainty arising from unreliable sensing of a continuous environment, or the explicit use of randomisation to break symmetry. It also includes *real-time* characteristics, such as time-outs or delays in communication or security protocols. To further complicate matters, such systems are often *nondeterministic* because their behaviour depends on inputs or instructions from some external entity such as a controller or scheduler.

Automated verification techniques such as probabilistic model checking have been successfully used to analyse quantitative properties of probabilistic, real-time systems across a variety of application domains, including wireless communication protocols, computer security and task scheduling. These systems are commonly modelled using *Markov decision processes* (MDPs), if assuming

© Springer International Publishing Switzerland 2015
S. Sankaranarayanan and E. Vicario (Eds.): FORMATS 2015, LNCS 9268, pp. 240–255, 2015.
DOI: 10.1007/978-3-319-22975-1_16

a discrete notion of time, or *probabilistic timed automata* (PTAs), if using a dense model of time. On these models, we can consider two problems: *verification* that it satisfies some formally specified property for any possible resolution of nondeterminism; or, dually, *synthesis* of a controller (i.e., a means to resolve nondeterminism) under which a property is guaranteed. For either case, an important consideration is the extent to which the system's state is *observable* to the entity controlling it. For example, to verify that a security protocol is functioning correctly, it may be essential to model the fact that some data held by a participant is not externally visible, or, when synthesising a controller for a robot, the controller may not be implementable in practice if it bases its decisions on information that cannot be physically observed.

Partially observable MDPs (POMDPs) are a natural way to extend MDPs in order to tackle this problem. However, the analysis of POMDPs is considerably more difficult than MDPs since key problems are undecidable [24]. A variety of verification problems have been studied for these models (see e.g., [1,3,11]) and the use of POMDPs is common in fields such as AI and planning [8], but there is limited progress in the development of practical techniques for probabilistic verification in this area, or exploration of their applicability.

In this paper, we present novel techniques for verification and control of probabilistic real-time systems under partial observability. We propose a model called *partially observable probabilistic timed automata* (POPTAs), which extends the existing model of PTAs with a notion of partial observability. The semantics of a POPTA is an infinite-state POMDP. We then define a temporal logic, based on [27], to express properties of POPTAs relating to the probability of an event or the expected value of various reward measures. Nondeterminism in a POPTA is resolved by a *strategy* that decides which actions to take and when to take them, based only on the history of observations (not states). The core problems we address are how to *verify* that a temporal logic property holds for all possible strategies, and how to *synthesise* a strategy under which the property holds.

In order to achieve this, we use a combination of techniques. First, we develop a *digital clocks* discretisation for POPTAs, which extends the existing notion for PTAs [20], and reduces the analysis to a *finite* POMDP. We define the conditions under which properties in our temporal logic are preserved and prove the correctness of the reduction. To analyse the resulting POMDP, we use grid-based techniques [23,29], which transform it to a fully observable but continuous-space MDP and then approximate its solution based on a finite set of grid points. We use this to construct and solve a strategy for the POMDP. The result is a pair of lower and upper bounds on the property of interest for the original POPTA. If the results are not precise enough, we can refine the grid and repeat.

We implemented these methods in a prototype tool based on PRISM [19], and investigated their applicability by developing three case studies: a non-repudiation protocol, a task scheduling problem and a covert channel prevention device (the NRL pump). Despite the complexity of POMDP solution methods, we show that useful results can be obtained, often with precise bounds. In each case study, nondeterminism, probability, real-time behaviour *and* partial observability are all crucial ingredients to the analysis, a combination not supported by any existing techniques or tools.

Related Work. POMDPs are common in fields such as AI and planning, and have many applications [8]. They have also been studied in the verification community, e.g. [1,3,11], establishing undecidability and complexity results for various qualitative and quantitative verification problems. Work in this area often also studies related models such as Rabin's probabilistic automata [3], which can be seen as a special case of POMDPs, and partially observable stochastic games (POSGs) [12], which generalise them. More practically oriented work includes: [15], which proposes a counterexample-driven refinement method to approximately solve MDPs in which components have partial observability of each other; and [10], which synthesises concurrent program constructs, using a search over memoryless strategies in a POSG. Theoretical results [6] and algorithms [9,14] have been developed for synthesis of partially observable timed games. In [6], it is shown that the synthesis problem is undecidable and, if the resources of the controller are fixed, decidable but prohibitively expensive. The algorithms require constraints on controllers: in [9], controllers only respond to changes made by the environment and, in [14], their structure must be fixed in advance. We are not aware of any work for probabilistic real-time models.

An extended version of this paper, with proofs, is available as [26].

2   Partially Observable Markov Decision Processes

We begin with background material on MDPs and POMDPs. Let $Dist(X)$ denote the set of discrete probability distributions over a set X, δ_x the distribution that selects $x \in X$ with probability 1, and $\mathbb{R}$ the set of non-negative real numbers.

Definition 1 (MDP). *An MDP is a tuple* $\mathsf{M}=(S, \bar{s}, A, P, R)$ *where: S is a set of states; $\bar{s} \in S$ an initial state; A a set of actions; $P : S{\times}A \rightarrow Dist(S)$ a (partial) probabilistic transition function; and $R : S{\times}A \rightarrow \mathbb{R}$ a reward function.*

Each state s of an MDP M has a set $A(s) \stackrel{\text{def}}{=} \{a \in A \mid P(s,a) \text{ is defined}\}$ of *enabled* actions. If action $a \in A(s)$ is selected, then the probability of moving to state s' is $P(s,a)(s')$ and a reward of $R(s,a)$ is accumulated in doing so. A *path* of M is a finite or infinite sequence $\omega = s_0 a_0 s_1 a_1 \cdots$, where $s_i \in S$, $a_i \in A(s_i)$ and $P(s_i, a_i)(s_{i+1}){>}0$ for all $i \in \mathbb{N}$. We write $FPaths_\mathsf{M}$ and $IPaths_\mathsf{M}$, respectively, for the set of all finite and infinite paths of M starting in the initial state $\bar{s}$.

A *strategy* of M (also called a *policy* or *scheduler*) is a way of resolving the choice of action in each state, based on the MDP's execution so far.

Definition 2 (Strategy). *A strategy of an MDP* $\mathsf{M}=(S, \bar{s}, A, P, R)$ *is a function* $\sigma : FPaths_\mathsf{M} \rightarrow Dist(A)$ *such that* $\sigma(s_0 a_0 s_1 \ldots s_n)(a){>}0$ *only if* $a \in A(s_n)$.

A strategy is *memoryless* if its choices only depend on the current state, *finite-memory* if it suffices to switch between a finite set of modes and *deterministic* if it always selects an action with probability 1. The set of strategies of M is denoted by Σ_{M}.

When M is under the control of a strategy σ, the resulting behaviour is captured by a probability measure Pr_{M}^{σ} over the infinite paths of M [18].

POMDPs. POMDPs extend MDPs by restricting the extent to which their current state can be observed, in particular by strategies that control them. In this paper (as in, e.g., [3,11]), we adopt the following notion of observability.

Definition 3 (POMDP). *A POMDP is a tuple* $\mathsf{M}=(S, \bar{s}, A, P, R, \mathcal{O}, obs)$ *where:* $(S, \bar{s}, A, P, R)$ *is an MDP;* $\mathcal{O}$ *is a finite set of observations; and obs :* $S \to \mathcal{O}$ *is a labelling of states with observations. For any states* $s, s' \in S$ *with* $obs(s)=obs(s')$, *their enabled actions must be identical, i.e.,* $A(s)=A(s')$.

The current state s of a POMDP cannot be directly determined, only the corresponding observation $obs(s) \in \mathcal{O}$. More general notions of observations are sometime used, e.g., that depend also on the previous action taken or are probabilistic. Our analysis of probabilistic verification case studies where partial observation is needed (see, e.g., Sec. 5) suggests that this simpler notion of observability will often suffice in practice. To ease presentation, we assume the initial state is observable, i.e., there exists $\bar{o} \in \mathcal{O}$ such that $obs(s)=\bar{o}$ if and only if $s=\bar{s}$.

The notions of paths, strategies and probability measures given above for MDPs transfer directly to POMDPs. However, the set Σ_{M} of all strategies for a POMDP M only includes *observation-based strategies*, that is, strategies σ such that, for any paths $\pi = s_0 a_0 s_1 \ldots s_n$ and $\pi' = s_0' a_0' s_1' \ldots s_n'$ satisfying $obs(s_i) = obs(s_i')$ and $a_i = a_i'$ for all i, we have $\sigma(\pi) = \sigma(\pi')$.

Key properties for a POMDP (or MDP) are the probability of reaching a target, and the expected reward cumulated until this occurs. Let O denote the target (e.g., a set of observations of a POMDP). Under a specific strategy σ, we denote these two properties by $Pr_{\mathsf{M}}^{\sigma}(\mathsf{F}\,O)$ and $\mathbb{E}_{\mathsf{M}}^{\sigma}(\mathsf{F}\,O)$, respectively.

Usually, we are interested in the *optimal* (minimum or maximum) values $Pr_{\mathsf{M}}^{opt}(\mathsf{F}\,O)$ and $\mathbb{E}_{\mathsf{M}}^{opt}(\mathsf{F}\,O)$, where $opt \in \{\min, \max\}$. For a MDP or POMDP M:

$$Pr_{\mathsf{M}}^{\min}(\mathsf{F}\,O) \stackrel{\text{def}}{=} \inf_{\sigma \in \Sigma_{\mathsf{M}}} Pr_{\mathsf{M}}^{\sigma}(\mathsf{F}\,O) \qquad \mathbb{E}_{\mathsf{M}}^{\min}(\mathsf{F}\,O) \stackrel{\text{def}}{=} \inf_{\sigma \in \Sigma_{\mathsf{M}}} \mathbb{E}_{\mathsf{M}}^{\sigma}(\mathsf{F}\,O)$$
$$Pr_{\mathsf{M}}^{\max}(\mathsf{F}\,O) \stackrel{\text{def}}{=} \sup_{\sigma \in \Sigma_{\mathsf{M}}} Pr_{\mathsf{M}}^{\sigma}(\mathsf{F}\,O) \qquad \mathbb{E}_{\mathsf{M}}^{\max}(\mathsf{F}\,O) \stackrel{\text{def}}{=} \sup_{\sigma \in \Sigma_{\mathsf{M}}} \mathbb{E}_{\mathsf{M}}^{\sigma}(\mathsf{F}\,O)$$

Beliefs. For POMDPs, determining the optimal probabilities and expected rewards defined above is undecidable [24], making exact solution intractable. A useful construction, e.g., as a basis of approximate solutions, is the translation from a POMDP M to a *belief MDP* $\mathcal{B}(\mathsf{M})$, an equivalent (fully observable) MDP, whose (continuous) state space comprises *beliefs*, which are probability distributions over the state space of M. Intuitively, although we may not know which of several observationally-equivalent states we are currently in, we can determine the likelihood of being in each one, based on the probabilistic behaviour of M. A formal definition is given below.

Definition 4 (Belief MDP). *Let* $\mathsf{M}=(S, \bar{s}, A, P, R, \mathcal{O}, obs)$ *be a POMDP. The belief MDP of* M *is given by* $\mathcal{B}(\mathsf{M})=(Dist(S), \delta_{\bar{s}}, A, P^{\mathcal{B}}, R^{\mathcal{B}})$ *where, for any beliefs*

$b, b' \in Dist(S)$ *and action* $a \in A$:

$$P^{\mathcal{B}}(b,a)(b') = \sum_{s \in S} b(s) \cdot \left(\sum_{o \in \mathcal{O} \wedge b^{a,o}=b'} \sum_{s' \in S \wedge obs(s')=o} P(s,a)(s') \right)$$
$$R^{\mathcal{B}}(b,a) = \sum_{s \in S} R(s,a) \cdot b(s)$$

and $b^{a,o}$ *is the belief reached from* b *by performing* a *and observing* o, *i.e.:*

$$b^{a,o}(s') = \begin{cases} \dfrac{\sum_{s \in S} P(s,a)(s') \cdot b(s)}{\sum_{s \in S} b(s) \cdot \left(\sum_{s'' \in S \wedge obs(s'')=o} P(s,a)(s'') \right)} & \text{if } obs(s')=o \\ 0 & \text{otherwise.} \end{cases}$$

The optimal values for the belief MDP equal those for the POMDP, e.g. we have:

$$Pr_{\mathsf{M}}^{\max}(\mathsf{F}\,O) = Pr_{\mathcal{B}(\mathsf{M})}^{\max}(\mathsf{F}\,T_O) \text{ and } \mathbb{E}_{\mathsf{M}}^{\max}(\mathsf{F}\,O) = \mathbb{E}_{\mathcal{B}(\mathsf{M})}^{\max}(\mathsf{F}\,T_O)$$

where $T_O = \{b \in Dist(S) \mid \forall s \in S. (b(s){>}0 \rightarrow obs(s) \in O)\}$.

3 Partially Observable Probabilistic Timed Automata

In this section, we define *partially observable probabilistic timed automata* (POP-TAs), which generalise the existing model of probabilistic timed automata (PTAs) with the notion of partial observability from POMDPs explained in Sec. 2. We define the syntax of a POPTA, explain its semantics (as an infinite-state POMDP) and define and discuss the *digital clocks* semantics of a POPTA.

Time and Clocks. As in classical timed automata [2], we model real-time behaviour using non-negative, real-valued variables called *clocks*, whose values increase at the same rate as real time. Assuming a finite set of clocks $\mathcal{X}$, a *clock valuation* v is a function $v : \mathcal{X} \rightarrow \mathbb{R}$ and we write $\mathbb{R}^{\mathcal{X}}$ for the set of all clock valuations. Clock valuations obtained from v by incrementing all clocks by a delay $t \in \mathbb{R}$ and by resetting a set $X \subseteq \mathcal{X}$ of clocks to zero are denoted $v{+}t$ and $v[X{:=}0]$, respectively, and we write $\mathbf{0}$ if all clocks are 0. A (closed, diagonal-free) *clock constraint* ζ is either a conjunction of inequalities of the form $x{\leqslant}c$ or $x{\geqslant}c$, where $x \in \mathcal{X}$ and $c \in \mathbb{N}$, or **true**. We write $v \models \zeta$ if clock valuation v satisfies clock constraint ζ and use $CC(\mathcal{X})$ for the set of all clock constraints over $\mathcal{X}$.

Syntax of POPTAs. To explain the syntax of POPTAs, we first consider the simpler model of PTAs and then show how it extends to POPTAs.

Definition 5 (PTA syntax). *A PTA is a tuple* $\mathsf{P}{=}(L, \bar{l}, \mathcal{X}, A, inv, enab, prob, r)$ *where:*

- L *is a finite set of* locations *and* $\bar{l} \in L$ *is an* initial location;
- $\mathcal{X}$ *is a finite set of* clocks *and* A *is a finite set of* actions;
- $inv : L \rightarrow CC(\mathcal{X})$ *is an* invariant condition;
- $enab : L{\times}A \rightarrow CC(\mathcal{X})$ *is an* enabling condition;
- $prob : L{\times}A \rightarrow Dist(2^{\mathcal{X}}{\times}L)$ *is a* probabilistic transition function;
- $r{=}(r_L, r_A)$ *is a* reward structure *where* $r_L : L \rightarrow \mathbb{R}$ *is a* location reward function *and* $r_A : L{\times}A \rightarrow \mathbb{R}$ *is an* action reward function.

A state of a PTA is a pair (l, v) of location $l \in L$ and clock valuation $v \in \mathbb{R}^{\mathcal{X}}$. Time $t \in \mathbb{R}$ can elapse in the state only if the invariant $inv(l)$ remains continuously satisfied while time passes and the new state is then $(l, v+t)$. An action a is enabled in the state if v satisfies $enab(l, a)$ and, if it is taken, then the PTA moves to location l' and resets the clocks $X \subseteq \mathcal{X}$ with probability $prob(l, a)(X, l')$. PTAs have two kinds of rewards: location rewards, which are accumulated at rate $r_L(l)$ while in location l and action rewards $r_A(l, a)$, which are accumulated when taking action a in location l. PTAs equipped with reward structures are a probabilistic extension of linearly-priced timed automata [5].

Definition 6 (POPTA syntax). *A partially observable PTA (POPTA) is a tuple* $\mathsf{P} = (L, \bar{l}, \mathcal{X}, A, inv, enab, prob, r, \mathcal{O}_L, obs_L)$ *where:*

- $(L, \bar{l}, \mathcal{X}, A, inv, enab, prob, r)$ *is a PTA;*
- $\mathcal{O}_L$ *is a finite set of observations;*
- $obs_L : L \rightarrow \mathcal{O}_L$ *is a location observation function.*

For any locations $l, l' \in L$ *with* $obs_L(l) = obs_L(l')$, *we require that* $inv(l) = inv(l')$ *and* $enab(l, a) = enab(l', a)$ *for all* $a \in A$.

The final condition ensures the semantics of a POPTA yields a valid POMDP: recall states with the same observation are required to have identical available actions. Like for POMDPs, for simplicity, we also assume that the initial location is observable, i.e., there exists $\bar{o} \in \mathcal{O}_L$ such that $obs_L(l) = \bar{o}$ if and only if $l = \bar{l}$.

The notion of observability for POPTAs is similar to the one for POMDPs, but applied to locations. Clocks, on the other hand, are always observable. The requirement that the same choices must be available in any observationally-equivalent states, implies the same delays must be available in observationally-equivalent states, and so unobservable clocks could not feature in invariant or enabling conditions. The inclusion of unobservable clocks would therefore necessitate modelling the system as a game with the elapse of time being under the control of a second (environment) player. The underlying semantic model would then be a partially observable stochastic game (POSG), rather than a POMDP. However, unlike POMDPs, limited progress has been made on efficient computational techniques for this model (belief space based techniques, for example, do not apply in general [12]). Even in the simpler case of non-probabilistic timed games, allowing unobservable clocks requires algorithmic analysis to restrict the class of strategies considered [9,14].

Encouragingly, however, we will later show in Sec. 5 that POPTAs with observable clocks were always sufficient for our modelling and analysis.

Restrictions on POPTAs. At this point, we need to highlight a few syntactic restrictions on the POPTAs treated in this paper. Firstly, we emphasise that clock constraints appearing in a POPTA, i.e., in its invariants and enabling conditions, are required to be *closed* (no strict inequalities) and *diagonal-free* (no comparisons of clocks). This is a standard restriction when using the digital clocks discretisation [20] which we work with in this paper.

Secondly, a specific (but minor) restriction for POPTAs is that resets can only be applied to clocks that are non-zero. The reasoning behind this is outlined later

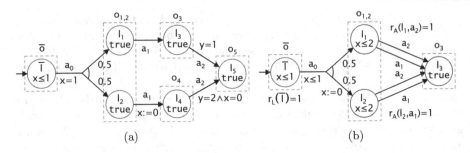

Fig. 1. Examples of partially observable PTAs (see Examples 1 and 2).

in Example 2. Checking this restriction can easily be done when exploring the discrete (digital clocks) semantics of the model – see below and Sec. 4.

Semantics of POPTAs. We now formally define the semantics of a POPTA P, which is given in terms of an infinite-state POMDP. This extends the standard semantics of a PTA [27] (as an infinite MDP) with the same notion of observability we gave in Sec. 2 for POMDPs. The semantics, $[\![P]\!]_{\mathbb{T}}$, is parameterised by a *time domain* $\mathbb{T}$, giving the possible values taken by clocks. For the standard (dense-time) semantics of a POPTA, we take $\mathbb{T} = \mathbb{R}$. Later, when we discretise the model, we will re-use this definition, taking $\mathbb{T} = \mathbb{N}$. When referring to the "standard" semantics of P we will often drop the subscript $\mathbb{R}$ and write $[\![P]\!]$.

Definition 7 (POPTA semantics). *Let* $P=(L,\bar{l},\mathcal{X},A,inv,enab,prob,r,\mathcal{O}_L,obs_L)$ *be a POPTA. The* semantics *of* P, *with respect to the time domain* $\mathbb{T}$, *is the POMDP* $[\![P]\!]_{\mathbb{T}}=(S,\bar{s},A \cup \mathbb{T},P,R,\mathcal{O}_L\times\mathbb{T}^{\mathcal{X}},obs)$ *such that:*

- $S = \{(l,v) \in L\times\mathbb{T}^{\mathcal{X}} \mid v \models inv(l)\}$ *and* $\bar{s}=(\bar{l},\mathbf{0})$;
- *for* $(l,v) \in S$ *and* $a \in A \cup \mathbb{T}$, *we have* $P((l,v),a) = \mu$ *if and only if:*
  - *(time transitions)* $a \in \mathbb{T}$, $\mu = \delta_{(l,v+a)}$ *and* $v+t \models inv(l)$ *for all* $0{\leqslant}t{\leqslant}a$;
  - *(action transition)* $a \in A$, $v \models enab(l,a)$ *and for* $(l',v') \in S$:

$$\mu(l',v') = \sum\nolimits_{X\subseteq\mathcal{X}\wedge v'=v[X:=0]} prob(l,a)(X,l')$$

- *for any* $(l,v) \in S$ *and* $a \in A \cup \mathbb{T}$, *we have* $R((l,v),a) = \begin{cases} r_L(l){\cdot}a & \textit{if } a \in \mathbb{T} \\ r_A(l,a) & \textit{if } a \in A \end{cases}$
- *for any* $(l,v) \in S$, *we have* $obs(l,v) = (obs_L(l),v)$.

Example 1. Consider the POPTA in Fig. 1(a) with clocks x,y. Locations are grouped according to their observations, and we omit enabling conditions equal to **true**. We aim to maximise the probability of observing o_5. If locations were fully observable, we would leave $\bar{l}$ when $x{=}y{=}1$ and then, depending on whether the random choice resulted in a transition to l_1 or l_2, wait 0 or 1 time units, respectively, before leaving the location. This would allow us to move immediately from l_3 or l_4 to l_5, meaning observation o_5 is seen with probability 1. However, in the POPTA, we need to make the same choice in l_1 and l_2 since they yield the same observation. As a result, at most one of the transitions leaving locations l_3 and l_4 is enabled, and the probability of observing o_5 is thus at most 0.5.

Digital Clocks. Since the semantics of a POPTA (like for a PTA) is an infinite-state model, for algorithmic analysis, we first need to construct a *finite* representation. In this paper, we propose to use the *digital clocks* approach, generalising a technique already used for PTAs [20], which in turn adapts one for timed automata [16]. In short, this approach discretises a POPTA model by transforming its real-valued clocks to clocks taking values from a bounded set of integers.

For clock $x \in \mathcal{X}$, let $\mathbf{k}_x$ denote the greatest constant to which x is compared in the clock constraints of POPTA P. If the value of x exceeds $\mathbf{k}_x$, its exact value will not affect the satisfaction of any invariants or enabling conditions, and thus not affect the behaviour of P. The digital clocks semantics, written $[\![P]\!]_\mathbb{N}$, can be obtained from Defn. 7, taking $\mathbb{T}$ to be $\mathbb{N}$ instead of $\mathbb{R}$. We also need to redefine the operation $v+t$, which now adds a delay $t \in \mathbb{N}$ to a clock valuation $v \in \mathbb{N}^{\mathcal{X}}$: we say that $v+t$ assigns the value $\min\{v(x)+t, \mathbf{k}_x+1\}$ to each clock $x \in \mathcal{X}$.

Under the restrictions on POPTAs described above, the digital semantics of a POPTA preserves the key properties required in this paper, namely optimal probabilities and expected cumulative rewards for reaching a specified observation. This is captured by the following theorem (the proof is available in [26]).

Theorem 1. *If* P *is a closed, diagonal-free POPTA which resets only non-zero clocks, then, for any set of observations* O *of* P *and* $opt \in \{\min, \max\}$, *we have:*

$$Pr_{[\![P]\!]_\mathbb{R}}^{opt}(\mathbf{F}\,O) = Pr_{[\![P]\!]_\mathbb{N}}^{opt}(\mathbf{F}\,O) \quad and \quad \mathbb{E}_{[\![P]\!]_\mathbb{R}}^{opt}(\mathbf{F}\,O) = \mathbb{E}_{[\![P]\!]_\mathbb{N}}^{opt}(\mathbf{F}\,O).$$

The proof relies on showing probabilistic and expected reward values agree on the belief MDPs underlying the POMDPs representing the dense time and digital clocks semantics. This requires introducing the concept of a belief PTA for a POPTA (analogous to a belief MDP for a POMDP) and results for PTAs [20].

Example 2. The POPTA P in Fig. 1(b) demonstrates why our digital clocks approach (Thm. 1) is restricted to POPTAs which reset only non-zero clocks. We aim to minimise the expected reward accumulated before observing o_3 (rewards are shown in Fig. 1(b) and are zero if omitted). If locations were fully observable, the minimum reward would be 0, achieved by leaving $\bar{l}$ immediately and then choosing a_1 in l_1 and a_2 in l_2. However, if we leave $\bar{l}$ immediately, l_1 and l_2 are indistinguishable (we observe $(o_{1,2}, (0))$ when arriving in both), so we must choose the same action in these locations, and hence the expected reward is 0.5.

Consider the strategy that waits $\varepsilon \in (0,1)$ before leaving $\bar{l}$, accumulating a reward of ε. This is possible only in the dense-time semantics. We then observe either $(o_{1,2}, (\varepsilon))$ in l_1, or $(o_{1,2}, (0))$ in l_2. Thus, we see if x was reset, determine if we are in l_1 or l_2, and take action a_1 or a_2 accordingly such that no further reward is accumulated before seeing o_3, for a total reward of ε. Since ε can be arbitrarily small, the minimum (infimum) expected reward for $[\![P]\!]_\mathbb{R}$ is 0. However, for the digital clocks semantics, we can only choose a delay of 0 or 1 in $\bar{l}$. For the former, the expected reward is 0.5, as described above; for the latter, we can again pick a_1 or a_2 based on whether x was reset, for a total expected reward of 1. Hence the minimum expected reward for $[\![P]\!]_\mathbb{N}$ is 0.5, as opposed to 0 for $[\![P]\!]_\mathbb{R}$.

4   Verification and Strategy Synthesis for POPTAs

We now present our approach for verification and strategy synthesis for POPTAs using the digital clock semantics given in the previous section.

Property Specification. First, we define a temporal logic for the formal specification of quantitative properties of POPTAs. This is based on a subset (we omit temporal operator nesting) of the logic presented in [27] for PTAs.

Definition 8 (Properties). *The syntax of our logic is given by the grammar:*

$$\phi ::= \mathsf{P}_{\bowtie p}[\psi] \mid \mathsf{R}_{\bowtie q}[\rho] \qquad\qquad \psi ::= \alpha\, \mathsf{U}^{\leqslant t}\, \alpha \mid \alpha\, \mathsf{U}\, \alpha$$
$$\alpha ::= \mathbf{true} \mid o \mid \neg o \mid \zeta \mid \alpha \wedge \alpha \mid \alpha \vee \alpha \qquad \rho ::= \mathsf{I}^{=t} \mid \mathsf{C}^{\leqslant t} \mid \mathsf{F}\,\alpha$$

where o is an observation, ζ is a clock constraint, $\bowtie\, \in \{\leqslant, <, \geqslant, >\}$, $p \in \mathbb{Q} \cap [0,1]$, $q \in \mathbb{Q}_{\geqslant 0}$ and $t \in \mathbb{N}$.

A property ϕ is an instance of either the probabilistic operator P or the expected reward operator R. As for similar logics, $\mathsf{P}_{\bowtie p}[\psi]$ means the probability of path formula ψ being satisfied is $\bowtie p$, and $\mathsf{R}_{\bowtie q}[\rho]$ the expected value of reward operator ρ is $\bowtie q$. For the probabilistic operator, we allow time-bounded ($\alpha\, \mathsf{U}^{\leqslant t}\, \alpha$) and unbounded ($\alpha\, \mathsf{U}\, \alpha$) until formulas, and adopt the usual equivalences such as $\mathsf{F}\,\alpha \equiv \mathbf{true}\, \mathsf{U}\, \alpha$ ("eventually α"). For the reward operator, we allow $\mathsf{I}^{=t}$ (location reward at time instant t), $\mathsf{C}^{\leqslant t}$ (reward accumulated until time t) and $\mathsf{F}\,\alpha$ (the reward accumulated until α becomes true). Our propositional formulas (α) are Boolean combinations of observations and clock constraints.

We omit nesting of P and R operators for two reasons: firstly, the digital clocks approach that we used to discretise time is not applicable to nested properties (see [20] for details); and secondly, it allows us to use a consistent property specification for either verification or strategy synthesis problems (the latter is considerably more difficult in the context of nested formulas [4]).

Definition 9 (Property semantics). *Let P be a POPTA with location observation function obs_L and semantics $[\![\mathsf{P}]\!]$. We define satisfaction of a property ϕ from Defn. 8 with respect to a strategy $\sigma \in \Sigma_{[\![\mathsf{P}]\!]}$ as follows:*

$$[\![\mathsf{P}]\!], \sigma \models \mathsf{P}_{\bowtie p}[\psi] \iff Pr^{\sigma}_{[\![\mathsf{P}]\!]}(\{\omega \in IPaths_{[\![\mathsf{P}]\!]} \mid \omega \models \psi\}) \bowtie p$$
$$[\![\mathsf{P}]\!], \sigma \models \mathsf{R}_{\bowtie q}[\rho] \iff \mathbb{E}^{\sigma}_{[\![\mathsf{P}]\!]}(rew(\rho)) \bowtie q$$

Satisfaction of a path formula ψ by path ω, denoted $\omega \models \psi$ and the random variable $rew(\rho)$ for a reward operator ρ are defined identically as for PTAs. Due to lack of space, we omit their formal definition here and refer the reader to [27]. For a propositional formula α and state $s = (l, v)$ of $[\![\mathsf{P}]\!]$, we have $s \models o$ if and only if $obs_L(l) = o$ and $s \models \zeta$ if and only if $v \models \zeta$. Boolean operators are standard.

Verification and Strategy Synthesis. Given a POPTA P and property ϕ, we are interested in solving the dual problems of *verification* and *strategy synthesis*.

Definition 10 (Verification). *The* verification *problem is: given a POPTA* P *and property ϕ, decide if* $[\![P]\!],\sigma \models \phi$ *holds for all strategies* $\sigma \in \Sigma_{[\![P]\!]}$.

Definition 11 (Strategy synthesis). *The* strategy synthesis *problem is: given POPTA* P *and property ϕ, find, if it exists, a strategy* $\sigma \in \Sigma_{[\![P]\!]}$ *such that* $[\![P]\!],\sigma \models \phi$.

The verification and strategy synthesis problems for ϕ can be solved similarly, by computing *optimal values* for either probability or expected reward objectives:

$$Pr_{[\![P]\!]}^{\min}(\psi) = \inf_{\sigma \in \Sigma_{[\![P]\!]}} Pr_{[\![P]\!]}^{\sigma}(\psi) \qquad \mathbb{E}_{[\![P]\!]}^{\min}(\rho) = \inf_{\sigma \in \Sigma_{[\![P]\!]}} \mathbb{E}_{[\![P]\!]}^{\sigma}(\rho)$$
$$Pr_{[\![P]\!]}^{\max}(\psi) = \sup_{\sigma \in \Sigma_{[\![P]\!]}} Pr_{[\![P]\!]}^{\sigma}(\psi) \qquad \mathbb{E}_{[\![P]\!]}^{\max}(\rho) = \sup_{\sigma \in \Sigma_{[\![P]\!]}} \mathbb{E}_{[\![P]\!]}^{\sigma}(\rho)$$

and, where required, also synthesising an *optimal strategy*. For example, verifying $\phi=P_{\geqslant p}[\psi]$ requires computation of $Pr_{[\![P]\!]}^{\min}(\psi)$ since ϕ is satisfied by all strategies if and only if $Pr_{[\![P]\!]}^{\min}(\psi) \geqslant p$. Dually, consider synthesising a strategy for which $\phi'=P_{\leqslant p}[\psi]$ holds. Such a strategy exists if and only if $Pr_{[\![P]\!]}^{\min}(\psi) \leqslant p$ and, if it does, we can use the optimal strategy that achieves the minimum value. A common practice in probabilistic verification to simply query the optimal values directly, using *numerical* properties such as $P_{\min=?}[\psi]$ and $R_{\max=?}[\rho]$.

As mentioned earlier, when solving POPTAs (or POMDPs), we may only be able to under- and over-approximate optimal values, which requires adapting the processes sketched above. For example, if we have determined lower and upper bounds $p^\flat \leqslant Pr_{[\![P]\!]}^{\min}(\psi) \leqslant p^\sharp$. We can verify that $\phi=P_{\geqslant p}[\psi]$ holds if $p^\flat \geqslant p$ or ascertain that ϕ does not hold if $p \geqslant p^\sharp$. But, if $p^\flat < p < p^\sharp$, we need to refine our approximation to produce tighter bounds. An analogous process can be followed for the case of strategy synthesis. The remainder of this section therefore focuses on how to (approximately) compute optimal values and strategies for POPTAs.

Numerical Computation Algorithms. Approximate numerical computation of either optimal probabilities or expected reward values on a POPTA P is performed with the sequence of steps given below, each of which is described in more detail subsequently. We compute both an under- and an over-approximation. For the former, we also generate a strategy which achieves this value.

(A) We modify POPTA P, reducing the problem to computing optimal values for a *probabilistic reachability* or *expected cumulative reward* property [27];
(B) We apply the *digital clocks* discretisation of Sec. 3 to reduce the infinite-state semantics $[\![P]\!]_\mathbb{R}$ of P to a *finite-state POMDP* $[\![P]\!]_\mathbb{N}$;
(C) We build and solve a *finite abstraction* of the (infinite-state) belief MDP $\mathcal{B}([\![P]\!]_\mathbb{N})$ of the POMDP from (B), yielding an *over-approximation*;
(D) We synthesise and analyse a strategy for $[\![P]\!]_\mathbb{N}$, giving an *under-approximation*;
(E) If required, we *refine* the abstraction's precision and repeat (C) and (D).

(A) Property Reduction. As discussed in [27] (for PTAs), checking P or R properties of the logic of Defn. 8 can always be reduced to checking either a probabilistic reachability ($P_{\bowtie p}[F\,\alpha]$) or expected cumulative reward ($R_{\bowtie q}[F\,\alpha]$) property on a modified model. For example, time-bounded probabilistic reachability

$(P_{\bowtie p}[F^{\leqslant t}\,\alpha])$ can be transformed into probabilistic reachability $(P_{\bowtie p}[F\,(\alpha \wedge y \leqslant t)])$ where y is a new clock added to the model. We refer to [27] for full details.

(B) Digital Clocks. We showed in Sec. 3 that, assuming certain simple restrictions on the POPTA P, we can construct a finite POMDP $[\![P]\!]_{\mathbb{N}}$ representing P by treating clocks as bounded integer variables. The translation itself is relatively straightforward, involving a syntactic translation of the PTA (to convert clocks), followed by a systematic exploration of its finite state space. At this point, we also check satisfaction of the restrictions on POPTAs described in Sec. 3.

(C) Over-approximation. We now solve the finite POMDP $[\![P]\!]_{\mathbb{N}}$. For simplicity, here and below, we describe the case of maximum reachability probabilities (the other cases are very similar) and thus need to compute $Pr_{[\![P]\!]_{\mathbb{N}}}^{\max}(F\,O)$. We first compute an *over-approximation*, i.e. an *upper* bound on the maximum probability. This is computed from an approximate solution to the belief MDP $\mathcal{B}([\![P]\!]_{\mathbb{N}})$, whose construction we outlined in Sec. 2. This MDP has a continuous state space: the set of beliefs $Dist(S)$, where S is the state space of $[\![P]\!]_{\mathbb{N}}$.

To approximate its solution, we adopt the approach of [29] which computes values for a finite set of representative beliefs G whose convex hull is $Dist(S)$. Value iteration is applied to the belief MDP, using the computed values for beliefs in G and interpolating to get values for those not in G. The resulting values give the required upper bound. We use [29] as it works with *unbounded* (infinite horizon) and *undiscounted* properties. There are many other similar approaches [28], but these are formulated for discounted or finite-horizon properties.

The representative beliefs can be chosen in a variety of ways. We follow [23], where $G = \{\frac{1}{M}v \mid v \in \mathbb{N}^{|S|} \wedge \sum_{i=1}^{|S|} v(i)=M\}$, i.e. a uniform *grid* with *resolution* M. A benefit is that interpolation is very efficient, using a process called triangulation [13]. A downside is that the grid size is exponential M.

(D) Under-Approximation. Since it is preferable to have two-sided bounds, we also compute an *under-approximation*: here, a lower bound on $Pr_{[\![P]\!]_{\mathbb{N}}}^{\max}(F\,O)$. To do so, we first synthesise a finite-memory strategy σ^* for $[\![P]\!]_{\mathbb{N}}$ (which is often a required output anyway). The choices of this strategy are built by stepping through the belief MDP and, for the current belief, choosing an action that achieves the values returned by value iteration in (C) above – see for example [28]. We then compute, by building and solving the finite Markov chain induced by $[\![P]\!]_{\mathbb{N}}$ and σ^*, the value $Pr_{[\![P]\!]_{\mathbb{N}}}^{\sigma^*}(F\,O)$ which is a lower bound for $Pr_{[\![P]\!]_{\mathbb{N}}}^{\max}(F\,O)$.

(E) Refinement. Finally, although no a priori bound can be given on the error between the generated under- and over-approximations (recall that the basic problem is undecidable), asymptotic convergence of the grid based approach *is* guaranteed [29]. In practice, if the computed approximations do not suffice to verify the required property (or, for strategy synthesis, σ^* does not satisfy the property), then we increase the grid resolution M and repeat steps (C) and (D).

5   Implementation and Case Studies

We have built a prototype tool for verification and strategy synthesis of POPTAs and POMDPs as an extension of PRISM [19]. We extended the existing modelling language for PTAs, to allow model variables to be specified as observable or hidden. The tool performs the steps outlined in Sec. 4, computing a pair of bounds for a given property and synthesising a corresponding strategy. We focus on POP-TAs, but the tool can also analyse POMDPs directly. The software, details of all case studies, parameters and properties are available online at:

http://www.prismmodelchecker.org/files/formats15poptas/

We have developed three case studies to evaluate the tool and techniques, discussed in more detail below. In each case, nondeterminism, probability, real-time behaviour *and* partial observability are all essential aspects required for analysis.

The NRL Pump. The NRL (Naval Research Laboratory) pump [17] is designed to provide reliable and secure communication over networks of nodes with 'high' and 'low' security levels. It prevents a covert channel leaking information from 'high' to 'low' through the *timing* of messages and acknowledgements. Communication is buffered and *probabilistic* delays are added to acknowledgements from 'high' in such a way that the potential for information leakage is minimised, while maintaining network performance. A PTA model is considered in [21].

We model the pump as a POPTA using a hidden variable for a secret value $z \in \{0, 1\}$ (initially set uniformly at random) which 'high' tries to covertly communicate to 'low'. This communication is attempted by adding a delay of h_0 or h_1, depending on the value of z, whenever sending an acknowledgement to 'low'. In the model, 'low' sends N messages to 'high' and tries to guess z based on the time taken for its messages to be acknowledged. We consider the maximum probability 'low' can (either eventually or within some time frame) correctly guess z. We also study the expected time to send all messages and acknowledgements. These properties measure the security and performance aspects of the pump. Results are presented in Fig. 2 varying h_1 and N (we fix $h_0=2$). They show that increasing either the difference between h_0 and h_1 (i.e., increasing h_1) or the number N of messages sent improve the chance of 'low' correctly guessing the secret z, at the cost of a decrease in network performance. On the other hand, when $h_0=h_1$, however many messages are sent, 'low', as expected, learns nothing of the value being sent and at best can guess correctly with probability 0.5.

Task-graph Scheduler. Secondly, we consider a task-graph scheduling problem adapted from [7], where the goal is to minimise the *time* or *energy consumption* required to evaluate an arithmetic expression on multiple processors with different speeds and energy consumption. We extend both the basic model of [7] and the extension from [27] which uses PTAs to model *probabilistic* task execution times. A new 'low power' state to one processor, allowing it to save energy when not in use, but which incurs a delay when waking up to execute a new task. This state is entered with probability *sleep* after each task is completed. We assume that the scheduler cannot observe whether the processor enters this lower power

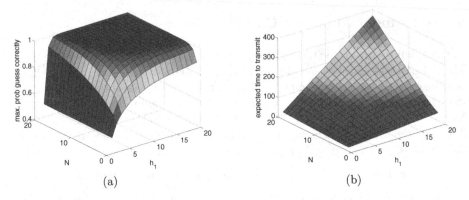

Fig. 2. Analysing security/performance of the NRL pump: (a) Maximum probability of covert channel success; (b) Maximum expected transmission time.

state, and hence the model is a POPTA. We generate optimal schedulers (minimising expected execution time or energy usage) using strategy synthesis.

Non-repudiation Protocol. Our third case study is a non-repudiation protocol for information transfer due to Markowitch & Roggeman [25]. It is designed to allow an originator O to send information to a recipient R while guaranteeing *non-repudiation*, that is, neither party can deny having participated in the information transfer. The initialisation step of the protocol requires O to *randomly* select an integer N in the range $1, \ldots, K$ that is never revealed to R during execution. In previous analyses [22,27], modelling this step was not possible since no notion of (non-)observability was used. We resolve this by building a POPTA model of the protocol including this step, thus matching Markowitch & Roggeman's original specification. In particular, we include a hidden variable to store the random value N. We build two models: a basic one, where R's only malicious behaviour corresponds to stopping early; and a second, more complex model, where R has access to a decoder. We compute the maximum probability that R gains an unfair advantage (gains the information from O while being able to deny participating). Our results (see Table 1) show that, for the basic model, this probability equals $1/K$ and R is more powerful in the complex model.

Experimental Results. Table 1 summarises a representative set of experimental results from the analysis of our three case studies. All were run on a 2.8 GHz PC with 8GB RAM. The table shows the parameters used for each model (see the web page cited above for details), the property analysed and various statistics from the analysis: the size of the POMDP obtained through the digital clocks semantics; number of observations; number of hidden values (i.e., the maximum number of states with the same observation); the grid size (resolution M and total number of points); the time taken; and the results obtained. For comparison, in the rightmost column, we show what result is obtained if the POPTA is treated as a PTA (by making everything observable).

On the whole, we find that the performance of our prototype is good, especially considering the complexity of the POMDP solution methods and the fact

Table 1. Experimental results from verification/strategy synthesis of POPTAs.

Case study (parameters)		Property	Verification/strategy synthesis of POPTA							PTA result
			States ($[\![P]\!]_N$)	Num. obs.	Num. hidd.	Res. (M)	Grid points	Time (s)	Result (bounds)	
pump (h_1 N)	16 2	$P_{\texttt{max}=?}[F\ guess]$	243	145	3	2	342	0.7	[0.940, 0.992]	1.0
	16 2		243	145	3	40	4,845	4.0	[0.940, 0.941]	1.0
	16 16		1,559	803	3	2	2,316	16.8	[0.999, 0.999]	1.0
pump (h_1 N D)	8 4 50	$P_{\texttt{max}=?}[F^{\leqslant D}\ guess]$	12,167	7,079	3	2	17,256	11.0	[0.753, 0.808]	1.0
	8 4 50		12,167	7,079	3	12	68,201	36.2	[0.763, 0.764]	1.0
	16 8 50		26,019	13,909	3	2	38,130	52.8	[0.501, 0.501]	1.0
	16 8 100		59,287	31,743	3	2	86,832	284.8	[0.531, 0.532]	1.0
scheduler basic (*sleep*)	0.25	$R_{\texttt{min}=?}[F\ done]$ (exec. time)	5,002	3,557	2	2	6,447	3.2	[14.69, 14.69]	14.44
	0.5		5,002	3,557	2	2	6,447	3.1	[17.0, 17.0]	16.5
	0.75		5,002	3,557	2	4	9,337	3.1	[19.25, 19.25]	18.5
scheduler basic (*sleep*)	0.25	$R_{\texttt{min}=?}[F\ done]$ (energy cons.)	5,002	3,557	2	4	9,337	3.1	[1.335, 1.335]	1.237
	0.5		5,002	3,557	2	2	6,447	3.1	[1.270, 1.270]	1.186
	0.75		5,002	3,557	2	2	6,447	3.2	[1.204, 1.204]	1.155
scheduler prob (*sleep*)	0.25	$R_{\texttt{min}=?}[F\ done]$ (exec. time)	6,987	5,381	2	2	8,593	5.8	[15.00, 15.00]	14.75
	0.5		6,987	5,381	2	2	8,593	5.8	[17.27, 17.27]	16.77
	0.75		6,987	5,381	2	4	11,805	5.0	[19.52, 19.52]	18.77
scheduler prob (*sleep*)	0.25	$R_{\texttt{min}=?}[F\ done]$ (energy cons.)	6,987	5,381	2	4	11,805	5.3	[1.335, 1.335]	1.3
	0.5		6,987	5,381	2	2	8,593	5.0	[1.269, 1.269]	1.185
	0.75		6,987	5,381	2	2	8,593	5.8	[1.204, 1.204]	1.155
nrp basic (*K*)	4	$P_{\texttt{max}=?}[F\ unfair]$	365	194	5	8	5,734	0.8	[0.25, 0.281]	1.0
	4		365	194	5	24	79,278	5.9	[0.25, 0.25]	1.0
	8		1,273	398	9	4	23,435	4.8	[0.125, 0.375]	1.0
	8		1,273	398	9	8	318,312	304.6	[0.125, 0.237]	1.0
nrp complex (*K*)	4	$P_{\texttt{max}=?}[F\ unfair]$	1,501	718	5	4	7,480	2.1	[0.438, 0.519]	1.0
	4		1,501	718	5	12	72,748	14.8	[0.438, 0.438]	1.0
	8		5,113	1,438	9	2	16,117	6.1	[0.344, 0.625]	1.0
	8		5,113	1,438	9	4	103,939	47.1	[0.344, 0.520]	1.0

that we use a relatively simple grid mechanism. We are able to analyse POPTAs whose integer semantics yields POMDPs of up to 60,000 states, with experiments usually taking just a few seconds and, at worst, 5-6 minutes. These are, of course, smaller than the standard PTA (or MDP) models that can be verified, but we were still able to obtain useful results for several case studies.

The values in the rightmost column of Table 1 illustrate that the results obtained with POPTAs would not have been possible using a PTA model, i.e., where all states of the model are observable. For the *pump* example, the PTA gives probability 1 of guessing correctly ('low' can simply read the value of the secret). For the *scheduler* example, the PTA model gives a scheduler with better time/energy consumption but that cannot be implemented in practice since the power state is not visible. For the *nrp* models, the PTA gives probability 1 of unfairness as the recipient can read the random value the originator selects.

Another positive aspect is that, in many cases, the bounds generated are very close (or even equal, in which case the results are exact). For the *pump* and *scheduler* case studies, we included results for the smallest grid resolution M required to ensure the difference between the bounds is at most 0.001. In many cases, this is achieved with relatively small values (for the *scheduler* example, in particular, M is at most 4). For *nrp* models, we were unable to do this when $K=8$ and instead include the results for the largest grid resolution for which POMDP solution was possible: higher values could not be handled within the memory constraints of our test machine. We anticipate being able to improve this in the future by adapting more advanced approximation methods for POMDPs [28].

6 Conclusions

We have proposed novel methods for verification and control of partially observable probabilistic timed automata, using a temporal logic for probabilistic, real-time properties and reward measures. We developed techniques based on a digital clocks discretisation and a belief space approximation, then implemented them in a tool and demonstrated their effectiveness on several case studies.

Future directions include more efficient approximation schemes, zone-based implementations and development of the theory for unobservable clocks. Allowing unobservable clocks, as mentioned previously, will require moving to partially observable stochastic games and restricting the class of strategies.

Acknowledgments. This work was partly supported by the EPSRC grant "Automated Game-Theoretic Verification of Security Systems" (EP/K038575/1). We also grateful acknowledge support from Google Summer of Code 2014.

References

1. de Alfaro, L.: The verification of probabilistic systems under memoryless partial-information policies is hard. In: Proc. PROBMIV 1999, pp. 19–32 (1999)
2. Alur, R., Dill, D.: A theory of timed automata. Theoretical Computer Science **126**, 183–235 (1994)
3. Baier, C., Bertrand, N., Größer, M.: On decision problems for probabilistic Büchi automata. In: Amadio, R.M. (ed.) FOSSACS 2008. LNCS, vol. 4962, pp. 287–301. Springer, Heidelberg (2008)
4. Baier, C., Größer, M., Leucker, M., Bollig, B., Ciesinski, F.: Controller synthesis for probabilistic systems (extended abstract). In: Levy, J.-J., Mayr, E.W., Mayr, J.C. (eds.) TCS 2004. IFIP, vol. 155, pp. 493–506. Springer, Heidelberg (2004)
5. Behrmann, G., Fehnker, A., Hune, T., Larsen, K., Pettersson, P., Romijn, J., Vaandrager, F.: Minimum-cost reachability for priced time automata. In: Di Benedetto, M.D., Sangiovanni-Vincentelli, A. (eds.) Hybrid Systems: Computation and Control. LNCS, vol. 2034, pp. 147–161. Springer, Heidelberg (2001)
6. Bouyer, P., D'Souza, D., Madhusudan, P., Petit, A.: Timed Control with partial observability. In: Hunt Jr., W.A., Somenzi, F. (eds.) CAV 2003. LNCS, vol. 2725, pp. 180–192. Springer, Heidelberg (2003)
7. Bouyer, P., Fahrenberg, U., Larsen, K., Markey, N.: Quantitative analysis of real-time systems using priced timed automata. Comm. of the ACM **54**(9), 78–87 (2011)
8. Cassandra, A.: A survey of POMDP applications. Presented at the AAAI Fall Symposium, 1998. http://pomdp.org/pomdp/papers/applications.pdf (1998)
9. Cassez, F., David, A., Larsen, K.G., Lime, D., Raskin, J.-F.: Timed Control with observation based and stuttering invariant strategies. In: Namjoshi, K.S., Yoneda, T., Higashino, T., Okamura, Y. (eds.) ATVA 2007. LNCS, vol. 4762, pp. 192–206. Springer, Heidelberg (2007)

10. Černý, P., Chatterjee, K., Henzinger, T.A., Radhakrishna, A., Singh, R.: Quantitative synthesis for concurrent programs. In: Gopalakrishnan, G., Qadeer, S. (eds.) CAV 2011. LNCS, vol. 6806, pp. 243–259. Springer, Heidelberg (2011)
11. Chatterjee, K., Chmelik, M., Tracol, M.: What is decidable about partially observable Markov decision processes with omega-regular objectives. In: CSL 2013. LIPIcs, vol. 23, pp. 165–180. Schloss Dagstuhl-Leibniz-Zentrum fuer Informatik (2013)
12. Chatterjee, K., Doyen, L.: Partial-observation stochastic games: How to win when belief fails. ACM Transactions on Computational Logic 15(2) (2014)
13. Eaves, B.: A course in triangulations for solving equations with deformations. Springer (1984)
14. Finkbeiner, B., Peter, H.-J.: Template-based controller synthesis for timed systems. In: Flanagan, C., König, B. (eds.) TACAS 2012. LNCS, vol. 7214, pp. 392–406. Springer, Heidelberg (2012)
15. Giro, S., Rabe, M.N.: Verification of partial-information probabilistic systems using counterexample-guided refinements. In: Chakraborty, S., Mukund, M. (eds.) ATVA 2012. LNCS, vol. 7561, pp. 333–348. Springer, Heidelberg (2012)
16. Henzinger, T.A., Manna, Z., Pnueli, A.: What good are digital clocks? In: Kuich, W. (ed.) ICALP 1992. LNCS, vol. 623, pp. 545–558. Springer, Heidelberg (1992)
17. Kang, M., Moore, A., Moskowitz, I.: Design and assurance strategy for the NRL pump. Computer 31(4), 56–64 (1998)
18. Kemeny, J., Snell, J., Knapp, A.: Denumerable Markov Chains (1976)
19. Kwiatkowska, M., Norman, G., Parker, D.: PRISM 4.0: verification of probabilistic real-time systems. In: Gopalakrishnan, G., Qadeer, S. (eds.) CAV 2011. LNCS, vol. 6806, pp. 585–591. Springer, Heidelberg (2011)
20. Kwiatkowska, M., Norman, G., Parker, D., Sproston, J.: Performance analysis of probabilistic timed automata using digital clocks. FMSD 29, 33–78 (2006)
21. Lanotte, R., Maggiolo-Schettini, A., Tini, S., Troina, A., Tronci, E.: Automatic analysis of the NRL pump. In: ENTCS, vol. 99, pp. 245–266 (2004)
22. Lanotte, R., Maggiolo-Schettini, A., Troina, A.: Automatic analysis of a non-repudiation protocol. In: Proc. QAPL 2004. ENTCS, vol. 112, pp. 113–129 (2005)
23. Lovejoy, W.: Computationally feasible bounds for partially observed Markov decision processes. Operations Research 39(1), 162–175 (1991)
24. Madani, O., Hanks, S., Condon, A.: On the undecidability of probabilistic planning and related stochastic optimization problems. Artif. Intell. 147(1–2), 5–34 (2003)
25. Markowitch, O., Roggeman, Y.: Probabilistic non-repudiation without trusted third party. In: Proc. Workshop on Security in Communication Networks (1999)
26. Norman, G., Parker, D., Zou, X.: Verification and control of partially observable probabilistic real-time systems (2015). http://arxiv.org/abs/1506.06419
27. Norman, G., Parker, D., Sproston, J.: Model checking for probabilistic timed automata. FMSD 43(2), 164–190 (2013)
28. Shani, G., Pineau, J., Kaplow, R.: A survey of point-based POMDP solvers. Autonomous Agents and Multi-Agent Systems 27(1), 1–51 (2013)
29. Yu, H.: Approximate Solution Methods for Partially Observable Markov and Semi-Markov Decision Processes. Ph.D. thesis, MIT (2006)

Deciding Concurrent Planar Monotonic Linear Hybrid Systems

Pavithra Prabhakar[1], Nima Roohi[2($\boxtimes$)], and Mahesh Viswanathan[2]

[1] IMDEA Software Institute, Madrid, Spain
pavithra.prabhakar@imdea.org
[2] Department of Computer Science, University of Illinois at Urbana-Champaign,
Champaign, USA
{roohi2,vmahesh}@illinois.edu

Abstract. Decidability results for hybrid automata often exploit subtle properties about dimensionality (number of continuous variables), and interaction between discrete transitions and continuous trajectories of variables. Thus, the decidability results often do not carry over to parallel compositions of hybrid automata, even when there is no communication other than the implicit synchronization of time. In this paper, we show that the reachability problem for concurrently running planar, monotonic hybrid automata is decidable. Planar, monotonic hybrid automata are a special class of linear hybrid automata with only two variables, whose flows in all states are simultaneously monotonic along some direction in the plane. The reachability problem is known to be decidable for this class. Our concurrently running automata synchronize with respect to a global clock, and through labeled discrete transitions. The proof of decidability hinges on a new observation that the timed trace language of a planar monotonic automaton can be recognized by a timed automaton, and the decidability result follows from the decidability of composition of timed automata. Our results identify a new decidable subclass of multi-rate hybrid automata.

1 Introduction

Hybrid automata [6] model the interaction between a discrete controller and a physical environment. Such automata have finitely many control locations, modeling the state of the discrete controller, and real-valued variables that evolve continuously with time, modeling the state of the physical environment. They exhibit hybrid behavior where control location changes influence the values of the real-valued variables and the physical laws governing their evolution. The safety verification of such systems can often be reduced to the reachability problem, wherein one asks if a certain state/set of states can be reached during an execution that starts from some initial state.

The reachability question for hybrid automata is in general undecidable [7], and special classes of decidable hybrid automata have been identified [2–4,7,8,11,13]. Small variations to the decidable classes are known to make the reachability problem undecidable [1,3,7,10,13]. The reason for this is because the decidability

S. Sankaranarayanan and E. Vicario (Eds.): FORMATS 2015, LNCS 9268, pp. 256–269, 2015.
DOI: 10.1007/978-3-319-22975-1_17

results exploit subtle properties about dimensionality (number of continuous variables in the hybrid automaton), and the interaction between the discrete transitions and the continuous dynamics of the variables. One consequence of this is that the reachability problem is often undecidable for parallel compositions of decidable automata. This is true even when the concurrently running automata do not communicate other than the implicit synchronization of time [5].

In this paper, we show that the reachability problem is decidable for parallel compositions of *planar monotonic linear hybrid systems*. Planar monotonic linear hybrid systems are hybrid systems with the following restrictions — the automaton has only two real-valued variables; the flows (continuous dynamics with time) of the variables are given by linear functions, and all the constraints describing the invariants, guards, and resets are linear functions; the flow in every control location is monotonic in some direction on the plane and the variables are reset on discrete transitions that either change this monotonic direction, or are labeled through actions that are used for communication between automata. The reachability problem for the subclass of the automata with no resets is known to be decidable [11].

Our proof proceeds as follows. For a planar monotonic linear hybrid system $\mathcal{H}$, let us consider $\mathtt{TReach}_{\mathcal{H}}$ to be the set of triples (x, t, y) such that there is an execution starting at x that reaches y at time t, and the variables are never reset along this execution. Our first observation is that $\mathtt{TReach}_{\mathcal{H}}$ is expressible in the first order theory of linear arithmetic. This requires us to adapt the decidability proof for reachability presented in [11] to consider timed reachability and representation in the theory of reals; the challenge in proving such an expressivity result is that executions of such automata can have an unbounded number of discrete transitions. One consequence of this is that the set of times at which one can reach a polyhedron P_2 when starting from a polyhedron P_1 can also be expressed in the theory of linear arithmetic. Since this theory is o-minimal [12], this means that this set of times can be expressed as a finite union of intervals. We use this conclusion to argue that the timed trace language of $\mathcal{H}$ (the sequence of visible synchronizable actions along with the time when they happen) can be generated by a timed automaton. Hence the parallel composition of planar monotonic linear hybrid automata is timed trace language equivalent to the parallel composition of timed automata, which can be effectively constructed from the component planar monotonic linear hybrid automata. Since the reachability question can be reduced to the emptiness of the timed trace language, our decidability result follows from the fact that the emptiness of the timed trace language of timed automata can be decided [2].

Our proof is inspired by ideas presented in [9] where a new decidability proof for initialized rectangular hybrid automata is obtained by viewing such an automaton as the parallel composition of 1-dimensional systems. Our proof and the results in [9] suggest a method to lift decidability results for low dimensional systems to higher dimensional systems. For example, one consequence of our results is the identification of new decidable subclass of multi-rate automata that we call *phased multi-rate automata*; reachability for the general class of multi-rate automata is known to be undecidable [7]. Our result is proved by demonstrating that phased multi-rate automata can be seen as the parallel composition of planar monotonic linear hybrid systems.

2   Preliminaries

Notations. $\mathbb{Q}$, $\mathbb{R}$, and $\mathbb{R}_{\geq 0}$ are, respectively, the set of *rational, real,* and *non-negative real* numbers. Given $\mathbf{u} \in \mathbb{R}^n$, we use $\mathbf{u}_i$ to denote the i-th component of $\mathbf{u}$. Given $\mathbf{u} \in \mathbb{R}^n$ and $\mathbf{v} \in \mathbb{R}^m$, we use $\mathbf{u} \circ \mathbf{v}$ to denote the *concatenation* of $\mathbf{u}$ with $\mathbf{v}$ in $\mathbb{R}^{n+m}$. Given two sets $U \subseteq \mathbb{R}^n$ and $V \subseteq \mathbb{R}^m$, $U \circ V = \{\mathbf{u} \circ \mathbf{v} \mid \mathbf{u} \in U, \mathbf{v} \in V\}$. For any two functions $f_1 \in [A_1 \to \mathbb{R}^n]$ and $f_2 \in [A_2 \to \mathbb{R}^m]$, their Cartesian product $f_1 \times f_2$ maps (a_1, a_2) to $f_1(a_1) \circ f_2(a_2)$. For any two functions $f_1 \in [A_1 \to 2^{\mathbb{R}^n}]$ and $f_2 \in [A_2 \to 2^{\mathbb{R}^m}]$, $f_1 \otimes f_2$ maps (a_1, a_2) to $f_1(a_1) \circ f_2(a_2)$. Given a function $f \in [A \to B]$ and $A' \subseteq A$, we denote the restriction of f to A' by $f[A']$ and the image of A' under f, that is, $\{f(a) \mid a \in A'\}$, by $f(A')$. Finally, id_A denotes the identity function on A.

Polyhedral Sets. Let $Poly(\mathbb{R}^n)$, $OpenPoly(\mathbb{R}^n)$ and $BOpenPoly(\mathbb{R}^n)$, respectively, denote the set of all polyhedral sets, open polyhedral sets and bounded open polyhedral sets in $\mathbb{R}^n$. We refer to $\mathbb{R}^2$ as the *plane,* and any polyhedral set in $\mathbb{R}^2$ is called a *planar* polyhedral set. Recall that a polyhedral set P is the set of all points $\mathbf{x}$ satisfying a finite set of linear constraints $\{\mathbf{u}_1 \cdot \mathbf{x} + b_1 \lhd_1 0, \ldots, \mathbf{u}_k \cdot \mathbf{x} + b_k \lhd_k 0\}$. where $\lhd_i \in \{<, \leq\}$, $\mathbf{u}_i \in \mathbb{R}^n$ and $b_i \in \mathbb{R}$. When the polyhedral set P is planar, we denote the lines corresponding to the constraints $\mathbf{u}_i \cdot \mathbf{x} + b_i = 0$ as $Lines(P)$.

An n-dimensional *rectangular set* is a polyhedral set which can be expressed as the cross product of intervals $I_1 \times \ldots \times I_n$. The set of all rectangular sets and open rectangular sets of dimension n are denoted as $Rect(\mathbb{R}^n)$ and $OpenRect(\mathbb{R}^n)$, respectively. In addition, $PBOpenRect(\mathbb{R}^n)$ is the set of all partially bounded rectangular sets, that is, rectangular sets $I_1 \times \ldots \times I_n$, where for every $i \in \{1, \ldots n\}$, either $I_i = (-\infty, \infty)$ or I_i is bounded.

3   Linear Hybrid Systems

Hybrid automata [6] are a popular formalism for modeling systems with mixed discrete continuous behaviors. The discrete behavior is captured by a finite state automaton, and the continuous behavior is captured by a finite set of continuously evolving variables.

Definition 1. *A* linear hybrid system *or a* linear hybrid automaton $\mathcal{H}$, *is a tuple* $(Loc, dim, Act, Inv, Flow, Edge, Init, Final)$, *where*

 - *Loc is a finite non-empty set of (discrete) locations.*
 - *dim is the* dimension *of the hybrid system $\mathcal{H}$ and represents the number of continuous variables of the system. $\mathbb{R}^{dim}$ is referred to as the continuous state-space.*

- *Act is a finite non-empty set of* actions *which does not contain a special symbol* τ *or the elements of* $\mathbb{R}_{\geq 0}$.
- *Inv* $\in \left[Loc \to Poly(\mathbb{R}^{dim}) \right]$ *maps each location* q *to a polyhedral set as the* invariant *of* q.
- *Flow* $\in \left[Loc \to \mathbb{Q}^{dim} \right]$ *maps each location* q *to a vector as the* flow *in* q.
- *Edge* $\subseteq Loc \times Loc \times (Act \cup \{\tau\}) \times Poly(\mathbb{R}^{2dim})$ *is a finite set of* edges. *Each* $e \in Edge$ *is a tuple* (q_1, q_2, l, r) *where*
  - $q_1 \in Loc$ *is the* source *of* e.
  - $q_2 \in Loc$ *is the* destination *of* e.
  - $l \in Act \cup \{\tau\}$ *is the* label *of* e.
  - $r \in Poly(\mathbb{R}^{2dim})$ *is the* reset *of* e *and captures a binary relation on the continuous state-space.*
  An edge labelled by an element of Act is called a visible *edge, and that labelled by* τ *is called an* invisible *or a* silent *edge. We denote the different elements of* e *by* $Src(e)$, $Dest(e)$, $Lab(e)$, *and* $Reset(e)$, *respectively.*
- *Init* $\in \left[Loc \to Poly(\mathbb{R}^{dim}) \right]$ *maps each location* q *to a polyhedral set representing the* initial *continuous states in* q.
- *Final* $\in \left[Loc \to Poly(\mathbb{R}^{dim}) \right]$ *maps each location* q *to a polyhedral set representing the* final *continuous states in* q.

We require that for all $q \in Loc$, $Init(q) \subseteq Inv(q)$ *and* $Final(q) \subseteq Inv(q)$.

We denote the different elements of $\mathcal{H}_\eta$ respectively by Loc_η, dim_η, Act_η, Inv_η, $Flow_\eta$, $Edge_\eta$, $Init_\eta$ and $Final_\eta$. From now on, a hybrid system will refer to a linear hybrid system. Finally, we require that all constants used in $\mathcal{H}$ are rationals.

3.1 Semantics

An execution of a hybrid system $\mathcal{H}$ starts in an initial state $(p, \mathbf{u})$, where $\mathbf{u} \in Init(p)$, and evolves through a sequence of continuous and discrete transitions. In any state $(q, \mathbf{v})$, a continuous transition corresponds to a continuous evolution of $\mathbf{v}$ using the rate $Flow(q)$ while remaining within the invariant $Inv(q)$; the location q does not change. On the other hand, a discrete transition from a state $(q, \mathbf{v})$ to a state $(q', \mathbf{v}')$ labelled by l is allowed if there is an edge (q, q', l, r) such that $(\mathbf{v}, \mathbf{v}') \in r$. Formally, the semantics of a linear hybrid system $\mathcal{H}$ is defined by the transition system $[\![\mathcal{H}]\!] = (S, S^{in}, S^{fin}, \to)$, where $S = Loc \times \mathbb{R}^n$ is the set of states, $S^{in} = \{(q, \mathbf{v}) \mid q \in Loc, \mathbf{v} \in Init(q)\}$ is the set of initial states, and $S^{fin} = \{(q, \mathbf{v}) \mid q \in Loc, \mathbf{v} \in Final(q)\}$ is the set of final states (note that $S^{in}, S^{fin} \subseteq S$). Finally, $\to \subseteq S \times (Act \cup \{\tau\} \cup \mathbb{R}_{\geq 0}) \times S$ is the union of discrete and continuous transitions that are defined as follows (we use $s \overset{l}{\to} s'$ to denote $(s, l, s') \in \to$):

- Discrete: $(q, \mathbf{v}) \overset{l}{\to} (q', \mathbf{v}')$ if $\mathbf{v} \in Inv(q)$, $\mathbf{v}' \in Inv(q')$, and there exists $e \in Edge$ such that $q = Src(e)$, $q' = Dest(e)$, $l = Lab(e)$, and $(\mathbf{v}, \mathbf{v}') \in Reset(e)$.
- Continuous: $(q, \mathbf{v}) \overset{t}{\to} (q', \mathbf{v}')$ if $q = q'$, $t \in \mathbb{R}_{\geq 0}$, $\mathbf{v}' = \mathbf{v} + t \cdot Flow(q)$ and $\forall t' \in [0, t] \bullet \mathbf{v} + t' \cdot Flow(q) \in Inv(q)$.

Path, Execution and Execution Fragment. A *path* of the hybrid system $\mathcal{H}$ is a sequence $\pi = e_1, e_2, \ldots, e_k$ such that for every j, $Dest(e_j) = Src(e_{j+1})$. An *execution fragment* of $\mathcal{H}$ is a sequence $\sigma = (q_0, \mathbf{v}_0)a_0(q_1, \mathbf{v}_1)a_1 \ldots (q_{m-1}, \mathbf{v}_{m-1})$ $a_{m-1}(q_m, \mathbf{v}_m)$, such that $(q_i, \mathbf{v}_i) \xrightarrow{a_i} (q_{i+1}, \mathbf{v}_{i+1})$, for $0 \leq i < m$. We call m the length of σ, and is denoted $|\sigma|$. Let $\sigma^s(i)$ denote the i-th state, namely, $(q_i, \mathbf{v}_i)$, and $\sigma^a(i)$ denote the i-th label, namely, a_i. Let $\sigma[i, j]$ denote the sequence from $(q_i, \mathbf{v}_i)$ to $(q_j, \mathbf{v}_j)$, namely, $(q_i, \mathbf{v}_i)a_i(q_{i+1}, \mathbf{v}_{i+1}) \ldots (q_{j-1}, \mathbf{v}_{j-1})a_{j-1}(q_j, \mathbf{v}_j)$. The *duration* of σ, denoted $Duration(\sigma)$, is given by $\sum_{0 \leq i < |\sigma|, \sigma^a(i) \in \mathbb{R}_{\geq 0}} \sigma^a(i)$. It taken to be 0 when the summation is over an empty set. We call the execution fragment σ an *execution* of $\mathcal{H}$ if $\sigma^s(0)$ is an initial state and $\sigma^s(|\sigma|)$ is a final state. Let $Exec(\mathcal{H})$ denote the set of all executions of $\mathcal{H}$.

Reachability Problem. The reachability problem asks, given a linear hybrid system $\mathcal{H}$, is $Exec(\mathcal{H})$ non-empty, i.e., is there an execution fragment of $\mathcal{H}$ from an initial state to a final state.

Timed Trace. A timed trace corresponding to an execution fragment is an alternating sequence of times (between consecutive visible transitions) and visible actions. First, we define a splitting of an execution. A *splitting* of an execution σ is a finite sequence of execution fragments $\sigma_0 \circ \sigma_1 \circ \sigma_2 \circ \ldots \circ \sigma_k$ such that there exists a sequence of indices $0 \leq i_0 \leq i_1 \leq i_2 \leq \ldots \leq i_k = |\sigma|$, where $\sigma_0 = \sigma[0, i_0]$, and for all $1 \leq j \leq k$, $\sigma_j = \sigma[i_{j-1}, i_j]$. A *visible splitting* of σ is a splitting $\sigma = \sigma_0 \circ \sigma_1 \circ \sigma_2 \circ \ldots \circ \sigma_k$ such that for all $0 \leq i < |\sigma_0|$, $\sigma_0^a(i) \notin Act$ and for all $1 \leq j \leq k$, $\sigma_j^a(i) \in Act$ if and only if $i = 0$. A *timed trace* of σ, denoted $TimedTrace(\sigma)$, is the sequence $t_0 a_1 t_1 \ldots a_k t_k$ in $(\mathbb{R}_{\geq 0} \cdot Act)^* \cdot \mathbb{R}_{\geq 0}$, such that $\sigma = \sigma_0 \circ \sigma_1 \circ \ldots \circ \sigma_k$ is a visible splitting of σ, for $0 \leq i \leq k$, $t_i = Duration(\sigma_i)$, and for $1 \leq i \leq k$, $a_i = \sigma_i^a(0)$ is the unique visible action in σ_i. We define the timed language of $\mathcal{H}$, denoted $TimedTrace(\mathcal{H})$, to be $\{TimedTrace(\sigma) \mid \sigma \in Exec(\mathcal{H})\}$. Furthermore, we call two hybrid systems $\mathcal{A}$ and $\mathcal{B}$ *timed language equivalent* (denoted by $\mathcal{A} \sim_{tt} \mathcal{B}$) if $TimedTrace(\mathcal{A}) = TimedTrace(\mathcal{B})$.

3.2   Special Subclasses of Linear Hybrid Automata

In this section, we present two subclasses of linear hybrid automata, namely, timed automata and planar monotonic linear hybrid automata. The decidability of the composition of the automata from the latter class is investigated in the paper, and the decidability proof reduces the reachability problem to that of timed automata.

Timed Automata. A timed automaton is a special type of linear hybrid automaton in which all the variables evolve at a constant rate of 1 in every location. The variables are referred to as clocks. The initial values of the clocks are 0. The resets are given by a pair of guard and zero sets. The guard is a rectangular set which specifies an enabling condition for the edge, and the zero set specifies a subset of the clocks that are reset to 0 with the remaining clock values unaltered during the discrete transition.

Definition 2. *A* timed automaton $\mathcal{H}$ *with* n *clocks is a linear hybrid system of dimension* n *with the following conditions:*
- *Flow maps each location to* 1^n.
- *Init maps each location to either the empty set or* $\{0^n\}$.
- *for every edge* $e \in Edge$, *there exists a* guard $Guard(e) \in Rect(\mathbb{R}^n)$ *and a zero set* $Zero(e) \subseteq \{1,\ldots,n\}$ *such that* $Reset(e) = \{(\boldsymbol{u},\boldsymbol{v})|\boldsymbol{u} \in Guard(e) \wedge \forall i \in \{1,\ldots,n\} \bullet [(i \in Zero(e) \Rightarrow v_i = 0) \wedge (i \notin Zero(e) \Rightarrow v_i = u_i)]\}$.
- *Inv, Final* $\in [Loc \to Rect(\mathbb{R}^n)]$.

Planar Monotonic Linear Hybrid System. The main result of the paper is to show that the reachability problem of parallel compositions of a class of two dimensional linear hybrid systems called planar monotonic linear hybrid systems is decidable. *Planar Monotonic Linear Hybrid Systems* were introduced in [11] and their reachability problem was shown to be decidable. A planar monotonic linear hybrid system is a two dimensional system such that all the flows are "monotonic", that is, all the flow vectors have a positive projection on some direction vector. There are no jumps in the system, that is, upon a discrete transition, the values of the continuous states remain the same. We present below a definition of planar monotonic linear hybrid systems which is slightly more general than the original version. In particular, we allow strong resets on edges, wherein the values of the continuous variables are non-deterministically reset to a polyhedral set. Strong resets essentially disengage the continuous states before and after the discrete transition. Also, we allow the flow vectors to be monotonic with respect to different direction vectors; however, we require strong resets on the edges whose source and target have different direction vectors. Further, we require that the edges with visible actions are also strongly reset.

Definition 3. *A planar monotonic linear hybrid system (PMHS for short)* $\mathcal{H}$ *is a linear hybrid system with the following constraints:*
- $\mathcal{H}$ *is 2 dimensional.*
- *Inv* $\in [Loc \to OpenPoly(\mathbb{R}^2)]$.
- *Init, Final* $\in [Loc \to BOpenPoly(\mathbb{R}^2)]$.
- $\mathcal{H}$ *is monotonic, that is, there exists a* monotonicity function *Mon* $\in [Loc \to \mathbb{Q}^2]$ *that maps each location* q *to a direction* f *such that* $f \cdot Flow(q) > 0$.
- *For every* $e \in Edge$, *one of the following is true:*
  1. *There exists* $Guard(e) \in OpenPoly(\mathbb{R}^n)$ *such that* $Reset(e) = \{(x,x)|x \in Guard(e)\}$. *This means that in order to traverse an edge, the current values of the variables must satisfy a guard* $Guard(e)$, *and the values of variables before and after traversing* e *are the same. We call* e *an* identity reset *edge.*
  2. *There exist* $Guard(e), Target(e) \in BOpenPoly(\mathbb{R}^n)$ *such that* $Reset(e) = Guard(e) \times Target(e)$. *This means that in order to traverse an edge, the current values of variables must satisfy a guard* $Guard(e)$ *(same as the previous case), but the values of variables after traversing* e *are reset to some values satisfying the reset* $Target(e)$. *We call* e *a* strong reset *edge.*

– *For every* $e \in Edge$, *if* $Lab(e) \neq \tau$ *(a visible edge) or* $Mon(Src(e)) \neq Mon(Dest(e))$ *(monotonicity function changes), then* e *must be a strong reset edge.*

We define the polyhedral sets associated with a *PMHS* $\mathcal{H}$, denoted $\mathcal{P}(\mathcal{H})$, to consist of polyhedral sets $Inv(q)$, $Init(q)$ and $Final(q)$ for every location q, and the sets $Guard(e)$ and $Target(e)$ appearing in the reset $Reset(e)$ for every edge e. The set of lines associated with $\mathcal{H}$, denoted $L_{\mathcal{H}}$, is $Lines(\mathcal{P}(\mathcal{H}))$. We call a planar linear hybrid system $\mathcal{H}$ *simple* if no three distinct lines in $L_{\mathcal{H}}$ intersect at a common point. We will assume that the planar linear hybrid systems are simple.

Example 1. Consider the example of a thermostat shown in Figure 1. There are two locations: ON and OFF. It has one variable x that keeps track of temperature. When thermostat is off, temperature decreases with constant rate 2, and when it is on, temperature increases with constant rate 3. If thermostat is off and temperature is less than

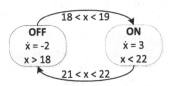

Fig. 1. Thermostat Example

19, we can turn it on by moving to location ON. Similarly, if the thermostat is on and temperature is above 21, we can turn it off by moving back to location OFF. When thermostat is off, temperature must always be above 18, and when it is on, temperature must always be below 22. This thermostat is an example of a *PMHS*. If we add an additional variable that behaves like a clock, then the automaton is monotonic.

3.3   Parallel Composition of Linear Hybrid Automata

The parallel composition of two linear hybrid automata corresponds to executing the two automata simultaneously with the restriction that they synchronize on common labels, that is, a transition labelled by a common label occurs only if both the automata execute a discrete transition labelled by the common label.

Definition 4. *For two linear hybrid systems* $\mathcal{H}_A$ *and* $\mathcal{H}_B$, *their parallel composition* $\mathcal{H}_A \parallel \mathcal{H}_B$ *is a linear hybrid system* $\mathcal{H}_C$ *which is defined as follows:*

- $Loc_C = Loc_A \times Loc_B$
- $dim_C = dim_A + dim_B$
- $Act_C = Act_A \cup Act_B$
- $Inv_C = Inv_A \otimes Inv_B$
- $Flow_C = Flow_A \times Flow_B$
- $Init_C = Init_A \otimes Init_B$
- $Final_C = Final_A \otimes Final_B$
- $Edge_C$ *is the set of edges* $((p_1, p_2), (q_1, q_2), l, r)$ *which satisfy the following:*

  P_1 : *If* $l \in Act_A \cap Act_B$, *then* $\exists r_1, r_2 \bullet (p_1, q_1, l, r_1) \in Edge_A \land (p_2, q_2, l, r_2) \in Edge_B \land r = r_1 \times r_2$

  P_2 : *If* $l \notin Act_B$, *then* $p_2 = q_2 \land \exists r_1 \bullet r = r_1 \times id_{\mathbb{R}^{dim_B}} \land (p_1, q_1, l, r_1) \in Edge_A$

  P_3 : *If* $l \notin Act_A$, *then* $p_1 = q_1 \land \exists r_2 \bullet r = id_{\mathbb{R}^{dim_A}} \times r_2 \land (p_2, q_2, l, r_2) \in Edge_B$

  P_1 *represents edges in both* $\mathcal{H}_A$ *and* $\mathcal{H}_B$ *such that their labels are in the common alphabet of* $\mathcal{H}_A$ *and* $\mathcal{H}_B$. P_2 (P_3) *represents edges in* $\mathcal{H}_A$ ($\mathcal{H}_B$) *such* *that their labels are not in the alphabet of $\mathcal{H}_\mathcal{B}$ ($\mathcal{H}_\mathcal{A}$). Note that when $l = \tau$, the premises of both P_2 and P_3 hold.*

Lemma 1 (Miller [9]). *For any linear hybrid automata $\mathcal{H}_1$, $\mathcal{H}_1'$, $\mathcal{H}_2$, and $\mathcal{H}_2'$ if $\mathcal{H}_1 \sim_{tt} \mathcal{H}_1'$ and $\mathcal{H}_2 \sim_{tt} \mathcal{H}_2'$ then $\mathcal{H}_1 \parallel \mathcal{H}_2 \sim_{tt} \mathcal{H}_1' \parallel \mathcal{H}_2'$.*

Lemma 2 (Alur et al. [2]). *For any finite set of timed automata $\mathcal{T}_1, \ldots, \mathcal{T}_n$, reachability problem for $\mathcal{T}_1 \parallel \ldots \parallel \mathcal{T}_n$ is decidable in* PSPACE.

4   Timed Language Equivalence of PMHS and Timed Automata

Before presenting our decidability result for reachability in Section 5, we present the key idea that enables this decidability result to go through, namely, that the timed language of any *PMHS* is equivalent to that of a timed automaton that can be effectively constructed.

Theorem 1. *The timed language of a PMHS $\mathcal{H}$ is equivalent to the timed language of a timed automaton $TA(\mathcal{H})$ computable from $\mathcal{H}$ in EXPSPACE.*

We will now sketch the ideas behind the proof of Theorem 1. Consider any execution σ of *PMHS* $\mathcal{H}$. The timed automaton $TA(\mathcal{H})$ will "simulate" this execution σ of $\mathcal{H}$ by an execution σ' such that the strong reset transitions taken in σ and σ' are the same, in the same order, and at the same times. Since every visible transition of $\mathcal{H}$ is a strong reset transition, this ensures that $TimedTrace(\sigma)$ is the same as $TimedTrace(\sigma')$. Now if $TA(\mathcal{H})$ simulates (in this manner) all executions of $\mathcal{H}$, and if $TA(\mathcal{H})$ only has such executions, then the timed languages of $\mathcal{H}$ and $TA(\mathcal{H})$ are the same. The executions of the timed automaton $TA(\mathcal{H})$ will only consist of a sequence of strong reset transitions of $\mathcal{H}$. If a strong reset edge e_2 is taken immediately after a strong reset edge e_1, then $TA(\mathcal{H})$ will ensure that the time elapsed between taking e_1 and e_2 is the same as the duration of some reset-free execution fragment of $\mathcal{H}$ that starts in some state in $Target(e_1)$ and ends in some state in $Guard(e_2)$. Notice, that this will immediately guarantee that the executions of $TA(\mathcal{H})$ "simulate" (in the sense outlined above) executions of $\mathcal{H}$. The automaton $TA(\mathcal{H})$ will maintain such constraints by having a clock variable that measures the time between successive transitions, and having locations that remember the last strong reset edge taken.

Before giving a formal definition, we introduce some concepts that will help us describe $TA(\mathcal{H})$ precisely. Given a *PMHS* $\mathcal{H}$, let us denote by $REdge(\mathcal{H})$, the strong reset edges of $\mathcal{H}$. We say that $\mathcal{H}$ is a *reset-free PMHS*, if $REdge(\mathcal{H}) = \emptyset$. For any *PMHS* $\mathcal{H} = (Loc, dim, Act, Inv, Flow, Edge, Init, Final)$ and $Init', Final' \in [Loc \to BOpenPoly(\mathbb{R}^2)]$, we define $ResetFree(\mathcal{H}, Init', Final')$ to be the *PMHS* $(Loc, dim, Act, Inv, Flow, Edge', Init', Final')$, where $Edge' = Edge \setminus REdge(\mathcal{H})$. Finally, for a *PMHS* $\mathcal{H}$, DReach($\mathcal{H}$) will denote the durations of all the executions of $\mathcal{H}$, i.e., DReach($\mathcal{H}$) = $\{t \mid \exists \sigma \in Exec(\mathcal{H}). \ t = Duration(\sigma)\}$.

Definition 5. *For a PMHS* $\mathcal{H} = (Loc, dim, Act, Inv, Flow, Edge, Init, Final)$, *define the timed automaton* $TA(\mathcal{H})$ *to be* $(Loc', dim' = 1, Act, Inv', Flow', Edge', Init', Final')$ *where*

- $Loc' = REdge(\mathcal{H}) \cup \{q_{Init}, q_{Final}\}$,
- *For every* $q \in Loc'$, $Inv'(q) = \mathbb{R}$, $Flow'(q) = 1$, $Init'(q) = \{0\}$ *if* $q = q_{Init}$ *and* $\emptyset$ *otherwise, and* $Final'(q) = \mathbb{R}$ *if* $q = q_{Final}$ *and* $\emptyset$ *otherwise,*
- $Edge'$ *is the set of all edges* e' *such that* $Zero(e') = \{1\}$ *(clock is always reset),* $(Src(e'), Dest(e')) \in (Loc' \setminus \{q_{Final}\}) \times (Loc' \setminus \{q_{Init}\})$ *and the following conditions hold:*
  1. *If* $Dest(e') \in REdge(\mathcal{H})$ *then* $Lab'(e') = Lab(Dest(e'))$ *and if* $Dest(e') = q_{Final}$ *then* $Lab'(e') = \tau$.
  2. $Guard(e') = \text{DReach}(ResetFree(\mathcal{H}, Init', Final'))$, *where*
     - *If* $Src(e') = q_{Init}$ *then* $Init' = Init$. *If* $Src(e') \in REdge(\mathcal{H})$ *then* $Init'(p) = Target(Src(e'))$, *if* $p = Dest(Src(e'))$, $Init'(p) = \emptyset$ *otherwise.*
     - *If* $Dest(e') = q_{Final}$ *then* $Final' = final$. *If* $Dest(e') \in REdge(\mathcal{H})$ *then* $Final'(p) = Guard(Dest(e'))$ *if* $p = Src(Dest(e'))$, *and* $Final'(p) = \emptyset$ *otherwise.*

Definition 5 formalizes the intuition outlined at the beginning of this section, and so, its timed language is equivalent to the timed language of $\mathcal{H}$. However, to finish the proof of Theorem 1, we still need to establish two facts. First, the automaton outlined above is a timed automaton only if the guards in the above definition are "nice" sets; in particular they need to be finite unions of intervals [1]. Second, to argue that $TA(\mathcal{H})$ can be effectively constructed from $\mathcal{H}$, we need to show that the transition guards can be computed. These two requirements do indeed turn out to be true, and is established in Lemma 3.

Lemma 3. *Given a reset-free PMHS* $\mathcal{H}$, *the set* $\text{DReach}(\mathcal{H})$ *is computable and is a finite union of intervals.*

The proof of Lemma 3 relies on the following key lemma. Define a timed reachability predicate for an automaton $\mathcal{H}$ as $\text{TReach}_{\mathcal{H}}^{q_1, q_2} = \{(\mathbf{u}, t, \mathbf{v}) \mid \exists \sigma \in Exec(\mathcal{H}), \sigma^s(0) = (q_1, \mathbf{u}), \sigma^s(|\sigma|) = (q_2, \mathbf{v}), Duration(\sigma) = t\}$.

Lemma 4. *For a reset-free PMHS* $\mathcal{H}$ *and* $q_1, q_2 \in Loc$, *there is a first order logic formula* $\varphi_{\mathcal{H}}^{q_1, q_2}(\boldsymbol{x}, \tau, \boldsymbol{y})$ *over* $(\mathbb{R}, +, <)$ *such that* $(\boldsymbol{v}, t, \boldsymbol{v}') \in \text{TReach}_{\mathcal{H}}^{q_1, q_2}$ *iff* $\varphi_{\mathcal{H}}^{q_1, q_2}(\boldsymbol{v}/\boldsymbol{x}, t/\tau, \boldsymbol{v}'/\boldsymbol{y})$ *holds. Further,* $\varphi_{\mathcal{H}}^{q_1, q_2}$ *is only existentially quantified and its length is bounded by an exponential in the size of* $\mathcal{H}$.

Proof. (Sketch.) The proof builds upon the results in [11], where it is shown that the problem of point-to-point and region-to-region reachability is decidable for the class of reset-free *PMHS*. Below we present briefly an overview of the proof in [11], and highlight the changes in extending it to prove the current lemma.

---

[1] Typically, the guards in a timed automaton are intervals. But transitions with finite unions of intervals as guards can be thought of as a set of finitely many nondeterministic transitions on intervals.

The first step in [11] is to divide the state-space of $\mathcal{H}$ into regions where each region is such that if it intersects with a guard or an invariant of $\mathcal{H}$, then it is contained in it. The maximal set of such regions can be uniquely determined for $\mathcal{H}$ and effectively computable. A tree is constructed which has as nodes subsets of edges of the regions. The children together capture the set of all states reached from the states in the parent by a "region-execution" — executions which remain within a single region. The main technical challenge lies in computing the children, since the number of mode switches in a region-execution between two edges of a region is not bounded. The challenging case is when the hybrid system restricted to the region has cycles. Hence, the problem is reduced to computing the reachable set of a hybrid automaton restricted to a region whose underlying graph is strongly connected. Here, it is shown that the following property P holds, that is, the reach set can be characterized by states reached by certain "executions" with bounded number of mode switches which can potentially violate the invariants and guards. The reach set can then be computed by a finite number of state-space exploration steps. More importantly, the monotonicity property of the flows ensures that the height of the tree is bounded, when the initial and final regions are bounded. And a final region is reachable if and only if one of the trees with root corresponding to an edge of the initial region, contains a node which has an edge of the final region.

In this paper, we extend the proof to compute the predicate $\varphi_{\mathcal{H}}^{q_1,q_2}(\mathbf{x}, \tau, \mathbf{y})$. Note that if node N_2 is a descendant of N_1, then there is an execution from every state in N_1 to some state in N_2. Our main idea is to extend the information along an edge in the tree to capture a ternary relation consisting of tuples $(\mathbf{u}, t, \mathbf{v})$ such that there is a region execution from $\mathbf{u}$ on node N_1 to node $\mathbf{v}$ on its child N_2 of duration t. Our main observation is that the boundedness property in P holds even when we require the executions to be of equal duration. More precisely, $\mathbf{v}$ can be reached from $\mathbf{u}$ by a region-execution of duration t if and only if there exists a certain "execution" with bounded number of mode switches from $\mathbf{u}$ to $\mathbf{v}$ of duration t potentially violating the invariants and guards. Further, we show that this predicate can be captured as an existentially quantified first-order logic formula over $(\mathbb{R}, +, <)$ with only conjunctions. The predicate $\varphi_{\mathcal{H}}^{q_1,q_2}(\mathbf{x}, \tau, \mathbf{y})$ is then constructed by composing the predicates corresponding to the edges.

Next, we provide an upper bound on the length of $\varphi_{\mathcal{H}}^{q_1,q_2}(\mathbf{x}, \tau, \mathbf{y})$. Let n be the size of the input representation of $\mathcal{H}$. Note that the number of constraints used in the description of the invariants and guards is at most n. Hence, the number of regions associated with it is at most 2^n, and the number of nodes in the tree is linear in the number of regions and is bounded by $O(2^n)$ [11]. If L is a bound on the length of the predicate corresponding to an edge, then the length of the predicate $\varphi_{\mathcal{H}}^{q_1,q_2}(\mathbf{x}, \tau, \mathbf{y})$ is bounded by $O(L2^n)$. L is bounded by a polynomial in the size of the automaton. Hence, $\varphi_{\mathcal{H}}^{q_1,q_2}(\mathbf{x}, \tau, \mathbf{y})$ is bounded by $2^{O(n)}$.

We now complete the proof of Lemma 3 (and therefore, Theorem 1). Recall that the first order theory of $(\mathbb{R}, +, <)$ is *o-minimal* [12]. Therefore, any set defined by a first order formula with one free variable in this structure is a finite union of intervals [12]. Finally, the theory of $(\mathbb{R}, +, <)$ has a *PSPACE* quantifier elimination procedure for existentially quantified formulas (formulas with no quantifier alternation), and hence, the intervals in the finite union are computable. Now since $\mathrm{DReach}(\mathcal{H}) = \exists \mathbf{x}, \mathbf{y}. \bigvee_{q_1, q_2} \varphi_{\mathcal{H}}^{q_1, q_2}(\mathbf{x}, \tau, \mathbf{y})$, we have established Lemma 3. Further, since, the length of the formula $\varphi_{\mathcal{H}}^{q_1, q_2}$ is at most exponential in the size of $\mathcal{H}$, $\mathrm{DReach}(\mathcal{H})$ can be computed in $EXPSPACE$, and hence $TA(\mathcal{H})$ can be computed in $EXPSPACE$.

5   Main Result

The timed trace equivalence of *PMHS* with timed automata (Theorem 1) allows us to prove the following main result of this paper.

Theorem 2. *The following problem is decidable in EXPSPACE: Given hybrid automata $\mathcal{H}_1, \mathcal{H}_2, \ldots, \mathcal{H}_k$ such that each $\mathcal{H}_i$ is either a PMHS or an initialized rectangular hybrid automaton, is $Exec(\mathcal{H}_1 \parallel \mathcal{H}_2 \parallel \ldots \parallel \mathcal{H}_k)$ empty?*

Proof. (Proof Sketch). Theorem 1 shows that any *PMHS* $\mathcal{H}$ is equivalent to the timed language of a timed automaton $TA(\mathcal{H})$ which can be constructed in $EXPSPACE$. Similarly, Miller [9] showed that any initialized rectangular hybrid automaton is also timed language equivalent to a timed automaton, constructible in $PSPACE$. Hence, for each $\mathcal{H}_i$, we can construct a timed automaton $TA(\mathcal{H}_i)$ such that $\mathcal{H}_i \sim_{\mathrm{tt}} TA(\mathcal{H}_i)$. From Lemma 1, $\mathcal{H}_1 \parallel \mathcal{H}_2 \parallel \ldots \parallel \mathcal{H}_k \sim_{\mathrm{tt}} TA(\mathcal{H}_1) \parallel TA(\mathcal{H}_2) \parallel \ldots \parallel TA(\mathcal{H}_k)$. Note that the latter is a composition of k timed automata. Therefore, from Lemma 2, the reachability problem, namely, if $Exec(TA(\mathcal{H}_1) \parallel TA(\mathcal{H}_2) \parallel \ldots \parallel TA(\mathcal{H}_k))$, is empty, is decidable in $PSPACE$. Equivalently, the emptiness of $Exec(\mathcal{H}_1 \parallel \mathcal{H}_2 \parallel \ldots \parallel \mathcal{H}_k)$, is decidable in $EXPSPACE$.

The above theorem, in particular, implies that the control state reachability problem is decidable for the composition of *PMHS*.

6   A Decidable Class of Multi-rate Automata

A multi-rate automaton is a generalization of timed automaton, where the continuous variables need not flow at rate 1. The reachability problem for general multi-rate automata is known to be undecidable [1,7]. In this section we identify a new subclass of multi-rate automata with a decidable reachability problem. The decidability result will be a consequence of our main result (Theorem 2). We begin by recalling what a multi-rate automaton is.

Definition 6. *A multi-rate automaton of dimension n is a linear hybrid system $\mathcal{H}$ with the restriction that*
  - *$Inv \in [Loc \rightarrow OpenRect(\mathbb{R}^n)]$,*
  - *$Init$ maps each location to either the empty set or $\{0^n\}$,*
  - *$Final \in [Loc \rightarrow PBOpenRect(\mathbb{R}^n)]$, and*

– *for each edge $e \in Edge$, there exists a* guard *$Guard(e) \in PBOpenRect(\mathbb{R}^n)$ and a zero set $Zero(e) \subseteq \{1,\ldots,n\}$ such that $Reset(e) = \{(u,v)|u \in Guard(e) \land \forall i \in \{1,\ldots,n\} \bullet [(i \in Zero(e) \Rightarrow v_i = 0) \land (i \notin Zero(e) \Rightarrow v_i = u_i)]\}$.*

In the above definition, we assume that variables reset on an edge are reset to 0. However, this condition can be relaxed to one where the variables are reset to any value in a bounded interval without affecting the decidability results. We make the simplifying assumption to make the presentation and notation simpler.

We identify a special subclass of multi-rate automata that we call phased multi-rate automata. Phased multi-rate automata are such that every execution of the machine can be divided into "phases". Each phase begins with a discrete transition that resets some set of variables, and every other discrete transition in the phase, leaves the continuous variables unchanged. In addition, during a phase, after the first transition, the flow of at most one variable can change. We will show that the reachability problem for such automata is decidable. Before defining this class, we introduce some definitions and notations that we will need.

Affected and Used Variables. Consider a multi-rate automaton $\mathcal{H}$ of dimension n and an edge e of $\mathcal{H}$. We will say that a variable $i \in \{1,\ldots n\}$ is *affected* by edge e, if either (a) i is reset, i.e., $i \in Zero(e)$, or (b) i's flow changes after taking the edge, i.e., $Flow(Src(e))_i \neq Flow(Dest(e))_i$. The set of variables affected by e will be denoted by $affect(e)$. A variable i is *used* by edge e if either (a) i is affected by e, i.e., $i \in affect(e)$, or (b) i appears in either $Inv(Src(e))$ or $Inv(Dest(e))$, i.e., I_i or I'_i not equal to $(-\infty,\infty)$, where $Inv(Src(e)) = I_1 \times \ldots \times I_n$ and $Inv(Dest(e)) = I'_1 \times \ldots \times I'_n$, or (c) variable i appears in $Guard(e)$, i.e., $I_i \neq (-\infty,\infty)$, where $Guard(e) = I_1 \times \ldots \times I_n$. The set of variables used by e is denoted by $use(e)$.

Phase Consistency. Consider a path $\pi = e_1, e_2, \ldots e_k$ of $\mathcal{H}$. A *phase* of π is a pair $(i,j) \in \{0,1,\ldots k+1\}^2$ with $i < j$ such that (a) if $i > 0$ then $Zero(e_i) \neq \emptyset$, (b) if $j < k+1$ then $Zero(e_j) \neq \emptyset$, and (c) for all ℓ, $i < \ell < j$, $Zero(e_\ell) = \emptyset$. In other words, (i,j) is a phase if e_i and e_j are successive reset edges in π. In the definitions that follow, we will find it convenient to take $Zero(e_0) = Zero(e_{k+1}) = \{1,\ldots n\}$. The path π is *phase consistent* for phase (i,j) if there is a variable $x_{ij} \in \{1,\ldots n\}$ such that (a) $x_{ij} \in Zero(e_i) \cap Zero(e_j)$, (b) for all $i < \ell < k$, $affect(e_\ell) \subseteq \{x_{ij}\}$ and $use(e_\ell) \subseteq Zero(e_i)$, and (c) $use(e_j) \setminus Zero(e_j) \subseteq Zero(e_i)$. When this happens, x_{ij} is said to be the *phase variable* of π in (i,j). We will say π is phase consistent if it is phase consistent for every phase (i,j).

Definition 7. *A phased multi-rate automaton (PMA) of dimension n is multi-rate automaton $\mathcal{H}$ with the following restrictions.*

– *For every edge e of $\mathcal{H}$, if $|affect(e)| > 1$ then $affect(e) \subseteq Zero(e)$. In other words, if more than one variable is affected, then all affected variables are reset.*
– *Every path π of $\mathcal{H}$ is phase consistent with respect to every phase.*

Theorem 3. *Reachability problem for phased multi-rate automata is decidable.*

Phased multi-rate automata are incomparable to the class of initialized multi-rate automata. Recall that in an initialized multi-rate automaton, a variable must be reset if its flow changes. This is not required in a phased multi-rate automaton as the phase variable can change its flow repeatedly without being reset. On the other hand, in phased multi-rate automata, the phase variable must be reset at the start and end of a phase; there is no analogous restriction in initialized multi-rate automata.

Example 2. Figure 2 shows an example of a water tank system. Here, we have two tanks and one hose. The hose could be on or off, and it could point to tank 1 or tank 2. Water is added at a constant rate to a tank when hose is on and pointing to that tank. Also, both tanks are leaking at a constant rate. One can turn the hose on and off at any time. However, to move the hose from

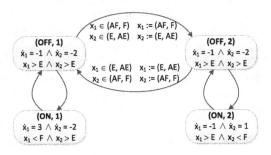

Fig. 2. Water Tank Example

tank 1 to tank 2, the tank 1 must have a sufficiently high level of water, and tank 2 must have a low level; similar constraints are required to be satisfied when moving the hose from tank 2 to tank 1. The level in a tank is considered "sufficiently high" if the level is between almost full (AF) and full (F), and it is low if it is between almost low (AL) and low (L). Observe that such a system is not initialized as the rate of change of level in a tank can change due to turning the hose on and off. However, it is a PMA as such changes to flow without resets are allowed. This automaton has the slightly more general form of resets where a variable can be reset to any value in a bounded set.

7 Conclusion

Our main result proved that the reachability problem is decidable for the parallel composition of a collection of planar monotonic linear hybrid systems. Our proof extends the observations in [11] to first showing that timed reachability (and not just reachability) is decidable by reducing it to the theory of linear arithmetic. This result allows us to conclude that the planar monotonic linear hybrid automata are timed trace equivalent to timed automata. Finally, our decidability result for concurrent planar monotonic linear hybrid systems follows from the decidability of the emptiness problem for timed trace language of concurrent timed automata. One consequence of our results is that it identifies a new decidable subclass of multi-rate automata, namely, phased multi-rate automata. Our results present a general technique of lifting decidability results for low dimensional systems to hybrid automata with many continuous variables.

A future direction of research would be to see if this idea can be applied to other decidable planar hybrid automata, i.e., automata with 2 variables.

References

1. Alur, R., Courcoubetis, C., Halbwachs, N., Henzinger, T.A., Ho, P.H., Nicollin, X., Olivero, A., Sifakis, J., Yovine, S.: The algorithmic analysis of hybrid systems. TCS **138**(1), 3–34 (1995)
2. Alur, R., Dill, D.L.: A theory of timed automata. Theoretical Computer Science **126**, 183–235 (1994)
3. Asarin, E., Maler, O., Pnueli, A.: Reachability analysis of dynamical systems having piecewise-constant derivatives. Theoretical Computer Science **138**(1), 35–65 (1995)
4. Asarin, E., Schneider, G., Yovine, S.: Algorithmic analysis of polygonal hybrid systems. Part I: Reachability. TCS **379**(1–2), 231–265 (2007)
5. Casagrande, A., Corvaja, P., Piazza, C., Mishra, B.: Decidable compositions of o-minimal automata. In: Cha, S.S., Choi, J.-Y., Kim, M., Lee, I., Viswanathan, M. (eds.) ATVA 2008. LNCS, vol. 5311, pp. 274–288. Springer, Heidelberg (2008)
6. Henzinger, T.A.: The theory of hybrid automata. In: Proceeding of IEEE Symposium on Logic in Computer Science, pp. 278–292 (1996)
7. Henzinger, T.A., Kopke, P.W., Puri, A., Varaiya, P.: What's decidable about hybrid automata? Journal of Computer and System Sciences **57**(1), 373–382 (1995)
8. Lafferriere, G., Pappas, G., Sastry, S.: o-minimal hybrid systems. MCSS **13**, 1–21 (2000)
9. Miller, J.S.: Decidability and complexity results for timed automata and semilinear hybrid automata. In: Lynch, N.A., Krogh, B.H. (eds.) HSCC 2000. LNCS, vol. 1790, pp. 296–309. Springer, Heidelberg (2000)
10. Mysore, V., Pnueli, A.: Refining the undecidability frontier of hybrid automata. In: Sarukkai, S., Sen, S. (eds.) FSTTCS 2005. LNCS, vol. 3821, pp. 261–272. Springer, Heidelberg (2005)
11. Prabhakar, P., Vladimerou, V., Viswanathan, M., Dullerud, G.: A decidable class of planar linear hybrid systems. Theoretical Computer Science **574**, 1–17 (2015)
12. L. van den Dries: Tame Topology and O-minimal Structures. Cambridge UnivesityPress (1998)
13. Vladimerou, V., Prabhakar, P., Viswanathan, M., Dullerud, G.E.: STORMED Hybrid Systems. In: Aceto, L., Damgård, I., Goldberg, L.A., Halldórsson, M.M., Ingólfsdóttir, A., Walukiewicz, I. (eds.) ICALP 2008, Part II. LNCS, vol. 5126, pp. 136–147. Springer, Heidelberg (2008)

Contracts for Schedulability Analysis

Philipp Reinkemeier[1]($\boxtimes$), Albert Benveniste[2], Werner Damm[1,3],
and Ingo Stierand[3]

[1] Offis, Oldenburg, Germany
philipp.reinkemejer@offis.de
[2] Inria-Rennes, Rennes, France
[3] Department of Computer Sciences, University of Oldenburg, Oldenburg, Germany

Abstract. In this paper we propose a framework of Assume / Guarantee contracts for schedulability analysis. Unlike previous work addressing compositional scheduling analysis, our objective is to provide support for the OEM / supplier subcontracting relation. The adaptation of Assume / Guarantee contracts to schedulability analysis requires some care, due to the handling of conflicts caused by shared resources. We illustrate our framework in the context of AUTOSAR methodology now popular in the automotive industry sector.

1 Introduction and Related Work

The focus of this work is the integration phase of a design process, where software components are allocated to a hardware platform. We consider scenarios

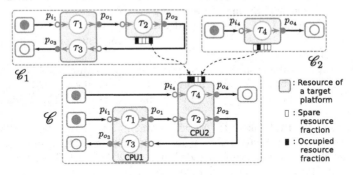

Fig. 1. Exemplary Integration Scenario using Resource Segregation

like the following. The bottom part of Figure 1 shows a target platform that is envisioned by, say, an Original Equipment Manufacturer (OEM). It consists of two processing nodes (CPU$_1$ and CPU$_2$). Suppose the OEM wants to implement

This work was partly supported by the Federal Ministry for Education and Research (BMBF) under support code 01IS11035M, *Automotive, Railway and Avionics Multi-core Systems* (ARAMiS), and by the German Research Council (DFG) as part of the Transregional Collaborative Research Center *Automatic Verification and Analysis of Complex Systems* (SFB/TR 14 AVACS).

S. Sankaranarayanan and E. Vicario (Eds.): FORMATS 2015, LNCS 9268, pp. 270–287, 2015.
DOI: 10.1007/978-3-319-22975-1_18

two applications, characterized by contracts $\mathscr{C}_1$ and $\mathscr{C}_2$, on this architecture and delegates their actual implementation to two different suppliers. Both applications share a subset of the resources of the target platform, e.g. tasks τ_2 and τ_4 are executed on CPU$_2$ after integration. Furthermore, we assume the system specification $\mathscr{C}$ shown in Figure 1 to be available from previous design phases. While some components together with their (local) contracts may also be known (e.g. in case of reuse), the OEM generally has to negotiate proper specifications with the suppliers, in our case the two contracts $\mathscr{C}_1$ and $\mathscr{C}_2$. In doing so, the scheduling of the software components delegated to each supplier must yield a satisfactory scheduling at system integration time, meaning that timing constraints are met given the performance characteristics of the computing and communication resources, even though the two designs compete for shared resources.

Quoted verbatim from [17] by Insup Lee et al.:[1] *Real-time systems could benefit from component-based design, only if components can be assembled without violating compositionality on timing properties. When the timing properties of components can be analyzed compositionally, component-based real-time systems allow components to be developed and validated independently and to be assembled together without global validation.* [17] develops a model of *scheduling interface* collecting the workloads, resources, and scheduling policy, addressing the above quoted objectives. Specific classes of hard real-time system scheduling problems are considered, namely periodic models and bounded-delay models. This group of authors has further developed the same track with the same techniques, making increasingly large classes of scheduling problems amenable for compositional analysis. This significant body of work is nicely summarized in the tutorial paper [3] and implemented through the CARTS tool for compositional analysis of real-time systems [14]. One interesting application case concerns the scheduling of ARINC partitions [10]. Compositional schedulability analyses have been proposed on top of the UPPAAL tool [5,6] with mixed scheduling policies and probabilistic evaluations. In a different direction, Lothar Thiele and co-workers have developed for real-time scheduling an algebraic framework called the *Real-Time Calculus* (RTC) [13,21,22]. Components of the RT Calculus are linear transfer functions in the max-plus algebra and interface behaviors are expressed as *arrival curves*, which specify lower and upper bounds for event arrivals. [20,21] considers real-time interfaces where assumptions and guarantees are expressed by means of arrival curves on inputs and outputs, respectively. Refinement of such interfaces is characterized and a parallel composition is defined; *adaptive interfaces* are proposed in which arrival curves are propagated throughout the network of components, compositionally. The above very elegant model captures timing and precedence constraints but does not consider conflicts due to shared resources. A blending of this model with timed automata is studied in [11] together with a mapping of RTC-based real-time interfaces to timed automata. The work [12] applies and develops similar techniques for distributed heterogeneous time-triggered automotive systems.

---

[1] The reader is referred to this paper for further discussion on related work from the real-time scheduling community. We discuss here the references that are directly relevant to our work.

Our work in this section has its roots in [15,16,18,19], which in turn are based upon the ideas underlying the interfaces for control and scheduling proposed in [1,2,23]. Contrary to these scheduling interfaces, we consider multiple resources and take task precedences into account. Our aim is different from the previous set of references and complements it nicely. In our work we assume that a procedure performing global scheduling analysis is available, so our focus is not on specific classes of schedulability analyses. Our aim is rather to lift such procedures to a contract framework supporting OEM-supplier relations in a supply chain. We first provide support for decomposing a system-level scheduling contract into subcontracts for suppliers, while guaranteeing safe system integration—this is different from the objectives of previous compositional schedulability studies. Second, our contract framework provides support for fusing different viewpoints on the system using contract conjunction. The model of *scheduling components* is presented in Section 2. Scheduling components capture implementations and environments for our *scheduling contracts,* developed in Section 3. Our approach is illustrated in Section 4 by an example in the context of the AUTOSAR methodology.

2   Scheduling Components

2.1   Our Approach: Building on Top of Assume/Guarantee Contracts

Recall that Assume/Guarantee contracts (A/G-contracts) are pairs of assumption and guarantees: $\mathscr{C} = (A, G)$. In the basic A/G-contract framework [4], A and G are assertions, i.e., sets of traces for system variables.[2] Components capturing legal implementations or environments of contracts are also modeled by assertions. Component E is a legal environment for $\mathscr{C}$ if $E \subseteq A$ and component M is an implementation for $\mathscr{C}$ if $A \times M \subseteq G$. In this writing, $\subseteq$ is simply set inclusion and component composition $\times$ is by intersection of sets of traces (assuming that the underlying set of system variables is universal and thus fixed): $A \times M =_{\text{def}} A \cap M$. One key notion of A/G-contracts is *saturation*: Contracts (A, G) and $(A, G \cup \neg A)$, where $\neg$ is set complement, possess identical sets of legal environments and implementations, so we consider them equivalent. The second one is called *saturated* and is a canonical form for the class of equivalent contracts. Also, $M_{\mathscr{C}} = G \cup \neg A$ is the maximal implementation for this contract. Thus, we need the operations $\cup$ and $\neg$, or at least we need the operation $(A, G) \rightarrow G \cup \neg A$, which is to be interpreted as "A entails G". Then for $\mathscr{C}$ and $\mathscr{C}'$ two saturated contracts, *refinement* $\mathscr{C}' \preceq \mathscr{C}$ holds iff $A' \supseteq A$ and $G' \subseteq G$ hold. The result of the composition $\mathscr{C}_1 \otimes \mathscr{C}_2$ of two saturated contracts, is a contract $((A_1 \cap A_2) \cup \neg(G_1 \cap G_2), G_1 \cap G_2)$.

Thus, as a first step, we need the counterpart of assertions for our scheduling component framework, with the associated algebra. Ingredients of scheduling problems are: *tasks* with their *precedence conditions* reflecting data dependencies and *resource allocation*. The sets of *timed traces* we are interested in are those

---

[2] These are typically specified using modeling tools such as Simulink/Stateflow.

satisfying the scheduling constraints, plus quantitative properties such as period, deadline conditions, etc. We call the resulting model *concrete scheduling components*. Unfortunately, no rich algebra with the requested operators $\subseteq, \times, \cup, \neg$ exists for concrete scheduling components.

By abstracting away part of the description of task activities in traces, we slightly abstract concrete scheduling components to so-called *abstract* ones. The idea is that we keep only what is essential for capturing interactions of scheduling problems, namely: 1) trigger and release events for tasks, and 2) busyness of resources. The abstraction map binds each concrete scheduling component to its abstraction and we will show that this binding is faithful with respect to composition and refinement. The framework of abstract scheduling components is simple enough so we manage to equip it with the wanted operations $\subseteq, \times, \cap, \cup, \neg$. A/G-contracts for abstract scheduling components follow then easily. The rest of this section is devoted to the introduction of concrete and abstract scheduling components. Then we study the relation between them.

2.2   Concrete Scheduling Components

For our model of scheduling components we assume the following:

- A slotted model of real-time, in which the real line $\mathbb{R}_+$ is divided into successive discrete time slots of equal duration. Successive slots are thus indexed by using natural numbers $1, 2, 3, \ldots, n, \ldots \in \mathbb{N}$.
- An underlying set $\mathcal{T}$ of *tasks*, generically denoted by the symbol τ. To describe events of interest for tasks, we consider the following alphabets: The *control alphabet* $\Sigma_c = \{i, o, io, aw, sl\}$ collects the *trigger, completion, trigger-and-completion, awake,* and *sleeping* events, for a task; this alphabet describes the triggering and completion of tasks; since we follow a slotted model of time, triggering and completion can occur within the same slot, which is indicated by the event io; The *busyness alphabet* $\Sigma_b = \{*, \bot\}$ collecting the *busy* and *idle* events; this alphabet indicates, for a task τ, its status busy/idle at a given time slot. On top of these alphabets, we build:

$$\Sigma_\tau =_{\text{def}} \{(c, b) \in \Sigma_c \times \Sigma_b \mid c = sl \Rightarrow b = \bot\} \tag{1}$$

reflecting that task τ can only be busy when it is not sleeping. The status of a task τ in each time slot is expressed by using alphabet Σ_τ.
In addition, each task τ comes equipped with a pair $(p^t(\tau), p^c(\tau)) \in \mathcal{P} \times \mathcal{P}$ of *trigger* and *completion* ports, where $\mathcal{P}$ is an underlying set of *ports*. For T a set of tasks, we will consider the set $P_T =_{\text{def}} \{p^t(\tau), p^c(\tau) \mid \tau \in T\}$.
- An underlying set $\mathcal{R}$ of *resources*, generically denoted by the symbol r. A resource can be either available or busy with executing a given task at a given time slot. Resources can run in parallel. Each resource $r \in \mathcal{R}$ is assigned the alphabet $\Sigma_r \subseteq \mathcal{T} \cup \{0\}$ of the tasks it can run, where the special symbol 0 indicates that r is idle.

Definition 1. *A concrete scheduling component is a tuple* $\mathbf{M} = (K, L)$, *where:*

- $K = (T, R, \rho)$ *is the* sort *of* $\mathbf{M}$, *where:* $T \subseteq \mathcal{T}$ *is the set of* tasks, $R \subseteq \mathcal{R}$ *is the set of* resources, *and* $\rho : T \to R$, *the* resource allocation map, *is a partial function satisfying* $\tau \in \Sigma_{\rho(\tau)}$.
  Say that tasks τ_1 *and* τ_2 *are* non-conflicting *if they do not use the same resource:* $\tau_1 \parallel_K \tau_2$ *if* $\rho(\tau_1)$ *is undefined, or* $\rho(\tau_2)$ *is undefined or* $\rho(\tau_1) \neq \rho(\tau_2)$.
- *For* $\tau_1, \tau_2 \in T$, *say that* τ_1 *precedes task* τ_2, *written* $\tau_1 \multimap \tau_2$, *if the completion port of* τ_1 *coincides with the start port of* τ_2: $p^c(\tau_1) = p^t(\tau_2)$.
  We require that this relation is cycle free and we denote by $\preceq$ *the partial order on* T *obtained by taking transitive closure of* $\multimap$ *and we call* $\preceq$ *the* precedence order.
  The dual order between ports will also be needed: for $p_1, p_2 \in P_T$, *say that* p_1 *precedes* p_2, *written* $p_1 \boxminus\!\rightarrow p_2$, *if there exists* $\tau \in T$ *such that* $p_1 = p^t(\tau)$ *and* $p^c(\tau) = p_2$; *relation* $\boxminus\!\rightarrow$ *is cycle free if so was* $\multimap$ *and, with no risk of confusion, we also denote by* $\preceq$ *the precedence order on* P_T *generated by* $\boxminus\!\rightarrow$.
- $L \subseteq \Sigma_T^\omega$ *is the* language *of* $\mathbf{M}$, *where* $\Sigma_T =_{\text{def}} T \to \Sigma_\tau$, *and* A^ω *denotes the set of all infinite words over alphabet* A. *Due to the decomposition* (1) *of* Σ_τ, *every word* $w \in L$ *can be equivalently seen as a pair of words* $w = (w_c, w_b)$ *describing the* control *and* busyness *history of* w.

Since a word $w \in L$ yields a history for each task, it induces, by picking the resource running that task, a corresponding *resource word* w^R, such that

$$w^R \text{ is the tuple collecting the } w^r \text{ for } r \in R, \text{ such that, for every slot} \qquad (2)$$
$$n\colon w^r(n) = \{\tau \in T \mid \rho(\tau) = r \text{ and } w(\tau, n) = (c, b) \text{ satisfies } b = *\}$$

i.e., $w^r(n)$ returns the set of tasks that resource r runs at slot n. This set is not a singleton if and only if a conflict occurs at slot n regarding resource r.

Whenever convenient, we will denote by T_K or T^K the set of tasks of sort K, and similarly for the other constituents of a sort. The events of a task τ will be denoted by i_τ, o_τ, etc. For w a word of Σ_K^ω, $T' \subseteq T$, and $R' \subseteq R$, we denote by

$$w^{T'} \text{ the } T'\text{-word of } w, \text{ and by } w^{R'} \text{ the } R'\text{-word of } w, \qquad (3)$$

obtained by projecting w to the sub-alphabet $\Sigma_{T'}$ and projecting the induced word w^R to the sub-alphabet $\Sigma_{R'}$, respectively.

Definition 2 (Semantics of concrete scheduling components). *Call* behavior *of sort* K *any infinite word* $w \in \Sigma_T^\omega$ *satisfying the following three* scheduling conditions:

1. *For each task* $\tau \in T$, *the control word* w_c *belongs to the language* $(sl^*.(io + i.aw^*.o))^\omega$, *where* $a^* =_{\text{def}} \epsilon + a + a.a + a.a.a + \ldots$ *is the Kleene closure starting at the empty word. Informally, the two events* i *and* o *alternate in* w, *with* i *occurring first;* io *is interpreted as the immediate succession of two* i *and* o *events at the same time slot.*

2. $\tau_1 \preceq \tau_2$ implies that, for every $n \geq 1$, the nth occurrence of event o_{τ_1} must have occurred in w strictly before i_{τ_2} (in words, τ_2 can only start after τ_1 has completed);

3. w is non-conflicting: for any two conflicting tasks τ_1 and τ_2 belonging to T (cf. Definition 1), it never happens that w^{τ_1} and w^{τ_2} are non-idle at the same time slot.

The semantics of $\mathbf{M}$ is the sub-language $[\![\mathbf{M}]\!] \subseteq L$ consisting of all behaviors of K belonging to L. Say that $\mathbf{M}$ is schedulable if $[\![\mathbf{M}]\!] \neq \emptyset$.

Due to the above Condition 2, tasks related by precedence conditions possess identical logical clocks—in particular, if they are specified periodic, their periods must be equal. This is not required for tasks not related by precedence conditions.

Comment 1. The pair $\mathbf{M} = (K, L)$ can be seen as the specification of a global scheduling problem. The sort K fixes the set of tasks and their precedence conditions, the set of resources, and the allocation of tasks to resources. The language L can serve to specify additional aspects of this scheduling problem, including task durations and/or minimum time interval between successive activation calls for a task. Semantics $[\![\mathbf{M}]\!]$ can be seen as the maximally permissive solution of the scheduling problem stated by $\mathbf{M}$.

Definition 3. Say that $\mathbf{M}_1$ and $\mathbf{M}_2$ are composable if their allocation maps ρ_1 and ρ_2 coincide on $T_1 \cap T_2$ and the relation $\dashrightarrow_1 \cup \dashrightarrow_2$ on $T_1 \cup T_2$ is cycle free. If $\mathbf{M}_1$ and $\mathbf{M}_2$ are composable, their composition $\mathbf{M}_1 \times \mathbf{M}_2 =_{\mathrm{def}} ((T, R, \rho), L)$ is defined as follows:

$$T = T_1 \cup T_2 , \quad R = R_1 \cup R_2 , \quad \forall \tau \in T : \rho(\tau) = \text{if } \tau \in T_1 \text{ then } \rho_1(\tau) \text{ else } \rho_2(\tau)$$
$$L = \mathbf{pr}_{T \to T_1}^{-1}(L_1) \cap \mathbf{pr}_{T \to T_2}^{-1}(L_2)$$

where $\mathbf{pr}_{T \to T_i}, i = 1, 2$, denotes the projection from T to T_i and $\mathbf{pr}^{-1}$ is its inverse.

Of course, the key to understand the meaning of composition $\times$ is the construction of the semantics $[\![\mathbf{M}_1 \times \mathbf{M}_2]\!]$. In the following lemma, for $\mathbf{M} = ((T, R, \rho), L)$ a scheduling component, we identify its semantics $[\![\mathbf{M}]\!]$ (which is a language) with the scheduling component $((T, R, \rho), [\![\mathbf{M}]\!])$. This gives a meaning to the expression $[\![\mathbf{M}_1]\!] \times [\![\mathbf{M}_2]\!]$.

Lemma 1. If $\mathbf{M}_1$ and $\mathbf{M}_2$ are composable, then $[\![\mathbf{M}_1 \times \mathbf{M}_2]\!] = [\![[\![\mathbf{M}_1]\!] \times [\![\mathbf{M}_2]\!]]\!]$.

As announced in the introductory discussion of Section 2, the model of concrete scheduling components is too complex and detailed as a model of components on top of which contracts can be built. We are unable to define the operations we need on components, particularly $\subseteq$ and $\cup \neg$ (in turn, parallel composition $\times$ was easy to define as we have seen). The notion of *abstract scheduling component* we develop in the forthcoming section will overcome these difficulties. Abstract scheduling components capture the architecture aspect of Figure 1, namely: ports carrying start and completion events of tasks, and resources—tasks themselves are, however, ignored.

2.3   Abstract Scheduling Components

Definition 4. *An* abstract scheduling component *is a language* $M \subseteq \mathcal{V}^\omega$, *where* $\mathcal{V} =_{\text{def}} (\{0,1\}^{\mathcal{P}}) \times (\prod_{r \in \mathcal{R}} \Sigma_r)$.

Recall that Σ_r is the alphabet of tasks that can be executed by resource r, see the beginning of Section 2.2. Symbol "1" indicates the occurrence of an event at the considered port. Abstract scheduling components come equipped with the following algebra:

- The Boolean algebra $\cap, \cup, \neg$, and the inclusion $\subseteq$ on sets;
- A *parallel composition* by intersection: $M_1 \times M_2 =_{\text{def}} M_1 \cap M_2$.

Thus, abstract scheduling components offer all the algebra required for a universe of components on top of which A/G-contracts can be built. It is therefore interesting to map concrete to abstract scheduling components.

Recall that, for $K = (T, R, \rho)$ a sort, we denote by $P_T =_{\text{def}} p^t(T) \uplus p^c(T) \subseteq \mathcal{P}$ the set of ports used by T, see the beginning of Section 2.2. Then, we set

$$\mathcal{V}_K =_{\text{def}} (\{0,1\}^{P_T}) \times (\prod_{r \in R} \Sigma_r) \tag{4}$$

Definition 5 (Mapping concrete to abstract scheduling components).
Each concrete scheduling component $\mathbf{M} = (K, L)$ *is mapped to a unique abstract scheduling component* $\llbracket \mathbf{M} \rrbracket^A$ *called its* abstract semantics, *defined as follows:*

1. *Pick any behavior* $w \in \llbracket \mathbf{M} \rrbracket$, *see Definition 2;*
2. *Denote by* $\pi_T(w)$ *the word over* $\{0,1\}^{P_T}$ *obtained from* w *as follows. For every* $p \in P_T$, *define* $^\bullet p = \{\tau \in T \mid p^c(\tau) = p\}$ *and* $p^\bullet = \{\tau \in T \mid p^t(\tau) = p\}$, *the sets of anterior and posterior tasks of* p. *The* nth *event of* p *is put nondeterministically after the* $n-1$st *event of* p, *when or after every task belonging to* $^\bullet p$ *has completed for the* nth *time in* w, *and strictly before every task belonging to* $p^\bullet$ *has started for the* nth *time in* w. *If* $^\bullet p = \emptyset$, *then the first condition is not considered and similarly if* $p^\bullet = \emptyset$.
3. *Denote by* $\pi_R(w)$ *the word over alphabet* $\prod_{r \in R} \Sigma_r$ *defined as follows: For every time slot* n *and every resource* $r \in R$, *set*

    $\pi_R(w)(r, n) = \tau$ *if and only if* $w(\tau, n) = (c, b)$ *satisfies* $b = *$ *and* $\rho(\tau) = r$.

    This part of word $\pi_R(w)$ *represents the "positive history" of* w, *i.e., the use of the resources belonging to* R *by tasks belonging to* T; *We complement* $\pi_R(w)$ *by describing the "negative history" of* w, *consisting of a description of all the possibilities left, for tasks not belonging to* T, *in using resources from* R:

    in all slots of $\pi_R(w)(r, n)$ *that are still idle, we set* $\pi_R(w)(r, n) = \tau'$ *where* $\tau' \in \Sigma_r, \tau' \notin T$ *is chosen nondeterministically.*

    Then, with reference to the sort $K = (T, R, \rho)$ *of* $\mathbf{M}$, *we set:*

    $$\eta_K(w) =_{\text{def}} (\pi_T(w), \pi_R(w)) \in \mathcal{V}_K^\omega$$

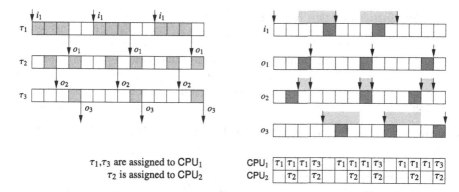

τ_1, τ_3 are assigned to CPU_1
τ_2 is assigned to CPU_2

Fig. 2. Showing a concrete behavior of **M** (left, with reference to Figure 1) and a corresponding abstract behavior of $[\![\mathbf{M}]\!]^A$ (right), by using $\mathcal{P} = \{i_1, o_1, o_2, o_3\}$ as underlying alphabet of ports. On the second diagram, blanks figure the slots left free for any external task to run on the referred resource. The yellow rectangles indicate the room for nondeterministic choices; bounds of these rooms are figured by pointing arrows; where such arrow is missing, the corresponding rectangle is unbounded on that side.

4. *Finally, we define*
$$[\![\mathbf{M}]\!]^A =_{\mathrm{def}} \mathbf{pr}^{-1}_{\mathcal{V}^\omega \to \mathcal{V}^\omega_K} \left(\{ \eta_K(w) \mid w \in [\![\mathbf{M}]\!] \} \right) \subseteq \mathcal{V}^\omega$$
where the quantification ranges over $w \in [\![\mathbf{M}]\!]$ and all instances of nondeterministic choices in step 2, and $\mathbf{pr}_{\mathcal{V}^\omega \to \mathcal{V}^\omega_K}$ denotes the projection, from $\mathcal{V}^\omega$ to $\mathcal{V}^\omega_K$.

Step 2 is sound since w is a behavior in the sense of Definition 2. Step 2 is the key step since it transforms a max-plus type of parallel composition (every task waits for all its preceding tasks having completed before starting) into a dataflow connection where data are communicated through the shared ports. The data communicated are the events carried by the ports. These events occur nondeterministically after all preceding tasks have completed for the nth time and before all succeeding tasks start for the nth time.

Step 3 complements the actual history of each task of **M** by an explicit description of all possibilities that are left to other scheduling components in using resources shared with **M**. The reason for doing this is that this allows to capture the interleaved use of shared resources by different components, by a simple parallel composition by intersection.

The above construction is illustrated in Figure 2. When hiding the tasks sitting inside the boxes, the architecture shown on Figure 1 is a dataflow representation of $[\![\mathbf{M}]\!]^A$: in interpreting this figure, one should consider that each task is free to start any time after it has received its triggering event, and free to wait for some time before emitting its completion event.

Lemma 2. *The mapping* $\mathbf{M} \to [\![\mathbf{M}]\!]^A$ *satisfies the following properties:* 1) *Schedulability is preserved in that* $[\![\mathbf{M}]\!] \neq \emptyset$ *if and only if* $[\![\mathbf{M}]\!]^A \neq \emptyset$; 2) *For every* $r \notin R$, *the set* $\{ v(r) \mid v \in [\![\mathbf{M}]\!]^A \}$ *is the free language* $(\mathcal{T} - T)^\omega$.

The special property 2) is not preserved under the Boolean set algebra. Therefore, the mapping $\mathbf{M} \to [\![\mathbf{M}]\!]^A$ is not surjective.

2.4   Faithfulness of the Mapping

Consider two concrete scheduling components $\mathbf{M}_1$ and $\mathbf{M}_2$, where $\mathbf{M}_i = (K_i, L_i)$ and $K_i = (T_i, R_i, \rho_i)$. It is difficult and generally undecidable to compare their abstract semantics: $[\![\mathbf{M}_1]\!]^A \subseteq [\![\mathbf{M}_2]\!]^A$. We will, however, need such checks in the sequel. We thus propose some effective sufficient conditions ensuring the inclusion of abstract semantics.

Lemma 3. *The following conditions on the pair* $(\mathbf{M}', \mathbf{M})$ *imply* $[\![\mathbf{M}']\!]^A \subseteq [\![\mathbf{M}]\!]^A$:

1. *There exists a surjective total map* $\psi : T' \to T$, *such that:*
   (a) *For every* $\tau \in T$: $p^t(\tau) = \min_{\psi(\tau')=\tau} p^t(\tau')$ *and* $p^c(\tau) = \max_{\psi(\tau')=\tau} p^c(\tau')$, *where min and max refer to the order* $\preceq'$ *generated by the precedence relation* $\multimap\!\!\to$ *on ports of* $\mathbf{M}'$, *see Definition 1;*
   (b) *The following holds, for every 4-tuple of tasks* $(\tau_1', \tau_2', \tau_1, \tau_2) \in T'^2 \times T^2$:
   $\psi(\tau_1')=\tau_1$ *and* $\psi(\tau_2')=\tau_2$ *together entail* $\tau_1' \parallel' \tau_2' \Rightarrow \tau_1 \parallel \tau_2$.
2. *For each task* $\tau \in T$, *there exists an injective total map* $\chi_\tau : \Sigma_\tau \to \biguplus_{\tau' \in \psi^{-1}(\tau)} \Sigma_{\tau'}$, *where the* $\Sigma_{\tau'}$ *are copies, for each referred task* τ', *of the alphabet defined in* (1); *set* $\chi =_{\mathrm{def}} \biguplus_{\tau \in T} \chi_\tau$. *The language* L *is defined through some temporal property* Timing_Prop *on the events from alphabet* $\biguplus_{\tau \in T} \Sigma_\tau$, *and, replacing, in* Timing_Prop, *every event* e *by its image* $\chi(e)$ *defines a language* L'' *such that* $L'' \supseteq L'$.

Say that $\mathbf{M}' \sqsubseteq \mathbf{M}$ *when the above three conditions hold.*

Observe that Conditions 1 involve only the sorts K_1 and K_2 of $\mathbf{M}_1$ and $\mathbf{M}_2$. Condition 2 formalizes the situation in which the language L_2 is specified through timing properties relating certain events of interest for tasks of $\mathbf{M}_2$ (duration between trigger and completion, end-to-end duration when traversing a set of successive tasks, etc.). The considered events are then mapped to some events of $\mathbf{M}_1$ and the timing property remains the same or is strengthened. The following results hold:

Lemma 4. *If* $\mathbf{M}_1$ *and* $\mathbf{M}_2$ *are composable, then* $[\![\mathbf{M}_1 \underline{\times} \mathbf{M}_2]\!]^A = [\![\mathbf{M}_1]\!]^A \times [\![\mathbf{M}_2]\!]^A$.

Lemma 5. *Let* $(\mathbf{A}, \mathbf{G})$ *be a composable pair of concrete scheduling components such that* $R_\mathbf{A} = \emptyset$. *Then, the following formulas define a concrete scheduling component* $\mathbf{M} = ((T, R, \rho), L)$ *such that* $[\![\mathbf{M}]\!]^A = [\![\mathbf{G}]\!]^A \cup \neg [\![\mathbf{A}]\!]^A$:

$$T = T_\mathbf{A} \cup T_\mathbf{G} \,, \ R = R_\mathbf{G} \,, \ \rho(\tau) = \text{if } \tau \in T_\mathbf{A} \text{ then } \rho_\mathbf{A}(\tau),$$
$$L = \mathbf{pr}^{-1}_{T \to T_\mathbf{G}}(L_\mathbf{G}) \cup \mathbf{pr}^{-1}_{T \to T_\mathbf{A}}(\neg L_\mathbf{A})$$

3   Scheduling Contracts

As recommended in Section 2.1, we first define what components are, and then we define contracts. Regarding components, the notations used here refer to the operations $\subseteq, \cap, \cup, \neg, \times$ introduced for abstract scheduling components in Section 2.3.

Definition 6 (Scheduling contracts). *A scheduling contract is a pair* $\mathscr{C} = (A, G)$ *of abstract scheduling components, called the* assumptions *and the* guarantees.

The set $\mathcal{E}_{\mathscr{C}}$ *of the legal environments for* $\mathscr{C}$ *collects all abstract scheduling components* E *with non-empty semantics such that* $E \subseteq A$. *The set* $\mathcal{M}_{\mathscr{C}}$ *of all implementations of* $\mathscr{C}$ *consists of all abstract scheduling components* M *with non-empty semantics such that* $A \times M \subseteq G$.

Each scheduling contract can be put in its equivalent saturated *form* $\mathscr{C} = (A, G \cup \neg A)$, *possessing the same sets of legal environments and implementations. Scheduling contract* $\mathscr{C}$ *is compatible if and only if* $A \neq \emptyset$ *and consistent if and only if* $G \cup \neg A \neq \emptyset$. *Say that scheduling contract* $\mathscr{C} = (A, G)$ *is* schedulable *if* $A \cap G \neq \emptyset$.

The background theory of A/G-contracts applies. Note that $A \cap G = A \cap (G \cup \neg A)$, hence checking schedulability does not require the contract to be saturated. The justification of this notion of schedulability for contracts is given in the next section.

In practice the designer will specify scheduling contracts using concrete, not abstract, scheduling components:

Definition 7 (Concrete scheduling contracts). *Call* concrete *scheduling contract (or concrete contract) a pair* $\mathbf{C} = (\mathbf{A}, \mathbf{G})$ *of composable concrete scheduling components called its* assumptions *and* guarantees.

See Definition 3 for the notion of composability. To contrast with concrete contracts, we will sometimes call *abstract scheduling contracts*, or *abstract contracts*, the scheduling contracts of Definition 6. The mapping from concrete to abstract scheduling components developed in Section 2.3 allows mapping concrete scheduling contracts to abstract ones:

$$\mathbf{C} = (\mathbf{A}, \mathbf{G}) \mapsto \mathscr{C}_{(\mathbf{A}, \mathbf{G})} =_{\mathrm{def}} (\llbracket \mathbf{A} \rrbracket^{\mathrm{A}}, \llbracket \mathbf{G} \rrbracket^{\mathrm{A}})$$

Say that $\mathbf{C}$ is *consistent, compatible, schedulable, or in saturated form, if so is* $\mathscr{C}_{(\mathbf{A}, \mathbf{G})}$.

Lemma 6 (Checking for contract refinement). *The following conditions imply refinement* $\mathscr{C}_{(\mathbf{A}, \mathbf{G})} \preceq \left(\bigwedge_{j \in J} \mathscr{C}_{(\mathbf{A}_j, \mathbf{G}_j)} \right)$: *for every* $j \in J$, $\mathbf{A}_j$ *is composable with* $\mathbf{G}$ *and the following two conditions hold:* $\mathbf{A}_j \times \mathbf{G} \sqsubseteq \mathbf{G}_j$ *and* $\mathbf{A}_j \sqsubseteq \mathbf{A}$.

3.1   Getting Sub-contracts in the AUTOSAR Development Process

In this section we develop techniques in support of the following design steps, which are advocated by the AUTOSAR methodology [7,8]:

Process 1 (AUTOSAR Development Process)

1. Start with a top-level, system wide, contract. At this level, only functions are considered whereas computing resources are ignored. Functions are abstracted as systems of tasks with their precedence constraints.

2. To prepare for subcontracting to different suppliers, decompose this functional top-level contract into functional sub-contracts.
3. At this step the computing resources are now taken into account. Perform system wide (global) schedulability analysis, thus inferring resource budgets.
4. Derive resource aware sub-contracts and submit them to the supplier.

This process is rather informal. It is thus tempting to interpret the above tasks as refinement steps, for scheduling contracts. With this in mind, Steps 1 and 2 exhibit no particular difficulty. Step 3, however, raises a problem. Adding the consideration of resources to a resourceless contract cannot be a refinement step. This can be seen from Lemma 3, which gives sufficient conditions for concrete contract refinement: referring to this lemma, there is no way that the resulting contracts $\mathbf{C}' = (\mathbf{A}', \mathbf{G}')$ can refine $\mathbf{C}$ since $[\![\mathbf{A}']\!]^A \supseteq [\![\mathbf{A}]\!]^A$ is not possible when resources are added, from $\mathbf{A}$ to $\mathbf{A}'$. This is no surprise in fact, since one cannot independently add *shared* resources to different contracts, and at the same time expect to be able to develop independently.

Of course, from a theoretical standpoint, there is an easy solution to this problem. One could argue that not considering resources and budgeting them from the very beginning is a mistake and cannot work. Following this argument we would need to consider resources already in the top-level contracts, and address budgeting right from the beginning. Unfortunately, this is in total disagreement with the AUTOSAR approach, which advocates at early stages the specification of software architectures consisting of software components, regardless of resources.

To overcome this difficulty, our approach is: 1) to precisely characterize the "illegal" development steps we perform that violate contract refinement, and 2) to precisely identify the resulting risks for later system integration. To this end we will use the weaker notion of *port-refinement*, for concrete contracts. Decompose the alphabet $\mathcal{V}$ introduced in Definition 4:

$$\mathcal{V} = \left(\{0,1\}^{\mathcal{P}} \right) \times \left(\prod_{r \in \mathcal{R}} \Sigma_r \right) = \mathcal{V}^{\mathcal{P}} \times \mathcal{V}^{\mathcal{R}}$$

For $\mathbf{M} = ((T, R, \rho), L)$ a concrete scheduling component, define

$$[\![\mathbf{M}]\!]^{\mathcal{P}} =_{\text{def}} \mathbf{pr}_{\mathcal{V}^{\mathcal{P}}} \left([\![\mathbf{M}_{\rho/\epsilon}]\!]^A \right), \text{ where } \mathbf{M}_{\rho/\epsilon} =_{\text{def}} ((T, \emptyset, \epsilon), L)$$

and ϵ is the allocation map with empty domain. In words, we first ignore the possible conflicts due to shared resources (replacing $\mathbf{M}$ by $\mathbf{M}_{\rho/\epsilon}$), we then take the abstract semantics $[\![\mathbf{M}_{\rho/\epsilon}]\!]^A$, and we finally project the resulting abstract semantics over the ports only (taking $\mathbf{pr}_{\mathcal{V}^{\mathcal{P}}}(\ldots)$). $[\![\mathbf{M}]\!]^{\mathcal{P}}$ captures the scheduling aspect of $\mathbf{M}$ while discarding the resource aspect of it. Observe that $[\![\mathbf{M}]\!]^{\mathcal{P}}$ contains the language obtained by projecting $[\![\mathbf{M}]\!]^A$ over the ports; this inclusion is generally strict. For $\mathbf{C} = (\mathbf{A}, \mathbf{G})$ a concrete scheduling contract, define

$$[\![\mathbf{C}]\!]^{\mathcal{P}} =_{\text{def}} ([\![\mathbf{A}]\!]^{\mathcal{P}}, [\![\mathbf{G}]\!]^{\mathcal{P}}) \text{ the } \textit{port-contract} \text{ associated with } \mathbf{C}$$

Despite the boldface notation used, port-contracts are abstract contracts. For $\mathbf{C}$ and $\mathbf{C}'$ two concrete contracts, say that

$\mathbf{C}'$ *port-refines* $\mathbf{C}$, written $\mathbf{C}' \preceq_{\mathcal{P}} \mathbf{C}$ if $[\![\mathbf{C}']\!]^{\mathcal{P}} \preceq [\![\mathbf{C}]\!]^{\mathcal{P}}$.

We will restrict the illegal steps of Process 1 to the following situation, which does not contradict the AUTOSAR methodology. Assume, from early design stages on, prior knowledge of the following property about a given set T of tasks—this does not require detailed knowledge of the computing resources:

Definition 8 (T-closed contracts). *Say that a set $T \subset \mathcal{T}$ of tasks is segregated if the set $\mathcal{R}$ of all resources partitions as follows: $\mathcal{R} = R \cup \overline{R}, R \cap \overline{R} = \emptyset$, and $T \subseteq \Sigma_R$ whereas $\mathcal{T} - T \subseteq \Sigma_{\overline{R}}$. For any segregated set of tasks T, say that concrete contract $\mathbf{C} = (\mathbf{A}, \mathbf{G})$ is T-closed if $T_{\mathbf{G}} \subseteq T$ and $T_{\mathbf{A}} \cap T = \emptyset$.*

If $\mathbf{C} = (\mathbf{A}, \mathbf{G})$ is T-closed, then $\rho_{\mathbf{G}}(T_{\mathbf{G}}) \cap \rho_{\mathbf{A}}(T_{\mathbf{A}}) = \emptyset$ holds. *Illegal steps* are performed on T-closed contracts only. An illegal step consists in replacing T-closed contract $\mathbf{C}$ by another T-closed contract $\mathbf{C}'$ port-refining it: $\mathbf{C}' \preceq_{\mathcal{P}} \mathbf{C}$.

Port-refinement being not a refinement, replacing $\mathbf{C}$ by $\mathbf{C}'$ *won't* ensure that any implementation of $\mathbf{C}'$ meets the guarantees of $\mathbf{C}$ under any legal environment for $\mathbf{C}'$—it should ensure this if it was a true refinement. Still, the following result holds, which precisely bounds the risks at system integration time:

Lemma 7. *Let be $\mathbf{C}' \preceq_{\mathcal{P}} \mathbf{C}$ satisfying the following conditions: $\mathbf{C}$ and $\mathbf{C}'$ are T-closed for a same segregated set T of tasks, $\mathbf{C}'$ is schedulable, $[\![\mathbf{A}']\!]^{\mathcal{P}} = [\![\mathbf{A}]\!]^{\mathcal{P}}$, $\mathbf{A}$ and $\mathbf{A}'$ both have their tasks pairwise non-conflicting, and $\mathbf{G}$ is resourceless. Then: $\emptyset \neq \mathbf{A} \times \mathbf{G}' \sqsubseteq \mathbf{G}$.*

Lemma 7 expresses that $\mathbf{G}'$ is an implementation of $\mathbf{C}'$ that, when put in the context of the most permissive environment of $\mathbf{C}$, meets the guarantee $\mathbf{G}$ and is schedulable. That $\mathbf{G}$ is met will remain valid for any legal environment of $\mathbf{C}$ and any implementation of $\mathbf{C}'$. Schedulability, however, is only ensured by the most permissive environment of $\mathbf{C}$ and implementation of $\mathbf{C}'$. This restriction is not surprising since schedulability is a liveness property whereas A/G-contracts support only safety properties.

We are now ready to explain how the AUTOSAR development process (Process 1) can be made safe by implementing the illegal development steps safely.

Process 2 (AUTOSAR Development Process Made Safe) We assume a segregated subset T of tasks.

1. Start with a top-level, T-closed, contract $\mathbf{C}_{\text{top}}^{\text{func}} = (A_{\text{top}}, G_{\text{top}})$. At this level, only functions are considered while computing resources are ignored. Functions are abstracted as systems of tasks with their precedence constraints. The top-level contract may be the conjunction of several viewpoints, and/or it may be specified by means of requirement tables.
   – *Comment*: No change with respect to Process 1 besides T-closedness.
2. To prepare for subcontracting to different suppliers, decompose the above functional contract $\mathbf{C}_{\text{top}}$ into functional, resource agnostic, sub-contracts in such a way that

$$\mathbf{C}_{\text{ref}}^{\text{func}} = (\mathbf{A}_{\text{ref}}, \mathbf{G}_{\text{ref}}) = \underset{i \in I}{\times} \mathbf{C}_i \text{ satisfies } \begin{cases} \mathbf{A}_{\text{top}} \times \mathbf{G}_{\text{ref}} \sqsubseteq \mathbf{G}_{\text{top}} \\ \mathbf{A}_{\text{ref}} \sqsupseteq \mathbf{A}_{\text{top}} \end{cases} \quad (5)$$

where the $\mathbf{C}_i$ are T-closed subcontracts for the different suppliers. In addition, we require that $\mathbf{A}_{\mathrm{ref}}$ and $\mathbf{A}_{\mathrm{top}}$ possess identical sets of tasks, i.e., map ψ of Lemma 3 is the identity. By Lemma 6, (5) ensures $\mathscr{C}_{\mathrm{ref}}^{\mathrm{func}} \preceq \mathscr{C}_{\mathrm{top}}^{\mathrm{func}}$. So far resources were not considered.

- *Comment*: No change so far, with respect to Process 1, besides naming contracts and making refinement step precise through (5). The first two steps make no reference to semantics, meaning that no scheduling analysis is required, cf. Comment 1. From the next step on, this process deviates from Process 1.

3. At this step the computing resources are now taken into account. Allocate a resource to each task of $\mathbf{A}_{\mathrm{ref}}$ and $\mathbf{G}_{\mathrm{ref}}$, in such a way that all tasks of $\mathbf{A}_{\mathrm{ref}}$ are pairwise non-conflicting, see Definition 1. Precedence constraints between tasks are not modified. This yields a resource aware T-closed contract $\mathbf{C}_{\mathrm{ref}}^{\mathrm{res}}$ such that

$$\mathbf{C}_{\mathrm{ref}}^{\mathrm{res}} = (\mathbf{A}_{\mathrm{ref}}^{\mathrm{res}}, \mathbf{G}_{\mathrm{ref}}^{\mathrm{res}}) \quad \preceq_{\mathcal{P}} \quad \mathbf{C}_{\mathrm{ref}}^{\mathrm{func}} \tag{6}$$

Since $\mathbf{A}_{\mathrm{ref}}^{\mathrm{res}}$ is free of conflict, only $\mathbf{G}_{\mathrm{ref}}^{\mathrm{res}}$ requires a non-trivial scheduling analysis, which result is specified through the semantics $[\![\mathbf{G}_{\mathrm{ref}}^{\mathrm{res}}]\!]$, cf. Comment 1. At this point, resources have been globally budgeted and scheduling analysis globally performed.

- *Comment*: This is the illegal step, which is protected by Lemma 7.

4. Continue by decomposing contract $\mathbf{C}_{\mathrm{ref}}^{\mathrm{res}}$ into resource aware sub-contracts $\mathbf{C}_i^{\mathrm{res}}$, following the architecture specified in Step 2, in such a way that $\bigotimes_{i \in I} \mathscr{C}_i^{\mathrm{res}} \preceq \mathscr{C}_{\mathrm{ref}}^{\mathrm{res}}$. The results of the next section can be used for this.

4   An Example in the Context of AUTOSAR

To illustrate the practical use of the framework of scheduling contracts in AUTOSAR, we consider as an example an excerpt of an exterior light management system for an automobile.[3] Regarding modeling methodology and notations, we will be using both concrete contracts (for the specification of contracts at early steps of the design) and abstract contracts (when using the contract algebra). We will use the symbols $\mathbf{C}$ and $\mathscr{C}$ to distinguish between them. The duration of the time slot is $1\mu s$.

Step 1 of Process 2: In this step a view of the Virtual Functional Bus System is created. It shows how the system functions interact regardless of any network topology or deployment across multiple ECUs. Step 1 of Process 2 is performed by considering resourceless contracts for this Virtual Functional Bus (*VFB*) view. All contracts created in this step have to be T-closed to prepare for the later steps where resources are added. In these contracts, functions provided by software components, are represented by means of tasks with precedence constraints. Typical constraints imposed by the language of contracts would be

---

[3] A case-study from the German SPES2020 project

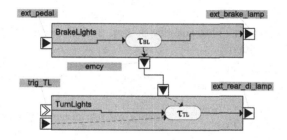

Fig. 3. Virtual Functional Bus (*VFB*) architecture

latency intervals, synchronization of events and event models. Figure 3 shows the VFB architecture of the exterior light management. The system shall control the brake lights in accordance with the driver pressing the brake pedal. The TurnLights component controls the direction indicator lights according to the position of the turn signal lever and the warn lights button. The system shall also implement an emergency stop signal, where warn lights flash in case of severe braking.

The graphical notations in Figure 3 distinguishes pure data flows (the dashed lines) from control flows (the solid lines), where the latter may also carry data items.

The languages $L_{\mathbf{A}}$ and $L_{\mathbf{G}}$ of a (concrete) scheduling contract can be specified by means of the AUTOSAR timing extensions [9]. The concept of *observable events* allows to derive sorts of scheduling components, as well as ports of their tasks. Precedence order $\multimap$ follows from the interconnection of ports of software components.

To avoid heavy textual notations, in the following we denote by the expression $\delta(\mathsf{X}, \mathsf{Y})$ the latency between occurrence of an event at port X and occurrence of an event at port Y. Further $\mathcal{S}(\mathsf{X}, T, J)$ denotes a periodic event model for occurrences of events at port X, where T is the period and J is the jitter. We will also write $\mathcal{S}(\mathsf{X}, T)$, if $J = 0$. We use boolean operators to combine such expressions.

In the case-study there is a maximum allowed latency between brake sensing and activating the brake lights. The same applies to flashing the warn lights in case of an emergency brake situation. The resulting top-level contract for the VFB is as follows:

$$\mathbf{C}_{\mathsf{top}} = (\mathbf{A}_{\mathsf{top}}, \mathbf{G}_{\mathsf{top}}) = \begin{pmatrix} \mathcal{S}(\mathsf{ext\_pedal}, 20ms) \wedge & \delta(\mathsf{ext\_pedal}, \mathsf{ext\_brake\_lamp}) \leq 25ms \wedge \\ \mathcal{S}(\mathsf{trig\_TL}, 20ms) & , & \delta(\mathsf{ext\_pedal}, \mathsf{ext\_rear\_di\_lamp}) \leq 60ms \end{pmatrix}$$

$\mathbf{A}_{\mathsf{top}}$ makes explicit an assumption about the frequency of sensor samples of the brake pedal position. These assumptions were not part of the requirements.[4]

Step 2 of Process 2: Assuming that components BrakeLights and TurnLights are implemented by two different suppliers, we propose sub-contracts specifying

---

[4] It is actually not uncommon that some critical assumptions are implicit in requirements documents, which may, at times, become a problem.

a time budgeting for them. Thereby a clear assignment of responsibilities to
the suppliers is achieved. This activity is step 2 of Process 2. In our case two
subcontracts are specified:

$$\mathbf{C_{BL}} = \left(\quad \mathcal{S}(\text{ext\_pedal}, 20ms) \quad , \begin{array}{l} \delta(\text{ext\_pedal}, \text{ext\_brake\_lamp}) \leq 25ms \wedge \\ \delta(\text{ext\_pedal}, \text{emcy}) \leq 5ms \end{array} \right)$$

$$\mathbf{C_{TL}} = \left(\begin{array}{l} \mathcal{S}(\text{emcy}, 20ms, 5ms) \wedge \\ \mathcal{S}(\text{trig\_TL}, 20ms) \end{array} , \delta(\text{emcy}, \text{ext\_rear\_di\_lamp}) \leq 50ms \right)$$

These contracts are still resourceless. To ensure that $\mathbf{C_{BL}}$ and $\mathbf{C_{TL}}$ are correct
with respect to the top-level contract, we must prove the refinement

$$\mathscr{C}_{BL} \otimes \mathscr{C}_{TL} \quad \preceq \quad \mathscr{C}_{top}$$

This can be performed by invoking Lemma 6.

Steps 3 and 4 of Process 2: The next step in the AUTOSAR methodology
consists in developing system and sub-system views, where the network topology and deployment of software components to ECUs is defined. Resource aware
contracts are now considered. A resource is allocated to each task of the contracts defined for the VFB description. Precedence constraints between tasks
are not modified. If tasks of the assumption are pair-wise non-conflicting (see
Definition 1), this yields a resource aware T-closed contract, that port-refines the
contract of the VFB.

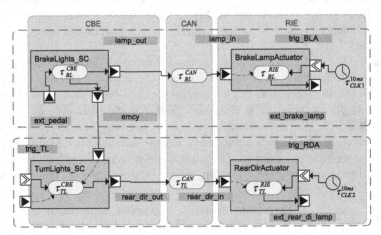

Fig. 4. Deploying *VFB* on computing and communication resources.

For the example, the VFB view is further refined and then deployed as the
architecture shown in Figure 4. The blue dashed boxes denote the previous
components BrakeLights and TurnLights from the architecture shown on Figure 3.
The brown boxes labeled CBE, CAN and RIE, indicate resources allocated to
tasks. Deployment is driven by the separation of the sensing and control parts

from the actuation part. In addition to allocating resources, execution budgets are specified per task. Mirroring the decomposition of the VFB description, the contract of the system view is the composition of the resource aware sub-contracts $\mathscr{C}_{BL'}$ and $\mathscr{C}_{TL'}$. Since contracts created in this step and in previous steps 1 and 2 are T-closed, Lemma 7 applies and we can bound the risks for later system integration.

5 Conclusion

We have developed a framework of Assume / Guarantee contracts for schedulability analysis. The methodological step of AUTOSAR suggesting a transition from a *Virtual Function Bus* view, which is independent of the target platform, to a system view where network topology and deployment across ECUs is considered, was particularly challenging. A strict contract based approach offering independent development was not feasible, since task scheduling is a resource allocation problem, which, by essence, can only be solved globally. However, our approach allows to properly bound the development steps of the AUTOSAR methodology that do not comply with the rules of contract based design, while avoiding risks at system integration with a clear and limited additional discipline regarding resource segregation. Within resource segregated subsystems, our contract framework enables compositional reasoning about scheduling of applications distributed over several resources.

References

1. Alur, R., Weiss, G.: Regular specifications of resource requirements for embedded control software. In: Proceedings of the 14th IEEE Real-Time and Embedded Technology and Applications Symposium, RTAS 2008, pp. 159–168. IEEE Computer Society (2008)
2. Alur, R., Weiss, G.: RTComposer: a framework for real-time components with scheduling interfaces. In: Proceedings of the 8th ACM & IEEE International Conference on Embedded Software, EMSOFT 2008, pp. 159–168. ACM (2008)
3. Anand, M., Fischmeister, S., Lee, I.: A Comparison of Compositional Schedulability Analysis Techniques for Hierarchical Real-Time Systems. ACM Trans. Embedded Comput. Syst. **13**(1), 2 (2013)
4. Benveniste, A., Caillaud, B., Ferrari, A., Mangeruca, L., Passerone, R., Sofronis, C.: Multiple viewpoint contract-based specification and design. In: de Boer, F.S., Bonsangue, M.M., Graf, S., de Roever, W.-P. (eds.) FMCO 2007. LNCS, vol. 5382, pp. 200–225. Springer, Heidelberg (2008)
5. Boudjadar, A., David, A., Kim, J.H., Larsen, K.G., Mikučionis, M., Nyman, U., Skou, A.: Widening the schedulability of hierarchical scheduling systems. In: Lanese, I., Madelaine, E. (eds.) FACS 2014. LNCS, vol. 8997, pp. 209–227. Springer, Heidelberg (2015)
6. Boudjadar, A., Kim, J.H., Larsen, K.G., Nyman, U.: Compositional schedulability analysis of an avionics system using UPPAAL. In: Proceedings of the 1st International Conference on Advanced Aspects of Software Engineering, ICAASE 2014, Constantine, Algeria, November 2–4, pp. 140–147 (2014)

7. AUTOSAR consortium: 10 years Autosar. Tech. rep., AUTOSAR (2013). http://www.autosar.org/fileadmin/files/events/10yearsautosar/ATZextra_AUTOSAR_-_THE_WORLDWIDE_AUTOMOTIVE_STANDARD_FOR_EE_SYSTEMS.pdf

8. AUTOSAR consortium: Methodology (Release 421, 2014). http://www.autosar.org/fileadmin/files/releases/4-2/methodology-templates/methodology/auxiliary/AUTOSAR_TR_Methodology.pdf

9. AUTOSAR consortium: Specification of Timing Extensions (Release 421, 2014). http://www.autosar.org/fileadmin/files/releases/4-2/methodology-templates/templates/standard/AUTOSAR_TPS_TimingExtensions.pdf

10. Easwaran, A., Lee, I., Sokolsky, O., Vestal, S.: A Compositional scheduling framework for digital avionics systems. In: 15th IEEE International Conference on Embedded and Real-Time Computing Systems and Applications, RTCSA 2009, Beijing, China, August 24–26, pp. 371–380 (2009)

11. Lampka, K., Perathoner, S., Thiele, L.: Component-based system design: analytic real-time interfaces for state-based component implementations. STTT 15(3), 155–170 (2013)

12. Lukasiewycz, M., Schneider, R., Goswami, D., Chakraborty, S.: Modular scheduling of distributed heterogeneous time-triggered automotive systems. In: Proceedings of the 17th Asia and South Pacific Design Automation Conference, ASP-DAC 2012, Sydney, Australia, January 30 - February 2, pp. 665–670 (2012)

13. Marimuthu, S.P., Chakraborty, S.: A Framework for compositional and hierarchical real-time scheduling. In: 12th IEEE Conference on Embedded and Real-Time Computing Systems and Applications (RTCSA 2006), August 16–18, Sydney, Australia, pp. 91–96 (2006)

14. Phan, L.T.X., Lee, J., Easwaran, A., Ramaswamy, V., Chen, S., Lee, I., Sokolsky, O.: CARTS: A Tool for Compositional Analysis of Real-Time Systems. SIGBED Review 8(1), 62–63 (2011)

15. Reinkemeier, P., Stierand, I.: Compositional timing analysis of real-time systems based on resource segregation abstraction. In: Schirner, G., Götz, M., Rettberg, A., Zanella, M.C., Rammig, F.J. (eds.) IESS 2013. IFIP AICT, vol. 403, pp. 181–192. Springer, Heidelberg (2013)

16. Reinkemeier, P., Stierand, I.: Real-Time Contracts - A Contract Theory Considering Resource Supplies and Demands. Reports of SFB/TR 14 AVACS 100, SFB/TR 14 AVACS, July 2014. http://www.avacs.org

17. Shin, I., Lee, I.: Compositional real-time scheduling framework. In: Proceedings of the 25th IEEE Real-Time Systems Symposium (RTSS 2004), December 5–8, Lisbon, Portugal, pp. 57–67 (2004)

18. Stierand, I., Reinkemeier, P., Bhaduri, P.: Virtual integration of real-time systems based on resource segregation abstraction. In: Legay, A., Bozga, M. (eds.) FORMATS 2014. LNCS, vol. 8711, pp. 206–221. Springer, Heidelberg (2014)

19. Stierand, I., Reinkemeier, P., Gezgin, T., Bhaduri, P.: Real-time scheduling interfaces and contracts for the design of distributed embedded systems. In: 8th IEEE International Symposium on Industrial Embedded Systems, SIES 2013, Porto, Portugal, June 19–21, pp. 130–139 (2013)

20. Stoimenov, N., Chakraborty, S., Thiele, L.: Interface-based design of real-time systems. In: Advances in Real-Time Systems (to Georg Färber on the occasion of his appointment as Professor Emeritus at TU München after leading the Lehrstuhl für Realzeit-Computersysteme for 34 illustrious years), pp. 83–101 (2012)

21. Thiele, L., Wandeler, E., Stoimenov, N.: Real-time interfaces for composing real-time systems. In: Proceedings of the 6th ACM & IEEE International Conference on Embedded Software, EMSOFT 2006, October 22–25, Seoul, Korea, pp. 34–43 (2006)

22. Wandeler, E., Thiele, L.: Interface-based design of real-time systems with hierarchical scheduling. In: 12th IEEE Real-Time and Embedded Technology and Applications Symposium (RTAS 2006), April 4–7, San Jose, California, USA, pp. 243–252 (2006)

23. Weiss, G., Alur, R.: Automata based interfaces for control and scheduling. In: Bemporad, A., Bicchi, A., Buttazzo, G. (eds.) HSCC 2007. LNCS, vol. 4416, pp. 601–613. Springer, Heidelberg (2007)

Bounded Determinization of Timed Automata with Silent Transitions

Florian Lorber[2](✉), Amnon Rosenmann[1], Dejan Ničković[1], and Bernhard K. Aichernig[2]

[1] AIT Austrian Institute of Technology GmbH Vienna, Vienna, Austria
rosenmann@math.tugraz.at, Dejan.Nickovic@ait.ac.at
[2] Institute for Software Technology, Graz University of Technology, Graz, Austria
{florber,aichernig}@ist.tugraz.at

Abstract. Deterministic timed automata are strictly less expressive than their non-deterministic counterparts, which are again less expressive than those with silent transitions. As a consequence, timed automata are in general non-determinizable. This is unfortunate since deterministic automata play a major role in model-based testing, observability and implementability. However, by bounding the length of the traces in the automaton, effective determinization becomes possible. We propose a novel procedure for bounded determinization of timed automata. The procedure unfolds the automata to bounded trees, removes all silent transitions and determinizes via disjunction of guards. The proposed algorithms are optimized to the bounded setting and thus are more efficient and can handle a larger class of timed automata than the general algorithms. The approach is implemented in a prototype tool and evaluated on several examples. To our best knowledge, this is the first implementation of this type of procedure for timed automata.

1 Introduction

The design of modern embedded systems often involves the integration of inter-acting components I_1 and I_2 that realize some requested behavior. In early stages of the design, I_1 and I_2 are high-level and partial models that allow considerable implementation freedom to the designer. In practice, this freedom is reflected in the non-deterministic choices that are intended to be resolved during subsequent design refinement steps. In addition, the composition of two components involves their synchronization on some shared actions. Typically, the actions over which the two components interact are *hidden* and become unobservable to the user. It follows that the overall specification $I = I_1 \parallel I_2$ can be a *non-deterministic partially observable* model. However, for many problems such as model-based testing, observability, implementability and language inclusion checking, it is desirable and in certain cases necessary to work with the deterministic model.

Many embedded systems must meet strict real-time requirements. Timed automata (TA) [3] are a formal modeling language that enables specification of

© Springer International Publishing Switzerland 2015
S. Sankaranarayanan and E. Vicario (Eds.): FORMATS 2015, LNCS 9268, pp. 288–304, 2015.
DOI: 10.1007/978-3-319-22975-1_19

complex real-time systems. In contrast to the classical automata theory, deterministic TA (DTA) are strictly less expressive than the fully observable non-deterministic TA (NTA) [3,12,17], whereas the latter are strictly less expressive than TA with silent transitions (eNTA) [5]. This strict hierarchy of TA with respect to determinism and observability has an important direct consequence - NTA are not determinizable in general. In addition, due to their complexity, it is rarely the case that exhaustive verification methods are used during the design of modern embedded systems. Lighter and incomplete methods, such as model-based testing [16] and bounded model checking [8] are used in practice in order to gain confidence in the design-under-test and effectively catch bugs.

In this paper, we propose a procedure for *bounded determinization* of eNTA. Given an arbitrary *strongly responsive*[1] eNTA A and a bound k, our algorithm computes a DTA $D(A)$ in the form of a timed tree, such that every timed trace consisting of at most k observable actions is a trace in A if and only if it is a trace in $D(A)$. It provides the basis for effectively implementing bounded refinement checking and test case generation procedures.

Our concrete motivation behind determinizing the model was induced by our previous model-based testing approach [2]. This approach uses fault-based techniques for the test generation and needs to perform language-inclusion between correct and faulty timed automata models. The language inclusion is implemented via SMT-solving and relies on deterministic models. Thus, the determinization enables the processing of a wider class of models and the restriction to bounded traces does not pose a problem, as testing only considers finite traces.

The proposed algorithms are performed in three steps: (1) we unfold the original automaton into a finite tree and rename the clocks in a way that only needs one clock reset per transition, (2) we remove the silent transitions from the tree, (3) we determinize it. Our determinization procedure results in a TA description which includes diagonal [9] and disjunctive constraints. Although non-standard, this representation is practical and optimized for the bounded setting – it avoids costly transformation of the TA into its standard form and exploits efficient heuristics in SMT solvers that can directly deal with this type of constraints. In addition, our focus on bounded determinization allows us to consider models, such as TA with loops containing both observable and silent transitions with reset, that could not be determinized otherwise. We implemented the procedure in a prototype tool and evaluated it on several examples. To our best knowledge, this is the first implementation of this type of procedure for timed automata.

Running Example. The different steps of the algorithms will be illustrated on a running example of a coffe-machine shown in Figure 1. After inserting a *coin*, the system heats up for zero to three seconds, followed by a *beep*-tone indicating its readyness. Alternatively, if there is no coffee or water left, the *beep* might occur after exactly two seconds, indicating that the *refunding* process has started and the coin will be returned within four seconds. Heating up and graining the coffee together may only take between one and two seconds. Then

---

[1] In model-based testing, strong responsiveness is the requirement that there are no silent loops, otherwise the tester cannot distinguish between deadlocks and livelocks.

the brewing process starts and finally the machine releases the *coffee* after one second of brewing. There is no observable signal indicating the transition from graining to brewing, thus this transition is silent.

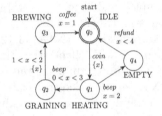

Fig. 1. Running example

The rest of the paper is structured as follows: First, we give the basic definitions and notation of TA with silent transitions (Section 2). Then, we illustrate the first step of our procedure, the bounded-unfolding of the automaton and the renaming of clocks (Section 3). This is followed by the second step, the removal of silent transitions (Section 4) and the final step, our determinization approach (Section 5). Section 6 summarizes the complexity of the different steps. In Section 7 we evaluate our prototype implementation and in Section 8 we address related work. Finally, in Section 9 we conclude our work. Complete proofs of the propositions and theorems can be found in our technical report [15].

2   Timed Automata with Silent Transitions

A timed automaton is an abstract model aiming at capturing the real-time behaviour of systems. It is a finite automaton extended with a set of clocks defined over $\mathbb{R}_{\geq 0}$, the set of non-negative real numbers. We may represent the timed automaton by a graph whose nodes are called *locations*, which are defined through a set of upper bounds put on the clock values. These bounds are restricted to non-negative integer values. While being at a location, all clocks progress at the same rate. The edges of the graph are called *transitions*. Each transition may be subject to constraints, called *guards*, put on clock values in the form of integer inequalities. At each such transition an *action* occurs and some of the clocks may be reset. The actions take values in some finite domain denoted by Σ. Here we are dealing with the class of timed automata with an extended set of actions including also *silent actions*, denoted by ϵ. hese are internal actions that are *non-observable* from the outside, and we distinguish them from the actions that are not silent and called *observable* actions. We call a TA without silent transitions *fully-observable*.

Let $\mathcal{X}$ be a finite set of *clock* variables. A clock *valuation* $v(x)$ is a function $v : \mathcal{X} \to \mathbb{R}_{\geq 0}$ assigning a real value to every clock $x \in \mathcal{X}$. We denote by $\mathcal{V}$ the set of all clock valuations and by $\mathbf{0}$ the valuation assigning 0 to every clock. For a valuation v and $d \in \mathbb{R}_{\geq 0}$ we define $v + d$ to be the valuation $(v + d)(x) = v(x) + d$ for all $x \in \mathcal{X}$. For a subset $\mathcal{X}_{rst}$ of $\mathcal{X}$, we denote by $v[\mathcal{X}_{rst}]$ the valuation such that for every $x \in \mathcal{X}_{rst}$, $v[\mathcal{X}_{rst}](x) = 0$ and for every $x \in \mathcal{X} \setminus \mathcal{X}_{rst}$, $v[\mathcal{X}_{rst}](x) = v(x)$. A *clock constraint* φ is a conjunction of predicates of the form $x \sim n$, where $x \in \mathcal{X}$, $n \in \mathbb{N}$ and $\sim \in \{<, \leq, =, \geq, >\}$. Given a clock valuation v, we write $v \models \varphi$ when v satisfies φ. We give now a formal definition of (non-deterministic) timed automata with silent transitions.

Definition 1 (eNTA). *A (non-deterministic) timed automaton with silent transitions A is a tuple* $(Q, q_{init}, \Sigma_\epsilon, \mathcal{X}, \mathcal{I}, \mathcal{G}, \mathcal{T}, Q_{accept})$, *where* Q *is a finite set of locations and* $q_{init} \in Q$ *is the* initial *location;* $\Sigma_\epsilon = \Sigma \cup \{\epsilon\}$ *is a finite set of actions, where* Σ *are the observable actions and* ϵ *represents a silent action, that is a non-observable internal action;* $\mathcal{X}$ *is a finite set of* clock *variables;* $\mathcal{I} : L \to LI$ *is a mapping from locations to* location invariants, *where each location invariant* $li \in LI$ *is a conjunction of constraints of the form true,* $x < n$ *or* $x \leq n$, *with* $x \in \mathcal{X}$ *and* $n \in \mathbb{N}$; $\mathcal{G}$ *is a set of* transition guards, *where each guard is a conjunction of constraints of the form* $x \sim n$, *where* $x \in \mathcal{X}$, $\sim \in \{<, \leq, =, \geq, >\}$ *and* $n \in \mathbb{N}$; $\mathcal{T} \subseteq Q \times \Sigma_\epsilon \times \mathcal{G} \times \mathcal{P}(\mathcal{X}) \times Q$ *is a finite set of* transitions *of the form* $(q, \alpha, g, \mathcal{X}_{rst}, q')$, *where* $q, q' \in Q$ *are the* source *and the* target *locations;* $\alpha \in \Sigma_\epsilon$ *is the transition* action; $g \in \mathcal{G}$ *is the transition* guard; $\mathcal{X}_{rst} \subseteq \mathcal{X}$ *is the subset of clocks to be* reset; $Q_{accept} \subseteq Q$ *is the subset of* accepting *locations.*

Example 1. For the eNTA illustrated in Figure 1 we have $Q = \{q_0, \ldots, q_4\}$, $q_{init} = q_0$, $\Sigma_\epsilon = \{\epsilon, coin, beep, refund, coffee\}$, $\mathcal{X} = \{x\}$, $\mathcal{I}(q_i) = true | q_i \in Q$, $\mathcal{G} = \{0 < x < 3, x = 2, x < 4, 1 < x < 2, x = 1\}$, $Q_{accept} = \{q_0\}$. $\mathcal{T}$ is the set containing all transitions, e.g. the transition from q_2 to q_3, with $\alpha = \epsilon$ (thus, it is a silent transition), $g = 1 < x < 2$ and $\mathcal{X}_{rst} = \{x\}$.

The *semantics* of an eNTA A is given by the *timed transition system* $[[A]] = (S, s_{init}, \mathbb{R}_{\geq 0}, \Sigma_\epsilon, T, S_{accept})$, where $S = \{(q, v) \in Q \times V \mid v \models \mathcal{I}(q)\}$; $s_{init} = (q_{init}, \mathbf{0})$; $T \subseteq S \times (\Sigma_\epsilon \cup \mathbb{R}_{\geq 0}) \times S$ is the transition relation consisting of *timed* and *discrete* transitions such that: *Timed transitions (delay):* $((q, v), d, (q, v+d)) \in T$, where $d \in \mathbb{R}_{\geq 0}$, if $v + d \models \mathcal{I}(q)$; *Discrete transitions (jump):* $((q, v), \alpha, (q', v')) \in T$, where $\alpha \in \Sigma$, if there exists a transition $(q, \alpha, g, \mathcal{X}_{rst}, q')$ in $\mathcal{T}$, such that: (1) $v \models g$; (2) $v' = v[\mathcal{X}_{rst}]$ and (3) $v' \models \mathcal{I}(q')$; $S_{accept} \subseteq S$ such that $(q, v) \in S_{accept}$ if and only if $q \in Q_{accept}$.

A *finite well-behaving run* ρ of an eNTA A is a finite sequence of alternating timed and discrete transitions, that ends with an observable action, of the form
$$(q_0, v_0) \xrightarrow{d_1} (q_0, v_0 + d_1) \xrightarrow{\tau_1} (q_1, v_1) \xrightarrow{d_2} \cdots \xrightarrow{d_n} (q_{n-1}, v_{n-1} + d_n) \xrightarrow{\tau_n} (q_n, v_n),$$
where $q_0 = q_{init}$, $v_0 = \mathbf{0}$, $\tau_i = (q_{i-1}, \alpha_i, g_i, \mathcal{X}_{rst(i)}, q_i) \in \mathcal{T}$ and $\alpha_i \in \Sigma$. In this paper we consider only finite and well-behaving runs. A run ρ is *accepting* if the last location q_n is accepting. The run ρ of A induces the *timed trace* $\sigma = (t_1, \alpha_1), (t_2, \alpha_2), \ldots, (t_n, \alpha_n)$ defined over Σ_ϵ, where $t_i = \Sigma_{j=1}^{i} d_j$. From the latter we can extract the *observable timed trace*, which is obtained by removing from σ all the pairs containing silent actions while taking into account the passage of time. A TA is called *deterministic* if it does not contain silent transitions and whenever two timed traces are the same then they are induced by the same run. Otherwise, the TA is *non-deterministic*. The *language* accepted by an eNTA A, denoted $\mathfrak{L}(A)$, is the set of observable timed traces induced by all accepting runs of A. Note, that the restriction to well-behaving runs is compatible with the definition of the language of the automaton, where silent actions that occur after the last observable action on a finite run are ignored. As a consequence, a location with in-going edges consisting of only silent transitions cannot be an accepting location.

3 k-Bounded Unfolding of Timed Automata

Given an eNTA A which is strongly responsive, its k-prefix language $\mathfrak{L}_k(A) \subseteq \mathfrak{L}(A)$ is the set of observable timed traces induced by all accepting runs of A which are of observable length bounded by k. That is,

$$\mathfrak{L}_k(A) = \{w \in \mathfrak{L}(A) \mid |w| \le k\}. \quad (1)$$

By unfolding A and cutting it at observable level k, the resulting TA, $U_k(A)$, satisfies

$$\mathfrak{L}(U_k(A)) = \mathfrak{L}_k(A). \quad (2)$$

$U_k(A)$ is in the form of a finite tree, where each path that starts at the root ends after at most k observable transitions, and we may also further cut A by requiring that all leaves are accepting locations. Note, that if we reach in $U_k(A)$ a copy of an accepting location q of A by a silent transition then it will not be marked as an accepting location (but another copy might be marked as an accepting location if reached by an observable transition).

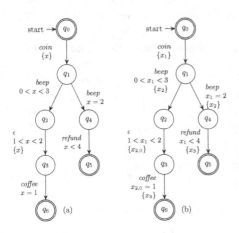

Fig. 2. Unfolding and clock renaming

Figure 2(a) shows the unfolding of the coffee-machine up to observable depth three. The left branch is longer than the right, as it contains a silent transition.

3.1   Renaming the Clocks

Every unfolded timed automaton can be expressed by an equivalent timed automaton that resets at most one clock per transition. This known normal form [4] crucially simplifies the next stages of our algorithm, where we do not need to bother with multiple clock resets in one transition. The basic idea is to substitute the clocks from the original automaton by new clocks, where multiple old clocks reset at the same transition are replaced by the the same new clock, as they measure the same time until they are reset again. The substitution of the clocks works straight forward: At each path from the root, at the i-th observable transition, a new clock x_i is introduced and reset, and if this transition is followed by $l > 0$ silent transitions then new clocks $x_{i,0}, \ldots, x_{i,l-1}$ are introduced and reset. A clock x that occurs in a guard is substituted by the new clock that was introduced in the transition where the last reset of x happened, or by x_0 if it was never reset. Let τ_i and τ_j be two transitions on the same path in the original automata at observable depth i, j, s.t. $i < j$. Furthermore, a clock x appearing in the guard of τ_j, is reset before in τ_i, but is not reset on any transition in between τ_i and τ_j. Then, x_i is introduced and reset at τ_i and the original clock variable x is substituted by x_i in the guard of τ_j. Figure 2(b) illustrates the clock renaming applied to the coffee machine. In the guards of the two *beep*-transitions starting at q_1, x is replaced by x_1, since the last reset of x in the original automata was at depth one, while in the *coffee*-transition from q_3 it is replaced by $x_{2,0}$, as x was reset in the first silent transition after depth two.

4 Removing the Silent Transitions

In this section we give an algorithm that removes the silent transitions from the eNTA A, which is in the form of a finite tree with renamed clocks. Thus, at each level i there will be a single clock x_i reset on all transitions of that level. Algorithm 1 shows the workflow and Figure 3 illustrates the general idea.

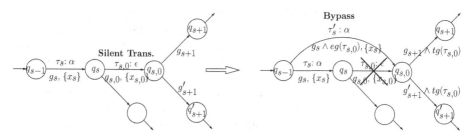

Fig. 3. Bypassing the silent transition

Algorithm 1. Removing the Silent Transitions

Input: $A \in \text{eNTA}_k$ in the form of a tree of observable depth k with renamed clocks
Output: $O(A) \in \text{NTA}_k$, such that $\mathcal{L}(O(A)) = \mathcal{L}(A)$
 1: **while** there are silent transitions **do**
 2:     FIND first (from root) silent transition $\tau_{s,0}$ from q_s to $q_{s,0}$
 3:     SET lower bound to the silent transition
 4:     CREATE bypass transition with enabling guard
 5:     AUGMENT transitions from $q_{s,0}$ with taken guard
 6:     UPDATE guards on paths from $q_{s,0}$
 7:     REMOVE $\tau_{s,0}$
 8: **end while**

We remove the silent transitions one at a time, where at each iteration we remove the first occurrence of a silent transition on some path from the root, until no silent transitions are left (e.g. we can pick a path and move one-by-one all its silent transitions, then move to another path, and so on). So, let $\tau_{s,0}$ be such a first silent transition found by Line 2 of the algorithm, leading from location q_s to location $q_{s,0}$ with guard $g_{s,0}$ and reset of clock $x_{s,0}$. Let q_s be reached from location q_{s-1} with an observable transition τ_s and with guard g_s. The case where q_s is the initial location is simpler, as it does not require building a bypass transition. In order to remove the silent transition $\tau_{s,0}$ after forming a transition that bypasses it, several steps are carried out, that will be explained in detail in the following subsections. First, we set an auxilliary lower bound on the clock that is reset on the silent transition by updating the guard (Line 3). Then, we create the bypass transition using an *enabling guard* $eg(\tau_{s,0})$ which represents the upper bound until when the silent transition $\tau_{s,0}$ is enabled (Line 4). In Line 5 we construct a *taken guard* $tg(\tau_{s,0})$ that ensures that the transitions from $q_{s,0}$ come after the necessary delay that is forced by the silent transition. The taken guard is added to all transitions leaving $q_{s,0}$. Finally, in Lines 6–7, we remove the silent transition $\tau_{s,0}$ and update all future guards referring to the deleted clock $x_{s,0}$.

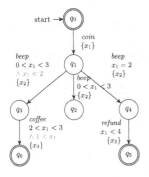

Fig. 4. Fully   observable non-deterministic TA

Setting a Lower Bound to the Silent Transition. We set a lower bound to the silent transition by augmenting the guard $g_{s,0}$ of $\tau_{s,0}$ to be $g'_{s,0} = g_{s,0} \wedge (0 \le x_s)$, where x_s is the clock that is reset on the transition τ_s that precedes the silent transition. This additional constraint per definition always evaluates to *true*, but it is used in the next step to compute the unary constraints of the enabling guard. The guard of the silent transition in Figure 2 (b) after setting the lower bound is $1 < x_1 < 2 \wedge 0 \le x_2$.

Creating a Bypass with the Enabling Guard. The enabling guard $eg(\tau_{s,0})$ guarantees that each clock's constraint that was part of the silent transition is satisfied at some nonnegative delay and that these constraints are satisfied simultaneously, thus at some point during the bypass transition the silent transition would have been enabled as well. We describe here how the enabling guards are defined for strict inequalities, as shown in the upper part of Table 1. The other cases are dealt similarly, as seen in the table, and the constraint $x_i = n_i$ is treated as $n_i \le x_i \le n_i$. For every pair of a lower bound constraint $m_i < x_i$ and an upper bound constraint $x_j < n_j$, where $i \ne j$ and $x_i, x_j \ne x_s$ (x_s is the clock that is reset at τ_s), that appear in $g'_{s,0}$ we form the enabling guard binary constraint $x_j - x_i < n_j - m_i$ as shown in the first line of Table 1.

The next two lines consider constraints that involve the clock x_s, where x_s will be removed as it is the clock that will be reset on the bypass and is considered of value 0. Note, that for each upper bound constraint $x_j < n_j$ we use the lower bound constraint $0 \le x_s$ that was added in the previous step of the algorithm to compute the enabling guard unary constraint $x_j < n_j$, which guarantees that at the time of the bypass x_j does not pass its upper bound constraint of the silent transition. An example of such a unary constraint is marked in red in the transition from q_1 to q_3 in Figure 4. The silent transition in the original automaton could not have been enabled if x_1 had already been higher than two

Table 1. Enabling guard constraints

Silent Trans. Constraints	Clock Reset	Enabling Guard Constraint
$(m_i < x_i) \wedge (x_j < n_j)$	x_s	$x_j - x_i < n_j - m_i$
$(m_s < x_s) \wedge (x_j < n_j)$	x_s	$x_j < n_j - m_s$
$(m_i < x_i) \wedge (x_s < n_s)$	x_s	$m_i - n_s < x_i$
$(m_i \leq x_i) \wedge (x_j < n_j)$	x_s	$x_j - x_i < n_j - m_i$
$(m_i < x_i) \wedge (x_j \leq n_j)$	x_s	$x_j - x_i < n_j - m_i$
$(m_i \leq x_i) \wedge (x_j \leq n_j)$	x_s	$x_j - x_i \leq n_j - m_i$
$(m_i = x_i) \wedge (x_j = n_j)$	x_s	$x_j - x_i = n_j - m_i$

after the *beep*-transition, thus the bypass can also only be enabled while x_1 is smaller than two. The running example does not contain any binary constraints.

To create the bypass, we split the paths through q_s in the original automaton A into two. Those that do not take the silent transition $\tau_{s,0}$ continue as before from q_{s-1} to q_s and then to some location different from $q_{s,0}$. The paths that went through $\tau_{s,0}$ are directed from q_{s-1} to $q_{s,0}$ and then continue as before. The bypass τ'_s from q_{s-1} to $q_{s,0}$ has the same observable actions as those of τ_s, the same new clock reset x_s, and the guard g'_s which is the guard g_s of τ_s augmented with the *enabling guard* $eg(\tau_{s,0})$ (see Figure 3). Figure 4 shows the removal of the silent transition illustrated on the coffee-machine. The transition from q_1 to q_3 is the bypass and the transition from q_1 to q_2 is the original transition. Since the silent transition was the only transition leaving q_2, q_2 does not contain any outgoing transitions anymore, once the bypass is generated.

Augmenting the Taken Guard. For each transition from $q_{s,0}$ to q_{s+1} we augment its guard g_{s+1} by forming $g'_{s+1} = g_{s+1} \wedge tg(\tau_{s,0})$ (see Figure 3), where $tg(\tau_{s,0})$ is the *taken guard*. $tg(\tau_{s,0})$ is composed of a single constraint: $0 \leq x_{s,0}$, where $x_{s,0}$ is the clock that is reset at the silent transition $\tau_{s,0}$. In the next stage of the algorithm of updating the future guards it will be transformed into the conjunction of the lower bound constraints $m_i < x_i$ or $m_i \leq x_i$ that appear in $g'_{s,0}$. These constraints make sure that we spend enough time at $q_{s,0}$ before moving to the next locations, as if we had taken the silent transition. The constraint is also used for synchronization of the future guards in the next step. In Figure 4, the red-marked part of the guard from transition q_3 to q_6 shows the taken guard that has already been updated from $0 \leq x_{2,0}$ to $1 < x_1$.

Table 2. Update rules for future guards after removing the silent transitions

Silent Trans. Constr.	Future Constr.	Replaced Constr.
$m_i < x_i, \{x_{s,0}\}$	$m_{s+j} < x_{s,0}$ or $m_{s+j} \leq x_{s,0}$	$m_i + m_{s+j} < x_i$
$m_i \leq x_i, \{x_{s,0}\}$	$m_{s+j} < x_{s,0}$	$m_i + m_{s+j} < x_i$
$m_i \leq x_i, \{x_{s,0}\}$	$m_{s+j} \leq x_{s,0}$	$m_i + m_{s+j} \leq x_i$
$x_i < n_i, \{x_{s,0}\}$	$x_{s,0} < n_{s+j}$ or $x_{s,0} \leq n_{s+j}$	$x_i < n_i + n_{s+j}$
$x_i \leq n_i, \{x_{s,0}\}$	$x_{s,0} < n_{s+j}$	$x_i < n_i + n_{s+j}$
$x_i \leq n_i, \{x_{s,0}\}$	$x_{s,0} \leq n_{s+j}$	$x_i \leq n_i + n_{s+j}$
$x_i = n_i, \{x_{s,0}\}$	$x_{s,0} \sim n_{s+j}$	$x_i \sim n_i + n_{s+j}$

Updating the Future Guards. The removal of the silent transition $\tau_{s,0}$ enforces updating of the guards in the paths that start at $q_{s,0}$ and that refer to the clock $x_{s,0}$, that is reset on the silent transition. The most simple case is when the the silent transition guard $g'_{s,0}$ contains an exact constraint $x_i = n_i$, because then any future constraint of the form $x_{s,0} \sim l$ can be replaced by $x_i \sim n_i + l$. So, let us assume that the silent transition does not contain an exact constraint. The rules for updating the future guards are summarized in Table 2. Note, that an equality constraint $x_{s,0} = n_{s+j}$ in a future guard may be treated as $n_{s+j} \leq x_{s,0} \leq n_{s+j}$.

Let $g_{s+1}, \ldots, g_{s+p}$ be the ordered list of guards of consecutive transitions $\tau_{s+1}, \ldots, \tau_{s+p}$ along a path that starts at $q_{s,0}$. Then, if g_{s+j} contains the constraint $m_{s+j} < x_{s,0}$, it is replaced by the conjunction of constraints $m_i + m_{s+j} < x_i$, for each constraint $m_i < x_i$ that appear in $g'_{s,0}$. Similarly, for upper bound constraints. In Figure 4, one future guard was updated in the transition from q_3 to q_6: The original guard of this transition was $x_{2,0} = 1$ (where $x_{2,0}$ was reset on the silent transition) and the guard of the silent transition was $1 < x_1 < 2$. Thus, according to the update rules, the updated future guard is $2 < x_1 < 3$ (written in black), conjuncted with the taken guard (marked in red).

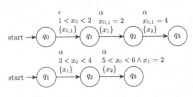

Fig. 5. Guard synchronization

These rules ensure that each future constraint on the clock $x_{s,0}$ separately conforms to and does not deviate from the possible time range of the silent transition. Yet, we need to satisfy a second condition: that along each path that starts at $q_{s,0}$ these future occurrences of $x_{s,0}$ are synchronized. This is achieved by augmenting the future guards with constraints of the form that appear in Table 3. No transition in our running example needs synchronization, hence we use a different example: the upper automaton in Figure 5 shows one silent transition followed by two observable transitions. Using only the previous update rules when removing the silent transition, the first observable transition might occur between three and four seconds, and the second one between five and six seconds. If the first transition occurs after three seconds and the second one after six, this would not conform to the original automaton which required exactly two seconds between them. Thus, applying the last synchronization rule of Table 3, the constraint $x_1 = 4 - 2$ is conjuncted to the second guard. The lower automaton in Figure 5 illustrates the synchronization. Note, we do not need a bypass transition here, since the silent transition starts in the initial state.

Removing the Silent Transition. Finally, we can safely remove the silent transition $\tau_{s,0}$ from q_s to $q_{s,0}$ after forming the bypass from q_{s-1} to $q_{s,0}$ with the necessary modifications to the transition guards.

Theorem 1 (Silent Transitions Removal). $\mathfrak{L}(O(A)) = \mathfrak{L}(A)$.

Table 3. Synchronization constraints for future guards after removing silent transitions

Constr. of g_{s+j}	Constr. of g_{s+i}, $\{x_{s+i}\}$, $i < j$	Sync. Constr. of g_{s+j}
$m_{s+j} < x_{s,0}$	$x_{s,0} < n_{s+i}$ or $x_{s,0} \leq n_{s+i}$	$m_{s+j} - n_{s+i} < x_{s+i}$
$m_{s+j} \leq x_{s,0}$	$x_{s,0} < n_{s+i}$	$m_{s+j} - n_{s+i} < x_{s+i}$
$m_{s+j} \leq x_{s,0}$	$x_{s,0} \leq n_{s+i}$	$m_{s+j} - n_{s+i} \leq x_{s+i}$
$x_{s,0} < n_{s+j}$	$m_{s+i} < x_{s,0}$ or $k_i \leq x_{s,0}$	$x_{s+i} < n_{s+j} - m_{s+i}$
$x_{s,0} \leq n_{s+j}$	$m_{s+i} < x_{s,0}$	$x_{s+i} < n_{s+j} - m_{s+i}$
$x_{s,0} \leq n_{s+j}$	$m_{s+i} \leq x_{s,0}$	$x_{s+i} \leq n_{s+j} - m_{s+i}$
$x_{s,0} = n_{s+j}$	$x_{s,0} = n_{s+i}$	$x_{s+i} = n_{s+j} - n_{s+i}$

5 Determinization

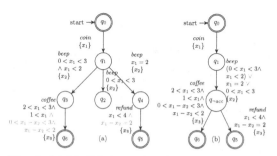

Fig. 6. (a) Modified guards added to future transitions (b) determinization via disjunction

Existing determinization algorithms (as e.g. applied in [18]) create the powerset of all transitions to be determinized, and build one transition for each subset in the powerset. We propose an alternative approach, that reduces the amount of locations and transitions in the deterministic automata, by shifting some complexity towards the guards. Our motivation is the use of SMT solvers for verifying the timed automata models. The larger guards can be directly converted into SMT-LIB formulas, and thus should not pose a problem.

The approach works under the following prerequisites: After the removal of the silent transitions the timed automaton A is in the form of a tree of depth k. At each level i the same new clock x_i is reset on each of the transitions of that level. This is the only clock reset on this level, and no clock is ever reset again.

The basic idea behind the determinization algorithm is to merge all transitions of the same source location and the same action via disjunction, and to push the decision which of them was actually taken to the following transitions. The postponed decision which transition was actually taken can be solved later on by forming diagonal constraints (as in zones) that are invariants of the time progress, and are conjuncted to immediately following transitions. Note that the distinction between accepting and non-accepting locations increases complexity slightly: the determinization of transitions leading to accepting locations and transitions leading to non-accepting locations can not be done exclusively by disjunction of their guards. We therefore need to add an accepting and a non-accepting location to the deterministic tree, and merge all transitions leading to non-accepting locations and all transitions leading to accepting locations separately. To ensure determinism for these transitions, we conjunct the negated guard of the accepting transition to the guard of the non-accepting transition.

Algorithm 2. Guard-Oriented Determinization

Input: $A \in \text{NTA}_k$ in the form of a tree of depth k with renamed clocks
Output: $D(A) \in \text{TA}_k$, such that $\mathfrak{L}(D(A)) = \mathfrak{L}(A)$
 1: $P \leftarrow \{(\mathcal{Q}_{init}, 0)\}$
 2: **while** $P \neq \emptyset$ **do**
 3:     PICK $(q_i, i) \in P$; $P \leftarrow P \backslash (q_i, i)$
 4:     **for** each $\alpha \in \Sigma$ **do**
 5:         **if** $\exists\ \tau_1(q_i, \alpha, g_1, \{x_{i+1}\}, q_1) \neq \tau_2(q_i, \alpha, g_2, \{x_{i+1}\}, q_2)$ **then**
 6:             $g_{acc} \leftarrow false$; $g_{\neg acc} \leftarrow false$
 7:             ADD new locations q_{acc}, $q_{\neg acc}$
 8:             **for** each transition $\tau_i(q_i, \alpha, g_{i+1}, \{x_{i+1}\}, q_{i+1})$ **do**
 9:                 $g' \leftarrow g_{i+1}$
10:                 **for** each clock x_j in g_{i+1} **do**
11:                     $g' \leftarrow g'[x_j := x_j - x_{i+1}]$
12:                 **end for**
13:                 **for** each transition $\tau_{i+1}(q_{i+1}, \beta, g_{i+2}, \{x_{i+2}\}, q_{i+2})$ **do**
14:                     ADD $\tau_{acc}(q_{acc}, \beta, (g_{i+2} \wedge g'), \{x_{i+2}\}, q_{i+2})$
15:                     ADD $\tau_{\neg acc}(q_{\neg acc}, \beta, (g_{i+2} \wedge g'), \{x_{i+2}\}, q_{i+2})$
16:                     REMOVE τ_{i+1}
17:                 **end for**
18:                 **if** $accepting(q_{i+1})$ **then** $g_{acc} \leftarrow g_{acc} \vee g_{i+1}$ **end if**
19:                 **if** $\neg accepting(q_{i+1})$ **then** $g_{\neg acc} \leftarrow g_{\neg acc} \vee g_{i+1}$ **end if**
20:                 REMOVE τ_i and q_{i+1}
21:             **end for**
22:             ADD transition $\tau_{acc}(q_i, \alpha, g_{acc}, \{x_{i+1}\}, q_{acc})$
23:             ADD transition $\tau_{\neg acc}(q_i, \alpha, (g_{\neg acc} \wedge \neg g_{acc}), \{x_{i+1}\}, q_{\neg acc})$
24:         **end if**
25:     **end for**
26:     **for** each transition $\tau_i(q_i, \alpha, g_{i+1}, \{x_{i+1}\}, q_{i+1})$ **do**
27:         $P \leftarrow P \cup (q_{i+1}, i+1)$
28:     **end for**
29: **end while**

A pseudo-code description is given in Algorithm 2. The determinization is done in several steps applied to every location q with multiple outgoing transitions with the same action (Line 5), starting at the initial location (Line 1). Let q_i be such a location with multiple α transitions (Line 8). First, we add an accepting and a non-accepting location q_{acc}, $q_{\neg acc}$ replacing the target locations of the multiple α transitions (Line 7). Then, for each τ_i in the α transitions with guard g from q_i to q_{i+1}, let g' be the result of subtracting the clock x_{i+1} that is reset on τ_i from all clocks that appear in g (Lines 9-12). Next, g' is conjuncted to the guards of each transition τ_{i+1} that follows τ_i and the source location of τ_{i+1} is set to either q_{acc} or $q_{\neg acc}$, depending on whether q_{i+1} is accepting or not. Transitions leaving $q_{\neg acc}$ are additionally copied to q_{acc}, in case the guards of α transitions overlap. (Lines 14,15). Note that g' evaluates to *true* in every branch below τ_i if τ_i was enabled, thus the conjunction does not change the language of the automaton. Figure 6(a) illustrates the conjunction of the modified guards on our running example, marked in red. Note that the determinization did not involve any accepting locations, thus there was no splitting into q_{acc} and $q_{\neg acc}$. Next, all the α-transitions from q leading to accepting locations are merged into a transition leading to q_{acc} (Line 22) and all others into a transition leading to $q_{\neg acc}$(Line 23), by disjuncting their guards (Lines 18,19). The guard of the transition leading to $q_{\neg acc}$ is conjuncted to the negation of the other guard, to ensure determinism (Line 23). Finally, all merged τ_i and their target locations can be removed (Line 20). Figure 6(b) shows the determinized coffee-machine.

Theorem 2 (Determinization). *The determinization algorithm constructs a deterministic timed automaton $D(A)$ such that $\mathfrak{L}(D(A)) = \mathfrak{L}(A)$.*

6   Complexity

Bounded Unfolding. We unfold the timed automaton A into a tree and cut it when reaching observable level k. Let us assume that the tree is of depth K, $K \geq k$, and of size $N = O(d^K)$, with $d \geq 1$ representing the approximate out-degree of the vertices in the graph of A. Since the analysis of the SMT solvers for different applications requires the exploration of all the transitions in the unfolded graph of A, the unfolding stage of our algorithm does not necessarily increase the overall time complexity of the algorithm.

Removing Silent Transitions. Our algorithm does not increase the size of the tree since we only substitute the silent transitions by the bypass transitions. We do add, however, constraints. The number of enabling-guard constraints that we add to each bypass transition is of order $O(K^2)$. Each updated future constraint is of order $O(K)$ (including on-the-fly simplification, so that each clock has at most one lower and one upper bound), and each future transition may be updated at most $O(K)$ times. Hence, the updating step is also of order $O(K^2)$, and the complexity of the whole algorithm is $O(NK^2)$. Note, we do not need to transform the diagonal constraints introduced in the algorithm into unary constraints, nor do they introduce problems in the next algorithm of determinization.

Determinization. decreases the size of the unfolded automaton, if non-determinism exists. The complexity gain can be exponential in the number of locations and transitions, but is lost by a proportional larger complexity in the guards.

7   Implementation and Experimental Results

The algorithms were implemented in Scala (Version 2.10.3) and integrated into the test-case generation tool MoMuT::TA[2], providing a significant increase in the capabilities of the tool. MoMuT::TA provides model-based mutation testing algorithms for timed automata [2], using UPPAAL's [14] XML format as input and output. The determinization algorithm use the SMT-solver Z3 [10] for

---

[2] https://momut.org/?page_id=355

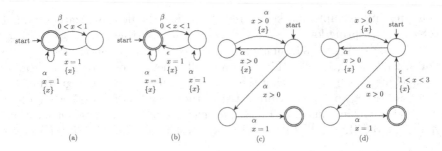

Fig. 7. The four timed automata used in Study 1 and Study 2

checking satisfiability of guards. All experiments were run on a MacBook Pro with a 2.53 GHz Intel Core 2 Duo Processor and 4 GB RAM.

The implementation is still a prototype and further optimizations are planned. One already implemented optimization is the "on-the-fly" execution of the presented algorithms, allowing the unrolling, clock renaming, silent transition removal and determinization in one single walk through the tree. The combined algorithm does not suffer from the full exponential blow-up of the unfolding: if the automaton contains a location that can be reached via different traces, yet with the same clock resets, the unfolding splits it into several, separately processed, locations, while the on-the-fly algorithm only needs to process it once.

The following studies compare the numbers of locations and the runtimes of *a*) the silent transition removal, *b*) a standard determinization algorithm that works by splitting non-deterministic transitions into several transitions that contain each possible combination of their guards, *c*) the new determinization algorithm introduced in Section 5 and *d*) its on-the-fly version.

Study 1. The first example, taken from Diekert et al. [11], is the timed automaton illustrated in Fig. 7 (a), which cannot be determinized. We then added another α-transition (Fig. 7 (b)), which causes non-determinism after removing the silent transition. The test results are shown in Table 4 (before and after modification).

Table 4. Runtime and number of locations for the automata of Fig. 7 (a) (first three rows) and Fig. 7 (b) (last three rows)

Depth	Number of locations				Runtime (sec.)			
	unfolded	std. det.	new det.	on-the-fly	ϵ-removal	std. det.	new det.	on-the-fly
2	8	7	7	7	0.1	0.3	0.1	0.1
5	78	63	63	63	0.4	0.5	0.4	0.2
9	1,278	1,023	1,023	1,023	16,011.2	6.7	7.2	1.0
2	9	8	8	8	0.2	0.2	0.2	0.1
5	177	135	84	63	0.8	0.9	1.3	0.7
9	8,361	4,364	3,609	1,023	20,969.0	71.2	88.3	9.6

Study 2. The second example is taken from Baier et al. [4] and is illustrated in Fig. 7(c). We modified the automaton by adding a silent transition (Fig. 7(d)). Table 5 shows the results of the two determinization approaches.

Table 5. Runtime and number of locations for the automata of Fig. 7 (c) (first three rows) and Fig. 7 (d) (last three rows)

Depth	Number of locations				Runtime (sec.)			
	unfolded	std. det.	new det.	on-the-fly	ϵ-removal	std. det.	new det.	on-the-fly
2	5	5	4	4	-	0.1	0.1	0.1
5	11	10	8	8	-	0.2	0.3	0.1
10	21	21	16	16	-	0.3	0.3	0.1
25	51	50	38	38	-	0.5	0.9	0.2
50	101	100	76	76	-	0.7	391.6	0.3
2	5	5	4	4	0.1	0.1	0.1	0.01
5	24	26	8	8	0.2	2.1	0.4	0.3
10	140	661	16	16	0.5	1,945.1	2.1	0.5

Study 3. This study is part of a model of an industrial application: it is based on a car alarm system that was already used as an example in our work on model-based mutation testing from timed automata (see [2] for the whole model). In this evaluation, we introduced a silent transition that adds a non-deterministic delay of up to two seconds before the timer of the alarm starts, and our results are given in Table 6. We were able to perform the removal of silent transitions and the guard-oriented determinization up to depth 12, and the location-oriented determinization up to depth 8.

As expected, the studies confirm that the complexity of the different algorithms depends vastly on the input models. For the current paper we picked two small examples that were introduced in previous papers on determinization and one example that was an industrial use case in a previous project. Our next step will be a stronger evaluation on a larger case study. The tool and the current examples are available[3].

8   Related Work

The main inspiration to our work comes from [5] and [4]. Bérard et al. [5] show that silent transitions extend the expressive power of TA and identify a sub-class of eNTA for which silent transitions can be removed. By restricting our selves to the bounded setting, we can remove silent transition of all strongly-responsive eNTAs. In addition, our approach for removing silent transitions preserves diagonal constraints in the resulting automaton, thus avoiding a potential exponential blow-up in the size of its representation (see [9] for the practical advantages of preserving diagonal constraints in TA). Baier et al. [4] propose a procedure

---

[3] https://momut.org/?page_id=394

Table 6. Runtime and number of locations for the Car Alarm System [2], modified by adding a silent transition causing a 0-2 seconds delay.

Depth	Number of locations				Runtime (sec.)			
	unfolded	std. det.	new det.	on-the-fly	ε-removal	std. det.	new det.	on-the-fly
2	8	8	8	8	0.108	0.2	0.1	0.0
5	153	139	83	81	0.4	1.0	0.8	0.2
8	2,062	1,973	757	739	4.1	129.0	11.6	0.9
12	78,847	-	14,009	13,545	10,592.3	-	4,832.1	10.2

for translating NTA to *infinite* DTA trees, and then identify several classes of NTA that can be effectively determinized into finite DTA. In contrast to our work, their procedure works on the region graph, which makes it impractical for implementation. In addition, we also allow in our determinization procedure disjunctive constraints which results in a more succint representation that can be directly handled by the bounded model checking tools. Both [5] and [4] tackle non-determinism and observabilty in TA from a general theoretical perspective. We adapt the ideas from these papers and propose an effective procedure for the bounded determinization of eNTA.

Wang et. al [18] use timed automata for language inclusion. Their procedure involves building a tree, renaming the clocks and determinization of the tree. Contrary to our work, they do not restrict themselves to the bounded setting, thus taking the risk that their algorithm does not terminate for some classes of timed automata. Also, they use the "standard" determinization method that involves splitting non-deterministic transitions into a possibly far larger set of deterministic transitions, whereas we join them into one transition.

Krichen and Tripakis [13] produce deterministic testers for non-deterministic timed automata in the context of model-based testing. They restrain the testers to using only one clock, which is reset upon receiving an input. The testers are sound, but not in general complete and might accept behavior of the system under test that should be rejected. Bertrand et al. [7] develop a game-based method for determinization of eNTA which generates either a language equivalent DTA when possible, or its approximation otherwise. A similar approach is proposed in [6] in the context of model-based testing, where it is shown that their approximate determinization procedure preserves the tioco relation. In contrast to our approach, which is language preserving up to a bound k, and thus appropriate for bounded model checking algorithms, determinization in the above-mentioned papers introduces a different kind of approximation than ours.

9   Conclusion

The bounded setting allows the handling of a larger class of TA and in a more efficient way than in the unbounded setting. The extension from standard unary constraints to diagonal and disjuncive constraints has a practical reason: it is more efficient to let the SMT solvers deal with them than to translate them into standard form. In this paper a novel procedure was presented, which transforms bounded, non-deterministic and partially-observable TA into deterministic and fully-observable TA with diagonal and disjunctive constraints. The procedure includes an algorithm for removing the silent transitions and a determinization algorithm. It was implemented, tested and integrated into a model-based test generation tool. Recently [1] we investigated ways of pruning the determinized tree, to reduce the state space of the unfolding. These appoaches look promising for applying the presented work to test-case generation in industrial studies.

Acknowledgments. The research leading to these results has received funding from the ARTEMIS Joint Undertaking under grant agreement N° 332830 and from the Austrian Research Promotion Agency (FFG) under grant agreement N° 838498 for the implementation of the project CRYSTAL, Critical System Engineering Acceleration.

References

1. Bernhard, K.: Aichernig and florian lorber. Towards generation of adaptive test cases from partial models of determinized timed automata. In: AMOST (2015)
2. Aichernig, B.K., Lorber, F., Ničković, D.: Time for mutants — model-based mutation testing with timed automata. In: Veanes, M., Viganò, L. (eds.) TAP 2013. LNCS, vol. 7942, pp. 20–38. Springer, Heidelberg (2013)
3. Alur, R., Dill, D.L.: A theory of timed automata. Theor. Comput. Sci. **126**(2), 183–235 (1994)
4. Baier, C., Bertrand, N., Bouyer, P., Brihaye, T.: When are timed automata determinizable? In: Albers, S., Marchetti-Spaccamela, A., Matias, Y., Nikoletseas, S., Thomas, W. (eds.) ICALP 2009, Part II. LNCS, vol. 5556, pp. 43–54. Springer, Heidelberg (2009)
5. Bérard, B., Petit, A., Diekert, V., Gastin, P.: Characterization of the expressive power of silent transitions in timed automata. Fundam. Inform. **36**(2–3), 145–182 (1998)
6. Bertrand, N., Jéron, T., Stainer, A., Krichen, M.: Off-line test selection with test purposes for non-deterministic timed automata. In: Abdulla, P.A., Leino, K.R.M. (eds.) TACAS 2011. LNCS, vol. 6605, pp. 96–111. Springer, Heidelberg (2011)
7. Bertrand, N., Stainer, A., Jéron, T., Krichen, M.: A game approach to determinize timed automata. In: Hofmann, M. (ed.) FOSSACS 2011. LNCS, vol. 6604, pp. 245–259. Springer, Heidelberg (2011)
8. Biere, A., Cimatti, A., Clarke, E.M., Strichman, O., Zhu, Y.: Bounded model checking. Advances in Computers **58**, 117–148 (2003)
9. Bouyer, P., Laroussinie, F., Reynier, P.-A.: Diagonal constraints in timed automata: forward analysis of timed systems. In: Pettersson, P., Yi, W. (eds.) FORMATS 2005. LNCS, vol. 3829, pp. 112–126. Springer, Heidelberg (2005)
10. de Moura, L., Bjørner, N.S.: Z3: An efficient SMT solver. In: Ramakrishnan, C.R., Rehof, J. (eds.) TACAS 2008. LNCS, vol. 4963, pp. 337–340. Springer, Heidelberg (2008)
11. Diekert, V., Gastin, P., Petit, A.: Removing epsilon-transitions in timed automata. In: STACS, pp. 583–594. Springer (1997)
12. Finkel, O.: Undecidable problems about timed automata. In: Asarin, E., Bouyer, P. (eds.) FORMATS 2006. LNCS, vol. 4202, pp. 187–199. Springer, Heidelberg (2006)

13. Krichen, M., Tripakis, S.: Conformance testing for real-time systems. Formal Methods in System Design **34**(3), 238–304 (2009)
14. Larsen, K.G., Pettersson, P., Yi, W.: Uppaal in a nutshell. STTT **1**(1–2), 134–152 (1997)
15. Lorber, F., Rosenmann, A., Ničković, D., Aichernig, B.K.: Bounded determinization of timed automata with silent transitions. Technical Report IST-MBT-2015-01. Graz University of Technology, Institute for Software Technology (2015). https://goo.gl/YTjjnF
16. Tretmans, Jan: Test generation with inputs, outputs, and quiescence. In: Margaria, Tiziana, Steffen, Bernhard (eds.) TACAS 1996. LNCS, vol. 1055, pp. 127–146. Springer, Heidelberg (1996)
17. Tripakis, S.: Folk theorems on the determinization and minimization of timed automata. Inf. Process. Lett. **99**(6), 222–226 (2006)
18. Wang, T., Sun, J., Liu, Y., Wang, X., Li, S.: Are timed automata bad for a specification language? language inclusion checking for timed automata. In: Ábrahám, E., Havelund, K. (eds.) TACAS 2014 (ETAPS). LNCS, vol. 8413, pp. 310–325. Springer, Heidelberg (2014)

A Score Function for Optimizing the Cycle-Life of Battery-Powered Embedded Systems

Erik Ramsgaard Wognsen[1]([⊠]), Boudewijn R. Haverkort[2], Marijn Jongerden[2],
René Rydhof Hansen[1], and Kim Guldstrand Larsen[1]

[1] Aalborg University, Aalborg, Denmark
{erw,rrh,kgl}@cs.aau.dk
[2] University of Twente, Enschede, The Netherlands
{b.r.h.m.haverkort,m.r.jongerden}@utwente.nl

Abstract. An ever increasing share of embedded systems is powered by rechargeable batteries. These batteries deteriorate with the number of charge/discharge cycles they are subjected to, the so-called cycle life. In this paper, we propose the wear score function to compare and evaluate the relative impact of usage (charge and discharge) profiles on cycle life. The wear score function can not only be used to rank different usage profiles, these rankings can also be used as a criterion for optimizing the overall lifetime of a battery-powered system.

We perform such an optimization on a nano-satellite case study provided by the company GomSpace. The scheduling of the system is modelled as a network of (stochastic) weighted timed games. In a stochastic setting, exact optimization is very expensive. However, the recently introduced UPPAAL STRATEGO tool combines symbolic synthesis with statistical model checking and reinforcement learning to synthesize near-optimal scheduling strategies subject to possible hard timing-constraints. We use this to study the trade-off between optimal short-term dynamic payload selection and the operational life of the satellite.

1   Introduction

Battery-powered devices are ubiquitous: Satellites, pacemakers, sensor networks, laptops, tablets, smartphones, etc. Electric cars are also becoming popular. But while batteries provide portable power, they only do this for a limited period of time, be it a day or several years. Primary (non-rechargeable) batteries by definition need replacement when they run out, but even secondary (rechargeable) batteries deteriorate with time and use. This is due to various unwanted chemical reactions which accompany the desired reactions that bind and release the chemically stored energy. Predicting this wear is important for battery-powered systems. For those systems that are not easily serviceable, such as unmanned spacecraft and sensors embedded in bridges and buildings, predicting the wear on secondary batteries is a central part of predicting the total system lifetime.

This work is supported by the 7th EU Framework Program under grant agreement 318490 (SENSATION — Self Energy-Supporting Autonomous Computation).

S. Sankaranarayanan and E. Vicario (Eds.): FORMATS 2015, LNCS 9268, pp. 305–320, 2015.
DOI: 10.1007/978-3-319-22975-1_20

For serviceable systems, prediction can be part of calculating the maintenance cost of the complete battery-powered system.

As part of design space exploration, a system designer may propose a set of possible system designs that use the battery differently. To help evaluate these designs, he or she may consult battery documentation and data sheets but will often find that the manufacturer has only included limited performance and endurance data. Another option is therefore to test the proposed designs in experiments with physical batteries. However, these tests can be prohibitively slow and expensive, even with accelerated testing techniques that wear out the battery faster at artificially high temperatures.

To greatly reduce the effort required for this part of the design space exploration, we propose a scoring function that takes as input a battery usage profile (state-of-charge time-series) obtained from system simulation, for example. To be able to analyze complicated workloads that cannot easily be decomposed into alternating phases of discharging and full recharging, we analyze the usage profile in the frequency domain. The advantage of our approach is that we provide a fully model-based evaluation approach for the performance and lifetime of battery-powered systems.

We demonstrate the feasibility of our approach on a nano-satellite case study, provided by the company GomSpace, in which we examine the trade-off between short-term dynamic payload selection and the operational life of the satellite. We do this by combining the wear score function with a timed automata-based system model, which is then subjected to near-optimization using reinforcement learning as provided by the new tool UPPAAL STRATEGO.

This paper is organized as follows. Section 2 introduces the UPPAAL STRATEGO tool, Section 3 introduces batteries and battery degradation, Section 4 introduces our wear score function, and Section 5 puts it all together in our case study. Section 6 discusses limitations and assumptions, Section 7 considers related work, and Section 8 concludes.

2   Uppaal Stratego

For the model-based evaluation we will use (weighted and stochastic) timed automata (and games), exploiting the tool UPPAAL STRATEGO [2] being a novel branch of the UPPAAL tool suite that allows to generate, optimize, compare and explore consequences and performance of strategies synthesized for stochastic priced timed games (SPTG) in a user-friendly manner. In particular, UPPAAL STRATEGO comes with an extended query language (see Appendix A), where strategies are first class objects that may be constructed, compared, optimized and used when performing (statistical) model checking of a game under the constraints of a given synthesized strategy.

To illustrate the features of UPPAAL STRATEGO, let us look at the example in Fig. 1, providing an "extended" timed automata model of a small task with two phases. In the first phase the task must choose between two treatments indicated by the location A and U differing in time (up to 100 time-units respectively 50

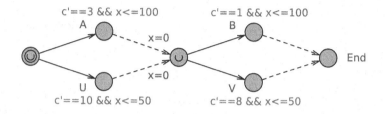

Fig. 1. A small task with two phases.

time-units) and cost-rate (3 respectively 10). Similarly, in the second phase, the task must choose between two treatments indicated by locations B and V again differing in time and cost-rate. Whereas the choice of treatment in the two phases is up to the task to control (indicated by the solid transitions), the actual time of the treatment is left to an uncontrollable environment (indicated by the dashed transitions). In one scenario, the objective of the task is to make choices that will ensure a given completion time regardless of a possible antagonistic environment. Under this interpretation, Fig. 1 represents a timed game. However, it may also be seen as a stochastic priced timed game (SPTG), assuming that the duration of the uncontrollable treatments are chosen by uniform distributions, and the objective of the control strategy is to optimize the expected completion time, or the expected completion cost (e.g. the cost-rate $c'==3$ in location A indicates that the cost variable c grows with rate 3 in this location).

We are interested in synthesizing strategies for various objectives. For example, the query **strategy** Opt = **minE**(c) [<=200]: <> Task.End will provide (by learning) the strategy Opt that minimizes the expected completion cost. The relativized query **E**[<=200; 1000] (**max:** c) **under** Opt estimates this expected cost to be 200.39. Figure 2(a) summarizes 10 random runs according to Opt, indicating that only cheap treatments (A and B) are chosen. Now, assume that the task *must* be completed before 150 time-units. From Fig. 2(a) the strategy Opt clearly does not guarantee this. However, we can generate the most permissive (non-deterministic) strategy Safe that guarantees this bound using the query **strategy** Safe = **control:** A<> Task.End **and** time<=150. Unfortunately, this has a high expected completion cost of 342.19, but the learning query **strategy** OptSafe = **minE**(c) [<=200]: <> Task.End **under** Safe

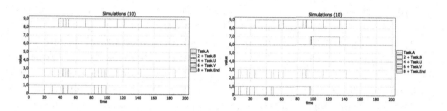

Fig. 2. (a) Runs under Opt. (b) Runs under OptSafe.

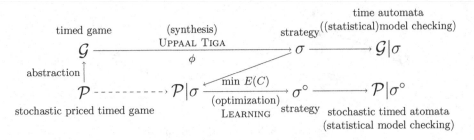

Fig. 3. Overview of UPPAAL STRATEGO

will provide a sub-strategy OptSafe optimizing the expected completion cost – here found to be 279.87 – subject to the constraints of Safe. Figure 2(b) summarizes 10 random runs according to SafeOpt, indicating that only the treatment U is never chosen. Model checking confirms that treatment B may only be chosen in case the first phase is completed before 50 time-units by the unsatisfiable query E<> Task.B **and** time>=51 **and** Task.x==0 **under** Safe.

As shown in the overview Fig. 3 UPPAAL STRATEGO will abstract a SPTG $\mathcal{P}$ into a timed game (TGA) $\mathcal{G}$ by simply ignoring prices and stochasticity in the model. Using $\mathcal{G}$, UPPAAL TIGA may now be used to (symbolically) synthesize a (most permissive) strategy σ meeting a required safety or (time-bounded) liveness constraint ϕ. The TGA $\mathcal{G}$ under σ (denoted $\mathcal{G}|\sigma$) may now be subject to additional (statistical) model checking. Similarly, the original STGA $\mathcal{P}$ under σ may be subject to statistical model checking. Now using reinforcement learning we may synthesize near-optimal strategies that minimizes (maximizes) the expectation of a given cost-expressions *cost*. In case the learning is performed from $\mathcal{P}|\sigma$, we obtain a sub-strategy σ^o of σ that optimizes the expected value of *cost* subject to the hard constraints guaranteed by σ. Finally, given σ^o, one may perform additional statistical model checking of $\mathcal{P}|\sigma^o$.

3   Battery Concepts

Electrochemical cells release chemically stored energy as electrical energy. In *primary* cells, the chemical reaction that enables this process irreversibly changes the chemical composition of the battery. However, in *secondary* cells, the reaction can be reversed, converting electrical energy back to chemical energy. Batteries consist of one or more electrochemical cells. When more severals cells are present, they can be connected in series for increased voltage, or in parallel for increased capacity, or a combination of connections for a combination of the properties. Small variations among the connected cells affect the performance and degradation of the overall battery and complicate charging and discharging procedures. Batteries can in turn be connected into battery packs with the same challenges. In this paper, we limit our attention to (single) batteries consisting of only one electrochemical cell.

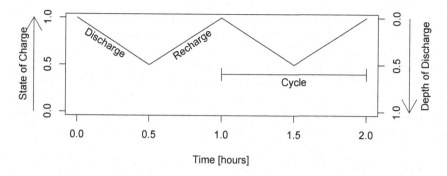

Fig. 4. Illustration of key battery concepts: State of charge (SOC), depth of discharge (DOD), discharge and recharge phases, and cycle.

Fig. 4 illustrates the fundamental battery concepts. The first one is **state of charge (SOC)**. Using a car analogy, a full tank corresponds to 100% SOC, and an empty tank corresponds to 0%. Driving speed and acceleration/breaking patterns affects wind and rolling resistance, and therefore the distance it is possible to travel with a given amount of fuel. Similarly for batteries, the load on the battery affects the amount of energy it can release before running dry. This is due to the *rate/capacity effect* [5]. (Note however, that the in the car, the energy stored is directly proportional to the amount of fuel in the tank. In the battery, the released energy itself varies with use.) Furthermore, a battery that runs dry is not really empty because the *recovery effect* [5] means that it will slowly regain some charge while resting. Last but not least, a battery can be charged above the design capacity if a higher voltage is applied (at the cost of faster wear of the battery).

Since both an empty and a full battery are not easily defined in practical usage, we refer to the battery datasheets to define the SOC. The battery is full when it is charged at the design charge voltage. The battery has reached a 0% SOC when it has delivered the nominal capacity. Some batteries are used for backup power and spend most of their lifetime near full SOC. In this work, we are interested in secondary batteries used in the typical cycling between charging and discharging.

A **cycle** in a system means returning to a state it has visited before. For a battery, it could, for example, be discharging a fully charged battery and then recharging it to its full capacity. **Depth of discharge (DOD)** = 1−SOC is another basic battery concept. It is often used in discussion of battery wear, and it is often used in the sense of maximal DOD. For example, "cycling at 80% DOD" means to repeatedly discharge to 80% DOD and recharge to 0% DOD (= 100% SOC).

The chemical reactions that store and release energy are, unavoidably, accompanied by other, unwanted chemical reactions and processes that slowly destroy the reactants or the electrodes. The main performance consequence is that with time and use, the capacity of the battery fades.

The rate of deterioration depends, among other things, on the maximal DOD reached, the rate of charge and discharge, temperature, dwelling at high and low SOC, and overcharging [3]. The maximal DOD that is discharged to is especially important, and can be the only focus of battery manufacturers' datasheets. For example, one battery is expected to reach end-of-life (80% capacity remaining) after 350 cycles at 100% DOD, 1000 cycles at 50%, and 1700 cycles at at 25%[1]. This kind of data can be good enough for simple workloads and system designs, but is not enough for advanced workloads, which motivates our approach.

4   The Wear Score Function for SOC-Profiles

In the discussion of battery powered systems with complicated workloads, the definition of a cycle from Section 3 often falls short because it is too precise. Consider, for example, a fully charged battery (100% SOC) that is discharged to 20%, recharged to 90%, discharged again to 20%, then recharged to 100%. According to the precise definition, this trajectory from 100% to 100% is one cycle, but from a battery application point of view, it is very close to being two cycles in the sense of "discharge-then-recharge".

Not only is this very likely usage of a battery difficult to discuss, but it is also unlikely that a battery data sheet will say anything about the expected battery lifetime for this type of load. To circumvent this issue, we propose to examine SOC profiles in the frequency domain. Using the discrete Fourier transform, we convert the SOC profile (time-series) into a frequency spectrum containing all component frequencies and their magnitudes. The discrete Fourier transform is computed by the Fast Fourier transform (FFT) algorithm, which outputs a sequence of complex numbers. The moduli (absolute values) of these numbers correspond to the magnitudes of the component frequencies. If the SOC profile is a sequence $S = s_1 s_2 \ldots s_n$ of SOC values sampled at frequency f, its score is

$$\mathrm{wsf}(S, f) = \frac{2f}{n} \sum_{i=0}^{\lfloor n/2 \rfloor} i |\mathcal{F}(S)_i|^2 \tag{1}$$

where $|\mathcal{F}(S)_i|$ is the modulus of the ith element of the output of the FFT function on S. The input consists only of real numbers, i.e., complex numbers with imaginary part zero. Therefore, only the first half of the FFT output (below the Nyquist frequency) is relevant to us. Hence, the sequence is summed up to index $\lfloor n/2 \rfloor$, and the multiplied by 2 to account for the frequencies lost above the Nyquist frequency. The fraction $\frac{fi}{n}$ (distributed inside and outside the sum) is the frequency corresponding to the FFT magnitude at index i. The outside fraction $\frac{2f}{n}$ does not affect ordering of scores, but it does bring them into a comfortable order of magnitude.

The wear score function is devised such that an SOC profile with a lower wear score is better for the longevity of the battery. Fig. 5 illustrates four different SOC profiles as well as their scores and intermediate results of the score

---

[1] http://www.gomspace.com/documents/gs-ds-batteries.pdf

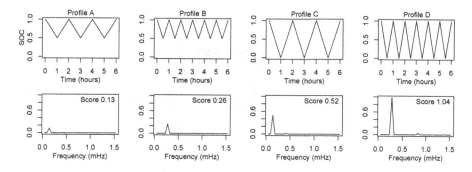

Fig. 5. Four example SOC profiles and their scores.

calculation. The FFT-like plots in fact show the magnitudes of the SOC oscillations at the component frequencies $\frac{fi}{n}$ for $i = 0, \ldots, \lfloor n/2 \rfloor$ (not to be confused with the sampling frequency, f). Each value is thus an element in the sequence $\frac{2fi}{n}|\mathcal{F}(S)|^2$, with modulus, exponentiation, and multiplication applied elementwise on the sequence. The wear score is the sum of this sequence. In the plot, the frequency axes are truncated to zoom in on the interesting harmonics.

Comparing profiles A and B, we see discharging to the same DOD (50%), but a doubling of the charge rate, discharge rate, the number of cycles that can be completed in the same time frame, and finally, the score. The same applies when comparing C and D. In these two simple comparisons, the score is proportional to the number of cycles/time, which conforms with the general idea that a battery can sustain a fixed number of cycles at a given DOD.

Comparing profiles B and C, we see that the same amount of charge is delivered — equivalent to three full capacities discharged in six hours. However, profile C discharges to twice the DOD while delivering this charge. This also increases the score because a higher DOD wears out the battery faster, even when the same charge is delivered. This matches what [3] cites as Symon's [7] Premise 2: "The charge life of the cell will always [...] be greater than [the rated charge life] when the battery is cycled less deeply." In other words, shallow DOD cycling improves the total amp-hour throughput in the lifetime of a battery.

The above examples serve only to test the wear score function on simple workloads, like those found in battery datasheets. The strength of the wear score function is however its ability to accept arbitrarily complicated workloads, including those mentioned at the beginning of this section. To demonstrate this, we turn to the nano-satellite case study in Section 5.

5   Nano-satellite Case Study

Our use case concerns the GOMX-3 satellite built by the company GomSpace. It is a nano-satellite with a volume of only three liters. Its purpose is two-fold. One subsystem tracks commercial aircraft, and two other subsystems are used to test improved forms of satellite-to-ground and satellite-to-satellite communication.

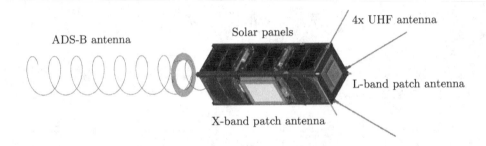

Fig. 6. The GOMX-3 nano-satellite

5.1 System Description

As you can see in Fig. 6, the satellite is covered in solar panels, and four different types of antennas for radio communication are attached. On the inside, it
packs circuitry for all the radios, reaction wheels and magnetic coils for attitude
(orientation) control, a main computer, and a battery.

The ADS-B system continuously tracks aircraft to assist ground-based systems, such as those in Europe and North America that cannot "see" the aircraft over the Atlantic Ocean. The UHF radio is the tried and tested means for
receiving commands from the ground station and sending measurements back.
The X-band radio is for experimenting with higher throughput ground communication. The L-band radio is for testing satellite-to-satellite communication.

Due to the locations of the antennas on the satellite body, only one of them
can be pointed towards its target at a time (using the attitude control system).
Therefore, for each orbit the satellite makes around the Earth, a single type of
communication is chosen, referred to as an orbit type. An orbit takes 90 minutes.

The four radios on the satellite consume a lot of energy, and the small number
of solar panels can only generate a limited amount of energy. The challenge is,
therefore, to do the most useful work with the available energy. Useful work can
be seen from different perspectives. From a short-term perspective, the focus is
on the number of experiments done in a short time-frame such as a week. But
as we know from Section 3, the battery wears out with use. So from a long-term
perspective, more work done every week means that the battery, and therefore
the satellite, will last fewer weeks. We model the aspects of the case relevant for
assessing battery wear and mission utility to study this trade-off as follows.

5.2 Satellite Model

The satellite is modelled in UPPAAL. The battery SOC is represented with a simple floating point percentage value using the declaration **double** soc = 80.0;.
The initial value is set to 80% SOC to represent the energy lost during the launch
and the storage period until the launch. The energy harvested from the solar panels, and the energy consumed by the subsystems and radios is represented by

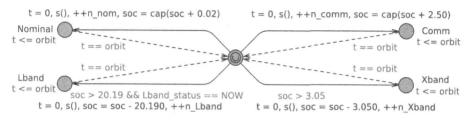

Fig. 7. Timed automaton describing the four orbit/experiment types. The controller only has influence over the solid edges; the dashed edges represent the environment.

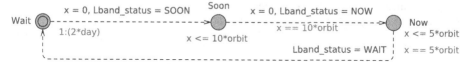

Fig. 8. Stochastic timed automaton controlling the L-band experiment window.

each orbit having and a net energy balance such as $+2.50$ or -20.19 percentage points SOC.

The automaton shown in Fig. 7 encodes the orbit types and energy balance. The initial, central location is the one from which experiments are chosen. It is urgent (marked by the rounded 'U'), which means that the choice must be made without delay. Edges in the automaton can have *guards*, which are conditions that must be satisfied to take a transition involving that edge. The Nominal and Communication (UHF) orbit types collect more energy than they consume, so these edges may always be chosen and have no guards. The X-band and L-band edges may only be taken when enough energy is available (e.g., `soc > 3.05`). The L-band experiment additionally can only be performed in specific time windows as indicated in the guard with `Lband_status == NOW`. The global variable `Lband_status` is controlled by a separate automaton, presented below.

Each of the four edges also has an *update* statement. Each edge (1) resets the clock t, (2) calls the function s which samples the SOC for use in the score calculation, (3) increments the relevant orbit type counter (which is used in the utility function), and (4) updates the SOC according to the energy balance of the relevant orbit type. For the two orbits with energy surplus, the `cap` function returns the minimum of its argument and 100.0, to prevent overcharging the batteries. In practice, this is achieved by disconnecting solar panels. Each experiment location has the *invariant* `t <= orbit`, and each edge returning to the central choice location has the guard `t == orbit`, ensuring that each orbit takes the orbit time, 90 minutes.

The arrival of the experiment windows for the L-band experiment are controlled by the automaton in Fig. 8. The time spent in the 'Wait' location follows an exponential probability distribution. Its rate λ is chosen such that the mean time between arrivals is two days (32 orbits). Once it is triggered, the automaton will spend ten orbits in the 'Soon' location, and then five orbits in the 'Now'

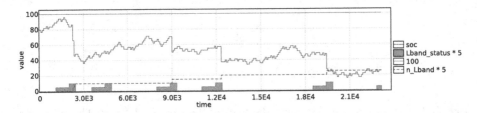

Fig. 9. Example simulation run of the system under no strategy: All nondeterministic choices are resolved using a uniform probability distribution. Note that increments of n_Lband only occur during the experiment window (the second step on the "staircase") and that it is accompanied by a large drop in state of charge.

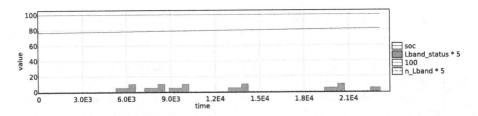

Fig. 10. Simulation of a strategy that minimizes the battery wear score. No L-band experiments are performed.

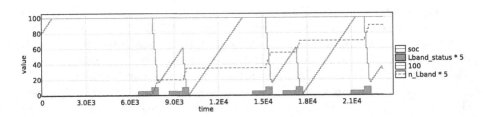

Fig. 11. Simulation of a strategy that maximizes the number of L-band experiments.

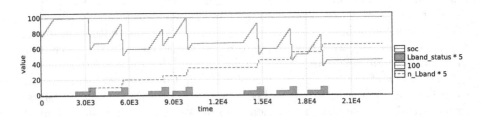

Fig. 12. Simulation of a strategy that minimizes 0.2*score - 0.8*n_Lband.

location, wherein the L-band orbits are possible. The purpose of the 'Soon' location is to give the reinforcement learning (see Section 5.3) the option of reacting to the upcoming experiment window.

An example simulation run of the system is shown in Fig. 9. The solid curve shows the evolution of the SOC between 0 and 100%. The solid "staircases" show the value of the variable Lband_status, as set in Fig. 8. The low step corresponds to the 'Soon' location, and the high step to the 'Now' location. The dashed line shows the accumulated number of L-band experiments performed, scaled by five to make the value more easily readable.

In addition to the two automata for the orbit type and the experiment window, the overall system model contains a separate automaton for calculating the wear score. This automaton waits until the end of the predefined system simulation period (16 days), and then calculates the score using (1) on the SOC samples taken by the orbit automaton's s function. Once the wear score has been calculated, the boolean done is set. Thus, the linear temporal logic (LTL) property "<> done" can be used as the requirement for the runs used in optimization.

5.3   Learning and Optimization

We use UPPAAL STRATEGO's "minimize expected value" query as follows:
    strategy s = **minE**(... *expression* ...) [<=nn*orbit]: <> done
The expression to minimize is our cost function. The first choice of cost function could be just the wear score. Fig. 10 shows a simulation run of the system under a strategy that minimizes the expected value of the score. The simulation is generated with the query **simulate** 1 [<=nn*orbit+1] {soc, Lband_status*5, 100, n_Lband*5} **under** s. The strategy almost always chooses the Nominal orbit because this orbit has the smallest effect on the SOC and will thus wear out the battery the least. The score is a low 0.003. But none of the L-band experiments are performed, so this is probably a bad strategy. It does not help if the battery will last for 15 years if nothing useful is done in those years!

In another extreme, we maximize the number of L-band experiments done. In the example simulation in Fig. 11, 18 L-band experiments were performed, and the sharp changes in SOC result in the high (bad) wear score of 73.5.

In between these two extremes, we might choose a cost function that combines the two previous in a weighted sum, e.g., 0.2*score - 0.8*n_Lband. The number of L-band experiments is subtracted rather than added because minimizing -n_Lband maximizes n_Lband. As we see in Fig. 12, the strategy has learned to choose the battery (wear) friendly Nominal orbit in waiting periods, save up energy with the Communication orbit just before the experiment window, and then do only a few L-band experiments, rather than almost depleting the battery as in Fig. 11. In this simulation, the number of L-band experiments was 13, and the wear score was 33.7.

The simulations discussed above only illustrate the strategies. To examine them more systematically, we find the mean value of the score from a number of runs (here, 25000) under the given strategy (here, s) with the query:
    E[<=nn*orbit+1; 25000] (**max:** score) **under** s

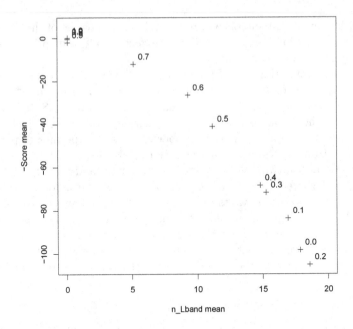

Fig. 13. Weighted sum optimizations of trade-offs between score and number of experiments done. The number next to each point is the parameter p in the expression being minimized, p `*score/6` - $(1 - p)$ `*n_Lband`.

We do this for both the `score` and `n_Lband` on a whole family of strategies[2] parameterized by $p \in [0, 1]$:

strategy s_p = **minE** (p `*score/6` - $(1 - p)$ `*n_Lband`) `[<=nn*orbit]`: `<>` done

Fig. 13 shows the Pareto-like frontier corresponding to this family of strategies. Note that the score axis is flipped such that the top right corner holds the most desirable values. The plot shows how improving one objective hurts the other. But going from $p = 0$ to $p = 0.1$ improves the wear score while only impacting the number of experiments minimally. Finding the largest number of experiments for $p = 0.2$ is unexpected. It is possible that the strategy that achieves this result is learned in a part of the state space that is, ironically, less likely to be explored thoroughly for the single objective optimization at $p = 0$.

6   Discussion of the Wear Score Function

Our score function is generic rather than tailored for a specific battery technology or application domain. We can see this, for example, when we consider the two profiles B and C in Section 4: The score doubles with a doubled DOD. The

---

[2]   The strategies are learned and evaluated using the command line version of UPPAAL, verifyta with the learning parameters `--learning-method 2 --filter 2 --good-runs 1000 --total-runs 1000 --runs-pr-state 500 --eval-runs 500`.

tendency in this is correct, but the wear may not be directly proportional to the DOD. To more exactly predict battery lifetime, the approach will have to be targeted to a specific battery technology.

However, obtaining wear data from battery manufacturers' datasheets can be very challenging. Petricca et al. [6] report that "from an extensive survey of more than 100 datasheets of commercial battery of different chemistries, sizes, energy and form factors, we did not find a single datasheet that report information about the following characteristics altogether in the same document: battery behavior due to constant current, pulse current, and aging effects."

However, we speculate that with enough data available for fitting, the following generalized form of (1), parameterized on p and q, could be relevant.

$$\text{wsf}'(\boldsymbol{S}, f) = \frac{2f^p}{n} \sum_{i=0}^{\lfloor n/2 \rfloor} i |\mathcal{F}(\boldsymbol{S})_i|^q \qquad (2)$$

Moreover, it seems to be not very well studied what happens when batteries are used in ways that are not simply repeating "charge fully, then immediately discharge to some depth". Drouilhet and Johnson [3] mention dwell time at low and high states of charge as a contributor to wear, implying that a medium SOC could be good for battery life. Similarly, the end of charge voltage, which also affects the SOC to which the battery is charged, is said to influence battery life[3]. Here, the DC component of the Fourier transform could be relevant to explore even though it is ignored in (1) and (2) due to being multiplied by zero.

We are starting work on experimental validation of the wear function with newly bought measurement equipment, and we are also interacting with battery manufacturers about this. Reporting on the results of this is future work.

Temperature is another wear factor that could be interesting to try to include. The correlation between temperature and wear is possibly complicated and the effect of temperature and charge/discharge rates may not be possible to consider separately. In this paper, we assume a constant temperature for the battery.

6.1   Limitations

Using a discrete Fourier transform imposes some limitations on the score function. The score is relevant for battery technologies for which charge and discharge rates can be considered to have symmetric effects on wear. With some technologies, this is not always the case for high currents, see, e.g., [1]. Drouilhet and Johnson [3] also cite a work saying that high charge rates at low and intermediate SOC may *increase* battery life, but they do not consider the evidence conclusive.

For our score function, we assume that the proposed SOC profile is to be repeated indefinitely. Therefore it should start and end at the same SOC to prevent an assumed discrete jump between SOCs when the profile is repeated. We also assume that the profile is of a short duration wherein the battery wear

---

[3] http://batteryuniversity.com/learn/article/how_to_prolong_lithium_based_batteries

can be ignored, i.e., the capacity remains close to constant. Such a profile could be on the order of weeks rather than months or years.

The sampling/simulation parameters f and n are chosen according to the speed of changes in the SOC. The sampling frequency f should be large enough that the oscillations of interest are slower than the Nyquist frequency $f/2$. Higher harmonics are negligible at realistic uses of batteries because they would not support sustained high currents (changes in SOC), which in turn give rise to strong high frequency harmonics. The sampling window n/f affects the lowest observable frequency, which is its reciprocal f/n. The lowest observable frequency should be low enough to observe the oscillations of interest. The score depends on the sampling parameters, so for now it only makes sense to compare scores calculated with the same parameters.

7   Related Work

Drouilhet and Johnson [3] in the context of energy storage describe a battery life prediction method that takes into account DOD and discharge rate. They propose a function for each of these to which manufacturer data can be fitted. Combining the two expressions, the effective discharge affecting the battery with respect to wear can be computed from a user-prescribed discharge profile consisting of a series of discharge events. The battery is seen as having a fixed charge life (lifetime Ampere-hour throughput until end-of-life), but relative to "effective" discharge, which depends on DOD and discharge rate. They apply their method to a case study of peak shaving in an Alaskan village powered by wind energy. By predicting the lifetime of different sizes of NiCd and VRLA batteries, they find the most cost effective battery technology and size for the given application. In our approach, we try to generalize from the focus on simple workloads wherein each discharge is followed by a full recharge.

Petricca et al. [6] describe an electrical circuit model of capacity fading due to cycling, as well as the increase of the internal resistance due to cycling. What is needed to build the model is manufacturer's data on capacity fading due to cycling at different temperatures and discharges rates (C-rates), and data on increase of the internal resistance at a reference discharge rate and for various DODs. It is questionable whether this data is always available to the user. As mentioned in Section 6, the authors had a hard time obtaining it. The capacity loss is based on an equation that takes as input the number of cycles. Again we encounter the concept of cycles that only works for simple workloads, where each discharge phase starts at 100% SOC.

Guena and Leblanc [4] in the context of backup power experimentally examine how DOD affects the cycle life of lithium-metal-polymer batteries. They test at 0.6%, 50%, 60%, 70%, 80%, and 100% DOD and find that reduced DOD improves cycle life and total charge throughput. This matches our expectations. They also test micro cycling (to 0.6% DOD) and find it to have no effect on cycle life, i.e., the micro cycled cell had the same capacity fade as one with a float charge (no cycling). Unfortunately the sample sizes are too small to say anything conclusive (one cycled cell compared to three floating cells), and more information would be interesting to have.

8 Conclusion

In this paper we have presented the wear score function, which ranks battery usage profiles according to their relative impact on the cycle life of the battery. The score function takes into account the workload characteristics that influence the cycle life the most: charge rate, discharge rate, and depth of discharge. The key strength of the score function is that it is not limited to standard regular charge-discharge profiles, but it allows comparison of complex workload profiles. This makes it a very useful tool in the design of battery powered devices, as we have shown in the GOMX-3 nano-satellite case study. In the case study, we have integrated the wear score function into an automata-based model of the satellite as a stochastic timed game. The wear score function is however suited for use with any system modelling formalism and field of application.

In its current form the wear score function allows ranking usage profiles and optimizing. The scores, however, may not be directly proportional to the actual battery life. We expect that the score function can be tailored to a specific battery type. However, in order to do this much experimental data is needed. Obtaining such data, and fitting the score function to match the real cycle life, is part of the future work.

Acknowledgments. This work has been done in cooperation with the partners of the EU FP7 project SENSATION. We would especially like to thank Peter Bak, David Gerhardt, and Morten Bisgaard of GomSpace ApS for our fruitful discussions about challenges of nano-satellites and the GOMX-3 project. We would also like to thank Gilles Nies, Jan Krčál, and Holger Hermanns of Saarland University for inspiring discussions of battery modelling and wear. Finally, our colleague at AAU Peter Gjøl Jensen has been helpful in explaining the inner workings of UPPAAL STRATEGO and its learning algorithm.

References

1. Choi, S.S., Lim, H.S.: Factors that affect cycle-life and possible degradation mechanisms of a Li-ion cell based on LiCoO2. Journal of Power Sources **111**(1), 130–136 (2002)
2. David, A., Jensen, P.G., Larsen, K.G., Mikučionis, M., Taankvist, J.H.: UPPAAL STRATEGO. In: Baier, C., Tinelli, C. (eds.) TACAS 2015. LNCS, vol. 9035, pp. 206–211. Springer, Heidelberg (2015)
3. Drouilhet, S., Johnson, B.L.: A battery life prediction method for hybrid power applications. In: AIAA Aerospace Sciences Meeting and Exhibit (1997)
4. Guena, T., Leblanc, P.: How depth of discharge affects the cycle life of lithium-metal-polymer batteries. In: 28th Annual International Telecommunications Energy Conference, INTELEC 2006, pp. 1–8, September 2006

5. Martin, T.L.: Balancing batteries, power, and performance: System issues in CPU speed-setting for mobile computing. PhD thesis, Carnegie Mellon (1999)
6. Petricca, M., Shin, D., Bocca, A., Macii, A., Macii, E., Poncino, M.: Automated generation of battery aging models from datasheets. In: Computer Design, pp. 483–488. IEEE (2014)
7. Symons, P.: Life estimation of lead-acid battery cells for utility energy storage. In: Proceedings of the Fifth conference on Batteries for Utility Storage, San Juan, Puerto Rico, July 1995

A   Appendix

Query Language of Uppaal Stratego

UPPAAL STRATEGO allows for strategy assignment "strategy S =" and strategy usage "under S", using strategy identifiers S. In particular, the queries of UPPAAL STRATEGO allow for constructing (and binding) strategies that guarantee safety or reachability objectives, or that optimize (minimize or maximize) the expected value of a given expression (within a given bound on time, steps or chosen cost). Constructed (and bound) strategies may now be used to relativize the queries already used in UPPAAL, UPPAAL TIGA and UPPAAL SMC.

Table 1. A non-comprehensive list of different types of now supported queries. *NS* (non-deterministic), *DS* (deterministic) and *SS* (stochastic) are used to signify the type of the strategy allowed in the given situation.

Strategy generators using UPPAAL OPT	
Minimize objective	`strategy DS = minE (expr) [bound]: <> prop`
Maximize objective	`strategy DS = maxE (expr) [bound]: <> prop under NS`
Strategy generators using UPPAAL TIGA	
Guarantee objective	`strategy NS = control: A<> prop`
Guarantee objective	`strategy NS = control: A[] prop`
Statistical Model Checking Queries	
Hypothesis testing	`Pr[bound](<> prop)>=0.1 under SS`
Evaluation	`Pr[bound](<> prop) under SS`
Comparison	`Pr[bound](<> prop1) under SS1 >=`
	`          Pr[bound](<> prop2) under SS2`
Expected value	`E[bound;int](min: prop) under SS`
Simulations	`simulate int [bound]{expr1,expr2} under SS`
Model checking queries	
Safety	`A[] prop under NS`
Liveness	`A<> prop under NS`

Author Index

Printed in the United States
By Bookmasters